Facts About
The Supreme Court
of the United States

Facts About The Supreme Court
OF THE UNITED STATES

By Lisa Paddock

Historical Overview by Paul Barrett,
Supreme Court correspondent for The Wall Street Journal

The H.W. Wilson Company
NEW YORK AND DUBLIN

A New England Publishing Associates Book
1996

Photo Credits
The photographs on pages 3, 21, 23, 28, 47, 122, 162, 167, 222, 225, 246, 250, 278, 374, and 422 are provided courtesy of the Library of Congress. The photographs on pages 5, 57, 80, 119, 138, 141, 200, 201, 223, 244, 280, 297, 301, 320, 323, 325, 328, 376, and 427 are provided courtesy of the Supreme Court of the United States.

NEW ENGLAND
PUBLISHING
ASSOCIATES

Copy-Editing: Karen Storo
Design and Page Composition: Teri Prestash
Editorial Administration: Dave Voytek
Proofreading: Margaret Heinrich Hand
Indexing: Miccinello Associates

Library of Congress Cataloging-in-Publication Data
    Paddock, Lisa.
    Facts about the Supreme Court of the United States / by Lisa Paddock.
    p. cm.
    Includes index.
    ISBN 0-8242-0896-X
    I. Title.
    KF8742.P32   1996
    347.73'26'09   dc20   95-53202
    [347.3073509]   CIP

Printed in the United States of America

CONTENTS

LIST OF ILLUSTRATIONS

PREFACE

Facts About the Supreme Court of the United States is a straightforward, chronologically organized reference compilation of essential historical information about one of the nation's oldest and most important institutions. By providing an historical and political context for the Supreme Court's most significant decisions and the lives of the men and women who have rendered them, the book illustrates how closely linked are the growth of the American republic and the development of its jurisprudence.

Facts About the Supreme Court of the United States is intended for a lay audience, and in order to make the cases more accessible, their analyses have been simplified in some respects. In particular, my restatement of the issues dealt with in the cases tends to reflect their underlying policy considerations rather than exactly mirroring the justices' own — often highly technical — phrasing of the legal questions presented at the time.

Under the subheading Opinions in the section of each chapter dealing with significant cases, wherever relevant I have reported as accurately and clearly as possible which justices concurred in and which dissented from the majority view. To avoid confusion, the reader should bear in mind the manner in which cases are decided and opinions written. In deciding a given case, the justices vote either to affirm or reverse the judgment of the court below. A justice who votes with the majority will then be assigned to write an opinion expressing the majority's rationale for its decision, and this opinion is then circulated among all the justices. Frequently, one or more of them will disagree with the reasoning of the majority opinion. In such cases, individually or jointly, justices may choose to write separate dissenting or concurring opinions. These opinions are circulated among the justices, who may join them in whole or in part. Sometimes a justice may even concur in part with the majority opinion while also joining in part in a dissenting view. Thus it is not uncommon for a justice to associate himself or herself with several opinions. Readers should remember, however, that each justice has only one vote, which — almost without exception — is finally registered as either supporting or opposing the majority view.

Throughout the book, all cases referenced are Supreme Court decisions unless otherwise noted. When the text refers to "the Court" with an upper case C, invariably the reference is to the United States Supreme Court.

In the sections devoted to judicial biographies, there is often overlap between the justices' occupations. All have been lawyers, and many acted simultaneously as lawyers and politicians, or lawyers and government officials, or lawyers and something else before and sometimes after they became justices. This last observation holds especially true in the early years of the Court, when justices — even chief justices — assumed nonjudicial duties or pursued political office while occupying the high bench. Indications that certain justices have written no significant opinions mean only that they did not author any of those analyzed in this volume. I should also note that I have calculated the justices' respective lengths of service beginning with the date each first took the oath of office.

For readers' convenience, some of the legal terms that appear most frequently in this book — those preceded by asterisks — are defined in a glossary at the back. The forms in which they appear in the text may not always exactly match those used in the glossary, but every effort has been made to prevent misleading disparities.

It is a pleasure to thank my knowledgeable and astute editor, Edward W. Knappman, whose guidance has been invaluable. Franz Jantzen and Derek Topham of the Supreme Court Curator's Office provided prompt, professional, and invariably gracious assistance. Finally, I want to thank my good-tempered, everlastingly supportive husband, Dr. Carl Rollyson — this book is for him.

Lisa Paddock
December 1995

INTRODUCTION

CREATION OF THE SUPREME COURT

When the framers of the Constitution met in Philadelphia, Pennsylvania, in the spring and summer of 1787, they knew they needed to formulate a document that would provide a framework for a national government more powerful than the government that had operated under the Articles of Confederation. The framers also knew that this new government needed a system of checks and balances policed by some form of court system. The new nation already had one such system in place, the state courts, and those members of the Constitutional Convention dedicated to preserving the power of the individual states argued that this was all that was necessary. Ultimately, the Federalists won the day, convincing the convention to endorse establishment of a federal court system — an institution that did not exist under the Articles of Confederation — to enforce federal law. However, the Federalist victory with regard to the judicial branch was only achieved — like that regarding the national legislature — by means of a compromise: although the Constitution would establish a federal judiciary, that system would coexist with state court systems.

Because at the time there was no body of federal law to enforce, Article III of the Constitution, which outlines the role of the federal judiciary, remained sketchy at best, merely touching on such matters as *original jurisdiction — the power to hear a case for the first time — versus *appellate jurisdiction, the power to hear appeals from those cases already tried. Article III is clear as to one issue, however: "The judicial Power of the United States shall be vested in one supreme court." What the exact powers of that supreme

court were to be would not be spelled out until Congress enacted the Judiciary Act of 1789.

THE STRUCTURE OF THE FEDERAL JUDICIAL SYSTEM

Article III also provides for "such inferior courts as the Congress may from time to time ordain and establish." In the 1789 Judiciary Act, Congress established a three-tiered system of federal courts that still endures today. At the top of this structure rested the United States Supreme Court, originally staffed by a chief justice and five associate justices (the size of the Court has varied over time, but since 1869, it has remained at nine seats, occupied by one chief justice and eight associate justices). The lowest tier was occupied by district courts, one in every state except Massachusetts and Virginia, which were each allotted two district courts (although neither was yet admitted to statehood, both the Maine district of Massachusetts and the Kentucky district of Virginia were granted their own district courts). Each district court bench was occupied by one judge, whose job it was to act as the primary trier of cases arising under general federal *jurisdiction. Between the Supreme Court and the district courts was an intermediate tier consisting of three *circuit courts, where three-judge panels decided both cases of original jurisdiction and those on appeal from the district courts. Decisions of these circuit courts were only reviewable by the Supreme Court.

The three original federal circuits were the Eastern Circuit, comprising New York, Connecticut, Massachusetts, and New Hampshire (Rhode Island and Vermont were added when they joined the Union in 1790 and 1791, respectively);

the Southern Circuit, which included South Carolina and Georgia (North Carolina was added when it joined the Union in 1790); and the Middle Circuit, made up of Pennsylvania, New Jersey, Delaware, Maryland, and Virginia. In the beginning, circuit courts had no staffs of their own; instead, each bench consisted of the district court judge from the state in which the circuit court had been convened, together with two Supreme Court justices traveling from state to state performing what was known as *circuit duty.

Today these circuit courts, now called courts of appeals, number 13. They have their own judges, who exercise only appellate jurisdiction over cases first heard in the 94 district courts around the nation, or in various federal administrative agencies and trial courts of limited and specialized jurisdiction, such as military courts and the Tax Court. In addition to the courts of appeals, the intermediate tier of courts today includes the Court of Appeals for the Federal Circuit, created in 1982 by combining the appellate jurisdictions of the United States Court of Claims, which heard cases concerning claims against the United States, and the Court of Customs and Patent Appeals.

Despite the changes in court names, the recombinations of jurisdictions, and the growth in the size of the system, the three-tiered structure and the geographic organizing principle of the federal judiciary called for in the 1789 Judiciary Act remain relatively unchanged.

THE RELATIONSHIP BETWEEN STATE COURTS AND THE FEDERAL JUDICIARY

Section 25 of the 1789 Judiciary Act contains its most important principle: even though state courts were to retain original jurisdiction over cases involving *federal questions — that is, cases requiring interpretation of some part of the Constitution, or of laws passed by Congress, or of treaties with foreign countries — the Supreme Court was to be the ultimate arbiter of such disputes. Article III of the Constitution had outlined situations in which the Supreme Court can review state court decisions, including contro-

versies "between Citizens of different States," where because neither state supreme court has jurisdiction, the U.S. Supreme Court will exercise what is known as its *diversity jurisdiction. Article III had also granted the federal judiciary power over "all Cases... arising under this Constitution, the Laws of the United States, and Treaties." To some, this vague language in the nation's foundation document about the power of the federal judiciary seemed overwhelming when combined with the final substantive portion of the Constitution, Article VI, which reads in part:

This Constitution, and the Laws of the United States which shall be made in Pursuance thereof ... shall be the supreme Law of the Land; and the Judges in every State shall be bound thereby, any Thing in the Constitution or Laws of any State to the Contrary notwithstanding.

Despite its endorsement of the principle of *judicial review, the Judiciary Act of 1789 went a long way towards calming the fears of *states' rights proponents, who were concerned with preserving the powers of the separate states. Under the act, the federal judiciary was not to have undefined and unrestricted power over state courts. While the act granted federal district courts original jurisdiction in such relatively minor matters as those concerning controversies arising at sea, petty crime, and revenue collection, it specified that a case involving a federal question could only reach the federal judicial system after the highest court of the applicable state had rendered a final decision. This decision could then be appealed to the U.S. Supreme Court (lower federal courts were not granted general trial jurisdiction over federal question cases until 1875). Furthermore, jurisdiction over diversity suits between *citizens of different states was made concurrent, meaning that plaintiffs in such cases could choose whether to proceed in state or federal court. The act added a further qualification to the pursuit in federal court of cases based on diversity: the amount of money at stake in such cases had to be at least $500 — a considerable amount of money at the time. (In 1989, this amount-in-controversy requirement reached $50,000).

SUPREME COURT JURISDICTION

Article III, section 2, spells out the Supreme Court's original jurisdiction, which is limited to cases involving such public officials as ambassadors, and cases in which a state is a named party. The Constitution restricts the remainder of the Court's jurisdiction to appeals from all Cases of admiralty or maritime Jurisdiction ... Controversies between two or more States; — between a State and Citizens of another State; — between Citizens of different States; — between Citizens of the same State claiming Lands under Grants of different States, and between a State, or the Citizens thereof, and foreign States, Citizens or Subjects.

The Supreme Court's original jurisdiction is not subject to alteration except by constitutional amendment. Such an alteration has occurred only once, when the Eleventh Amendment, prohibiting federal courts from hearing suits against states brought by citizens of other states or of foreign countries, was adopted expressly to reverse *Chisholm v. Georgia* (1793), the first landmark case heard by the Court. On the other hand, the Court's appellate jurisdiction is subject to "such Exceptions, and under such Regulations as the Congress shall make" — such as the judiciary act passed in 1789 and others that have followed it.

Other constitutional provisions also restrict the Supreme Court's — indeed, all federal courts' — jurisdiction. The language of Article III, section 2, limits federal jurisdiction to "Cases" and "Controversies," which the Supreme Court has interpreted to mean that its proper role is to address real controversies having genuine repercussions for the parties, rather than to issue merely *advisory opinions. In 1793, for example, the Jay Court declined President George Washington's request that it render a legal opinion regarding America's neutrality in the face of war between England and France. Citing the framers' intent that there be *separation of powers between the branches of the federal government, the Court stated that this issue was one for the national executive to decide for itself. This disinclination on the part of the Court to entertain issues more

properly resolved by the executive or legislative branches later came to be known as the *political question doctrine.

The cases and controversies requirement of Article III also gave rise to the doctrines of *ripeness, *mootness, and *standing. Ripeness and mootness concern the timing of a case. The ripeness doctrine provides that a federal court will not entertain a case until the issues it involves can be addressed in terms of actual occurrences. Conversely, the mootness doctrine provides that a federal court will dismiss a case if what is at stake is merely academic or has ceased to be a live issue for any reason. The concept of standing concerns the identity of the party seeking redress for unconstitutional governmental actions. If the plaintiff in such an action has no clear stake in its outcome, that plaintiff has no standing, and the case will be dismissed.

Undoubtedly, the most important aspect of the Supreme Court's jurisdiction is its power of judicial review, the authority to review decisions of the highest state courts and to determine the constitutionality of actions taken by other branches of the federal government. The Constitution itself grants no interpretative authority to any person or entity. Rather, it was Chief Justice John Marshall, in the seminal *Marbury v. Madison* (1803) case, who stated, "It is emphatically the province and duty of the judicial department to say what the law is." Marshall argued that only the Supreme Court had final authority to judge legislative and executive actions because, of all three branches of government, the judiciary alone was granted the power to decide cases according to the law, and the source of federal law was the Constitution. Furthermore, the Constitution makes the Supreme Court the ultimate arbiter not only of federal government actions, but also those of state government, including state court decisions based on federal law. The Marshall Court settled this issue in *Martin v. Hunter's Lessee* (1816) by upholding section 25 of the Judiciary Act of 1789, which endowed the Supreme Court with final authority to decide federal questions.

HOW CASES ARRIVE AT THE SUPREME COURT

As noted above, the Constitution severely limited the types of cases over which the Supreme Court can preside as a trial court. The number of original cases coming before the Court was restricted further when Congress granted federal district courts concurrent original jurisdiction over all cases except those between states. And rather than treating a suit between two states strictly as an original case, in such instances the Supreme Court now customarily appoints a judicial officer known as a special master to hear the facts and recommend a decision, which the justices then address as if it were an appeal from a decision of a lower federal court. It is hardly surprising, then, that the number of original cases the Supreme Court disposes of annually has been in the single digits for more than a quarter of a century.

The vast majority of cases come before the Court after either a state court or a lower federal court has already ruled on the factual and legal issues they present. When the Court considers an appeal, it rarely reviews issues of fact. Instead, the Court concentrates on disputes over legal matters, relying on the findings of the lower courts as to the events that generated the case, which are contained in the court record. Often, cases appealed to the Supreme Court have already been through several appeals in either the state or federal court system, or both.

Early in the history of the federal judiciary, when the judges of a lower appellate court were evenly divided as to the outcome of a case, *certification to the Supreme Court for review was mandatory. For state court decisions involving federal questions, a court order known as a *writ of error served as the procedural vehicle for obtaining Supreme Court review. And under the Habeas Corpus Act of 1867, state prisoners could apply directly to federal courts — including the Supreme Court — for issuance of a *writ of habeas corpus to obtain judicial determination of the legality of their detention.

In more recent Supreme Court history, three basic methods of requesting review became available to *appellants: they could petition for *certiorari, they could appeal, or they could request *certification of particular questions. By petitioning for certiorari, any party to a civil or criminal action in which either a federal district or appellate court had rendered a final decision could ask the Supreme Court to make a preliminary review of its case. The Court would then either grant or deny a writ of certiorari, which is an order to the court below to forward a record of the case. This method was not used with any frequency, however, until the Judiciary Act of 1925, in an effort to reduce the Court's workload, replaced obligatory review — invoked by means of appeal or writ of error — in most instances with discretionary review, which was achieved by petition for certiorari.

A right of appeal, a second method of obtaining Supreme Court review, was available when a federal appellate court invalidated a state statute on the basis of federal law or, in civil cases where the United States was a party, when federal legislation was held unconstitutional. However, this avenue of appeal, like the others, was limited: the Supreme Court could only review claims arising under federal law. If the lower court also decided state law issues, the aggrieved party was obliged to petition for certiorari to achieve complete review of its case.

Less often, a party who lost at the federal court of appeals level would invoke the Court's ostensibly obligatory appeal jurisdiction to review decisions using federal law to invalidate statutes. Rarely, however, did the Court grant jurisdiction in such cases, most of which were disposed of summarily, just like petitions for certiorari.

In 1988 Congress revised the statutes governing Supreme Court appellate jurisdiction, eliminating virtually all of the Court's previously mandatory federal appeal jurisdiction and making certiorari the only procedure available to most appellants seeking Supreme Court review. Direct appeals from district court decisions are still available, but they rarely occur. Such appeals can only be taken from decisions rendered by three-judge district court panels, but in 1976 most of these were abolished by Congress. Instead, because petitions for certiorari can now be filed before a circuit court of appeals has rendered its decision, aggrieved parties seeking Supreme Court review of final district court decisions need only file an appeal in the circuit court before filing a petition for certiorari. In the preponderance of cases, the Court denies certiorari, allowing the decision below to stand. Such a ruling has no value as *precedent, however: the denial of "cert" in a given case cannot be used as a basis for deciding subsequent similar cases along the lines of the lower court ruling the Supreme Court has left in place.

The third — and rarest — modern method of invoking the Court's appellate jurisdiction, certification, also remains intact. This review procedure requires that a federal circuit court of appeals certify that certain questions raised by a case are so pressing and so vital to the public welfare that they require immediate Supreme Court review. Although consideration of certified questions is mandatory, the Supreme Court may dismiss the lower court's certification, or it may issue binding instructions with regard to the certified questions requiring the lower court to rule in a certain way. The Supreme Court may also require that the entire case, and not just the certified questions arising from it, be sent up for decision.

Appeals from decisions of state courts usually come from the states' highest courts, which are also customarily referred to as supreme courts. Occasionally, however, the U.S. Supreme Court hears appeals from lower state appellate courts — usually called courts of appeals or superior courts — or from state trial courts. The avenues of appeal from state courts were until recently generally equivalent to those available to appellants seeking review of federal court decisions — with the added provision that certiorari and appeal were only available for review of decisions on federal questions. Since 1988, however, Supreme Court review of state court decisions has been limited to petitions for certiorari concerning federal questions on which a state's highest court has already rendered judgment.

Restrictions on Supreme Court review of state court decisions have been generated in part by concerns about the strength of the federal government and the preservation of state power, but like the statutes controlling review of federal court decisions, these constraints are also intended to reduce the Court's ever-increasing workload, which was reaching unmanageable proportions. Since passage of the Judiciary Act of 1925, the Court, by exercising its discretionary review powers, has cut the number of full, signed opinions it issues almost in half. Before 1925 the Court averaged 200 such opinions per term; since then the average has dropped to 125.

THE CASE SELECTION PROCESS

One consequence of the enormous growth in the number of cases filed with the Supreme Court is the justices' increased reliance on their law clerks, usually recent graduates of top law schools, each of whom is employed by an individual justice for one or two years. This practice began in 1882 when Justice Horace Gray hired temporary clerks at his own expense. Other justices followed suit, but it was not until 1922 that Congress passed an appropriation act permitting each justice to employ one clerk. Today each justice may employ as many as four law clerks.

One of the clerks' primary jobs is to evaluate the volume of certiorari petitions that flood the Court each year — in 1992 the number reached 7,233 — and help winnow out those cases that are worthy of review. Petitions for certiorari are initially screened by the clerk of the court, a permanent administrator, who places those petitions that appear to be acceptable on the *docket. It is then the responsibility of the justices, in conjunction with their law clerks, to determine which of the docketed petitions are "certworthy." Since 1972 most of the justices have participated in a "cert pool," in which the petitions are divided equally among their clerks, who draft memoranda on their assigned cases, evaluating each and recommending that certiorari be granted or denied. The memoranda are then circulated among all the participating justices, each of whose own law clerks further evaluate the cases.

The ultimate decisions about which cases the

Court will hear rest with the justices themselves. These decisions are made in judicial conferences, which for docket review take place on Fridays during the Court's annual term, which begins in October and customarily ends in May. Sometimes the judicial conferences continue until July — well after the term's scheduled cases have been disposed of. In the 1970s the Court also added a series of conferences in late September, prior to the opening of its regular term, to consider petitions that have accumulated over the summer recess. Before convening the judicial conference, the chief justice distributes a "discuss list" of cases that have made it through the initial screening process — usually fewer than one-quarter of those filed. At the conference, which is held in strict secrecy and attended only by the justices themselves, the chief justice initiates discussion of the merits of those petitions on the list. In order of seniority, the associate justices then add their own comments and indicate tentative votes. If four or more justices vote in favor of granting certiorari to a case, the clerk of the court schedules it for *briefing and *oral argument. Only a fraction of those cases that make it onto the docket are granted review. The "orders list," consisting of those petitions for certiorari and appeal that have been granted review, is released in open court the following Monday.

BRIEFING AND ORAL ARGUMENT

Customarily, there is an interval of several months between the Court's announcement of its decision to hear a case and the actual appearance in court of the attorneys representing the parties. In the interim, the parties must meet a predetermined schedule in filing their briefs, which are written statements outlining the facts and legal arguments supporting their respective views of their cases. The appellant (sometimes referred to as the petitioner) is required to file the first brief, which must be submitted within 45 days of the Court's granting review. The *appellee (or respondent) must in turn file a brief within the following 30 days. The appellant is then given the opportunity to file a reply brief rebutting argu-

ments raised in the appellee's brief. At any time before oral argument either party may file a supplemental brief addressing legislation or other matters that have arisen since the initial briefs were filed. In addition, amicus curiae (friend of the court) briefs may be filed by individuals or organizations that are not parties to the case, but which nonetheless have an interest in how its outcome might affect them. Almost invariably, an amicus curiae will be aligned with one side of the case or the other.

Before 1821, Court rules did not require parties to submit briefs. Over time, however, the practice became such a significant part of the litigation process that by the middle of the twentieth century the Court was obliged to place a page limit on briefs. Supreme Court rules now restrict an initial brief on the merits of a party's case to fifty printed pages and allow fewer pages for other types of briefs.

Similarly, there once were no restrictions on the length of lawyers' oral arguments before the Court. The introduction of briefs, and the Court's increasing workload, however, did away with the early custom of allowing counsel to argue indefinitely, resulting in a 1849 rule limiting each side to two hours of oral argument. This limit remained in effect until early in the twentieth century, when it was cut down to one hour. Today, each side is allotted only a half hour for oral argument, a limitation strictly observed. In fact, the time actually devoted to presenting the case is less, for justices can — and do — frequently interrupt counsel with questions. Some justices have suggested that the submission of briefs, which permit them to become familiar with each side's arguments in advance, makes oral argument dispensable. Other justices, however, look on oral argument as an opportunity to test the soundness of a party's case in ways the opposing brief might have overlooked.

CONFERENCING AND OPINIONS

The Court typically hears from two to four cases per day, Mondays, Tuesdays, and Wednesdays during seven two-week sessions scheduled from October through April. On Wednesday afternoons and on Fridays, the chief justice convenes the judicial conference to discuss cases heard that week and to take tentative votes on them. During these sessions the justices observe the same secrecy and seniority rules that apply to discussion and voting on petitions. The protocol associated with the judicial conference has not always been so strictly observed. In the early years of the Court, the justices often discussed cases in the evenings and on weekends, sometimes at the boarding houses where they shared lodgings.

A case can be decided only when a majority vote is achieved among the justices participating (a *quorum of six is currently required to conduct Court business). If a majority cannot be reached, or if some of the justices remain undecided, the case can be set down for reargument. Once a majority is achieved, responsibility for writing the majority opinion is assigned. If the chief justice voted with the majority, he can assume this responsibility himself or he can assign it to another justice who voted with the majority. If the chief justice is among the minority, the senior associate justice voting with the majority assigns the opinion.

During its early years, the Supreme Court did not issue joint opinions; instead, all of the justices prepared separate opinions, which they then delivered in reverse order of their seniority. When John Marshall became chief justice in 1801, as part of his effort to increase the Court's authority in the new nation, he strove to achieve unanimity and to issue single opinions of the Court. The bulk of such opinions issued by the Marshall Court were signed by Marshall himself, although almost certainly he did not write them all.

It is also true today that the justices often do not write their own opinions. One of the most important — and most controversial — duties of the law clerks is to draft opinions for the justices they serve. The justices do, however, make final decisions about the opinions that bear their names. After a justice is satisfied with his or her opinion, it is circulated among the other justices so that they can join it if they wish.

In controversial cases, it is not uncommon for an opinion to be in production for months while the author rewrites it in order to accommodate those justices who disagree with points in the initial draft. Even then, justices may disagree and sometimes change their votes on a case. Not even the great John Marshall was able to rein in his associate William Johnson, one of the earliest practitioners of what is now a long tradition of dissent in the Supreme Court. Other justices, such as Sandra Day O'Connor, regularly issue concurrences in order to spell out alternative grounds for reaching the same result the majority endorses. The contemporary Court rarely issues unanimous opinions and is often so splintered that *plurality opinions — those joined by less than a majority of participating justices, but receiving more endorsements than any concurring opinion — have become commonplace. And sometimes the Supreme Court will issue an unsigned *per curiam opinion joined by the whole Court or a majority of its members, but not attributed to any individual. Such opinions usually announce judgments in uncomplicated matters, but they have been used in major cases, such as the important 1969 First Amendment case, *Brandenburg v. Ohio*.

ANNOUNCING AND ISSUING OPINIONS

Before 1965, decisions of the Court were traditionally announced on Mondays. Since then, however, the Court has announced its decisions as they become ready. Announcement of opinions can occur whenever the Court is in session, although in practice the bulk of its decisions are delivered towards the end of the term.

Until 1930 the justices customarily read their entire opinions from the bench, a time-consuming exercise. When the Taney Court delivered its decision in the *Dred Scott* case (1857), it took two days for the justices to read through seven separate opinions. Today the author of the majority opinion usually delivers only a summary, occasionally followed by dissenting justices who also summarize their views.

Recording of Supreme Court opinions only began in 1791, when Alexander J. Dallas appointed himself the Court's first reporter and publisher. Even today not all of the Court's opinions are formally reported. There is no constitutional requirement that opinions be written down, and indeed, the justices did not commit their views to paper until the second reporter of decisions, William Cranch, took over from Dallas in 1801. Early reporting of Supreme Court decisions was a commercial venture on the part of the reporter, who bore the expense of editing and publishing them — as well as the responsibility for selling them to what was then a limited market. Prior to 1817 Supreme Court reporters received no salary, and until the advent of the official series of volumes entitled United States Reports in 1874, reports bore the names of their respective reporters.

Today, initial "slip opinions," copies of Court decisions, are distributed to the lawyers and others present in the courtroom as the opinion is being delivered. Slip opinions contain only a proofread text of the justices' opinions, to which the official reporter of decisions adds a headnote summarizing the decision, together with the voting lineup. Edited, preliminary texts of the opinions appear within a few months, issued as United States Reports and bearing a legend requesting users to notify the reporter of any errors. Final versions of United States Reports opinions are later bound together in chronological order and printed by the U.S. Government Printing Office. This process can sometimes take years to complete, and in the interim commercial printers make opinions publicly available. Annotated texts are available in two unofficial series, Supreme Court Reporter and United States Supreme Court Reports, Lawyers' Edition. Since 1931 the periodical United States Law Week has also pub-

lished full texts of decisions within days of their announcement. Quickest access to the most recent opinions is obtained through such on-line computer services as WESTLAW and LEXIS and the Project Hermes database.

INTERPRETING CASE CITATIONS

Citations of Supreme Court cases typically contain five elements: the title of the case (usually consisting of some form of the names of the principal appellants and appellees); the volume of the reporter series being cited; an abbreviated form of the name of the reporter series being cited; the page of the volume on which the Court's opinion commences; and, parenthetically, the year in which the case was decided. For example, *Brown v. Board of Education,* 347 U.S. 483 (1954), indicates that the Court's opinion in the case, which was decided in 1954, begins on page 483 of volume 347 of *United States Reports.* The same format would be followed in citing from the two unofficial reporters, *Supreme Court Reporter* and *United States Supreme Court Reports, Lawyers' Edition.* All but the most recent cases generally cite just the official *United States Reports,* but citations to cases decided before 1874, such as *Chisholm v. Georgia,* 2 Dall. (2 U.S.) 419 (1793), customarily contain an additional, parallel citation to a nominative reporter — in this instance, volume 2 of the opinions originally published by Alexander Dallas under his surname (2 Dall.), which now also constitutes volume 2 of *United States Reports.*

Historical Overview
OF THE SUPREME COURT OF THE UNITED STATES

By Paul M. Barrett
Supreme Court correspondent for *The Wall Street Journal*

Of all the experiments in government sketched by the United States Constitution, the Supreme Court was perhaps the least well defined. Most of the founding fathers did not know what to expect from a national judiciary. Alexander Hamilton predicted that it would be the weakest of the three branches. At the same time, he anticipated that it would possess the awesome power to strike down acts of the popularly elected legislature or executive branch if, in the Court's view, the acts conflicted with the Constitution. As it turned out, the Supreme Court's use of this authority, known as *judicial review, would make it the most powerful judicial entity in the world, exerting a degree of influence far beyond that of comparable bodies in other countries.

This book explains how the Court's role has evolved over more than two centuries. From its uncertain beginnings, the Court spent decades getting itself into working order and helping to define the relationships among the different elements of the new and distinctively American form of government. Under the leadership of a far-sighted chief justice, John Marshall, it responded to pressures for expanded economic activity by facilitating commerce among the states and curbing parochialism. When regional rivalries and the confrontation over slavery fractured the country, the Supreme Court found itself forced to rule on disputes that could not be settled by mere judicial pronouncements. Sadly, the Court made matters worse with its pro-slavery decisions, culminating in the infamous *Dred Scott* case of 1857.

The story of the Supreme Court is mostly one of an institution reacting to — rather than creating — the aspirations and anxieties of American society. For example, when late 19th century industry organized itself on a national level, the Court fashioned new constitutional doctrines to protect property rights and limit progressive regulation. The Court maintained a rigid antiregulatory mindset even as the country slid into the Great Depression and the other branches of government tried to respond with more aggressive management of the economy. Under tremendous political pressure, the Court finally relented, ceasing to pass judgment on economic policy and shifting its attention from property rights to personal rights. Later, the Court found itself in the unusual position of helping to lead the nation in addressing long-neglected problems stemming from slavery's legacy.

The desegregation rulings of the 1950s recast the Court in a more active role, celebrated by liberals and reviled by conservatives. The activist drive eventually decelerated, but not before the Court had embroiled itself in controversies ranging from criminal rights to abortion, from school prayer to affirmative action. The Court of the late 1980s and 1990s has moved to the right, striving fitfully to reduce its role in resolving societal controversies. Although they have returned to a more reactive role, the members of the current Court remain among the most scrutinized players on the political stage. To understand the ideas and traditions that influence these nine people in black robes, it is vital to understand the history of the institution they control.

UNCERTAIN BEGINNINGS

The classical grandeur of the Supreme Court's pillared marble building in Washington, D.C., expresses a sense of permanence and prestige. But it was far from obvious at the time of the country's founding that the Court would become an important institution.

Delegates to the Constitutional Convention of 1787 spent relatively little time debating the nature of the new nation's judiciary. Article III, the section of the Constitution that describes the judicial branch, is far less detailed than the constitutional provisions on Congress and the presidency, leaving the task of completing the design to Congress, and, by implication, to the Supreme Court itself. Most notably, the Constitution did not address one way or the other whether the nation's top court could use judicial review to void legislation. That critical issue would be left for a later day.

Uncertainty over the Supreme Court's role in the new national government contributed to a lack of popular interest in the Court's early activity. Some of the men chosen by President George Washington to serve as the first justices were themselves less than enthusiastic about the honor. The first chief justice, John Jay, complained bitterly about the burden of riding *circuit, which required the individual justices to travel long distances on rough roads to preside over lower-court cases. Despite repeated pleas from the justices, it was not until 1891 that Congress eliminated this responsibility. Jay, who called his post "intolerable", quit in 1795 to become governor of New York and refused to return when the chief justice's chair became vacant again in 1800.

Although they were not anywhere close to the center of political action in the 1790s, the early justices did slowly begin the work of carving out a place for the Supreme Court in American govern-

ment. The Court clarified that the judiciary was to be an independent branch. Still, the early *precedents lacked an overall coherence or sense of purpose. The Court needed a leader with a broader view of its mission and the skills to forge consensus.

ESTABLISHING AUTHORITY

John Marshall, a politician and diplomat from Virginia not known for his technical legal prowess, was appointed to the High Court in 1801, served until his death 34 years later, and is commonly recognized by scholars as "the great chief justice." He saw the potential power in the post that his two predecessors, John Jay and Oliver Ellsworth, had not been able to imagine. By the force of his personality and the clarity of his thought, he dominated the Court and won the respect of his colleagues. A commander in the Revolutionary War, he felt loyalty to the new nation as a whole, beyond any attachment to his home state. In this critical way, among others, he differed from his fellow Virginian, Thomas Jefferson, the great skeptic of strong national government, who was elected president at the dawn of the new century. Before President John Adams left office, he named Marshall to lead the Supreme Court in what would be a dynamic era of expanding judicial authority.

The government moved from Philadelphia to its permanent home in Washington the same year that Marshall assumed the chief justiceship. But in a reflection of the Court's modest stature in 1801, no one thought to provide it with a space of its own. Eventually it was allotted cramped quarters in the still-incomplete Capitol. The justices at that time met for only a few months each year, living together in a boardinghouse, where they also took their meals, and, after dinner, discussed pending cases. In this intimate setting, Marshall was apparently masterful in persuading his housemates to go along with decisions strengthening the Court as an institution. He convinced his colleagues to end the practice of each justice issuing a separate opinion so that the Court could speak through one authoritative opinion, typically signed by Marshall himself.

Dissents soon resurfaced, but Marshall achieved his basic goal of forging a more unified Court. Also early in the Marshall years, regular publication of the Court's decisions got under way, making its work better known among lawyers and at least some members of the public.

President Jefferson had reason to fear that John Adams had used his lame duck power to seed the judiciary with Federalists devoted to bolstering the national government — none with more determination than Chief Justice Marshall. Indeed, Marshall saw his fundamental task as the establishment of the Supreme Court's authority in relation to the other two branches and to the states. Beyond that, he led the justices in clearing traditional legal obstacles to the growth of commerce in a young nation just beginning to realize its economic potential.

Neither the Constitution nor Congress had originally granted the Supreme Court the authority to determine whether legislative acts conflicted with the Constitution and were therefore void. However, in 1803, the Court, led by Marshall, simply declared that it possessed this power of judicial review. Alexander Hamilton, arguing for ratification of the Constitution, had contended that the judiciary generally would be the weakest branch, lacking control as it did over either a treasury or an army. But he added that at critical moments it would serve as an independent bulwark against overreaching by the people's elected representatives. The Constitution created a potentially strong federal government, but one whose powers were limited. In Hamilton's view, it would be the Supreme Court's job to say when ordinary laws exceeded these limitations.

Marshall adopted and applied this theory in the seminal case of *Marbury v. Madison* (1803). At issue was the refusal of Secretary of State James Madison to deliver a commission as justice of the peace to William Marbury, one of the "midnight judges" appointed by outgoing President Adams. The confrontation reflected the tense standoff between the electorally defeated Federalists, who nevertheless dominated the judiciary, and their wary foes, the Jeffersonians. Executing an artful political compromise at the same time that he set the foundation for American constitutional *jurisprudence, Chief Justice Marshall wrote for the Court that Marbury should have gotten his commission, but that the Supreme Court lacked authority to order it handed over. The section of the Judiciary Act of 1789 that Marbury invoked was invalid, Marshall reasoned, because Congress had tried to give the Supreme Court power that had not been authorized by the Constitution. Marshall declared that it was the Court's distinctive role to determine when a statute collided with the Constitution and to assert the Constitution's supremacy. The Supreme Court would not strike down another act of Congress for more than a half-century, but Marshall had secured for his institution an essential role in maintaining the balance among the branches of national government.

The judiciary had to define its authority not only in relation to the other two branches of the federal government, but also to the states. Marshall spoke for the Court when in 1810 it asserted its authority to strike down a state law as unconstitutional. The decision in a case from Georgia was the first in a series of rulings that inhibited state legislative power by giving a broad reading to the Constitution's provision protecting the sanctity of contracts. State authorities, particularly in the South, resented this assertion of federal authority, but the Supreme Court held firm. In 1816 the Court slapped down the rambunctious state judiciary of Virginia, which had insisted that the Supreme Court could not tell state courts what to do. On the contrary, the Supreme Court ruled, Congress was within its rights to give the nation's top judicial body *appellate jurisdiction over state court rulings involving questions of federal law. Three years later, the Supreme Court extended its interpretation of the Constitution's *Commerce Clause to protect corporate charters against meddling by state governments.

While constraining state lawmakers from interfering with commercial relations, the Marshall Court boosted congressional efforts to fuel the expanding economy. In the landmark 1819 case of *McCulloch v. Maryland*, the chief justice led his colleagues in ruling that the Congress could charter a national bank and that the states could not tax its operations. The Constitution did not speak specifically of chartering banks, but Marshall interpreted broadly the constitutional provision giving Congress authority to pass laws "which shall be necessary and proper" for carrying out its enumerated duties. A bank, for instance, would be needed for the financing of the central government. Marshall deftly transformed Hamiltonian arguments for a strong national government into constitutional law. The Jeffersonian view that the Constitution should be construed strictly, with Congress allowed only those powers explicitly assigned to it, was decimated. The related *holding in the case — that states cannot tax a federal body such as the bank — only further exacerbated southern resentment of the Supreme Court's imposition of federal limits on state *sovereignty.

The themes of federal primacy over the states and the protection of commercial networks from local interference were intertwined in Marshall's thinking. In the 1824 case of *Gibbons v. Ogden*, the Court, speaking through Marshall, struck down a New York law granting a steamboat monopoly on key interstate routes. The monopoly excluded from New York waterways boats licensed under a federal law, which Congress had enacted pursuant to its constitutional power to oversee interstate commerce. Commerce, the chief justice explained, went beyond traditional buying and selling to include transportation. Implicit in the ruling was one side in an emerging debate on the American economy. Some leaders of the time believed that officially granted monopolies were needed to give investors security. Without saying so explicitly, Marshall lent support to the opposing view — that competition, not monopoly, would strengthen the country. The rulings in *Gibbons v. Ogden* and in other cases that followed encouraged the development of major waterways and railroads, which would become the indispensable arteries of the American economy.

After a period of extraordinary dynamism, the Marshall Court moved more cautiously during its final decade, consolidating authority and even making some concessions to state power. Hamilton had observed that the judiciary would need the support of the political branches if it hoped to see its decisions followed. The wisdom of that observation was illustrated when Marshall uncharacteristically misjudged the reach of the Court's practical influence in the *Cherokee Cases* of the early 1830s. Georgia had defied a Supreme Court ruling growing out of disputes over the state's *jurisdiction over Indians and their land. President Andrew Jackson sided with the state and is credited (perhaps inaccurately) with making the famous remark, "Well, John Marshall has made his decision; now let him enforce it."

Overall, however, the Marshall legacy was a judiciary that enjoyed the power and prestige of a co-equal branch of government. In addition, Marshall helped nurture the national government, promoting its powers over those of the states and giving substance to the Hamiltonian vision of a strong central structure. The 19th century French political observer Alexis de Tocqueville noted that several European states had adopted representative systems of government, but that he was "unaware that any nation of the globe has hitherto organized a judicial power in the same manner as the Americans . . . . A more imposing judicial power was never constituted by any people."

COMMERCE, SLAVERY, AND CIVIL WAR

In the decades that followed John Marshall's death in 1835, the Supreme Court began to recalibrate the balance of the federal system, giving more weight to the concerns of the states. Although arguably sensible in the realm of commerce, this approach had disastrous results when applied to the institution of slavery.

Marshall's successor, Roger Taney of Maryland, was the fourth of President Andrew Jackson's High Court appointees. A former attorney general and treasury secretary, Taney was a partisan Jacksonian Democrat who aided in his president's attack on the Bank of the United States, an institution that the Marshall Court had protected. Conservatives feared that Taney would threaten private property interests, but this concern turned out to be excessive. While he interpreted state powers more generously than Marshall, there were crucial elements of continuity between the Marshall and Taney Courts — most notably, the steady expansion of federal judicial power. Assessments of Taney's 28-year tenure as chief justice are understandably colored by the *Dred Scott* slavery case. But most of the Taney Court's activity actually was consistent with positions established by the Marshall Court during the first third of the 19th century.

By 1836, in Taney's first term, the Court had grown to nine justices from the original number of six. In this era, the Court's docket was still small, and oral arguments in a single case could go on for days at a time; masterful orators such as Daniel Webster and Henry Clay argued major cases before the Taney Court and kept the proceedings lively. In 1860 the Supreme Court left its basement room in the Capitol for a more dignified courtroom in the refurbished former Senate chamber. The Court would remain there for 75 years, until it moved across the street to its majestic Corinthian-style building.

The enlarged bench led by Chief Justice Taney continued to confront problems stemming from economic growth, and, on the whole, it maintained the course of encouraging competition and the development of new technology. In the *Charles River Bridge* case (1837), Taney spoke for the Court when it rejected the argument that a charter granted by Massachusetts included an implied right to monopoly — in this instance, to provide a crossing over Boston's Charles River. Allowing implied advantages like monopoly status or freedom from taxation to be read into corporate charters, Taney warned in his opinion, would reward old, inefficient entities such as turnpike corporations, and impede the development of railroad and canal transportation.

Without disturbing the main precedents of the Marshall era, the Taney Court made room for state regulation that it found reasonable and not in conflict with federal law. In 1852, for example, the Court qualified the broad principles of *Gibbons v. Ogden* in a challenge to a Philadelphia ordinance requiring certain ships to take on pilots to navigate the city's port. Upholding the ordinance, the Supreme Court said that some aspects of interstate and foreign commerce — such as harbor navigation — are local in character and therefore could be regulated by states or cities.

Increasingly, however, the Supreme Court found that questions of regulating commerce became intertwined with disputes over slavery. Cases touching on state authority were inevitably scrutinized for their effects on southern efforts to expand slavery in the face of mounting calls for its abolition. Supreme Court decisions began to produce more confusion than clarity. In the 1840s the Court upheld the federal Fugitive Slave Act when it conflicted with state personal liberty laws. Then, in 1856 the justices heard the case of *Dred Scott v. Sandford*, which, by the time it reached the Supreme Court, was seen by many southerners as an opportunity for the judiciary to insulate slavery once and for all. Taney, one of five justices from slaveholding states, shared this dubious view. The case received intense public attention, with one New York newspaper observing, "The court, in trying this case, is itself on trial."

Scott, a slave from Missouri, claimed that he should be considered free because he and his family were taken for a time to a free state and free territory. Taney led a divided Court in rejecting Scott's plea, holding that African Americans, whether slaves or free, were not citizens, and therefore did not deserve to be heard in federal courts. Striking down an act of Congress as unconstitutional for the first time since *Marbury v. Madison*, the majority said Congress had lacked authority when it enacted the Missouri Compromise in 1820, stopping the spread of slavery to the territories. Therefore a slave taken to a "free" territory was not legally liberated. The ruling inflamed emotions on both sides of the slavery debate and hastened the Civil War. By splitting Democrats in the North from those in the South, it also helped put Republican Abraham Lincoln in the White House.

One Supreme Court scholar, Carl B. Swisher, has written that "the Taney Court fell upon evil times... because it was caught in the grinding pressures of sectional conflict." Even so, the *Dred Scott* decision, and more pointedly, Taney's opinion, reached further than necessary to reject Scott's claim, invalidating the Missouri Compromise as well as Scott's suit for freedom. The consequences for the Court, as for the nation, were devastating. For the first time in decades, the Court found itself under broad public attack. The Civil War and its immediate aftermath saw the Court's reputation sink even further amid general disregard for the rule of law. Consumed by bloodshed, the nation did not pay much attention when President Lincoln, defying objections by Chief Justice Taney, suspended procedural legal protections for prisoners captured by the Union army. Years later, after both men were dead, Supreme Court rulings vindicated Taney on this point.

RECONSTRUCTION

As they launched their program to remake the defeated South, many northern politicians viewed the Supreme Court as a potential enemy. Their main concern was that the Court would rule unconstitutional the provisional military governments established in the South as part of the Republican program of Reconstruction. This suspicion was fueled by the Court's decisions limiting the use of military courts martial in civilian matters and striking down loyalty-oath requirements for office holders. But whatever distaste some members of the Supreme Court may have had for aspects of Reconstruction, there was not a judicial consensus to resist directly the Republican majority in Congress. Southern legal challenges to the Reconstruction regime were rejected or dodged by the High Court. Still, in its interpretation of the Reconstruction-era amendments to the Constitution, the Supreme Court illustrated a desire to reassert state sovereignty and repel broad assertions of civil rights.

The amendments rang notes of liberty. The Thirteenth abolished slavery. The Fourteenth gave more protection against state actions threatening individual rights. The Fifteenth guaranteed African Americans the right to vote. Yet, in what has become a symbol of promises unkept, the fortunes of former slaves were not even the issue in the first Supreme Court case testing the Fourteenth Amendment. Instead, the Court heard the claim of a group of butchers that the state of Louisiana was interfering with their right to do business. In the *Slaughterhouse Cases* (1873), the Supreme Court interpreted the Fourteenth Amendment's protection so narrowly that it would remain an almost useless weapon against oppressive state action for years to come. In 1880 the Court did say that states could not restrict jury service to whites only. But three years later, in the *Civil Rights Cases*, it emphasized that the Fourteenth Amendment covered only official, not private, discrimination against African Americans. This line of decisions culminated in the 1896 case of *Plessy v. Ferguson*, in which the Supreme Court articulated more fully the racist social assumptions that underpinned its constricted view of the Fourteenth Amendment. Upholding a Louisiana law requiring railroads to provide separate cars for African Americans and whites, the 7 to 1 ruling stated that "if one race be inferior to the other socially, the Constitution... cannot put them upon the same plane." It was not until the 1950s that the Court admitted its mistake in championing the doctrine of "separate but equal" in race relations.

THE ECONOMY AND PROPERTY RIGHTS

In the decades after the Civil War, the Supreme Court had become a less personal and more institutional place. The justices, for example, no longer lived together in a common rooming house. At the Court, the focus in their cases was not personal rights, but the nation's booming economy. The Civil War accelerated the nationalization of industry, transportation, and communication. When state and federal authorities tried to police the effects of these changes, businesses went to the judiciary seeking protection. And in most instances, the Supreme Court adopted a pro-business view of postwar industrialization.

The Court sustained some states' efforts to regulate commerce within their borders and, at first, upheld far-reaching laws limiting railroad rates for shipping farm products. But by the 1880s, the Court was emphasizing that states could not interfere with any business activities crossing state lines — a major victory for the railroads and their allies. The Court was equally skeptical of new federal regulatory efforts. In a triumph for the monopolies, or "trusts," that dominated entire industries, the Court initially limited the Sherman Antitrust Act to cover only trading activities, not manufacturing.

The Supreme Court had at first resisted the notion of protecting business interests under the Fourteenth Amendment, but this hesitance soon faded. In 1886 it declared that corporations would be considered "persons" for purposes of Fourteenth Amendment challenges; four years later, it introduced the peculiar idea that there was a "substantive" component to the constitutional guarantee of procedural justice. The Fifth and Fourteenth Amendments prohibit federal and state governments, respectively, from depriving any person of "life, liberty, or property, without due process of law." Under the doctrine of *substantive due process, the Court said these provisions gave federal judges authority to scrutinize the substance of laws, not merely the procedures they establish. The judiciary assumed responsibility for approving the economic wisdom of regulatory legislation: an open-ended invitation for conservative jurists to knock down what they saw as intrusions on the free market.

Before the turn of the century, the Supreme Court added another weapon to its antiregulatory arsenal: a freedom-of-contract principle derived from the constitutional protection of liberty. Announcing that individuals had the right to make any economic arrangements they chose, the Court used this doctrine for four decades to strike down state worker-protection laws setting maximum hours, minimum pay, and safety standards. The Court embraced the idea that the Constitution embodied moral and economic principles of *laissez faire and that government should not interfere with the "natural" distribution of wealth. In its best-known application of this approach, *Lochner v. New York* (1905), the Court ruled that a New York law limiting the workday for bakers violated the freedom of contract. For the Court to uphold health or safety regulations, it had to be convinced that the law served the "general welfare," rather than interests of a favored group, such as the New York bakery workers.

The *Lochner* decision sparked sharp criticism from progressive leaders and from advocates of *judicial restraint, including a relatively new justice, Oliver Wendell Holmes, who filed a sharp dissent in the case. The former chief judge of the Massachusetts Supreme Judicial Court, Holmes would serve for 29 years on the U.S. Supreme Court and is almost universally considered to be one of its greatest justices. In unusually piquant prose, he questioned whether the Constitution actually did incorporate the social Darwinism fashionable among captains of industry and their attendants. The strong popular reaction against *Lochner* was reflected in the redoubled trust-busting efforts of Theodore Roosevelt and his successor, William Howard Taft. However, it seemed to have only a temporary effect on the Court, which engaged in a liberal interlude of a dozen years, during which some wage and hour laws for women and children, as well as worker's compensation statutes, were upheld.

The Court majority's essential conservatism reemerged, however, during World War I, and grew stronger after the armistice. In 1918 the Court struck down a federal child-labor law that prohibited goods made by underage workers from being shipped across state lines. The Court revived the rigid distinction between manufacturing and commerce, concluding that Congress had overreached by regulating production by child workers.

Former President William Howard Taft, appointed the tenth chief justice by President Warren Harding in 1921, served for nine years, during which the Court strongly reaffirmed its conservative pro-business stance. But interestingly, the Court in this period also showed some early signs of interest in civil liberties claims — a subtle development that foreshadowed the liberal "due process revolution" of the 1960s.

"The business of America is business," President Calvin Coolidge said, and the Supreme Court seemed to take the admonition to heart. The conservative majority undercut the Federal Trade Commission's investigative power and undermined federal legislation aimed at curbing judicial use of antilabor *injunctions. The full force of *Lochner v. New York* was revived in 1923, when the Court ruled that Washington, D.C.'s minimum-wage law for women interfered with liberty of contract enjoyed by worker and employer. In subsequent years, the Court struck down more than one hundred state laws in the name of property and contract rights, often with Justices Holmes and Louis Brandeis in dissent. Brandeis, a progressive Jew portrayed as a dangerous radical by the establishment attorneys who opposed his 1916 confirmation, became Holmes's ally-in-dissent in both the economic rights cases and some important individual rights cases.

The economic collapse of the 1930s brought forth a wave of federal legislative activity designed to rescue and regulate American capitalism. But a Supreme Court dominated by conservatives born in the 19th century viewed President Franklin D. Roosevelt's New Deal as extremist, and they set about to stop it.

The "Four Horseman" of the right — Justices James McReynolds, Willis Van Devanter, George Sutherland, and Pierce Butler — were generally able to pick up the fifth vote they needed to strike down federal laws and their state equivalents. The Court voided the oil-regulation section of the National Recovery Act, invalidated the Railroad Retirement Act, and struck down the National Industrial Recovery Act. It likewise dispatched New York's model minimum-wage law.

After his reelection in 1936, FDR responded to this judicial obstructionism with his "court-packing" plan: a clumsily disguised threat to add as many as six additional justices to the Supreme Court, purportedly to relieve its cluttered *docket. Members of the Court, including the liberal Brandeis, attacked the scheme, and the Senate rejected it in 1937. But in the midst of the furor, FDR got the breakthrough he was after; the Court, in the 1937 case of *West Coast Hotel Co. v.*

Parrish, upheld a Washington state minimum-wage law similar to the one from New York it had struck down in 1936. As a famous quip put it: a "switch in time saved the nine."

From then on, the Court sustained every New Deal measure that came before it. And FDR was able to influence the direction of the Court by means of ordinary appointments. These included Hugo Black, Felix Frankfurter, William O. Douglas, and Robert Jackson. The new justices typically took a broad view of Congress's power under the *commerce and *taxing authority, making almost any economic activity, no matter how local it might seem, subject to congressional regulation. Under the new approach, the Court was inclined to uphold any federal economic law that had some *rational basis — an extremely deferential standard. Similar respect was accorded state economic legislation. And in a series of cases beginning in 1937, the Court upheld revised versions of most of the significant New Deal legislation it had struck down earlier.

LIBERTIES STIRRING

Once the Roosevelt justices had steered the Supreme Court away from close supervision of economic lawmaking, a new concern captured the Court's attention: the degree to which the Constitution protected individual rights and liberties. This interest had surfaced first during the generally conservative era of the 1920s, although not in a simple or straightforward fashion. Justice Brandeis had suggested that the individual liberties that were secured against state infringement by the Fourteenth Amendment included not only property rights but also rights such as *freedom of speech. In its boldest form, Brandeis's theory held that the Fourteenth Amendment should be understood to have "incorporated" the guarantees of the first eight amendments to the Constitution and made them applicable to the states as well as to the federal government. In 1925 the Court upheld the conviction of socialist Benjamin Gitlow under New York's criminal anarchy law, but acknowledged in its decision, almost casually, that the First Amendment freedoms of speech and the press "are among the personal rights and 'liberties' protected by the due process clause of the Fourteenth Amendment from impairment by the states." This *due process concept became the basis for the Court's rulings in the 1930s striking down state laws as violating the First Amendment.

Meanwhile there were other rumblings on individual rights. In 1923 the High Court struck down a state law forbidding the teaching of a foreign language in elementary schools, finding that the Fourteenth Amendment protection of liberty applies not just against bodily restraint, but also guards "those privileges long recognized at common law as essential to the orderly pursuit of happiness by free men." A 1925 decision invalidating a state requirement that children attend public schools asserted that parents' right to educate their kids as they saw fit also was an aspect of constitutionally protected personal liberty. Progress on the individual rights front was not uniform, however. In 1926 the Court refused to invalidate racially *restrictive covenants discouraging the sale of real estate to African Americans. Federal law enforcement tactics also withstood constitutional attack — for example, in a case holding that *warrantless wiretapping did not violate the Fourth Amendment's restrictions on search and seizure. In this case, Justice Brandeis dissented, claiming that the Constitution protected privacy — the right to be let alone — an idea that a court majority later adopted in 1965 in the context of the freedom to use contraceptives, and later expanded in the abortion cases.

By the late 1930s, a steady stream of cases on constitutional liberties was reaching the Court, forcing a major debate over the reach of Brandeis's *incorporation doctrine. Would the justices permit the wholesale incorporation into the Fourteenth Amendment of all the guarantees in the Bill of Rights, thereby providing vast new protection against intrusive state action? In 1937 the Court answered no; instead, it would selectively incorporate only those rights that are "of the very essence of a scheme of ordered liberty" and so deeply rooted in American traditions as to be considered "fundamental." While the justices

continued in subsequent decades to argue over the wisdom of broad-versus-selective incorporation, case by case the Court found that almost all of the individual protections in the Bill of Rights were essential and therefore applicable to the states as well as to the federal government.

Feeling a need to rationalize its shift of attention from economic rights to individual liberties, the Court announced in 1938 that henceforth it would apply starkly different constitutional standards to claims asserting each of the two types of rights. In a ruling upholding a federal milk regulation, the Court said that it would assume the validity of such economic restrictions unless a challenger could meet the difficult test of proving the law irrational. In contrast, laws that allegedly trampled individual rights guaranteed by the Bill of Rights would be scrutinized closely by the judiciary, because such restrictions on rights potentially shut off the political processes that provided the only other means of attacking repressive legislation.

By the 1940s, the Supreme Court was unabashedly charting a new course in constitutional law, but the new course required numerous adjustments and corrections. The flag-salute cases illustrate the point. In 1940 Justice Frankfurter spoke for the Court in an 8 to 1 ruling that said schools could require children to pledge allegiance to the flag, even if the patriotic ritual impinged on their religious beliefs. By 1943, in the middle of World War II, the Court reversed itself and ruled 6 to 3 that the First Amendment's religion clause protected believers from being forced to compromise their faith. Justice Jackson captured the Court's emerging libertarian spirit: "If there is any fixed star in our constitutional constellation, it is that no official, high or petty, can prescribe what shall be orthodox in politics, nationalism, religion, or other matters of opinion or force citizens to confess by word or act their faith therein."

In time, the anxieties related to World War II and the subsequent cold war confrontation with Communism had a distorting effect on the Court's constitutional vision, resulting in decisions that were viewed later as embarrassing mistakes. None was more egregious than the 1944 ruling upholding internment of Japanese Americans. Aside from fears of enemies abroad and at home, however, a basic disagreement was developing among the New Deal justices. As the Vinson Court encountered new constitutional claims of personal rights, Felix Frankfurter called for fidelity to the philosophy of judicial restraint, which had guided the Court when it stopped obstructing Congress from regulating the economy. The Court must move cautiously, Frankfurtuer urged, assuming that the political process would eventually address most forms of societal injustice. Opposing him with growing passion were Justices Hugo Black and William O. Douglas, who openly advocated *judicial activism to right the wrongs brought to the Court's attention. This division would remain a source of tension on the Court — and a basic theme in political debate over its proper role — from the 1940s to the present.

Frankfurter's theory of restraint probably reached its high point during the cold war years, when the Court took a relatively passive approach in upholding prosecutions of purported subversives in the face of First Amendment free-speech challenges. Frankfurter similarly deterred the Court from expanding enforcement of the protections in the Bill of Rights as they affected criminal suspects, including restrictions on police searches and interrogations. Since 1914 the Supreme Court had held that evidence gathered in violation of the Fourth Amendment guarantee of personal security against unreasonable searches could not be used in federal prosecutions. The idea behind the "*exclusionary rule" was to discourage police misconduct. But under Frankfurter's restraining influence, the High Court resisted extending the rule from federal to state cases. In the areas of free speech and criminal rights, Frankfurter's positions ultimately were overturned by liberal activist decisions. However, his contention that judges ordinarily should refrain from second-guessing legislative and executive-branch judgments could not be dismissed altogether. Judicial restraint became a persistent subtheme in the country's political and legal debates, raising doubts about the propriety of an increasingly adventurous Supreme Court.

CIVIL RIGHTS AND RACE

The Supreme Court had in effect endorsed racial segregation with its separate-but-equal *Plessy v. Ferguson* ruling in 1896. But as African Americans and their liberal allies campaigned against this situation after World War II, the Court signaled that legal changes were coming. In an initial tentative move, the justices had ruled in *Missouri *ex rel. Gaines v. Canada* (1938), that if the southern states wanted to maintain segregated schools for whites, it had to provide "equal" facilities for African Americans. Then, in 1950 the High Court said that Oklahoma had violated the Fourteenth Amendment's *Equal Protection Clause by forcing an African American student admitted to a graduate program in education to sit in the hall outside his class. The same year, the justices ordered the University of Texas Law School to admit an African American student because a newly created black law school did not offer a comparable education.

These *test cases, orchestrated by the National Association for the Advancement of Colored People, chipped away at the foundation of the separate-but-equal concept and gradually prepared the Supreme Court for the day the doctrine would be confronted head-on. In 1952 the Court agreed to decide five cases on the issue of racial segregation in public schools. The five cases came to be known by the name of one: *Brown v. Board of Education of Topeka, Kansas*. The chief justice at the time, Fred Vinson, a Truman appointee, died before the cases were resolved. So it fell to his replacement, Earl Warren, a Republican politician appointed in 1953 by President Dwight Eisenhower, to lead the Court toward what would be its most important decision of the 20th century. Warren, the governor of California when he was nominated as chief justice, was known as a moderate pragmatist with an instinct for coalition-building.

In *Brown v. Board of Education*, the justices were nearly unanimous on the question of jettisoning separate-but-equal, but there was dissension over how to put the decision into effect in the public school cases. Seeking a unanimous court, Chief Justice Warren split the issues so they could be dealt with one by one. First, in 1954 he spoke for the Court in overturning the 58-year-old precedent of *Plessy v. Ferguson.* "We conclude that in the field of public education the doctrine of 'separate-but-equal' has no place," he wrote. "Separate educational facilities are inherently unequal." Then the next year, in a case known as *Brown II*, the Court addressed the question of implementing the decision, declaring with notable ambiguity that states should end segregation in public schools with "all deliberate speed." Again, the Court was unanimous.

The effects of the *Brown* decisions gradually undermined official segregation not just in schools but also in many other aspects of public life. Resistance — both in the states and in Congress — was fierce. Earl Warren was vilified, and southern governors stood in schoolhouse doors to block African American students. Nevertheless, in a 1958 case from Arkansas, the Supreme Court insisted that the states had to follow its orders on desegregation, and in a courageous endorsement of judicial authority, President Eisenhower dispatched Army troops to Little Rock to enforce the Court's decision.

The Supreme Court had unmistakably transformed its role from that of a reactive force to one of helping to galvanize social change. Critics of the Court in the 1920s and 1930s had demanded judicial restraint so that popularly elected legislators could try to solve the country's massive economic problems. The philosophy of restraint, eloquently promoted by New Dealer Felix Frankfurter, had often prevailed on questions of economic regulation. By the 1950s, however, there was a new demand on the Court — at least from the liberal establishment — that it use the Constitution as a hammer to break up the political stalemate on race relations. Under Earl Warren's leadership, the Court accepted that challenge and, through the 1960s, grew ever bolder in asserting itself as the protector of individual liberties. Our assumptions today about the Supreme Court's place in society are based largely on the image of intrepid jurists demanding an end to state-sponsored subordination of the descendants of slaves.

DUE PROCESS REVOLUTION

To the dismay of political conservatives, the Warren Court in the 1960s continued its course of expanding individual rights at the expense of government authority. It launched a "due-process revolution" to reform state law enforcement and criminal court procedures. The exclusionary rule was now extended to the states so that improperly gathered evidence was kept out of prosecutions. After *Gideon v. Wainwright* (1963) indigent defendants accused of serious crimes were guaranteed lawyers. State authorities had to refrain from coercing suspects into making confessions or other self-incriminating statements. Under the hotly debated *Miranda v. Arizona* (1966) decision, police were required to inform people in custody that they had the right to remain silent, that their words could be used against them, and that they also had a right to an attorney. By 1969 the Supreme Court had declared that the states must follow almost all of the major parts of the Bill of Rights.

The Warren Court did not limit itself to criminal law. Enforcing the First Amendment prohibition against the "establishment" of religion by government, it ignited new explosions of conservative outrage with rulings against officially sponsored school prayer. With *New York Times v. Sullivan* (1964), the Court expanded the First Amendment protection of the press by insulating the news media from most libel suits by public figures. Striking down a Connecticut law banning the sale of contraceptives, the Court announced a hazily defined constitutional right to privacy that barred the state's intrusion into at least some aspects of the marital relationship. In another area, voting rights, the Court abandoned the long-held Frankfurtian view that claims challenging the fairness of gerrymandered or disproportionate electoral districts were, by definition, *political questions and therefore beyond the purview of the judiciary. For example, in decisions during the early 1960s, the Warren Court forbade states from rigging electoral districts in order to exclude African Americans. It also said that districts could not have grossly unequal voting populations. Political equality required "one person, one vote," the Court declared in a decision that required a vast redistribution of power in Congress and state legislatures.

After its breakthrough with the *Brown* cases, the Court's role in the race relations debate became one of reinforcing congressional action and prodding the states into following through on their obligations to desegregate. Congress, by passing the 1964 Civil Rights Act and similar legislation, finally gave some teeth to the Reconstruction-era amendments — Thirteenth, Fourteenth, and Fifteenth — which had promised to make the former slaves and their descendants full citizens. In a series of decisions beginning in the mid-1960s, the Court upheld these statutes and amplified their message. Separately, in cases such as *Edwards v. South Carolina* (1963), the Court invalidated some southern efforts to interfere with the activities of civil rights organizers. The justices also tried, with mixed success, to bolster desegregation by ruling that states could not simply close their public schools or use other delaying tactics.

REPUBLICAN REACTION

The most recent 25 years of the Court's history has in many ways consisted of a prolonged struggle over the Warren Court's liberal legacy. Despite the efforts of three Republican presidents — Richard Nixon, Ronald Reagan, and George Bush — who appointed a total of nine justices to the Supreme Court, the political right failed to sweep away the major precedents of the Warren era. The momentum of the due process revolution, ignited by Louis Brandeis in the 1920s, eventually dwindled, and some liberal emphases on individual rights were contained and qualified. But the conservative counter-revolution predicted by many experts did not occur. Even with a conservative majority on the Court by the late 1980s, moves toward the right tended

to be incremental rather than dramatic. Examined closely, most of the conservative victories in recent years, such as *Freeman v. Pitts* (1992) and *Adarand Constructors, Inc. v. Pena* (1995), have rolled back liberal advances made in the 1970s and 1980s, leaving in place the earlier landmarks of the Warren years.

It had appeared that critics of the Warren Court would finally have their day when Earl Warren retired in 1969. Newly elected President Richard Nixon vowed to make good on his "law-and-order" campaign speeches attacking the liberal trend of Court decisions, and over the course of his first term he filled a total of four seats. But things did not work out as Nixon planned.

The new Nixon-appointed chief justice, Warren Burger, lacked Earl Warren's leadership ability. Justice William Brennan, architect of some key Warren Court decisions, continued to find five votes for liberal rulings, even as Nixon's nominees joined the Court. While some criminal rights precedents were trimmed a bit, the overall thrust of the Court's work continued to be progressive, often bold. New limits were imposed on state death-penalty laws, and during the same period the Supreme Court began striking down state rules that discriminated against women. In the 1973 case of *Roe v. Wade*, the Court expanded on the Warren-era privacy right to grant constitutional protection to women seeking abortions and overturn state laws that prohibited them from doing so. Over the next dozen years, the Court fortified *Roe v. Wade* and expanded its protections, striking down a variety of state abortion regulations. As a result, the antiabortion movement grew in size and tenaciousness, once again making the Court the object of severe criticism.

The debate over race relations, meanwhile, was moving away from the issue of individual equality to questions of "group rights": to what degree could the courts or other arms of government order race-conscious remedies — such as school busing or "affirmative action" hiring — in order to make up for past discrimination? The Supreme Court imposed limits on these remedies, but resisted conservative demands that racial classifications be abandoned altogether in responding to bias. In 1978, in *Regents of the University of California v. Bakke*, an ambivalent Court ruled that racial "quotas" in public university admissions were invalid, but that some consideration of race was permissible. The next year, the Court said that private companies could adopt voluntary racial preference policies in hiring to address imbalances in certain categories of jobs. Under continual pressure from those who perceived affirmative action as reverse discrimination, the Court ultimately restricted government programs reserving a specific percentage of public contracts for minorities, saying that such special treatment would be allowed only when it was a "narrowly tailored" response to specific, provable past discrimination. The Court also put limits on cases from the 1970s that broadly interpreted federal civil rights statutes as they applied to the workplace. Despite these rulings, which provoked strong popular and political reactions, new federal legislation continued to be enacted that largely reversed conservative precedents and even expanded some of the remedies available for job bias.

In 1986 President Ronald Reagan elevated Justice William Rehnquist to replace retiring Chief Justice Burger. Rehnquist, a midwesterner transplanted to Arizona, had flourished in that state's hard-right Republican Party. He had joined the High Court in 1971, determined to redress what he saw as the Warren Court's liberal excesses. As an associate justice in the 1970s, he had dissented frequently from the Court's majority opinions, earning himself the nickname "the Lone Ranger" among some of his admirers. A more sophisticated legal mind and better writer than Burger, Rehnquist toned down his rhetoric somewhat when he moved into the chief justice's chair but did not abandon his basic point of view. As a result, the general direction of the Rehnquist Court has been unmistakably conservative. However, moderating political forces outside the Court and concern among some of Rehnquist's fellow justices about the institution's image and stability have weighed against a more dramatic conservative transformation.

Liberals, with the Democratic Party locked out of the White House during the 1980s, became alarmed at the explicit threat of the Rehnquist Court to Warren Court precedents. In 1987 resistance from the left doomed the nomination of the brilliant and markedly conservative Robert Bork. In his place, the more moderate Anthony Kennedy was eventually appointed. Kennedy's uneasiness over dramatic changes in precedent — reinforced by similar cautiousness on the part of Reagan appointee Sandra Day O'Connor and Bush appointee David Souter — has hindered the Rehnquist Court's efforts to undermine the landmarks of the Warren era. The 1992 election of Democrat Bill Clinton to the White House suspended, at least temporarily, the Republican program of trying to use the appointment power to remake the High Court.

If one area of controversy epitomized the state of the Supreme Court in the first half of the 1990s, it was abortion. By 1989 a clear majority of justices opposed the idea that the U.S. Constitution—specifically the Due Process Clause—guaranteed women the right to have an abortion despite state restrictions. But there were not five votes for overturning *Roe v. Wade*. Under continual pressure from the Reagan and Bush administrations — not to mention the "right-to-life" movement — in cases such as *Webster v. Reproductive Health Services* (1989) the Rehnquist Court reinterpreted *Roe* to make room for more aggressive state regulation of abortion procedures, but refused to completely overturn the 1973 ruling that had become a symbol of independence for many women. In 1992 a splintered five-justice majority further trimmed the abortion right but called for a truce in the fight over *Roe*. Rejecting sharply-worded dissents by the chief justice and his allies, the majority left *Roe* in place. The controlling opinion of the Court, authored jointly by Justices O'Connor, Kennedy and Souter, invoked the need for continuity in constitutional law and respect for the Supreme Court as an institution that operates above the ordinary political fray. *Roe v. Wade*, though not admired by most of the justices, was not to be discarded as finally as were *Plessy v. Ferguson*, the 1896 separate-but-equal case, and *Lochner v.*

New York, the 1905 exemplar of judicial defiance of economic regulation.

The Supreme Court of the 1990s is a fractured, at times unpredictable institution. Given the uncertainty of national politics and thus of future appointments, it would be foolish to try to predict precisely where the Court will go in coming years. But the benefit of an historical perspective allows a couple of observations about the Court today.

Perhaps most importantly, the Supreme Court of this era, or of any other, should not be evaluated exclusively in comparison with the still vivid experiences of the Warren Court. Contemporary analysis of the Court — on television, in newspapers, and even in many scholarly works — tends too often to assume that the Supreme Court's natural and appropriate role is to be in the vanguard in addressing questions of social injustice. Some commentators imply that anything less than such an activist role on the part of the Court bespeaks conservative extremism or even simple incompetence. This slant ignores the Court's history and the central fact that, as an institution, it has tended most often to respond to social, economic, and political developments, rather than initiate them.

The Supreme Court is best understood as reacting to what Oliver Wendell Holmes termed the "felt necessities" of the times. The Marshall Court, for example, helped establish the authority of the new national government — including that of the Court itself — and protected an emerging national economy from excessive state interference. The Taney Court further encouraged the growth of business while adjusting the balance of power more in favor of the states. In the late 19th century, the Court forged constitutional doctrines to benefit industrialization. The twentieth-century Court, in the name of protecting property rights, at first resisted progressive management of economic relations. But in the face of a depression and an ascendant liberalism in the country, the Court eventually changed its course. While making way for far-reaching government economic regulation, the Court became increasingly concerned about official intrusions on personal liberties. Several decades spent creating and expanding protections for those liberties have ended in the current period, one of conservative modification of — and ambivalence toward — the liberal agenda of the mid-1950s through the mid-1980s.

The purpose of this book is to provide a sense of the Supreme Court's shifting priorities and its role in striving to maintain what Justice Robert Jackson called "the great system of balances upon which our free government is based": the balances between the branches of the federal government, between the federal government and the states, and between official authority and the rights of the individual.

The Jay Court 1790-1795

BACKGROUND

A NEW CONSTITUTION

The Articles of Confederation, creating the political entity called the United States of America, were drawn up by the Continental Congress in 1777 and ratified by the states in 1781. However, the Articles were found to be inadequate to govern the complex nation that was emerging in the wake of the Revolutionary War. The Articles had reserved *sovereignty to the individual states, impeding both political consensus and foreign relations. Furthermore, they concentrated all governmen-tal power in a single body, a one-house Congress; there was no national executive or judiciary, and the only federal courts were those set up to adjudicate piracy cases and appeals of decisions regarding vessels taken as prizes in time of war.

To remedy the situation, the Confederation Congress called for a constitutional convention, to take place in Philadelphia during the spring and summer of 1787. From the outset, the framers of the new constitution agreed that their foundation document must be based on the concept of *separation of powers. Accordingly, they adopted the so-called Virginia Plan, drafted by James Madison, which specifically provided "[t]hat a national govern-ment ought to be established consisting of a supreme legislative, judiciary and executive."

The Virginia Plan envisioned a legislative branch composed of two houses, with voting power in both *apportioned among the states according to their respective populations. Delegates from larger, more populous states tended to favor the plan, while delegates from smaller states, not surprisingly, did not. William Paterson (later Justice Paterson) of New Jersey offered an alternate plan that was little more than a revision of the Articles of Confederation, and his New Jersey Plan was voted down. A solution was found in the Connecticut Compromise, which proposed that voting be proportional according to popu-lation in one house and equal in the other. Further debate concerning the right of southern states to include slaves in their population counts for pur-poses of representation resulted in another com-promise, whereby each slave would count as three-fifths of a person.

MEMBERS Of the Court 1790–1795

(In Order of Seniority)

John Jay (Chief Justice)	(1789-1795)
John Rutledge (resigned)	(1790-1791)
William Cushing	(1790-1795)
James Wilson	(1789-1795)
John Blair Jr.	(1790-1795)
James Iredell	(1790-1795)
Thomas Johnson (replaced John Rutledge; resigned)	(1791-1793)
William Paterson (replaced Thomas Johnson)	(1793-1795)

An asterisk (*) before a word or phrase indicates that a definition will be found in the glossary at the end of this volume.

The Convention went on to adopt the broad outlines of Madison's original proposal, but when it came time to finalize the new document, delegates fearful of the power of the new centralized government and proponents of *states' rights rallied behind George Mason and his demand for a bill of rights. Mason was joined by his fellow Virginian, Edmund Randolph, and Elbridge Gerry of Massachusetts in refusing to sign.

Before going into effect, the constitution had to be ratified by special conventions elected for this purpose by the people of each state. In the debate surrounding ratification, Constitutional supporters, who called themselves Federalists, found articulate spokesmen in James Madison, Alexander Hamilton, and John Jay, who published a series of explanatory essays that came to be known as *The Federalist Papers*. Those opposing the Constitution were tagged Anti-Federalists. The Anti-Federalists lacked any real alternative to the Constitution, but they did manage to secure a commitment for the addition of a bill of rights. In September 1787 all 12 state delegations at the Convention (Rhode Island did not send a delegation) approved the Constitution, and Congress fowarded it to the states for ratification. Ratification by the requisite nine states was finally achieved after Congress submitted 12 proposed amendments to the states in September 1789. Two of the 12 failed. The tenth, by stating that those powers not enumerated by the Constitution are retained by the states and by the people, made explicit the balance between national government and the states in the new federation.

CREATING A FEDERAL JUDICIARY

Article III of the Constitution created a Supreme Court with both *original and *appellate jurisdiction over legal controversies. It also gave Congress the power to create inferior federal courts. The national judiciary was thus modeled on colonial and state courts, both of which had employed a comparable system of inferior and superior courts.

Although the *jurisdiction of the Supreme Court was made subject to "Exceptions" and "Regulations" that Congress might choose to

make, the framers of the Constitution, led by Oliver Ellsworth (who would become the Court's third chief justice), concentrated on making the federal courts independent. The Constitution gave the president power to appoint federal judges, but his choices were subject to confirmation by the Senate. Similarly, federal judges were not subject to arbitrary removal; they would serve indefinitely "during good Behavior," and they could not have their pay reduced. The framers were also concerned that the federal judiciary be strong. Mindful of such assaults on judicial authority as Shays's Rebellion of 1786-1787—which sought to aid debtors by forcibly closing courts that foreclosed on their property—the Constitution invested federal courts with the judicial power of the nation.

Little of the debate at the Convention, however, focused on the judiciary, and the Constitution is itself surprisingly short on detail. The work of fleshing out the skeletal structure of Article III was left to the First Congress. With the Judiciary Act of 1789, authored largely by Oliver Ellsworth and William Paterson (also to become a Supreme Court justice), the federal court system took shape. The Supreme Court would have six justices and dominate a three-tiered structure. A district court was established in each state, and the nation as a whole was divided into three *circuits, each presided over by two Supreme Court justices and one district court judge.

CIRCUIT RIDING

*Circuit riding was unquestionably the most onerous duty imposed on the justices by the first judiciary act, requiring each of them to travel one of the three circuits twice every year. Justices undertook this duty at some risk to their well-being; traveling the Southern Circuit, for instance, required them to cover 1,800 miles over poor or nonexistent roads.

The circuit riding requirement was one of the main impediments to filling vacancies on the Court, and it was so unpopular among sitting justices that they constantly lobbied for its repeal. Congress ignored their entreaties, however, convinced that the presence of judges on their circuits

Royal Exchange Building, New York City, where the Supreme Court first convened in 1790

was one of the most effective means of impressing the weight of federal authority directly on the people. Congress abolished the practice in 1801, but only temporarily; the next year circuit riding was restored. The justices were not permanently relieved of this responsibility until after the Civil War. The Judiciary Act of 1869 first established a separate circuit court judiciary, but the justices retained some circuit duties until the 1891 Judiciary Act was passed. Congress finally declared an official end to circuit riding in 1911.

THE QUESTION OF JURISDICTION

Article III of the Constitution states that "[t]he judicial Power [of the United States] shall extend to all Cases… arising under this Constitution, the Laws of the United States, and Treaties," and to controversies "between Citizens of different States… and between… the Citizens [of a State], and foreign… Citizens or Subjects." However, with the Judiciary Act of 1789, Congress adopted restrictions to this sweeping language that helped to quell Anti-Federalist concerns that federal courts would usurp state court authority.

Section 25 of the 1789 Judiciary Act restricted federal jurisdiction over cases involving the Constitution and the laws and treaties of the United States (*federal question cases). Only after the highest court of a state had rendered a final decision could such cases be appealed to a federal court. Furthermore, in cases involving citizens of different states (*diversity cases) and in cases between United States citizens and foreign citizens (*alienage cases), the jurisdiction of federal courts was made concurrent with that of state courts; that is, plaintiffs had their choice of a federal or a state court in which to air their grievances. Ordinary civil and criminal matters remained under state jurisdiction.

THE SUPREME COURT CONVENES

The Judiciary Act of 1789 also stipulated that the Supreme Court would consist of a chief justice and five associate justices who were to meet twice yearly, once in February and once in August. On February 1, 1790, the date of the Court's opening session, only three of the five justices who had been confirmed (James Iredell's confirmation would not come until February 10 that year) were present. For lack of a designated courthouse, they met in the Royal Exchange Building in New York City, which was the nation's capi-

JUDICIAL BIOGRAPHY
John Jay

PERSONAL DATA
Born: December 12, 1745, in New York, New York
Parents: Peter Jay, Mary Van Cortlandt Jay
Higher Education: King's College, now Columbia University (undergraduate degree, 1764)
Bar Admission: New York, 1768
Political Party: Federalist
Marriage: April 28, 1774, to Sarah Van Brugh Livingston, who bore Jay two sons and five daughters, and who died in 1802
Died: May 17, 1829, in Bedford, Westchester County, New York
Buried: Jay family churchyard, Rye, New York

PROFESSIONAL CAREER
Occupations: Lawyer, 1768-1773; Politician, 1773-1777, 1778-1779, 1795-1801; Diplomat, 1774, 1779-1789, 1794-1795; Serviceman, 1776-1778; Judge, 1777-1778, 1789-1795
Official Positions: Secretary, Royal Boundary Commission, 1773; Member, New York Committee of Correspondence with Britain, 1774; Delegate, Continental Congress, 1774, 1775, 1777; Delegate, New York Provincial Congress, 1776-1777; Chief Justice, New York State, 1777-1778; President, Continental Congress, 1778-1779; Minister Plenipotentiary to Spain, 1779; Joint Commissioner for what became the Treaty of Paris, 1782-1783; Secretary for Foreign Affairs, 1784-1789; Chief Justice, United States Supreme Court, 1789-1795; United States Envoy to Great Britain, 1794-1795; Governor, New York State, 1795-1801; President, American Bible Society, 1821

SUPREME COURT SERVICE
Nominated: September 24, 1789
Nominated By: George Washington
Confirmed: September 26, 1789
Confirmation Vote: Voice vote
Oath Taken: October 19, 1789
Significant Opinions: *Chisholm v. Georgia.* (1793); *Glass v. The Sloop Betsy* (1794)
Left Court: Resigned June 29, 1795
Length of Service: 5 years, 8 months, 10 days
Replacement: Acting Chief Justice John Rutledge

Some years later, without consulting Jay, President John Adams nominated him for a second term as chief justice. The Senate confirmed the nomination on December 19, 1800, but Jay formally declined the position on January 2, 1801, without having taken up any of its duties.

---

tal. The next day, Chief Justice John Jay and Associate Justices James Wilson and William Cushing were joined by Associate Justice John Blair, and the Court now had a *quorum. As no cases were before them, the justices spent their time on organizational matters and adjourned on February 10. The second term lasted from August 2 to August 3, 1790.

The next year, the Court, along with the rest of the government, moved to the new capital, Philadelphia, where it shared quarters in City Hall. No cases were brought before the Court until 1793. Justice Rutledge, never having attended a Court session, resigned in March 1791 to become a state judge. Thomas Johnson took Rutledge's place September 19, 1791, but Johnson served only 16 months before resigning for reasons of poor health, exacerbated by the rigors of circuit riding. He was succeeded in March 1793 by William Paterson.

JOHN JAY AS DIPLOMAT

Many points of friction remained between Britain and her former North American colonies even

John Jay

after the signing of the Treaty of Paris in 1783, which formally concluded the Revolutionary War. For instance, Britain prohibited Americans from engaging in the lucrative West Indian trade. Americans attempted to circumvent this prohibition by trading with French colonies in the West Indies during hostilities between France and England in 1793-1794. Britain retaliated by seizing American vessels on the high seas. Also, in blatant violation of the 1783 peace treaty, the British continued to maintain garrisons in American territory along the Great Lakes, even supplying Indians with guns and ammunition during the uprisings of the early 1790s. For its part, Britain maintained that the United States violated the terms of the peace treaty, most egregiously in the failure of many Americans (the majority of them southern planters) to pay prewar debts owed Britons.

Fearful of a fresh Anglo-American conflict, President George Washington sent Chief Justice John Jay to London to negotiate a new treaty with the British. Unfortunately, Jay arrived at an inopportune time, when Britain was winning its war with France and dominating the seas.

Although he was able to secure Britain's agreement to surrender its northwest posts and to grant limited trading privileges in India and the West Indies, Jay in return had to agree to the creation of an international commission to oversee repayment of American debts.

The short-term domestic political impact of the Jay Treaty, signed in November 1794, was enormous. Southerners observed that most of Britain's concessions favored the North, while they themselves were the hardest hit by America's agreement to see that its citizens paid off their British debtors. The nation rapidly became polarized into two political factions, as the South vocally declared its support for the Anti-Federalists, soon to be called Republicans.

JAY'S EARLY LIFE

John Jay was the descendant of two prominent colonial families, the sixth son and eighth child of Peter Jay, a wealthy merchant of French Huguenot ancestry, and Mary Jay, the daughter of one of New York's most powerful families, the Dutch Van Cortlandts. Jay received his early education from his mother, who tutored him in French and Latin, and from the French Huguenot Church in New Rochelle, New York, where he boarded for three years. At the age of 14, Jay entered King's College, which later became Columbia University. Some evidence of his later revolutionary spirit is suggested by an episode that occurred shortly before he graduated in 1764, when Jay was temporarily suspended for refusing to testify against fellow students charged with destroying collège property.

Jay had decided upon a career in law, and following the custom of his day, he apprenticed himself to the prominent attorney Benjamin Kissim for four years before being admitted to practice in New York State in 1768. While continuing his association with Kissim, Jay formed a partnership with Robert R. Livingston and quickly gained success in the private practice of law.

On April 28, 1774, at Liberty Hall in Elizabeth, New Jersey, Jay married Sarah Van Brugh Livingston. William Livingston, the bride's father, was to become governor of New Jersey during the Revolution. John and Sarah Jay would have seven children together.

JAY'S PUBLIC LIFE

Reports of Jay's wedding referred to him as an eminent barrister. The reference doubtless pertained to his achievements as a lawyer, but it also had something to do with the fact that at the early age of 28, he had already entered public service, acting as secretary of a royal commission arbitrating a boundary dispute between New York and New Jersey. The year of his marriage, he also served as a member of the New York Committee of Correspondence, whose job it was to maintain diplomatic relations with England.

As the American colonies moved toward independence from the mother country in the period from 1774 to 1776, Jay abandoned not only his private law practice, but also his hope for a gradual break with England. In 1774 and 1775 he was elected a New York delegate to the First and Second Continental Congresses, held in Philadelphia. He was not among the signers of the Declaration of Independence in 1776 because he had returned to serve in the New York Provincial Congress, where he helped draft his state's constitution. Jay did, however, actively work for the adoption of the Declaration of Independence. Shortly after his return to Philadelphia in December 1778, he was elected president of the Continental Congress.

The negotiating experience Jay had acquired while serving on the boundary commission was put to the test in 1779, when Congress appointed him Minister Plenipotentiary to Spain, where his mission was to obtain official recognition and monetary support for the United States. Jay had only modest success in persuading the Spanish to continue their secret support of the new nation, but Congress trusted his diplomatic skills, and in the spring of 1782, he was sent to assist John Adams and Benjamin Franklin in formulating the terms of the Treaty of Paris, which officially ended the Revolutionary War the following year. Jay's insistence that England recognize the "United States," rather than its former colonies, and his willingness to withdraw Congress's demand that England relinquish Canada, greatly contributed to the successful completion of the treaty. In recognition of his services, Jay was named secretary of foreign affairs (for the Confederation) upon his return in 1784, a post he retained until 1789.

Jay's dealings with foreign powers strengthened his belief in his country's need for a strong central government and, correspondingly, for a federal constitution. After the Constitutional Convention in 1787, he joined with Alexander Hamilton and James Madison to produce *The Federalist Papers*, which sought to persuade the American people to elect delegates who would support the proposed federal Constitution at state ratification conventions. Poor health, which had dogged Jay since childhood, permitted him to contribute only five essays to the political treatise, but his persuasiveness helped bring New York into the union.

JAY AS CHIEF JUSTICE

After Jay had refused George Washington's initial offer of the post of secretary of state, Washington nominated him as the first chief justice of the Supreme Court on September 24, 1789, the same day the president signed into law the judiciary act establishing the Court. The Senate confirmed Jay two days later.

The Court did not convene until February 1, 1790, and it stayed in session only ten days. Jay, and all of his associate justices, devoted the bulk of their time to serving on lower federal circuit courts, as little business came before the Supreme Court in its early years. Some of Jay's most significant contributions to American jurisprudence came about as a consequence of his circuit duties. In *Hayburn's Case* (1791), Jay upheld the constitutionally mandated *separation of powers by rejecting an act of Congress that required Supreme Court justices sitting in circuit court to rule on invalid pension claims. The same year, in a case that was not officially recorded, Jay and his colleagues, sitting in circuit court in Connecticut, upheld the supremacy of federal treaties over state legislation. Jay's dissent in a circuit court decision in Virginia in the 1796 case of *Ware v. Hylton* took the same attitude towards the supremacy of the Treaty of Paris over state law, a point of view later adopted by the Ellsworth Court when the case went up on appeal. State compliance with federal law was also upheld in *Champion and Dickason v. Casey* (1792), in which Jay and his fellow judges, in circuit court in Rhode Island, invalidated a state law which would have violated the constitutional prohibition against impairing the power of contractual obligations.

The first significant case to come before the Jay Court was *Chisholm v. Georgia* (1793), in which the issue was whether a state can be sued by *citizens of another state. Jay's opinion, and that of every member of the Court but one, was that the Constitution permitted such a suit. The state of Georgia disagreed with the Court's dismissal of its *sovereign immunity to suit, however, and led a campaign for the Eleventh Amendment, restricting the power of federal courts to hear suits against states brought by citizens of other states. Its adoption overturned *Chisholm*. Jay had more lasting success with *Glass v. The Sloop Betsy* (1794), in which he led a unanimous Court in ruling that U.S. federal courts, not French *admiralty courts, had *jurisdiction over claims concerning captured vessels brought into American ports by French ships. With this ruling, Jay helped the Court, and his country, gain respect.

The same year, while still sitting as chief justice, Jay traveled to England at the request of President Washington to negotiate a settlement of trade disputes and other differences that had arisen in the wake of the Treaty of Paris. The resulting agreement, which came to be known as the Jay Treaty, provided that the British would withdraw their soldiers from their remaining North American garrisons, but maintained restrictions on American trade with British colonies in the West Indies. Although highly controversial, the Jay Treaty was ratified by the Senate in 1795 and possibly prevented another war with England. It also marked the end of Jay's tenure on the Supreme Court.

In 1792 Jay had permitted his name to be submitted as the Federalist candidate for governor of New York; however, because of his position as chief justice, he declined to participate actively in the election. On returning from England in 1795, he discovered that not only had he been nominated once again for governor of his home state, this time he had won. Jay tendered his resignation as chief justice to President Washington in June 1795.

Jay served as governor of New York for two three-year terms, distinguishing himself by revising the New York penal code, building a model penitentiary, and supporting and signing into law anti-slavery legislation. When Oliver Ellsworth resigned as chief justice in 1800, John Adams named Jay to succeed him, and the Senate confirmed the nomination the next day. Jay declined to resume his old post, however, in part because the Federalists' power was waning. In the presidential election of 1800, Jay had received electoral votes from four states, but the office went to Thomas Jefferson, the Republican leader.

In 1801 Jay retired from public view, spending the remainder of his long life as a gentleman farmer at his estate in Bedford, New York. His only public pronouncements after his wife's death in 1802 concerned his opposition to the War of 1812 and his condemnation of slavery, voiced in 1819 at the time of the Missouri Compromise. Jay was active in the Episcopal Church and helped establish the American Bible Society, which he served as president in 1821. The last survivor of the First Continental Congress, Jay died on May 17, 1829, at the age of 83.

ASSOCIATE JUSTICES

For a biography of Associate, then Acting Chief Justice **John Rutledge,** see entry under **THE RUTLEDGE COURT.**

WILLIAM CUSHING

PERSONAL DATA
Born: March 1, 1732, in Scituate, Massachusetts
Parents: John Cushing, Mary Cotton Cushing
Higher Education: Harvard College (B.A., 1751)
Bar Admission: Massachusetts, 1755
Political Party: Federalist

Marriage: 1774 to Hannah Phillips, who died in 1834
Died: September 13, 1810, in Scituate
Buried: Family graveyard, Scituate

PROFESSIONAL CAREER

Occupations: Educator, 1751-1752; Lawyer, 1755-1772; Judge, 1760-1761, 1772-1810; Politician, 1776, 1779, 1788
Official Positions: Justice of the Peace and Judge of Probates, Lincoln County, Massachusetts (then a district of Maine), 1760-1761; Associate Justice, Superior Court of Massachusetts Bay Province, 1772-1775; Senior Associate Justice, Superior Court of the Commonwealth of Massachusetts, 1775-1777; Chief Justice, Superior Court of the Commonwealth of Massachusetts, 1777-1780; Member, Massachusetts Constitutional Convention, 1779; Chief Justice, Massachusetts Supreme Judicial Court, 1780-1789; Vice President, Massachusetts convention to ratify the federal constitution, 1788; Delegate, Electoral College, 1788; Associate Justice, United States Supreme Court, 1790-1810

SUPREME COURT SERVICE

Nominated: September 24, 1789
Nominated By: George Washington
Confirmed: September 26, 1789
Confirmation Vote: Voice vote
Oath Taken: February 2, 1790
Significant Opinions: *Chisholm v. Georgia* (1793); *Ware v. Hylton* (1796); *Calder v. Bull* (1798); *Fowler v. Lindsay* (1799)
Left Court: Died September 13, 1810
Length of Service: 20 years, 7 months, 11 days
Replacement: Joseph Story

On January 26, 1796, Washington nominated William Cushing to replace John Rutledge as chief justice after the Senate refused to confirm Rutledge, who had been serving in an acting capacity. The Senate confirmed Cushing's nomination to the post the next day, but Cushing declined, pleading age and ill health. He nonetheless remained on the bench as an associate justice.

William Cushing was born in Scituate, Massachusetts, on March 1, 1732, of an old and distinguished colonial family. Both his father and his paternal grandfather had served in the government of the Massachusetts Bay Province, and

his mother was a descendant of the famous Puritan minister John Cotton. After graduating from Harvard College in 1751, Cushing taught for a year in Roxbury, Massachusetts, then clerked in the offices of a prominent Boston lawyer, Jeremiah Gridley, becoming a member of the bar three years later. In 1760, unable to make a living in Massachusetts, Cushing moved to the frontier settlement of Pownalborough (now Dresden, Maine) where, as the only lawyer in newly created Lincoln County, he was appointed both justice of the peace and registrar of probates.

Cushing did not, however, know any real financial or professional success until 1772, when he was appointed to succeed his father as judge of the Massachusetts Bay Province Superior Court upon the elder Cushing's retirement. In 1774 Cushing was well enough established to marry Hannah Phillips of Middletown, Connecticut.

In 1775 Cushing became the only judge appointed by the previous colonial government to be granted a seat on the reorganized Superior Court of the new Commonwealth of Massachusetts. He served as an associate justice there until he succeeded John Adams as the court's chief justice in 1777, a post he held until 1780. During this same period he was active in revolutionary politics; in 1776 he drafted the resolutions of Scituate, which instructed Massachusetts delegates to the Continental Congress to vote in favor of independence. He also helped draft the Massachusetts state constitution in 1779.

In 1780 Cushing became chief justice of the Massachusetts Supreme Judicial Court where, in 1783, he presided over the abolition of slavery in the Commonwealth and, in 1787, tried the leaders of Shays's Rebellion. The next year, Cushing served as vice president of the Massachusetts convention to ratify the federal Constitution and was a powerful advocate of a strong federal government, a role President Washington clearly remembered when making Cushing one of his first nominees to the United States Supreme Court.

At the age of 57, Cushing was the oldest appointee to the Jay Court, yet when he died in 1810, he had served longest of all of Washington's original appointees. During his tenure on the Court he maintained a relatively conservative judicial posture, writing only 19 opinions.

JAMES WILSON

PERSONAL DATA

Born: September 14, 1742, in Caskardy, Fifeshire, Scotland
Parents: William Wilson, Alison Lansdale Wilson
Higher Education: University of St. Andrews, 1756-1760; University of Glasgow, ca. 1760-1763; University of Edinburgh, 1763-1765
Bar Admission: Pennsylvania, 1767
Political Party: Federalist
Marriages: November 5, 1771, to Rachel Bird, who bore Wilson six children, and who died in 1786; September 19, 1793, to Hanna Gray, who bore Wilson one son, who died in infancy
Died: August 21, 1798, in Edenton, North Carolina
Buried: Originally Hayes Plantation, Edenton; reburied November 1906 in Christ Church, Philadelphia, Pennsylvania

PROFESSIONAL CAREER

Occupations: Educator, 1762-1763, 1766; Lawyer, 1767-1789; Politician, 1775-1789; Businessman, 1777-1787; Judge, 1789-1798
Official Positions: Chairman, Pennsylvania Committee of Correspondence with Britain, 1774; Delegate, Pennsylvania Provincial Congress, 1774; Delegate, Second Continental Congress, 1775-1776; Member, Committee of Detail, Constitutional Convention, 1787; Member, Pennsylvania convention to ratify the federal Constitution, 1787; Associate Justice, United States Supreme Court, 1789-1798

SUPREME COURT SERVICE

Nominated: September 24, 1789
Nominated By: George Washington
Confirmed: September 26, 1789
Confirmation Vote: Voice vote
Oath Taken: October 5, 1789
Significant Opinion: *Chisholm v. Georgia* (1793)
Left Court: Died August 21, 1798
Length of Service: 8 years, 10 months, 16 days
Replacement: Bushrod Washington

Born in the Scottish lowlands on September 14, 1742, James Wilson came from a family of poor Calvinist farmers. His parents were determined that he study for the ministry, and he entered divinity school at St. Andrews University, only to be forced, when his father died, to leave for financial reasons prior to graduation. Wilson worked as a private tutor, then studied accounting, again without taking a degree. In 1765, at the age of 23, he emigrated to America.

Settling in Philadelphia, Wilson first took a tutor's position at the College of Pennsylvania in 1766, then shortly thereafter began to read law in the offices of John Dickinson. Admitted to the bar in 1767, Wilson quickly became the leading attorney in central Pennsylvania. He also began to pursue business opportunities, chiefly in real estate.

Like many of his contemporaries, Wilson used his status as a lawyer as a vehicle for political advancement. He began his quest for public recognition with the pamphlet *Considerations on the Nature and Extent of the Legislative Authority of the British Parliament*, which he wrote in 1768 and published in 1774. In his writings, and in his public pronouncements, Wilson identified himself with the American revolutionaries' belief that the British Parliament should have no say in American affairs. In 1775 Pennsylvania elected him a delegate to the Second Continental Congress, where he signed the Declaration of Independence. In 1787 he was again elected to represent his adopted state's interests at the Constitutional Convention, becoming one of only six Americans whose names grace both of the nation's most important foundational documents. Wilson believed strongly in principles of popular *sovereignty and democracy, advocating that the Constitution, like the institutions of the presidency and Congress, be approved by popularly elected conventions. When the Constitution came before Pennsylvania's ratification convention, he fought for and helped achieve a Federalist victory.

As one of the foremost theoreticians and framers of the Constitution, Wilson had every reason to hope for public office. He knew, however, that his highly visible personal investments—

which were sometimes tainted by conflicts of interest and often debt-producing—probably made him unelectable. He offered himself to Washington as chief justice. The president passed him over for that post in 1789 and again in 1796, but did nominate him as an associate justice.

Wilson served almost nine years as an associate justice, and during most of that time he continued to speculate in land. Although he is acknowledged as a brilliant legal theoretician, his record on the bench is fairly undistinguished, with the notable exception of his opinion in *Chisholm v. Georgia* (1793), where he elaborated on his philosophy of popular sovereignty. In the 1790s Wilson's investments began to fail. He was frequently pursued by creditors while riding *circuit duty and was even jailed because of his debts. In 1798, amid rumors of *impeachment, he sought refuge with fellow justice James Iredell in Edenton, North Carolina, where at the age of 55 he died at an inn adjacent to the Edenton Court House.

JOHN BLAIR JR.

PERSONAL DATA
Born: 1732 in Williamsburg, Virginia
Parents: John Blair, Mary Munro Blair
Higher Education: College of William and Mary (undergraduate degree with honors, 1754); Middle Temple, London, England, 1755-1756
Bar Admission: Virginia, 1756
Political Party: Federalist
Marriage: 1756 to Jean Balfour, who died November 22, 1792
Died: August 31, 1800, in Williamsburg
Buried: Bruton Parish churchyard, Williamsburg

PROFESSIONAL CAREER
Occupations: Lawyer, 1756-1766; Politician, 1766-1777, 1786-1787; Judge, 1777-1795
Official Positions: Member, Virginia House of Burgesses, 1766-1769; Clerk, Virginia Governor's Council, 1770-1775; Delegate, Virginia Constitutional Convention, 1776; Member, Virginia Privy Council, 1776-1777; Judge, Virginia General Court, 1777-1778; Chief Justice, Virginia General Court, 1779; Judge, Virginia Court of Appeals, 1779-1789; Chancellor, Virginia High Court of Chancery, 1780-1789; Delegate, Constitutional Convention, 1786-1787; Associate Justice, United States Supreme Court, 1789-1795

SUPREME COURT SERVICE
Nominated: September 24, 1789
Nominated By: George Washington
Confirmed: September 26, 1789
Confirmation Vote: Voice vote
Oath Taken: February 2, 1790
Significant Opinions: None
Left Court: Resigned October 25, 1795
Length of Service: 5 years, 8 months, 23 days
Replacement: Samuel Chase

John Blair Jr. was born in 1732 in Williamsburg, Virginia, into a wealthy and prominent family. His father, a member of the Virginia House of Burgesses and the governor's counsel, once served as acting governor of the state. In addition to a tradition of public service, the family had a strong commitment to education. Blair graduated with honors from the College of William and Mary in 1754, and studied law at the Middle Temple in London from 1755 to 1756.

Upon his return, Blair practiced law before the General Court of Virginia for a decade. In 1766 he began his public career by assuming a seat in the Virginia House of Burgesses where, as a political conservative, he opposed Patrick Henry's resolutions against the Stamp Act, under which Britain unilaterally imposed taxes on its North American colonies. Gradually, however, Blair came to support the revolutionary cause. In 1777 the state legislature elected him a judge in the General Court, of which he became chief justice two years later. When the state's first Court of Appeals was organized in 1779, Blair also became a member of that bench, from which he issued what is arguably his most influential decision. In *Commonwealth of Virginia v. Canon* (1782), he led the state court in ruling that it had the power to invalidate an unconstitutional Virginia statute, setting a crucial precedent for the doctrine of *judicial review, later embodied in the famous Supreme Court opinion, *Marbury v. Madison* (1803).

Blair was the last of George Washington's initial nominees for associate justice actually to serve on the court. He was selected not so much for his public service or judicial acumen, but because he was a personal friend of the president and was a resident of the new nation's largest and most influential state, which expected to be represented on the Court. Blair served on the Court for almost six years, during which service he seemed to suffer more than his fellow justices from the rigors of *circuit riding, particularily after his wife died in 1792. The August 1795 Supreme Court term was his last.

JAMES IREDELL

PERSONAL DATA

Born: October 5, 1751, in Lewes, England
Parents: Francis Iredell, Margaret McCulloh Iredell
Higher Education: None
Bar Admission: North Carolina, 1770
Political Party: Federalist
Marriage: July 18, 1773, to Hannah Johnston, who bore Iredell three children
Died: October 20, 1799, in Edenton, North Carolina
Buried: Governor Samuel Johnston's private cemetery, Hayes Plantation, North Carolina

PROFESSIONAL CAREER

Occupations: Government Official, 1768-1776; Lawyer, 1770-1790; Judge, 1777-1778, 1790-1799; Politician, 1779-1781, 1787-1788
Official Positions: Comptroller of Customs, Edenton, North Carolina, 1768-1774; Collector of Customs, Port of Edenton, North Carolina, 1774-1776; Judge, Superior Court of North Carolina, 1777-1778; Attorney General, North Carolina, 1779-1781; Member, Governor's Council of North Carolina, 1787; Delegate, North Carolina convention to ratify the federal Constitution, 1788; Associate Justice, United States Supreme Court, 1790-1799

SUPREME COURT SERVICE

Nominated: February 8, 1790
Nominated By: George Washington
Confirmed: February 10, 1790
Confirmation Vote: Voice vote
Oath Taken: May 12, 1790

Significant Opinion: *Chisholm v. Georgia* (1793)
Left Court: Died October 20, 1799
Length of Service: 9 years, 5 months, 8 days
Replacement: Alfred Moore

President George Washington nominated his old friend Robert Hanson Harrison as an associate justice on September 24, 1789. Harrison, who had been chief judge of the General Court of Maryland, was confirmed by the Senate two days later, but he declined because of poor health. At Washington's urging, Harrison reconsidered and was on his way to New York City to accept when a sudden illness caused him to cancel his trip and any plans of serving on the Supreme Court. In his place, Washington chose James Iredell.

James Iredell was born on October 5, 1751, in Lewes, England, one of two members of the original Supreme Court to have been born in the British Isles. After his father died, Iredell, then 17, sailed to Edenton, North Carolina, to assume the post of comptroller of His Majesty's Customs, a position purchased for him by his mother's wealthy relatives. While he performed his duties, he also studied law under Samuel Johnston, whose sister he married in 1773, three years after he began practicing law.

Although Iredell continued to serve the Crown from 1774 to 1776 as collector of customs for the Port of Edenton, he embraced the patriot cause. His first service to the revolutionary movement was to help revise North Carolina law to conform to the state's new independent status. In recognition of this service, North Carolina named Iredell one of three superior court judges in 1777. Within a year, however, Iredell tired of the *circuit riding duties that were a part of the job and resigned. Shortly thereafter, however, he was appointed state attorney general, a post he held until 1781, when he resumed the private practice of law.

In 1787 Iredell went back into public service, first as a member of the North Carolina Governor's Council, then, more significantly, by publishing under the name "Marcus" a pamphlet supporting the new federal Constitution and answering George Mason's widely publicized objections to it. This pamphleteering, together with his role as Federalist floor leader at the North

Carolina convention to ratify the Constitution, brought him to the attention of President Washington. When Robert Hanson Harrison, one of Washington's original nominees for associate justice, was unable to accept the post, the president named Iredell in his stead.

At the age of 38, Iredell was the youngest member of the Jay Court. As its newest member, he was required to deliver his opinion first when in 1793 the Court decided its first significant case, *Chisholm v. Georgia.* Iredell led with a dissent, arguing that under *common law principles a state court could not be sued by a citizen of another state. His argument did not carry the day, but Iredell was later vindicated when Congress overruled *Chisholm* by enacting the Eleventh Amendment.

Iredell served on the Court for nine years, during which he rode the Southern Circuit five times. It was on the last of these journeys that he died, at the age of 48, at his home in Edenton.

THOMAS JOHNSON

PERSONAL DATA

Born: November 4, 1732, in Calvert County, Maryland

Parents: Thomas Johnson, Dorcas Sedgwick Johnson

Higher Education: None

Bar Admission: Maryland, 1760

Political Party: Federalist

Marriage: February 16, 1766, to Ann Jennings, who bore Johnson three boys and five girls, and who died in 1794.

Died: October 26, 1819, in Frederick, Maryland

Buried: Mount Olivet Cemetery, Frederick

PROFESSIONAL CAREER

Occupations: Lawyer, 1760-1776; Serviceman, 1776-1777; Politician, 1762, 1774-1780, 1786-1788; Businessman, 1780-1785; Judge, 1790-1793; Public Servant, 1791-1794

Official Positions: Delegate, Maryland Provincial Assembly, 1762; Delegate, Annapolis Convention, 1774; Member, Continental Congress, 1774-1777; Delegate, first Maryland constitutional convention, 1776; First Brigadier General, Maryland Militia,

1776-1777; Governor of Maryland, 1777-1779; Member, Maryland House of Delegates, 1780, 1786, 1787; Delegate, Maryland convention to ratify the federal Constitution, 1788; Chief Judge, General Court of Maryland, 1790-1791; Chairman, Board of Commissioners of the Federal City (Washington, D.C.), 1790-1791; Associate Justice, United States Supreme Court, 1791-1793; Member, Board of Commissioners of the Federal City, 1791-1794

SUPREME COURT SERVICE

Appointed: August 5, 1791 (recess appointment)

Appointed By: George Washington

Oath Taken: September 19, 1791

Nominated: October 31, 1791

Confirmed: November 7, 1791

Confirmation Vote: Voice vote

Oath Retaken: August 6, 1792

Replaced: John Rutledge

Significant Opinion: *Georgia v. Brailsford* (1792)

Left Court: Resigned January 16, 1793

Length of Service: 1 year, 3 months, 28 days

Replacement: William Paterson

Born of an old Puritan family on November 4, 1732, in Calvert County, Maryland, Thomas Johnson was first educated at home. He clerked at the Maryland Provincial Court and read law with attorney Stephen Bordley before being admitted to practice in 1760. He began his public career at the age of 29, when he was elected to the provincial assembly. He emerged as a force in national politics in 1774 when, as a member of the First Continental Congress, he helped draft a petition of grievances against George III. At the Second Continental Congress, at which he again served as a delegate from Maryland, it was he who nominated his old friend George Washington to be commander in chief of the Continental army.

Johnson himself served as the first brigadier general of Maryland's militia during the Revolution. Starting in 1777, he served three consecutive three-year terms as governor of Maryland, a post that allowed him to play a crucial part in keeping General Washington supplied with troops and equipment.

After the Treaty of Paris ended the war in 1783,

Johnson and Washington entered into a business partnership called the Potomac Company, whose aim was to increase river trade. Johnson continued to serve as a state legislator, and he refused Washington's offer of a federal judgeship when the new government was organized. Instead, Johnson assumed the role of chief judge of the General Court of Maryland, where he began his long involvement in the planning of the nation's new capital in the federal District of Columbia.

When John Rutledge resigned from the Supreme Court in mid-1791, Washington temporarily appointed Johnson as Rutledge's replacement. When Congress reconvened in the autumn, it confirmed the president's recess appointment. Johnson's service as an associate justice was brief, and his contribution to the Court was minimal, as he wrote only one opinion (as the most junior justice, his opinion was the first to appear in the Court's first recorded case, *Georgia v. Brailsford* [1792]). Johnson had not wished to take on *circuit riding duties and had agreed to serve only because Chief Justice Jay assured him that every effort would be made to lighten his burden. Unsuccessful, however, in persuading Jay to rotate him out of the Southern Circuit, Johnson resigned from the Court in January 1793, a mere 14 months after being confirmed.

Although he refused Washington's offer of the post of secretary of state in 1795, Johnson continued to serve his old friend indirectly through his efforts as a board member of the Federal City Commission. When Johnson died in December 1799, Washington honored him by delivering the funeral oration.

WILLIAM PATERSON

PERSONAL DATA

Born: December 24, 1745, in County Antrim, Ireland
Parents: Richard Paterson, Mary Paterson
Higher Education: College of New Jersey, now Princeton University (undergraduate degree, 1763; M.A., 1766)
Bar Admission: New Jersey, 1769
Political Party: Federalist

Marriages: February 9, 1779, to Cornelia Bell, who bore Paterson three children, and who died in November 1783; September 9, 1785, to Euphemia White
Died: September 9, 1806, in Albany, New York
Buried: Albany Rural Cemetery, Menands, New York

PROFESSIONAL CAREER

Occupations: Lawyer, 1769-1789; Politician, 1775-1777, 1787-1793; Businessman, 1791-ca. 1793; Judge, 1790-1806
Official Positions: Member, New Jersey Provincial Congress, 1775-1776; Delegate, New Jersey state constitutional convention, 1776; Attorney General, New Jersey, 1776-1783; Member, New Jersey Council of Safety, 1777; Delegate, Constitutional Convention, 1787; Member, United States Senate, 1789-1793; Governor, New Jersey, 1790-1793; Chancellor, New Jersey, 1790-1793; Associate Justice, United States Supreme Court, 1793-1806

SUPREME COURT SERVICE

Nominated: February 27, 1793 (nomination withdrawn February 28, 1793)
Nominated By: George Washington
Renominated: March 4, 1793
Confirmed: March 4, 1793
Confirmation Vote: Voice vote
Oath Taken: March 11, 1793
Replaced: Thomas Johnson
Significant Opinions: *Penhallow v. Doane's Administrator* (1795); *Ware v. Hylton* (1796); *Hylton v. United States* (1796); *Calder v. Bull* (1798); *Stuart v. Laird* (1803)
Left Court: Died September 9, 1806
Length of Service: 13 years, 5 months, 29 days
Replacement: Brockholst Livingston

William Paterson was born in County Antrim, Ireland on December 24, 1745, and emigrated to the United States with his parents when he was two years old. By 1750 the family had settled in Princeton, New Jersey, where Paterson's father opened a store and established a tin plate factory. The proceeds of his father's successful real estate investments provided Paterson with a good education; he received both a bachelor's degree and a master's degree at the local College of New Jersey. Afterward, he read law in the offices of Richard

Stockton and was admitted to practice in 1769.

Paterson was an early and outspoken supporter of independence from the mother country. From 1775 to 1776 he was a member of New Jersey's Provincial Congress, where he helped draft the first state constitution. Immediately thereafter, he was chosen to be New Jersey's first attorney general, a position he held for six years. During the same period, he also served his state as a member of the Council of Safety and as a member of the local militia. In 1780 Paterson was elected to serve as a delegate to the Second Constitutional Congress, but he refused the honor.

Paterson's political interests were originally strictly local. When elected to represent New Jersey at the Constitutional Convention, he assumed the task of representing the interests of small states like his own, initiating the New Jersey Plan, under which the legislative branch of the federal government would consist of a single body in which each state had a single vote. After the Connecticut Compromise, which established the bicameral Congress (consisting of a lower house in which representation is based on population, and an upper house, where each state is represented equally), Paterson became a strong advocate of centralized authority. One of the signers of the Constitution in 1787, he was chosen two years later as one of New Jersey's first two senators in the new federal government.

As a member of the first Senate Judiciary Committee, Paterson, together with Oliver Ellsworth, helped write the Judiciary Act of 1789, which created the third branch of the new government and gave it real force by implicitly affording federal courts the power of *judicial review. He supported Alexander Hamilton's fiscal plans, and he participated in negotiations resulting in the transfer of the nation's capital southward from New York in return for southern states' compliance with a strengthened federal government.

In 1790 Paterson was chosen to succeed William Livingston as governor of New Jersey. Concurrently, he acted as state chancellor, codifying state law in *Public Laws of the State of New Jersey* (1800), a work that significantly influenced the formalization of other states' laws in the nineteenth century. During this period, Paterson also continued his long association with Hamilton, forming in 1791 the Society for Establishing Useful Manufacturers, which led to the development of the industrial New Jersey town later known as Paterson.

Paterson was first nominated as a Supreme Court justice by President Washington on February 27, 1793, but the nomination was withdrawn the next day because the Constitution prohibits such an appointment while the appointee is serving in the United States Senate. He was renominated four days later, after his Senate term of office expired. An active and—as one of the authors of the Constitution—a knowledgeable advocate of the supremacy of the federal government, Paterson presided over trials of anti-tax insurgents after the Whiskey Rebellion and later over the *sedition trials of outspoken Anti-Federalists. Paterson's pronounced partisanship and his association with Hamilton probably cost him the nomination for chief justice to succeed Oliver Ellsworth in 1800. In the wake of both that rejection and the victory of Thomas Jefferson in the presidential election of 1800, Paterson muffled his Federalist opinions. He died in 1806, still a member of the Court.

SIGNIFICANT CASES

HAYBURN'S CASE

Citation: 2 Dall. (2 U.S.) 409 (1792)
Argued: August term, 1792
Decided: Decision never rendered because issue was *mooted by congressional action.
Court Below: Circuit Court for the District of Pennsylvania
Basis for Review: Motion for *mandamus
Facts: On March 23, 1792, Congress passed an act requiring circuit court judges, who were often also Supreme Court justices, to act as commissioners to rule on applications for federal pensions by disabled war veterans, their decisions subject to review by the secretary of war and by Congress. The New York District Court, led by Jay, declared the law unconstitutional. The Pennsylvania District Court, led by Justice

Wilson, was of the same opinion.

Issue: Was the pension act passed by Congress in 1791 unconstitutional in that it required federal judges to perform *extrajudicial duties and make decisions that were subject to further congressional review?

Outcome: The Court agreed to hold the motion for *mandamus under advisement until the next term, but in the interim Congress revised the pension act to do away with the constitutional difficulties it had posed.

Vote: None

Participating: Jay, Cushing, Wilson, Blair, Iredell, (Johnson not participating)

Opinions: In the form of protest letters sent by the five participating justices to President Washington

Significance: This case marked the first time that the Court considered the issues of *separation of powers and *justiciability and asserted its right to declare acts of Congress unconstitutional. Although all of the justices except Wilson consented voluntarily to perform the commissioners' duties, they remained firm in their opposition to the congressional requirement. Anti-Federalists supported the justices in the belief that if the Court could invalidate one law, it might do the same for other laws passed by the Federalist Congress.

GEORGIA V. BRAILSFORD

Citation: 2 Dall. (2 U.S.) 402 (1792)
Argued: August term, 1792
Decided: August 11, 1792
Court Below: None
Basis for Review: *Original Supreme Court jurisdiction

Facts: The State of Georgia enacted a law permitting confiscation of Loyalist property after the Revolutionary War, but Brailsford — a British subject at the time of the suit — had already won a lower court action to recover his property. Georgia now sought to bar his recovery.

Issue: Can a state be sued by a citizen of another state?

Outcome: Georgia was granted an *injunction barring Brailsford's recovery.

Vote: 4-2

Participating: Jay, Cushing, Wilson, Blair, Iredell, Johnson

Opinions: Johnson (dissenting), Iredell, Blair, Wilson, Cushing (dissenting), Jay

Significance: This was the Court's first recorded opinion. The Court followed the English custom of justices delivering serial opinions (one by one in reverse order of seniority) until the time of the Marshall Court. As the most junior justice, Johnson was accorded first place. His opinion, a dissent, thus established the tradition of dissent that has been one of the hallmarks of the Supreme Court throughout its history. The injunction granted Georgia in this case was permitted to stand until 1794, when the case was tried before a jury specially convened by the Court. In the wake of the decision against Georgia in *Chisholm v. Georgia* (1793), which the Court had rendered in the interim, Chief Justice Jay felt at liberty to instruct the jury in such a manner that their eventual finding for Brailsford was a foregone conclusion.

CHISHOLM V. GEORGIA

Citation: 2 Dall. (2 U.S.) 419 (1793)
Argued: February 5, 1793
Decided: February 18, 1793
Court Below: None
Basis for Review: *Motion of the attorney general

Facts: The heirs of a South Carolina merchant, themselves citizens of that state, sued the state of Georgia for the value of clothing supplied to Georgia by the merchant during the Revolutionary War.

Issue: Is a state a *sovereign entity immune to suit brought in federal court by citizens of another state?

Outcome: Deciding that Georgia, which did not appear as a party to the case, could be sued without its consent, the Court entered a default judgment for the plaintiff.

Vote: 4-1

Participating Justices: Jay, Cushing, Wilson, Blair, Iredell

Opinions: Iredell (dissenting), Blair, Wilson, Cushing, Jay

Significance: Interpreting Article II, Section 2, of the Constitution strictly, a majority of the jus-

POLITICAL COMPOSITION
of the Jay Court

Justice & Total Term	Courts Served	Appointing President	Political Party
John Jay 1789-1795	Jay	Washington	Federalist
John Rutledge 1790-1791 1795	Jay Rutledge	Washington Washington	Federalist
William Cushing 1790-1810	Jay Rutledge Ellsworth Marshall	Washington	Federalist
James Wilson 1789-1798	Jay Rutledge Ellsworth	Washington	Federalist
John Blair Jr. 1790-1795	Jay Rutledge	Washington	Federalist
James Iredell 1790-1799	Jay Rutledge Ellsworth	Washington	Federalist
Thomas Johnson 1791-1793	Jay	Washington	Federalist
William Paterson 1793-1806	Jay Rutledge Ellsworth Marshall	Washington	Federalist

tices found that federal judicial power extended to controversies between "a State and Citizens of another State," and that, in the words of Justice Wilson, "[a]s to the purposes of the Union, Georgia is not a sovereign state." During the Constitutional Convention the Federalists had countered objections from their critics to the wording of Article II, section 2, by promising that the clause would never be interpreted to mean that the citizens of one state could sue another state. Anti-Federalists — those in southern states in particular — feared loss of their sovereignty through just such a decision as *Chisholm*. Consequently, Georgia led the movement, backed by other southern states, for passage of the Eleventh Amendment. This amendment — ratified in 1798 and the first to be added after the Bill of Rights — was adopted explicitly to overturn *Chisholm* and marked the first instance in which a Supreme Court decision was superseded by a constitutional amendment.

GLASS V. THE SLOOP BETSY

Citation: 3 Dall. (3 U.S.) 6 (1794)
Argued: February 8 & 10-12, 1794
Decided: February 18, 1794
Court Below: United States Circuit Court for the District of Maryland

Basis for Review: Appeal *in scriptis* taken before a notary and probably filed directly with the Court, an irregular procedure

Facts: A Swedish ship, its cargo owned by Swedes and Americans, was captured as a wartime prize by French warships, which towed it into port at Baltimore.

Issue: Does an American federal court, acting as an *admiralty court, have *jurisdiction over prize vessels brought into American ports, or does this authority belong to foreign consular officers stationed in the United States?

Outcome: The Supreme Court overruled the lower court's finding that it had no power to adjudicate disputes over ownership of foreign ships and cargo captured by alien warships as prizes.

Vote: 5-0

Participating: Jay, Cushing, Wilson, Blair, Paterson

Opinion: Jay for the Court

Significance: In addition to the specific holding noted above, Jay stated unequivocally that in the absence of a treaty granting it such authority, no foreign power has the right to establish courts on American soil. This opinion, the last Chief Justice Jay ever wrote, was probably also his most important. His ruling not only helped to maintain President Washington's policy of strict neutrality in the struggle then going on between Britain and France, but also increased respect internationally for the new nation and its courts.

PENHALLOW V. DOANE'S ADMINISTRATOR

Citation: 3 Dall. (3 U.S.) 54 (1795)

Argued: February 6-17, 1795

Decided: February 24, 1795

Court Below: United States Circuit Court for the District of New Hampshire

Basis for Review: *Writ of error

Facts: A decree of the Court of Appeals in Cases of Capture, established under the Articles of Confederation, had twice been declared invalid by New Hampshire state courts, but it was upheld by the district court.

Issue: Do the federal courts have *jurisdiction over the case?

Outcome: The decree, and the district court, were upheld.

Vote: 4-0

Participating: Cushing, Blair, Iredell, Paterson

Opinions: Paterson, Iredell, Blair, Cushing

Significance: Even though the Court of Appeals had been ordained by the defunct Continental Congress, its logical successor was the district court, not the state court. The New Hampshire legislature, which was outraged by what it saw as the district court's violation of its *sovereignty, had twice formally protested the federal court's judgment in the United States Senate. Once the matter had been settled by the Supreme Court, however, the decision was universally acknowledged as final.

VOTING PATTERNS

Chief Justice Jay, as well as all of the associate justices who served with him, were Federalists appointed by President Washington. As Federalists, the members of the Court were strongly predisposed to strengthen the authority of the central government — including the Court's own power of *judicial review. During its early years, the Court decided few cases, spending most of the time it was in session organizing this new and important branch of the national government.

The most pressing task facing the Jay Court was to define the functions of the federal judiciary with respect to the other branches of the new government. Thus in *Hayburn's Case* (1792), members of the court asserted that Congress could not ask them to rule on the validity of pensioners' claims while the justices were acting in their official capacities. To assign federal courts duties that were not properly judicial, they declared, was unconstitutional. Similarly, in 1793, the Court declined to honor Washington's request that it render *advisory opinions regarding a treaty with France. The nationalistic justices were highly ingenious, however; in the charges they issued to juries while on *circuit, they found a means of supporting the administration within the boundaries of their sphere. In opening proceedings at the Wake County Court House in

North Carolina on June 2, 1794, for example, Justice Iredell took the opportunity to educate his audience as to the necessity of supporting the federal government's position of neutrality during the hostilities between Britain and France.

The Court's attempt to assert its constitutional mandate over the states in *Chisholm v. Georgia* (1793) was less successful. Although Justice Iredell dissented from the Court's judgment that it had *jurisdiction over this dispute between *citizens of South Carolina and the State of Georgia, his opinion marked the only time in the history of the Jay Court that one of its members sided strongly with the states in their struggle for power with the federal government. Iredell's vote, however, accorded with public sentiment. Set against the Court's view of what was at stake in the case — as Justice Wilson saw it, the case raised no less a question than "[D]o the people of the United States form a nation?" — was the states' concern about confiscation and debt repudiation during the Revolution. The Eleventh Amendment followed almost immediately upon the heels of *Chisholm*, overturning it with finality.

The Rutledge Court 1795

BACKGROUND

The history of the Rutledge Court, which lasted for only the August 1795 term, is that of its acting chief justice, John Rutledge. The Court heard few cases during its early years; only two cases, neither of lasting significance, were heard during Rutledge's tenure as chief justice.

Rutledge's career on the Supreme Court is full of distinctions, few of them estimable. He was the first justice to resign from the Court, quitting his post as senior associate justice on the Jay Court 13 months after taking the oath of office and without ever having attended a session. No other justice resigned in order to take up a state court judgeship. No justice served a shorter term than Rutledge's single month of service during his second tenure on the Supreme Court when he was chief justice. He was the only nominee for chief justice ever rejected by a vote of the

Senate.[†] He was the first justice to resign from the Court and be reappointed, and the first Supreme Court appointee not to be confirmed.

Rutledge was, nonetheless, an admirable figure whose public career — the Supreme Court aside — was marked by greatness. And what made him great — his instinctive assumption of leadership, his allegiance to his native South Carolina — also in a sense generated his downfall. After playing prominent roles in both state and national government for virtually his entire adult life, and on the eve of achieving a kind of professional apotheosis as chief justice of the United States Supreme Court, Rutledge destroyed his career and almost destroyed himself as well.

It is unclear whether Rutledge received President Washington's letter dated July 1, 1795, which offered him the position of chief justice, before or after a July 16, 1795, public meeting in Charleston, South Carolina, called to protest the Jay Treaty. The treaty was highly controversial, nowhere more so than in the southern states, which by its terms would be required to repay the bulk of the pre-Revolutionary War debt still owed the British. In South Carolina, which the British had plundered during its 1780-1781 occupation, public sentiment against the Jay Treaty was pronounced. Rutledge, assuming his usual leadership role, took control of the July 16 meeting, delivering an hour-long harangue during which he called the treaty a "prostitution of the dearest rights of free men."

Rutledge had apparently suffered some severe mental disturbances as the result of financial setbacks and the death of his wife in 1792. After

---

MEMBERS Of the Court 1795	
(In Order of Seniority)	
John Rutledge (Acting Chief Justice)	1795
William Cushing	1795
James Wilson	1795
John Blair Jr.	1795
James Iredell	1795
William Paterson	1795

An asterisk (*) before a word or phrase indicates that a definition will be found in the glossary at the end of this volume.

† Abe Fortas's nomination was withdrawn by President Lyndon B. Johnson in 1968 when it became apparent the Senate would refuse to confirm him.

JUDICIAL BIOGRAPHY
John Rutledge

PERSONAL DATA

Born: September 1739 in Charles Town (later Charleston), South Carolina
Parents: Dr. John Rutledge, Sarah Hext Rutledge
Higher Education: Middle Temple, London, England, 1758-1760
Bar Admission: England, 1760
Political Party: Federalist
Marriage: May 1, 1763, to Elizabeth Grimke, who bore Rutledge ten children, and who died in 1792
Died: June 21, 1800, in Charleston, South Carolina
Buried: St. Michael's churchyard, Charleston

PROFESSIONAL CAREER

Occupations: Lawyer, 1761-1764, 1765-1774; Politician, 1764, 1774-1784, 1787-1788; Judge, 1784-1795
Official Positions: Member, South Carolina Commons House of Assembly, 1761-1764; Attorney General, South Carolina, 1764; Delegate, Stamp Act Congress, 1765; Delegate, Continental Congress, 1774-1776; President, South Carolina General Assembly, 1776-1778; Governor of South Carolina, 1779-1781; Member, United States Congress, 1782-1784; Chief Judge, South Carolina Court of Chancery, 1784-1791; Delegate and Chairman, Committee on Detail, Constitutional Convention, 1787; Member, South Carolina convention to ratify the federal Constitution, 1788; Associate Justice, United States Supreme Court, 1789-1791; Chief Justice, South Carolina Court of Common Pleas, 1791-1795; Acting Chief Justice, United States Supreme Court, 1795

SUPREME COURT SERVICE

As Associate Justice:
Nominated: September 24, 1789
Nominated By: George Washington
Confirmed: September 26, 1789
Confirmation Vote: Voice vote
Oath Taken: February 15, 1790
Significant Opinions: None
Left Court: Resigned March 5, 1791
Length of Service: 1 year, 18 days
Replacement: Thomas Johnson
As Chief Justice:
Appointed: July 1, 1795 (recess appointment)
Appointed By: George Washington
Oath Taken: August 12, 1795
Replaced: John Jay
Rejected: December 15, 1795
Rejection Vote: 14-10
Significant Opinions: None
Length of Service: 4 months, 3 days
Replacement: Chief Justice Oliver Ellsworth

---

his July 1795 performance, Federalist leaders speculated openly about his sanity. Apparently, concerns about both Rutledge's politics and his person contributed to the Senate vote to reject his appointment to the Court later that year.

RUTLEDGE'S EARLY LIFE

John Rutledge was born, probably in late September 1739, into an old aristocratic family in what is now Charleston, South Carolina. His father, Dr. John Rutledge, died in 1750. Fortunately for the son, however, his mother was left one of the wealthiest widows in the state.

Rutledge was privately tutored, then studied law in the offices of his Uncle Andrew Rutledge, speaker of the South Carolina Commons House of Assembly. After his uncle died, Rutledge first read law with James Parsons (who later became speaker of the United States House of Representatives), and then at the Middle Temple in London. He was called to the English bar in 1760.

RUTLEDGE'S PUBLIC LIFE

Rutledge's public life began almost immediately upon his return from England. His family con-

John Rutledge

nections assured that the legal practice he set up would be successful, and within three months of his homecoming, at the age of 21, he was elected to the South Carolina Assembly. He rapidly advanced in both careers, becoming the first lawyer in the colonies to bring an action for *breach of promise, and being appointed South Carolina's attorney general in 1764. In 1763 he married Elizabeth Grimke, and the couple produced ten children, including John Rutledge Jr., who would continue the family dynasty by serving as a member of the United States House of Representatives from 1797 to 1803.

In 1765, at the age of 25, Rutledge was the youngest delegate to the Stamp Act Congress, which colonial leaders had called in an attempt to address the stamp tax recently imposed by Britain. As chairman of Congress's Committee on Resolutions, Rutledge drafted the respectful position paper presented to the English House of Lords, evincing what would become a lifelong fondness for British law and government. Rutledge would manifest the same attitude when, as leader of the South Carolina delegation to the First Continental Congress, he supported accommo-

dation with the mother country.

In the Continental Congress, Rutledge also displayed a tenacious ability to defend the interests of his state and his class. Although the Congress was successful in organizing an economic boycott of Britain, the price of Rutledge's vote was a concession that permitted continued trade in rice, South Carolina's principal export.

Rutledge's service in the Continental Congress continued, but his primary focus was on South Carolina, whose constitution he helped draft in 1775. When the newly formulated state assembly met the next year, Rutledge was elected its first president. In that role, Rutledge made a crucial decision to defend Fort Moultrie against the British attack on Charleston in 1776, a move that brought America its first substantial victory in the Revolutionary War. When South Carolina adopted a new, more democratic constitution in 1778, Rutledge resigned. His departure from state politics lasted only a year, however, as the assembly elected him governor in 1779. South Carolina fell to the British in 1780, but the next year, after the British moved on to Virginia, Rutledge was active in restoring civil authority.

Rutledge returned to federal government from 1782 to 1784, when he served as a member of Congress. He declined offers to serve on a federal court or as minister to the Netherlands, choosing instead to take his first judicial post as chief judge of South Carolina's new Court of Chancery. When South Carolina chose a delegation to attend the Constitutional Convention in 1787, it chose Rutledge as the delegation's chief. Once there, Rutledge distinguished himself by participating in the select committee that devised the Great Compromise giving all states an equal voice in federal government through creation of the Senate, where each state had equal representation. He also served as chairman of the Committee on Detail, which authored the first draft of the Constitution, and proposed the *supremacy clause, which states that the Constitution and laws of the United States "shall be the supreme law of the land." Rutledge then worked tirelessly for adoption of the Constitution in South Carolina.

POLITICAL COMPOSITION
of the Rutledge Court

Justice & Total Term	Courts Served	Appointing President	Political Party
John Rutledge 1790-1791 1795	Jay Rutledge	Washington Washington	Federalist
William Cushing 1790-1810	Jay Rutledge Ellsworth Marshall	Washington	Federalist
James Wilson 1789-1798	Jay Rutledge Ellsworth	Washington	Federalist
John Blair Jr. 1790-1795	Jay Rutledge	Washington	Federalist
James Iredel 1790-1799	Jay Rutledge Ellsworth	Washington	Federalist
William Paterson 1793-1806	Jay Rutledge Ellsworth Marshall	Washington	Federalist

Rutledge's home state honored him for his services by casting its electoral vote for him as vice president in the 1788 national presidential election. Rutledge lost to John Adams, but his eyes were actually focused on the position of chief justice of the Supreme Court. President Washington's appointment of John Jay to the post disappointed Rutledge, who nevertheless accepted Washington's offer of senior associate justice. Although he rode the Southern Circuit for two years, Rutledge never sat on the Supreme Court bench, and he resigned his position there in March 1791 to take what he considered a more prestigious one, chief justice of the South Carolina Court of Common Pleas.

RUTLEDGE AS CHIEF JUSTICE

In June 1795, learning that John Jay had resigned as chief justice, Rutledge wrote to Washington requesting appointment to the vacancy. By return letter, dated July 1, Washington eagerly agreed, asking Rutledge to preside over the Court's August term. On July 16, 1795, before joining the Court, Rutledge led a public meeting called in Charleston to condemn the Jay Treaty. His remarks, together with subsequent rumors about his mental instability, doomed his career. As his was a recess appointment, confirmation had to be put before the Senate when it reconvened later in the year. On December 15, 1795, Rutledge was rejected by a vote of 14 to 10.

Before his rejection, Rutledge did preside over the Court's August 1795 term. Only two cases were heard and decided that term: *United States v. Richard Peters* and *Talbot v. Jansen*. Both cases concerned France's practice of seizing U.S. and neutral vessels with largely American crews and using them to attack British merchant ships.

Old City Hall, Philadelphia, where the Supreme Court met 1791–1800

Rutledge issued brief opinions in both cases.

Rutledge, disabled from *circuit riding, returned to Charleston in November 1795. After learning of his rejection by the Senate, he attempted to commit suicide by jumping off a wharf into Charleston Bay on December 26, 1795. Although he was saved from drowning, Rutledge spent the remainder of his life as an eccentric — although probably not insane — recluse. He died in Charleston on June 21, 1800.

ASSOCIATE JUSTICES

For biographies of Associate Justices **William Cushing, James Wilson, John Blair Jr., James Iredell,** and **William Paterson,** see entries under **THE JAY COURT.**

SIGNIFICANT CASES

The Rutledge Court tried only two cases during the one term it met (August 1795). Both *United States v. Richard Peters* (3 Dall. [3 U.S.] 121 [1795]) and *Talbot v. Jansen* (3 Dall. [3 U.S.] 133 [1795]) concerned the French practice, during its hostilities with Britain, of seizing U.S. and other neutral vessels and enlisting their American crews to capture British ships in North American waters. Although important at the time because of concerns about maintaining United States neutrality, neither case has had lasting import.

VOTING PATTERNS

The political makeup of the Court remained unchanged under Rutledge, who inherited from Jay the same uniformly Federalist associate justices. Rutledge was himself at least nominally a Federalist, and despite the strong pro-French feeling that characterized his native South Carolina during this period, he voted with the other justices to restore a French prize ship to its Dutch owners in *Talbot v. Jansen* (1795).

The Ellsworth Court 1796-1800

BACKGROUND

FEDERALISTS V. REPUBLICANS

The tenure of the Ellsworth Court was marked by the development of party politics. Although initially the government of the new nation was composed mostly of Federalists (who favored strong central authority and a liberal interpretation of the Constitution), Anti-Federalists (who emphasized the empowerment of individual states and the need for a bill of rights to protect individuals from potential abuse by the central government) had existed from the nation's inception. A committed Federalist, President George Washington nonetheless remained above the fray. The rift reached his own cabinet, however, where Secretary of the Treasury Alexander Hamilton led the Federalists and Secretary of State Thomas Jefferson headed the Anti-Federalists.

WASHINGTON'S FAREWELL AND THE ELECTION OF JOHN ADAMS

Having decided against running for a third term, President Washington composed a farewell address to the American people, which was published in September 1796. In his address, he cautioned against the kind of regional divisions that were fueling the country's growing partisan debate. He also warned his countrymen that their diplomatic efforts abroad should remain independent of alliances with other countries.

As the presidential election of 1796 drew near, France—now at war with Britain and looking for support—was endeavoring to influence the American political process in the hope that its efforts might result in the election of the †Republican candidate, Thomas Jefferson, who was a supporter of the French Republic. However, Jefferson finished second to the Federalist candidate, John Adams, and owing to the election rules of the day, became Adams's vice president for the next four years.

Although Federalists constituted the majority of the presidential electors, Adams defeated Jefferson by only three votes, an indication of how divided the Federalist Party had become in

MEMBERS Of the Court 1796–1800

(In Order of Seniority)

Oliver Ellsworth (Chief Justice)	(1796-1800)
William Cushing	(1796-1800)
James Wilson (died)	(1796-1798)
James Iredell (died)	(1796-1799)
William Paterson	(1796-1800)
Samuel Chase	(1796-1800)
Bushrod Washington (replaced James Wilson)	(1798-1800)
Alfred Moore (replaced James Iredell)	(1800-)

An asterisk (*) before a word or phrase indicates that a definition will be found in the glossary at the end of this volume.

† Anti-Federalists now referred to themselves as Republicans to distinguish them from those favoring a strong executive — in some cases, even a monarchy — instead of the democratic ideal, which they believed could be achieved only through strict interpretation of the Constitution and stricter limitations on federal government.

the aftermath of Washington's retirement from public life. Some of the electors pledged to Adams refused to vote for his vice presidential nominee, Thomas Pinckney, and some of Pinckney's electors refused to vote for Adams. Adams had been a compromise candidate, selected in part because while serving as Washington's vice president, he had not been directly associated with such Federalist initiatives as Alexander Hamilton's plan for a centralized banking system. Adams would increasingly become the target of "high" Federalist defenders like Hamilton and, ultimately, a one-term president.

FOREIGN AFFAIRS AND THE QUASI WAR WITH FRANCE

The development of partisan politics in the United States was partly related to its foreign policy. Fears that the Federalists wanted to reinstitute the monarchy on American soil were heightened by the signing in 1794 of the Jay Treaty, in which Supreme Court Chief Justice—and Federalist—John Jay was seen to have capitulated to British demands, thereby jeopardizing American neutrality in the war between monarchical Britain and republican France. To make matters worse, those treaty issues on which Jay had prevailed—trading concessions and the surrender of British forts—were interpreted as favoring the northern states, where the Federalists held sway.

Initially, the Republicans sympathized with the internal struggles of the new French Republic, which had overthrown the Bourbon monarchy of Louis XVI. This enthusiasm was dampened, however, when the ideals of the French Revolution degenerated into the Reign of Terror, during which thousands—including the king—were guillotined.

In the wake of the Jay Treaty, France perceived America to be a British ally and therefore began seizing American ships and confiscating their cargoes. America's response to the French actions was to send a negotiating team to Paris in the fall of 1797. Finding French Foreign Minister Charles Maurice de Talleyrand unwilling to meet with them, the team was preparing to return to America when it encountered three agents of the French government. The agents suggested that diplomacy between the two nations might be improved if the American government would give $250,000 to certain French officials and loan the French government $12 million. Repelled by such a suggestion and unwilling to jeopardize their nation's neutrality with a loan, the Americans reported the details of the matter to President Adams.

When, in the spring of 1798, Adams published the diplomats' dispatches —which referred to the French agents only as X, Y and Z—the American public was outraged. The XYZ affair had, in effect, ended American neutrality in the contest between Britain and France. The nation began to arm itself as it settled into a state of undeclared war with its former ally, France.

THE ALIEN AND SEDITION ACTS

In addition to legislation increasing the nation's armed forces in order to combat the French, Congress passed a series of Alien and Sedition Acts in 1798. The acts were intended to quell political dissent, particularly from the Republican Party, which was decidedly pro-French.

The Alien Enemies Act aroused little Republican ire, as it merely gave the president the power to expel from America citizens of any country with which the United States might be at war. The Alien Friends Act, however, was more alarming to the Republicans, as it permitted the president to expel any alien and seemed to be politically motivated, designed to keep out foreign nationals (French and Irish immigrants were then flocking to American shores) who might express anti-British sentiments. Also, it concentrated a dangerous amount of power in the hands of one individual, the president. Republicans also objected to a third piece of legislation, the Naturalization Act, which extended the waiting period for citizenship—and hence eligibility to vote—from 5 to 14 years.

Republican dissent largely took the form of published criticism of President Adams, who was struggling against pressure from the hawkish wing of his own Federalist Party to undertake an expen-

JUDICIAL BIOGRAPHY
Oliver Ellsworth

PERSONAL DATA
Born: April 29, 1745, in Windsor, Connecticut
Parents: Captain David Ellsworth, Jemima Leavitt Ellsworth
Higher Education: Yale University, 1762-1764; College of New Jersey, now Princeton University (B.A., 1766)
Political Party: Federalist
Bar Admission: Connecticut, 1771
Marriage: 1772 to Abigail Wolcott, who bore Ellsworth four sons and three daughters
Died: November 26, 1807, in Windsor
Buried: Palisado Cemetery, Windsor

PROFESSIONAL CAREER
Occupations: Farmer, 1770-1773; Lawyer, 1771-1785; Politician, 1773-1796, 1801-1807; Judge, 1785-1789, 1796-1800, 1807; Diplomat, 1799-1800
Official Positions: Windsor Representative, Connecticut General Assembly, 1773-1776; State's Attorney, Hartford County, Connecticut, 1777-1785; Delegate, Continental Congress, 1777-1783; Member, Connecticut Council of Safety, 1779; Member, Connecticut Governor's Council, 1780-1785; Judge, Connecticut Supreme Court of Errors, 1785; Judge, Connecticut Superior Court, 1785-1789; Delegate, Constitutional Convention, 1787; Member, United States Senate, 1789-1796; Chief Justice, United States Supreme Court, 1796-1800; United States Commissioner to France, 1799-1800; Member, Connecticut Governor's Council, 1801-1807; Chief Justice, Connecticut Supreme Court of Appeals, 1807

SUPREME COURT SERVICE
Nominated: March 3, 1796
Nominated By: George Washington
Confirmed: March 4, 1796
Confirmation Vote: 21-1
Oath Taken: March 8, 1796

Replaced: Acting Chief Justice John Rutledge
Significant Opinions: *United States v. La Vengeance* (1796); *Moodie v. The Ship Phoebe Anne* (1796); *Wiscart v. Dauchy* (1796)
Left Court: Resigned December 15, 1800
Length of Service: 4 years, 9 months, 7 days
Replacement: Chief Justice John Marshall

Washington's first choice to fill the vacancy left by Chief Justice Jay's resignation was former Associate Justice John Rutledge, whom he appointed on July 1, 1795. Rutledge served as chief justice from the time he was sworn in on August 12, 1795, until the Senate reconvened and voted on his nomination, which was rejected 14 to 10. Washington next nominated Associate Justice William Cushing on January 26, 1796. Cushing was confirmed the next day, but declined the promotion.

sive war against France that the nation could scarcely afford. The publishers and editors of several Republican publications—among them Matthew Lyon, a Republican member of Congress from Vermont—were prosecuted under the Sedition Act of 1798, which made opposition to the national government, in word or in deed, a punishable offense. The fact that the act was scheduled to expire in 1800 made it clear that its purpose was solely to quiet political dissent during the presidential campaign. During the four years the Sedition Act was in force, 25 people were arrested under this statute, of whom 14 were indicted and 10 convicted—primarily by Federalist Supreme Court justices while on *circuit duty.

FEDERAL POWER V. STATES' RIGHTS

The *sovereignty of individual states, a Republican cause, was strengthened early in 1798

Oliver Ellsworth

with passage of the Eleventh Amendment which, in response to the Supreme Court's decision to the contrary in *Chisholm v. Georgia* (1793), provided that no state could be sued by a citizen of another state. Republicans, led by Jefferson and Madison, then drafted two sets of resolutions, adopted by the legislatures of Kentucky and Virginia, which argued that the states themselves—rather than the uniformly Federalist Supreme Court—should have the power to decide the constitutionality of federal legislation. In particular, the resolutions called on all states to nullify the Alien and Sedition Acts.

While no other states joined with Kentucky and Virginia, the resolutions were significant because their emphasis on *states' rights remained a beacon for southern states and served as a political platform for the Republicans, who won the election of 1800. The election of Jefferson as president marked the end of Federalist rule and the beginning of southern domination of the federal government that was to last, largely uninterrupted, until 1860.

ELLSWORTH'S EARLY LIFE

Oliver Ellsworth was a third-generation American of English stock, born to Captain David Ellsworth and Jemima Leavitt Ellsworth on April 29, 1745, in Windsor, Connecticut, where his great-grandfather settled upon emigrating from Yorkshire in the mid-seventeenth century. Ellsworth's father, a war hero, lived on a farm, where Ellsworth grew up.

Ellsworth received his early education at home from the Reverend Joseph Bellamy. The senior Ellsworth hoped that his son would become a minister and enrolled him at Yale. Ellsworth left Yale at the end of his sophomore year and enrolled at Princeton, from which he received a B.A. degree in 1766. To honor his father's wishes, Ellsworth began studying for the ministry, but his interests turned to law and he began to train for the Connecticut bar, to which he was admitted in 1771. When his father refused to subsidize him, Ellsworth turned to cutting and selling timber from a piece of inherited woodland to support himself and his wife, Abigail Wolcott, whom he had married in 1772 when she was 16 and he 26.

During the early years of his legal practice, Ellsworth's earnings were meager—during his first three years as a lawyer his income totaled a mere three pounds in Connecticut currency. With his appointment in 1773 to the Connecticut General Assembly, however, his reputation and law practice grew. Over the next few years his fortunes increased to the point that he was one of the wealthiest men in Connecticut.

ELLSWORTH'S PUBLIC LIFE

As a member of the Connecticut Assembly, Ellsworth was inevitably drawn into the Revolutionary War. In 1775 he became a member of the Assembly's Committee of the Pay Table, which supervised the state militia's expenditures. Two years later he was named state attorney for Hartford County.

During the Revolutionary War, Ellsworth acted as his state's delegate to the Continental Congress, where he served on a number of committees, the most important of which was the

Committee of Appeals. This committee represented the first exercise of Congress's legal *jurisdiction and was, in a sense, the precursor of the Supreme Court. While serving on the Committee of Appeals, Ellsworth heard a number of appeals from *admiralty courts on maritime matters. This experience was to serve Ellsworth well when he was elevated to the nation's highest court.

When the war ended in 1783, Ellsworth resigned from the Continental Congress to resume practicing law full time in his home state. He again served on Connecticut's Governor's Council, and when the state Supreme Court of Errors was formed in 1785, Ellsworth became one of its judges. Shortly thereafter, he was elevated to the state superior court.

In 1787 Ellsworth was selected as one of Connecticut's three delegates to the Constitutional Convention. He played a role in devising the Connecticut Compromise, which ended the dispute about representation between small states and large states by establishing two federal legislative branches, the Senate and the House of Representatives. Ellsworth may have been the first delegate to propose "United States" as the official name for the new nation. He also participated in the creation of a judicial branch for the new government, and it is clear that even from this early stage, he regarded the Supreme Court as having the power to interpret the Constitution and overrule state and federal statutes not in accord with it.

In the congressional elections of 1789, the first ever held, Ellsworth was chosen by the Connecticut legislature as one of his state's two United States senators (election of U.S. senators occurred in state legislatures until adoption of the Seventeenth Amendment in 1913). During his seven-year tenure in the Senate, Ellsworth worked prodigiously, being involved with the drafting of the first set of Senate rules, and the organization of the army, the post office, the diplomatic service, and a national census. Most importantly, he coauthored the Judiciary Act of 1789, which established the structure of the federal court system.

ELLSWORTH AS CHIEF JUSTICE

In 1795 John Jay resigned as the Supreme Court's first Chief Justice to become governor of New York. When the Senate subsequently refused to confirm President Washington's appointment of John Rutledge as chief justice, and after Associate Justice William Cushing declined the office, Washington appointed Oliver Ellsworth on March 3, 1796. He was confirmed by the Senate the next day and took his seat as chief justice of the Court four days later.

Ellsworth's appointment to the Court came too late for him to participate in two important cases. *Hylton v. United States* (1796) was a significant case in that it marked the first time the Court had ruled on the constitutionality of a congressional act. *Ware v. Hylton* (1796) was significant in that it involved the fundamental issue of the relationship of the states to the federal government. Ellsworth, nonetheless, presumably agreed with the outcome in both cases. During his tenure as a delegate to the Constitutional Convention he had made no secret of his support for the Supreme Court's power of review. Later, in such circuit court opinions as *Hamilton v. Eaton* (1797), he affirmed his belief in the primacy of the federal government.

Ellsworth wrote three important decisions during his first year on the Court, two of which concerned disputes over warships. In *United States v. La Vengeance* (1796) and *Moodie v. The Ship Phoebe Anne* (1796), he was able to draw on past experience with admiralty cases which he had garnered working on the Committee of Appeals. *United States v. La Vengeance* was significant in that it extended the federal government's maritime authority to inland waterways. In *Moodie v. The Ship Pheobe Anne*, Ellsworth led the Court in affirming the precedence of international treaties over national laws. In a third case, *Wiscart v. Dauchy* (1796), Ellsworth arguably made his greatest contribution to *jurisprudence by defining the Supreme Court's *appellate jurisdiction as limited to *questions of law, rather than review of both the facts of the case and the law that might apply to them.

In 1799 President Adams selected Ellsworth as part of a commission to negotiate with America's Revolutionary War ally, France, with whom relations had deteriorated during the Quasi War. Ellsworth was instrumental in ending hostilities with France with the signing of the Treaty of Morfontaine in 1800. The rigors of foreign travel affected his health, however, and on September 30, 1800, before Ellsworth returned home, he conveyed his resignation as chief justice, effective December 15, to the president.

Ellsworth returned to his home in Windsor, Connecticut, after retiring from national service at the age of 56. While he accepted an appointment to the Governor's Council and agreed to serve as the first chief justice of the state Supreme Court of Appeals, poor health never permitted him to take his seat on that bench. Ellsworth died on November 26, 1807, at the age of 62.

ASSOCIATE JUSTICES

For biographies of Associate Justices **William Cushing, James Wilson, James Iredell,** and **William Paterson,** see entries under **THE JAY COURT.**

SAMUEL CHASE

PERSONAL DATA

Born: April 17, 1741, in Somerset County, Maryland
Parents: Rev. Thomas Chase, Martha Walker Chase
Higher Education: None
Bar Admission: Maryland, 1761
Marriages: May 21, 1762, to Anne Baldwin, who bore Chase three children, and who died ca. 1779; March 3, 1784, to Hannah Kitty Giles, who bore Chase four children
Died: June 19, 1811, in Baltimore, Maryland
Buried: St. Paul's Cemetery, Baltimore

PROFESSIONAL CAREER

Occupations: Lawyer, 1761-1791; Politician, 1764-1784; Judge, 1788-1811
Official Positions: Member, Maryland General Assembly, 1764-1784; Member, Maryland Committee of Correspondence, 1774; Delegate, Continental Congress, 1774-1780; Member, Maryland Convention and Council of Safety, 1775; Chief Judge, Baltimore Criminal Court, 1788-1796; Chief Judge, General Court of Maryland, 1791-1796; Associate Justice, United States Supreme Court, 1796-1811

SUPREME COURT SERVICE

Nominated: January 26, 1796
Nominated By: George Washington
Confirmed: January 27, 1796
Confirmation Vote: Voice vote
Oath Taken: February 4, 1796
Replaced: John Blair Jr.
Significant Opinions: *Hylton v. United States* (1796); *Ware v. Hylton* (1796); *Calder v. Bull* (1798)
Left Court: Died June 19, 1811
Length of Service: 15 years, 4 months, 5 days
Replacement: Gabriel Duvall

Samuel Chase was the only Supreme Court justice ever to be *impeached. He was impeached by the House of Representatives on March 12, 1804, by a vote of 73 to 32. He was tried before the Senate early the next year, and on March 1, 1805, he was acquitted. Although a majority of senators voted against him, the vote fell short of the two-thirds required for conviction.

Samuel Chase, whose mother died when he was a child, was raised in Baltimore by his father, an Episcopalian rector who tutored his son in the classics. At the age of 18, Chase began his legal studies in the offices of Hammond and Hill in Annapolis, Maryland. He was admitted to the Maryland bar two years later. At the age of 23, he was elected to the Maryland Assembly, where he spent 20 years as the representative for Annapolis.

Chase was an ardent supporter of the revolutionary cause, joining the militant Sons of Liberty organization, which demonstrated actively against British rule. In 1774, at the age of 33, he became one of the youngest members of the First Continental Congress, where he was among the signers of the Declaration of Independence. In the Second Continental Congress, he served energetically on more than 50 committees.

In the early 1780s, however, Chase was dropped from the Maryland delegation to Congress for two years after being accused of war profiteering for attempting to corner the flour market. During that decade, he continued to pursue his legal practice, while other unfortunate investments caused him to declare personal bankruptcy in 1789.

Meanwhile, his public life likewise continued to be controversial. In 1787 he publicly opposed adoption of the Constitution, publishing a series of articles against ratification under the pen name "Caution." In 1788 he was appointed chief judge of the Baltimore Criminal Court, and two years later became chief judge of the General Court of Maryland, thus holding two judgeships simultaneously. When the state assembly tried to remove him from both offices, the vote went in his favor by the narrowest of margins.

After considering Chase briefly as a replacement for Acting Chief Justice John Rutledge, whom the Senate had refused to confirm, President Washington instead nominated Chase on January 26, 1796, to replace retiring Associate Justice John Blair Jr. Chase was confirmed the next day and took his seat in time to hear arguments in the seminal case, *Hylton v. United States* (1796). As the most junior justice, his written opinion about the case appeared first, and in it he not only raised the question of *judicial review, but also provided a definition of a *direct tax, which the framers of the Constitution had left ambiguous. In *Ware v. Hylton* (1796), Chase continued to establish himself as the intellectual leader of the Ellsworth Court by arguing forcefully and convincingly for the supremacy of national treaties over state laws. In *Calder v. Bull* (1798), Chase provided a definition of *ex post facto laws that has survived into modern times. In *Hollingsworth v. Virginia* (1798), he noted that it was not necessary to submit constitutional amendments to the president, an observation that became the rule. And while sitting in *circuit court in 1789, he argued his opinion in *United States v. Worrell* (1789) that federal courts lack the *jurisdiction to try *common law crimes

like *seditious libel. Chase was the only Federalist judge to express this view, but it was upheld by the Supreme Court in the 19th century and is still the predominant rule.

Chase's attitude towards common law crime may seem ironic in view of his later harsh enforcement of the Alien and Sedition Acts of 1798 when he presided over such notorious trials as that of tax rebel John Fries. But Chase was a political conservative and an ardent Federalist partisan, and he did not hesitate to use all his judicial authority to support the Adams administration's fight for survival. He continued to wage war against the Republicans even after Jefferson won the election of 1800, in 1803 delivering a passionate tirade before a grand jury in which he denounced democracy as "mobocracy." This speech led to Chase's impeachment by the House of Representatives in 1804. When he was tried before the Senate, however, there were not enough votes to convict him. Thereafter, Chase's presence on the Supreme Court bench was a subdued one. During the ten years he served under Chief Justice John Marshall, Chase was often absent due to poor health. He died at the age of 70 in 1811, while still serving on the court.

BUSHROD WASHINGTON

PERSONAL DATA

Born: June 5, 1762, in Westmoreland County, Virginia

Parents: John Augustine Washington, Hannah Bushrod Washington

Higher Education: College of William and Mary, (undergraduate degree, Phi Beta Kappa, 1778)

Bar Admission: Virginia, 1784

Political Party: Federalist

Marriage: 1785 to Julia Ann Blackburn, who died in 1829

Died: November 26, 1829, in Philadelphia, Pennsylvania

Buried: Family vault, Mount Vernon, Virginia

PROFESSIONAL CAREER

Occupations: Serviceman, 1780-1781; Lawyer, 1784-1789; Politician, 1787-1788; Judge, 1798-1829

Official Positions: Member, Virginia House of Delegates, 1787; Delegate, Virginia convention to ratify the federal Constitution, 1788; Associate Justice, United States Supreme Court, 1798-1829

SUPREME COURT SERVICE
Appointed: September 29, 1798 (recess appointment)
Appointed By: John Adams
Oath Taken: November 9, 1798
Nominated: December 19, 1798
Confirmed: December 20, 1798
Confirmation Vote: Voice vote
Oath Retaken: February 4, 1799
Replaced: James Wilson
Significant Opinions: *Dartmouth College v. Woodward* (1819); *Green v. Biddle* (1823); *Ogden v. Saunders* (1827)
Left Court: Died November 26, 1829
Length of Service: 31 years, 17 days
Replacement: Henry Baldwin

Often recalled as George Washington's favorite nephew, Bushrod Washington was born into the American aristocracy, with both his father and mother belonging to what has come to be known as the First Families of Virginia. As a boy, he was privately tutored. At the age of 16, he graduated from the College of William and Mary, where he had been a founding member of Phi Beta Kappa, then a secret social club.

Washington enlisted as a private in the Continental army towards the end of the Revolutionary War. After demobilization, he traveled to Philadelphia to study law under James Wilson, whom he would later replace on the Supreme Court. He was admitted to the Virginia bar in 1784 and practiced law privately in Westmoreland County, Virginia, and later in Alexandria and Richmond, Virginia. In 1787, encouraged by his uncle, he ran for and won a seat in the Virginia House of Delegates. The next year he was sent as a delegate to the state convention to ratify the federal Constitution.

Washington had a decidedly scholarly bent. In addition to training many law students, he published two volumes of Virginia Court of Appeals cases. Later, while serving on the Supreme Court,

he published four additional volumes of reports of decisions of the federal Third Circuit Court.

In September 1798 George Washington again convinced his nephew to run for political office (this time for Congress), but before beginning his campaign, he was appointed to the Supreme Court by President Adams. Because his was a recess appointment, made while Congress was adjourned, Washington had to be formally confirmed later that year. He rode the Southern *Circuit that fall before the Senate confirmed him in December.

Washington remained on the Court for 31 years, but he played only a small role in shaping it. He spent the bulk of his days on the bench echoing Chief Justice John Marshall's opinions. He wrote 70 of the Marshall Court's majority decisions but only one dissent. He found himself in disagreement with Marshall only three times during the 28 years they shared the high bench. Washington played a more prepossessing role while sitting in circuit court as a trial judge. In the 1809 treason case, *United States v. Bright,* he ordered state military officers who had resisted a federal court decree to be jailed. The trial was fraught with a high degree of political tension, but Washington managed to maintain calm and uphold the power of national government by pardoning the officers on humanitarian grounds. It is for such tact and judiciousness that Washington is best remembered.

ALFRED MOORE

PERSONAL DATA
Born: May 21, 1755, in Brunswick County, North Carolina
Parents: Judge Maurice Moore, Anne Grange Moore
Higher Education: None
Bar Admission: North Carolina, 1775
Political Party: Federalist
Marriage: 1775 to Susanna Elizabeth Eagles, who bore Moore four children
Died: October 15, 1810, in Bladen County, North Carolina
Buried: St. Philip's Churchyard, Southport, North Carolina

PROFESSIONAL CAREER

Occupations: Lawyer, 1775-late 1770s, 1777-1798; Serviceman, 1776-1777; Politician, 1782-1794, 1798; Diplomat, 1798; Public Servant, 1789-1807; Judge, 1798-1804

Official Positions: Representative for Brunswick County, North Carolina Legislature, 1782; Attorney General, North Carolina, 1782-1791; Trustee, University of North Carolina, 1789-1807; Member, North Carolina House of Commons, 1792-1794; Commissioner, Federal commission to negotiate peace with the Cherokee Nation, 1798; Judge, Superior Court of North Carolina, 1798-1799; Associate Justice, United States Supreme Court, 1800-1804

SUPREME COURT SERVICE

Nominated: December 4, 1799
Nominated By: John Adams
Confirmed: December 10, 1799
Confirmation Vote: Voice vote
Oath Taken: April 21, 1800
Replaced: James Iredell
Significant Opinion: *Baas v. Tingy* (1800)
Left Court: Resigned January 26, 1804
Length of Service: 3 years, 9 months, 5 days
Replacement: William Johnson

Alfred Moore was born into a distinguished family headed by one of the three colonial judges in North Carolina. Although he was sent to Boston to receive his education, when it came time for him to read law, Moore returned home to study law under his father, with whom he entered into practice in 1775. During the Revolution, which saw the deaths of his father, brother, and uncle, Moore served first as a captain of Continental troops, then, after his father's death in 1777, as a colonel of the local militia. In the latter capacity, he participated in raids against British troops, who in retaliation plundered his property.

Moore's reputation for leadership resulted in his election to the North Carolina legislature in 1782. In the same year, he was elected his state's attorney general, replacing James Iredell, whom he would later succeed on the United States Supreme Court. Moore served eight years as attorney general for North Carolina, resigning only

when the state created the position of solicitor general, which Moore viewed as a competing office. He then served one term, from 1792 to 1794, in the North Carolina House of Commons. In 1794 Moore ran for the United States Senate, only to be defeated in the North Carolina legislature by one vote. In 1798 President Adams appointed him one of three commissioners to negotiate peace with the Cherokee Nation, but he resigned before a treaty was signed. In 1798 he began his judicial career when the North Carolina General Assembly elected him to the state's superior court.

When Justice Iredell died in October 1799, President Adams wanted to replace him with another North Carolinian. His first choice was not available, so Adams chose Moore. Moore took his seat in time to hear arguments in *Baas v. Tingy* (1800) during the August term. As the most junior justice, Moore delivered his opinion first, declaring that a state of war existed with France, justifying retaliative measures on the part of the United States. It was the only Supreme Court opinion Moore ever wrote. Citing ill health, Moore resigned in 1804 and returned to his home state to pursue his most abiding passion, establishing the University of North Carolina.

SIGNIFICANT CASES

HYLTON V. UNITED STATES

Citation: 3 Dall. (3 U.S.) 171 (1796)
Argued: February 23-25, 1796
Decided: March 8, 1796
Court Below: United States Circuit Court for the District of Virginia
Basis for Review: *Writ of error
Facts: A 1794 congressional act levied a national tax on carriages.
Issue: Are such taxes * "direct" within the meaning of Article I, section 8, of the Constitution and therefore required to be *apportioned, or allocated, among the states in proportion to their respective populations?
Outcome: Congress's right to levy this tax was found to be constitutional.
Vote: 3-0

Participating: Iredell, Paterson, Chase (Cushing and Wilson not participating)
Opinions: Chase, Paterson, Iredell
Significance: The Constitution delegates the power to enact and collect taxes to the federal government. However, because arbitrary taxation by the British had given rise to the Revolutionary War, and because southern states feared that their lands and slaves would be subject to special taxes not equally charged to northern states, the Constitution limited Congress's power by stating that direct taxes (a term left undefined) can only be levied in proportion to the population of each state. By finding the carriage tax case involved an *excise tax, the Court narrowed the meaning of direct taxes and made way for an unapportioned national income tax program, which remained in effect until the Court's 1895 ruling in *Pollock v. Farmers' Loan & Trust Co. Pollock* in turn led to adoption and ratification in 1913 of the Sixteenth Amendment, which exempted income taxes from the constitutional requirement for apportionment of direct taxes.

Hylton is equally important because of Justice Chase's statement that "it is unnecessary, at this time, for me to determine, whether this court constitutionally possesses the power to declare an act of Congress void, on the ground of its being made contrary to, and in violation of, the constitution." While the Court was still some years away from formally declaring its power of *judicial review, *Hylton* was an early indication that it intended to assert this authority.

WARE V. HYLTON

Citation: 3 Dall. (3 U.S.) 199 (1796)
Argued: February 6-7, 1796
Decided: March 7, 1796
Court Below: United States Circuit Court for the District of Virginia
Basis for Review: *Writ of error
Facts: The 1783 Treaty of Paris, which ended the Revolutionary War, provided that neither the United States nor Britain would on its own soil obstruct citizens of the other country in their efforts to collect debts. Virginia, nonetheless, passed legislation allowing its citizens to repay these debts in depreciated currency, and numerous British creditors brought suit. The lower court upheld the Virginia statute.
Issue: Do the provisions of the Treaty of Paris supersede state law?
Outcome: Finding that federal treaties are the law of the land, *preempting conflicting state laws, the Ellsworth Court declared the Virginia law invalid.
Vote: 4-0
Participating: Cushing, Wilson, Paterson, Chase (Iredell not participating)
Opinions: Chase, Paterson, Iredell (who did not participate in deciding the case, but read his dissenting lower court opinion into the court record), Wilson, Cushing
Significance: Justice Iredell registered his dissent in *Ware* by reading into the record his circuit court opinion in the case, which had upheld the Virginia statute. When the case came before the Supreme Court, the minority circuit court opinion, which was originally expressed by former Chief Justice John Jay, was endorsed. Between the time of the circuit court decision in *Ware* and its rejection by the Supreme Court, Jay had left the Court to negotiate a treaty with Britain, which also addressed the debt problem existing between Britain and the United States. In upholding the superiority of treaties, the Court established an important legal principle; at the same time the Federalists on the bench were not above giving a boost to Jay's highly unpopular treaty.

UNITED STATES V. LA VENGEANCE

Citation: 3 Dall. (3 U.S.) 297 (1796)
Argued: August 10, 1796
Decided: August 11, 1796
Court Below: United States Circuit Court for the District of New York
Basis for Review: *Writ of error
Facts: A vessel was accused of illegally exporting arms from Sandy Hook, New Jersey, to France, and the lower court's *jurisdiction over the matter was challenged.
Issue: Because the ship was loaded on inland American waterways rather than the high seas, was this an *admiralty case which the federal

courts had the power to decide?

Outcome: The Supreme Court affirmed the circuit court's assertion of *appellate jurisdiction over the matter.

Vote: 6-0

Participating: Ellsworth, Cushing, Wilson, Iredell, Paterson, Chase

Opinion: Ellsworth for the Court

Significance: This case strengthened federal authority by extending federal admiralty jurisdiction to inland waterways. Prior to this decision, the jurisdiction of federal courts in admiralty cases had only applied to cases arising out of incidents that occurred on the high seas. Cases arising out of incidents occurring on navigable inland waterways, such as the Great Lakes, had previously been deemed to fall under state court jurisdiction. *United States v. La Vengeance* thus added considerably to the power of federal courts at the expense of state judiciaries.

MOODIE V. THE SHIP PHOEBE ANNE

Citation: 3 Dall. (3 U.S.) 319 (1796)

Argued: August 6, 1796

Decided: August 9, 1796

Court Below: United States Circuit Court for the District of South Carolina

Basis for Review: *Writ of error

Facts: A French warship, damaged in a storm, sought safety and made repairs in an American port.

Issue: In permitting the *Phoebe Anne* to reequip in one of its ports, did the United States violate its national neutrality laws?

Outcome: Reasoning that treaties supersede federal legislation, the Supreme Court affirmed the circuit court's decree upholding the ship's right to make repairs.

Vote: 6-0

Participating: Ellsworth, Cushing, Wilson, Iredell, Paterson, Chase

Opinion: Ellsworth for the Court

Significance: At issue in this case were two seemingly conflicting laws: the 1778 Treaty with France that granted a right to repair ships in port, and the federal neutrality laws that were designed to keep America out of the conflict that began in

1793 between Britain and France. In upholding the supremacy of international treaties over federal legislation, the Federalist Court displayed uncharacteristic impartiality, as their decision clearly favored France, then a U.S. enemy.

WISCART V. DAUCHY

Citation: 3 Dall. (3 U.S.) 321 (1796)

Argued: August 10, 1796

Decided: August 12, 1796

Court Below: United States Circuit Court for the District of Virginia

Basis of Review: *Writ of error

Facts: A suit, seeking to have certain deeds transferring slaves and personal property from one individual to another, was *removed, or transferred, from the Virginia Circuit Court to the Supreme Court by writ of error, rather than as a formal appeal.

Issue: In civil cases, is the Supreme Court permitted to rule on *questions of fact as well as *questions of law?

Outcome: The circuit court's judgment was allowed to stand, as Congress empowered the Court only to rule on questions of law in civil— as opposed to criminal—cases, which are properly removed to the higher court by writ of error.

Vote: 4-2

Participating: Ellsworth, Cushing, Wilson, Iredell, Paterson, Chase

Opinions: Ellsworth for the Court; Wilson dissenting

Significance: This case helped to define the Supreme Court's *appellate jurisdiction in civil cases which, by act of Congress, was—and is to this day—limited in civil cases to review of legal issues. The argument between Chief Justice Ellsworth and Justice Wilson in this case centered on the question of whether Article III of the Constitution or the Judiciary Act of 1789 controlled the Court's appellate jurisdiction. As Ellsworth wrote in his opinion: "If Congress had provided no rule to regulate our proceedings, we cannot exercise an appellate jurisdiction; and if the rule is provided, we cannot depart from it. The question, therefore, on the constitutional point of an appellate jurisdiction, is simply,

POLITICAL COMPOSITION
of the Ellsworth Court

Justice & Total Term	Courts Served	Appointing President	Political Party
Oliver Ellsworth 1796-1800	Ellsworth	Washington	Federalist
William Cushing 1790-1810	Jay Rutledge Ellsworth Marshall	Washington	Federalist
James Wilson 1789-1798	Jay Rutledge Ellsworth	Washington	Federalist
James Iredell 1790-1799	Jay Rutledge Ellsworth	Washington	Federalist
William Paterson 1793-1806	Jay Rutledge Ellsworth Marshall	Washington	Federalist
Samuel Chase 1796-1811	Ellsworth Marshall	Washington	Federalist
Bushrod Washington 1798-1829	Ellsworth Marshall	J. Adams	Federalist
Alfred Moore 1800-1804	Ellsworth Marshall	J. Adams	Federalist

whether Congress has established any rule for regulating its exercise?"

Despite Wilson's vigorous dissent, the majority of the Court agreed with Ellsworth that the vague parameters of Article III were not controlling, since Congress had spelled out the Court's appellate jurisdiction in the Judiciary Act. These rules clearly indicated that in civil cases, removal to the Supreme Court was to be achieved by writ of error, which presented the Court with a record of the proceedings below in order that it might examine errors allegedly committed there. Such a procedure barred review of the lower courts' determinations of the facts that were at issue when they originally heard the cases.

CALDER V. BULL

Citation: 3 Dall. (3 U.S.) 386 (1798)
Argued: February 8 & 13, 1798
Decided: August 8, 1798
Court Below: Connecticut Court of Errors
Basis for Review: *Writ of error
Facts: A resolution of the Connecticut state legislature set aside a decree of a state probate court that refused to record a will and granted the losing litigant a new trial.

Issue: Was the state legislature's action an unconstitutional *ex post facto law?

Outcome: The decree of the Connecticut Court of Errors affirming the legislature's resolution was affirmed.

Vote: 4-0

Participating: Cushing, Iredell, Paterson, Chase (Ellsworth not participating)

Opinions: Chase, Paterson, Iredell, Cushing

Significance: The Constitution's ban on ex post facto laws was determined to apply only to criminal statutes; it was not intended to protect property rights. While the Constitution clearly bans the enactment of laws—by federal or state legislatures—declaring certain acts to be criminal after they have been committed, this ban does not prohibit a state from nullifying an individual's right to property. In permitting the losing litigant to attempt to reclaim his property by means of another probate hearing, therefore, the Connecticut legislature did not violate the federal Constitution. Whether the enactment of such legislation in the wake of a state court finding is permissible is therefore not within the Supreme Court's authority to decide; it is, rather, a question for Connecticut courts.

BAAS V. TINGY

Citation: 4 Dall. (4 U.S.) 37 (1800)
Argued: August 14, 1800
Decided: August 15, 1800
Court Below: United States Circuit Court for the District of Pennsylvania
Basis for Review: *Writ of error
Facts: An American warship recaptured an American merchant vessel from a French privateer, which was authorized by the French government to seize enemy vessels.
Issue: Was France an enemy of the United States within the meaning of the law, thus validating the rights Americans claimed in the recaptured American ship and its cargo?
Outcome: The decree of the circuit court granting the Americans their salvage rights was affirmed.
Vote: 4-0
Participating: Paterson, Chase, Washington, Moore

Opinions: Moore, Washington, Chase, Paterson
Significance: In deciding that the conflict between France and the United States amounted to a state of war, the Supreme Court was in effect usurping Congress's constitutionally guaranteed right to declare war. The hostilities that took place from 1797 to 1800 between France and the United States, largely on the high seas, were given the title Quasi War because the United States never formally declared war against France. Two acts of Congress, both pertaining to salvage rights in recaptured American ships, were at issue in this case. By endorsing the application of the act granting the larger salvage right—a right enforceable only against enemies of the United States—the Court acknowledged that America and France were in a state of war. Such an acknowledgement, Republicans argued, amounted to an unauthorized exercise of power on the part of the Federalist Supreme Court.

VOTING PATTERNS

As Federalists, the justices of the Ellsworth Court were inclined to strengthen the authority of the central government—including the Court's own powers of *judicial review. In most of the cases it decided between 1796 and 1800, the Court took the opportunity to affirm the supremacy of federal law over conflicting state laws. Of the seven significant cases heard by the Ellsworth Court, only two featured dissenting opinions, those of Justice Iredell in *Ware v. Hylton* (1796) and of Justice Wilson in *Wiscart v. Dauchy* (1796). Iredell's disagreement with the majority of the Court (rather than dissenting, he abstained, having written the circuit court opinion) may have been a reaction against Justice Chase's profoundly nationalistic opinion upholding the supremacy of United States treaties over states' laws, but it did reflect his continuing interest in safeguarding the rights of states. Wilson's dissent in *Wiscart v. Dauchy* would have expanded the Supreme Court's *appellate jurisdiction beyond that prescribed by the Judiciary Act of 1789. It is significant, perhaps, that the Federalist Court, so determined to establish its authority and prestige with the American people, declined to enlarge its powers at the expense of Congress.

SPECIAL FEATURES OF THE ELLSWORTH COURT

ENFORCEMENT OF THE ALIEN AND SEDITION ACTS

It was not surprising that the justices of the Ellsworth Court—Federalists all—supported legislation collectively known as the Alien and Sedition Acts of 1798. What was surprising was the blatant lack of equitableness with which they enforced these laws. The prosecutorial roles played by Justices Iredell and Chase, in particular, in *seditious libel trials wreaked havoc on the judicial ideal of impartiality.

In 1798 in anticipation of war with France, Congress passed not only the Alien and Sedition Acts, but also a revenue-raising tax based on assessed value of residential property. When John Fries led a revolt against this tax by freeing two tax evaders from prison, he was accused of treason. At Fries's first trial, in Pennsylvania Circuit Court in 1799, Justice Iredell used the occasion to defend the Alien and Sedition Acts in his jury charge. Iredell's clear implication that the defendant was guilty as charged resulted in a guilty verdict and a death sentence. Because of the alleged bias of one juror, however, Iredell granted Fries a new trial.

Fries's second trial took place in 1800 in Pennsylvania Circuit Court, this time presided over by Justice Chase, the most ardent Federalist on the federal bench. Chase's behavior was more outrageous than Iredell's had been. Chase issued a written opinion on Fries's case before the trial even began. Although Chase was persuaded to withdraw his opinion, it was clear that his mind was already made up and that a fair trial for Fries was impossible. Frustrated by their inability to perform their jobs, Fries's attorneys withdrew, leaving Chase to act as their client's counsel and judge. The result was predictable: Fries was sentenced to death by hanging.

In another sedition case tried during the same court term, Chase employed the same tactics to defeat any attempt to defend Thomas Cooper, a Republican editor, whose sedition trial also resulted in a guilty verdict. Fries ultimately received a presidential pardon from John Adams, as did Cooper. Chase, however, pursued his partisan approach to dispensing justice, which devalued the federal courts and sealed his own reputation as a "hanging judge."

The Naturalization Act and the two Alien Acts are today regarded as having been legitimate legislation in time of war—even an undeclared one. The infamous Sedition Act, in contrast, was probably unconstitutional. Although the justices of the Ellsworth Court consistently upheld the Alien and Sedition Acts when ruling from lower court benches while on *circuit duty, none of the statutes was ever tested by the Supreme Court before the acts expired in 1800. We shall never be entirely certain, therefore, how the Ellsworth Court would have ruled on these acts in the atmosphere of wartime excess that characterized its tenure.

DEVELOPMENT OF JUDICIAL REVIEW

During the years Oliver Ellsworth headed the Supreme Court, the Court was still defining its role in the tripartite structure of federal government. *Marbury v. Madison,* decided by the Marshall Court in 1803, remains the best known expression by the Supreme Court of its power to determine what the law is by judging the constitutionality of decisions made by the states and by the other branches of the federal government. However, as early as *Hayburn's Case,* which the Jay Court deliberated in 1792, the Supreme Court was beginning to articulate its attitude toward *judicial review, a concept rooted in the traditions of English *common law but only implicit in the Constitution.

Three cases decided by the Ellsworth Court were particularly important to the development of judicial review. While in *Hayburn's Case* the justices had expressed their opposition to being obliged by Congress to act as pension commissioners while sitting as judges, the statute at issue was revised before the Supreme Court actually ruled on it. *Hylton v. Ware* (1796) marked the first time the Supreme Court considered the constitutionality of a federal law, finding a 1794 congressional tax act valid. The power of judicial review also extends to state legislation and judicial decisions. In both *Ware v. Hylton* (1796) and *Calder v. Bull* (1798), the Ellsworth Court asserted its authority to determine the validity of state laws under the Constitution. And it was in the latter case that Justice Iredell provided an institutional basis for the Court's supreme authority, arguing that the only justification for striking down a statute created "by the legislature of the Union, or the legislature of any member of the Union" is its potential violation of the federal Constitution in a "clear and urgent case."

The Marshall Court 1801-1835

BACKGROUND

THE ELECTION OF 1800

By the time of the fourth presidential election, the Federalists, who had dominated national politics up to that point, were in disarray. The high Federalists, a faction of the party led by Alexander Hamilton, actively worked against the reelection of John Adams, their party's nominee. The Republicans renominated Thomas Jefferson and Aaron Burr, who had been their candidates in the 1796 election. The Republicans won handily, with 73 electoral votes to the Federalists' 65.

Naming the next president, however, was a complicated business. The electoral rules of the time dictated that whoever came in second, regardless of party affiliation, would be named vice president. Republican unity was so strong that each Republican elector cast one vote for Jefferson and one for Burr. The Constitution mandated that in the case of such a tie, the House of Representatives would break the deadlock. Early in 1801, however, the House was dominated by Federalists who had been elected in 1798. Although this was a lame-duck session of Congress, the Federalists seized the opportunity to derail the Republican victory by supporting Burr in the belief that he would be more malleable, an impression Burr encouraged. Jefferson was declared the winner after the 35th ballot, but in the aftermath of the chaos surrounding the election, Congress passed the Twelfth Amendment, requiring that nominees for presi-

---

An asterisk (*) before a word or phrase indicates that a definition will be found in the glossary at the end of this volume.

dent and vice president be specifically designated by their parties.

Jefferson took the oath of office on March 4, 1801, one month after the swearing in of John Marshall as chief justice of the Supreme Court. When Oliver Ellsworth resigned late in 1800, President Adams turned first to former Chief Justice John Jay, who was a popular choice but who turned down the appointment. Another popular candidate for elevation to the chief justiceship was Justice William Paterson, but as an adherent of the Hamiltonian faction, he was unacceptable to Adams, who refused to appoint him. Instead, Adams nominated his secretary of state, Marshall, on January 20, 1801. The Senate, hoping that Adams could be persuaded to reconsider Paterson for the post, suspended consideration of Marshall's nomination for a week, but finding the president inflexible and fearing that someone more objectionable might be named if they rejected Marshall, finally confirmed him on January 27.

THE JUDICIARY ACT OF 1801 AND THE "MIDNIGHT JUDGES"

In February 1801, only days before Jefferson's inauguration, the Federalist Congress passed a new judiciary act. The 1801 Judiciary Act reduced the number of Supreme Court justices to five and eliminated one vacancy. It also ended *circuit duty for the justices and created six new *circuit courts which were to be staffed by newly appointed judges. Outgoing President John Adams quickly filled the new posts from among the ranks of the Federalist faithful, and by March 2, two days before Jefferson took office, the Senate had confirmed the appointments. The newly elected Republicans rightly saw this as a plan to pack the federal judiciary with Federalist loyalists and to protect the political composition of the Supreme Court by forestalling any immediate appointments by the new president. On March 8, 1802, the Republicans repealed the 1801 Judiciary Act.

A second late session law, passed in the final days of the Adams administration, had created a number of justice of the peace positions in the District of Columbia. President Adams made his appointments to these posts on March 2, 1801, and his appointees were confirmed the next day. Not all of the appointees' commissions, however, were delivered before midnight on March 3, when the new administration took over. President Jefferson subsequently ordered his secretary of state, James Madison, to hold back the signed and sealed commissions still in his possession. One of these named William Marbury who, later that year, petitioned the Supreme Court for a writ of *mandamus requiring Madison to surrender his commission, thus giving rise to one of the most significant cases in Supreme Court history, *Marbury v. Madison* (1803).

THE CHASE IMPEACHMENT

Jefferson's war on the Federalist judiciary rose to new heights in 1804, when the House of Representatives *impeached Justice Chase by a vote of 73 to 32. Chase was widely hated for his harsh enforcement of the Sedition Act of 1798, and a particularly prejudicial speech to a grand jury in 1803 provided the occasion for a drive to impeach him. Still, his misconduct fell far short of the high crimes and misdemeanors required to impeach a government official; his active campaigning for John Adams during the election of 1800 was more probably to blame for his impeachment trial. In the end, although a majority of the Senate voted on March 1, 1805, to remove Chase, the vote fell short of the two-thirds required for conviction.

Chase's acquittal quelled rumors of Republican plans to impeach the other four remaining Federalist judges: John Marshall, William Cushing, William Paterson, and Bushrod Washington (indeed, some historians of the Court believe the Chase acquittal permanently secured the Court from impeachment threats based on essentially political grounds). Jefferson's animosity towards Marshall — whom he regarded as yet another "midnight judge" appointed in the waning days of the Adams administration — remained personal, but by 1805, having won reelection with little opposition, his attention turned away from partisan bickering and toward foreign affairs.

THE BURR CONSPIRACY

Jefferson and Marshall were cousins and bitter enemies. The suspicion with which they regarded one another was heightened when Aaron Burr was brought to trial in 1807. Burr, whose activities during the election of 1800 made him both Jefferson's vice president for a term and politically suspect, was permanently exiled from the national arena when he killed Alexander Hamilton in a duel in 1804. After leaving the vice presidency, Burr led a military expedition in the West, where he advocated secession and formation of a western confederacy. Burr and his co-conspirators were arrested for treason.

The Marshall Court reacted to the Jefferson administration's prosecution of the Burr conspiracy by issuing a writ of *habeas corpus, finding that there was insufficient evidence to detain two of Burr's accomplices. After the Supreme Court term ended, the chief justice declared his opposition more openly by traveling to Richmond to preside personally over Burr's trial in circuit court, where he threw out much of the government's testimony. Largely as a result of such rulings, Burr was acquitted. Jefferson, outraged by the outcome, suggested that the Constitution be amended to provide for some means other than impeachment to remove justices, but no such amendment passed.

THE WAR OF 1812

A large part of Jefferson's landslide victory in 1804 can be attributed to his administration's purchase from France the previous year of the Louisiana Territory, which increased the size of the country nearly 150 percent. Relations between the United States and Britain, however, worsened during Jefferson's second term and resulted in outright warfare during the tenure of his successor, James Madison.

Animosity between America and Britain grew out of a renewal of hostilities between Britain and France, starting in 1803. Both the French and the British seized American vessels, but the British violated international law by performing their seizures on the high seas, rather than in their own ports. Britain maintained a blockade around Europe, stopping and searching every American ship that penetrated its unilaterally declared sphere of control. Britain often pressed American seamen into service to reinforce decimated English crews. As many as ten thousand Americans may have been serving on British warships by 1811. At the same time, the British were inciting rebellion among the Indians of the American Northwest. On June 1, 1812, President Madison asked Congress for a formal declaration of war.

For two and a half years the war raged on, with the great Shawnee chief Tecumseh driving the Americans out of the Northwest, but with the Americans winning most of their naval battles against the British. The British attacked by land as well, however, and in August 1814 they managed to reach Washington, D.C., where they burned government buildings, including the White House. Then, in January 1815, Andrew Jackson's Tennessee irregulars, together with two regiments of free blacks and a band of Louisiana pirates, scored a stunning victory over the British in the Battle of New Orleans. Shortly thereafter, word reached the capital that a treaty ending the war had been signed in Ghent, Belgium, a few days before Jackson's success.

THE FEDERALISTS AND THE HARTFORD CONVENTION

The pro-British Federalists had opposed the Madison administration's declaration of war. In December 1814 New England delegates of the party met in Hartford, Connecticut, to consider methods of resisting the war. The convention resulted in a proposal for seven constitutional amendments reflecting Federalist ethnocentrism, the most important of which would have repealed the Great Compromise of 1787 granting the South additional power by allowing slaves to be counted as three-fifths of a person for purposes of representation in Congress. By the time these proposals reached the nation's capital, the war had ended, and the convention only succeeded in branding the Federalists as disloyal. The Hartford Convention marked the Federalists' final, abortive attempt to dominate national politics.

THE ERA OF GOOD FEELINGS AND THE MONROE DOCTRINE

The collapse of the Federalists left the country dominated by one-party rule for nearly a decade, during which the absence of partisan tensions contributed to a sense of national well-being. James Monroe was elected president in 1816. He presided over a country that was experiencing a tremendous postwar boom. In March 1816 Congress chartered the Second Bank of the United States (the charter of the first national bank had been allowed to expire in 1811) to help regulate the nation's money supply. Congress also established the nation's first tariff, and such protective measures, together with the Marshall Court's willingness to put law at the service of enterprise in such cases as *Dartmouth College v. Woodward* (1819) and *Gibbons v. Ogden* (1824), helped fuel rapid economic growth.

At the same time, the nation was expanding geographically, appropriating Florida (with the help of war hero Andrew Jackson) and extending the nation westward to include the Oregon Country. Territorial expansion during the two-term Monroe administration was achieved largely through the efforts of Monroe's secretary of state, John Quincy Adams. Fueled by a vision of America as a powerful nation extending across the continent, Adams pursued the national interest in the realm of foreign affairs, encouraging President Monroe to issue a public statement that would let the world know of the nation's economic and political strength.

The policy statement Monroe inserted into his annual message to Congress in December 1823 asserted that the American continents were no longer "to be considered as subjects for future colonization by any European power." The two hemispheres of the earth, Monroe declared unequivocally, were separated by politics as well as geography. The United States lacked the military might to enforce the nonintervention policy he announced, but what was later known as the Monroe Doctrine became an integral part of American foreign policy.

THE MISSOURI COMPROMISE

With the defeat of the Western Indian tribes in the War of 1812, areas in the Mississippi Valley were opened up to settlers. Within four years, four new states were admitted to the Union: Indiana, Illinois, Alabama, and Mississippi. In February 1819 when the House of Representatives was considering a bill to permit Missouri to draft a state constitution, Congressman James Tallmadge of New York proposed that this bill be amended so that no more slaves could be imported into the state, and that children born to slaves be freed upon reaching 25 years of age. Southerners viewed the proposed amendment as a frontal attack on slavery and on *states' rights; in their view, Missouri as a *sovereign entity should be able to choose its own social system.

The northern-dominated House passed Tallmadge's amendment, but the Senate, which was equally divided between slave-holding and free states, defeated it. The stalemate was ended the next year when Maine's admission to the Union as a free state was tied to approval of Missouri's admission as a slave-holding state. The Missouri Compromise, which became law in March 1820, also stipulated that slavery would be prohibited in the remainder of the land constituting the Louisiana Purchase above 36° 30' north latitude. Southern states did not come immediately to the realization that this prohibition meant they would quickly become a minority, but the Missouri Compromise marked the beginning of the serious division between North and South which, four decades later, would result in the Civil War.

THE ELECTION OF 1824 AND THE BIRTH OF THE DEMOCRATIC PARTY

As Republicans during the Jefferson, Madison, and Monroe administrations worked to consolidate federal power, they began to adopt the perspective of their old rivals, the Federalists. After the election of John Quincy Adams in 1824, the party assumed a new identity as National Republicans.

The election of 1824 was the second and last

to be decided in the House of Representatives. Andrew Jackson won the popular vote, but no one had a majority of the electoral vote. In the House, Jackson, a military hero but a political unknown, was defeated by the combined forces of Adams and Speaker of the House Henry Clay, whom Adams then named as his secretary of state. Jackson, a southerner and a slave owner, proclaimed that a conspiracy of eastern aristocrats had robbed him of his victory. While it is probable that Adams and Clay had struck no bargain and that Jackson was finally undone by his own lack of political acumen, Jackson managed to paint himself as a virtuous representative of the common man and, with the help of consummate politician Martin Van Buren, to found a new party, the Democratic Republicans. Forging an alliance between southerners and old-style Republicans, Van Buren played a pivotal role in winning the election of 1828 for Jackson and his supporters, who soon shortened their name to the Democratic Party.

INDIAN REMOVAL

Jackson's first priority upon election was to remove the Creek and Cherokee Indians from the prime farmland they occupied in Georgia. In his first annual message to his countrymen, he outlined a plan setting aside a tract of land west of the Mississippi that would be exchanged with the tribes for their eastern landholdings. Congress in turn passed the Indian Removal Act of 1830, mandating tribal migration to new Indian lands in Oklahoma, Kansas, and Nebraska.

Jackson undertook his program of Indian removal in the name of *states' rights, specifically endorsing Georgia's position that those Indians remaining within its borders were subject to state laws. The Cherokees responded by filing a series of *original jurisdiction suits with the Supreme Court to prevent Georgia from enforcing stringent new state laws affecting Indians and their lands. While in *Cherokee Nation v. Georgia* (1831) Chief Justice Marshall, writing for the Court, found the Cherokees subject to state laws because they were not a *sovereign nation, one year later, in *Worcester v. Georgia*, Marshall in

effect reversed himself, finding that federal *jurisdiction over Indian affairs was exclusive. The Cherokees' victory was a hollow one, however, for Jackson sided openly with Georgia, allegedly declaring, "John Marshall has made his decision, now let him enforce it."

THE NULLIFICATION CRISIS

Although Jackson espoused *states' rights, he also believed strongly in preservation of the Union, as became abundantly clear in 1832 at the height of his battle with South Carolina and with Vice President John C. Calhoun. Jackson had inherited from the previous administration a tariff that protected manufacturers at the expense of farmers. The almost entirely agricultural south viewed the 1828 tariff as an unconstitutional exercise of federal power, and nowhere was opposition greater than in South Carolina, where resistance was fueled by fear that the national government might grow so powerful as to emancipate the large slave population on which the state's economy depended.

In December 1828 the South Carolina legislature published an *Exposition and Protest* against the "tariff of abominations," an anonymous essay which was nevertheless known to be written by Vice President Calhoun. The tract argued that the Constitution was a pact between *sovereign states, any of which could declare an act of the national government null and void. If the federal government should amend the Constitution in response to such nullification, the state could either assent or secede from the Union.

Jackson managed to purge his cabinet of Calhoun allies (Calhoun himself was succeeded by Martin Van Buren as Jackson's running mate in 1832) and to quell temporarily the nullification controversy. Nonetheless, for the next three decades leading up to the Civil War, nullification, with its emphasis on secession as a constitutional right, remained a part of the national debate concerning states' rights and slavery.

THE BANK WAR

Jackson's distrust of centralized power culminated in his assault on the Second Bank of the United

JUDICIAL BIOGRAPHY
John Marshall

PERSONAL DATA

Born: September 24, 1755, near Germantown (now Midland), Virginia

Parents: Thomas Marshall, Mary Randolph Keith Marshall

Higher Education: College of William and Mary, 1780

Bar Admission: Virginia, 1780

Political Party: Federalist

Marriage: January 3, 1783, to Mary Willis Ambler, who bore Marshall seven sons and three daughters (five sons and one daughter survived to adulthood), and who died December 25, 1831

Died: July 6, 1835, in Philadelphia, Pennsylvania

Buried: Shockoe Hill Cemetery, Richmond, Virginia

PROFESSIONAL CAREER

Occupations: Serviceman, 1776-1781; Lawyer, 1780-1797; Politician, 1782-1786, 1787-90, 1795-1801; Judge, 1785-1788, 1801-1835; Diplomat, 1797-1798

Official Positions: Member, Virginia House of Delegates, 1782-1785, 1787-1790, 1795-1796; Member, Virginia Executive Council of State, 1782-1784; Recorder, Richmond, Virginia, City Hustings Court, 1785-1788; Delegate, Virginia convention to ratify the federal Constitution, 1788; Special Envoy to France, 1797-1798; Member, United States House of Representatives, 1799-1800; United States Secretary of State, 1800-1801; Chief Justice, United States Supreme Court, 1801-1835

SUPREME COURT SERVICE

Nominated: January 20, 1801

Nominated By: John Adams

Confirmed: January 27, 1801

Confirmation Vote: Voice vote

Oath Taken: February 4, 1801

Replaced: Chief Justice Oliver Ellsworth

Significant Opinions: *Marbury v. Madison* (1803); *Bank of the United States v. Deveaux* (1809); *Fletcher v. Peck* (1810); *Martin v. Hunter's Lessee* (1816); *Dartmouth College v. Woodward* (1819); *McCulloch v. Maryland* (1819); *Sturges v. Crowninshield* (1819); *Cohens v. Virginia* (1821); *Gibbons v. Ogden* (1824); *Osborn v. Bank of the United States* (1824); *Wayman v. Southard* (1825); *Brown v. Maryland* (1827); *Weston v. Charleston* (1829); *Willson v. Blackbird Creek Marsh Co.* (1829); *Craig v. Missouri* (1830); *Providence Bank v. Billings* (1831); *Cherokee Nation v. Georgia* (1831); *Worcester v. Georgia* (1832); *Barron v. Baltimore* (1833)

Left Court: Died July 6, 1835

Length of Service: 34 years, 5 months, 2 days

Replacement: Chief Justice Roger Brooke Taney

States, which was administered by his political enemies. In his first message to Congress, he made his doubts about the necessity — even the constitutionality — of the bank clear. The issue remained alive throughout Jackson's first administration and became a political issue in the election of 1832. Nicholas Biddle, then president of the bank and a supporter of Jackson's National Republican opponent, Henry Clay, asked Congress to renew the bank's charter in January 1832, even though it was not due to expire for four more years. The bank had strong support in Congress, which would certainly vote to renew.

And, as Clay saw it, he would profit from whatever action Jackson took in response to a congressional renewal bill. If Jackson signed it, Clay, a longtime supporter of the bank, would benefit from the institution's continuation. If, on the other hand, Jackson vetoed the bill, Clay had a campaign issue.

Congress did vote to renew the bank's charter. For his part, Jackson responded with a ringing veto and went on to win the election in a landslide. His reelection meant the end of the Second Bank of the United States. Although it continued to exist until the date its new charter ran out,

John Marshall

Jackson took swift action to rob it of power, ordering that all government moneys be removed from the bank. When the secretary of the treasury and his successor both protested that the president's plan was unconstitutional, Jackson found a man who would execute his wishes, Roger Brooke Taney. When the great nationalist and Jackson opponent John Marshall died two years later, Taney was rewarded with the chief justiceship.

MARSHALL'S EARLY LIFE

John Marshall, the eldest of 15 children, was born in a log cabin on the northwestern frontier of Virginia. His formal education lasted only two years; the bulk of what he learned came from his father, who first taught him math and English literature, then schooled him in *Blackstone's Commentaries on the Laws of England* (1765).

Marshall's father, who served in the Virginia House of Burgesses and as George Washington's assistant surveyor, also introduced his son to politics. When the Revolutionary War broke out, father and son enlisted together. As a member of the Culpepper Minute Men and later the Continental army, Marshall saw action at the battles of Great Bridge, Brandywine, Germantown, and Monmouth Courthouse. He also wintered with Washington at Valley Forge where, it is said, his lifelong commitment to a strong national government grew as he and his fellow soldiers froze owing to congressional impotence and inaction.

After the war, Marshall went to Williamsburg, Virginia, where he met his future wife and, for six weeks, attended law lectures given by the distinguished scholar George Wythe at the College of William and Mary. After these short weeks, he was admitted to both Phi Beta Kappa and the Farquier County bar.

MARSHALL'S PUBLIC LIFE

In 1783 he married Mary Willis Ambler, daughter of the Virginia state treasurer, and set up practice in Richmond. His law practice was an active one, devoted largely to defense of Virginia debtors trying to avoid prewar obligations to British creditors, the same issue that gave rise to *Ware v. Hylton* (1796), the only case Marshall argued before the Supreme Court. Like many young lawyers, Marshall became active in state and local politics, serving several terms in the Virginia House of Delegates. In 1788 he distinguished himself as a Federalist leader at the Virginia ratifying convention, where he spoke out ardently and eloquently in support of federal judicial authority. Shortly thereafter, President Washington, a friend of the family, offered Marshall a commission as the first United States attorney for the District of Columbia. Marshall declined this offer, along with offers to serve as a minister to France and as an associate justice of the U.S. Supreme Court.

Marshall's main reason for refusing such honors seems to have been financial. Between 1796 and 1806, he was preoccupied with meeting debts he had incurred in land speculation. Financial considerations weighed heavily in his decision to accept a commission to write the *Life of George Washington*, which appeared in five volumes between 1805 and 1807. When Marshall finally did accept a government appointment, an offer in 1797 to serve as a special envoy to France, he did so because it promised a substantial financial reward. This mission, which precipitated the XYZ affair (see p. 26), was unsuccessful because the French government demanded a bribe before it would negotiate. However, Marshall's services, including a published response to the blackmailers, earned him $20,000 and public acclaim.

Shortly thereafter, at Washington's urging, Marshall ran for and won a seat in the House of Representatives. While a member of the House, he successfully defended the Adams administration when it was attacked by Republicans for surrendering Thomas Nash, an English murderer masquerading as an American sailor, to the British minister for trial. A grateful president offered Marshall the portfolio of the War Department, which Marshall declined, then the position of secretary of state, which he accepted in 1800. For the last month of the Adams administration, Marshall served simultaneously as both secretary of state and chief justice.

MARSHALL AS CHIEF JUSTICE

When Oliver Ellsworth resigned as chief justice in September 1800, President Adams first nominated former Chief Justice John Jay. Jay was quickly confirmed by the Senate, but he declined the position. Sentiment was strong among the Hamiltonian wing of the Federalist Party to replace Ellsworth with Associate Justice William Paterson, whom Marshall, too, favored. Adams, however, turned to Marshall himself, a man who had served him faithfully during the waning days of his administration.

Marshall was nominated on January 20, 1801, and confirmed one week later. Only Justice William Cushing was present at the opening, on February 2, 1801, of the Supreme Court's first term in its new quarters in Washington, D.C. Two days later, however, the appearance of Justices Samuel Chase and Bushrod Washington made a *quorum, and Marshall was sworn in as chief justice.

The strongly Federalist Marshall was the first justice to serve simultaneously with a president from the opposition party. Jefferson and Marshall were arch antagonists throughout Jefferson's two terms, but Marshall succeeded in resisting the president's attempts to diminish the power of the Supreme Court. Marshall succeeded in dominating the Court as no other justice has ever done, and he did so through a combination of diplomacy, personality, and sheer hard work. During his 34 years as chief justice, he wrote roughly half of the 1,106 opinions issued by the Court.

Marshall's first real opportunity to express his judicial philosophy came in 1803 in *Marbury v. Madison*, which has gained lasting significance as the Supreme Court's first clear statement of its power of *judicial review. In *Marbury*, Marshall amply demonstrated those qualities that made him such a powerful leader on the Court. The plaintiff in the case, William Marbury, was one of the "midnight" justices of the peace who, because of the change in administrations, never received his commission. He applied directly to the Supreme Court for a writ of *mandamus, as was his right under the Judiciary Act of 1789, commanding the secretary of state to deliver his commission. Marshall's dilemma was this: if he ordered Secretary Madison to deliver the commission and Madison refused, the authority of the Court would be undermined; if he found that Marbury had no case, he would be accused of ingratiating himself with the Republicans — and the Court's authority would still be weakened. Instead of choosing either option, Marshall devised an ingenious third course. While finding that Marbury was deserving of his commission, Marshall ruled it could not be delivered because the applicable section of the 1789 Judiciary Act was an unconstitutional enlargement of the Court's *original jurisdiction. Marshall thus managed to avoid a confrontation between the executive and the judiciary, and at the same time firmly establish the Supreme Court's role as final arbiter of the constitutionality of legislation.

Marshall went on to expand the Supreme Court's review powers in *Fletcher v. Peck* (1810), in which the Court first found a state law unconstitutional, and in *Martin v. Hunter's Lessee* (1816) and *Cohens v. Virginia* (1821), both of which affirmed the Supreme Court's *appellate power over the decisions of state courts. In *McCulloch* *v. Maryland* (1819), Marshall led the Court in reinforcing the strength of the entire national government by means of a liberal reading of the *Necessary and Proper Clause of the Constitution, which endows Congress with the capacity to create substantive laws enabling exercise of its *enumerated powers. The power of the federal government to regulate commerce with foreign nations and between states was the subject of *Gibbons v. Ogden* (1824), in which Marshall limited state power by creating what amounted to a powerful basis for federal regulation of all commerce. Marshall employed the law to protect private property and promote the growth of American business in such cases as *Dartmouth College v. Woodward* (1819).

For the last decade that Marshall presided over the Court, the nation—and the Court—were confronted with the steadily increasing power of the *states' rights movement. During this period, Marshall modified some of his earlier holdings, and he also experienced his first outright defeat when, after he wrote the opinion upholding the *sovereignty of the Cherokee Nation in *Worcester v. Georgia* (1832), President Jackson refused to enforce the Court's decision. By that time, however, Marshall had irrevocably changed the status of the Supreme Court, fashioning it into the ultimate interpreter of the Constitution—which itself gained new life because of Marshall's written opinions.

After the election of Andrew Jackson, Marshall found himself surrounded on the Court by Republicans sympathetic to states' rights arguments, but he refused to resign, hoping to outlast Jackson so that the next chief justice appointed could help maintain balance on the Court. In 1831, however, Marshall lost his wife and underwent a serious operation to remove bladder stones. On July 6, 1835, following an injury from a stage coach accident and suffering from a liver ailment, Marshall became the first chief justice to die while still on the bench.

ASSOCIATE JUSTICES

For biographies of Associate Justices **William Cushing** and **William Paterson,** see entries under

THE JAY COURT. For biographies of Associate Justices **Samuel Chase, Bushrod Washington,** and **Alfred Moore,** see entries under **THE ELLSWORTH COURT.**

WILLIAM JOHNSON

PERSONAL DATA

Born: December 27, 1771, in St. James Goose Creek Parish, South Carolina, near Charleston
Parents: William Johnson, Sarah Nightingale Johnson
Higher Education: College of New Jersey, now Princeton University (undergraduate degree, with honors, 1790)
Bar Admission: South Carolina, 1793
Political Party: Democratic Republican
Marriage: March 20, 1794, to Sarah Bennett, who bore Johnson eight children (six of whom died in childhood), and who, with her husband, adopted two children from Santo Domingo (now the Dominican Republic)
Died: August 4, 1834, in Brooklyn, New York
Buried: It is not known where, but a monument to him was erected in St. Philips churchyard, Charleston

PROFESSIONAL CAREER

Occupations: Lawyer, 1793-1799; Politician, 1794-1798; Judge, 1799-1834
Official Positions: Member, South Carolina House of Representatives, 1794-1798; Speaker, South Carolina House of Representatives, 1798; Judge, South Carolina Court of Common Pleas, 1799-1804; Associate Justice, United States Supreme Court, 1804-1834

SUPREME COURT SERVICE

Nominated: March 22, 1804
Nominated By: Thomas Jefferson
Confirmed: March 24, 1804
Confirmation Vote: Voice vote
Oath Taken: May 8, 1804
Replaced: Alfred Moore
Significant Opinions: *United States v. Hudson and Goodwin* (1812); *Ogden v. Saunders* (1827)
Left Court: Died August 4, 1834
Length of Service: 30 years, 2 months, 27 days
Replacement: James M. Wayne

William Johnson was born into a family of modest means headed by a man who was a blacksmith by trade, but who was also a patriot during the Revolutionary War and later a legislator. After attending grammar school in Charleston, South Carolina, Johnson enrolled at the College of New Jersey, from which he graduated at the head of his class in 1790. Johnson read law with Federalist leader Charles Cotesworth Pinckney, and he was admitted to the bar in 1793.

The next year, Johnson was elected to the first of three consecutive terms in the South Carolina House of Representatives, where he served as cashier and was later chosen as Speaker. While serving in these positions, Johnson converted to Jeffersonian republicanism and the view that the legislature served as the engine of government. Johnson began his judicial career in 1799, when the state assembly selected him to serve as a judge on South Carolina's highest tribunal.

When Thomas Jefferson appointed him to the Supreme Court in 1804, Johnson at the age of 32 was much younger than the other justices and came from a considerably less privileged background. His initial status as the first and only Republican on the Court also set him apart. As a member of the majority party in the South Carolina Court of Common Pleas, he had become accustomed to issuing *seriatim opinions, and he did not fall readily into line with Chief Justice Marshall's attempts to present unanimous opinions which he himself authored. Instead, Johnson became known as the Court's first great dissenter. Johnson began first by disagreeing with Justice Marshall's chief surrogate, Justice Story, perhaps most noticeably in *United States v. Hudson and Goodwin* (1812), in which he refused to endorse federal *jurisdiction over criminal cases. In 1822 he published a two-volume work on Revolutionary War General Nathanael Greene, a Jeffersonian rebuttal to Marshall's Federalist biography of George Washington, and began a lengthy correspondence with then ex-President Jefferson. After 1823 he frequently broke with the unified front the chief justice tried to maintain, writing 9 of the Court's 11 concurring opinions and 18 of 42 dissents. Other new appointees to the Marshall

Court soon followed his example, and the Court ceased to speak as one.

Thomas Jefferson was Johnson's hero, and in 1826, after the former president's death, Johnson published a *Eulogy of Thomas Jefferson*. Johnson was an independent, even erratic thinker who managed to affront Federalists and Republicans alike. He had a restless mind, and was easily distracted by activities outside the law, such as the American Philosophical Society, which he actively supported, and the University of South Carolina, which he helped found. On August 4, 1834, following jaw surgery in New York, Johnson died, apparently of exhaustion.

HENRY BROCKHOLST LIVINGSTON

PERSONAL DATA

Born: November 25, 1757, in New York, New York
Parents: William Livingston, Susanna French Livingston
Higher Education: College of New Jersey, now Princeton University (undergraduate degree, 1774)
Bar Admission: New York, 1783
Political Party: Democratic Republican
Marriages: Catharine Keteltas, who bore Livingston five children; Ann Ludlow, who bore him three children; Catharine Seaman Kortright, who bore him three children
Died: March 18, 1823, in Washington, D.C.
Buried: Trinity Church churchyard, New York, New York

PROFESSIONAL CAREER

Occupations: Serviceman, 1776-1779; Diplomat, 1779-1782; Lawyer, 1783-1802; Politician, 1786-1802; Judge, 1802-1823
Official Positions: Member, New York Assembly, 1786-1789; Judge, New York Supreme Court, 1802-1806; Associate Justice, United State Supreme Court, 1807-1823

SUPREME COURT SERVICE

Appointed: November 10, 1806 (recess appointment)
Appointed By: Thomas Jefferson
Oath Taken: January 20, 1807
Nominated: December 13, 1806

Confirmed: December 17, 1806
Confirmation Vote: Voice vote
Oath Retaken: February 2, 1807
Replaced: William Paterson
Significant Opinions: None
Left Court: Died March 18, 1823
Length of Service: 16 years, 1 month, 26 days
Replacement: Smith Thompson

Henry Brockholst Livingston — who dropped his first name to distinguish himself from prominent relatives of the same name — grew up in New Jersey, where his father had served as governor during the Revolution. After graduating from the College of New Jersey, where he was a classmate of James Madison, Livingston joined the Continental army and was commissioned as an officer. He served under Generals Schuyler and St. Clair, and acted as Benedict Arnold's aide.

After the war, Livingston went to Spain to serve as private secretary to his brother-in-law, John Jay, then American minister to that country. It was during this period that Livingston began to develop an antipathy toward Jay that would evolve into open political warfare and result in Livingston's conversion to republicanism. Nonetheless, after he returned to the United States to pursue a legal career, he began working closely with Alexander Hamilton, who was renowned for his devotion to Federalist principles.

Livingston pursued state office, serving three terms in the New York Assembly. By 1791 he was recognized as an Anti-Federalist leader, and he helped Jefferson carry New York in the election of 1800. He was rewarded with a position on the New York Supreme Court bench. When Justice Alfred Moore died in 1804, President Jefferson considered Livingston as his replacement. William Johnson was chosen instead, but when another vacancy occurred on the Supreme Court two years later, Jefferson turned to Livingston. Livingston's was a recess appointment which first occurred on November 10, 1806. He first took the oath of office on January 20, 1807, by which time he was involved in the official confirmation process.

Although Livingston had an outgoing, ani- mated personality and approached his judicial duties energetically, he soon fell under the sway of Chief Justice Marshall, eventually reverting to his Federalist sympathies. He was widely acknowledged to be an expert on commercial law, but with the appointment of Justice Story in 1811, even this distinction was eclipsed.

Livingston's life was marred by an attempt to assassinate him in 1785, and a 1798 duel in which he killed a man. He was also implicated in violations of judicial ethics: first, when he informed John Quincy Adams of the Court's intended decision in *Fletcher v. Peck* (1810), and again in 1819 when he reportedly succumbed to influence peddling in *Dartmouth College v. Woodward* (1819). On the positive side, he devoted himself to support of the New York Historical Society, Columbia University, and free public schooling, which he helped to establish in New York City.

THOMAS TODD

PERSONAL DATA

Born: January 23, 1765, in King and Queen County, Virginia
Parents: Robert Todd, Elizabeth Richards Todd
Higher Education: Liberty Hall, now Washington and Lee University (undergraduate degree, 1783)
Bar Admission: Virginia, 1788
Marriages: 1788 to Elizabeth Harris, who bore Todd five children, and who died in 1811; 1812 to Lucy Payne, who bore him two sons and a daughter
Political Party: Democratic Republican
Died: February 7, 1826, in Frankfort, Kentucky
Buried: Frankfort Cemetery

PROFESSIONAL CAREER

Occupations: Serviceman, 1779, 1781; Educator, 1783-1784; Government Official, 1784-1801; Lawyer, 1788-1801; Judge, 1801-1826
Official Positions: Clerk, conventions on Kentucky statehood, 1784-1792; Clerk, Kentucky House of Representatives, 1792-1801; Clerk, Kentucky constitutional conventions, 1792, 1799; Clerk, Lexington Democratic Society, 1793-1794; Clerk, Kentucky Court of Appeals, 1799-1801; Judge, Kentucky Court of Appeals, 1801-1806; Chief Judge, Kentucky Court

of Appeals, 1806-1807; Associate Justice, United States Supreme Court, 1807-1826

SUPREME COURT SERVICE
Nominated: February 28, 1807
Nominated By: Thomas Jefferson
Confirmed: March 3, 1807
Confirmation Vote: Voice vote
Oath Taken: May 4, 1807
Replaced: No one; filled newly created seat
Significant Opinions: None
Left Court: Died February 7, 1826
Length of Service: 18 years, 9 months, 3 days
Replacement: Robert Trimble

Born to a Kentucky family of wealthy landowners, Thomas Todd was orphaned by the time he was 11 years old. During the Revolution, he enlisted twice, at the age of 14 and again at the age of 16, in the Continental army, eventually serving as a private during the last year of the conflict. Although most of his inheritance had been squandered by his guardian, he managed to obtain a good classical education, and upon graduation from Liberty Hall in 1783, he served as tutor to the daughters of Harry Innes, a Virginia legislator and distant relative.

Through Innes, Todd became involved in Kentucky's movement for separation from Virginia, working as the official recorder for all ten Kentucky statehood conventions. He served a similar function for the new Kentucky legislature and for the state constitutional conventions. Again because of Innes's good offices, Todd — who had been admitted to the bar in 1788 and subsequently developed a thriving practice in property law — was appointed clerk of the Kentucky Court of Appeals, on whose bench Innes sat. Two years later, Todd was himself elevated to a judgeship on that court, where he later became chief judge.

Throughout his life, Todd benefited from his reputation for fairness — and from his connections. After his first wife died, Todd married Dolley Madison's sister, Lucy Payne, in the East Room of the White House. And in 1807, when a new federal *circuit, comprising Tennessee, Kentucky and Ohio, was created, the senators and representatives from those states recommended to President Jefferson that Todd be appointed to fill the seventh seat on the Supreme Court that had been created to service the new circuit.

Once on the Supreme Court, Todd, like so many others, fell under the sway of Chief Justice Marshall's Federalist consensus building. Owing to illness and the distance between Washington, D.C., and his home, Todd was absent for six terms of the Court. He wrote only 14 opinions of his own during his 18-year tenure: eleven for the majority (ten of them concerning land claims, his area of expertise), two concurrences, and just one dissent — the last of which happened also to be his first written Supreme Court opinion.

GABRIEL DUVALL

PERSONAL DATA
Born: December 6, 1752, in Prince Georges County, Maryland
Parents: Benjamin Duvall, Susanna Tyler Duvall
Higher Education: None
Bar Admission: Maryland, 1778
Political Party: Democratic Republican
Marriages: July 24, 1787, to Mary Bryce, who bore Duvall one son, before she died on March 24, 1790; May 5, 1795, to Jane Gibbon, who died in April 1834
Died: March 6, 1844, in Prince Georges County
Buried: Glen Dale, Prince Georges County (family estate)

PROFESSIONAL CAREER
Occupations: Serviceman, 1776-1771; Government Official, 1775-1787, 1802-1811; Politician, 1782-1796, 1800, 1802-1811; Judge, 1796-1802, 1811-1835
Official Positions: Clerk, Maryland Convention, 1775-1777; Clerk, Maryland House of Delegates, 1777-1787; Member, Maryland State Council, 1782-1785; Member, Maryland House of Delegates, 1787-1794; Member, United States House of Representatives, 1794-1796; Chief Justice, General Court of Maryland, 1796-1802; Member, Electoral College, 1796, 1800; Comptroller, United States Treasury, 1802-1811; Associate Justice, United States Supreme Court, 1811-1835

SUPREME COURT SERVICE

Nominated: November 15, 1811
Nominated By: James Madison
Confirmed: November 18, 1811
Confirmation Vote: Voice Vote
Oath Taken: November 23, 1811
Replaced: Samuel Chase
Significant Opinions: None
Left Court: Resigned January 14, 1835
Length of Service: 23 years, 1 month, 22 days
Replacement: Philip Barbour

Gabriel Duvall was born into a family of French Huguenots at Marietta, their ancestral Maryland estate. He was privately educated in the classics and also read law, which resulted in his bar admission in 1778. Even before he completed his legal studies, he was active in the Revolution, acting as muster-master and commissary of stores for the Maryland forces, and later serving as a private in the Maryland militia. His political career also began during the war, when he was made clerk of the Maryland Convention, the governing state body. When the state government was formally organized into the House of Delegates, Duvall served as clerk for that body as well. He was later elected to the State Council, the Maryland House of Delegates, and the United States House of Representatives. He was also selected as a delegate to the Constitutional Convention in 1787, a position he declined.

Duvall began his judicial career in 1796, when he was elected chief judge of the General Court of Maryland. In 1806 he was elevated to a seat on the Court of Appeals of Maryland, but again for unknown reasons, he declined. Duvall's status as a loyal Democratic Republican was acknowledged by President Jefferson in 1802, when the president selected him as the first comptroller of the federal treasury, a post he held until 1811. Presumably his long career in public service contributed to his appointment that year to the Supreme Court, where he filled the vacancy created by the death of Samuel Chase, another Maryland native.

Duvall failed to distinguish himself on the Marshall Court, customarily falling into line with the chief justice's nationalistic interpretations of the Constitution. Duvall is known to have dissented only once during his 23 years on the High Court, and even in that instance — *Dartmouth College v. Woodward* (1819) — he failed to write an opinion. Apparently he did write proficient opinions in some minor cases involving *maritime and commercial law, but in the company of such strong minds and personalities as Justices Marshall and Story, he failed to make an impact. In later years, increasingly deaf and disabled, he became an embarrassment to other members of the Court, who were grateful for his resignation in 1835. He lived nine more years, which he devoted to ancestral history and enjoyment of his family.

JOSEPH STORY

PERSONAL DATA

Born: September 18, 1779, in Marblehead, Massachusetts
Parents: Elisha Story, Mehitable Pedrick Story
Higher Education: Harvard College, (undergraduate degree, with honors, 1798)
Bar Admission: Massachusetts, 1801
Political Party: Democratic Republican
Marriages: December 9, 1804, to Mary Lynde Oliver, who died in June 1805; August 27, 1808, to Sarah Waldo Wetmore, who bore Story seven children, two of whom survived to adulthood
Died: September 10, 1845, in Cambridge, Massachusetts
Buried: Mount Auburn Cemetery, Cambridge

PROFESSIONAL CAREER

Occupations: Lawyer, 1801-1812; Politician, 1805-1809, 1811, 1820; Judge, 1812-1845; Educator, 1829-1845
Official Positions: Member, Massachusetts Legislature, 1805-1808; Member, United States House of Representatives, 1808-1809; Speaker, Massachusetts House of Representatives, 1811; Associate Justice, United States Supreme Court, 1812-1845; Delegate, Massachusetts Constitutional Convention, 1820; Dane Professor, Harvard Law School, 1829-1845

SUPREME COURT SERVICE

Nominated: November 15, 1811

Nominated By: James Madison

Confirmed: November 18, 1811

Confirmation Vote: Voice Vote

Oath Taken: February 3, 1812

Replaced: William Cushing

Significant Opinions: *Martin v. Hunter's Lessee* (1816); *Martin v. Mott* (1827); *New York v. Miln* (dissent) (1837); *Briscoe v. Commonwealth Bank of Kentucky* (dissent) (1837); *Charles River Bridge v. Warren Bridge* (dissent) (1837); *Swift v. Tyson* (1842); *Prigg v. Pennsylvania* (1842)

Left Court: Died September 10, 1845

Length of Service: 33 years, 7 months, 7 days

Replacement: Levi Woodbury

James Madison first tried to replace Justice Cushing with Massachusetts attorney Levi Lincoln. Owing to ill health and poor eyesight, Lincoln declined, but on January 2, 1811, Madison nevertheless submitted his name to the Senate. The Senate confirmed Lincoln the next day by voice vote, but Lincoln only repeated his decision not to sit on the High Court. Madison turned next to Alexander Wolcott of Connecticut, whom he nominated on February 4, 1811, but owing to serious doubts about Wolcott's judicial abilities, the Senate rejected him by a vote of 24 to 9 on February 13. John Quincy Adams, then serving as minister to Russia, was Madison's next choice, but Adams too declined after being confirmed by voice vote the day after his nomination on February 21, 1811. Finally, the seat went to Joseph Story.

Joseph Story, the most influential member of the Marshall Court after the chief justice himself, was born in the fishing village of Marblehead, Massachusetts. His father was a physician and a patriot who had served in George Washington's army during the War of Independence. Story's early education took place at Marblehead Academy, but owing to an altercation with a classmate, he was forced to leave prior to graduation. Exhibiting the tenacity and motivation that were to be hallmarks throughout his life, Story mastered — on his own and in six months' time — the remainder of his preparatory studies, as well

as the course work for the first semester of college, after which he was admitted to Harvard College.

After graduating second in his class from Harvard in 1798, Story pursued legal studies in the offices of Congressman Samuel Sewall. When Sewall was appointed a judge, Story continued reading law under the tutelage of Samuel Putnam. Admitted to the bar in 1801, Story became active in state politics, despite his minority status as a Jeffersonian Democratic Republican in Federalist-dominated Massachusetts. After serving in the Massachusetts legislature, he was elected to the United States House of Representatives in 1808, but he resigned after a single term, having been accused of party disloyalty for opposing President Jefferson's embargo on the importation of foreign goods. He returned then to the Massachusetts legislature, where he was elected Speaker of the House in 1811.

That same year, after President Madison's first three attempts to fill a vacant Supreme Court seat failed, Madison turned to Story. Story had by that time gained a considerable reputation for his legal skills (he argued successfully for the land speculators before the Supreme Court in 1810 in *Fletcher v. Peck*), and for his scholarship, having published American editions of various English legal tracts, and he was easily confirmed.

At the age of 32, Story was the youngest justice to be appointed to the Supreme Court. Like most of the other justices serving with John Marshall, he was convinced of the rightness of the chief justice's liberal approach to the Constitution. The man whom Jefferson had labeled a "pseudo-republican" soon exhibited, in opinions such as the one he wrote for *Martin v. Hunter's Lessee* (1816), a desire to enhance national power equivalent to that of the Federalist Marshall. In *Martin*, Story established the *appellate supremacy of the Supreme Court over state courts, and throughout his tenure on the Court, he worked steadily for the expansion of federal *jurisdiction — most notably, perhaps, in *Swift v. Tyson* (1842).

When Marshall died in 1835 Story was his obvious successor, but President Jackson regarded him as "the most dangerous man in America," and passed him over in favor of the Democratic loyalist Roger Brooke Taney. Thereafter, Story usually found himself dissenting from the majority of the Court. He became so disillusioned that he was planning to resign when, in 1845, he suddenly died.

Story is remembered today as much for his activities off the Court as on. He played a pivotal role in the formation of Harvard Law School, where he served as a professor even while he performed a disproportionately large share of the Supreme Court's duties, writing 286 opinions during his tenure. At Harvard, he helped develop the national, institutionalized approach to legal education still followed today. His work at Harvard also resulted in a series of highly esteemed legal treatises. Through his combined roles as judge, educator and commentator, Story arguably exerted more influence on the evolution of American law than any of his contemporaries.

SMITH THOMPSON

PERSONAL DATA

Born: January 17, 1768, in Dutchess County, New York
Parents: Ezra Thompson, Rachel Smith Thompson
Higher Education: College of New Jersey, now Princeton University (undergraduate degree, 1788)
Bar Admission: New York, 1792
Political Party: Democratic Republican
Marriages: 1794 to Sarah Livingston, who bore Thompson two sons and two daughters, and who died September 12, 1833; 1836 to Eliza Livingston, who bore Thompson one son and two daughters
Died: December 18, 1843, in Poughkeepsie, New York
Buried: Poughkeepsie Cemetery

PROFESSIONAL CAREER

Occupations: Lawyer, 1793-1800; Politician, 1800-1801, 1813; Judge, 1802-1818, 1824-1843; Government Official, 1819-1823
Official Positions: Member, New York State Legislature, 1800; Delegate, New York Constitutional Convention, 1801; Associate Justice, New York

Supreme Court, 1802-1814; Member, New York State Board of Regents, 1813; Chief Justice, New York Supreme Court, 1814-1818; United States Secretary of the Navy, 1819-1823; Associate Justice, United States Supreme Court, 1824-1843

SUPREME COURT SERVICE

Appointed: September 1, 1823 (recess appointment)
Appointed By: James Monroe
Nominated: December 8, 1823
Confirmed: December 19, 1823
Confirmation Vote: Voice Vote
Oath Taken: February 10, 1824
Replaced: Brockholst Livingston
Significant Opinions: Ogden v. Saunders (1827); Cherokee Nation v. Georgia (dissent) (1831); Kendall v. United States *ex rel. Stokes (1838)
Left Court: Died December 18, 1843
Length of Service: 19 years, 10 months, 8 days
Replacement: Samuel Nelson

The politically ambitious Smith Thompson was born to an Anti-Federalist father well known in New York political circles. Smith strengthened his political connections when, after joining the law practice of James Kent and Gilbert Livingston, he joined the powerful Livingston family by marrying Livingston's daughter (after her death, he married her first cousin).

Thompson's entry into politics as a member of the New York state legislature was certainly helped by his family ties. Other political offices followed quickly. In fact, when he was appointed district attorney for the Middle District of New York, he was forced to decline the position in favor of another appointment to the state supreme court. On the court, where he eventually succeeded his old friend James Kent to become chief justice, he served with two cousins by marriage, including Brockholst Livingston, whom he would later replace on the United States Supreme Court. Probably through the influence of rising political star Martin Van Buren, Thompson was appointed secretary of the navy by President Monroe who, when a seat on the Supreme Court became available in 1823, again turned to Thompson. Thompson had long cherished hopes of higher office, however, and he delayed his acceptance in hopes of mounting a presidential campaign for the 1824 election. When it became apparent that he could not count on the aid of Van Buren, he accepted a position on the High Court. Van Buren was to disappoint Thompson again. Still nursing his political ambitions while serving on the Court, Thompson campaigned for the office of governor of New York in 1828. Not only did he incur much criticism for his *extrajudicial political activity, but he lost to Martin Van Buren.

Unlike many Republicans appointed to the Marshall Court, Thompson managed to hang on to his Anti-Federalist views. Perhaps his most significant disagreement with the chief justice occurred in *Ogden v. Saunders* (1827), when he joined the majority in forcing Marshall to write his only constitutional dissent. Thompson frequently found himself at odds with Marshall's nationalistic interpretation of the *Commerce Clause, believing that states should have the right to regulate their own commerce unless prohibited from doing so by federal legislation. Although he wrote 85 opinions for the Court, perhaps Thompson's finest hour came with his dissent in *Cherokee Nation v. Georgia* (1831), in which he argued for the *sovereignty of the Indian tribe. For all his political maneuvering, he did not lack independence: writing for the majority in *Kendall v. United States* (1838), he opposed President Jackson with his finding that the executive branch was not immune to judicial authority.

ROBERT TRIMBLE

PERSONAL DATA

Born: November 17, 1776, in Augusta County, Virginia (now West Virginia)
Parents: William Trimble, Mary McMillan Trimble
Higher Education: Kentucky Academy, now Transylvania University, 1796–1797
Bar Admission: Kentucky, 1800
Marriage: August 18, 1803, to Nancy Timberlake, who bore Trimble ten children
Political Party: Democratic Republican
Died: August 25, 1828, in Paris, Kentucky
Buried: Paris Cemetery

PROFESSIONAL CAREER

Occupations: Lawyer, 1800-1807, 1808-1817; Politician, 1802, 1808, 1812-1817; Judge, 1807-1808, 1810, 1817-1828; Government Official, 1813-1817, 1820
Official Positions: Member, Kentucky House of Representatives, 1802; Judge, Kentucky Court of Appeals, 1807-1808; Member, Electoral College, 1808, 1812, 1816; Chief Justice, Kentucky Court of Appeals, 1810; United States District Attorney for Kentucky, 1813-1817; Judge, United States District Court for the District of Kentucky, 1817-1826; Member, Commission to resolve boundary dispute between Kentucky and Tennessee, 1820; Associate Justice, United States Supreme Court, 1826-1828

SUPREME COURT SERVICE

Nominated: April 11, 1826
Nominated By: John Quincy Adams
Confirmed: May 9, 1826
Confirmation Vote: 27-5
Oath Taken: June 16, 1826
Replaced: Thomas Todd
Significant Opinions: None
Left Court: Died August 25, 1828
Length of Service: 2 years, 2 months, 9 days
Replacement: John McLean

Robert Trimble was born to a Kentucky pioneer family, the oldest of seven children. He himself fathered ten children, and the size of his family contributed to the financial considerations that both motivated him to build his successful law practice and kept him from devoting his life to public service. After being admitted to the bar in 1800, he did serve a single term as a Kentucky state representative. When he was appointed to the Kentucky Court of Appeals in 1807, he resigned the next year, citing the poverty resulting from his one thousand dollar annual salary. He did, however, agree to serve briefly as chief justice in 1810.

Trimble reentered the judiciary in 1817, when he became Kentucky's second federal court judge, appointed by President James Madison. He held that post until, eight years later, he became John Quincy Adams's only successful Supreme Court appointee. Adams chose Trimble for his strong

Old Supreme Court Chamber, which the Court occupied 1810–1814 & 1819–1860

nationalist beliefs. In the 16 opinions Trimble wrote during his two years on the Court, he generally concurred with Chief Justice Marshall. One notable exception came in the case of *Ogden v. Saunders* (1827), where Trimble joined the majority (Marshall dissented) that found states have the right to enact bankruptcy laws. Trimble, aged 51, died suddenly of a fever on August 25, 1828.

JOHN MCLEAN

PERSONAL DATA
Born: March 11, 1785, in Morris County, New Jersey
Parents: Fergus McLean, Sophia Blockford McLean
Higher Education: None
Bar Admission: Ohio, 1807
Political Party: Democrat
Marriages: 1807 to Rebecca Edwards, who bore McLean three sons and four daughters, and who died in December 1840; 1843 to Sarah Bella Ludlow Garrard, who bore McLean one son, and who died in childbirth
Died: April 4, 1861, in Cincinnati, Ohio
Buried: Spring Grove Cemetery, Cincinnati

PROFESSIONAL CAREER
Occupations: Publisher, 1807-1810; Lawyer, 1810-1812; Goverment Official, 1811-1812, 1822-1829; Politician, 1812-1816; Judge, 1816-1822, 1830-1861
Official Positions: Examiner, United States Land Office, Cincinnati, Ohio, 1811-1812; Member, United States House of Representatives (Chairman, Committee on Accounts) 1812-1816; Judge, Ohio Supreme Court, 1816-1822; Commissioner, General Land Office, 1822-1823; Postmaster General, United States Post Office, 1823-1829; Associate Justice, United States Supreme Court, 1830-1861

SUPREME COURT SERVICE
Nominated: March 6, 1829
Nominated By: Andrew Jackson
Confirmed: March 7, 1829
Confirmation Vote: Voice vote
Oath Taken: January 11, 1830
Replaced: Robert Trimble
Significant Opinions: *Briscoe v. Commonwealth Bank of Kentucky* (1837); *Prigg v. Pennsylvania* (dissent) (1842); *License Cases* (1847); *Pennsylvania v. Wheeling and Belmont Bridge Co.* (1852); *Scott v. Sandford* (1857)
Left Court: Died April 4, 1861
Length of Service: 31 years, 2 months, 24 days
Replacement: Noah H. Swayne

John Quincy Adams's first choice to fill the

Court vacancy left by Robert Trimble's death was John Crittenden, a Kentucky lawyer and statesman nominated December 17, 1828, on the eve of Andrew Jackson's election. On February 12, 1829, the Senate postponed the nomination, which then died, leaving it to Jackson to appoint the next justice, John McLean.

Born to a family of Irish immigrants which, when he was a child, moved west (finally settling in Ohio), John McLean received only a spotty formal education. Nonetheless, he worked as a farmhand to earn enough to hire Presbyterian ministers as tutors. When he was 18, he apprenticed with the clerk of Hamilton County Court in Cincinnati as a means of studying for the bar.

McLean initially chose to pursue journalism, publishing the Democratic *Western Star* in his hometown of Lebanon, Ohio, from 1807 to 1810, when he turned the business over to his brother so that he could pursue private legal practice. Starting in 1811 he held his first public office as an examiner for the local federal land office, and in 1812 he was elected to the House of Representatives. Elected as a "war hawk," once in Congress he supported the Madison administration's war effort in his role as Chairman of the Committee on Accounts by organizing financial backing.

McLean resigned his position in 1816 when he was elected a judge of the Ohio Supreme Court, but before leaving, he supported the presidential candidacy of James Monroe in congressional caucus. In 1822 Monroe rewarded McLean by appointing him to the more lucrative office of commissioner of the General Land Office. McLean, always eager for political advancement, launched a failed bid for the Senate. Monroe consoled him by making him postmaster general the next year. Monroe's successor, John Quincy Adams, was so impressed by McLean's administrative skills in overseeing the post office's rapid expansion that he granted the office of postmaster general cabinet status.

In the election of 1828 McLean publicly supported his benefactor Adams, but behind the scenes he courted the Jackson camp. On the eve of the election, Adams nominated John J. Crittenden to replace the recently deceased Justice Trimble, but the Senate tarried, ultimately declining to consider the appointment. McLean's political gamble paid off when, shortly after his inauguration, Jackson tapped him for the High Court.

While on the Supreme Court bench, McLean continued to hunger for political power, but was hampered by his inability to campaign actively and by his eventual alienation of President Jackson. Nonetheless, McLean continued his flirtation with a variety of political parties. After his dissent in the *Dred Scott* case in 1857 made him one of the few anti-slavery voices on the Taney Court, he was considered as a presidential candidate, first by the antislavery Free-Soil Party in 1848, then by the Republicans in 1856 and again in 1860. While McLean's ongoing quest for the White House stained his reputation, his dissent in *Dred Scott* forced the Taney Court to confront the issue of slavery head-on — a confrontation that ultimately precipitated the Civil War — and clearly left his mark on posterity.

HENRY BALDWIN

PERSONAL DATA

Born: January 14, 1780, in New Haven, Connecticut
Parents: Michael Baldwin, Theodora Wolcott Baldwin
Higher Education: Yale College (undergraduate degree, 1797)
Bar Admission: Pennsylvania, 1798
Political Party: Democrat
Marriages: 1802 to Marianna Norton, who bore Baldwin one son, and who died in 1803; 1805 to Sally Ellicott
Died: April 21, 1844, in Philadelphia, Pennsylvania
Buried: Oak Hill Cemetery, Washington, D.C. (there is some evidence of a later transfer to Greendale Cemetery, Meadville, Pennsylvania)

PROFESSIONAL CAREER

Occupations: Lawyer, 1798-1830; Publisher, early 1800s; Businessman, early 1800s; Politician, 1817-1822; Judge, 1830-1844
Official Positions: Member, United States House of Representatives (Chairman, Committee on Domestic

Manufactures) 1817-1822; Associate Justice, United States Supreme Court, 1830-1844

SUPREME COURT SERVICE

Nominated: January 4, 1830
Nominated By: Andrew Jackson
Confirmed: January 6, 1830
Confirmation Vote: 41-2
Oath Taken: January 18, 1830
Replaced: Bushrod Washington
Significant Opinions: None
Left Court: Died April 21, 1844
Length of Service: 14 years, 3 months, 3 days
Replacement: Robert C. Grier

Henry Baldwin was born into an aristocratic New England family whose roots in America dated back to the seventeenth century. Although he grew up near New Haven, Connecticut, and attended Yale, when it came time to read law, he did so in the Philadelphia offices of prominent attorney Alexander J. Dallas. He later set up his own practice in Pittsburgh. There he built a thriving practice with two partners, with whom he also published a newspaper, *The Tree of Liberty*, which became a mouthpiece for a Republican party faction. Baldwin also became a prominent business leader, with part ownership in rolling mills in Pennsylvania and a woolen mill in Ohio.

It was as a manufacturer and a Federalist that Baldwin was elected in 1816 to the United States House of Representatives, where he served as Chairman of the Committee on Domestic Manufactures. Although ill health forced him to resign in 1822, while in the House he worked hard on behalf of Pennsylvania business interests and became an ardent supporter of Andrew Jackson. He supported Jackson's presidential bid in 1828, and after the death of Bushrod Washington, Jackson rewarded Baldwin with a seat on the Supreme Court.

On the Court, Baldwin proved to be unpredictable. While his views on constitutional issues remained middle-of-the-road and fairly consistent throughout his tenure (he supported unobstructed interstate commerce as well as the preservation of *states' rights), he served as a divisive force on the generally consensual Marshall Court,

dissenting seven times from the majority in only his second year on the Court. During that same period, he threatened to resign because of the chief justice's expansion of federal power, but President Jackson intervened. Thirteen years prior to his death, Baldwin began to suffer from paralysis, and what had at first appeared to be independence deteriorated into abrasiveness and possibly madness, which manifested itself in occasional violent outbursts from the bench. Baldwin stayed on the Court until his death in 1844.

JAMES MOORE WAYNE

PERSONAL DATA

Born: 1790 in Savannah, Georgia
Parents: Richard Wayne, Elizabeth Clifford Wayne
Higher Education: College of New Jersey, now Princeton University (undergraduate degree, 1808)
Bar Admission: Georgia, 1810
Political Party: Democrat
Marriage: 1813 to Mary Johnston Campbell, who bore Wayne three children
Died: July 5, 1867, in Washington, D.C.
Buried: Laurel Grove Cemetery, Savannah

PROFESSIONAL CAREER

Occupations: Lawyer, 1810-1812, ca. 1815-1820; Serviceman, 1812; Politician, 1815-1819, 1829-1835; Judge, 1820-1828, 1835-1867
Official Positions: Member, Georgia House of Representatives, 1815-1816; Member, Savannah Board of Aldermen, ca. 1816; Mayor, Savannah, Georgia, 1817-1819; Judge, Savannah Court of Common Pleas, 1820-1822; Judge, Georgia Superior Court, 1822-1828; Member, United States House of Representatives (Chairman, Committee on Foreign Relations), 1829-1835; Associate Justice, United States Supreme Court, 1835-1867

SUPREME COURT SERVICE

Nominated: January 6, 1835
Nominated By: Andrew Jackson
Confirmed: January 9, 1835
Confirmation Vote: Voice vote
Oath Taken: January 14, 1835
Replaced: William Johnson
Significant Opinions: *Dobbins v. Erie* (1842);

Louisville Railroad Co. v. Letson (1844); *Dodge v. Woolsey* (1856)

Left Court: Died July 5, 1867

Length of Service: 32 years, 5 months, 21 days

Replacement: No one; under the terms of the 1866 Judiciary Act, the Court was to decrease by attrition from ten to seven members; the 1869 Judiciary Act restored two seats for a total of nine

James M. Wayne was the son of a British immigrant army officer who owned a rice plantation near Savannah, Georgia. His early education came at home at the hands of an Irish tutor, but he chose to pursue formal education in the North, entering what is now Princeton University at the age of 14. After graduating at the age of 18, he first studied law under a prominent Savannah attorney and then at Yale. He was admitted to the bar in 1810.

Wayne had barely started to practice law when the War of 1812 broke out. He interrupted his legal career to serve in the Chatham Light Dragoons, a volunteer Georgia militia, where he gained the rank of captain. After the war, he reentered private practice, but in 1815 he was elected to the Georgia house. Following two terms there, he became at the age of 27 the mayor of Savannah, a position he resigned in 1819 because of low pay. The next year he began his judicial career when the state legislature elected him to the Savannah Court of Common Pleas. He went on to serve on the Georgia Superior Court before entering national politics in 1829.

During his three terms in the United States House of Representatives, Wayne proved to be a loyal supporter of Andrew Jackson. Considered a party loyalist and a Unionist, he was rewarded by Jackson with a seat on the Supreme Court in 1835.

Wayne served with Chief Justice Marshall only a few months before Marshall died, but in many areas — particularly *admiralty law — Wayne continued to manifest the same expansive nationalism that had marked Marshall's tenure. His support for the national government was sorely tested in *Scott v. Sandford* (1857), in which he was the only justice to endorse — and perhaps even

drafted — Chief Justice Taney's opinion for the Court that Congress lacked the authority to abolish slavery. Wayne was himself a slaveholder, but when the Civil War erupted after the *Dred Scott* decision, he remained on the bench, more committed to the Union than to the institution of slavery. While the war raged on and his son joined the Confederate forces, Wayne, who was branded a traitor in his native Georgia and had his property confiscated, upheld President Lincoln's war measures. After the war, however, Wayne opposed the harsh measures of Reconstruction and refused to hold *circuit court in states under military rule. He died in 1867 of typhoid, never seeing the end of Reconstruction.

SIGNIFICANT CASES

MARBURY V. MADISON

Citation: 1 Cr. (5 U.S.) 137 (1803)

Argued: February 11, 1803

Decided: February 24, 1803

Court Below: *Original Supreme Court jurisdiction

Basis for Review: Application for writ of *mandamus

Facts: William Marbury, who had been appointed a justice of the peace by the outgoing Adams administration, was denied the post when newly elected President Jefferson ordered that Marbury's commission (as well as those of a number of other Federalists) not be delivered.

Issue: Is the grant of original jurisdiction to the Supreme Court in section 13 of the Judiciary Act of 1789, authorizing the Court to issue writs of mandamus, within the scope of its powers as outlined in Article III of the Constitution?

Outcome: Although Marbury was due his commission, because the judiciary act was an unconstitutional enlargement of the Court's jurisdiction, the Supreme Court lacked the power to order delivery of the commission.

Vote: 5-0

Participating: Marshall, Cushing, Paterson, Chase, Washington (Moore not participating)

Opinion: Marshall for the Court

Significance: Although *Marbury v. Madison* was not the Supreme Court's first exercise of its power of *judicial review —the authority to decide the constitutionality of presidential or legislative acts — this case marked the first time the Court actually declared an act of Congress unconstitutional (it would not do so again until *Scott v. Sandford* in 1857). By declaring that the Constitution does not authorize Congress to enlarge upon the powers it grants the Supreme Court, Marshall firmly established two things: first, that the Supreme Court's jurisdiction is based primarily on the Constitution and only secondarily on legislative authorization, and second, that the Court itself is the final arbiter of constitutional questions.

STUART V. LAIRD

Citation: 1 Cr. (5 U.S.) 299 (1803)
Argued: February 23-24, 1803
Decided: March 2, 1803
Court Below: United States Circuit Court for the District of Virginia
Basis for Review: *Writ of error
Facts: In 1801 a plaintiff obtained a judgment in a federal court, which was subsequently abolished by the 1802 Repeal Act. The defendant questioned the constitutionality of the Repeal Act before Justice Marshall, hearing the case on *circuit, who rejected this argument.
Issues: Can Congress abolish courts it created by the 1801 statute? Can Congress require Supreme Court justices to perform circuit duties?
Outcome: The judgment of the lower court was affirmed. Justice Paterson narrowed the first issue in the case by declaring that Congress had the power to require transfer of a case from a court existing under the 1801 Judiciary Act to one created by the 1802 Repeal Act. In addition, he added that because Supreme Court justices had always acquiesced in circuit duties, such duties had become firmly established.
Vote: 4-0
Participating: Paterson, Chase, Washington, Moore (Marshall and Cushing not participating)
Opinion: Paterson for the Court

Significance: By upholding the 1802 Repeal Act, the Federalist-dominated Supreme Court avoided a confrontation with the Republican Congress, which had recently passed the legislation. Coming just six days after the assertion of Supreme Court authority in *Marbury v. Madison*, *Stuart v. Laird* was probably a politically wise decision, even though it side-stepped the constitutional questions raised.

BANK OF THE UNITED STATES V. DEVEAUX

Citation: 5 Cr. (9 U.S.) 61 (1809)
Argued: February 10-11, 1809
Decided: March 15, 1809
Court Below: United States Circuit Court for the District of Georgia
Basis for Review: *Writ of error
Facts: The Bank of the United States sued Deveaux, a Georgia tax collector, in federal court to recover cash he had seized when the bank refused to pay a state tax.
Issue: Can a corporation be a party to a federal law suit based on *diversity jurisdiction (i.e., one where the parties are citizens of different states), and if so, how is the *citizenship of the corporation to be decided?
Outcome: A corporation is a citizen for purposes of diversity jurisdiction, but there was no diversity in this case because some of the bank's shareholders resided in Georgia, which was also the defendant's residence.
Vote: 6-0
Participating: Marshall, Cushing, Chase, Washington, Johnson, Todd (Livingston not participating)
Opinion: Marshall for the Court

Significance: In *Deveaux*, the Marshall Court offered a very narrow interpretation of the diversity requirement for federal cases, thus limiting corporations' access to federal courts and, consequently, the federal judicial power. Little corporate litigation took place until 1844, when *Louisville Railroad Co. v. Letson* overruled *Deveaux* by holding that for purposes of diversity, corporate citizenship is determined by where the corporation was chartered.

FLETCHER V. PECK

Citation: 6 Cr. (10 U.S.) 87 (1810)
Argued: February 15, 1810
Decided: March 16, 1810
Court Below: United States Circuit Court for the District of Massachusetts
Basis for Review: *Writ of error
Facts: After bribing many government officials to look the other way, the Georgia legislature sold a large tract of land for a scandalously low price to four land companies. Two years later, the state legislature rescinded the sale. Meanwhile, however, one of the initial purchasers, Robert Fletcher, had sold his holdings to Robert Peck, who sued to regain title to the land he had bought. The lower court found for Peck.
Issue: Does the Georgia legislature's act revoking its initial grant of sale violate the *Contracts Clause of the Constitution?
Outcome: The legislative repeal of the land grant and the titles granted under it were declared unconstitutional.
Vote: 4-1
Participating: Marshall, Washington, Johnson, Livingston, Todd (Cushing and Chase not participating)
Opinions: Marshall for the Court; Johnson dissenting in part
Significance: *Fletcher v. Peck* marked another milestone in the evolution of the doctrine of *judicial review, as it was the first time the Supreme Court exercised its power to nullify a state law by declaring it unconstitutional. Chief Justice Marshall avoided the corruption issue, focusing instead on the second legislative enactment, which the Court found violated the Constitution's prohibition on state acts which impair the obligation of contracts. *Fletcher v. Peck*, which was successfully argued by future Supreme Court Justice Joseph Story, reflected Marshall's commitment to the security of property rights as an instrument of national economic advancement.

UNITED STATES V. HUDSON & GOODWIN

Citation: 7 Cr. (11 U.S.) 32 (1812)
Argued: Submitted without oral argument

Decided: February 13, 1812
Court Below: United States Circuit Court for the District of Connecticut
Basis for Review: *Certificate of division of opinion
Facts: The codefendants were convicted in federal court of having published a *seditious libel on President Jefferson, accusing him of conspiring with Napoleon Bonaparte.
Issue: Does the Constitution grant federal courts the right to create or enforce *common law crimes?
Outcome: The *indictments against the defendants were dismissed, the Court holding that federal courts could not exercise *jurisdiction over common law crimes.
Vote: 6-0
Participating: Marshall, Johnson, Livingston, Todd, Duvall, Story (Washington not participating)
Opinion: Johnson for the Court
Significance: Although federal courts had long upheld convictions for common law crimes, Republicans argued that this was an unlawful exercise of power not explicitly granted by the Constitution or bestowed by Congress. This ruling, declaring there is no federal common law of crimes, remains valid today.

MARTIN V. HUNTER'S LESSEE

Citation: 1 Wheat. (14 U.S.) 304 (1816)
Argued: March 12, 1816
Decided: March 20, 1816
Court Below: Virginia Court of Appeals
Basis for Review: *Writ of error
Facts: During the Revolution, Virginia passed a law confiscating Loyalists' property. In an earlier Supreme Court case, *Fairfax's Devisee v. Hunter's Lessee* (1813), this legislation was ruled incompatible with the provisions of the Treaty of Paris and the Jay Treaty, which protected Loyalists' property rights. The Virginia courts, however, refused to enforce the Court's ruling.
Issue: Does the Supreme Court have *appellate review power over all decisions — regardless of their courts of origin — involving federal laws and treaties, and over state court rulings reject-

ing federal constitutional challenges to state laws?
Outcome: Section 25 of the Judiciary Act of 1789, empowering the Supreme Court to review the decisions of even the highest state courts, when they concern such matters, was upheld.
Vote: 6-0
Participating: Washington, Johnson, Livingston, Todd, Duvall, Story (Marshall not participating)
Opinions: Story for the Court; Johnson concurring
Significance: Story's opinion was the most important of his nearly 34 years on the Supreme Court. Rejecting the *states' rights theory that the Constitution represented a compact between *sovereign states granting the federal government only certain *enumerated powers (which section 25 of the 1789 act clearly exceeded), Story endorsed not only the Supreme Court's power to review state court opinions, but also the theory of *implied powers, which Justice Marshall was to elaborate on in *McCulloch v. Maryland* (1819).

DARTMOUTH COLLEGE V. WOODWARD

Citation: 4 Wheat. (17 U.S.) 518 (1819)
Argued: March 10-11, 1818
Decided: February 2, 1819
Court Below: New Hampshire Supreme Court
Basis for Review: *Writ of error
Facts: The New Hampshire legislature passed statutes revising the college's 1769 royal charter, attempting to impose external, public regulation on the institution's governing procedures. The lower court upheld the statutes.
Issue: Is a corporate charter a contract within the meaning of Article I, section 10, of the Constitution, and therefore protected from state legislative interference?
Outcome: The Court found Dartmouth College to be a private, not a public, institution, one whose charter constituted a contract between the college and the state as successor to the colonial government that issued the original charter. The lower court's ruling was reversed, with costs awarded to the college.
Vote: 5-1
Participating: Marshall, Washington, Johnson,

Livingston, Duvall, Story (Todd not participating)
Opinions: Marshall for the Court; Washington and Story concurring; Duvall dissenting (without written opinion)
Significance: *Dartmouth College* marked the first time that the Constitution's prohibition on *state action "impairing the Obligation of Contracts" was applied to legislation directed at a corporate charter. The Marshall Court's finding that under the terms of its charter the college was a private, not a public institution was crucial because, in the chief justice's view, the *Contracts Clause of the Constitution was intended solely to protect private property rights. Because the college charter could then be deemed a contract between the state and an unregulated, autonomous entity, the case cleared the way for subsequent corporations to pursue their economic interests relatively free of constraints imposed by state authorities.

STURGES V. CROWNINSHIELD

Citation: 4 Wheat. (17 U.S.) 122 (1819)
Argued: February 8, 1819
Decided: February 17, 1819
Court Below: United States Circuit Court for the District of Massachusetts
Basis for Review: *Certificate of division of opinion
Facts: New York's 1811 bankruptcy statute freed debtors from prison and released them from their debts if they signed their property over to their creditors.
Issue: Does the New York insolvency law violate the *Contracts Clause of the Constitution by interfering with preexisting obligations?
Outcome: The statute was voided.
Vote: 6-0
Participating: Marshall, Washington, Johnson, Livingston, Duvall, Story (Todd not participating)
Opinion: Marshall for the Court
Significance: Because the New York bankruptcy statute discharged debtors from liabilities incurred before its passage, it violated the Constitution's ban on state interference with contracts. This was the first Supreme Court test of the constitutionality of state insolvency laws, an issue that remained unresolved until *Ogden v. Saunders*

(1827) and which was not finally put to rest until the passage of federal bankruptcy legislation in 1898.

MCCULLOCH V. MARYLAND

Citation: 4 Wheat. (17 U.S.) 316 (1819)
Argued: February 22-27 & March 1-3, 1819
Decided: March 7, 1819
Court Below: Maryland Court of Appeals
Basis for Review: *Writ of error
Facts: Although a national bank was opposed by Jeffersonians as unconstitutional and unnecessary, Congress chartered the First Bank of the United States in 1791. The Republican-dominated Congress refused to renew the charter in 1811, but then reversed itself in 1816, creating the Second Bank of the United States. To demonstrate their opposition, many states imposed taxes upon branches of the bank operating within their boundaries. The head cashier of the Baltimore branch, James McCulloch, refused to pay the Maryland tax. The decision of the Baltimore county court upholding the law was quickly affirmed by the Maryland Court of Appeals.
Issues: Does the Constitution empower Congress to incorporate a national bank? Do states have the right to tax instruments of the federal government?
Outcome: The opinion of the lower court upholding the Maryland law authorizing taxation of the bank was reversed.
Vote: 6-0
Participating: Marshall, Washington, Johnson, Livingston, Duvall, Story (Todd not participating)
Opinion: Marshall for the Court
Significance: *McCulloch* was one of Chief Justice Marshall's most significant opinions, in that it defined the *Necessary and Proper Clause of the Constitution. Under his liberal interpretation, Congress was not restricted to ratifying only essential legislation, but could adopt any legitimate and appropriate means of achieving national goals. This view powerfully counteracted the emphasis *states' rights advocates placed on another section of the Constitution, the Tenth Amendment, which stipulates that those powers not enumerated in the Constitution are reserved

to the states. While Marshall granted that the Constitution did not specifically grant Congress the power to incorporate a bank, neither did it prohibit such an exercise, which would itself enable the federal government to execute its delegated rights, such as collecting taxes. The bank, as an agency of the federal government, was not subject to state taxation, as states have no *sovereignty over entities governed by the superior authority of the Constitution and federal law.

COHENS V. VIRGINIA

Citation: 6 Wheat. (19 U.S.) 264 (1821)
Argued: February 18, 1821
Decided: March 3, 1821
Court Below: Quarterly Session Court for the Borough of Norfolk, State of Virginia
Basis for Review: *Writ of error
Facts: The Cohens were convicted in Virginia of violating state law prohibiting the sale of lottery tickets, although such sales were authorized by an act of Congress.
Issue: Does the Supreme Court have *appellate power over state court decisions involving federal laws?
Outcome: The lower court's conviction of the Cohens was affirmed, Marshall holding that because the federal lottery statute applied only in the District of Columbia, Virginia had the right to rule on its own state laws.
Vote: 6-0
Participating: Marshall, Johnson, Livingston, Todd, Duvall, Story
Opinion: Marshall for the Court
Significance: *Cohens,* which some regarded as a concocted case, marked the second time (the first occurred in *Martin v. Hunter's Lessee* in 1816) that the Marshall Court addressed the question of the Supreme Court's *appellate jurisdiction over state court decisions. Typically politic, Marshall avoided the issue of Virginia's noncompliance with federal law, but his opinion unequivocally settled the authority of the High Court under section 25 of the Judiciary Act of 1789 to review state court decisions. To argue otherwise, Marshall said, was unconstitutional, because the states are not independent *sovereigns, but members of a

greater union governed by a single document designed to advance national goals. Virginia's apparent attempt — in the wake of *McCulloch v. Maryland (1819)* — to challenge federal authority by citing the Eleventh Amendment prohibition barring suits against states did not apply to cases involving *federal questions.

GIBBONS V. OGDEN

Citation: 9 Wheat. (22 U.S.) 1 (1824)
Argued: February 4-6, 1824
Decided: March 2, 1824
Court Below: Court for the Trial of Impeachments and Correction of Errors of the State of New York
Basis for Review: Appeal
Facts: Robert Fulton had been granted a monopoly to operate steamboats in New York waterways, and the New York courts had repeatedly rejected challenges to his exclusive right. *Gibbons v. Ogden* involved Aaron Ogden, who held a license granted by Fulton, and Thomas Gibbons, who operated a competing steamboat line.
Issue: Under the *Commerce Clause (Article I, section 8) of the Constitution, who has the power to regulate commerce — the federal government or the states?
Outcome: The decree of the lower court was reversed on grounds that Gibbons's federally-granted steamboat license superseded New York's grant of monopoly.
Vote: 6-0
Participating: Marshall, Washington, Johnson, Todd, Duvall, Story
Opinions: Marshall for the Court; Johnson concurring
Significance: Marshall characteristically chose narrow grounds for reaching his desired conclusion, managing to assert federal authority over interstate commerce while refraining from alienating southern states by declaring federal authority exclusive in this sphere. Nonetheless, he defined commerce in broad terms, to include not just exchanges of goods, but all sorts of commercial "inter-course" — such as navigation on state waterways — when it affects more than one state. Together with *McCulloch v. Maryland* (1819), this

case provides the Marshall Court's most enduring legacy to American life, extending federal superiority to the economic realm, and thereby spurring the growth of business by clarifying the regulatory environment.

OSBORN V. BANK OF THE UNITED STATES

Citation: 9 Wheat. (22 U.S.) 738 (1824)
Argued: March 10-11, 1824
Decided: March 19, 1824
Court Below: United States Circuit Court for the District of Ohio
Basis for Review: Appeal
Facts: Ohio imposed a prohibitive tax on the Bank of the United States. Ralph Osborn, the state's auditor, defied a federal *injunction prohibiting its collection.
Issue: Is a state official carrying out state law immune from suit in federal court under the Eleventh Amendment which limited the role of the federal courts in suits against the states?
Outcome: The circuit court ruling ordering Osborn to return the monies he had impounded was upheld.
Vote: 6-1
Participating: Marshall, Washington, Johnson, Todd, Duvall, Story, Thompson
Opinions: Marshall for the Court; Johnson dissenting
Significance: Although Osborn was acting under state law, that law was unconstitutional under *McCulloch v. Maryland* (1819). Accordingly, Osborn could not assert immunity from suit under the Eleventh Amendment. Marshall used his opinion to enlarge federal *jurisdiction to include virtually every case involving the bank, a proposition Johnson objected to for fear that it would expand *federal question jurisdiction too much.

WAYMAN V. SOUTHARD

Citation: 10 Wheat. (23 U.S.) 1 (1825)
Argued: March 15, 1824
Decided: February 12, 1825
Court Below: United States Circuit Court for the District of Kentucky
Basis for Review: *Certificate of division of opinion

Facts: Certain Kentucky statutes required losing defendants to post bonds to satisfy judgments against them.

Issue: Are state procedural rules binding on federal courts?

Outcome: Federal courts may fashion their own practices and are not bound by the procedural rules applicable to the courts of states in which they are located.

Vote: 6-0

Participating: Marshall, Washington, Johnson, Duvall, Story, Thompson (Todd not participating)

Opinion: Marshall for the Court

Significance: Marshall reasoned that Article III of the Constitution gave Congress the power to establish federal courts, and that the 1789 Judiciary Act in turn gave federal courts the power to make rules necessary to carry out their functions. In essence, the Supreme Court was recognizing for the first time Congress's authority under the Constitution to delegate aspects of its legislative power, a finding that cleared the way for establishment of federal regulatory agencies.

MARTIN V. MOTT

Citation: 12 Wheat. (25 U.S.) 19 (1827)

Argued: January 17, 1827

Decided: February 2, 1827

Court Below: Court for the Trial of Impeachments and Correction of Errors of the State of New York

Basis for Review: *Writ of error

Facts: During the War of 1812, President Madison ordered some states to assemble their militias because of the danger of British invasion. Jacob Mott, a private in the New York militia, refused his governor's order to appear and was subsequently fined. When he refused to pay, Martin, a United States marshall, seized Mott's goods. Mott filed suit to recover his property and a New York court awarded him judgment.

Issue: Is the president, as commander in chief, endowed with the sole authority to determine when it is appropriate to exercise the *military power granted by the Constitution?

Outcome: The lower court's ruling was reversed, with the result that the president's military power

was not only defined but made binding on state authorities.

Vote: 7-0

Participating: Marshall, Washington, Johnson, Duvall, Story, Thompson, Trimble

Opinion: Story for the Court

Significance: This was the first in a line of cases broadly defining the president's *executive power and set a precedent for Abraham Lincoln's actions in the early days of the Civil War.

OGDEN V. SAUNDERS

Citation: 12 Wheat. (25 U.S.) 213 (1827)

Argued: February term, 1824; reargued January 19, 1827

Decided: February 19, 1827

Court Below: United States District Court for the District of Louisiana

Basis for Review: *Writ of error

Facts: A New York insolvency law passed after *Sturges v. Crowninshield* (1819) provided debtors with relief from obligations incurred after passage of the bill.

Issue: Do laws that relieve debtors of obligations incurred after passage of such insolvency legislation impair the obligations of contracts?

Outcome: The insolvency law was upheld.

Vote: 4-3

Participating: Marshall, Washington, Johnson, Duvall, Story, Thompson, Trimble

Opinions: Washington, Thompson, and Trimble *seriatim; Johnson concurring (without written opinion); Marshall, joined by Duvall and Story, dissenting

Significance: Although *Sturges* had outlawed retroactive bankruptcy laws, *Ogden* demonstrated that the *Contracts Clause was not an absolute bar to state debtor relief legislation. *Ogden* was the only case involving an important constitutional issue in which Marshall found himself in dissent. The case was again reargued on March 6, 1827, and when the Court issued a second opinion on March 13, Justice Johnson had joined the original dissenters to provide an additional holding in the case: state bankruptcy laws do not apply to out-of-state debtors who had no contracts in that state other than the original one.

BROWN V. MARYLAND

Citation: 12 Wheat. (25 U.S.) 419 (1827)
Argued: February 28, 1827
Decided: March 12, 1827
Court Below: Maryland Court of Appeals
Basis for Review: *Writ of error
Facts: Importers of foreign goods challenged a state law requiring them to buy licenses.
Issue: Does such a statute violate the constitutional ban on import taxes, as well as interfere with federal authority over commerce?
Outcome: The lower court ruling upholding the statute was reversed.
Vote: 6-1
Participating: Marshall, Washington, Johnson, Duvall, Story, Thompson, Trimble
Opinion: Marshall for the Court; Thompson dissenting
Significance: *Brown v. Maryland* found that a licensing requirement for foreign goods was equivalent to an unconstitutional tax and reinforced the Marshall Court's broad interpretation of federal *commerce powers. Chief Justice Marshall's opinion also included a formulation of the "original package" doctrine whereby state taxing power does not apply to imports from foreign countries as long as they remain in their original wrappings and do not become intermingled with general property already located in the state.

WESTON V. CHARLESTON

Citation: 2 Pet. (27 U.S.) 449 (1829)
Argued: February 28 & March 10, 1829
Decided: March 18, 1829
Court Below: Constitutional Court of South Carolina
Basis for Review: *Writ of error
Facts: The city of Charleston imposed a tax on debt certificates held by creditors of the federal government.
Issue: Do cities and states have the power to tax United States debt instruments?
Outcome: The lower court ruling upholding the tax was reversed.
Vote: 4-2
Participating: Marshall, Washington, Johnson, Duvall, Story, Thompson
Opinion: Marshall for the Court; Johnson and Thompson dissenting
Significance: The tax was struck down as an impermissible interference with the power granted the federal government "To borrow Money on the credit of the United States" in Article I, section 8, of the Constitution. The chief justice's opinion reinforced his strong defense of federal power against state encroachment in *McCulloch v. Maryland* (1819) by quoting a terse statement from the latter, "the power to tax involves the power to destroy."

WILLSON V. BLACK BIRDCREEK MARSH CO.

Citation: 2 Pet. (27 U.S.) 245 (1829)
Argued: March 17, 1829
Decided: March 20, 1829
Court Below: Delaware High Court of Errors and Appeals
Basis for Review: *Writ of error
Facts: A Delaware statute permitted the construction of a dam across a minor navigable waterway to drain a swamp.
Issue: Does such legislation interfere with the federal *commerce power?
Outcome: The lower court ruling upholding the statute was affirmed.
Vote: 6-0
Participating: Marshall, Washington, Johnson, Duvall, Story, Thompson
Opinion: Marshall for the Court
Significance: In *Willson* and other cases decided late in Marshall's tenure, the chief justice retreated from the strict nationalism he had demonstrated in earlier years. While he could have followed *Gibbons v. Ogden* (1824) in finding the Delaware statute unconstitutional, Marshall instead suggested that where Congress had not enacted any legislation directly applicable with regard to an aspect of interstate commerce, the state could exercise its concurrent powers. Thus was born the doctrine known as the *dormant commerce power.

CRAIG V. MISSOURI

Citation: 4 Pet. (29 U.S.) 410 (1830)
Argued: March 2-3, 1830

Decided: March 12, 1830
Court Below: Missouri Supreme Court
Basis for Review: *Writ of error
Facts: A Missouri statute authorized the state to issue its own loan certificates.
Issue: Does the statute violate the constitutional ban on state bills of credit?
Outcome: The judgment of the court below upholding the statute was reversed.
Vote: 4-3
Participating: Marshall, Johnson, Duvall, Story, Thompson, McLean, Baldwin
Opinions: Marshall for the Court; Johnson, Thompson, and McLean dissenting
Significance: Marshall spoke for a bare majority in ruling against state issuance of paper money. The dissenters apparently found the language of the statute vague enough that it did not violate the ban against state currency in Article I, section 10. The Taney Court, in *Briscoe v. Bank of Kentucky* (1837), upheld such a scheme, undoubtedly fueling the increasing power of the *states' rights movement.

PROVIDENCE BANK V. BILLINGS

Citation: 4 Pet. (29 U.S.) 514 (1830)
Argued: February 11, 1830
Decided: March 22, 1830
Court Below: Rhode Island Supreme Court
Basis for Review: *Writ of error
Facts: Rhode Island granted a charter to the Providence Bank in 1791. In 1822 the state sought to tax the stock of every bank in Rhode Island, but the Providence Bank protested that its charter implicitly exempted it from taxation.
Issue: Is such a tax an unconstitutional impairment of the obligations of the bank's original contract with the state?
Outcome: The lower court's ruling upholding the tax was affirmed.
Vote: 7-0
Participating: Marshall, Johnson, Duvall, Story, Thompson, McLean, Baldwin
Opinion: Marshall for the Court
Significance: *Providence Bank* marked further retrenchment by the Marshall Court in the face of Jacksonian democracy and the increasing power

of *states' rights advocates. Rejecting the bank's assertion that the state tax impaired its contractual obligations, Marshall argued that in order to be valid, any special corporate privilege must be expressly stated in its charter. The Taney Court would enlarge upon this ruling in *Charles River Bridge v. Warren Bridge* (1837) by stating explicitly that corporate charters are to be *strictly construed.

CHEROKEE NATION V. GEORGIA

Citation: 5 Pet. (30 U.S.) 1 (1831)
Argued: March 5, 1831
Decided: March 18, 1831
Court Below: None; *original Supreme Court jurisdiction
Basis for Review: Motion for *subpoena
Facts: Although the Cherokees were by treaty an independent nation with rights of self-determination, Georgia convicted a Cherokee in state court for a murder committed on a reservation. The Cherokee Nation filed an original case with the Supreme Court seeking an order directing the federal government to compel the state to cease violations of tribal *sovereignty.
Issue: Does the Supreme Court have *jurisdiction over the Cherokees' request for an *injunction?
Outcome: Finding that the Cherokees constituted a "domestic, dependent nation," the Court declared it lacked jurisdiction over their case.
Vote: 4-2
Participating: Marshall, Johnson, Story, Thompson, McLean, Baldwin (Duvall not participating)
Opinions: Marshall for the Court; Johnson and Baldwin concurring; Thompson, joined by Story, dissenting
Significance: *Cherokee Nation* pitted the authority of the Supreme Court against that of the executive branch. If Marshall ruled in favor of the Indians and President Jackson then refused to force Georgia (and, by failing to send a legal representative, flouted the Court's authority) to comply — as was probable, given Jackson's history as an Indian fighter — the Court's prestige would have suffered. As it happened, the Court modified the holding of *Cherokee Nation* the next year

POLITICAL COMPOSITION
of the Marshall Court

Justice & Total Term	Courts Served	Appointing President	Political Party
John Marshall 1801-1835	Marshall	J. Adams	Federalist
William Cushing 1790-1810	Jay Rutledge Ellsworth Marshall	Washington	Federalist
William Paterson 1793-1806	Jay Rutledge Ellsworth Marshall	Washington	Federalist
Samuel Chase 1796-1811	Ellsworth Marshall	Washington	Federalist
Bushrod Washington 1798-1829	Ellsworth Marshall	J. Adams	Federalist
Alfred Moore 1800-1804	Ellsworth Marshall	J. Adams	Federalist
William Johnson 1804-1834	Marshall	Jefferson	Democratic Republican
Brockholst Livingston 1807-1823	Marshall	Jefferson	Democratic Republican
Thomas Todd 1807-1826	Marshall	Jefferson	Democratic Republican
Gabriel Duvall 1811-1835	Marshall	Madison	Democratic Republican
Joseph Story 1812-1845	Marshall Taney	Madison	Democratic Republican
Smith Thompson 1824-1843	Marshall Taney	Monroe	Democratic Republican
Robert Trimble 1826-1828	Marshall	J.Q. Adams	Democratic Republican
John McLean 1830-1861	Marshall Taney	Jackson	Democrat
Henry Baldwin 1830-1844	Marshall Taney	Jackson	Democrat
James M. Wayne 1835-1867	Marshall Taney Chase	Jackson	Democrat

in *Worcester v. Georgia*, precipitating precisely this result.

WORCESTER V. GEORGIA

Citation: 6 Pet. (31 U.S.) 515 (1832)
Argued: February 20, 1832
Decided: March 3, 1832
Court Below: Superior Court for the County of Gwinnett, State of Georgia
Basis for Review: *Writ of error
Facts: A white missionary defied a Georgia ordinance requiring him to obtain a license in order to live on an Indian reservation. He was convicted and sentenced to hard labor by a Georgia state court.
Issue: Does the federal government have exclusive *jurisdiction over disputes involving the Indian nations?
Outcome: The ruling of the lower court was reversed.
Vote: 5-1
Participating: Marshall, Duvall, Story, Thompson, McLean, Baldwin
Opinion: Marshall for the Court; McLean concurring; Baldwin dissenting (without written opinion)
Significance: Although Georgia refused once again (as it had in *Cherokee Nation v. Georgia* [1831]) to acknowledge a Supreme Court proceeding which concerned the state, this time the Court found the state had infringed on federal jurisdiction by violating the national government's treaties with the Indian nation, guaranteeing them autonomy in their own territories. Although Marshall did not explicitly overrule *Cherokee Nation v. Georgia*, this time he emphasized the independence of Indian nations. President Jackson, as expected, refused to enforce the Court's ruling, with the eventual result that Georgia drove the Cherokees and other tribes from its borders.

BARRON V. BALTIMORE

Citation: 7 Pet. (32 U.S.) 243 (1833)
Argued: February 11, 1833
Decided: February 16, 1833
Court Below: Court of Appeals for the Western Shore of Maryland
Basis for Review: *Writ of error
Facts: A wharf owner sued the city of Baltimore for lowering the water level around his property, thereby reducing his property's value. This, he claimed, was a violation of the Fifth Amendment, which prevents government from *taking private property without providing just compensation.
Issue: Is the Fifth Amendment applicable to state and local governments?
Outcome: The case was dismissed for lack of *jurisdiction.
Vote: 6-0
Participating: Marshall, Johnson, Duvall, Story, Thompson, McLean (Baldwin not participating)
Opinion: Marshall for the Court
Significance: Owing to the changed composition of the Court and the increasing influence of *states' rights advocates, Marshall retreated in *Barron* from his pronounced nationalism, claiming that Americans must look to their state constitutions for the kinds of protections offered at the federal level by the Bill of Rights. Today state constitutions do incorporate most of the government restraints memorialized in the first ten amendments to the federal Constitution.

VOTING PATTERNS

Until Jacksonian democracy began to make inroads during the last years of his tenure as chief justice, John Marshall dominated the Court. Marshall was a staunch Federalist dedicated to building the nation and filled with the mission of building the prestige of the Court and making it into an equal branch of the federal government. To that end, he instituted the custom of unified — and preferably unanimous — opinions issued by the Court, rather than serial opinions delivered by each of the justices. Most of these opinions were written by — or at least attributed to — Marshall himself. As a result, it almost appears as if most of Marshall's brethren on the Court wrote little or nothing.

While it is true that Marshall was prodigiously prolific, writing almost half of the 1,106 opinions issued by the Court between 1801 and 1835, it is not true that he did all his Court's work or that every associate justice shared his views. William Johnson, Thomas Jefferson's first Supreme Court appointee, profoundly challenged the relationship of the colleagues on the Marshall Court and their unanimity. Marshall and his distant cousin Jefferson were lifelong personal and philosophical enemies, and Johnson — who maintained a close relationship with Jefferson even after the latter left office — served as a Jefferson surrogate, becoming known as the Court's first great dissenter. The other Federalist justices — Cushing, Paterson, Chase, Washington, and Moore — usually agreed with Marshall's strong nationalist line, as did Democratic Republican Justice Story, who functioned as a kind of lieutenant to the chief justice. With few exceptions, most of the Republicans appointed to the Court also fell under Marshall's sway. During his brief time on the Court Robert Trimble generally concurred with Marshall, while Brockholst Livingston reverted to his earlier Federalist orientation. Thomas Todd and Gabriel Duvall spoke out in dissent only once each during their many years on the Marshall Court. Smith Thompson's Anti-Federalist origins, in contrast, were clearly apparent in his opposition to Marshall's crafting of the *commerce power into a tool for increased federal power.

Only once was Marshall himself forced to dissent (in defense of creditors' rights) on a major constitutional issue. This dissent occurred in *Ogden v. Saunders* (1827), which is also notable because it was one of the few times that Justice Washington, who sided with the majority, disagreed with Marshall. Serious discontent with Marshall's liberal approach to the Constitution, however, did not set in until the last decade of his tenure, which saw the increasing power of the *states' rights movement and the addition of Andrew Jackson's appointees to the Court. While John McLean was a maverick Democrat who could disagree with both Marshall and Jackson, and James M. Wayne only served a few months under Marshall, Henry Baldwin represented all that Marshall had worked to overcome. Baldwin so opposed Marshall's expansion of federal powers at the expense of the states that he threatened to resign, and unlike Johnson,

he never acquiesced in the Marshall Court's nationalism. Baldwin represented the reactionary element of democracy that was to lead, during the next Court, to Civil War.

SPECIAL FEATURES OF THE MARSHALL COURT

SHIFTING QUARTERS

Although the federal government was transferred from Philadelphia to new quarters in Washington, D.C. — the newly designed "Federal City" — in 1800, no provision had been made for housing the Supreme Court. Before the first session of the Marshall Court, which convened February 2, 1801, Congress hurriedly passed a resolution providing that the Court could use a room on the first floor of the Capitol. The Court met in a 24 by 30 foot room off the entrance hall until renovations forced its removal to the former library of the House of Representatives. The Court met in the former library for both of its 1808 terms, but because of the lack of adequate heat, the justices repaired to Long's Tavern during 1809.

In February 1810 the Court met for the first time in a courtroom specifically designed for it. The justices convened in this room, located in the basement beneath the Senate chamber, until the Capitol was burned by the British during the War of 1812. While the Capitol was being restored, the Court met first in the temporary "Brick Capitol," then in a rented private residence, returning in 1817 to occupy an undestroyed section of the Capitol. In February 1819 the basement courtroom was once again ready for occupancy, and the Supreme Court met there until 1860.

CHANGES IN COURT SCHEDULE AND NUMBER OF JUSTICES

While the Judiciary Act of 1801 changed the start of the two Court terms from February and August to June and December, when the act was repealed the next year, only the February term was retained. Because the single annual term was enacted after February 1802, the next meeting of the Court was delayed for 14 months. The Court did not convene between December 1801 and February 1803.

The 1801 Judiciary Act also reduced the number of justices to five, in an effort to prevent President Jefferson from filling vacancies immediately. The 1802 Judiciary Act reconstituted the six-member Court, but in 1807, because of the nation's westward expansion, a new federal circuit was created, consisting of Tennessee, Kentucky, and Ohio. Owing to the still existing *circuit duty requirement and the Supreme Court's increasing case load, a seventh seat, filled by Thomas Todd of Kentucky, was created on the Court.

OFFICIAL REPORTS

Alexander J. Dallas, a Philadelphia lawyer and journalist, began voluntarily recording the Supreme Court's decisions in 1790. Over the next 17 years Dallas was to publish four volumes of his *Reports of Cases Ruled and Adjudged in the Courts of Pennsylvania, Before and Since the Revolution*, which covered the decade. Although the Supreme Court began meeting in Philadelphia in 1791, the first of Dallas's volumes included only Pennsylvania decisions, as the Supreme Court had not yet decided any cases. Dallas was succeeded by William Cranch, a Washington, D.C. circuit court judge, whose volumes cover the years 1801-1815.

Although both Dallas's and Cranch's reports were sanctioned by the Court and together make up the first 13 volumes of the Court's official reporter (a series known as *United States Reports*), the Supreme Court had no official court reporter until Congress authorized the post in 1816. Henry Wheaton was appointed to fill the now salaried post. Wheaton was succeeded in 1828 by Richard Peters Jr., who served as the Court's reporter for the remainder of Chief Justice Marshall's tenure.

Court appointed reporters still prepare the official versions of Supreme Court decisions for publication, but only the first 90 volumes of *United States Reports* continue, after the English fashion, to be known by the surnames of their respective reporters (in addition to Dallas, Cranch, Wheaton, and Peters, these include

Benjamin C. Howard, Jeremiah S. Black, and John W. Wallace, whose tenure lasted until 1874).

OPINIONS OF THE COURT

Prior to John Marshall's tenure as chief justice, each justice had delivered his opinion aloud *seriatim, starting with the most junior member of the Court. At the urging of a reporter, William Cranch, the justices began submitting written texts of their oral opinions. Then at the insistence of the chief justice, these submissions were usually combined into a single majority opinion written by — or at least attributed to — Marshall himself.

When Marshall assumed his post, the Supreme Court was held in low esteem by the rest of the federal government and by the American people. Before Marshall accepted his appointment, John Jay had in 1800 refused a second term as chief justice because the Court lacked "energy, weight and dignity," as well as the "public confidence and respect which, as the last resort of the justice of the nation, it should possess." By urging his colleagues to speak with one voice in an "opinion of the court," customarily delivered by him, Marshall was able to increase not only his own authority, but that of the Court as a whole. Recognizing the powerful sway exercised by his rival Marshall and the anonymity afforded by univocal opinions, Thomas Jefferson advocated a return to seriatim opinions, which would almost certainly have shattered the harmony of the Marshall Court and the unified nationalist front it presented to the American public. Like most of Jefferson's attempts to curtail the authority of the Supreme Court, his campaign against unified opinions failed. Until Harlan Fiske Stone assumed the chief justiceship in 1941, the Court continued to speak as one.

WILLIAM JOHNSON AND THE TRADITION OF DISSENT

Jefferson's entreaties may have had some effect on one member of the Marshall Court, William Johnson, the first Republican appointee to the Supreme Court, named by Jefferson himself. In a series of letters to Johnson written in 1822 and 1823, the former president urged his appointee to persuade his fellow justices to express themselves individually when delivering opinions. Afterward, Johnson, always an independent spirit — criticized for both anti-Unionism and faint-hearted support of *states' rights — separated himself further from the influential chief justice, delivering 9 of 11 concurring opinions and 18 of 42 dissents, for a career total of 21 concurrences and 34 dissents on the Court. Almost single-handedly, Johnson destroyed the unity of the Marshall Court and entrenched the Supreme Court tradition of dissent that lasts to this day.

The Taney Court 1836-1864

BACKGROUND

THE RISE OF THE WHIGS

Opposition to President Jackson and the Democrats centered around Henry Clay of Kentucky, a presidential hopeful. In 1834 a New York newspaper christened the opposition party Whigs, after Britain's traditional foes of royal authority, for this American group was united by its antagonism to "King Andrew" Jackson and his assertion of executive power. Whigs were essentially a coalition party consisting of National Republicans, southerners whose support for Jackson had waned, and Anti-Masons, a group unified by opposition to the Freemasons, an elitist secret society with origins in Europe.

In 1836 the Whigs attempted to defeat the Democratic incumbency by nominating a series of regional candidates. Their effort failed, and Jackson's heir apparent, Martin Van Buren, won the presidential election. Van Buren, however, was to be a one-term president. Owing primarily to a financial panic which hit the country in 1837 and which Van Buren was unable to end, he was defeated in 1840 by Whig candidate William Henry Harrison, also known as "Old Tippecanoe," the Indian fighter. Harrison's presidency was to be even shorter than his predecessor's: after only one month in office, he died of pneumonia. He was succeeded by his vice president, John Tyler.

EXPANSIONISM

Tyler's presidency was marred by antagonism with the Whig-dominated Congress, which was led by his chief political opponent, Henry Clay. The Whig Party ultimately ousted Tyler from its ranks, and the president, left without a party and without congressional allies, was unable to pursue a domestic agenda. Tyler compensated by embarking on an aggressive program of territorial expansionism that irrevocably altered the face of the nation.

Tyler's preferred target for annexation was Texas, which had gained its independence from Mexico in 1836. Tyler saw an advantage for the South in the addition of what he presumed would be another slaveholding state, and consequently he found an election issue. Texas desired statehood, and in the spring of 1844, Texas President Sam Houston signed an annexation treaty with the United States. When the Senate learned of Tyler's intention to add to the nation's slaveholding territory, however, it refused to grant the treaty the two-thirds majority needed for passage.

Henry Clay, the Whig's presidential candidate in the 1844 election, opposed Texas annexation on grounds that it would provoke war with Mexico. The Democratic candidate, James K. Polk, was an ardent expansionist who adopted the position that admission of Texas should be balanced with that of Oregon as a free state. The Democratic election slogan, promoting annexation of all the Oregon Territory up to the latitude of fifty-four degrees, forty minutes, "Fifty-Four Forty or Fight," proved to be a winner. Although a shift in popular sentiment and a changed political strategy enabled Tyler to sign a measure admitting Texas to the Union three days before he left office, President Polk would preside over the nation's last great territorial acquistion pursued under the rubric of "manifest destiny."

An asterisk (*) before a word or phrase indicates that a definition will be found in the glossary at the end of this volume.

MEMBERS Of the Court 1836–1864

(In Order of Seniority)

Roger Brooke Taney *(Chief Justice)*	*(1836-1864)*
Joseph Story *(died)*	*(1836-1845)*
Smith Thompson *(died)*	*(1836-1843)*
John McLean *(died)*	*(1836-1861)*
Henry Baldwin *(died)*	*(1836-1844)*
James M. Wayne	*(1836-1864)*
Philip P. Barbour *(died)*	*(1836-1841)*
John Catron *(filled newly created seat)*	*(1837-1864)*
John McKinley *(filled newly created seat; died)*	*(1838-1852)*
Peter V. Daniel *(replaced Philip P. Barbour; died)*	*(1842-1860)*
Samuel Nelson *(replaced Smith Thompson)*	*(1845-1864)*
Levi Woodbury *(replaced Joseph Story; died)*	*(1845-1851)*
Robert C. Grier *(replaced Henry Baldwin)*	*(1846-1864)*
Benjamin R. Curtis *(replaced Levi Woodbury; resigned)*	*(1851-1857)*
John A. Campbell *(replaced John McKinley; resigned)*	*(1853-1861)*
Nathan Clifford *(replaced Benjamin R. Curtis)*	*(1858-1864)*
Noah H. Swayne *(replaced John McLean)*	*(1862-1864)*
Samuel F. Miller *(replaced Peter V. Daniel)*	*(1862-1864)*
David Davis *(replaced John A. Campbell)*	*(1862-1864)*
Stephen J. Field *(filled newly created seat)*	*(1863-1864)*

THE PACIFIC COAST

In December 1845 President Polk asked Congress for authority to give Britain one year's notice, as required under the treaty of 1818, to end their occupation of Oregon. While Polk publicly postured about the necessity of reaching a settlement within the next year, privately he informed the British ambassador that, despite his election slogan, he was willing to compromise on an extension of the 49th parallel as the dividing line between British and American holdings in the Pacific Northwest. The two sides quickly and amicably agreed on this boundary, and the Senate approved their treaty on June 15, 1846. On the same day, American settlers living in the Mexican territory of California raised a homemade flag emblazoned with a grizzly bear as an emblem of their independence from their Mexican sovereign. The Bear Flag Revolt was born.

In May 1845 the federal government had sent John C. Fremont, a former army captain, to map the Nevada Basin for potential trails and railroad routes westward. Fremont and his suspiciously large band of hearty Mountain Men did very little exploration of the supposed route, instead moving on — doubtless with the government's knowledge — to Sutter's Fort, California, near the homes of American settlers. His presence provoked the already agitated settlers into open revolt against Mexico.

The Mexican government expelled Fremont, but he left California only for a month, returning in mid-June 1846 to lead the revolutionaries, then occupying a Mexican outpost in Sonoma, to the capital in Monterey. Seven United States vessels already lay anchored in Monterey Bay, and the stars and stripes flew over the former Mexican capital of California. The Bear Flag Revolt was merged with a wider conflict, now two months old, that was raging between the United States and Mexico.

WAR WITH MEXICO

In the autumn of 1845 President Polk sent an emissary to Mexico City with an offer to purchase California and New Mexico. The Mexican government, as expected, declined. Polk countered by sending General Zachary Taylor with 1500 troops to the banks of the Rio Grande, to occupy a narrow strip of land whose ownership had been in dispute when Texas was still a republic. This attempt to provoke an attack by the Mexicans eventually succeeded and, claiming that the Mexicans had "shed American blood upon American soil," Polk on May 11, 1846, asked Congress for a declaration of war.

Although Congress passed the declaration by wide margins the next day, many were troubled by Polk's tactics, fearing that he had provoked a war with Mexico strictly in order to seize territory that would prove fertile ground for an extension of slavery. The war ended a year and a half after it began, with the Treaty of Guadalupe Hidalgo, signed in February 1848, ceding to the United States Mexican lands from the Rio Grande to the Pacific. By that time, the war had ceased to be a popular issue, but it had created a popular hero, General Taylor. Polk, now universally distrusted, did not seek renomination, and the winner of the 1848 election was the Whig candidate, Taylor.

FREE SOIL

Although the abolitionists had long been active on the American scene, founding antislavery newspapers and flooding the mails with antislavery tracts, they remained largely without a popular constituency and without political representation. Then, in 1846, abolition came to the forefront of the political stage. The war with Mexico was only three months old when David Wilmot, a Democratic member from Pennsylvania, proposed an amendment in the House of Representatives that would bar slavery from any territory acquired from Mexico as a result of war.

The proposal, which came to be known as "Free Soil," essentially accepted the status quo, merely seeking to prevent the growth of slavery. Nonetheless, it provoked heated debates in Congress, which voted the proposal down in 1846, as well as twice more in the two succeeding years. The main opposition came from a united block of southern states, which offered the alternative of popular *sovereignty, allowing the citizens of ter-

ritories seeking admission to the Union to vote as to whether they wished to be slaveholding or nonslaveholding.

In the election of 1848, the Free-Soilers developed into a party, with Martin Van Buren as its presidential candidate. The Democrats, rallying around popular sovereignty, nominated Lewis Cass. The Whigs refrained from adopting a platform, simply nominating Zachary Taylor. Taylor won the election, and the slavery issue remained unaddressed and unresolved.

THE COMPROMISE OF 1850

Congressional dispute over the fate of the new territories continued to escalate, as first California, then New Mexico, applied for admission as free states. Southern states, feeling embattled, called in January 1850 for a June convention to consider secession. On January 29, 1850, Henry Clay jumped into the fray with a legislative package that proposed to resolve the impasse, First, the North would agree to abandon the Wilmot Free Soil Proviso. In return, the South would not insist on the right of slaveholders to transport slaves to the new territories. California would be admitted as a free state, and territorial governments without restrictions would be created in the rest of the area formerly ruled by Mexico. In addition, Congress would be allowed to terminate the slave trade in Washington, D.C., but slavery itself would be allowed to continue in the District and in Maryland. Finally, Congress would pass a new fugitive slave law that would make it easier for southerners to recover runaways.

Recognizing that Clay's proposal would still allow California and New Mexico to be admitted as free states, the South still balked. Stephen A. Douglas of Illinois, leader of the Western Democrats, proposed a solution: the remainder of the Mexican cession should be divided between two territorial governments, New Mexico and Utah, and each would be permitted to determine its own fate. With the addition of popular sovereignty, the southern states agreed to the compromise. President Taylor, who had favored the admission of California without concessions to the South, died of cholera on July 9, 1850. After

Douglas shepherded the bills constituting the compromise through Congress, in September 1850 they were signed into law by Taylor's successor, Millard Fillmore.

The Compromise of 1850 proved to be merely a temporary truce in the escalating war of words between North and South. The presidential election of 1852 was in effect a referendum on the compromise. The Whigs nominated Winfield Scott and generally supported the compromise. The Free Soil Party chose John P. Hale and condemned it. The Democrats nominated Franklin Pierce, a New Englander who supported the revised, harsher Fugitive Slave Act, popular sovereignty in the Mexican cession, *states' rights and the continued existence of slavery. He, together with a large majority of congressional Democrats, was swept into office with strong southern support.

BLEEDING KANSAS

The antagonism between North and South that eventually led to the Civil War first erupted as a surrogate brawl over the route to be taken by the proposed transcontinental railroad. Southerners favored a route originating in Memphis or New Orleans, traveling south of the Rocky Mountains via the Rio Grande and Gila Rivers and ending in Los Angeles or San Diego. President Pierce indicated his tacit agreement by engineering the Gadsden Purchase in 1854, whereby the United States acquired from Mexico a strip of land along the Gila. Northerners wanted a route that began in St. Louis or Chicago and passed through the unorganized Indian territory west of the Missouri River to terminate in San Francisco or Sacramento.

Stephen Douglas, as chairman of the Senate Committee on Territories, proposed a plan for organizing the western Indian lands and permitting them to be received into the Union with or without slavery. Douglas's plan came under fire for undermining the Missouri Compromise, which dictated that all lands north of latitude 36° 30' would be free soil. Douglas first attempted to remedy his plan by introducing popular *sovereignty to the unorganized territory. Because this change still left his plan at odds with the Missouri Compromise, he proposed two further amend-

ments. The first amendment would effectively repeal the Missouri Compromise. The second amendment would split the area in question into two territories, Kansas and Nebraska, with the implication that ultimately one would be free and the other a slave state. President Pierce signed the amended bill into law in May 1854.

The immediate effect of the Kansas-Nebraska Act was to give rise to a new antislavery political party calling itself Republican and consisting of Free-Soilers, Whigs, anti-Nebraska Democrats, and so-called "Know Nothings," originally a secretive political party made up of nativist white Protestants. The act also marked the beginning of the end of Stephen Douglas's political fortunes, as it exposed the vagueness that doomed his cherished popular sovereignty. If there were any hopes for this doctrine, they were dashed as the fight for Kansas escalated into bloodshed.

In 1854 a territorial government election resulted in a large proslavery majority, but when the election results were compared with census figures, it was clear that this outcome was achieved through fraud. Free-Soilers set up a rival government, and the two factions began what amounted to a guerilla war, with each side being supplied by outsiders. The battle by proxy quickly spread to the rest of the nation. After delivering a tirade against the South titled "The Crime Against Kansas," Senator Charles Sumner was severely beaten by Congressman Preston S. Brooks on the floor of the Senate for alleged insults to Brooks's absent South Carolina kinsman, Senator Andrew P. Butler. Two days later, abolitionist zealot John Brown, who had immigrated to Kansas from Ohio a year earlier, set out with six others to avenge an earlier attack, known as the "Sack of Lawrence," on a Free-Soil settlement. Brown and his men retaliated with the "Pottawatomie Massacre," during which five proslavery partisans were hacked to death with broadswords.

THE ELECTION OF 1856 AND
THE DRED SCOTT DECISION

The 1856 presidential election is most notable for the geographic division it revealed in the nation. The Republican Party, which nominated

John Fremont, was supported exclusively by the northern tier of states, while the Democrats dominated the South. Every slaveholding state — save Maryland, which went for Know Nothing nominee Millard Fillmore — voted for Democratic candidate James Buchanan, who became the country's 15th president. The Democrats also managed to hang on to four northern states, New Jersey, Pennsylvania, Indiana and Illinois, but only by the slimmest of margins — due in large part to the new Republicans' lack of organization. The controversy over slavery was on the verge of dividing the nation.

Loath to associate themselves with such an unmanageable problem, politicians left the issue to the courts. In his inaugural address, President Buchanan informed his countrymen that the Supreme Court would soon resolve the question of territorial status regarding slavery. In doing so, Buchanan inadvertently indicated that he had had some illegitimate conversations with members of the Court about a pending case. Dred Scott, the African American *appellant in the case, *Scott v. Sandford* (*appellee John Sanford's name was misspelled in the official reports), had long been pursuing his case through the courts, and it was well known to the American public. Scott, who once lived several years with his master in the Wisconsin Territory, from which the Missouri Compromise had banished slavery, claimed that his residency there had made him a free man. However, because he had returned with his master to Missouri, the Missouri courts ruled that he was still a slave. While the Supreme Court could — and almost did — find that Missouri law governed the case and that, as a consequence, Scott was not free, Chief Justice Roger Brooke Taney, at President Buchanan's urging, chose instead to attempt to resolve the larger question of territorial status. Through some very convoluted reasoning, the Court ruled that the Missouri Compromise provision prohibiting slavery north of latitude 36° 30', was unconstitutional because it deprived citizens of their property — i.e., their slaves — without just compensation. Minnesota Territory, and other northern territories, had therefore never been free soil, the Court stated, and Scott could thus have

no claim to freedom. Moreover, because he was a slave, not a citizen, he had no *standing to sue, and the Court dismissed his case.

While the Buchanan administration, and its southern supporters, gloried in the decision, *Scott v. Sandford* convinced northerners that there was a conspiracy afoot in the federal government. Far from settling the controversy over territorial status, the Taney Court in effect opened the entire nation up to slavery.

KANSAS REVISITED

Scott v. Sandford did not end the conflict over slavery, neither did it end Buchanan's attempts to manipulate the issue. A few months after the Supreme Court handed down the decision, Kansas applied for statehood. Buchanan appointed Robert J. Walker to serve as state governor and to preside over the constitutional convention called by proslavery forces. Free-Soilers generally boycotted the convention, and they roundly denounced the document it produced, which protected current slaves as property but — in a parody of popular *sovereignty — left it to the voters to decide if slavery would be expanded in the state.

Free-Soilers managed to have the entire state constitution put to a popular vote. The issue, however, was phrased in such a way that Kansas was forced to accept the constitution and, consequently, slavery. Buchanan announced his support for the document, which was sent to Congress for approval. The Senate passed it, but a majority in the House, led by Stephen Douglas, opposed it. After weeks of bitter struggle, Congress compromised and sent the constitution back to Kansas for a new referendum. One condition of the compromise was that if voters rejected the constitution, they would have to wait for admission to statehood. Kansans did not flinch. They unequivocally voted down the constitution, and Kansas did not enter the Union until 1861, after the Civil War had begun.

THE ELECTION OF 1860

Political conventions for the 1860 presidential election took place against a backdrop of enormous social turmoil. Although she was not, as

Roger Brooke Taney

Abraham Lincoln later said of her, the woman who started the Civil War, Harriet Beecher Stowe had managed to reach an enormous popular audience with her novel, *Uncle Tom's Cabin; or Life Among the Lowly*, published in 1852. The book sold in the millions and for the first time lent the controversy over slavery an air of immediacy the American public — which up to that time had been largely indifferent — took to heart. In October 1859 John Brown attempted to provoke a slave uprising by seizing the federal arsenal at Harpers Ferry, Virginia. The revolt did not follow, but Brown's capture and subsequent execution for treason made him a martyr to the abolitionist cause and a rallying point for northerners.

The fate of the Democratic Party mimicked that of the nation. Its first nominating convention, meeting in April 1860 in Charleston, South Carolina, broke up when southern delegates walked out after the convention refused to pass a platform that included a guarantee of slavery in the territories. The scene was repeated at a second convention in Baltimore in May. Recognition of the party's irrevocable split resulted in two nominees: Stephen A. Douglas, representing northern Democrats, and John C. Breckinridge, representing southern Democrats.

The Republican convention, meeting in Chicago in May, resulted in the third-ballot nomination of Abraham Lincoln. The Democratic split guaranteed a Republican victory, and Lincoln carried the entire North, together with Oregon and California.

SECESSION AND CIVIL WAR

Six weeks after the results of the presidential election became known, South Carolina called a convention of southern states, at which it announced its withdrawal from the Union. Within another six weeks, it was followed by the remaining states constituting the deep south: Alabama, Mississippi, Florida, Georgia, Louisiana, and Texas. In February 1861 these states drew up a constitution and proclaimed themselves the Confederate States of America.

When Abraham Lincoln took office on March 4, 1861, the only bastion of federal authority remaining in the deep south was a garrison of 100 soldiers at Fort Sumter, South Carolina, located in Charleston Bay. The next day, March 5, Fort Sumter's commander, Major Robert Anderson, called for reinforcements and supplies. Lincoln sent only the latter, but the South interpreted Lincoln's gesture as a provocation, and on the morning of April 12, Confederate President Jefferson Davis ordered an attack on the fort. The Civil War had begun.

Virginia, North Carolina, Tennessee, and Arkansas soon joined the Confederacy, but the balance between North and South was a lopsided one. To the Confederacy's 11 states, the Union had 23. To a Confederate population of nine million (more than a third of whom were slaves), the Union had 21 million. The bulk of the nation's resources, and nearly all of its factories, were located in the North. Nonetheless, the Civil War dragged on for four long years, resulting in more American casualties than occurred in all other American wars combined.

JUDICIAL BIOGRAPHY
Roger Brooke Taney

PERSONAL DATA
Born: March 17, 1777, in Calvert County, Maryland
Parents: Michael Taney, Monica Brooke Taney
Higher Education: Dickinson College, (undergraduate degree, class valedictorian 1795)
Bar Admission: Maryland, 1799
Political Party: Democrat
Marriage: January 7, 1806, to Anne P. C. Key, who bore Taney six daughters and one son, who died in infancy, and who herself died in 1855
Died: October 12, 1864, in Washington, D.C.
Buried: St. John the Evangelist Cemetery, Frederick, Maryland

PROFESSIONAL CAREER
Occupations: Lawyer, 1799-1835; Politician, 1799-1800, 1816-1821, 1827-1826; Government Official, 1826-1831,

1831-1834; Judge, 1836-1864
Official Positions: Member, Maryland House of Delegates, 1799-1800; Member, Maryland State Senate, 1816-1821; Maryland Attorney General, 1826-1831; Chairman, Jackson Central Committee for Maryland, 1827-1828; United States Attorney General, 1831-1833; Acting United States Secretary of War, 1831; Acting United States Secretary of the Treasury, 1833-1834; Chief Justice, United States Supreme Court, 1836-1864

SUPREME COURT SERVICE
Nominated: January 15, 1835
Nominated By: Andrew Jackson
To replace: Gabriel Duvall
Nomination Postponed: March 3, 1835
Renominated: December 28, 1835

Confirmed: March 15, 1836
Confirmation Vote: 29-15
Oath Taken: March 28, 1836
Replaced: Chief Justice John Marshall
Significant Opinions: *Charles River Bridge v. Warren Bridge* (1837); *Bank of Augusta v. Earle* (1839); *Holmes v. Jennison* (1840); *Prigg v. Pennsylvania* (concurrence) (1842); *License Cases* (1847); *Luther v. Borden* (1849); *Genesee Chief v. Fitzhugh* (1852); *Scott v. Sandford* (1857); *Abelman v. Booth, United States v. Booth* (1859); *Kentucky v. Dennison* (1861)
Left Court: Died October 12, 1864
Length of Service: 28 years, 6 months, 14 days
Replacement: Chief Justice Salmon P. Chase

THE EMANCIPATION PROCLAMATION

Although the Civil War had not begun as a war over slavery per se, it became one. In the summer of 1862, with the war at a stalemate, President Lincoln sought any means to resolve the conflict. Lincoln was personally opposed to slavery and had long been looking for a constitutional means of ending it. He began to see emancipation as a military necessity. His status as commander in chief thus permitted him to free the slaves. The southern economy was dependent on slavery; by ending the "peculiar institution," Lincoln could at once undermine the Confederacy's economic base and give the war a wider purpose. On September 23 he proclaimed that as of January 1, 1863, slaves residing in rebel states would be free.

TANEY'S EARLY LIFE

Roger Brooke Taney was descended from prominent families who first settled in the Maryland tidewater area in the 1650s and 1660s. His mother's family had always been aristocratic, but his father's forebear was an indentured servant who managed to work his way up in the world, eventually becoming a member of the local gentry. Taney's own father was a tobacco planter who, by means of private tutoring, secured an excellent education for his second son. Because of such tutoring by a Princeton undergraduate, Taney was able to enter Dickinson College in Pennsylvania at the age of 15. He graduated as class valedictorian in 1795.

As a second son, Taney was not in line to inherit property, so he pursued a legal career, reading law in the Annapolis, Maryland, offices of Judge Jeremiah Chase. Three years later, Taney was admitted to the Maryland bar, having won his first case two days earlier. Despite this early success, however, he was unable to make a living in Annapolis and returned home.

TANEY'S PUBLIC LIFE

Taney seems to have had better success on home turf. A year after his return home, he was elected to the state House of Delegates. At this point in his life, however, Taney was a Federalist, and the Jeffersonian juggernaut that swept through American politics in 1800 put him out of office. Moving to Frederick, Maryland, which would be his home for the next 20 years, Taney developed a successful legal practice and pursued local politics. Another attempt at the House of Delegates in 1803 was frustrated, as were several runs for the state senate and one attempt at election to the Maryland slate of presidential electors. Finally, in 1816, he was elected as a Federalist to the Maryland senate for a five-year term. Left adrift by the dissolution of his party, Taney joined the Democrats, becoming chairman of the local committee to elect Jackson and establishing himself among local party leaders.

Taney was serving as state attorney general when a shakeup in Andrew Jackson's first cabinet in 1831 occasioned Taney's move to Washington, D.C., where he assumed the position of attorney general. Taney was a Jackson stalwart, and during the president's bank war, Taney came into his own as a partisan politician, supporting Jackson's veto of the bill to recharter the Bank of the United States and helping to draft the veto message. When Jackson decided to kill the bank by

removing its federal funds deposits, he went through two successive secretaries of the Treasury, who refused to carry out his orders, before settling on Taney as hatchet man.

Jackson wanted to reward Taney's services to him, but he knew that the now alienated Senate would oppose Taney's nomination as secretary of the Treasury (he had been serving on an interim basis). Jackson held off putting Taney's name forward as long as possible, and when the nomination finally was made in the Senate, it was soundly rejected. Taney resigned in 1834. The next year, Gabriel Duvall's retirement from the Supreme Court offered Jackson a second chance to reward Taney. This time, instead of rejecting Taney outright, the Senate indefinitely postponed a decision on his nomination. A few months later, upon the death of Chief Justice Marshall, Jackson tried again, nominating Philip Barbour for Duvall's still-unfilled seat on the Court and Taney as chief justice. Once again, the Senate delayed, but this time, after an executive session during which no records were kept, the senators approved both of the president's nominees.

TANEY AS CHIEF JUSTICE

Coming directly after the great and much loved Marshall, Taney had large shoes to fill. It did not help that he had a reputation as a political hack. Yet it is interesting to note that Marshall himself had tried to help Taney's first nomination to the Court. And although initially it was feared that the Democratic loyalist would try to undo all of the advances in constitutional nationalism made by the Marshall Court, the Taney Court in fact helped to balance the federal bias developed during Marshall's leadership by emphasizing a more equitable *sovereignty shared with the states.

The first three cases that came before the Taney Court all had been argued during Marshall's tenure, but they were held over for decision because of a spate of resignations and deaths among the justices. In the first of these, *City of New York v. Miln* (1837), the ideological fault lines in the Taney Court were clear, as Justice Barbour, writing for the Court, upheld a state regulation requiring reporting of all passengers brought into the port of New York. Justice Joseph Story strongly dissented, claiming that the *commerce power rested solely with the federal government. In *Briscoe v. Bank of the Commonwealth of Kentucky* (1837), the Taney Court again upheld a state law, this time one authorizing a state-chartered bank to issue bank notes.

Taney himself wrote the opinion in the most famous of these early decisions, *Charles River Bridge v. Warren Bridge* (1837), which set rights of private property against societal good by challenging an act of the Massachusetts legislature that permitted the construction of a second bridge across the Charles River, possibly violating the charter for the first bridge. Introducing some tenets of Jacksonian democracy, Taney stated that although "private property rights are sacredly guarded," the community too has rights, which are promoted by the *police powers vested in the states. Of these three early cases, this one marked the clearest departure from the Marshall tradition, emphasizing that in some situations rights vested in the states can override the prohibitions of the *Contracts Clause.

The Taney Court's modifications of prior constitutional readings proceeded gradually and, over time, resulted in an increase in the Supreme Court's prestige. Unfortunately, towards the end of his tenure, Taney was to preside over the infamous *Dred Scott* (1857) decision. Whereas the Court, like the remainder of the federal government, had up to that time managed to sidestep the slavery question, deciding all cases touching on the issue on narrow grounds, this time the aged Taney let his *states' rights orientation interfere with his judicial temperament — to his own detriment and that of the entire nation. Although each justice wrote a separate opinion in the case, the chief justice delivered the inflammatory opinion of the Court.

Taney lived for seven years after *Scott v. Sandford*, during which his prestige and that of his Court steadily diminished as the Civil War raged on. Although the Court decided a number of important cases after 1857, its effectiveness had been undermined. Taney died a frustrated, angry man whose tainted legacy long survived him.

Much of the overreaction to *Dred Scott* has since been corrected, with the result that a century after his death, Justice Taney is once again valued as one of the Court's greatest jurists.

ASSOCIATE JUSTICES

For biographies of Associate Justices **Joseph Story, Smith Thompson, John McLean, Henry Baldwin** and **James M. Wayne,** see entries under **THE MARSHALL COURT.**

PHILIP PENDLETON BARBOUR

PERSONAL DATA
Born: May 25, 1783, in Orange County, Virginia
Parents: Thomas Barbour, Mary Pendleton
Thomas Barbour
Higher Education: College of William and Mary, 1801
Bar Admission: Virginia, 1800
Political Party: Democrat
Marriage: 1804 to Frances Todd Johnson, who bore Barbour seven children
Died: February 25, 1841, in Washington, D.C.
Buried: Congressional Cemetery, Washington D.C.

PROFESSIONAL CAREER
Occupations: Lawyer, 1800-1801, 1802-1812, 1825-1827; Politician, 1812-1825, 1827-1830; Judge, 1825-1827, 1830-1841
Official Positions: Member for Orange County, Virginia House of Delegates, 1812-1814, 1830; Member, United States House of Representatives, 1814-1825, 1827-1830, (Speaker, 1821-1823); Judge, General Court for the Eastern District of Virginia, 1825-1827; Member, then President, Virginia Constitutional Convention, 1829-1830; Judge, United States District Court for Eastern Virginia, 1830-1836; Associate Justice, United States Supreme Court, 1836-1841

SUPREME COURT SERVICE
Nominated: December 28, 1835
Nominated By: Andrew Jackson
Confirmed: March 15, 1836
Confirmation Vote: 30-11
Oath Taken: May 12, 1836

Replaced: Gabriel Duvall
Significant Opinion: *New York v. Miln* (1837)
Left Court: Died February 25, 1841
Length of Service: 4 years, 9 months, 13 days
Replacement: Peter V. Daniel

Philip Barbour was born into an aristocratic family of Virginia planters. By the time of his birth, however, much of the family fortune had been spent by his politically active father, and Barbour received a less rigorous education than would normally be accorded the son of such a prominent family. Nevertheless, Barbour was conspicuously intelligent, and after serving less than a year as a law clerk, he moved to Kentucky to practice law. His only college-level education came after this year, when he returned to Virginia to study for one term at the College of William and Mary.

Barbour devoted ten years to developing his Virginia legal practice, then he followed the example of his father and his older brother James, who figured prominently on the state and national political stages, and entered politics. In 1812, at the age of 29. Barbour ran successfully for the Virginia legislature. Scarcely two years later, he was elevated to the United States House of Representatives, where he distinguished himself as a *strict constructionist, *states' rights Republican, and where he served for two years as speaker. His first tenure in the House was notable for his defense of then General Andrew Jackson's overly enthusiastic military campaign against the Spanish in Florida, and for his outspoken support for state *sovereignty in the debate over admission of Missouri.

Barbour spent two years as a state judge before returning to the House in 1827. That same year he sought to make the Bank of the United States a political issue by calling for the federal government to sell its interest in the institution. The bank was not an issue in the 1828 presidential campaign, but Barbour's position regarding it would later make him a force in the Jackson camp.

After Jackson's victory in the 1828 campaign, Barbour — now unquestionably a Jacksonian Democrat — was frequently mentioned as a possible cabinet nominee. Instead, he accepted a

federal judgeship in 1830. During the election of 1832, Barbour received considerable popular support as a vice presidential candidate. Initially he did nothing to quell the movement that sought to place him, rather than Jackson's chosen successor, Martin Van Buren, on the ticket with Jackson. When Barbour finally asked the Jackson-Barbour committee to support the regular nominees, his relationship with the president was salvaged.

Barbour's reward came in 1836, when Jackson named him to replace Justice Gabriel Duvall, who had recently resigned from the Supreme Court. Although Barbour was certainly anathema to National Republicans and Whigs in the Senate, their attention was focused on the — to them — more shocking nomination of Roger Brooke Taney to replace Chief Justice Marshall.

Barbour joined the Court within two months of the chief justice. His tenure there was brief, however, and he wrote only one important majority opinion, *New York v. Miln* (1837), which he authored during his second year on the Court. During the February 1841 term, Barbour was temporarily absent from the Court due to illness, but he resumed his seat on February 24, apparently recovered. That evening he convened with his brethren until ten in the evening, only to die in his sleep later that night of a sudden heart attack.

JOHN CATRON

PERSONAL DATA

Born: ca. 1786 in Pennsylvania
Parents: Peter Catron (mother's name unknown)
Higher Education: None
Bar Admission: Tennessee, 1815
Political Party: Democrat
Marriage: 1807 to Mary Childress
Died: May 30, 1865, in Nashville, Tennessee
Buried: Mount Olivet Cemetery, Nashville

PROFESSIONAL CAREER

Occupations: Serviceman, 1812; Lawyer, 1815-1824, 1834-1837; Judge, 1824-1834, 1837-1865; Businessman, 1827-1833; Politician, 1836-1837
Official Positions: Prosecuting Attorney, Tennessee, ca. 1815-1817; Judge, Tennessee Supreme Court,

1824-1831; Chief Justice, Tennessee Supreme Court, 1831-1834; Associate Justice, United States Supreme Court, 1837-1865

SUPREME COURT SERVICE
Nominated: March 3, 1837
Nominated By: Andrew Jackson
Confirmed: March 8, 1837
Confirmation Vote: Voice vote
Oath Taken: May 1, 1837
Replaced: No one; filled newly created seat
Significant Opinion: *License Cases* (1847)
Left Court: Died May 30, 1865
Length of Service: 28 years, 29 days
Replacement: No one; under the terms of the 1866 Judiciary Act, the Court was to decrease by attrition from ten to seven members; the 1869 Judiciary Act restored two seats for a total of nine.

Little is known about John Catron's personal life. He was of German ancestry on his father's side, and was probably born in 1786 in Pennsylvania. After spending some of his childhood in Virginia, he moved with his family to Kentucky, where he lived until 1812. His family was poor, and he appears to have been self-taught.

Moving to the Cumberland Mountain area of Tennessee with his wife, Mary Childress Catron, whom he married in 1807, Catron served under General Andrew Jackson in the War of 1812. After the war, Catron was admitted to the bar and entered private practice, also serving occasionally as a public prosecutor. In 1818 he moved to Nashville, where he developed a reputation for his litigation of land claims and became one of the leaders of the local bar. In 1824 he was appointed to Tennessee's highest court, and in 1831, when the state legislature created the office of chief justice, Catron was elevated to that post. Later, when the Tennessee judicial system was reorganized, he left the bench to resume private practice and pursue business interests.

Much of what is known about Catron comes from the opinions he wrote while serving in the state judiciary. What emerges is the very picture of a Jacksonian Democrat, an advocate of *states' rights and the institution of slavery. Catron was indeed a party loyalist, serving as a stalking horse

for Jackson's criticisms of the Bank of the United States and echoing the President's views on the expendability of the Cherokees. In 1836 he took charge of Martin Van Buren's presidential campaign in Tennessee.

There is reason to believe that President Jackson, himself a Tennessean, influenced Catron's appointment as chief justice of the state supreme court. And, on his last day in office, Jackson nominated Catron to fill one of two newly-created seats on the United States Supreme Court.

On the Court, Catron continued to curry favor with the administration, conferring privately — and improperly — with President Buchanan about the *Dred Scott* (1857) case while it was still before the Court. In the decision itself, Catron sided with the "southern" majority, finding the Missouri Compromise unconstitutional. And yet, when the Civil War came, Catron remained a true Jacksonian, demonstrating a profound commitment to preserving the Union. After the Supreme Court adjourned on March 14, 1861, he attempted to perform his *circuit duties in Kentucky, Tennessee, and Missouri. Although the legislature of his home state had already made a military commitment to the Confederacy, Catron tried to hold federal court in Nashville, only to leave when the federal marshall warned him his life was in danger. A second trip to Nashville after denying writs of *habeas corpus to detained secessionists in St. Louis resulted in an ultimatum: he must either resign his seat on the Court or leave town within 24 hours without his ailing wife and despite his advanced years (he was in his seventies at the time).

Catron lived just long enough to see the Union restored with Robert E. Lee's surrender at Appomattox. Catron died, still on the High Court, on May 30, 1865.

JOHN MCKINLEY

PERSONAL DATA
Born: May 1, 1780, in Culpepper County, Virginia
Parents: Doctor Andrew McKinley, Mary Logan McKinley

Higher Education: None
Bar Admission: Kentucky, 1800
Political Party: Democrat
Marriages: Juliana Bryan; Elizabeth Armistead
Died: July 19, 1852, in Louisville, Kentucky
Buried: Cave Hill Cemetery, Louisville

PROFESSIONAL CAREER

Occupations: Lawyer, 1800-1820, 1821-1826; Politician, 1820, 1826-1831, 1833-1837; Judge, 1837-1852
Official Positions: Member, Alabama Legislature, 1820, 1831, 1836; Member, United States Senate, 1826-1831, 1837; Member, United States House of Representatives, 1833-1835; Associate Justice, United States Supreme Court, 1838-1852

SUPREME COURT SERVICE

Appointed: April 22, 1837 (recess appointment)
Appointed By: Martin Van Buren
Nominated: September 18, 1837
Confirmed: September 25, 1837
Confirmation Vote: Voice vote
Oath Taken: January 9, 1838
Replaced: No one; filled newly created seat
Significant Opinions: None
Left Court: Died July 19, 1852
Length of Service: 14 years, 6 months, 10 days
Replacement: John A. Campbell

When Congress created two new seats on the Supreme Court in 1837, President Andrew Jackson, on his last day in office, nominated John Catron and William Smith, the latter from Alabama. He had previously offered to nominate Smith in 1829. Both times Smith declined, the second time after he had been confirmed on March 8, 1837, by a vote of 23 to 18. Because these events occurred after Jackson had stepped down, it was left to his successor, Martin Van Buren, to nominate McKinley, another staunch Jacksonian, instead.

Shortly after his birth in 1780, John McKinley moved with his family from Virginia to Lincoln County, Kentucky. His father was a physician, and although McKinley did not follow him in that profession, he too became a professional, studying law. He was admitted to the bar in 1800 and practiced in Kentucky, in Frankfort and

Louisville, before moving to Huntsville, Alabama, in 1818 to seek his fortune.

McKinley quickly became one of the ruling elite, and his political ambitions surfaced immediately. As early as 1819 he was running for elected office, a state judgeship. He lost that contest, but the next year he was elected to the first of three terms he served in the state legislature. In 1822 he pursued, but lost, nomination to the United States Senate.

Early in his political career, McKinley was a follower of perpetual presidential hopeful Henry Clay. Although Clay was a powerful individual, in 1826 his star was waning as Andrew Jackson's rose. That year, McKinley became a Jacksonian, and he obtained a seat in the United States Senate. In 1830 he was defeated in his attempt to keep the seat, but he won other elections, at both the state and federal levels, before regaining his Senate seat in the 1836 election. He never actually served his second term as a senator, for he was offered a Supreme Court seat before Congress convened. Although he complained in advance of the vast new *circuit (including Alabama, Louisiana, Mississippi, and Arkansas) he would be required to travel, he nevertheless accepted President Van Buren's nomination.

McKinley's record on the Court was undistinguished. In his 15 years on the High Court, he wrote only 20 majority opinions and two concurrences. He is most remembered for his dissent in *Bank of Augusta v. Earle* (1839), in which he ardently defended his circuit court opinion holding that corporations could not make contracts or otherwise operate in a state without the state's express permission. He was alone in this dissent, which expressed an extremist view of *states' rights. He never again dissented on his own.

Eighteen forty-five marked McKinley's most productive year on the Court, during which he wrote ten opinions. During the next seven years, he became increasingly obscure. McKinley was often absent from the Supreme Court and finally ceased participating in district court in Arkansas altogether as a means of cutting down on travel. He died in 1852, apparently a victim of the rigors of the 10,000 miles of circuit riding that annually had been required of him.

PETER VIVIAN DANIEL

PERSONAL DATA

Born: April 24, 1784, in Stafford County, Virginia

Parents: Travers Daniel, Frances Moncure Daniel

Higher Education: College of New Jersey, now Princeton University, 1802-1803

Bar Admission: Virginia, 1808

Political Party: Democrat

Marriages: April 1809 to Lucy Randolph, who bore Daniel three children and who died in 1847; 1853 to Elizabeth Harris, who bore Daniel two children

Died: May 31, 1860, in Richmond, Virginia

Buried: Hollywood Cemetery, Richmond

PROFESSIONAL CAREER

Occupations: Lawyer, 1808-1809; Politician, 1809-1835; Judge, 1836-1860

Official Positions: Member, Virginia House of Delegates, 1809-1812; Member, Virginia Privy Council, 1812-1835; Lieutenant Governor, Virginia, 1818-1835; Judge, United States District Court for the Eastern District of Virginia, 1836-1841; Associate Justice, United States Supreme Court, 1842-1860

SUPREME COURT SERVICE

Nominated: February 26, 1841

Nominated By: Martin Van Buren

Confirmed: March 2, 1841

Confirmation Vote: 22-5

Oath Taken: January 10, 1842

Replaced: Philip P. Barbour

Significant Opinions: *License Cases* (1847); *West River Bridge Co. v. Dix* (1848)

Left Court: Died May 31, 1860

Length of Service: 18 years, 4 months, 21 days

Replacement: Samuel F. Miller

Peter V. Daniel came from a family that had lived for several generations in Virginia, where they owned a plantation called Crow's Nest. Like most young Virginia gentlemen of his status, Daniel was privately educated. At the age of 18 he attended the College of New Jersey for one year as a junior, but he returned home to read law with Edmund Randolph.

Daniel made a judicious choice in selecting Randolph as his mentor. As one of the founding fathers and George Washington's attorney general, Randolph was one of the preeminent members of the bar. In 1809 Daniel improved his prospects further by marrying Randolph's daughter, Lucy.

Daniel began his political career immediately after being admitted to the bar. In 1809 his county sent him to the Virginia House of Delegates, where he served until he became a member of the state privy council in 1812. Four years later he was elevated to the status of state lieutenant governor. By then, he long had been a member of the Richmond Junto, Virginia's ruling elite, and a close friend of Martin Van Buren of New York, whose political supporters banded together with the Junto to promote the Democratic Party.

Because of his ties with Van Buren, Daniel was a Jackson partisan. While many Democrats deserted their leader during Jackson's bank war, Daniel did not, and in 1835 he paid a price for his loyalty when the Whig-controlled Virginia legislature removed him from the privy council. One year later, Jackson compensated Daniel with a federal judgeship in the Eastern District of Virginia.

When Justice Philip Barbour died in 1841, Van Buren had only a week remaining in his presidency. Lest the nomination for Barbour's replacement fall to the incoming Whigs, Van Buren rushed his old friend Daniel's nomination through even before Barbour was buried. Daniel was confirmed on March 2, two days before the inauguration of William Henry Harrison as the nation's ninth president.

Daniel and Van Buren had a falling out, however, when Van Buren ran for president in 1848 on the Free-Soil ticket. Daniel's support of *states' rights and slavery seemed only to become more absolute during his tenure on the Supreme Court, where he seemed to be constantly writing in dissent. The one notable majority opinion he authored, *West River Bridge Co. v. Dix* (1848), concerned the issue of states' powers of *eminent domain over real estate, and in this instance the other justices agreed with Daniel that the *Contracts Clause might, in some instances, be subordinated to the states' power to condemn privately held property for public use. The facts of this case made it an exception, however, and the rest of the Court seldom agreed with Daniel's extreme antagonism towards any enlargement of federal power. In Daniel's final opinion, a dissent submitted on the last day of the Court's 1858-1859 term, he insisted that federal courts have no *jurisdiction over divorce and alimony contests. He died on May 31, 1860, in Richmond, less than a year before his native Virginia seceded from the Union, a development he doubtless would have approved.

SAMUEL NELSON

PERSONAL DATA

Born: November 10, 1792, in Hebron, New York
Parents: John Rogers Nelson, Jean McCarter (some sources cite McArthur) Nelson
Higher Education: Middlebury College (undergraduate degree, 1813)
Bar Admission: New York, 1817
Political Party: Democrat
Marriages: 1819 to Pamela Woods, who bore Nelson one son, and who died in 1822; 1825 to Catherine Ann Russell, who bore Nelson one son and two daughters
Died: December 13, 1873, in Cooperstown, New York
Buried: Lakewood Cemetery, Cooperstown

PROFESSIONAL CAREER

Occupations: Lawyer, 1817-1820; Government Official, 1820-1823; Politician, 1820-1823; Judge, 1823-1872; Diplomat, 1871
Official Positions: Postmaster, Cortland, New York, 1820-1823; Presidential Elector, 1820; Representative for Cortland County, New York State Constitutional Convention, 1821; Judge, Sixth Circuit Court of New York, 1823-1831; Associate Justice, New York Supreme Court, 1831-1837; Chief Justice, New York Supreme Court, 1837-1845; Associate Justice, United States Supreme Court, 1845-1872; Member, Alabama Claims Commission, 1871

SUPREME COURT SERVICE

Nominated: February 4, 1845
Nominated By: John Tyler
Confirmed: February 14, 1845
Confirmation Vote: Voice Vote
Oath Taken: February 27, 1845
Replaced: Smith Thompson
Significant Opinion: *Collector v. Day* (1871)
Left Court: Retired November 28, 1872
Length of Service: 27 years, 9 months, 1 day
Replacement: Ward Hunt

When Justice Thompson, a New Yorker, died on December 18, 1843, President Tyler was predisposed to nominate another New Yorker. Initially, he thought of naming Martin Van Buren, thereby eliminating him as a political opponent. This suggestion went nowhere, so on January 9, 1844, Tyler turned to John C. Spenser, a maverick New York Whig, whom the Senate rejected by a vote of 21 to 26 on January 31. Next, Tyler approached two Philadelphia lawyers, John Sergeant and Horace Binney, both of whom declined. Tyler twice offered the position to Senator Silas Wright of New York, but he, too, declined. On March 13, 1844, Tyler nominated New York Chancellor Reuben H. Walworth, but Walworth proved unpopular, and Tyler ultimately withdrew his name on June 17. When Tyler then named Nelson, the Senate confirmed him quickly — probably out of relief.

Samuel Nelson spent his childhood on a farm in upstate New York. Early on, he impressed his elders with his scholarship, and it was determined that he would pursue a career in the ministry. After graduating from Middlebury College, however, he settled on law, studying in the offices of Judges Savage and Woods. Upon being admitted to the bar in 1817, he moved westward to Madison County, New York, where he went into partnership with Woods and married Woods's daughter.

Around 1820, however, Nelson moved to Cortland, New York, where he went into solo practice, emphasizing litigation, real estate, and commercial law. In Cortland, he apparently established himself quickly in local politics, becoming in 1820 a presidential elector and, the next year, Cortland County's representative to the state constitutional convention. At the convention, he distinguished himself by his support for restructuring the state judicial system and expanding suffrage.

In 1823 Nelson began his career as a judge. Although he was widely known among his contemporaries for his judicial temperament, when he left the judiciary after almost 50 years, he seems to have left no mark. Perhaps Nelson's lack of distinction arises primarily from his penchant for *judicial restraint, a quality much in evidence during the *Dred Scott* (1857) controversy.

Loath to find the Missouri Compromise unconstitutional, Nelson drafted what originally was intended to be the Taney Court's opinion in *Scott v. Sandford*, affirming the lower court's decision and deferring to Missouri state law on the question of Scott's citizenship. Because the Court was divided as to whether or not it had *jurisdiction over the case, Nelson suggested a postponement in delivering the opinion and a reargument of the case. Following a series of delays, the Court determined it would decide all the issues raised by the case. Nelson refused to change his views, and he refused to change his opinion — even retaining the original use of the pronoun "we," despite the fact that he no longer was speaking for his brethren. Nelson's was only one of nine separate opinions finally delivered in the case.

Although Nelson consequently was criticized in the northern antislavery press, he considered himself a patriot. In March 1861 he remained in Washington, D.C., after the close of the Court term to negotiate with Confederate representatives. And in 1871 he accepted a post on the Alabama Claims Commission in an attempt to settle differences with Britain arising out of its support of the South during the Civil War. This work proved difficult for Nelson who, owing to old age and illness, resigned his seat on the Supreme Court in November 1872, only to die a year later.

LEVI WOODBURY

PERSONAL DATA

Born: December 22, 1789, in Francestown, New Hampshire

Parents: Peter Woodbury, Mary Woodbury

Higher Education: Dartmouth College (undergraduate degree, with honors, 1809); Tapping Reeve Law School, 1810

Bar Admission: New Hampshire, 1812

Political Party: Democrat

Marriage: June 1819 to Elizabeth Williams Clapp, who bore Woodbury one son and four daughters

Died: September 4, 1851, in Portsmouth, New Hampshire

Buried: Harmony Grove Cemetery, Portsmouth

PROFESSIONAL CAREER

Occupations: Lawyer, 1812-1816, 1824-1825; Politician, 1816, 1823-1845; Judge, 1817-1823, 1845-1851

Official Positions: Clerk, New Hampshire Senate, 1816; Associate Justice, New Hampshire Superior Court, 1817-1823; Governor, New Hampshire, 1823-1824; Speaker, New Hampshire Legislature, 1825; Member, United States Senate, 1825-1831, 1841-1845; United States Secretary of the Navy, 1831-1834; United States Secretary of the Treasury, 1834-1841; Associate Justice, United States Supreme Court, 1845-1851

SUPREME COURT SERVICE

Appointed: September 20, 1845 (recess appointment)

Appointed By: James K. Polk

Oath Taken: September 23, 1845

Nominated: December 23, 1845

Confirmed: January 3, 1846

Confirmation Vote: Voice vote

Oath Retaken: January 3, 1846

Replaced: Joseph Story

Significant Opinions: *Jones v. Van Zandt* (1847); *License Cases* (1847)

Left Court: Died September 4, 1851

Length of Service: 5 years, 11 months, 12 days

Replacement: Benjamin R. Curtis

Levi Woodbury was the second of ten children born to an old New England family whose forebears were among the earliest settlers of the region. After an education in the public schools and at the hands of a private tutor, he attended Dartmouth College, from which he graduated with honors in 1809. He next briefly attended the Tapping Reeve Law School in Litchfield, Connecticut — making him the first Supreme Court justice to have studied at a law school — but, as was the custom of the day, he completed his legal education by reading law in the offices of well-known jurists.

Woodbury was admitted to the bar in 1812, but almost immediately he turned his attention to politics. Politics, rather than law, was his true interest, and he held a nearly uninterrupted series of political offices until his appointment to the Supreme Court in 1845. The one exception occurred in 1817 when he began serving as an associate justice of the New Hampshire Supreme Court, but he made it clear that he probably would not sit long on the bench. Six years later, he did indeed leave to become governor of New Hampshire.

In 1819 Woodbury married Elizabeth Clapp, the daughter of a wealthy New England merchant with powerful political connections. His father-in-law seems to have used his money and his connections to advance Woodbury's career, first on the local scene, and then nationally. When the New Hampshire legislature sent Woodbury to the United States Senate (election of U.S. senators then occurred in state legislatures) in 1825, he immediately allied himself with Andrew Jackson. It is worth noting that although he was at that time a Republican and could have been expected, like most New England party regulars, to have supported the new administration of John Qunicy Adams, he owed his arrival on the national scene to Asa Clapp's Jacksonian allies.

Woodbury's transformation into a Jacksonian Democrat almost immediately paid off. When his Senate term expired in 1831, he went home to Portsmouth, New Hampshire, but he was soon called back to Washington, D.C., by President Jackson, who offered him the post of secretary of the navy. Then in 1834, after Roger Brooke Taney's role in Jackson's bank war caused the Senate to reject Taney's nomination as secretary of the Treasury, Jackson offered the position to Woodbury. He left that office in 1841 and, once again, returned to New Hampshire. Within the year, however, he was back in Washington as a senator.

Although Woodbury had been elected as a Democrat, his stance in the Senate was more that of a conservative Republican, as he espoused *states' rights doctrine with increasing vigor. Such views brought him to the attention of southerners, and in the election of 1844 his name was mentioned as a vice presidential candidate, one who would presumably be acceptable to all sections of an increasingly divided nation. The nomination went to another, however, and the next year President Polk nominated Woodbury as Justice Story's replacement.

Woodbury never entirely gave up politics, even after he reached the Supreme Court. In 1848 he was a contender for the Democratic presidential nomination. The time he spent on the Court was almost too brief for him to have made an impact, and during those six years he did little to distinguish himself from the other justices, consistently supporting Chief Justice Taney's positions. In the one significant opinion he authored for the Court, *Jones v. Van Zandt* (1847), he ruled in favor of a slaveowner who had sued a northerner for illegally harboring a fugitive slave, a stance that temporarily increased his stature with southern electors, although not his prominence as a Supreme Court justice.

ROBERT COOPER GRIER

PERSONAL DATA

Born: March 5, 1794, in Cumberland County, Pennsylvania

Parents: Reverend Isaac Grier, Elizabeth Cooper Grier

Higher Education: Dickinson College (undergraduate degree, 1812)

Bar Admission: Pennsylvania, 1817

Political Party: Democrat

Marriage: 1829 to Isabella Rose, who bore Grier two children

Died: September 25, 1870, in Philadelphia, Pennsylvania

Buried: West Laurel Hill Cemetery, Bala-Cynwyd, Pennsylvania

PROFESSIONAL CAREER

Occupations: Educator, 1812-1817; Lawyer, 1817-

1833; Judge, 1833-1870

Official Positions: Judge, Allegheny County, Pennsylvania, District Court, 1833-1846; Associate Justice, United States Supreme Court, 1846-1870

SUPREME COURT SERVICE

Nominated: August 3, 1846

Nominated By: James K. Polk

Confirmed: August 4, 1846

Confirmation Vote: Voice vote

Oath Taken: August 10, 1846

Replaced: Henry Baldwin

Significant Opinions: *License Cases* (1847); *Prize Cases* (1863)

Left Court: Retired January 31, 1870

Length of Service: 23 years, 5 months, 21 days

Replacement: William Strong

After Pennsylvania Justice Henry Baldwin died in 1844, it took more than two years to replace him, owing in part to John Tyler's lack of support among Whigs and Democrats. President Tyler first nominated Edward King, a Philadelphia judge, on June 5, 1844, but ten days later the Senate postponed consideration of his appointment by a vote of 29 to 18 On December 4, 1844, Tyler tried again, and again the Senate postponed consideration. King eventually withdrew his nomination on February 7, 1845. That same day, Tyler nominated John M. Read of Pennsylvania, but his nomination died when Congress adjourned without acting on it.

The seat remained empty when President Polk took office in March 1845. Future President James Buchanan's name then was circulated as a potential nominee, but he declined. On December 23, 1845, Polk then nominated George W. Woodward, a Pennsylvania jurist, but on January 22 of the next year, the Senate rejected him by a vote of 29 to 20 — in part, apparently, because of his anti-immigrant leanings. Buchanan surfaced again, but when he could not make up his mind, Polk turned to Grier, an uncontroversial but virtually unknown candidate from Pennsylvania.

Robert C. Grier was the eldest of 11 children born to a Presbyterian minister married to the daughter of a Presbyterian minister. Grier's father, Reverend Isaac Grier, also operated a grammar school and eventually supervised an academy.

Grier himself, after graduating in one year from Dickinson College (he was admitted as a junior), and staying on there for a year as an instructor, came home to assist his father with the academy. When his father died three years later, Grier assumed his father's position, studying law in his off hours and finally being admitted to the bar in 1817.

Grier practiced law successfully for 16 years, earning enough money to help support his mother and his ten younger siblings. When in 1833 the various political factions could not agree on an appointee for judge of the Allegheny County district court, the governor offered the position to Grier, who was expected to decline. Instead, he accepted. This appointment seemed to set a precedent for the later set of political misadventures that led to his appointment to the Supreme Court.

Grier seems to have functioned as a competent, if unremarkable state judge, but within a short while after joining the High Court, he established himself in a position of some influence. Chief Justice Taney often gave him responsibility for drafting opinions in prestigious cases concerning constitutional questions. In the *License Cases* (1847), decided soon after he joined the Supreme Court, Grier strongly defended the states' *police powers in upholding their right to pass laws restricting the interstate flow of liquor. His opinion in the *Dred Scott* case (1857), which consisted of less than half a page concurring with Justices Taney and Nelson, was considerably less eloquent and influential. Nonetheless, Grier played a pivotal role in the whole imbroglio surrounding that decision.

When the Court reached a stalemate in February 1856 regarding the issue of citizenship of free blacks, Justices Nelson and Grier were the ones intent on a strategy of *judicial restraint that avoided this question. Justice Catron then wrote to President-elect Buchanan to suggest that Buchanan write Grier in an effort to influence the latter to rule on the constitutionality of the Missouri Compromise. While Grier was not persuaded by Buchanan's attentions to alter his own strategy, he did supply the president-elect with crucial information about the judicial lineup favoring his position, and assured him that decision would not be rendered until two days after his inauguration.

Despite Grier's questionable role in the *Dred Scott* decision and his general support for the *states' rights, proslavery faction in the Court, his opinion in the *Prize Cases* (1863) revealed him to be a Unionist. A week after the Confederate assault on Fort Sumter in April 1861, before a formal declaration of war, President Lincoln had ordered a blockade of southern ports and seized neutral ships carrying Confederate cargo. Two years later, Grier, writing for the Court, upheld the president's right to prosecute the war even without congressional authorization.

Only a few years later, Justice Grier's ability to continue on the Court came into question. His mind had begun to wander, and he was prone to vote on cases in a contradictory manner. In 1862 he gave up his *circuit duties, and his apparent disabilities figured in the congressional debates about the proposed Judiciary Act of 1869. All of his brethren, led by Justice Stephen J. Field, urged him to resign, and in December 1869 Justice Grier agreed. The resignation became effective in January 1870, and Grier died nine months later.

BENJAMIN ROBBINS CURTIS

PERSONAL DATA

Born: November 4, 1809, in Watertown, Massachusetts
Parents: Benjamin Curtis III, Lois Robbins Curtis
Higher Education: Harvard College (undergraduate degree, with highest honors, 1829); Harvard Law School (law degree, 1832)
Bar Admissions: Massachusetts, 1832
Political Party: Whig
Marriages: May 1833 to Eliza Maria Woodward, who bore Curtis five children, and who died in 1844; January 1846 to Anna Wroe Curtis, a cousin, who bore Curtis three children, and who died in 1860; 1861 to Maria Malleville Allen, who bore Curtis four children
Died: September 15, 1874, in Newport, Rhode Island
Buried: Mount Auburn Cemetery, Cambridge, Massachusetts

PROFESSIONAL CAREER

Occupations: Lawyer, 1831-1849, 1857-1874; Politician, 1849-1851; Judge, 1851-1857
Official Positions: Representative, Massachusetts General Court (state legislature), 1849-1851; Chairman, Commission to Reform Judicial Proceedings, Massachusetts General Court, 1849-1851; Associate Justice, United States Supreme Court, 1851-1857

SUPREME COURT SERVICE

Appointed: September 22, 1851 (recess appointment)
Appointed By: Millard Fillmore
Oath Taken: October 10, 1851
Nominated: December 11, 1851
Confirmed: December 20, 1851
Confirmation Vote: Voice Vote
Replaced: Levi Woodbury
Significant Opinions: *Cooley v. Board of Wardens* (1852); *Murray's Lessee v. Hoboken Land & Improvement Co.* (1856)
Left Court: Resigned September 30, 1857
Length of Service: 5 years, 11 months, 20 days
Replacement: Nathan Clifford

Benjamin Curtis's father was a ship's captain who was lost at sea when the future justice was only five years old. Curtis's mother started a dry goods store and circulating library in their hometown of Watertown, Massachusetts, to support her two sons. When Curtis entered Harvard College in 1825, she moved with him to Cambridge, where she opened a boarding house to help pay her son's tuition.

Immediately after graduating with honors in 1829, Curtis entered Harvard Law School, which had recently — thanks in large part to Justice Joseph Story — been transformed into the first academic professional school in the country. Curtis left law school in March 1831, 18 months before graduating, to take over a law practice in Northfield, Massachusetts, but he returned for four months in 1832 to complete his degree.

Dissatisfied with small town practice, in October 1834 Curtis joined the prominent Boston law firm of a distant cousin. He remained there for the next 17 years, after which he sought, and won, election to the Massachusetts legislature for the specific purpose of reforming state judicial proceedings. His work saw fruition with publication in 1851 of the Massachusetts Practice Act.

Politically, Curtis was a loyal Whig. When Daniel Webster came under severe criticism for his role in formulating the Compromise of 1850, Curtis publicly supported Webster and spoke out in favor of sectional accommodation as the means of preserving the Union. When Webster later served as secretary of state, he did not forget his former ally, suggesting Curtis to President Fillmore as Justice Woodbury's replacement.

Thus far, Curtis had had a highly successful legal career. He quickly established himself as a force on the Taney Court with his majority opinion in _Cooley v. Board of Wardens_ (1852), written during his first term on the bench. _Cooley_, which concerned an act passed by the Pennsylvania legislature to regulate pilotage in the port of Philadelphia, raised the issue of whether the state had authority over this matter in the absence of congressional action. Upholding the act, Curtis elaborated the doctrine of *selective exclusiveness, whereby the states could regulate interstate commerce in areas where no uniform national rule was required.

During Curtis's six years on the Court, he wrote 53 majority opinions and seldom dissented. One of his dissents, however, was historic, and ultimately resulted in his resignation. Justices Curtis and McLean were the only members of the Taney Court to dissent in the _Dred Scott_ case in 1857. Curtis's dissent was foursquare against the chief justice's opinion, rejecting the notion that an African American person could not be a citizen, affirming the proposition that a slave's entrance onto free soil could free him, and finally, upholding Congress's authority to prohibit slavery in the territories under the Missouri Compromise. Curtis breached judicial decorum by providing a Boston newspaper with a copy of his dissent prior to publication of the other justices' opinions and without informing them. The cycle of blame and dissension that followed in the wake of _Scott v. Sandford_ resulted in Curtis's res-

ignation on September 30, 1857.

Curtis resumed his law practice, subsequently arguing 54 cases before the Supreme Court. In 1864 and 1873 he was considered as a candidate for chief justice, but passed over. He came to national prominence again during the *impeachment trial of President Andrew Johnson in 1868, when he served as defense counsel. By convincing the Senate, which was acting as a jury, that impeachment should be a judicial, not a political process, he helped to achieve a verdict of not guilty. A grateful Johnson offered him the post of attorney general, but Curtis declined, preferring his private legal practice. When he died in 1874 at the age of 64, his passing was widely lamented in the press.

JOHN ARCHIBALD CAMPBELL

PERSONAL DATA

Born: June 24, 1811, in Washington, Georgia
Parents: Duncan Green Campbell, Mary Williamson Campbell
Higher Education: Franklin College, now the University of Georgia (undergraduate degree, with high honors, 1825); United States Military Academy at West Point, 1825-1828
Bar Admission: Georgia, 1829
Political Party: Democrat
Marriage: Early 1830s to Anna Esther Goldthwaite, who bore Campbell five children
Died: March 12, 1889, in Baltimore, Maryland
Buried: Green Mountain Cemetery, Baltimore

PROFESSIONAL CAREER

Occupations: Educator, 1928-1829; Lawyer, 1829-1853, 1865-1889; Politician, 1837, 1843, 1850, 1862-1865; Judge, 1853-1861
Official Positions: Representative, Alabama State Legislature, 1837, 1843; Delegate-at-Large, Southern Convention, 1850; Associate Justice, United States Supreme Court, 1853-1861; Assistant Secretary of War, Confederate States of America, 1862-1865

SUPREME COURT SERVICE

Nominated: March 22, 1853
Nominated By: Franklin Pierce

Confirmed: March 25, 1853
Confirmation Vote: Voice vote
Oath Taken: April 11, 1853
Replaced: John McKinley
Significant Opinions: None
Left Court: Resigned April 30, 1861
Length of Service: 8 years, 19 days
Replacement: David Davis

Lame duck Whig President Millard Fillmore tried unsuccessfully four times to fill the seat left vacant by the death in July 1852 of Justice McKinley. The Democratically controlled Senate rejected all three nominees. Prominent Louisiana attorney Edward A. Bradford was nominated on August 16, 1852, but the Senate adjourned without acting on his nomination. The Senate rejected one of its own on February 11, 1853, by voting 26 to 25 to postpone action on Fillmore's nomination of North Carolina Senator George E. Badger, whose name had been placed before it on January 10, 1853. Fillmore then offered the position to Judah P. Benjamin, a newly elected Louisiana Whig senator, but he declined. At Benjamin's suggestion, on February 24, 1853, Fillmore named Benjamin's law partner, William C. Micou, to fill the vacancy, but again the Senate failed to take action. It was left to the incoming Democratic president, Franklin Pierce, to name McKinley's successor, John A. Campbell.

John A. Campbell was a prodigy who enrolled in college at the age of 11 and graduated with high honors three years later. His performance at West Point was considerably less stellar, and after three years there he withdrew upon the death of his father in 1828. To help support his family, he taught for a year, then began studying law in 1829. That same year, he was admitted to the Georgia bar at the age of 18 by a special act of the state legislature.

Campbell continued to distinguish himself, quickly becoming the state's leading attorney. Twice he was offered a seat on the state supreme court — the first time when he was only 24 — but both times he declined. He did, however, serve two terms in the Alabama legislature which, in 1850, elected him to serve as a delegate to a convention of southern states in Nashville,

Tennessee, called to discuss the North's perceived encroachment on southern *states' rights.

After Millard Fillmore's three nominees for the Supreme Court were rejected, in an unprecedented maneuver, a committee from the Taney Court, consisting of Justices John Catron and Benjamin R. Curtis, approached newly elected President Pierce to advise him that John Campbell should be appointed. Campbell, a respected attorney and states' rights Jacksonian Democrat, suited the Democratic Senate, which quickly confirmed him. On the Court, Campbell was known more for his dissents than his majority opinions. While the Taney Court left largely undisturbed the expanded reach of the *Contracts Clause established by John Marshall, Campbell disagreed, most memorably in *Dodge v. Woolsey* (1856), where he opposed the expansion of federal *jurisdiction over state-chartered corporations. Predictably, in *Scott v. Sandford* (1857), Campbell voted with the majority.

Campbell was, however, a moderate on slavery, having himself freed all his slaves after his Supreme Court appointment. And when Confederate commissioners arrived in Washington, D.C., to try to negotiate the surrender of Fort Sumter, Campbell acted as an intermediary with Secretary of State William H. Seward. After his home state of Alabama seceded from the Union, Campbell ultimately resigned from the Court, but he delayed four months before doing so. The delay, together with his previous participation in the Fort Sumter negotiations, cost Campbell mightily with Confederate firebrands, who threatened him with lynching when he returned home to Mobile, Alabama. Campbell moved to New Orleans, where the atmosphere was more relaxed. He practiced law there for a year before agreeing to become Confederate assistant secretary of war in charge of conscription. His position in the Confederate cabinet caused him to be jailed for four months after Appomattox.

Following the Civil War, Campbell returned to New Orleans and his lucrative legal practice, which involved him in the most significant legal argument of his life when he appeared before the Supreme Court in the *Slaughterhouse Cases* (1873).

Here he presented the first legal construction of the Fourteenth Amendment, passed in the wake of the Civil War. Campbell lost the case in a close 5 to 4 decision, but the Supreme Court reversed itself 20 years later, adopting his interpretation.

NATHAN CLIFFORD

PERSONAL DATA

Born: August 18, 1803, in Rumney, New Hampshire
Parents: Deacon Nathaniel Clifford,
Lydia Simpson Clifford
Higher Education: None
Bar Admission: New Hampshire, 1827
Political Party: Democrat
Marriage: 1828 to Hannah Ayer, who bore Clifford
six children
Died: July 25, 1881, in Cornish, Maine
Buried: Evergreen Cemetery, Portland, Maine

PROFESSIONAL CAREER

Occupations: Lawyer, 1827-1831, 1834-1838, 1846-1848, 1849-1858; Politician, 1831-1834, 1839-1843; Government Official, 1834-1838, 1846-1848, 1877; Diplomat, 1848-1849; Judge, 1858-1881
Official Positions: Member, Maine Legislature, 1831-1834; Speaker, Maine House of Representatives, 1833-1834; Attorney General, Maine, 1834-1838; Member, United States House of Representatives, 1839-1843; United States Attorney General, 1846-1848; United States Minister to Mexico, 1848-1849; Associate Justice, United States Supreme Court, 1858-1881; Chairman, Electoral Commission to Decide the 1876 Presidential Election, 1877

SUPREME COURT SERVICE

Nominated: December 9, 1857
Nominated By: James Buchanan
Confirmed: January 12, 1858
Confirmation Vote: 26-23
Oath Taken: January 21, 1858
Replaced: Benjamin R. Curtis
Significant Opinions: None
Left Court: Died July 25, 1881
Length of Service: 23 years, 6 months, 4 days
Replacement: Horace Gray

Nathan Clifford was the only son and the oldest of seven children born to a subsistence farmer. The family's lack of means prevented him from receiving a good elementary and secondary education, and his father's early death made it impossible for Clifford to pursue his goal of attending Dartmouth College.

Clifford studied law in the office of a prominent local attorney before being admitted to the New Hampshire bar in 1827. He then improved his lot by moving to Newfield, Maine, where he was the only attorney and where he married Hannah Ayer, the daughter of a prominent and influential family. Clifford's political sensibilities, however, were formed during his impoverished rural childhood, and he remained an ardent Jacksonian Democrat all his life. This party orientation served him well prior to his arrival at the Supreme Court, for he served three terms in the Maine legislature and two in the United States House of Representatives. He also acted as attorney general at both the state and federal levels, and as President Polk's minister to Mexico in 1848, he managed to gain ratification of the treaty that ended that country's war with the United States.

Despite Clifford's loyalty to, and long service with, Democratic administrations, his political career was hardly one of consistent advancement. Twice, he was forced by political reverses to leave Washington and return to his law practice in Maine. When a New England vacancy opened on the Supreme Court following Justice Curtis's resignation, President Buchanan considered a number of candidates from the region, as well as a southerner, before settling on his old stalwart, Clifford. The nomination resulted in a storm of protest; not only was Clifford unqualified, he was widely perceived to be a hack whose blind obedience to the party line brought him perilously close to being a "doughface," a northerner with southern sympathies. The Senate dragged its feet for 34 days, finally approving the nomination by the narrowest of margins.

Once on the Court, Clifford unfortunately lived up to his reputation. He seemed out of his depth, writing a disproportionate number of dissents — one-fifth of all his opinions — most of them remarkable only for their ponderous length. He never authored a major constitutional opinion, and one of his later chiefs, Morrison Waite, calculated that of the 66 opinions he assigned between 1874 and 1881, Clifford wrote only one.

Clifford's Democratic constancy led to his appointment as head of an electoral commission Congress created to decide the disputed presidential election of 1876. Whereas Democratic candidate Samuel J. Tilden had won a popular majority over Republican Rutherford B. Hayes, the electoral vote was in doubt. Clifford vigorously supported Tilden, but Hayes won by a single electoral vote. Clifford felt that Hayes had gained the presidency illegitimately, and consequently refused to attend Hayes's inauguration or to enter the White House while Hayes resided there.

Clifford outlasted his Democratic brethren, and by 1872 the Republican majority on the Court tended to outvote him. Despite failing health, frequent absences, and memory lapses, Clifford refused to resign, hoping for the election of a Democratic president who could name his successor. In 1880 he suffered a severe and debilitating stroke, but still he stubbornly refused to leave the Court. He died in 1881.

NOAH HAYNES SWAYNE

PERSONAL DATA
Born: December 7, 1804, in Frederick County, Virginia
Parents: Joshua Swayne, Rebecca Smith Swayne
Higher Education: None
Bar Admission: Virginia, 1823
Political Party: Republican
Marriage: 1832 to Sarah Ann Wager, who bore Swayne four sons and one daughter
Died: June 8, 1884, in New York, New York
Buried: Oak Hill Cemetery, Washington, D.C.

PROFESSIONAL CAREER
Occupations: Lawyer, 1823-1860; Government Official, 1825-1829, 1830-1841, 1850s, 1861; Politician, 1829, 1836; Judge, 1862-1881
Official Positions: Prosecuting Attorney, Coshocton

County, Ohio, 1825-1829; Member, Ohio Legislature, 1829, 1836; United States District Attorney for Ohio, 1830-1841; Member, Columbus, Ohio, City Council, 1834; Ohio Fund Commissioner, 1850s; Assistant to the Governor of Ohio, 1861; Associate Justice, United States Supreme Court, 1862-1881

SUPREME COURT SERVICE
Nominated: January 22, 1862
Nominated By: Abraham Lincoln
Confirmed: January 24, 1862
Confirmation Vote: 38-1
Oath Taken: January 27, 1862
Replaced: John McLean
Significant Opinion: *Gelpcke v. Dubuque* (1864)
Left Court: Retired January 24, 1881
Length of Service: 18 years, 11 months, 28 days
Replacement: Stanley Matthews

Noah Swayne's parents were both Quakers, and they seem to have instilled in him an opposition to slavery that guided many of his personal and professional decisions. His education was scattered and constantly interrupted. He devoted himself first to medicine and then to classical studies, but he was unable to see either course of study through to its end. Finally he settled on law and was admitted to the Virginia bar in 1823, but he left Virginia almost at once for Ohio because of his antislavery views. During his long legal career in Ohio, he frequently defended fugitive slaves, and when he married Sarah Ann Wager of Virginia in 1832, he forced her to free her slaves.

Swayne became involved in politics almost immediately upon his arrival in Ohio. He was then a Jacksonian Democrat, and in 1830 President Jackson appointed him United States attorney for the district of Ohio, a post he held for ten years. During the public debate over free soil that dominated national politics during the 1850s, however, Swayne became a Republican Party convert.

Swayne was a close friend of Justice John McLean of Ohio, who openly supported Swayne as his successor on the Supreme Court. When McLean died in April 1861 Swayne mounted an all-out campaign for his seat, enlisting support from the entire Ohio congressional delegation and such prominent easterners as Samuel J. Tilden. Swayne himself traveled to Washington "to learn the lay of the land," and was disappointed when President Lincoln did not react immediately to his openly expressed desire for appointment. Finally, however, Lincoln was convinced by Swayne's antislavery convictions and his dedication to both the Union and the Republican Party. Noah Swayne was nominated for the Supreme Court on January 22, 1862, and confirmed two days later with only one senator voting against him.

Once on the High Court, Swayne proved a disappointment. Although he supported the emergency measures Lincoln took in prosecuting the Civil War, lobbied for passage of the Fifteenth Amendment, and wrote the majority opinion in the important case, *Gelpcke v. Dubuque* (1864), his record in constitutional law was unimpressive. Swayne seems to have remained most interested in politics, maneuvering vigorously but unsuccessfully for the chief justiceship when it became vacant in 1864 and again in 1873. He lingered on the bench long after his effectiveness had waned, and only retired because of a combination of pressure from President Hayes, the promise of appointment of Swayne's friend, Stanley Matthews, as his successor, and an agreement for the simultaneous retirement of fellow justice William Strong.

SAMUEL FREEMAN MILLER

PERSONAL DATA

Born: April 5, 1816, in Richmond, Kentucky
Parents: Frederick Miller, Patsy Freeman Miller
Higher Education: Transylvania University (M.D., 1838)
Bar Admission: Kentucky, 1847
Political Party: Republican
Marriages: 1839 to Lucy Ballinger, who bore Miller three children, and who died in 1854; 1857 to Elizabeth Winter Reeves, who bore Miller two children
Died: October 13, 1890, in Washington, D.C.
Buried: Oakland Cemetery, Keokuk, Iowa

PROFESSIONAL CAREER

Occupations: Physician, 1838-1850; Government Official, 1840s; Lawyer, 1850-1862; Judge, 1862-1890
Official Positions: Justice of the Peace and Member of Knox County, Kentucky Court (an administrative body), 1840s; Associate Justice, United States Supreme Court, 1862-1890

SUPREME COURT SERVICE

Nominated: July 16, 1862
Nominated By: Abraham Lincoln
Confirmed: July 16, 1862
Confirmation Vote: Voice Vote
Oath Taken: July 21, 1862
Replaced: Peter V. Daniel
Significant Opinions: *Test Oath Cases* (dissent)(1867); *Woodruff v. Parham* (1869); *Slaughterhouse Cases* (1873); *Bradwell v. Illinois* (1873); *Kilbourn v. Thompson* (1881); *Ex parte Yarbrough* (1884); *Head Money Cases* (1884); *Wabash, St. Louis & Pacific Railway Co. v. Illinois* (1886); *In re Neagle* (1890)
Left Court: Died October 13, 1890
Length of Service: 28 years, 2 months, 22 days
Replacement: Henry B. Brown

President Buchanan had made an earlier attempt to fill the vacancy on the Court created by the death on May 31, 1860, of Justice Daniel. Buchanan's nomination of Secretary of State Jeremiah S. Black on February 5, 1861, was rejected by the Senate on February 21 by a vote of 26 to 25. It was left to Abraham Lincoln to replace Justice Daniel two years later with Samuel F. Miller.

Samuel F. Miller began his professional life in medicine, an interest sparked when he left school as a boy to work at a relative's pharmacy. After earning an M.D. in 1838 from Transylvania University in Lexington, Kentucky, Miller practiced medicine for 12 years in the mountains in the southeastern corner of the state. He shared an office with a lawyer, and when he grew tired of medicine, his interest turned to law. He studied for the bar examination on his own, and in 1847, at the age of 31, he was admitted to practice.

Miller was an enthusiastic advocate of emancipation, and when a new Kentucky state constitution strengthened slavery in his state in 1850, he left for free soil in Iowa. Originally a Whig and a supporter of Henry Clay, after the chaos engendered by passage of the Kansas-Nebraska Act, Miller switched to the new Republican Party, which he helped to organize in Iowa. Miller was a strong Lincoln supporter, and when the Civil War broke out, he gave his own money to help pay and equip Union soldiers.

In 1862 there were three vacancies on the Supreme Court. Also in that year, Miller's congressional supporters lobbied successfully for creation of a judicial *circuit west of the Mississippi and for the appointment of their man to the High Court, despite his lack of judicial experience. The Senate confirmed Miller's nomination within a half hour after Lincoln named him. He was the first justice appointed from a state west of the Mississippi.

Throughout the war, Miller's judicial stance was unequivocally pro-Union, and he supported both Lincoln's suspension of *habeas corpus and the president's trials of treasonous civilians in courts martial. Miller left his strongest mark on the Court, however, in his interpretations of those constitutional amendments passed after the war, particularly the Fourteenth Amendment. In the *Slaughterhouse Cases* (1873), he construed the amendment narrowly, stating that it was intended to provide former slaves with some equality, but not to expand the rights of the rest of the population. In *Ex parte Yarbrough* (1884), he adopted a somewhat more liberal attitude toward the Fifteenth Amendment, writing for a unanimous Court that voting in national elections was a federally protected right. Commentators have cited *Yarbrough* as the foundation for the later Civil Rights movement of the 1960s.

Miller exerted considerable influence on the Court, in part because he was so prolific, writing 616 opinions, more than any justice before him. In addition, he concentrated his efforts on the important area of constitutional law. Twice (in 1873 and 1888) he was considered for the position of chief justice, but both times he was passed over. In 1880 and again in 1884, he was also discussed as a Republican presidential candidate. Instead, he served with dedication on the

Supreme Court for 28 years, working almost up to the day he died.

DAVID DAVIS

PERSONAL DATA
Born: March 9, 1815, in Cecil County, Maryland
Parents: Dr. David Davis, Ann Mercer Davis
Higher Education: Kenyon College (undergraduate degree, 1832); New Haven Law School (associated with Yale Law School), 1835
Bar Admission: Illinois, 1835
Political Party: Republican
Marriages: October 30, 1838, to Sarah Woodruff Walker, who died in 1879; March 14, 1883, to Adeline Burr, who bore Davis two daughters
Died: June 26, 1886, in Bloomington, Illinois
Buried: Evergreen Cemetery, Bloomington

PROFESSIONAL CAREER
Occupations: Lawyer, 1835-1845; Politician, 1845-1848, 1877-1883; Judge, 1848-1877
Official Positions: Member, Illinois Legislature, 1845-1847; Member, Illinois State Constitutional Convention, 1847; Judge, Illinois Eighth Circuit Court, 1848-1862; Associate Justice, United States Supreme Court, 1862-1877; United States Senator, 1877-1883; President Pro Tem, United States Senate, 1881-1883

SUPREME COURT SERVICE
Appointed: October 17, 1862 (recess appointment)
Appointed By: Abraham Lincoln
Nominated: December 1, 1862
Confirmed: December 8, 1862
Confirmation Vote: Voice vote
Oath Taken: December 10, 1862
Replaced: John A. Campbell
Significant Opinion: *Ex parte Milligan* (1866)
Left Court: Resigned March 4, 1877
Length of Service: 14 years, 2 months, 22 days
Replacement: John Marshall Harlan

David Davis, the son of a physician who died before Davis was born, directed his early career toward law — even studying law for a time in an academic setting, a practice unusual in his day —

but it was politics that consumed his life. In 1836 he purchased a law practice in Bloomington, Illinois (which became his lifelong home), and became directly involved in Whig politics. He lost his first bid for the state senate in 1840, but won a seat in the state house in the next election. It was during this period that he began a crucial association with another Illinois attorney, Abraham Lincoln, who was also a Whig at that time.

In 1848 he was elected as judge of the new Illinois eighth *circuit, a position he held for the next 14 years, during which Lincoln frequently appeared before him as counsel. Davis and Lincoln became close friends and, upon the Whigs' demise in the 1850s, the two joined the Republican Party. As Lincoln's campaign manager in 1860, Davis was pivotal in securing the presidency for his friend. After Lincoln's election, Davis served him further by helping him form a cabinet and draft his inaugural address.

Davis's hopes for political patronage in return for his services were modest. Initially he asked only to be considered for the position of federal district judge. After Congress reorganized the judicial circuits so that midwestern states were better represented, however, Davis lobbied for a position on the Supreme Court. Lincoln appointed him in the fall of 1862.

Davis saw himself as a trial judge, and he was never comfortable with his position on the nation's highest *appellate court. He is best remembered on the Court for his majority opinion in _Ex parte Milligan_ (1866), in which he wrote that the military trial of a Confederate civilian during the Civil War was unconstitutional because it took place in Indiana, where civil courts were available to try cases involving allegedly treasonous activities. Although _Milligan_ is regarded as a landmark of American constitutional liberty, it has been largely disregarded by the other branches of government. Even as it was handed down, Congress was putting a military scheme of government in place as part of its reconstruction plan for the South — seemingly in violation of _Milligan_.

Davis continued to dabble in politics while sitting on the High Court. In 1872 he was nominated for president by a splinter political party, the Labor Reform Party. He hoped to parlay this nomination into that of a larger group, the Liberal Republicans, but when they nominated newspaperman Horace Greeley, Davis withdrew his name. Then, in 1877, while still on the Court, Davis was elected to the United States Senate by the Illinois legislature. He saw this as his opportunity to resign from a position in which he had never felt comfortable.

Davis's resignation came at a particularly bad time for the nation, as he was widely expected to serve as the 15th — and more importantly, only nonpartisan — member of an electoral commission established to decide the presidential election of 1876, which was still in dispute. His replacement was Republican Justice Joseph P. Bradley, who voted, as expected, for Republican Rutherford B. Hayes. While Democrats denounced Davis for irresponsibility, Davis himself said after the fact that he, too, would have voted for Hayes.

Davis served one term in the Senate. In 1881 when Vice President Chester A. Arthur became president upon the assassination of James A. Garfield, Davis served for two years as president pro tem, next in the line of presidential succession. Chief Justice Morrison Waite sardonically declared that this was "as near to the Presidency as [Davis] can get."

STEPHEN JOHNSON FIELD

PERSONAL DATA

Born: November 4, 1816, in Haddam, Connecticut
Parents: Reverend David Dudley Field, Submit Dickinson Field
Higher Education: Williams College (undergraduate degree, class valedictorian, 1837)
Bar Admission: New York, 1841
Political Party: Democrat
Marriage: June 2, 1859, to Virginia Swearingen
Died: April 9, 1899, in Washington, D.C.
Buried: Rock Creek Cemetery, Washington, D.C.

PROFESSIONAL CAREER

Occupations: Lawyer 1841-1848, 1851-1857;

Politician, 1850-1851; Judge, 1857-1897
Official Positions: *Alcalde* of Marysville, California, 1850; Member, California Legislature, 1850-1851; Justice, California Supreme Court, 1857-1863; Associate Justice, United States Supreme Court, 1863-1897

SUPREME COURT SERVICE
Nominated: March 6, 1863
Nominated By: Abraham Lincoln
Confirmed: March 10, 1863
Confirmation Vote: Voice vote
Oath Taken: May 20, 1863
Replaced: No one; filled newly created seat
Significant Opinions: *Test Oath Cases* (1867); *Paul v. Virginia* (1869); *Slaughterhouse Cases* (dissent) (1873); *Mugler v. Kansas* (dissent)(1887); *Chae Chan Ping v. United States* (1889); *De Geofroy v. Riggs* (1890); *Virginia v. Tennessee* (1893)
Left Court: Retired December 1, 1897
Length of Service: 34 years, 6 months, 12 days
Replacement: Joseph McKenna

Stephen J. Field was born into a family headed by a Congregational clergyman of Puritan stock whose uncompromising theology Field would later reflect in the extreme degree of righteous independence he exhibited on the bench. Field was one of eight children. After graduating from Williams College, Field read law in the offices of his brother David, who was already established as a noted New York attorney and politician. After Field was admitted to the bar, he and his brother practiced law together until 1848, when Field's restlessness led him to travel to Europe.

Eventually, Field settled in California, where he helped to establish the town of Marysville, soon becoming its *Alcalde*, the chief civil magistrate and administrative officer under the old Mexican system of government. During this same period Field also practiced law and speculated in land, but he remained focused on politics. After serving a term in the new state house, he ran for the state senate in 1851. His bid for this office was unsuccessful, but in 1857 he was elected to the California Supreme Court, where he commenced his 40-year judicial career.

As a legislator and jurist in the rough-and-

tumble atmosphere of California, Field learned to be both decisive and adaptable, qualities that led President Lincoln to nominate him when in 1863 Congress created a tenth seat on the Supreme Court — partly to serve the new Pacific Coast *circuit, and partly to ensure that during wartime the Court had a majority dedicated to the Union. Field filled both requirements: he was familiar with the singular water and mineral rights issues originating in California, and he was a firm supporter of the Union.

On the Court, Field was a proponent of the ideal of unalienable rights. Initially, his conception of these rights had a civil libertarian cast to them, but over time they came to stand for the protection of private property. Field would become the most uncompromising proponent of constitutional *laissez faire the Court has ever seen, shaping the *Due Process Clause of the Fourteenth Amendment into a doctrine known as *substantive due process. The doctrine, which in modern times has served to protect rights of privacy, grew almost entirely out of Field's dissent in the *Slaughterhouse Cases* (1873).

Like other members of the High Court, Field did not abandon politics when he assumed his seat. California put his name forward as a presidential candidate in 1868, in 1880, and again in 1884, during which he openly campaigned for office. All his nominations fared badly. When Chief Justice Morrison Waite died in 1888, Field felt that as the only Democrat on the Court — and one whom Democratic President Grover Cleveland owed political favors — he was Waite's natural successor. Again, Field was bitterly disappointed by dashed ambitions. (It is worth noting that Field seemed to have a gift for making enemies, a gift that led, in 1889, to an attempt on his life, making him one of only two Supreme Court justices to have survived assassination attempts, the other being Brockholst Livingston.)

Throughout his tenure on the Supreme Court, Field exhibited an unshakable belief in the rightness of his beliefs, and he was undaunted by the prospect of being the only dissenter. Altogether he dissented 220 times, 68 times alone. His final tally on the Court, a total of 640 opinions, appears to be a record. The length of his tenure, 34 years, 6 months, 12 days from the date of swearing in, is another record. Towards the end of his service, Field began to fail badly, both physically and mentally, but he could not be persuaded to leave until he had surpassed the service record set by John Marshall.

SIGNIFICANT CASES

BRISCOE V. BANK OF THE COMMONWEALTH OF KENTUCKY

Citation: 11 Pet. (36 U.S.) 257 (1837)
Argued: January term, 1834; reargued January 28-February 1, 1837
Decided: February 11, 1837
Court Below: Kentucky Court of Appeals
Basis for Review: *Writ of error
Facts: A Kentucky statute permitted a state-chartered bank, owned and controlled by the state, to issue interest-bearing loan certificates. The case arose when a debtor tried to avoid repaying debts incurred by borrowing state bank notes issued by the bank.
Issue: Does the Kentucky statute violate Article I, section 10, of the Constitution, which prohibits states from issuing "bills of credit"?
Outcome: The statute, and the lower court ruling, were upheld because the Court narrowly defined bills of credit to mean notes issued by the state, whereas in this case the notes were redeemable by the bank.
Vote: 6-1
Participating: Taney, Story, Thompson, McLean, Baldwin, Wayne, Barbour
Opinions: McLean for the Court; Thompson concurring; Story dissenting
Significance: *Briscoe* represented the Taney Court's retreat in the area of banking and currency from the economic nationalism of the Marshall era. Whereas the Marshall Court had decided in a similar case, *Craig v. Missouri* (1830), that state-issued interest-bearing loan certificates were impermissible, the Taney Court took advantage of the imprecise meaning of bills of credit in the Constitution to complete the financial rev-

olution begun by Andrew Jackson's refusal to recharter the Second Bank of the United States.

CHARLES RIVER BRIDGE V. WARREN BRIDGE

Citation: 11 Pet. (36 U.S.) 420 (1837)
Argued: March 7-11, 1831; reargued January 19-26, 1837
Decided: February 12, 1837
Court Below: Massachusetts Supreme Judicial Court
Basis for Review: *Writ of error
Facts: In 1785 the Massachusetts legislature incorporated a body for purposes of building a bridge connecting Boston with its northern neighbor, Charleston. In 1828 when the legislature authorized another bridge across the Charles River, the Charles River Bridge proprietors sought to halt construction, claiming that their charter implicitly granted them a monopoly on foot traffic (and the tolls it generated) over the river. The Massachusetts Supreme Judicial Court affirmed a lower court's denial of an *injunction.
Issue: Does Massachusetts's Warren Bridge charter violate the constitutional ban on state action impairing the obligations of contracts?
Outcome: Upholding the lower court's refusal to enjoin the building of a second bridge, the Court ruled that the grant of a charter for the Warren Bridge was within the authority of the Massachusetts legislature.
Vote: 4-3
Participating: Taney, Story, Thompson, McLean, Baldwin, Wayne, Barbour
Opinions: Taney for the Court; McLean, Story, Thompson dissenting
Significance: *Charles River Bridge* was argued first before the Marshall Court, but absences and vacancies on the Court, as well as a lack of consensus regarding vested property rights, delayed decision for six years. The most senior associate justices, holdovers from the glory days of the Marshall Court, with its nationalistic capitalism, dissented, upholding the inviolability of the *Contracts Clause. But Chief Justice Taney's concessions to states' powers carried the day. The state legislature, representing the *sovereign power of the peo-

ple, had chartered the first bridge for the public good; a second bridge was now needed for the same purpose. Absent an express grant of monopoly, the Charles River Bridge proprietors had no exclusive right to control public travel and — implicitly — no right to impede the implementation of technological and economic progress.

NEW YORK V. MILN

Citation: 11 Pet. (36 U.S.) 102 (1837)
Argued: January term, 1834; reargued January 27-28, 1837
Decided: February 16, 1837
Court Below: United States Circuit Court for the Southern District of New York
Basis for Review: *Certificate of division of opinion
Facts: A New York statute required that all ships arriving in the state provide a list of passengers, post a bond for indigent passengers, and remove all undesirable aliens.
Issue: Does the state law interfere with federal power to regulate foreign commerce under the *Commerce Clause?
Outcome: The statute was upheld, as it was a legitimate exercise of the state's *police powers regulating the human cargo of ships plying interstate waterways.
Vote: 6-1
Participating: Taney, Story, Thompson, McLean, Baldwin, Wayne, Barbour
Opinions: Barbour for the Court; Thompson concurring; Story dissenting
Significance: The Court decided as it did largely because the statute involved the interstate transportation and admission of persons rather than goods, and thus raised the controversial issue of slavery. This was the first *Commerce Clause case to come before the Taney Court, and it sidestepped the complex area of concurrent federal and state commerce powers by emphasizing instead New York's *police powers, which permit the state to protect the welfare of its citizens. This was the first time in the history of the Court that state police powers were invoked as justification for state regulation of interstate waterways, and *Miln* seemed to contradict the recent

precedent of *Gibbons v. Ogden* (1824). Nonetheless, *Miln* remained valid until 1941, when the Court found that it impermissibly used economic criteria as a means of restricting individual travel.

KENDALL V. UNITED STATES *EX REL. STOKES

Citation: 12 Pet. (37 U.S.) 524 (1838)
Argued: February 13, 19-24, 26-27, 1838
Decided: March 12, 1838
Court Below: United States Circuit Court for the District of Columbia
Basis for Review: *Writ of error
Facts: Congress passed first an act, then a resolution, requiring newly appointed Postmaster General Kendall to obey an order from the solicitor general of the Treasury requiring Kendall to honor a contract negotiated by his predecessor. When he refused, the claimants on the contract acquired a writ of *mandamus from the circuit court requiring Kendall to act.
Issue: Is the congressional act an unconstitutional infringement on the executive branch?
Outcome: A unanimous Supreme Court upheld Congress's right to order executive branch officials not under the exclusive control of the president to perform nondiscretionary, ministerial duties. Furthermore, a majority of the Court found that such duties can be enforced by writs of mandamus issued by federal courts.
Vote: 9-0
Participating: Taney, Story, Thompson, McLean, Baldwin, Wayne, Barbour, Catron, McKinley
Opinion: Thompson for the Court; Taney, Barbour, and Catron dissenting in part
Significance: *Kendall* resolved a conflict regarding the *separation of powers between the executive and legislative branches of the federal government, and at the same time established a role for the federal judiciary in resolving such conflicts.

BANK OF AUGUSTA V. EARLE

Citation: 13 Pet. (38 U.S.) 519 (1839)
Argued: January 30-February 1, 1839
Decided: March 9, 1839
Court Below: United States Circuit Court for

the Southern District of Alabama

Basis for Review: *Writ of error

Facts: Three banks chartered outside Alabama that bought financial instruments in that state sued when the makers of these bills of exchange refused to pay on them. The lower court ruled that the banks were not entitled to recover their investment because they were not authorized to conduct such business in Alabama.

Issue: Can a corporation, chartered in one state, enter into contracts enforceable in another state?

Outcome: The lower court's ruling was struck down because, although a state can exclude a foreign corporation from doing business within its boundaries, or impose reasonable restrictions on such business, Alabama failed to indicate clearly that it subscribed to any such prohibitions.

Vote: 8-1

Participating: Taney, Story, Thompson, McLean, Baldwin, Wayne, Barbour, Catron, McKinley

Opinions: Taney for the Court; Baldwin concurring (without written opinion); McKinley dissenting

Significance: This marked the first time the Supreme Court ruled on the powers of a state over private corporations chartered in other states. By finding for the banks, the Court undoubtedly forestalled financial chaos that would have worsened the depression. *Bank of Augusta v. Earle* remains in force, but the Court subsequently modified its holding by ruling that state restrictions may not impose undue burdens on *foreign corporations.

HOLMES V. JENNISON

Citation: 14 Pet. (39 U.S.) 540 (1840)

Argued: January 24-25, 1840

Decided: Dismissed March 4, 1840

Court Below: Vermont Supreme Court

Basis for Review: *Writ of error

Facts: The governor of Vermont, Silas H. Jennison, ordered George Holmes, a Quebec fugitive detained in Vermont, sent back to Canada for trial on murder charges, despite the fact that the United States had no extradition treaty with that country. Holmes sought release by petitioning the state supreme court for a writ of *habeas corpus, but the court denied his petition.

Issue: Does the Supreme Court have *jurisdiction in this case?

Outcome: Because the Court was evenly divided on the question of jurisdiction, the case was dismissed. Five of the eight justices sitting on the Court decided that Governor Jennison lacked authority to surrender Holmes, however, and the Vermont Supreme Court subsequently ordered his release.

Vote: 4-4

Participating: Taney, Story, Thompson, McLean, Baldwin, Wayne, Barbour, Catron (McKinley not participating)

Opinions: Taney writing for himself, Story, McLean, and Wayne; Thompson, Baldwin, Barbour, and Catron disagreeing

Significance: Reasoning that the federal government had exclusive powers over relations with foreign powers, Chief Justice Taney found that the Court had jurisdiction over the case. The significant aspect of his opinion, however, is its declaration that states are forbidden to engage independently in foreign affairs.

GROVES V. SLAUGHTER

Citation: 15 Pet. (40 U.S.) 449 (1841)

Argued: February 12-13, 15-18, 1841

Decided: March 10, 1841

Court Below: United States Circuit Court for the Eastern District of Louisiana

Basis for Review: *Writ of error

Facts: In 1832, by constitutional amendment, Mississippi prohibited the importation of slaves for purposes of sale. The state did not, however, pass *enabling legislation. Subsequently, a purchaser of slaves defaulted on payment for imported slaves. The federal circuit court found for the seller.

Issue: Is the Mississippi constitutional amendment void owing to a conflict with the federal *commerce power?

Outcome: The lower court was overruled on the basis that the Mississippi amendment was not self-executing and therefore unenforceable.

Vote: 5-2

Participating: Taney, Story, Thompson, McLean, Baldwin, Wayne, McKinley (Catron not participating)

Opinion: Thompson delivering the judgment of the Court, but in fact writing only for himself and Wayne; McLean, Taney, and Baldwin concurring; McKinley and Story dissenting (without written opinions)

Significance: In retrospect, the significance of *Groves* lies in what the Court did not say. The case demonstrates the Court's fragmentation — and evasiveness — with regard to the slavery question.

SWIFT V. TYSON

Citation: 16 Pet. (41 U.S.) 1 (1842)
Argued: January 14, 1842
Decided: January 25, 1842
Court Below: United States Circuit Court for the Southern District of New York
Basis for Review: *Certificate of division of opinion
Facts: New York defendants were sued in federal court in New York over payment due on a bank draft they wrote to a nonresident of the state. While the payee plaintiffs argued that general commercial law made the draft good, the defendants cited New York decisions which would argue for the instrument's defectiveness.
Issue: Are state court decisions "laws" that federal courts are required to follow under section 34 of the 1789 Judiciary Act, mandating that federal courts follow state laws wherever applicable?
Outcome: Because state court decisions are themselves interpretations of general commercial law and not fixed pronouncements of an independent body of laws, the instrument was valid.
Vote: 9-0
Participating: Taney, Story, Thompson, McLean, Baldwin, Wayne, Catron, McKinley, Daniel
Opinion: Story for the Court; Catron concurring
Significance: By limiting the impact of local precedent, *Swift* preserved the reasonable expectations of parties to interstate commercial transactions and encouraged the development of national and international commercial law. At a later date, the Court would repudiate the resolution of conflicts through recourse to custom and general principles, opting instead, in *Erie Railroad Co. v. Tompkins* (1938), for a stricter application of state laws in *diversity cases.

PRIGG V. PENNSYLVANIA

Citation: 16 Pet. (41 U.S.) 539 (1842)
Argued: February 8-10, 1842
Decided: March 1, 1842
Court Below: Pennsylvania Supreme Court
Basis for Review: *Writ of error
Facts: Edward Prigg seized a runaway slave living in Pennsylvania and applied for certificates allowing removal under the federal Fugitive Slave Act and the state's personal liberty law. A state magistrate refused to issue the certificate, and Prigg took the slave to Maryland anyway. Prigg was indicted in Pennsylvania on charges of kidnapping, and the state legislature arranged for an expedited trial that would find him guilty and occasion an appeal to the Supreme Court.
Issue: In view of the Fugitive Slave Act of 1793, do states have the power to legislate with regard to runaway slaves?
Outcome: The Pennsylvania law concerning fugitive slaves was struck down, the Court declaring that federal *jurisdiction over returns of runaways was exclusive. State officials, however, could not be forced to comply with the federal law requiring restoration of runaways.
Vote: 8-1
Participating: Taney, Story, Thompson, McLean, Baldwin, Wayne, Catron, McKinley, Daniel
Opinions: Story for the Court; Taney, Thompson, Baldwin, Wayne, and Daniel concurring; McLean dissenting
Significance: In his concurring opinion, Chief Justice Taney mischaracterized Story's opinion, objecting that Story released state judges from enforcing the federal law. Later, some northern states took up Taney's view and used *Prigg* as justification for refusing to hear fugitive slave cases or prohibiting the use of state facilities for return of runaways.

DOBBINS V. ERIE COUNTY

Citation: 16 Pet. (41 U.S.) 435 (1842)
Argued: February 14, 1842
Decided: March 4, 1842
Court Below: Pennsylvania Supreme Court
Basis for Review: *Writ of error

Facts: Pennsylvania taxed the income of the captain of a United States revenue cutter stationed in that state. When the captain challenged the validity of the tax, it was upheld in the state supreme court.

Issue: Can a state tax the federal government's constitutionally sanctioned means of executing its constitutionally granted powers?

Outcome: The lower court's ruling was unanimously overruled, owing to the doctrine of *intergovernmental immunities, whereby states are prohibited from taxing the income of federal officials.

Vote: 9-0

Participating: Taney, Story, Thompson, McLean, Baldwin, Wayne, Catron, McKinley, Daniel

Opinion: Wayne for the Court

Significance: Starting with John Marshall's opinion in *McCulloch v. Maryland* (1819), the Supreme Court began to interpret broadly the doctrine of intergovernmental immunity. *Dobbins*, together with *Collector v. Day* (1871), which held that the federal government cannot tax the income of state officials, stretched the doctrine of reciprocal immunity to its limits, and both were overruled by the Supreme Court's decision in *Graves v. New York *ex rel. O'Keefe* (1939).

LOUISVILLE RAILROAD CO. V. LETSON

Citation: 2 How. (43 U.S.) 497 (1844)

Argued: February 20, 1843

Decided: March 7, 1844

Court Below: United States Circuit Court for the District of South Carolina

Basis for Review: *Writ of error

Facts: Letson, a New York citizen, sued the railroad, chartered by South Carolina, in federal circuit court under *diversity jurisdiction.

Issue: For purposes of diversity jurisdiction, how is a corporation's citizenship determined?

Outcome: The lower court's decision upholding *jurisdiction was itself upheld, as a corporation is deemed for diversity purposes to be a citizen of the state in which it is chartered.

Vote: 5-0

Participating: Story, McLean, Baldwin, Wayne, Catron (Taney, McKinley, and Daniel not participating)

Opinion: Wayne for the Court

Significance: Overturning its earlier decision in *Bank of the United States v. Deveaux* (1809), the Supreme Court now declared that for diversity purposes a corporation is no longer a citizen of those states in which its shareholders reside. By making a corporation a citizen of a single state, the Court enabled more corporations to avail themselves of the federal courts. In 1958 Congress would modify the holding of *Letson* by providing that in diversity cases a corporation should be deemed a citizen not only of the state which chartered it, but also of the state which is its principle place of business.

JONES V. VAN ZANDT

Citation: 5 How. (46 U.S.) 215 (1847)

Argued: Not argued; decided on the basis of papers submitted February 1, 1847

Decided: March 5, 1847

Court Below: United States Circuit Court for the District of Ohio

Basis for Review: *Certificate of division of opinion

Facts: Van Zandt, a conductor of the Underground Railroad, was charged with civil liability for harboring a slave. After the jury instructions were delivered, Salmon P. Chase, acting as counsel for the defendant abolitionist, moved for a new trial. Although it was granted, no new trial was held, and the circuit court judges — despite having no real difference of opinion — certified the points made on behalf of the new trial as a division of opinion.

Issue: Is the Fugitive Slave Act of 1793 unconstitutional because it is at odds with the Bill of Rights and the principle of *due process?

Outcome: The Court voted unanimously to hold Van Zandt liable and to uphold the Fugitive Slave Act as the law of the land, adding that slavery was not a moral issue but a *political question for the state to resolve.

Vote: 9-0

Participating: Taney, McLean, Wayne, Catron, McKinley, Daniel, Nelson, Woodbury, Grier

Opinion: Woodbury for the Court

Significance: As in *Prigg v. Pennsylvania* (1842), the Taney Court upheld the Fugitive Slave Act, adding to an unbroken succession of such decisions, which had the effect of supporting the institution of slavery and exacerbating the tensions that resulted in the Civil War.

LICENSE CASES (THURLOW V. MASSACHUSETTS; FLETCHER V. RHODE ISLAND; PEIRCE V. NEW HAMPSHIRE)

Citation: 5 How. (46 U.S.) 504 (1847)
Argued: January 29-31, 1846 (*Thurlow*); *Thurlow* reargued, together with original arguments in the other two cases, January 12, 14-15, 20-21, 1847
Decided: March 6, 1847
Court Below: Massachusetts Supreme Court (*Thurlow*); Rhode Island Supreme Court (*Fletcher*); Superior Court of Judicature for the First Judicial District of New Hampshire (*Peirce*)
Bases for Review: *Writs of error
Facts: All three cases — separate in the lower courts, but heard together in the Supreme Court — concerned the legality of state statutes requiring the licensing of intoxicating beverages imported into these states. Lower courts had upheld the statutes in each case.
Issue: Do the state laws violate federal control of interstate commerce, or do they represent legitimate exercises of state *police power?
Outcome: The Taney Court unanimously upheld the statutes and the lower courts' rulings; however, six separate opinions were filed by the nine justices taking part in the decision, indicating dissension regarding state powers with respect to the slavery issue, an issue raised in the *Fletcher* case.
Vote: 9-0
Participating: Taney, McLean, Wayne, Catron, McKinley, Daniel, Nelson, Woodbury, Grier
Opinions: Taney, McLean, Catron, Daniel, Woodbury, and Grier delivered separate opinions; Taney, Daniel, and Grier addressed all three cases in one opinion each, while McLean wrote three separate opinions and Catron wrote two, one addressing *Pierce* and one *Thurlow*.
Significance: The compromise reached in the *License Cases* helped to shape the Taney Court's doctrine of *selective exclusiveness, which influenced decisions regarding application of the *commerce power until the New Deal era of the

1930s, when the balance of this power tipped decidedly in favor of the federal government.

WEST RIVER BRIDGE CO. V. DIX

Citation: 6 How. (47 U.S.) 507 (1848)
Argued: January 5-7, 1848
Decided: January 31, 1848
Court Below: Vermont Supreme Court
Basis for Review: *Writ of error
Facts: Vermont granted a corporation the exclusive right to maintain a toll bridge for one hundred years, but the state subsequently decided to create a free public highway that crossed the bridge. The bridge company was granted compensation for the state's appropriation of its franchise.
Issue: Does the state's action constitute an impairment of contract in violation of the *Contracts Clause?
Outcome: The state's exercise of *eminent domain was upheld as superior to the corporation's private property rights, embodied in its contract.
Vote: 7-1
Participating: Taney, McLean, Wayne, Catron, Daniel, Nelson, Woodbury, Grier (McKinley not participating)
Opinions: Daniel for the Court; McLean and Woodbury concurring; Wayne dissenting (without written opinion)
Significance: This decision established the principle that a state may legitimately exercise its power of eminent domain to promote public welfare, even when such an exercise interferes with an earlier grant or franchise. The use of eminent domain was thus liberalized.

LUTHER V. BORDEN

Citation: 7 How. (48 U.S.) 1 (1849)
Argued: January 24-28, 1848
Decided: January 3, 1949
Court Below: United States Circuit Court for the District of Rhode Island
Basis for Review: *Writ of error
Facts: Article IV, section 4 of the Constitution ensures that the federal government guarantees each state a "Republican Form of Government." The Dorr Rebellion brought about by urban Rhode Islanders politically disenfranchised by an anti-

quated state constitution, tested the meaning of the *Guarantee Clause. In 1842, Rhode Island split into two governments dominated by competing political groups. In the resulting chaos, the sitting state government imposed martial law, during which the home of Martin Luther, a supporter of reform Governor Thomas Wilson Dorr, was entered and searched. Luther sued the militiaman who searched his premises, (Luther Borden) as did Luther's wife, Rachel, in a separate case, claiming that the state's undemocratic constitution provoked the rebellion, which was justified as an exercise of political *sovereignty. Therefore, he claimed, Bordon's search was illegitimate. The lower court found for the defendant.

Issues: Does political frustration with state government justify revolution? What level of popular participation in state government is ensured by the Constitution? Is the *Guarantee Clause enforceable through the federal courts?

Outcome: The Court affirmed the lower court's ruling but refused to resolve what was essentially a political dispute, stating that such conflicts must be resolved by the legislative and executive branches of government.

Vote: 8-1

Participating: Taney, McLean, Wayne, Catron, McKinley, Daniel, Nelson, Woodbury, Grier

Opinions: Taney for the Court; Woodbury dissenting

Significance: *Luther* articulated the *political question doctrine, and in doing so, indicated that the *Guarantee Clause was only enforceable by legislative and executive means. Still, the Taney Court side-stepped the issue of what level of republicanism is ensured by the Constitution.

PASSENGER CASES (*SMITH V. TURNER;
NORRIS V. BOSTON*)

Citation: 7 How. (48 U.S.) 283 (1849)

Argued: December term, 1845 (*Smith*); December term, 1846 (*Norris*); both reargued December term, 1847 and December 19-22, 1848

Decided: February 7, 1949

Courts Below: New York Court for the Trial of Impeachments and Corrections of Errors (*Smith*); Massachusetts Supreme Court (*Norris*)

Bases for Review: *Writs of error

Facts: New York and Massachusetts both taxed passengers coming into their ports, with the proceeds intended for the welfare of indigent passengers.

Issue: Are the states' tax statutes impermissible infringements of the federal *commerce power?

Outcome: Both tax laws were struck down.

Vote: 5-4

Participating: Taney, McLean, Wayne, Catron, McKinley, Daniel, Nelson, Woodbury, Grier

Opinions: No opinion of the Court; McLean, Wayne, Catron, Grier, and McKinley constituted the majority; Taney, joined by Nelson, dissenting, Daniel and Woodbury dissenting

Significance: The decision in the *Passenger Cases* would seem to contradict the Taney Court's earlier decision in *New York v. Miln* (1837), but the plethora of opinions filed in this case is an indication of the factionalism that had developed with regard to states' control of slavery. This factionalism would continue on the Court until *Cooley v. Board of Wardens* (1852) provided partial resolution.

COOLEY V. BOARD OF WARDENS

Citation: 12 How. (53 U.S.) 299 (1852)

Argued: February 9-11, 1852

Decided: March 2, 1852

Court Below: Pennsylvania Supreme Court

Basis for Review: *Writ of error

Facts: A Pennsylvania statute required any vessel entering or leaving the port of Philadelphia to pay half the customary pilotage fee if the ship did not employ a local pilot. The lower court upheld the statute.

Issue: Does the statute affect interstate and international commerce so as to constitute an infringement of Congress's power under the *Commerce Clause?

Outcome: The Court upheld the statute because it regulated a sphere of commerce that was merely local in scope.

Vote: 6-2

Participating: Taney, McLean, Wayne, Catron, Daniel, Nelson, Grier, Curtis (McKinley not participating)

Opinions: Curtis for the Court; McLean dissenting, Wayne dissenting (without written opinion); Daniel concurring

Significance: Owing to the invariable connection between such cases as *Cooley* and the states' control of slavery, the Taney Court previously had been unable to issue definitive decisions in Commerce Clause cases that had come before it. In *Cooley*, Justice Curtis fashioned a doctrine called *selective exclusiveness that divided regulation of commerce according to the subject matter of the regulation rather than the nature of the commerce power. Certain subjects were of necessity national in scope and therefore regulated by Congress; other subjects, like that of the pilotage act, were primarily local in nature and could be regulated by the states. The selective exclusiveness doctrine has proven to be enduring, and *Cooley*, together with *Gibbons v. Ogden* (1824), ranks at the forefront of Commerce Clause cases.

PENNSYLVANIA V. WHEELING AND BELMONT BRIDGE CO.

Citation: 13 How. (54 U.S.) 518 (1852)
Argued: December 1, 1851
Decided: February 6, 1852
Court Below: None
Basis for Review: *Original Supreme Court jurisdiction
Facts: The Virginia legislature chartered the Wheeling and Belmont Bridge Company to build a bridge across the Ohio River to provide access to the West. The state of Pennsylvania invoked the Court's original jurisdiction to *enjoin completion of the bridge because its low height obstructed river traffic and constituted a impediment to interstate commerce.
Issues: Does Pennsylvania have *standing to sue? Does the bridge constitute an impediment to interstate commerce?
Outcome: The Court found that Pennsylvania had cause to sue owing to economic losses it had suffered because of curtailment of river traffic. The Court then ordered that the bridge either be removed or raised to accommodate higher vessels.
Vote: 7-2

Participating: Taney, McLean, Wayne, Catron, McKinley, Daniel, Nelson, Grier, Curtis
Opinions: McLean for the Court; Taney and Daniel dissenting
Significance: Six months after the Court's ruling, Congress passed legislation declaring the bridge's original height legal, marking the first time that Congress reversed a Supreme Court decision. In a suit of the same name brought before the Court in 1856, it was decided, based on a federal statute, that the bridge did not obstruct interstate commerce. Subsequently, the height of the Wheeling Bridge set the standard for river bridge clearances for the remainder of the century.

GENESEE CHIEF V. FITZHUGH

Citation: 12 How. (53 U.S.) 443 (1852)
Argued: January 2, 5-6, 1852
Decided: February 20, 1852
Court Below: United States Circuit Court for the Northern District of New York
Basis for Review: Appeal
Facts: In an 1825 *admiralty decision, *The Thomas Jefferson*, the Supreme Court adopted the English rule regarding navigable waterways, which restricted *jurisdiction to tidal waters. In 1845, however, Congress passed legislation extending federal court jurisdiction to include cases arising on the Great Lakes.
Issue: Is the 1845 act within the federal admiralty power as defined by the Constitution?
Outcome: The 1845 act was sustained because, the Court reasoned, the English rule was inappropriate to America's vast network of navigable rivers and lakes.
Vote: 8-1
Participating: Taney, McLean, Wayne, Catron, McKinley, Daniel, Nelson, Grier, Curtis
Opinions: Taney for the Court; Daniel dissenting
Significance: By rejecting the English rule, the Court enabled Congress to regulate uniformly the traffic, which now included steamboats, throughout the nation's waterways. *Genesee Chief* demonstrates the Court's willingness to interpret the Constitution broadly to accommodate changes in technology so as to encourage economic growth.

MURRAY'S LESSEE V. HOBOKEN LAND & IMPROVEMENT CO.

Citation: 18 How. (59 U.S.) 272 (1856)
Argued: January 30-31 & February 4, 1856
Decided: February 19, 1856
Court Below: United States Circuit Court for the District of New Jersey
Basis for Review: *Certificate of division of opinion
Facts: An embezzler used stolen customs receipts to purchase land, and the Treasury Department employed an administrative procedure to void the sale and recover the stolen funds. The embezzler challenged the proceeding as a violation of *due process and the doctrine of *separation of powers.
Issue: Can the federal government — specifically, the executive branch — resort to such non-judicial procedures?
Outcome: The procedure was upheld under the Due Process Clause of the Fifth Amendment.
Vote: 9-0
Participating: Taney, McLean, Wayne, Catron, Daniel, Nelson, Grier, Curtis, Campbell
Opinion: Curtis for the Court
Significance: *Murray's Lessee* provided the occasion for the Court's first interpretation of the Due Process Clause of the Fifth Amendment. Due process, Justice Curtis proclaimed, "is a restraint on the legislative as well as on the executive and the judicial powers of the government, and cannot be construed as to leave Congress free to make any process 'due process of law.'" Curtis's opinion is widely held to contain a suggestion of what would later in the century evolve into *substantive due process.

DODGE V. WOOLSEY

Citation: 18 How. (59 U.S.) 331 (1856)
Argued: February 6, 1856
Decided: April 8, 1856
Court Below: United States Circuit Court for the District of Ohio
Basis for Review: Appeal
Facts: In 1851 Ohio adopted a new constitution which effectively repealed the tax immunity that was granted banks in an 1845 statute. John W. Woolsey, a Connecticut resident and a shareholder in an Ohio bank, brought suit to prevent George C. Dodge, an Ohio county treasurer, from collecting tax on the bank. The lower federal court took *jurisdiction of the case and *enjoined collection.
Issue: Does the bank tax unconstitutionally impair the contractual obligation between the state and the bank contained in the 1845 act?
Outcome: The Court upheld the injunction.
Vote: 6-3
Participating: Taney, McLean, Wayne, Catron, Daniel, Nelson, Grier, Curtis, Campbell
Opinions: Wayne for the Court; Catron, Daniel, and Campbell dissenting (all without written opinions)
Significance: *Dodge* marks the first time the Court nullified a section of a state constitution. Later decisions would restrict the holding in *Dodge* by limiting it to instances where such tax exemptions were specifically laid out in the corporate charter.

SCOTT V. SANDFORD

Citation: 19 How. (60 U.S.) 393 (1857)
Argued: February 11-14, 1856; reargued December 15-18, 1856
Decided: March 6-7, 1857
Court Below: United States Circuit Court for the District of Missouri
Basis of Review: *Writ of error
Facts: Dred Scott was a slave born in Virginia who moved with his master to St. Louis, where he was sold to a Dr. Emerson. Emerson's military career took them to the free soil of both Illinois and Wisconsin. Emerson married Eliza Sanford, who remained in St. Louis along with the family slaves while her husband served with the army in Florida. Emerson died shortly after returning home in 1843. In 1846 Scott sued for his freedom in a Missouri court, claiming that his sojourn on free soil qualified him to be freed under the state legal principle of "once free, always free."

Scott's original suit resulted in a *mistrial, but when the case was retried in 1850, he was awarded his freedom. During the years between the two state trials, Scott's wages were held in escrow, pending a decision as to his freedom. Meanwhile, Mrs. Emerson remarried, leaving her affairs in St. Louis under control of her brother, John Sanford (whose name was misspelled in the official reports). With Scott awarded his freedom, Sanford stood to lose control of the escrow funds, and he appealed to the Missouri Supreme Court to reverse the decision favoring Scott. The state supreme court overruled the lower court decision, as well as its own legal *precedents. Scott could have appealed the state court decision to the United States Supreme Court, but he ran the risk that the Court would merely endorse the Missouri decision without reconsidering the merits of the case. Instead, Scott's lawyers began a new suit in federal court, naming Sanford, a New York resident, as the defendant for purposes of *diversity jurisdiction. It was Sanford's lawyers who raised the issues of the citizenship of African Americans and the constitutionality of the Missouri Compromise.

The Taney Court was initially prepared to avoid these controversies by simply affirming the decision of the Missouri Supreme Court. In conference, however, a bare majority of five justices, all from southern states, approved Justice Wayne's proposal that the Court resolve the issues Sanford raised. Although Chief Justice Taney wrote an opinion for the Court, each member of the Court drafted his own opinion. It took two days for five of the justices to deliver their opinions orally (four eventually submitted their opinions without reading them).

Issues: Is Scott a citizen of the United States entitled to *standing in a federal court? Is the Missouri Compromise constitutional?

Outcome: Scott's case was dismissed for lack of *jurisdiction. Taney's opinion contained the following findings: 1) African Americans could be state citizens, but not citizens of the United States possessing the right to sue in federal court; 2) Scott had never been free, because Congress lacked authority under the Constitution to abolish slavery in certain territories under the terms of the Missouri Compromise; 3) because slaves were property protected by the Constitution, the

Missouri Compromise was invalidated; 4) if a slave voluntarily returned to a slave state from free soil, his or her status depended upon the law of the former, and since Missouri had found Scott to be a slave, the United States Supreme Court was obliged to do the same.

Vote: 7-2

Participating: Taney, McLean, Wayne, Catron, Daniel, Nelson, Grier, Curtis, Campbell

Opinions: Taney for the Court; Wayne, Nelson, Daniel, Grier, Campbell, and Catron concurring; McLean and Curtis dissenting

Significance: Universally agreed to be the worst decision ever delivered by the Supreme Court, *Dred Scott* undermined not only the prestige of the Court, but the delicate balance between North and South that had thus far maintained the Union. It would take a Civil War and the passage of two Civil War amendments — the Thirteenth, which abolished slavery, and the Fourteenth, declaring all persons born in the United States citizens — to undo the damage wrought by this ill-considered and wretchedly executed decision.

ABLEMAN V. BOOTH;
UNITED STATES V. BOOTH

Citation: 21 How. (62 U.S.) 506 (1859)
Argued: January 19, 1859
Decided: March 7, 1859
Courts Below: Wisconsin Supreme Court (*Ableman v. Booth*); United States Circuit Court for the District of Wisconsin (*United States v. Booth*)
Basis for Review: *Writs of error
Facts: In 1854 a slaveowner from Missouri traveled to Wisconsin to capture a slave who had escaped from him two years earlier. The slave was found and, owing to the Fugitive Slave Act of 1850, imprisoned on the basis of a warrant issued by a federal commissioner. Meanwhile, Sherman M. Booth, editor of an abolitionist newspaper, obtained a writ of *habeas corpus for the slave's release from a Wisconsin county court. Federal officials would not acknowledge the authority of the local court and refused to release their prisoner. However, a crowd broke into the jail and released

the prisoner, who escaped and permanently disappeared. Booth and the others involved in the jailbreak were indicted for violating federal law.

Booth was tried twice for his offenses, once in state court, which upheld his release from detention on the basis of the unconstitutionality of the federal Fugitive Slave Act, and once in federal court, which found Booth guilty. Both cases were appealed to the United States Supreme Court and subsequently tried together.

Issue: Do state courts have the power to issue writs of habeas corpus for the release of prisoners detained by federal authorities?

Outcome: A unanimous Taney Court upheld the finding of the lower federal court denying Booth a writ of habeas corpus. The Wisconsin court, which refused to return the United States Supreme Court's writ of error in the appeal of Booth's state court trial, was denounced.

Vote: 9-0

Participating: Taney, McLean, Wayne, Catron, Daniel, Nelson, Grier, Campbell, Clifford

Opinion: Taney for the Court

Significance: The two *Booth* cases, with their emphasis on *jurisdictional conflict, demonstrate the depth of division within the country regarding slavery and the low level of respect accorded the Taney Court in the wake of the *Dred Scott* decision. When Booth was retried in 1860, the Wisconsin Supreme Court split once again on the issue of whether or not Booth was entitled to a writ of habeas corpus, despite the Taney Court's unanimous ruling a year earlier. And although the *Booth* cases established that states lack the authority to issue writs of habeas corpus for federal prisoners, the issue was relitigated after the Civil War.

KENTUCKY V. DENNISON

Citation: 24 How. (65 U.S.) 66 (1861)

Argued: February 20, 1861

Decided: March 14, 1861

Court Below: None

Basis for Review: *Original Supreme Court jurisdiction

Facts: In 1859 a free African American living in Ohio helped a Kentucky slave escape to Ohio.

Kentucky indicted the Ohioan for theft, and the Kentucky governor asked the Ohio governor, then Salmon P. Chase, to *extradite the freed man for trial in Kentucky. Chase refused, as did a subsequent Ohio governor, William Dennison, and Kentucky sued in the Supreme Court for a writ of *mandamus ordering Dennison to comply with the state's request.

Issue: Does the United States Supreme Court have the power to force states to comply with constitutionally imposed obligations?

Outcome: While recognizing a state's moral responsibility to honor extradition requests from other states, the Supreme Court refused to issue a writ of mandamus.

Vote: 8-0

Participating: Taney, McLean, Wayne, Catron, Nelson, Grier, Campbell, Clifford

Opinion: Taney for the Court

Significance: Chief Justice Taney was clearly proslavery and in favor of *states' rights, as were other members of his Court, yet the only way to enforce Kentucky's right was through the use of federal power, which with the onset of secession, the Court would not risk. This case remained valid as precedent until it was reversed in 1987 by *Puerto Rico v. Branstad.*

PRIZE CASES

Citation: 2 Black (67 U.S.) 635 (1863)

Argued: February 10-13, 16-20, 23-25, 1863

Decided: March 10, 1863

Courts Below: United States District Court for Massachusetts (re: *The Amy Warwick*); United States District Court for the Southern District of New York (re: *The Hiawatha* and *The Crenshaw*); and United States District Court for the Southern District of Florida (re: *The Brilliante*)

Bases for Review: Appeal

Facts: On April 19, 1861, after the Confederate attack on Fort Sumter, President Lincoln ordered a blockade of Confederate ports, resulting in the immediate capture as wartime prizes of numerous ships attempting to use these ports. However, Congress did not authorize an official declaration that a state of war existed until July 13, 1861, after the capture of the four ships that were the subjects of these combined cases.

Issue: Did the president have the authority to impose a wartime blockade without prior congressional approval?

Outcome: A bare majority of the Supreme Court affirmed the decisions of the lower courts that upheld seizure of the ships. As commander in chief, Lincoln was the proper party to proclaim the blockade.

Vote: 5-4

Participating: Taney, Wayne, Catron, Nelson, Grier, Clifford, Swayne, Miller, Davis

Opinions: Grier for the Court; Nelson, joined by Taney, Catron, and Clifford, dissenting

Significance: By approving Lincoln's methods of prosecuting the Civil War — as if it were a domestic insurrection with the character of an international war — the Court implicitly suggested that other unorthodox presidential acts, such as the Emancipation Proclamation and the suspension of *habeas corpus, constitutionally were permissible. Because a state of war already existed, Justice Grier wrote, the president had "to meet it in the shape it presented itself, without waiting for Congress to baptize it with a name..."

VOTING PATTERNS

When Roger Brooke Taney became chief justice, the only real holdover from the protracted Marshall era was Joseph Story. Smith Thompson, who joined the Court midway through Marshall's tenure, had opposed Marshall's Federalist expansion of centralized power and had more in common with the incoming Jacksonian Democrats than with his Democratic Republican brother, Story. To John McLean, Henry Baldwin, and James M. Wayne, all of whom Andrew Jackson had appointed toward the end of the Marshall Court, Jackson quickly added Philip P. Barbour and John Catron, as well as the august chief justice. Jackson had the opportunity to appoint six members to the nation's highest tribunal — more than any president since George Washington — and to shape it to suit his own ends. With the swearing in of John Catron just months after Jackson left office, a majority of the Court consisted of Southern Democrats.

Jackson's appointees were followed by John McKinley and Peter V. Daniel, nominated by Jackson's protege, Martin Van Buren. Five more Democrats (Samuel Nelson, Levi Woodbury, Robert C. Grier, John A. Campbell, and Nathan Clifford), plus one Whig (Benjamin R. Curtis), would be added before Abraham Lincoln's election and the outbreak of the Civil War. By the late 1850s the Whigs had reorganized and became known as Republicans. Republican President Lincoln would, toward the end of Taney's leadership, appoint three Republicans (Noah H. Swayne, Samuel F. Miller, and David Davis) as well as one Democrat (the maverick Stephen J. Field) to help uphold legislation vital to the Union cause.

By the time of Lincoln's appointments, Taney and his Court were badly weakened, having undermined their authority with the 1857 *Dred Scott* decision, the product of a generations' old debate between *federalism and *states' rights and two decades of Democratic control of the Supreme Court. Prior to *Dred Scott*, however, Taney exercised an authority nearly equal to that of his predecessor, John Marshall, which added to the imposing institution Marshall had built. Taney's approach to *jurisprudence, emphasizing *judicial restraint, differed markedly from Marshall's, but it was one that appealed to a majority of his brethren through most of his tenure. When that emphasis shifted too far toward preservation of state, versus federal power, however, Jacksonian Democratic holdovers from the Marshall Court — McLean and Wayne, in addition to Jeffersonian Democrat Story — became, as they did in *Cooley v. Board of Wardens* (1852), neo-Federalist dissenters.

In was *Scott v. Sandford*, however, that most clearly showed the Taney Court's ideological fault lines. In its declaration that slaves are not citizens and its invalidation of the Missouri Compromise, the seven-member majority clearly revealed its proslavery stance, while McLean, together with Curtis, passionately dissented. (While McLean partially was responsible for forcing the Court to address the slavery issue directly, Curtis's resignation directly resulted from the fallout of his historic dissent.) It would take a civil war to redress

POLITICAL COMPOSITION
of the Taney Court

Justice & Total Term	Courts Served	Appointing President	Political Party
Roger B. Taney 1836-1864	Taney	Jackson	Democrat
Joseph Story 1812-1845	Marshall Taney	Madison	Democratic Republican
Smith Thompson 1824-1843	Marshall Taney	Monroe	Democratic Republican
John McLean 1830-1861	Marshall Taney	Jackson	Democrat
Henry Baldwin 1830-1844	Marshall Taney	Jackson	Democrat
James M. Wayne 1835-1867	Marshall Taney Chase	Jackson	Democrat
Philip P. Barbour 1836-1841	Taney	Jackson	Democrat
John Catron 1837-1865	Taney Chase	Jackson	Democrat
John McKinley 1838-1852	Taney	Van Buren	Democrat
Peter V. Daniel 1842-1860	Taney	Van Buren	Democrat
Samuel Nelson 1845-1872	Taney Chase	Tyler	Democrat
Levi Woodbury 1845-1851	Taney	Polk	Democrat

(continued on page 114)

the discord aggravated by this decision and to correct the political imbalance on the Court.

SPECIAL FEATURES OF THE TANEY COURT

REORGANIZATION

Owing to the growth of the nation and the not unrelated growth of the Court's *docket during Taney's tenure as chief justice, the Supreme Court underwent a number of structural changes dur-

ing the years 1836 through 1864. Nine states located in the Mississippi Valley were admitted to the Union after passage of the 1802 Judiciary Act. The increase in the size of the *circuits made *circuit riding more and more onerous; Justice Todd, for example, was required to travel 2,600 miles yearly to serve courts in Ohio, Kentucky, and Tennessee, as well as the Supreme Court in Washington, D.C.

The Judiciary Act of 1837 created three new circuits and added two seats to the Court. On the last day of his presidency, Andrew Jackson

POLITICAL COMPOSITION
of the Taney Court

Justice & Total Term	Courts Served	Appointing President	Political Party
Robert C. Grier 1846-1870	Taney Chase	Polk	Democrat
Benjamin R. Curtis 1851-1857	Taney	Fillmore	Whig
John A. Campbell 1853-1861	Taney	Pierce	Democrat
Nathan Clifford 1858-1881	Taney Chase Waite	Buchanan	Democrat
Noah H. Swayne 1862-1881	Taney Chase Waite	Lincoln	Republican
Samuel F. Miller 1862-1890	Taney Chase Waite Fuller	Lincoln	Republican
David Davis 1862-1877	Taney Chase Waite	Lincoln	Republican
Stephen J. Field 1863-1897	Taney Chase Waite Fuller	Lincoln	Democrat

thus was enabled to name two Supreme Court appointees. One of these men, William Smith of Alabama, declined, but John Catron of Tennessee accepted. Between Catron and Alabamian John McKinley, the nominee of Jackson's successor, Martin Van Buren, the continuance of a Supreme Court dominated by Southern Democrats was assured.

Then, in March 1863, largely in order to accommodate President Lincoln's desire for a Supreme Court majority that would support his war policies, Congress added a tenth seat. This increase was accomplished through the creation of a tenth Pacific Coast circuit, and was accompanied by a reorganization of the other circuits which resulted in the reduction of the southern circuits from five to three.

In 1844 Congress made another attempt to offset the Court's increasing work load by lengthening its term, moving opening day backward from the second Monday in January to the first Monday in December. In 1839 the Court had attempted to cut down on its record keeping by requiring that all *motions be filed in writing with the clerk of the Court. In 1849 the length of *oral argument was limited for the first time, with each side allotted only two hours to present its case.

In December 1860 the Taney Court moved from the basement of the Capitol to new quarters, upstairs in the old Senate chamber, which had been refurbished specifically for the Supreme Court. The Court would occupy this chamber for the next 75 years until it moved into its own building, where it continues to meet.

Court-appointed reporter Richard Peters was succeeded in 1843 by former Congressman Benjamin Chew Howard. When Howard resigned in 1861 to run unsuccessfully for governor of Maryland, he was followed by Jeremiah S. Black, an unsuccessful nominee for the Daniel seat on the Court. Black served for only two years before resigning to resume private legal practice. Nominative Supreme Court reports ended with John William Wallace, who took over in 1863 and served until 1875.

TOWARD A DEFINITION OF DUE PROCESS

The lopsided political composition that prevailed for most of the tenure of Chief Justice Taney (a majority of justices from below the Mason-Dixon line dominated the Court from the time of Justice McKinley's appointment in 1837 until 1862) and the resulting disaster of the *Dred Scott* (1857) decision can be said to have hastened the Civil War. Justice Curtis's opinion in *Murray's Lessee v. Hoboken Land & Development Co.* (1856) addressed the concept of *due process in terms that foreshadowed the later development of the doctrine of *substantive due process, although Taney ignored the earlier decision the subsequent year in his *dicta about due process in *Dred Scott*. The issue confronting the Court in *Murray's Lessee* (1856) concerned the more traditional notion of *procedural due process, but Curtis's language regarding restrictions on Congress's power to declare any process due process presaged later Courts' uses of substantive due process to uphold equality and individual liberty in the face of government intrusion.

CONSTITUTIONAL LAW AND PRESIDENTIAL WAR POWERS

For the most part, civil liberties suffered greatly during the years of the Taney Court. Not only was the Court dominated by proslavery sentiment for most of the period, in its waning years it was generally unable to address President Lincoln's unprecedented — and unilateral — exercise of emergency executive powers to combat the secessionists. Lincoln suspended the writ of *habeas corpus, ordering arrests without warrants and detentions without trials. Sitting as a circuit judge in Baltimore, Taney did declare such actions unconstitutional in *Ex parte Merryman* (1861), finding that only Congress has the right to suspend habeas corpus. After the Civil War ended, the Supreme Court confirmed this view in *Ex parte Milligan* (1866). Meanwhile, however, Lincoln continued to ignore Taney's opinion, just as the military refused to obey the writ Taney issued.

In the *Prize Cases* (1863), concerning Lincoln's emergency measures, a bare 5 to 4 majority — consisting of Lincoln's first three nominees, plus Justices Wayne and Grier — supported the president's imposition of a blockade on southern ports. The proclamation was itself a belligerent act which, to the Supreme Court, legally constituted the legal commencement of the Civil War. In deciding that the president's actions constituted a recognition of a existing situation, rather than an attempt to circumvent Congress's mandate to issue a formal declaration of war, the Court afforded Lincoln a constitutional sanction for prosecuting this extraordinary war with extraordinary measures — including the Emancipation Proclamation which, like his other wartime maneuvers, he had come to regard as a military necessity.

The Chase Court 1864-1873

BACKGROUND

THE ELECTION OF 1864, THE END OF THE CIVIL WAR, AND THE ASSASSINATION OF PRESIDENT LINCOLN

Leading up to the election of 1864, Lincoln's Republican Party was divided. The radicals believed that President Lincoln was moving too slowly to implement emancipation and that his post-war plan for the South, called Reconstruction, was too lenient. In an effort to counteract these criticisms, Lincoln's supporters promoted Andrew Johnson of Tennessee as Lincoln's running mate. Although a Democrat, Johnson was virulent and outspoken in his hatred of the southern aristocracy, which he believed bore responsibility for the Civil War.

A turn of the war in favor of the North helped to assure Lincoln's reelection. General William Tecumseh Sherman's capture and destruction of Atlanta and ensuing march to the sea, together with the success of new offensives by General Ulysses S. Grant in Virginia, rapidly brought the war to an end. On April 9, 1865, Confederate Commander Robert E. Lee surrendered to Grant at Appomattox Courthouse, Virginia. Six days later, on April 15, Lincoln lay dead, shot on April 14 while watching a performance of *Our American Cousin* at Ford's Theatre in Washington, D.C. His assassin was actor John Wilkes Booth, a sympathizer with the lost southern cause.

An asterisk (*) before a word or phrase indicates that a definition will be found in the glossary at the end of this volume.

PRESIDENT JOHNSON AND RECONSTRUCTION

As early as December 8, 1863, Lincoln had announced his program for Reconstruction of the South once the war ended. Lincoln's plan consisted of four basic parts: 1) all southerners, with the exception of Confederate government officials and high-ranking military officers, would be offered amnesty; 2) upon swearing loyalty to the United States, southerners would regain full citizenship and control of their property; 3) when, in any given southern state, the percentage of population willing to take such a loyalty oath equaled ten percent of the votes cast in the 1860 election, that state could elect its own government; and 4) as soon as such new civil regimes abolished slavery, they would receive federal recognition.

After Vice President Johnson took the oath of office in the wake of Lincoln's assassination, it quickly became apparent that he planned to follow his predecessor's plan for southern Reconstruction. Johnson accepted Reconstruction as complete in the four states — Virginia, Arkansas, Tennessee, and Louisiana — that had fulfilled Lincoln's requirements by the time of his death. Johnson then moved to carry out the plan in the seven other formerly Confederate states.

Johnson announced his reconstruction plan in May 1865, after Congress had adjourned. He made it clear that he regarded restoration of the Union as an executive function. When Congress reconvened that December, moderate Republicans allied themselves with the Radicals, united by their belief that Congress, not the president, should oversee reorganization of the South. Refusing to seat the senators and representatives elected in the four states that had followed the Lincoln-Johnson plan, Congress instead appointed a Joint Committee on Reconstruction to investigate conditions in the South and drafted legislation for a civil rights act and a freedman's bureau, which would oversee aid to former slaves.

Johnson reacted swiftly with a veto of the Civil Rights Act and a condemnation of the Freedman's Bureau as an intrusion on *states' rights. Congress responded with equal furor, overriding the presidential veto (the first time this had happened to a major piece of legislation), and drafting an amendment to the Constitution that would make civil rights a part of the nation's fundamental law. Both houses of Congress adopted the Fourteenth Amendment in June 1866. Johnson, not surprisingly, campaigned against its ratification and succeeded in convincing southern states to reject it.

Johnson's — and the South's — uncompromising ways became the central issue in the 1866 off-year elections. Attempting to prevent his opponents from gaining control of Congress, Johnson managed instead to diminish his presidency further by embarking on a "Swing Around the Circle," an unprecedented and ill-advised campaign tour during which his stubborn and eccentric temperament was on public display. The Republicans won the election, gaining a two-thirds majority in both houses.

IMPEACHMENT AND RADICAL RECONSTRUCTION

Finally in control of Congress, Johnson's opponents moved swiftly to undermine him and to take control of southern Reconstruction. Even before the new Congress met, its lame-duck predecessor enacted a variety of legislative measures designed to counter the president, the most significant of which proved to be the Tenure of Office Act, prohibiting the president from dismissing any member of his cabinet without prior consent of the Senate. In August of 1867, with the new Congress in recess, Johnson dismissed Secretary of War Edwin M. Stanton, persuading General Grant to take his place. When Congress reconvened, it refused to approve Stanton's removal. Grant resigned, and Stanton barricaded himself in the War Department, resisting all attempts to remove him.

Because Stanton was a Lincoln appointee, his dismissal did not technically violate the Tenure of Office Act. Nonetheless, Johnson's attempt to remove him provoked the House of Representatives to vote that the president be *impeached for "high crimes and misdemeanors

Salmon Portland Chase

in office." Johnson was forced to reinstate Stanton when the Senate refused to approve the latter's removal. On March 30, 1868, the impeachment trial opened in the Senate, with Chief Justice Salmon P. Chase presiding. Although the final vote, 35 in favor of conviction and 19 against, fell one vote short of the two-thirds majority required to remove Johnson from office, the trial irrevocably undermined his authority.

With Johnson effectively out of the way, Radical Reconstruction took over in the South. The Radicals saw the southern states as conquered provinces and instituted military rule in the ten former Confederate states they regarded as unreconstructed (Tennessee, which had already ratified the Fourteenth Amendment, was an exception). In every state but Virginia, Republicans took control. These Republican regimes proved to be short-lived, however. As southern states were readmitted to the Union, Radical reforms gave way to southern "Redeemers," whose mission it was to reestablish white control under the auspices of the Democratic Party.

THE ELECTION OF 1868

Overseeing Radical Reconstruction was to be the principal occupation of the Republicans' suc-

cessful 1868 presidential candidate, Ulysses S. Grant. Grant, formerly a Democrat, was a reluctant politician, and his chosen subordinates managed to mar his eight-year administration with a series of scandals. As Republican dominion waned in the South, Grant's tenure in office also became associated with the appearance of opportunistic northern "carpetbaggers" and southern "scalawags" and with the rise of the Ku Klux Klan. The depression of 1873, hastened by the drain on social services occasioned by emancipation, put an end to northern idealism.

THE CIVIL WAR AMENDMENTS

The three constitutional amendments — the Thirteenth, Fourteenth, and Fifteenth — passed after the Civil War, constituted the first substantive alterations of the Constitution in 60 years. The Thirteenth Amendment, abolishing slavery in the United States, ultimately became law in 1865 after Republican electoral victories that year assured passage in both houses of Congress. (Its passage was also helped by the requirement that formerly Confederate states had to ratify the Thirteenth Amendment, and later the Fourteenth Amendment, as conditions for readmission to the Union.)

Most civil rights laws for the next century focused on the Fourteenth Amendment, ratified in 1866. Reversing the *Dred Scott* (1857) decision, the Fourteenth Amendment makes all persons born in the United States citizens of both the nation and of the states in which they reside. The Fourteenth Amendment goes on to prohibit states from abridging *privileges or immunities of citizens and from depriving citizens of *due process of law or *equal protection under the law. While the initial thrust of the Republican-sponsored Fourteenth Amendment may have been to codify racial equality, in the period of rapid industrialization that followed Reconstruction, the Fourteenth Amendment — particularly its Due Process Clause — was primarily applied to protect and promote private enterprise by restricting the right of the state to regulate business activity.

The Fifteenth Amendment, ratified in 1870, was intended to enfranchise most of the nation's

JUDICIAL BIOGRAPHY

Salmon Portland Chase

PERSONAL DATA

Born: January 13, 1808, in Cornish, New Hampshire

Parents: Ithamar Chase, Janette Ralston Chase

Higher Education: Dartmouth College (undergraduate degree, 1826)

Bar Admission: Ohio, 1830

Political Party: Republican

Marriages: March 4, 1834, to Katharine Jane Garniss, who bore Chase one daughter who did not survive into adulthood, and who herself died on December 1, 1835; September 26, 1839, to Eliza Ann Smith, who died September 29, 1845; November 6, 1846, to Sara Belle Dunlop Ludlow, who bore Chase five daughters, two of whom survived beyond infancy, and who herself died January 13, 1852

Died: May 7, 1873, in New York, New York

Buried: Spring Grove Cemetery, Cincinnati, Ohio

PROFESSIONAL CAREER

Occupations: Lawyer, 1830-1850s; Politician, 1849-1864; Judge, 1864-1873

Official Positions: Member, United States Senate, 1849-1855, 1861; Governor of Ohio, 1856-1860; United States Secretary of the Treasury, 1861-1864; Chief Justice, United States Supreme Court, 1864-1873

SUPREME COURT SERVICE

Nominated: December 6, 1864

Nominated By: Abraham Lincoln

Confirmed: December 6, 1864

Confirmation Vote: Voice vote

Oath Taken: December 15, 1864

Replaced: Chief Justice Roger Brooke Taney

Significant Opinions: *Mississippi v. Johnson* (1867); **Ex parte McCardle* (1869); *Texas v. White* (1869); *Veazie Bank v. Fenno* (1869); *Hepburn v. Griswold* (1870)

Left Court: Died May 7, 1873

Length of Service: 8 years, 4 months, 23 days

Replacement: Chief Justice Morrison R. Waite

---

population. Its genesis lay in the presidential election of 1868, which Ulysses S. Grant won with 73 percent of the electoral vote, but only 52 percent of the popular vote. In order to forestall a Democratic resurgence, abetted by intimidation of southern African American voters predisposed to cast their ballots for the party of Lincoln, the Republicans yoked their egalitarian idealism to practical politics, granting African Americans the right to vote.

CHASE'S EARLY LIFE

Orphaned at an early age, Salmon P. Chase was raised by an uncle, Philander Chase, an Episcopal bishop in Ohio, whose influence filled young Chase with a strong religious sense that would direct much of his future. Chase was dedicated to his studies, and his family saw to it that he went to Dartmouth College. After completing his undergraduate education, Chase appealed for help to another famous uncle, Dudley Chase, a United States senator from Vermont, who arranged for his nephew to study law under United States Attorney General William Wirt.

After completing his legal training, Chase returned to Ohio, where he set up a law practice in Cincinnati. Chase devoted a great deal of his attention during the early part of his career to legal writing, compiling *The Statutes of Ohio* (1835). He quickly developed an interest in the most significant political issue of the day, slavery — an interest spurred both by Chase's religious fervor and by his political ambition. He devoted a significant amount of his practice to defending fugitive slaves and those assisting them, appearing before the Supreme Court for the defendant in *Jones v. Van Zandt* (1847) and eventually acquiring a reputation as the "attorney general for runaway slaves."

CHASE'S PUBLIC LIFE

Revealing the political opportunism that was later to become one of his hallmarks, Chase was first a Whig and then a leader of the Liberal Party which, aligned with the Free-Soil Party, dominated Ohio politics in the late 1840s. When the Free-Soilers agreed to let the Democrats organize the Ohio legislature, they did so with the understanding that the Democrats would in return elect a Free-Soiler to the United States Senate (at the time, U.S. senators were elected by state legislatures). Salmon Chase was thus elected to his first term as a senator from Ohio. In 1855 he returned to state politics, serving two terms as governor of Ohio. In 1860 he was reelected to the United States Senate.

In the Senate, Chase devoted himself to the antislavery movement. When the controversy over passage of the Kansas-Nebraska Bill erupted in 1854, giving birth to the Republican Party, Chase immediately became one of the movement's leaders. During the 1860 Republican Convention, Chase and his fellow abolitionist, William Seward, were considered to be the front-runners for the party's presidential nomination. On the third ballot, however, the balance swung over to Abraham Lincoln. After his election, Lincoln nominated Chase as his treasury secretary; after serving only two days of his second term in the Senate, Chase accepted.

Chase's primary responsibility as a member of Lincoln's Civil War cabinet lay in funding the Union's military effort, which he did by establishing a national banking system and gaining acceptance for the nation's first effective paper currency not backed by coin (gold or silver). Chase did far more, however, often filling in for Lincoln's incompetent secretary of war, Simon Cameron. Then, in 1864, he used his influence to become Lincoln's political rival, lobbying behind the scenes for the Republican presidential nomination. Chase, who had used the threat of resignation as a means of resolving his frequent disagreements with the president, may not have been surprised when this time Lincoln accepted his offer.

CHASE AS CHIEF JUSTICE

Lincoln was not a man to hold a grudge, however. When Chase actively campaigned to succeed Chief Justice Roger Brooke Taney after Taney died in 1864, the president appointed Chase. Lincoln was frank, however, about the reasons for Chase's appointment: he needed support in the Supreme Court for his emancipation and legal tender programs. Although Chase would stoutly support the emancipation program, he never entirely was comfortable with the financial system he himself had put in place, and when the issue of the legality of the Legal Tender Act, which permitted paper money to be used for public or private debts, came before the Court in 1870, Chase would decide against it.

Shortly after Chase's appointment, Lincoln was assassinated, and Chase, like Lincoln's successor, Andrew Johnson, fell victim to a resurgent Congress which, after 1866, was dominated by Republican Radicals. While Chase sympathized with the Radicals' attempts to enforce racial equality and African American voter enfranchisement, on other occasions he resisted their extremism, refusing, for example, to ride *circuit in his judicial district until martial law had been lifted. And during President Johnson's *impeachment trial before the Senate, over which Chase presided, Chase battled with the Radicals, insisting upon following proper courtroom procedures, rather than ignoring them in a headlong rush to unseat the president.

Chase's management of Johnson's impeachment trial was probably his finest hour, and the increase in his public esteem that followed encouraged Chase once again to seek the presidency. While in 1868 his own party clearly had settled on Ulysses S. Grant, Chase saw that he still had an opportunity to run as a Democrat. And so, despite his lifelong opposition to the racism with which the Democrats were then associated, Chase was willing to compromise. In the end, the Democratic nomination went to another, and Chase had lost more than a chance to occupy the White House.

Chase's leadership of the Court was weakened by such displays of opportunism. His brethren,

The Chase Court, 1865. From left: Court Clerk Daniel W. Middleton (standing), David Davis, Noah H. Swayne, Robert C. Grier, James M. Wayne, Salmon P. Chase, Samuel Nelson, Nathan Clifford, Samuel F. Miller, Stephen J. Field

like the rest of the country, came to see his every decision as governed primarily by political expediency. Consequently, Chase frequently found himself a dissenter, perhaps most notably in the *Legal Tender Cases* (1871), which reversed his own opinion in *Hepburn v. Griswold* (1870), decided just 15 months earlier. In hindsight, Chase appears frequently to have been on the right side of the issues of his day. In the *Slaughterhouse Cases* (1873), for example, he insisted that the majority's restricted interpretation of the *Privileges and Immunities Clause of the Fourteenth Amendment would erode rights African Americans had gained only recently and through much suffering (an argument validated during the many decades that passed before the Civil Rights movement reclaimed these rights). Chase's tenure as chief justice was not only one of the briefest in the history of the Court, but also one of the most undistinguished, marked by little judicial activity and a lack of leadership that contributed to congressional dominance over the judiciary.

Chase never gave up hope of achieving the presidency, but on May 7, 1873, shortly after a decision was handed down in the *Slaughterhouse Cases*, he died of a massive stroke.

ASSOCIATE JUSTICES

For a biography of Associate Justice **James M. Wayne,** see entry under **THE MARSHALL COURT.** For biographies of Associate Justices **John Catron, Samuel Nelson, Robert C. Grier, Nathan Clifford, Noah H. Swayne, Samuel F. Miller, David Davis,** and **Stephen J. Field,** see entries under **THE TANEY COURT.**

WILLIAM STRONG

PERSONAL DATA
Born: May 6, 1808, in Somers, Connecticut
Parents: Rev. William Lighthouse Strong, Harriet Deming Strong
Higher Education: Yale College (B.A., 1828; M.A., 1831); Yale Law School, 1832
Bar Admissions: Pennsylvania, 1832
Political Party: Republican
Marriages: November 28, 1836, to Priscilla Lee Mallery, who bore Strong two daughters and one son, and who died in 1844; November 22, 1849, to Rachel Davies Bull, who bore Strong two daughters and two sons

Died: August 19, 1895, in Lake Minnewaska, New York
Buried: Charles Evans Cemetery, Reading, Pennsylvania

PROFESSIONAL CAREER

Occupations: Educator, 1828-1832; Lawyer, 1832-1847, 1851-1857, 1868-1870; Politician, 1830s-1851; Judge, 1857-1868, 1870-1880; Religious Activist, 1871-1895
Official Positions: Member, Reading, Pennsylvania, City Council and Board of Education, ca. 1830s-1840s; Member, United States House of Representatives, 1847-1851; Associate Justice, Pennsylvania Supreme Court, 1857-1868; Associate Justice, United States Supreme Court, 1870-1880; Vice President, American Bible Society, 1871-1895; President, American Tract Society, 1873-1895; Vice President, American Sunday School Union, 1883-1895

SUPREME COURT SERVICE

Nominated: February 7, 1870
Nominated By: Ulysses S. Grant
Confirmed: February 18, 1870
Confirmation Vote: Voice vote
Oath Taken: March 14, 1870
Replaced: Robert C. Grier
Significant Opinions: *Legal Tender Cases* (1871); *Strauder v. West Virginia* (1880)
Left Court: Retired December 14, 1880
Length of Service: 10 years, 9 months
Replacement: William B. Woods

On April 16, 1866, Andrew Johnson nominated Henry Stanbery of Ohio to fill the vacancy created by the death of Justice John Catron. The Senate took no action on the nomination. Furthermore, congressional Republicans reduced the number of justices from ten to seven, thereby preventing Johnson from filling any vacancies on the Court. (Another unfilled vacancy was created by Justice James M. Wayne's death on July 5, 1867.) Stanbery then served as Johnson's attorney general.

In the spring of 1869, however, Congress passed legislation increasing the number of justices to nine. On December 15, 1869, Ulysses S. Grant nominated Ebenezer R. Hoar, his attorney general, to fill one of these seats. Hoar's nomination precipitated a bitter confirmation battle in the Senate, owing to his ear-

lier insistence that newly created federal *circuit court appointments not be filled via patronage. On February 3, 1870, his appointment was rejected by a vote of 33 to 24.

Upon Justice Robert Grier's December 15, 1869, announcement that he would retire as of January 31 the next year, President Grant nominated former Secretary of War Edwin M. Stanton on December 20, 1869, and the Senate confirmed him the same day by a vote of 46 to 11. Four days later, however, Stanton died from a heart attack, never having assumed the bench. William Strong took his place.

William Strong was the eldest of 11 children born to a Presbyterian minister and his wife. After receiving bachelor's and master's degrees from Yale, Strong taught school in Burlington, New Jersey for four years, during which time he also studied law. In 1832 he returned to Yale, this time to the Law School, where he was enrolled for a short time before being admitted to the bar.

Strong set up practice in Reading, Pennsylvania, where he prospered as both an attorney and a civic leader. In 1846 he entered national politics as a "Locofoco" Democrat (the radical, equal rights, wing of Jacksonian Democrats) and was elected to the House of Representatives. He was reelected two years later, but declined a third nomination. In 1857, again as a Democrat, he was elected to a 15-year term on the Pennsylvania Supreme Court. He resigned in 1868, citing financial reasons.

With the outbreak of the Civil War, Strong allied himself with the Union and the Republican Party. It is possible that President Lincoln considered Strong as Chief Justice Taney's replacement in 1864, but six years would pass before Strong was actually nominated by Ulysses S. Grant to replace retiring Justice Grier. Grant seems to have delayed Strong's nomination for a time in order to avoid a repetition of "the curious spectacle of a Judge dead and buried in state [Stanton] while his predecessor [Grier] sits on the Bench and goes to the funeral." The same day that Strong's name was put before the Senate, the Chase Court announced its decision in *Hepburn v. Griswold* (1870), declaring the Legal

Tender Act unconstitutional. Because this outcome was unacceptable to Grant, and because Congress had created another vacancy on the Court for Grant to fill, Strong's appointment, together with the simultaneous appointment of Joseph P. Bradley, gave the appearance of an attempt to "pack" the Court. This impression received further support from the fact that Strong was known to support legal tender laws (having previously upheld them while on the Pennsylvania Supreme Court). When a new majority of the Chase Court overruled *Hepburn* 15 months later in the *Legal Tender Cases* (1871), Strong's authorship of the majority opinion only added to the cloud under which he began his tenure on the High Court.

With the exception of his opinion in *Strauder v. West Virginia* (1880), a case that was unusual in that it was one of the few instances when an African American individual won a legal victory in the post-Civil War period, the remainder of Strong's time on the Court was unremarkable. His leave-taking, however, was as exceptional as his arrival. In 1880, still in good health and intellectually strong, he tendered his resignation, perhaps, it has been conjectured, as an example to Justices Nathan Clifford, Ward Hunt, and Noah H. Swayne, who remained on the Court despite their various disabilities. For the next 15 years, Strong devoted himself to Presbyterian Church matters, finally succumbing to illness in his 88th year.

JOSEPH P. BRADLEY

PERSONAL DATA
Born: March 14, 1813, in Berne, New York
Parents: Philo Bradley, Mercy Gardner Bradley
Higher Education: Rutgers College (undergraduate degree, 1836)
Bar Admission: New Jersey, 1839
Political Party: Republican
Marriage: 1844 to Mary Hornblower, who bore Strong seven children, four of whom survived into adulthood
Died: January 22, 1892, in Washington, D.C.
Buried: Mount Pleasant Cemetery, Newark, New Jersey

PROFESSIONAL CAREER
Occupations: Educator, ca. 1829-1833, 1836; Journalist, ca. 1836; Lawyer, 1839-1870; Judge, 1870-1892
Official Positions: Associate Justice, United States Supreme Court, 1870-1892

SUPREME COURT SERVICE
Nominated: February 7, 1870
Nominated By: Ulysses S. Grant
Confirmed: March 21, 1870
Confirmation Vote: 46-9
Oath Taken: March 23, 1870
Replaced: No one; filled newly created seat
Significant Opinions: *Ex parte Siebold* (1880); *Civil Rights Cases* (1883); *Boyd v. United States* (1886)
Left Court: Died January 22, 1892
Length of Service: 21 years, 9 months, 30 days
Replacement: George Shiras Jr.

Born into a family of subsistence farmers, Joseph P. Bradley came to epitomize the American ideal of advancement through hard work. Bradley was entirely self-educated until the age of 16, when a Dutch Reformed Church minister took an interest in him, tutored him, arranged a teaching job for him, then secured his enrollment at Rutgers.

At Rutgers, Bradley was once again fortunate in his friends, which included a future leader of the New Jersey bar and a future United States secretary of state, both of whom would help him advance in life. And Bradley's career was probably furthered by his marriage in 1844 to Mary Hornblower, the daughter of the chief justice of New Jersey's supreme court.

Bradley ran unsuccessfully for Congress in 1862, and this seems to have been his only flirtation with politics. Instead, he focused his energies on his burgeoning legal practice, which was for the most part devoted to representing railroads. He was nonetheless known as a loyal Unionist and Republican, and when Congress created a new seat on the Court for President Grant to fill, Bradley's friends campaigned successfully for his nomination. Bradley became, together with Justice Strong, who was nominated the same day, a part of the new Chase Court majority that overturned *Hepburn v. Griswold*

(1870) in 1871. Like Strong, Bradley always denied charges that he was chosen solely because he had committed himself in advance to support the Legal Tender Act.

Bradley's only other involvement in politics came in 1877, when he was chosen to replace Justice David Davis, who recently had resigned from the Court, on the committee deciding the 1876 presidential election outcome. When Bradley was appointed, the commission was split evenly between Republicans and Democrats, so Bradley alone was seen to carry the burden of deciding between Samuel Tilden and Rutherford B. Hayes. Bradley cast his vote for Hayes and was denounced by the Democrats. Although Bradley always maintained that he did not vote on a partisan basis, there is some evidence to suggest that his vote may have been influenced by his powerful friends.

As a jurist, Bradley was known for the thoroughness of his research (Chief Justice Morrison R. Waite, in particular, seems to have depended on Bradley's skills in this area) and for his expertise in such technical areas as patent law. He worked steadily on the Court almost until the day he died at the age of 78.

WARD HUNT

PERSONAL DATA

Born: June 14, 1810, in Utica, New York
Parents: Montgomery Hunt,
Elizabeth Stringham Hunt
Higher Education: Union College (undergraduate degree, with honors, 1828); Litchfield Law School, 1831
Bar Admission: New York, 1831
Political Party: Republican
Marriages: 1837 to Mary Ann Savage, who bore Hunt three children and who died in 1845; 1853 to Marie Taylor
Died: March 24, 1886, in Washington, D.C.
Buried: Forest Hill Cemetery, Utica

PROFESSIONAL CAREER

Occupations: Lawyer, 1831-1844, 1845-1865; Politician, 1838, 1844; Judge, 1865-1869, 1873-1882; Government Official, 1869-1873
Official Positions: Member, New York State

Assembly, 1838; Mayor of Utica, New York, 1844; Judge, New York Court of Appeals, 1865-1868; Chief Judge, New York Court of Appeals, 1868-1869; Commissioner of Appeals, New York State, 1869-1873; Associate Justice, United States Supreme Court, 1873-1882

SUPREME COURT SERVICE

Nominated: December 3, 1872
Nominated By: Ulysses S. Grant
Confirmed: December 11, 1872
Confirmation Vote: Voice vote
Oath Taken: January 9, 1873
Replaced: Samuel Nelson
Significant Opinions: None
Left Court: Retired January 27, 1882
Length of Service: 9 years, 18 days
Replacement: Samuel Blatchford

Ward Hunt had a conventional upbringing and education, after which he developed an extensive legal practice in his home town of Utica, New York. He entered politics as a Jacksonian Democrat in 1838, when he was elected to the state legislature, where he served one term. Six years later he served one term as Utica's mayor. Opposed to the expansion of slavery into the territories, he supported Martin Van Buren's Free-Soil presidential bid in 1848. Then, in 1855, Hunt helped organize the Republican Party in New York State.

Hunt's true ambitions were judicial rather than political. After two failed attempts to be elected to the bench, in 1865 he was finally elected to New York's highest court, the Court of Appeals, probably with the backing of his political ally, Roscoe Conkling, then the New York Republican boss. Hunt served on the Court of Appeals for a total of four years, sitting his last year as its chief judge. In 1869, when a state constitutional amendment resulted in reorganization of the New York judiciary, Hunt stayed on as the state commissioner of appeals.

Hunt's old friend Conkling was probably responsible for bringing him to the attention of President Grant as a potential successor to retiring Supreme Court Justice Samuel Nelson. Once on the Court, Hunt remained politically loyal to

Grant and voted consistently to uphold the Republican *enabling legislation behind the Civil War amendments. His performance during his nine years as a High Court justice was workmanlike: he wrote 149 opinions for the Court and four of his own dissents. Otherwise, his career was undistinguished except for the manner in which he left it.

Six years after his arrival, he suffered a disabling stroke. Although he never returned to the bench, he refused to resign because he had served less than the ten years required to receive a pension. Eventually, former Justice David Davis sponsored congressional legislation granting Hunt special early retirement, with receipt of his pension conditioned on his resigning within 30 days. Hunt did so the day the bill was signed into law.

SIGNIFICANT CASES

*EX PARTE MILLIGAN

Citation: 4 Wall. (71 U.S.) 2 (1866)
Argued: March 5-13, 1866
Decided: April 3, 1866
Court Below: United States Circuit Court for the District of Indiana
Basis for Review: *Certificate of division of opinion
Facts: Military officials arrested Lambdin P. Milligan in Indiana in 1864 for alleged anti-Union activities. Although Indiana was not a theater of battle, and the civil courts were open there, Milligan was tried in military court, where he was found guilty and sentenced to hang.
Issue: What is the extent of military authority over civilians and of the government's emergency powers in time of war?
Outcome: A unanimous Court agreed that the military court lacked *jurisdiction over the case, and that Milligan and two others must be released. The justices disagreed, however, as to the basis for this outcome.
Vote: 9-0
Participating: Chase, Wayne, Nelson, Grier, Clifford, Swayne, Miller, Davis, Field

Opinions: Davis for the Court; Chase, joined by Wayne, Swayne, and Miller, concurring
Significance: Although *Milligan* is frequently cited as a landmark case for civil liberties, it often has been ignored. In *Duncan v. Kahanamoku* (1946), for example, the Supreme Court ignored its own *precedent by basing its opposition to the imposition of martial law in Hawaii on legislation specific to the state, rather than the constitutional principles elaborated in *Milligan*. And the Court again ignored the case when consenting to the internment of Japanese Americans during the Second World War. The weakness of *Milligan* as precedent doubtless has something to do with the division in the Chase Court's reasoning. While Davis argued that constitutional guarantees of *indictment by *grand jury and trial by jury were not suspended in time of war, Chase and the other concurring justices based their opinions on statutory grounds, citing the *Habeas Corpus Act of 1863 as a guarantee to civilians of trial in civil courts, where they are available.

TEST OATH CASES (CUMMINGS V. MISSOURI; *EX PARTE GARLAND)

Citation: *Cummings*, 4 Wall. (71 U.S.) 277 (1867); *Garland*, 4 Wall. (71 U.S.) 333 (1867)
Argued: *Cummings*, March 15-16, 19-20, 1866; *Garland*, March 13-15, 1866
Decided: January 14, 1867
Courts Below: *Cummings*, Missouri Supreme Court ; *Garland*, None
Bases for Review: *Cummings*, *Writ of error; *Garland*, *Original Supreme Court jurisdiction
Facts: *Cummings* concerned a Missouri regulation requiring individuals involved in certain occupations to swear that they had not sympathized with or aided the Confederacy during the Civil War. *Garland* involved a federal statute requiring that lawyers wishing to practice before federal courts take a similar oath.
Issue: Are such retrospective loyalty oaths constitutional?
Outcome: Both oaths were found to violate constitutional prohibitions against *ex post facto laws and *bills of attainder.

Vote: *Cummings*, 5-4; *Garland*, 5-4
Participating: Chase, Wayne, Nelson, Grier, Clifford, Swayne, Miller, Davis, Field
Opinions: *Cummings*: Field for the Court; Miller dissenting; Chase, Swayne, and Davis dissenting (without written opinions); *Garland*: Field for the Court; Miller, joined by Chase, Swayne, and Davis, dissenting
Significance: The split within the Chase Court reflected that of post-war society in general. While some felt that former Confederates should be reintegrated into the Union as quickly as possible, others, like Justice Miller, felt that such persons lacked the moral qualifications to resume respected positions in society. The principles laid out in the *Test Oath Cases* remain valid and were invoked in 1965 in *United States v. Brown* to strike down a federal statute prohibiting former Communists from holding union offices.

MISSISSIPPI V. JOHNSON

Citation: 4 Wall. (71 U.S.) 475 (1867)
Argued: April 12, 1867
Decided: April 15, 1867
Court Below: None
Basis for Review: *Original Supreme Court jurisdiction
Facts: In March 1867 Congress passed a Reconstruction Act over President Johnson's veto. Mississippi filed a motion with the Court, seeking to prevent Johnson from enforcing what it saw as the punitive measures of the act. Because Johnson saw the motion as a threat to executive power, he opposed it through his attorney general.
Issue: Does the judiciary have power to *enjoin the president from performing executive duties?
Outcome: The Court voted unanimously that it lacked *jurisdiction over the exercise of such duties, owing largely to the doctrine of *separation of powers.
Vote: 9-0
Participating: Chase, Wayne, Nelson, Grier, Clifford, Swayne, Miller, Davis, Field
Opinion: Chase for the Court
Significance: Chase's opinion distinguished this case from *Marbury v. Madison* (1803) on the basis that the earlier case concerned only ministerial duties of the executive branch, while this case concerned executive duties involving the discretionary exercise of political judgment. Because the Constitution assigns specific tasks to the president, the Court cannot restrain him from enforcing acts of Congress, even when, as here, they are allegedly unconstitutional.

*EX PARTE MCCARDLE

Citation: 7 Wall. (74 U.S.) 506 (1869)
Argued: March 2-4, 9, 1868
Decided: April 12, 1869
Court Below: United States Circuit Court for the Southern District of Mississippi
Basis for Review: Appeal
Facts: A Mississippi journalist, William McCardle, was arrested by military officials for publishing editorials allegedly inciting insurrection again the occupying northern army, which now proposed to try McCardle in military court under the provisions of the Reconstruction Act of 1867. Because the Reconstruction Act permitted such trials even when civil courts were available, McCardle challenged its constitutionality under *Ex parte Milligan* (1866) and invoked the *Habeas Corpus Act of 1867, which directs federal courts to issue *writs to individuals detained in violation of their constitutional rights. When the circuit court refused to issue the writ, McCardle invoked another provision of the Habeas Corpus Act granting *appellate jurisdiction in such cases to the Supreme Court. After the Court had heard arguments in the case, but before it had rendered decision, Congress, controlled by Radical Republicans who feared that the Reconstruction Act would be struck down, passed legislation repealing the provision of the Habeas Corpus Act that permitted such appeals to the High Court.
Issue: Does Congress have the power to curtail the Supreme Court's *jurisdiction?
Outcome: The case was dismissed for lack of jurisdiction.
Vote: 8-0
Participating: Chase, Nelson, Grier, Clifford, Swayne, Miller, Davis, Field
Opinion: Chase for the Court

Significance: In *McCardle* the Chase Court seems to have yielded to the dominance of the Reconstruction Congress. The Chase opinion notes that the Constitution limits the Supreme Court's appellate jurisdiction "with such exceptions, and under such regulations as the Congress shall make," obliging the Court to accept the 1868 repeal measure. The suggestion that congressional power over the Court is unlimited, however, contradicts the doctrine of separation of powers, and subsequent commentators on the case have seen it as an example of the Court's (perhaps excessive) flexibility, pointing to another challenge to the Reconstruction Act, *Ex parte Yerger* (1869), in which the Court granted jurisdiction only months after dismissing *McCardle*.

TEXAS V. WHITE

Citation: 7 Wall. (74 U.S.) 700 (1869)
Argued: February 5, 8, & 9, 1869
Decided: April 12, 1869
Court Below: None
Basis for Review: *Original Supreme Court jurisdiction
Facts: The Reconstruction government of the state of Texas brought suit to recover bonds that had been sold during the war by the state's Confederate government. Defendants in the suit countered that because Texas had seceded from the Union and had not yet been readmitted, it had no *standing to sue in federal court.
Issues: Did Texas's secession deprive it of incidents of membership in the Union, such as the right to sue in federal court?
Outcome: The Court found that the state was entitled to recover its securities.
Vote: 5-3
Participating: Chase, Nelson, Grier, Clifford, Swayne, Miller, Davis, Field
Opinions: Chase for the Court; Grier dissenting and Swayne, joined by Miller, dissenting
Significance: Chase's opinion contained perhaps his most memorable words: "The Constitution, in all its provisions, looks to an indestructible Union, composed of indestructible states." While the Court's majority held that Texas never had really left the Union because it lacked the power

to do so, the three dissenting justices pointed to this assertion as the ultimate *legal fiction. But as Chase argued, although the Civil War temporarily had deprived Texas of a lawful government, under the *Guarantee Clause, Congress was granted the authority to reestablish such a government. This Congress had done by establishing a Reconstruction government in Texas which, although it still was provisional, nonetheless had the right of access to federal courts.

PAUL V. VIRGINIA

Citation: 8 Wall. (75 U.S.) 168 (1869)
Argued: October 12, 1869
Decided: November 1, 1869
Court Below: Virginia Supreme Court
Basis for Review: *Writ of error
Facts: Many states imposed a variety of taxes and license fees on insurance companies chartered in other states. *Paul*, a *test case financed by the National Board of Fire Underwriters, involved an agent for New York insurance companies who was convicted in Virginia of selling insurance without a state license. The lower court fined agent Paul $50 for selling out-of-state insurance without a license.
Issues: Are corporations "citizens" as defined by the *Privileges and Immunities Clause of Article IV of the Constitution and therefore immune to state discrimination against nonresidents? Can insurance sales constitute interstate commerce as defined by Article I, section 8, of the Constitution and therefore be exempted from state regulation?
Outcome: The lower court's ruling was affirmed.
Vote: 8-0
Participating: Chase, Nelson, Grier, Clifford, Swayne, Miller, Davis, Field
Opinion: Field for the Court
Significance: The Court's decision, which reflected then current belief that corporations were not citizens for purposes of the *Privileges and Immunities Clause, resulted in continued state regulation of the insurance industry. The Court reversed itself in 1944 in *United States v. South-Eastern Underwriters Association*, but because state regulatory agencies were so

entrenched, Congress returned authority to the states with the McCarran-Ferguson Act of 1945.

WOODRUFF V. PARHAM

Citation: 8 Wall. (75 U.S.) 123 (1869)
Argued: October 13, 1869
Decided: November 8, 1869
Court Below: Alabama Supreme Court
Basis for Review: *Writ of error
Facts: Mobile, Alabama, imposed a tax on auction sales of goods brought in from other states in their original packages. The lower court upheld the tax.
Issue: Are states constitutionally prohibited from taxing goods brought in from other states?
Outcome: The lower court ruling was affirmed.
Vote: 7-1
Participating: Chase, Nelson, Grier, Clifford, Swayne, Miller, Davis, Field
Opinions: Miller for the Court; Nelson dissenting
Significance: *Brown v. Maryland*, an 1827 case that established the "original package" doctrine, held that states can control such commerce when a commodity, by changing its packaging, changes its character as an import. *Woodruff* read this *precedent narrowly, stating that "imports" refers only to goods from foreign countries. Goods from other states, in contrast, can be taxed at the state level, even when they remain in their original packaging. The Court stressed, however, that such taxes cannot discriminate against interstate commerce. Because the Mobile tax applied to all goods, not just those brought in from other states, it was constitutional.

VEAZIE BANK V. FENNO

Citation: 8 Wall. (75 U.S.) 533 (1869)
Argued: October 18, 1869
Decided: December 13, 1869
Court Below: United States Circuit Court for the District of Maine
Basis for Review: *Certificate of division of opinion
Facts: In order to pay the Union war debt, Congress passed legislation in 1866 increasing a tax on state bank notes from one to ten percent, thereby giving untaxed national bank notes a competitive advantage. The Veazie Bank of Maine refused to pay the tax, and this controversy arose when Fenno, an internal revenue collector, forced the bank to pay under protest. The bank sued for reimbursement.
Issue: Is such a tax void because it is a *direct tax, then disallowed by the Constitution, or because it impermissibly taxes a state agency, i.e., the state chartered bank?
Outcome: The tax was upheld.
Vote: 6-2
Participating: Chase, Nelson, Grier, Clifford, Swayne, Miller, Davis, Field
Opinions: Chase for the Court; Nelson, joined by Davis, dissenting
Significance: The tax was found to be a constitutional means for Congress to control national currency, one of its functions. The Court also stated that the remedy for excessive taxation is political, not judicial. Nelson's dissenting view that Congress had overreached itself by intruding into the realm of state authority has become more and more discounted by the emergence of the *taxing power as an instrument of public policy.

HEPBURN V. GRISWOLD

Citation: 8 Wall. (75 U.S.) 603 (1870)
Argued: December 10, 1869
Decided: February 7, 1870
Court Below: Kentucky Court of Appeals
Basis for Review: *Writ of error
Facts: Hepburn, a debtor on a note made prior to passage of the Legal Tender Act, which substituted paper money for gold as legal tender, used treasury notes to pay the debt, and the creditor sued for payment in coin. The lower court, finding the act unconstitutional, held for the creditor.
Issues: Is the Legal Tender Act unconstitutional? Is the Constitution to be applied according to its *original intent, or adapted judicially to accommodate developments unforeseen when the document was written?
Outcome: The lower court's ruling was upheld and the Legal Tender Act declared unconstitutional as applied to contracts made prior to its passage.
Vote: 4-3

Participating: Chase, Nelson, Clifford, Swayne, Miller, Davis, Field
Opinions: Chase for the Court; Miller, joined by Swayne and Davis, dissenting
Significance: As secretary of the Treasury, Chase had devised a system of funding the Civil War through issuance of paper money not redeemable in gold. However, when Congress made these greenbacks official currency by passing the Legal Tender Act in 1862, Chase was reluctant to endorse it, on the basis that the Constitution clearly intended to banish paper currency unless it was backed by silver or gold. With *Hepburn* his reluctance became law, but only temporarily, as the same day the decision was announced, President Grant nominated two Republicans who supported his legal tender policies to fill existing vacancies on the Court.

COLLECTOR V. DAY

Citation: 11 Wall. (78 U.S.) 113 (1871)
Argued: February 3, 1871
Decided: April 3, 1871
Court Below: United States Circuit Court for the District of Massachusetts
Basis for Review: *Writ of error
Facts: Protesting a federal tax on his salary, Day, a Massachusetts probate judge, sued the tax collector and won in the lower court.
Issue: Can the federal government tax the income of a state official?
Outcome: The lower court ruling was upheld.
Vote: 7-1
Participating: Nelson, Clifford, Swayne, Miller, Davis, Field, Strong, Bradley (Chase not participating)
Opinions: Nelson for the Court; Bradley dissenting
Significance: In *Dobbins v. Erie County* (1842), the Court held that the state could not tax the income of a federal official, and here, again because of the Tenth Amendment and the doctrine of dual *sovereignty, the Court made a reciprocal finding, barring the federal government from taxing the income of state officials. This mutual tax immunity was eventually overruled by *Graves v. O'Keefe* (1939).

LEGAL TENDER CASES (KNOX V. LEE; PARKER V. DAVIS)

Citation: 12 Wall. (79 U.S.) 457 (1871)
Argued: *Knox*, November 17, 1869, reargued February 23, 1871; *Parker*, April 18, 1871
Decided: May 1, 1871
Court Below: *Knox*, United States Circuit Court for the Western District of Texas; *Parker*, Massachusetts Supreme Court
Basis for Review: *Knox*, *Writ of Error; *Parker*, Appeal
Facts: In *Knox v. Lee*, Lee was the owner of a flock of sheep confiscated by the Confederacy and sold to Knox. Lee then attempted to recover the value of his property in coin. In *Parker v. Davis*, Davis bought a lot from Parker on installments. Parker refused payments made in legal tender. In both cases judgment required acceptance of payment in paper money.
Issue: Is the Legal Tender Act constitutional?
Outcome: The Court overruled *Hepburn v. Griswold* (1870), declaring the act legitimate and applicable even retroactively.
Vote: 5-4
Participating: Chase, Nelson, Clifford, Swayne, Miller, Davis, Field, Strong, Bradley
Opinions: Strong for the Court; Bradley concurring; Chase, joined by Nelson, dissenting, Clifford and Field dissenting
Significance: The *Legal Tender Cases* reinforced Congress's control over the currency but had the net effect of weakening the Supreme Court's authority. The swift reversal of *Hepburn* in the wake of the recent, seemingly engineered judicial appointments of Justices Strong and Bradley, undermined the Court's reputation for consistency and political autonomy in its decisions.

SLAUGHTERHOUSE CASES

Citation: 16 Wall. (83 U.S.) 36 (1873)
Argued: February 3-5, 1873
Decided: April 14, 1873
Court Below: Louisiana Supreme Court
Basis for Review: *Writ of error
Facts: Louisiana incorporated the Crescent City Live-Stock Landing and Slaughtering Company,

requiring that all butchering in New Orleans take place at that facility. The Butchers' Benevolent Association sued Crescent City in Louisiana Supreme Court, which rejected the butchers' claim that the monopoly violated the Fourteenth Amendment by depriving them of their right to labor freely. This case was joined with three others at the United States Supreme Court.

Issue: Does the Louisiana monopoly violate the Fourteenth Amendment's prohibition against state laws which "abridge the privileges or immunities of citizens of the United States"?

Outcome: By a bare majority, the Court upheld the lower court's ruling that the *Privileges and Immunities Clause was not intended to protect such fundamental rights as that to labor freely.

Vote: 5-4

Participating: Chase, Clifford, Swayne, Miller, Davis, Field, Strong, Bradley, Hunt

Opinions: Miller for the Court; Field, joined by Chase, dissenting; Bradley and Swayne dissenting

Significance: Although the three constitutional amendments passed after the Civil War by the Republican Congress were intended primarily to insure civil and political rights for African Americans, the amendments were framed in such a way that states remained the primary insurers of individual rights, with the federal government retaining the right to intervene should the states fail in their responsibilities. What was at issue in the *Slaughterhouse Cases* was not a matter of individual civil rights, but a health regulation establishing a butchering monopoly—an area well within the province of the state's *police powers. In this first Supreme Court interpretation of the Fourteenth Amendment, the majority found that the Privileges and Immunities Clause was not intended to protect such rights as that asserted by the butchers, but Justice Miller's opinion narrowed the scope of the amendment to such an extent that this decision limited the power of the federal government to intervene in abuses of fundamental freedoms. Ultimately, the Court did overrule the kinds of state regulations found constitutional in the *Slaughterhouse Cases* in decisions that reflect the reasoning of the strong dissenting opinions — particularly that of Justice

Field — filed in this landmark case.

BRADWELL V. ILLINOIS

Citation: 16 Wall. (83 U.S.) 130 (1873)
Argued: January 18, 1873
Decided: April 15, 1873
Court Below: Illinois Supreme Court
Basis for Review: *Writ of error
Facts: Myra Bradwell, who had studied law and founded a leading Midwestern legal periodical, applied for admission to the Illinois bar and was refused admission by the state supreme court on the basis of her gender.

Issue: Does the state's ruling violate the *Privileges and Immunities Clause of the Fourteenth Amendment?

Outcome: The lower court's denial of Bradwell's admission was upheld.

Vote: 8-1

Participating: Chase, Clifford, Swayne, Miller, Davis, Field, Strong, Bradley, Hunt

Opinions: Miller for the Court; Bradley, joined by Swayne and Field, concurring; Chase dissenting (without written opinion)

Significance: The Court's opinion in *Bradwell* reflected not only the prevailing views of the day regarding women, but also the restrictive reading given the Fourteenth Amendment just the preceding day in the *Slaughterhouse Cases*. It would be another century before the Supreme Court began to undo sexually discriminatory state laws, and the Court would do so based on the *Equal Protection Clause of the amendment, rather than its Privileges and Immunities Clause. In *Bradwell*, the majority of the Court contended that the right to practice law is neither a privilege nor an immunity connected with United States citizenship.

VOTING PATTERNS

President Lincoln chose Samuel Chase as chief justice not because he would be a great leader, but because his political career had proven that he could be led. Lincoln's primary consideration in selecting Justice Taney's successor was finding a chief who would bend — and who would allow

POLITICAL COMPOSITION
of the Chase Court

Justice & Total Term	Courts Served	Appointing President	Political Party
Salmon P. Chase 1864-1873	Chase	Lincoln	Republican
James M. Wayne 1835-1867	Marshall Taney Chase	Jackson	Democrat
John Catron 1837-1865	Taney Chase	Jackson	Democrat
Samuel Nelson 1845-1872	Taney Chase	Tyler	Democrat
Robert C. Grier 1846-1870	Taney Chase	Polk	Democrat
Nathan Clifford 1858-1881	Taney Chase Waite	Buchanan	Democrat
Noah H. Swayne 1862-1881	Taney Chase Waite	Lincoln	Republican
Samuel F. Miller 1862-1890	Taney Chase Waite	Lincoln	Republican
David Davis 1862-1877	Taney Chase Waite	Lincoln	Republican
Stephen J. Field 1863-1897	Taney Chase Waite Fuller	Lincoln	Democrat
William Strong 1870-1880	Chase Waite	Grant	Republican
Joseph P. Bradley 1870-1892	Chase Waite Fuller	Grant	Republican
Ward Hunt 1873-1882	Chase Waite	Grant	Republican

the Court to be bent — to the will of the other branches of government. After the debacle of the *Dred Scott* (1857) decision, the Supreme Court was in such a weakened state that Lincoln prob-ably thought this stratagem would not be hard to execute.

Instead, other justices stepped into the lead-ership void at the top of the Court. Samuel F.

Miller, in particular, assumed a leadership role during the Chase years, playing a crucial part in shaping the Chase Court's most important decision, the *Slaughterhouse Cases* (1873), in which the legislative intent behind the Fourteenth Amendment was interpreted as leaving enormous power with the states. Although the Court divided 5 to 4 on this outcome, it had a profound and long-lasting effect on the federal government's authority to enforce civil rights. If Lincoln's goal in choosing Chase was, as he said, to install "a Chief Justice who will sustain what has been done in regard to emancipation and the legal tenders," he was sorely mistaken about Chase's ability to support legislation passed specifically to protect the rights of African Americans.

Lincoln was wrong, too, about Chase's commitment to legal tender. Although as secretary of the Treasury Chase had been responsible for crafting the 1862 Legal Tender Act, he wrote the majority opinion in *Hepburn v. Griswold* striking it down as unconstitutional in 1870. Because *Hepburn* was decided by less than a full court, President Grant could and did immediately remedy the situation by appointing two Republican stalwarts and legal tender supporters, William Strong and Joseph P. Bradley. Chase's lack of authority was underscored when the Court overruled *Hepburn*, just 15 months after it was handed down, in the *Legal Tender Cases* (1872). This turn of events demonstrated the post-Civil War ascendancy of the other branches of the federal government, which not only enacted the legal tender legislation, but made certain it was upheld.

During this period both the White House and Congress were dominated by the Republican Party, as was the Chase Court which, by February 1870, included only two Democrats. One of these, Stephen J. Field, cannot be characterized by party affiliation. Field, who led the dissenters in the *Slaughterhouse Cases*, was to come into his own in the Waite and Fuller Courts, when his formulation in that dissent of the doctrine of *substantive due process, as it came to be called, would preoccupy the Court and lend it a radical — and conservative — new orientation.

SPECIAL FEATURES OF THE CHASE COURT

DECIDING THE NATURE OF THE NATION

During Chief Justice Chase's tenure, the Supreme Court was confronted in *Texas v. White* (1869) with the problem of defining the legal nature of the Union. While the debate over *states' rights and *federalism that engendered the Civil War had been going on since the formation of the nation and the drafting of its founding document, never before had the Supreme Court been called upon to rule on the southern conception of the Constitution. Because *Texas v. White* found Texas to be a state with *standing to sue in federal court, the case acted as a kind of legal Appomattox, marking an end to the Confederacy and to the Confederate heresy that saw the Constitution as a kind of revocable contract between the Union and its constituent states. More than a pro forma recognition of the reality of the end of the Civil War, *Texas v. White* marked the end of a long legal controversy about national identity.

JUDICIAL ACTIVISM V. JUDICIAL SUBSERVIENCE

Whereas prior to 1862 only two acts of Congress of any consequence had been overruled by the Supreme Court (section 13 of the Judiciary Act of 1789 in *Marbury v. Madison* [1803] and the Missouri Compromise in *Scott v. Sandford* [1857]), fully ten congressional acts were found to be unconstitutional during the tenure of the Chase Court. In addition to overruling 11 minor pieces of legislation, the Chase Court invalidated parts of the *Habeas Corpus Act of 1863 as well as the Legal Tender Act, declared a congressional test oath unconstitutional, and outlawed a federal tax on state officials' salaries.

Nonetheless, the Chase Court is remembered less for its *judicial activism than for its submission to the Republican Congress that dominated the Reconstruction period. Jealously guarding its power, Congress proposed various means of forestalling adverse Supreme Court decisions. Congress considered, then discarded, a proposal that decisions striking down any of its acts be supported by two-thirds of the justices, as well as a bill denying the Court *jurisdiction over any case arising out of the Reconstruction Acts. Instead, between the time that the Court heard arguments in *Ex parte McCardle* in March 1868 and April 1869, when decision was rendered in the case, Congress repealed an 1867 statute authorizing appeals to the Supreme Court in *habeas corpus cases — in effect, depriving the Court of jurisdiction. The Chase Court reacted by dismissing the case. *McCardle* marks the only time in the history of American jurisprudence that Congress blatantly acted to curtail Supreme Court authority in order to prevent the Court from ruling on the constitutionality of a particular statute.

COURT "PACKING"

Congress made another attempt to control the Court when it increased the number of justices from seven — the number decreed by the 1866 Judiciary Act — to nine with the Judiciary Act of 1869. President Grant, the choice of the Radical Republicans then controlling Congress, had an opportunity to fill one vacancy on the Court, which then consisted of eight members. Grant was given a second seat to fill when the infirm Justice Grier announced his retirement effective January 31, 1870.

On February 7, 1870, Justice Chase read his opinion for the Court in *Hepburn v. Griswold*, effectively striking down the Legal Tender Act which the Union had used to finance its war effort. At practically the same moment, Grant submitted the names of William Strong and Joseph P. Bradley to the Senate for confirmation to the Supreme Court. Fifteen months later, *Hepburn* was overturned by a new majority, consisting of Grant's appointees and the *Hepburn* dissenters, in a set of new *Legal Tender Cases* brought before the Court by Grant's attorney general within weeks of Strong's and Bradley's confirmations. Although it is not known if the Grant administration had advance word of the decision in *Hepburn*, which was adverse to the government's interests, speculation that Grant and the Congress conspired to pack the Court persisted, further undermining the Chase Court's authority.

The Waite Court 1874-1888

BACKGROUND

THE CIVIL RIGHTS ACT OF 1875

The Republican attempt to codify racial equality in the postbellum period culminated in the Civil Rights Act of 1875, the legacy of Senator Charles Sumner of Massachusetts, who did not live to see either the act's passage or its subsequent evisceration. The act, which prohibited discrimination at inns, in public conveyances, and at places of amusement, was meant to implement the rights guaranteed by the Civil War amendments, but it proved to be nearly a century ahead of its time.

In the 1883 *Civil Rights Cases*, the Waite Court struck the act down on grounds that it attempted to reach purely private conduct not within the scope of the *Equal Protection Clause. The principle that the Fourteenth Amendment addresses only *state action thus made its way into American *jurisprudence, and it was not until 1964, when Congress passed another civil rights act based on the federal government's *commerce power, that the courts were able to deal with the kinds of discrimination Senator Sumner's bill was intended to correct.

THE ELECTION OF 1876 AND THE COMPROMISE OF 1877

The presidential election of 1876 saw Samuel J. Tilden, Democratic governor of New York, pitted against the Republican governor of Ohio, Rutherford B. Hayes. In the election aftermath,

---

An asterisk (*) before a word or phrase indicates that a definition will be found in the glossary at the end of this volume.

it appeared that the popular vote had gone for Tilden, who won 184 uncontested electoral votes to Hayes's 165. The number required for election was 185. Twenty electoral votes, however, were disputed; nineteen involved electors from the three southern states (Florida, Louisiana, and South Carolina) still under Republican Reconstruction rule, and one was from an Oregon elector.

In case of such a contested presidential election, the Twelfth Amendment provides that, "The President of the Senate shall, in the presence of the Senate and the House of Representatives, open all the certificates, and the votes shall then be counted." Because this instruction fails to stipulate who shall count the votes, and because Congress was itself equally divided, with the Senate controlled by Republicans and the House by Democrats, an electoral commission was set up. The commission consisted of five senators, five representatives, and five Supreme Court justices. The Senate selected three Republicans and two Democrats, while the House selected three Democrats and two Republicans. The bill setting up the commission designated four of the justices who were to serve, two of whom were Republicans and two Democrats. These four justices were to select a fifth, nonpartisan justice, with whom, of necessity, the ultimate decision would rest.

It was expected that Republican Justices Samuel Freeman Miller and William Strong, together with Democratic Justices Stephen J. Field and Nathan Clifford, would choose Justice David Davis, the only truly neutral member of the Court, as the commission's nonpartisan justice. Davis unexpectedly resigned from the Court in 1877, however, leaving the commission with only Republican justices from which to choose. Justice Joseph P. Bradley, seemingly the most nonpartisan of the group, was chosen as the commission's 15th man. Although there is some evidence that Bradley may have been influenced by political pressure, the vote divided, not surprisingly, along party lines, with Hayes elected by a margin of one vote.

The Democrats — primarily southerners — cried foul and threatened to delay Hayes's inauguration indefinitely. A compromise, engineered by Justice Stanley Matthews (who was appointed to the Supreme Court by Hayes in the aftermath of the election), was finally struck on the eve of the inauguration whereby the Democrats agreed to let Hayes peacefully assume office. In return, the Republicans promised to withdraw federal troops from the South, to appropriate funds for internal improvements in the region, and to appoint at least one southerner to the cabinet.

THE ASSASSINATION OF PRESIDENT GARFIELD

The presidential election of 1880, by another close vote, went to Republican James A. Garfield of Ohio. Four months after his inauguration, Garfield was shot and mortally wounded by Charles J. Guiteau, a man with a history of mental problems who was also a disappointed office seeker. Garfield was succeeded by his vice president, Chester A. Arthur of New York. Following the assassination, civil service reform, which had been a plank of the Republican platform that helped elect Garfield, was quickly implemented. The Pendleton Act of 1883 enabled future chief executives to combat graft and cronyism — which had assumed crisis proportions during Reconstruction — by establishing a merit system governing appointments and promotions.

THE GRANGER MOVEMENT AND THE INTERSTATE COMMERCE COMMISSION

After the Civil War, the railroads, like many other corporations, grew explosively, with competition among various railroad companies resulting in monopolies, discriminatory pricing, and variable access to rail lines. Complaints against the railroads were especially pronounced in the Midwest, where farmers were dependent upon railroad-owned storage elevators and on rail lines for moving their harvested crops. The Grange, a farmers' organization established by the United States Department of Agriculture in 1867, lobbied state legislatures to pass laws prohibiting rate discrimination and to set up commissions to enforce them. Several states — Illinois, Iowa, Minnesota, and Wisconsin — passed laws regulating the railroads. These so-called Granger laws were challenged in court.

The decisions in the *Granger Cases* (1877)

were probably the most important handed down by the Waite Court, which pronounced that any business, such as the railroads, which is "clothed with a public interest" is subject to regulation. Government was thus given unprecedented power over enterprise. However, this ruling was quickly diluted by another stating that rate-setting by states must be "reasonable," and that only courts can determine reasonableness. Railroads responded by challenging in court each rate set by state commissions. The Supreme Court in *Wabash, St. Louis & Pacific Railway Co. v. Illinois* (1886) killed the Granger laws by declaring that states have no power to regulate railroad rates for interstate shipments — which constituted nearly all cargo transports.

Wabash, St. Louis & Pacific Railway ceded regulation of the railroads to Congress, and Congress responded the next year by creating the Interstate Commerce Commission (ICC), the first modern independent regulatory agency. The act that created the ICC, however, stated that rates must be "reasonable and just," and because the Supreme Court had already appointed federal courts as the arbiters of what is reasonable, the railroads again responded with a flurry of litigation. In the 1890s the Court deprived the ICC of its rate-setting authority and made it solely an instrument for information gathering, after which the railroads resumed their unfair practices.

THE ELECTION OF 1880

After the election of James Garfield in 1880, the presidency alternated every four years between Democrats and Republicans for the remainder of the century. Having narrowly lost the two previous elections, the Democrats, supported by Republican independents known as "Mugwumps" (after an Indian name for young warriors), nominated Grover A. Cleveland of New York. Cleveland, too, was elected by a narrow margin (consisting almost entirely of New York's 36 electoral votes). When he took up residence in the White House in 1885, he was the first Democrat to do so in nearly a quarter of a century.

Cleveland's rise to power had been meteoric. He only made his appearance on the political scene in the early 1880s, when he was elected mayor of Buffalo, New York. His reputation as a reformer carried him into the New York governor's mansion in 1882, where he served for only two years before assuming the presidency. The Mugwumps, discomforted by what they saw as the growing closeness between the Republicans and big business, backed Cleveland because of his reputation as a social crusader. Once in office, Cleveland proved a disappointment. Although he approved two important pieces of legislation during his first term, the Dawes Severalty Act and the Interstate Commerce Act, neither originated with him. In 1888 the presidency swung back to the Republican camp.

THE DAWES ACT

By the late 1880s virtually all of the Indian tribes had been subdued and relegated to reservations. Most of the reformers felt that the impoverished Indians should be assimilated into the larger white society. They formulated a plan to break up the reservation lands held collectively by Indian tribes and to redistribute them to individuals, a plan adopted by Congress in 1887 as the Dawes Severalty Act.

Under the Dawes Act, while each individual's land allotment was to be held in trust by the government for 25 years (ostensibly to forestall speculation), it could be leased. This last provision had the opposite effect of what was intended, and by 1900 Indian holdings in the West amounted to half what they had been in 1887, with some tribes facing the prospect of extinction.

IMMIGRATION

While many among the American populace wanted to assimilate the Indians, others wanted to stem the tide of immigrants from other parts of the world. Between 1870 and 1900 nearly twelve million immigrants came to the shores of the United States from abroad. More than one hundred American cities — where immigrants tended to settle — at least doubled in size during the 1880s.

Immigrant groups treated with the most hostility tended to be those most dissimilar from the majority population, which had its origins in

Morrison R. Waite

Western Europe. Perhaps the most egregious example of America's growing nativism during this period was a series of laws directed at the Chinese. By 1880 approximately seventy-five thousand Chinese lived in California, more than half of them in San Francisco. Chinese continued to come to San Francisco despite enactment of such ordinances as the 1870 Cubic Air Ordinance restricting the number of Chinese occupants per apartment building, the 1876 Queue Ordinance requiring all Chinese prisoners to have their hair cut, and the 1878 No Special Police for Chinese Quarter Ordinance denying the Chinese police protection. With passage of the 1882 Exclusion Act, the Chinese became the only group in the world excluded from the United States by an act of Congress.

WAITE'S EARLY LIFE

Morrison R. Waite was the eldest son of a gentleman farmer and lawyer who became chief justice of Connecticut. After graduating from Yale, Waite studied law briefly with his father, then migrated westward to Ohio. In Maumee, Waite completed his legal studies with Samuel D. Young, a prominent attorney with whom Waite, upon

being admitted to the bar, formed a partnership. In 1840 Waite married his second cousin, Amelia Warner, who had followed him to Ohio, and in 1850 the couple moved to Toledo, where Waite established himself as a prominent — though never wealthy — railroad attorney.

WAITE'S PUBLIC LIFE

Active in Whig politics, Waite reluctantly ran for Congress in 1846 and was defeated. In 1849, however, he did gain a seat in the state assembly, where he served one term. With the demise of the Whigs in the mid-1850s, Waite helped to organize the Republican Party in Ohio and, at the urging of party leaders, ran — once again unsuccessfully — for Congress in 1862. In the Ohio gubernatorial race the next year, Waite campaigned intensely for Republican candidate John Brough who, upon carrying the state, offered Waite a seat on the Ohio Supreme Court. Characteristically, Waite demurred, preferring instead to play an unofficial advisory role.

Waite came to national prominence with the 1871 Geneva Arbitration Tribunal, in which he acted as one of three United States counsels. The tribunal was convened to resolve antagonism between the United States and Britain resulting from the latter's outfitting Confederate commerce raiders — the most infamous was the *Alabama* — intended to destroy Union shipping during the Civil War. When the tribunal awarded the United States $15.5 million, the counsels returned home covered with glory. Rejecting a nomination for Congress, Waite once again immersed himself in state politics, serving as president of Ohio's 1873 constitutional convention. While at the convention, he received word that President Grant had nominated him as chief justice of the Supreme Court. The nomination came as a complete surprise to him, as well as to others. Given Grant's troubles in filling the post up to that point, Waite's relative obscurity seemed his primary recommendation.

WAITE AS CHIEF JUSTICE

Waite, who had never argued a case before the Supreme Court or acted in a judicial role, was

JUDICIAL BIOGRAPHY
Morrison Remick Waite

PERSONAL DATA

Born: November 29, 1816, in
Lyme, Connecticut
Parents: Henry Matson Waite,
Maria Selden Waite
Higher Education: Yale College
(undergraduate degree, 1837)
Bar Admission: Ohio, 1839
Political Party: Republican
Marriage: September 21, 1840,
to Amelia C. Warner, who bore
Waite five children
Died: March 23, 1888, in
Washington, D.C.
Buried: Woodlawn Cemetery,
Toledo, Ohio

PROFESSIONAL CAREER

Occupations: Lawyer, 1839-
1874; Politician, 1850-1852,
1873-1874; Diplomat, 1871-
1872; Judge, 1874-1888
Official Positions: Member,
Ohio General Assembly, 1850-
1852; United States Counsel,
Geneva Arbitration Tribunal,
1871-1872; President, Ohio State
Constitutional Convention,

1873-1874; Chief Justice, United
States Supreme Court, 1874-
1888

SUPREME COURT SERVICE

Nominated: January 19, 1874
Nominated By: Ulysses S. Grant
Confirmed: January 21, 1874
Confirmation Vote: 63-0
Oath Taken: March 4, 1874
Replaced: Chief Justice Salmon
P. Chase
Significant Opinions: *Minor v.
Happersett* (1875); *United States
v. Reese* (1876); *United States v.
Cruikshank* (1876); *Munn v.
Illinois* (1877); *Hall v. DeCuir*
(1878); *Reynolds v. United States*
(1879); *Stone v. Mississippi*
(1880)
Left Court: Died March 23,
1888
Length of Service: 14 years, 19
days
Replacement: Chief Justice
Melville W. Fuller

After the death of Chief
Justice Chase, President Grant
nominated as his replacement
New York's political boss, Roscoe
Conkling, but Conkling declined
the offer to become chief justice
in the belief that his political
destiny lay in replacing Grant
himself. Grant then resorted to
cronyism, with disastrous results.
On December 1, 1873, he nominated his attorney general,
George H. Williams, but
Williams was forced to withdraw
his name the following January 8
when it was revealed that his
wife had bartered immunity from
federal prosecution for $30,000.
Grant next nominated former
Attorney General Caleb Cushing
on January 21, 1874. Widely perceived as a political opportunist,
Cushing was denounced in the
press and in the Senate. At
Cushing's request Grant withdrew his name four days later.
Grant then nominated Morrison
R. Waite.

initially treated with condescension by his
brethren. Senior Associate Justice Nathan
Clifford, who had presided over the Court in the
interval after Chase's death, presumed that Waite
lacked familiarity with Court procedure and suggested that the new chief justice might wish to
spend his first few days simply observing. Waite,
however, quickly took command, becoming an
able — if not inspiring — administrator. To his
credit, he spurned any suggestion that he might
be a presidential candidate, thereby avoiding the
political distractions that had compromised Chief

Justice Chase's tenure. He also managed to sidestep any involvement with the 1876 electoral
commission, another misguided foray into politics
that detracted from the justices' authority.

Although he lacked the stature of many of his
predecessors, Waite, who drafted more than a thousand opinions during his 14 years as chief justice,
presided over a Court that delivered a series of
decisions which have had long range effects on
American life. These decisions primarily concerned
two areas, civil rights and economic regulation.
In both of these areas Waite's views more closely

resembled Taney's than Marshall's. In cases like *Minor v. Happersett* (1875) and *United States v. Cruikshank* (1876), Waite wrote opinions for the Court that restricted the rights of women and African Americans, fostering constitutional interpretations that were to last into the next century. On the issue of regulation of business, as demonstrated by his most important decision, *Munn v. Illinois* (1877), Waite favored state over federal controls. While the rationale for regulation offered in the latter case was almost immediately undone by the *laissez faire interpretations of *due process fostered by Justices Stephen J. Field and Joseph P. Bradley, it provided the framework for the complex regulatory environment that developed in the second half of the 20th century.

Waite's death, which occurred while he was presiding over the Supreme Court, happened unexpectedly and reflected the modesty and responsibility that characterized his life. Having caught a chill while helping his coachman in inclement weather, Waite continued to appear on the bench for fear that news of his absence might alarm his wife, who was vacationing in California. The chill rapidly developed into pneumonia, which caused his death on March 23, 1888.

ASSOCIATE JUSTICES

For biographies of Associate Justices **Nathan Clifford, Noah H. Swayne, Samuel F. Miller, David Davis,** and **Stephen J. Field,** see entries under **THE TANEY COURT.** For biographies of Associate Justices **William Strong, Joseph P. Bradley,** and **Ward Hunt,** see entries under **THE CHASE COURT.**

JOHN MARSHALL HARLAN

PERSONAL DATA

Born: June 1, 1833, in Boyle County, Kentucky
Parents: James Harlan, Eliza Shannon Davenport Harlan
Higher Education: Centre College (A.B., 1850); Transylvania University, 1851-1853
Bar Admission: Kentucky, 1853

Political Party: Republican
Marriage: December 23, 1856, to Malvina F. Shanklin, who bore Harlan six children
Died: October 14, 1911, in Washington, D.C.
Buried: Rock Creek Cemetery, Washington, D.C.

PROFESSIONAL CAREER

Occupations: Lawyer, 1850-1867; Government Official, ca. 1850-1851, 1863-1867, 1877; Judge, 1858, 1877-1911; Serviceman, 1861-1863; Educator, 1889-1911; Diplomat, 1893
Official Positions: City Attorney, Frankfort, Kentucky, ca. 1850; Judge, Franklin County, Kentucky, 1858; Attorney General of Kentucky, 1863-1867; Member, Louisiana Reconstruction Committee, 1877; Associate Justice, United States Supreme Court, 1877-1911; Professor of Law, Columbian University (later George Washington University), 1889-1911; Member, Bering Sea Arbitration Tribunal, 1893

SUPREME COURT SERVICE

Nominated: October 16, 1877
Nominated By: Rutherford B. Hayes
Confirmed: November 29, 1877
Confirmation Vote: Voice vote
Oath Taken: December 10, 1877
Replaced: David Davis
Significant Opinions: *Civil Rights Cases* (dissent) (1883); *Hurtado v. California* (dissent) (1884); *Santa Clara County v. Southern Pacific Railroad Co.* (1886); *Mugler v. Kansas* (1887); *Pollock v. Farmers' Loan & Trust Co.* (dissent) (1895); *United States v. E.C. Knight Co.* (dissent) (1895); *Plessy v. Ferguson* (dissent) (1896); *Chicago, Burlington & Quincy Railroad Co.v. Chicago* (1897); *Smyth v. Ames* (1898); *Maxwell v. Dow* (dissent) (1900); *Champion v. Ames* (1903); *Northern Securities Co. v. United States* (1904); *Adair v. United States* (1908)
Left Court: Died October 14, 1911
Length of Service: 33 years, 10 months, 4 days
Replacement: Mahlon Pitney

John Marshall Harlan was born to a prominent Kentucky family. Harlan's father was a friend of politician Henry Clay and an admirer of Chief Justice John Marshall, after whom he named his son. The elder Harlan served as a United States

The Waite Court, 1882. From left: Joseph P. Bradley, William B. Woods, Samuel F. Miller, Horace Gray, Morrison R. Waite, John Marshall Harlan, Stephen J. Field Samuel Blatchford, Stanley Matthews

congressman and in his home state as attorney general, legislator, and secretary of state. Justice Harlan's grandson and namesake, John Marshall Harlan II, was himself a Supreme Court justice.

Harlan was raised an archetypal Kentuckian, supporting both slavery and the Union. After graduating from Centre College and studying law, first at Transylvania University, then with his father, he followed his father's example by entering the political arena as a Whig. With the devolution of the Whigs, both Harlans became Know-Nothings. It was as a Know-Nothing nativist that Harlan gained his first elective office as a county judge, the only judicial experience he had prior to his Supreme Court appointment. Also as a Know-Nothing, Harlan delivered a number of racist and *states' rights speeches that would embarrass him in later life.

With the onset of secession, however, Harlan discovered that his higher allegiance was to the Union. Forming the 10th Kentucky Volunteers, he served with distinction in Tennessee and was recommended for the rank of brigadier general before his father's death in 1863 forced him to retire from the military to care for his family.

During and after the Civil War, Harlan continued to pursue political office. Gradually drifting into the Republican Party, he campaigned in 1868 for Ulysses S. Grant.

Harlan stepped permanently into national politics during the 1876 presidential campaign, at first backing his former legal partner, Benjamin Bristow, but at the crucial moment leading the Kentucky delegation into the Hayes camp. Hayes did not forget Harlan, naming him to a commission which, as part of the Compromise of 1877, was charged with ending Republican rule in Louisiana. And after Justice David Davis resigned — in part to avoid serving on the electoral commission that was to declare Hayes president — Hayes named Harlan as Davis's successor.

Harlan served nearly 34 years on the Court, almost as long as Chief Justice John Marshall and Justice Stephen J. Field. During that time, he was involved in approximately 14,226 cases — in 13,074 of which he formed part of the Court majority. He wrote 745 decisions of the Court, 100 concurrences, and 316 dissents. It is for his dissenting opinions that Harlan is most remembered.

Because of his colorful personality and the unorthodox — often extemporaneous — delivery of his opinions, Justice Harlan was known as an eccentric. His historical reputation has reflected his own erratic nature. His differences with the majority's findings that monopolies are not by definition malignant in *Standard Oil Co. v. United States* and *United States v. American Tobacco Co.*, both decided in 1911 shortly before his death, made him popular at the time but have since proven outmoded. On the other hand, his dissenting opinions in landmark civil rights cases such as the *Civil Rights Cases* of 1883 and *Plessy v. Ferguson* (1896), which established the doctrine of "separate but equal," have since become law and secured his status as a civil rights prophet.

WILLIAM BURNHAM WOODS

PERSONAL DATA

Born: August 3, 1824, in Newark, Ohio
Parents: Ezekiel S. Woods, Sarah J. Burnham Woods
Higher Education: Western Reserve College, now Case Western Reserve University, 1841-1844; Yale College (undergraduate degree, class valedictorian, 1845)
Bar Admission: Ohio, 1847
Political Party: Republican
Marriage: June 21, 1855, to Anne E. Warner, who bore Woods one son and one daughter
Died: May 14, 1887, in Washington, D.C.
Buried: Cedar Hill Cemetery, Newark, Ohio

PROFESSIONAL CAREER

Occupations: Lawyer, 1847-1856, 1866-1868; Politician, 1856, 1857-1861; Serviceman, 1862-1866; Judge, 1868-1887
Official Positions: Mayor, Newark, Ohio, 1856; Speaker, Ohio legislature, 1857-1859; Minority leader, Ohio legislature, 1860-1861; Chancellor, Middle Chancery Division of Alabama, 1868-1869; Judge, United States Fifth Circuit Court, 1869-1880; Associate Justice, United State Supreme Court, 1881-1887

SUPREME COURT SERVICE

Nominated: December 15, 1880
Nominated By: Rutherford B. Hayes
Confirmed: December 21, 1880
Confirmation Vote: 39-8
Oath Taken: January 5, 1881
Replaced: William Strong
Significant Opinion: *Presser v. Illinois* (1886)
Left Court: Died May 14, 1887
Length of Service: 6 years, 4 months, 9 days
Replacement: Lucius Q.C. Lamar

William B. Woods was the first southern justice appointed in the post-Civil War era. Often recalled as a "carpetbagger" judge, Woods in fact played a pivotal role in committing Ohio to the Union cause after the outbreak of hostilities. A native Ohioan, Woods was popular among his early political constituency, which elected him first as mayor of his hometown of Newark, then sent him to the state legislature. At the beginning of Abraham Lincoln's first administration, Woods, a Democrat, opposed Republican war policy. Soon thereafter, however, he committed himself to the survival of the Union, politically and personally. He publicly defended a loan bill opposed in the House of Representatives by his own party. In 1861 he joined the Union army, and he distinguished himself at the battles of Shiloh and Vicksburg and marched with General William T. Sherman through Georgia.

When the war ended, Woods settled in Alabama, where in addition to practicing law, he planted cotton and invested in iron works — and switched to the Republican Party. He was quickly elected to the state judiciary and then, in 1869, named by President Grant as a federal circuit court judge. His *circuit, the Fifth, included Louisiana and Texas, thus requiring him to become familiar with the intricacies of French and Spanish legal *precedents.

Although the electoral votes of two states within his circuit, Florida and Louisiana, were among those disputed in the 1876 presidential election, Woods refused to become involved in the chaos surrounding the commission formed to decide the election. President Hayes did not hold this reticence against him, and when Hayes sought a southerner to replace resigning Justice William Strong, he turned to the former Democratic

Unionist Woods, by then a resident of Georgia.

On the high bench, Woods's tenure was brief and undistinguished. He customarily formed part of the majority in decisions made by the Waite Court. He wrote 218 opinions altogether, most of which concerned *equity matters, his specialty. In his most significant opinion, *Presser v. Illinois* (1886), for which he wrote the opinion of the Court, he demonstrated that he shared the restricted view of the Fourteenth Amendment that was a hallmark of the Supreme Court in the years following Reconstruction. That same year, he became incapacitated by illness and played little part on the Court from that time until his death the following year.

THOMAS STANLEY MATTHEWS

PERSONAL DATA

Born: July 21, 1824, in Cincinnati, Ohio
Parents: Thomas Johnson Matthews, Isabella Brown Matthews
HIgher Education: Kenyon College (B.A., 1840)
Bar Admissions: Tennessee, 1842; Ohio, 1844
Political Party: Republican
Marriages: February 1843 to Mary Ann Black, who bore Matthews eight children, three of whom died in childhood, and who died herself in 1885; 1887 to Mary Theaker
Died: March 22, 1889, in Washington, D.C.
Buried: Spring Grove Cemetery, Cincinnati

PROFESSIONAL CAREER

Occupations: Educator, 1842-1844; Journalist, 1842-1848; Lawyer, 1842-1848, 1849-1850, 1853-1855, 1865-1877, 1879-1881; Politician, 1848-1849, 1855-1861, 1864, 1868, 1872, 1877-1879; Judge, 1851-1853, 1863-1865, 1881-1889; Serviceman, 1861-1863
Official Positions: Assistant Prosecuting Attorney, Hamilton County, Ohio, 1845; Clerk, Ohio House of Representatives, 1848-1849; Judge, Ohio Court of Common Pleas, 1851-1853; Member, Ohio Senate, 1855-1858; United States Attorney for the Southern District of Ohio, 1858-1861; Judge, Superior Court of Cincinnati, Ohio, 1863-1865; Presidential elector, 1864, 1868; Temporary Chairman, Liberal Republican convention, 1872; Counsel, Hayes-Tilden Electoral Commission, 1877; Member, United States Senate, 1877-1879; Associate Justice, United States Supreme Court, 1881-1889

SUPREME COURT SERVICE

Nominated: January 26, 1881 (no action)
Nominated By: Rutherford B. Hayes
Renominated: March 14, 1881
Renominated By: James A. Garfield
Confirmed: May 12, 1881
Confirmation Vote: 24-23
Oath Taken: May 17, 1881
Replaced: Noah H. Swayne
Significant Opinions: *Ex parte Crow Dog* (1883); *Hurtado v. California* (1884); *Yick Wo v. Hopkins* (1886)
Left Court: Died March 22, 1889
Length of Service: 7 years, 10 months, 5 days
Replacement: David J. Brewer

Thomas Stanley Matthews, who dropped his first name later in life, entered Kenyon College as a junior in 1839. At Kenyon he befriended another student, Rutherford B. Hayes, whose destiny would have a profound effect on his own. Matthews's early career consisted of an unusual mix of lawyering, politics, and journalism, all of which made him a prominent figure at an early age. His anti-slavery stance as editor of the *Cincinnati Herald* brought him election in 1848 as clerk of the Ohio House of Representatives. After Matthews served as a state judge and state senator, President Buchanan appointed him a United States attorney. Despite his own belief in abolitionism, Matthews was obliged in this post to prosecute a Cincinnati reporter for violating the Fugitive Slave Act, and the apparent incongruity of this action would later come back to haunt him.

With the outbreak of the Civil War, Matthews and his old friend Hayes joined the army together, and both achieved officer rank. Matthews resigned his commission in 1863 after being elected a judge of the Cincinnati Superior Court. He held that position only two years before resigning to resume private legal practice.

Matthews became a highly successful railroad attorney, but at the same time remained politically active. In 1876 when Hayes asked him to aid in his presidential bid, Matthews agreed. In the aftermath of the election, he also agreed to aid Hayes by arguing the Republican case before the electoral commission. After the contest was finally settled in Hayes's favor, Matthews assisted again by helping to negotiate the Compromise of 1877 which permitted Hayes to assume the presidency.

When a vacancy on the Supreme Court came up in 1881, Hayes rewarded Matthews by nominating him to the post. This first nomination was not, however, to result in Matthews's confirmation. He was assailed from all quarters: for his hypocrisy in upholding the Fugitive Slave Act, for conflicts of interest arising from his representation of big business, for depriving Samuel Tilden of the presidency, and for benefitting from cronyism (in addition to their friendship, Matthews and Hayes were distantly related by marriage). The Judiciary Committee refused to bring Matthews's appointment to the Senate floor, and Hayes, having lost the 1880 election, had to leave office before seeing Matthews established on the High Court. Before leaving office, however, Hayes secured a promise from his successor, James A. Garfield, that the latter would put Matthews's name forward again. The same arguments against Matthews were revived; however, this time he was confirmed by a one-vote margin.

Matthews's contributions to the Court were curtailed by the relatively brief time he served there. In somewhat under eight years, however, he authored 232 opinions and five dissents. Two of his opinions for the Court, *Hurtado v. California* (1884) and *Yick Wo v. Hopkins* (1886), remain undisturbed as *precedents more than a century after they were delivered. Matthews's primary legacy to American law probably comes from the latter case — one of the only post-Reconstruction cases to strengthen minority rights — in which he set the standard for all future public civil rights *disparate impact suits.

HORACE GRAY

PERSONAL DATA

Born: March 24, 1828, in Boston, Massachusetts

Parents: Horace Gray, Harriet Upham Gray
Higher Education: Harvard College (B.A., 1845); Harvard Law School (LL.B., 1849)
Bar Admission: Massachusetts, 1851
Political Party: Republican
Marriage: June 4, 1889, to Jane Matthews
Died: September 15, 1902, in Nahant, Massachusetts
Buried: Mount Auburn Cemetery, Cambridge, Massachusetts

PROFESSIONAL CAREER

Occupations: Lawyer, 1851-1864; Legal Reporter, 1854-1964; Judge, 1864-1902
Official Positions: Reporter, Massachusetts Supreme Judicial Court, 1854-1864; Associate Justice, Massachusetts Supreme Judicial Court, 1864-1873; Chief Justice, Massachusetts Supreme Judicial Court, 1873-1881; Associate Justice, United States Supreme Court, 1882-1902

SUPREME COURT SERVICE

Nominated: December 19, 1881
Nominated By: Chester A. Arthur
Confirmed: December 20, 1881
Confirmation Vote: 51-5
Oath Taken: January 9, 1882
Replaced: Nathan Clifford
Significant Opinion: *United States v. Wong Kim Ark* (1898)
Left Court: Died September 15, 1902
Length of Service: 20 years, 8 months, 6 days
Replacement: Oliver Wendell Holmes

Horace Gray was born into one of Boston's leading commercial families, and he had an upbringing typical of the social stratum to which he belonged. Following his early education at private school and Harvard College, he was making a leisurely grand tour of Europe when he received news of his father's business reversals. Gray, exhibiting the unerring instinct for proper behavior that would become his trademark, came home immediately and took up a profitable career in the law.

In the legal sphere, Gray's early interest in natural history and taxonomy translated into an affinity for legal history and the minute particulars of *precedent. His careful attention to detail served him well when, as a young lawyer, he was appointed as the Massachusetts Supreme Court's official reporter. This position proved a stepping stone, first to appointment as associate justice (at the age of 36, he was the youngest man ever to serve in this position), then as chief justice of the state's highest court. As a state supreme court justice, Gray instituted the practice of hiring outstanding law students as clerks (one such student was future Supreme Court Justice Louis D. Brandeis), a custom which has since become the rule in American federal courts.

Gray's demeanor on the bench was one of overwhelming attention to detail, and one is tempted to speculate that this, his most pronounced characteristic, made him a good judge but a poor politician — his one attempt to run for office, as state attorney general, ended in defeat. He nonetheless made friends in high places, and it was probably Massachusetts Senator George F. Hoar who suggested him as a replacement for Justice Nathan Clifford. President Garfield considered naming Gray to the High Court and, as was the custom, requested that Gray forward sample opinions for evaluation. Gray, considering this gesture to be too much like self-promotion, declined. Garfield died before he could act on Gray's appointment, but his successor, Chester A. Arthur, followed up quickly, and Gray was speedily confirmed for a seat which had been empty for five months following Justice Clifford's death.

Gray was disinclined to dissent, believing that to do so was to weaken a court's authority. As a state supreme court justice he did so only once in 17 years. On the High Court he dissented more frequently, but his voice was seldom heard separately, either in dissent or speaking for the Court as a whole. In part because of his heavy reliance on precedent, none of his decisions was overruled in his lifetime, yet he is remembered for few of them. His greatest impact on the Court may have come in the highly controversial *Pollock v. Farmers' Loan & Trust Co.* (1895), in which either he or Justice George Shiras changed his vote after a rehearing of the case, invalidating a national income tax.

Gray's second decade on the Court was marred by frequent illness, and after a stroke left him partially paralyzed, he tendered his resignation on July 9, 1902. The resignation was contingent upon the accession of a successor, but Gray died before Oliver Wendell Holmes could be confirmed.

SAMUEL BLATCHFORD

PERSONAL DATA
Born: March 9, 1820, in New York, New York
Parents: Richard M. Blatchford, Julia Ann Mumford Blatchford
Higher Education: Columbia College (A.B., first in his class, 1837)
Bar Admission: New York, 1842
Political Party: Republican
Marriage: December 17, 1844, to Caroline Appleton, who bore Blatchford two children
Died: July 7, 1893, in Newport, Rhode Island
Buried: Green Wood Cemetery, Brooklyn, New York

PROFESSIONAL CAREER
Occupations: Lawyer, 1842-1867; Judge, 1867-1893
Official Positions: Judge, United States District Court for the Southern District of New York, 1867-1872; Judge, United States Second Circuit Court, 1872-1882; Associate Justice, United States Supreme Court, 1882-1893

SUPREME COURT SERVICE
Nominated: March 13, 1882
Nominated By: Chester A. Arthur
Confirmed: March 27, 1882
Confirmation Vote: Voice vote
Oath Taken: April 3, 1882
Replaced: Ward Hunt
Significant Opinions: *Chicago, Milwaukee & St. Paul Railway Co. v. Minnesota* (1890); *Counselman v. Hitchcock* (1892); *Budd v. New York* (1892)
Left Court: Died July 7, 1893
Length of Service: 11 years, 3 months, 4 days
Replacement: Edward Douglass White

President Arthur first attempted to fill Justice Hunt's seat with New York political boss Roscoe Conkling, whom he nominated on February 24, 1882. Conkling was confirmed by a vote of 39 to 12 on March 2, 1882, but ultimately he declined the appointment, as did Arthur's second choice for the position, Vermont Senator George F. Edmunds.

Samuel Blatchford was Arthur's third, and finally successful, candidate for the position.

The son of a prominent New York lawyer and politician, Samuel Blatchford was something of a prodigy, entering Columbia College at the age of 13 and graduating at the head of his class four years later. He prepared for the bar while acting as private secretary to his father's good friend, New York Governor William H. Seward. After being admitted to the bar, Blatchford practiced with his father for three years, then joined Seward's law firm before setting up his own practice in New York City in 1854.

In 1885 Blatchford declined a seat on the state supreme court, preferring to devote himself to his growing practice, which consisted mainly of *admiralty and international cases. At the same time, he began publishing a series of legal reports memorializing important cases tried in various New York federal courts. These reports doubtless helped recommend him as a candidate for a federal judgeship, and in 1867 President Johnson appointed him to the bench of the U.S. District Court for Southern District of New York. Five years later President Hayes elevated him to the federal Second Circuit Court where, in addition to utilizing his expertise in admiralty law, he developed a specialty in patent law.

For the first eight years after President Arthur appointed him to the Supreme Court, Blatchford continued to work pretty much as he had on the lower federal benches. He enhanced his areas of expertise, rarely dissented, and was not assigned to write many opinions on constitutional law. During this period, he developed a position as a centrist on the Court, a position that was to change dramatically during his last two years as a Supreme Court justice.

During the 1890s, the Court turned the *Due Process Clause of the Fourteenth Amendment into a means of judicially evaluating state regulation, a process Blatchford fostered with his opinions in Chicago, Milwaukee & St. Paul Railway Co. v. Minnesota (1890) and Budd v. New York (1892). Unfortunately, these two opinions — the first striking down state regulation of business

and the second upholding it — are contradictory, resting on procedural details that would seem to make no constitutional difference. Like other justices of the day, Blatchford apparently was employing his judicial skills to achieve desired social ends. In his case, however, the effort was especially strained, and the seeming irreconcilability of Chicago, Milwaukee and Budd has detracted from his reputation.

LUCIUS QUINTUS CINCINNATUS LAMAR

PERSONAL DATA
Born: September 17, 1825, in Eatonton, Georgia
Parents: Lucius Quintus Cincinnatus Lamar, Sarah Bird Lamar
Higher Education: Emory College, now Emory University (B.A., 1845)
Bar Admission: Georgia, 1847
Political Party: Democrat
Marriages: July 15, 1847, to Virginia Longstreet, who bore Lamar one son and three daughters and who died in 1884; January 5, 1887, to Henrietta Dean Holt
Died: January 23, 1893, in Vineville, Georgia
Buried: Riverside Cemetery, Macon, Georgia; an alternative claim is made for St. Peter's Cemetery, Oxford, Mississippi

PROFESSIONAL CAREER
Occupations: Lawyer, 1847-1857, 1863-1873; Educator, 1849-1853, 1866-1870; Politician, 1853, 1857-1860, 1873-1888; Serviceman, 1861-1865; Diplomat, 1862-1863; Judge, 1888-1893
Official Positions: Professor, University of Mississippi, 1849-1853, 1866-1870; Member, Georgia House of Representatives, 1853; Member, United States House of Representatives, 1857-1860, 1873-1877; Confederate Commissioner to Russia, 1862-1863; Colonel and Advocate General, Confederate Army, 1863-1865; Member, United States Senate, 1877-1885; United States Secretary of the Interior, 1885-1888; Associate Justice, United States Supreme Court, 1888-1893

SUPREME COURT SERVICE
Nomination: December 6, 1887

Nominated By: Grover Cleveland
Confirmed: January 16, 1888
Confirmation Vote: 32-28
Oath Taken: January 18, 1888
Replaced: William B. Woods
Significant Opinion: *Kidd v. Pearson* (1888)
Left Office: Died January 23, 1893
Length of Service: 5 years, 5 days
Replacement: Howell E. Jackson

Lucius Q. C. Lamar, a descendant of French Huguenots, was born into the southern landed aristocracy, to which he always retained a clear allegiance. His father, who committed suicide when Lamar was nine years old, was a plantation owner and Georgia circuit judge. Other relatives were, like Lamar, members of the federal Supreme Court. His cousin, John A. Campbell, who sat on the High Court from 1853 to 1861, was the last southerner appointed to the Court before Lamar, and in 1911 another relative, Joseph Rucker Lamar, became an associate justice of the Supreme Court.

Lamar, whose lifelong bouts of apoplexy may have reflected the trauma occasioned by his father's death, formed his strongest emotional bond with Reverend Augustus B. Longstreet, Lamar's father-in-law and later the president of the University of Mississippi in Oxford. Lamar followed Longstreet there in 1849 to take up a position teaching mathematics. In 1860 the university elected him to the position of professor of ethics, although politics and the Civil War intervened, preventing Lamar from assuming the post until 1866. The next year he was elected to a legal professorship, during which he pioneered the case method, which remains the standard approach to legal education.

Throughout much of his academic and early political career, Lamar kept up a successful legal practice. In the years leading up to and including the Civil War, however, he was too engaged in engineering and defending secession to pursue a private career. Elected to Congress in 1857, he resigned before his term expired, taking up the *states' rights banner and drafting the Ordinance of Secession at the Mississippi Secession

Convention of 1861. During the Civil War, he served first as a Confederate officer, then as a Confederate diplomat, and finally, as an aide to Jefferson Davis and Robert E. Lee.

After Appomattox, however, Lamar became one of the leading southern statesmen favoring national reconciliation. His reinstatement in national politics commenced with reelection to the federal Congress and was cemented by his delivery of a eulogy for Massachusetts Unionist Charles Sumner so stirring that Lamar became known as the "Great Pacificator." Lamar went on to serve in all three branches of the government, becoming first a senator, then President Cleveland's secretary of the Interior, and finally a Supreme Court justice.

To be sure, Lamar's path to the High Court was not without controversy. The Senate Judiciary Committee, controlled by Republicans, voted against him, citing lack of legal experience and advanced age. Finally, however, he was narrowly confirmed at the age of 62, making him at the time the second oldest individual (after Ward Hunt) to assume the Supreme Court bench. On the Court he customarily voted with the majority, but he was generally assigned relatively inconsequential cases. In 1892 his health began to deteriorate, and he would write only two more opinions before his death in 1893.

SIGNIFICANT CASES

MINOR V. HAPPERSETT

Citation: 21 Wall. (88 U.S.) 162 (1875)
Argued: February 9, 1875
Decided: March 9, 1875
Court Below: Missouri Supreme Court
Basis for Review: *Writ of error
Facts: Virginia Louise Minor, an adherent of the feminist cause, was denied the right to vote, a judgment upheld by the supreme court of her state.
Issue: Can a state constitutionally prohibit a woman from voting?
Outcome: Finding that the right to vote is not among the *privileges and immunities guaranteed citizens by the Fourteenth Amendment, the

Waite Court affirmed the lower court's ruling.
Participating: Waite, Clifford, Swayne, Miller, Davis, Field, Strong, Bradley, Hunt
Vote: 9-0
Opinion: Waite for the Court
Significance: In addition to being a reflection of the paternalistic attitude towards women prevalent at the time, *Minor* is a near-contemporary interpretation of the *original intent behind the Fourteenth Amendment. The definition of citizenship in that amendment, the Waite Court declared, "convey[s] the idea of membership in a nation, nothing more." The right to vote, the justices decided, is not among the privileges and immunities granted by the Fourteenth Amendment. *Minor* was effectively overruled by *Reynolds v. Sims* (1964) and *Harper v. Virginia State Board of Elections* (1966).

UNITED STATES V. REESE

Citation: 92 U.S. 214 (1876)
Argued: January 13-14, 1875
Decided: March 27, 1876
Court Below: United States Circuit Court for the District of Kentucky
Basis for Review: *Writ of error
Facts: A Kentucky election official, Hiram Reese, had refused to register an African American voter for a municipal election. Because the two judges sitting in circuit court had different opinions in the matter, that of the presiding judge prevailed, sustaining a *demurrer to the official *indictment, with the result that Reese was released on bond.
Issue: Does the Fifteenth Amendment guarantee the right to vote?
Outcome: The Fifteenth Amendment does not give anyone the right to vote, reasoned the Waite Court; therefore, the lower court's ruling was affirmed.
Vote: 8-1
Participating: Waite, Clifford, Swayne, Miller, Davis, Field, Strong, Bradley, Hunt
Opinions: Waite for the Court; Clifford concurring; Hunt dissenting
Significance: The right to vote, reasoned the Waite Court, is granted under state, not federal laws. The function of the Fifteenth Amendment, the justices

found, was to provide the federal government with the power to prevent voters from being disenfranchised on racial grounds. Because of this highly technical reading of the Fifteenth Amendment (this was the Court's first voting rights case arising out of the amendment), southern states remained free for decades to prevent African Americans from voting by such means as literacy tests and other methods not strictly dependent on race.

UNITED STATES V. CRUIKSHANK

Citation: 92 U.S. 542 (1876)
Argued: March 30-31 & April 30, 1875
Decided: March 27, 1876
Court Below: United States Circuit Court for the District of Louisiana
Basis for Review: *Writ of error
Facts: An armed group of white individuals killed more than one hundred African Americans over a disputed Louisiana gubernatorial election.
Issue: Is interference with the right to vote a federal offense under the Enforcement Act of 1870, intended to *enable enforcement of the Civil Rights amendments?
Outcome: Because the *indictments against the accused offenders did not allege that their actions were motivated by race, the indictments were dismissed.
Vote: 9-0
Participating: Waite, Clifford, Swayne, Miller, Davis, Field, Strong, Bradley, Hunt
Opinions: Waite for the Court; Clifford concurring
Significance: By concluding that responsibility for punishing the offenders in *Cruikshank* lay with the state, rather than the federal government, the Court deliberately retreated from the tenets of Reconstruction and inadvertently encouraged violence against African Americans in the South.

MUNN V. ILLINOIS

Citation: 94 U.S. 113 (1877)
Argued: January 14 & 18, 1876
Decided: March 1, 1877
Court Below: Illinois Supreme Court
Basis for Review: *Writ of error
Facts: In 1875 the Illinois legislature passed a bill

setting rates that grain elevator operators could charge their customers in Chicago. On the basis of the 1873 *Slaughterhouse Cases*, the Illinois Supreme Court upheld the legislation as constitutional.

Issue: Is regulation of business by a state a permissible exercise of its *police power?

Outcome: The Supreme Court affirmed the finding of the lower court that the Illinois statute was constitutional because it gave the state control over property dedicated to the public interest.

Vote: 7-2

Participating: Waite, Clifford, Swayne, Miller, Davis, Field, Strong, Bradley, Hunt

Opinions: Waite for the Court; Field, joined by Strong, dissenting

Significance: In this, the most important of the so-called *Granger Cases*, the Waite Court found that state legislation meant to regulate business "in which the public has an interest," neither infringes Congress's *commerce power nor violates the *Due Process Clause of the Fourteenth Amendment, intended to prevent the state from depriving persons of their property without due process of law. Furthermore, Waite's opinion stated, while it is the judiciary's role to determine the legitimacy of such exercises of state *police powers, if the state was acting properly, "the people must resort to the polls, not the courts." Justice Field's dissent from this view was as important as the majority's opinion. Field, arguing that the Constitution protects certain rights from all legislative interference, introduced a legal theory that would come to be known as *substantive due process. In addition, his farsighted opinion predicted the more activist role the judiciary would assume in adjudicating policy questions concerning the economy.

HALL V. DECUIR

Citation: 95 U.S. 485 (1878)

Argued: April 17, 1877

Decided: January 14, 1878

Court Below: Louisiana Supreme Court

Basis for Review: *Writ of error

Facts: Owing to a state statute, the Louisiana Supreme Court awarded damages to an African American woman, Josephine DeCuir, who had not been permitted to enter a stateroom during a voyage from New Orleans to Hermitage, Louisiana, on a vessel that also traveled between Louisiana and Mississippi.

Issue: Is regulation of public conveyances engaged in interstate commerce within the purview of the states?

Outcome: Arguing that the Louisiana anti-discrimination statute impermissibly burdened interstate commerce, the Waite Court overturned the lower court ruling.

Vote: 8-0

Participating: Waite, Clifford, Swayne, Miller, Field, Strong, Bradley, Hunt

Opinions: Waite for the Court; Clifford concurring

Significance: Because the steamship that carried DeCuir from one point in Louisiana to another also crossed state lines, the Waite Court was able to argue that the statute interfered with Congress's power to regulate interstate commerce by requiring such carriers to provide integrated facilities. Justice Clifford's concurring opinion made it clear that the Court's underlying concern was preserving segregationist custom by introducing a doctrine that would later become known as "separate but equal." The speciousness of the majority's reasoning was revealed a few years later in *Louisville, New Orleans & Texas Railway Co. v. Mississippi* (1890), in which the Supreme Court upheld state legislation requiring segregation in interstate commerce.

REYNOLDS V. UNITED STATES

Citation: 98 U.S. 145 (1879)

Argued: November 14-15, 1878

Decided: May 5, 1879

Court Below: Supreme Court of the Territory of Utah

Basis for Review: *Writ of error

Facts: George Reynolds, secretary to Mormon Church leader Brigham Young, was the *appellant in this *test case brought in an attempt to invalidate a federal antibigamy statute that was part of President Grant's campaign to stamp out Mormon polygamy. Reynolds's conviction by the territorial district court was upheld by the Utah

Territorial Supreme Court.

Issue: Is polygamy a religious practice protected by the First Amendment?

Outcome: Finding polygamy a punishable criminal offense, the Waite Court upheld the statute and the conviction.

Vote: 9-0

Participating: Waite, Clifford, Swayne, Miller, Field, Strong, Bradley, Hunt, Harlan

Opinion: Waite for the Court; Field concurring

Significance: Although stating that "a wall of separation between church and state" exists, Waite's opinion looked beyond the language of the First Amendment to *original intent to find that religious practices not in accord with the public interest cannot be protected. While a person cannot be punished for religious beliefs, he or she is accountable for illegal actions. With the development of this "belief-action" doctrine in *Reynolds*, the Supreme Court foreclosed the possibility of constitutionally mandated exceptions to unlawful activity.

STRAUDER V. WEST VIRGINIA

Citation: 100 U.S. 303 (1880)

Argued: October 21, 1879

Decided: March 1, 1880

Court Below: West Virginia Supreme Court

Basis for Review: *Writ of error

Facts: A West Virginia statute limited jury service in state courts to white males. An African American man, Taylor Strauder, who was being tried in West Virginia state court, petitioned for *removal of his case on grounds that he would not receive a fair trial because of the statute, but his petition was denied, and he was tried and convicted. His conviction was upheld by the state supreme court.

Issue: Does the West Virginia statute violate the *Equal Protection Clause of the Fourteenth Amendment?

Outcome: Because of the express language of the West Virginia statute, the Supreme Court struck it down, reversing the judgment below.

Vote: 6-2

Participating: Waite, Clifford, Swayne, Miller, Field, Strong, Bradley, Harlan (Hunt

not participating)

Opinions: Strong for the Court; Field, joined by Clifford, dissenting

Significance: *Strauder* was one of four cases the Supreme Court decided in 1880 that involved exclusion of African Americans from juries. In two other cases, which were less straightforward, the Court held that all deliberate exclusion of African Americans from jury duty, whether statutorily mandated or not, was prohibited. However, in the fourth, *Virginia v. Rives*, the Court undermined any potential benefit to African Americans by finding that their mere absence from juries was not in itself a violation of the Fourteenth Amendment. Southern courts took advantage of the loophole thus created until the Supreme Court found, in *Taylor v. Louisiana* (1975), that the Sixth Amendment's guarantee of an impartial jury protects the right to jury service.

*EX PARTE SIEBOLD

Citation: 100 U.S. 371 (1880)

Argued: October 24, 1879

Decided: March 8, 1880

Court Below: United States Circuit Court for the District of Maryland

Basis for Review: *Writ of error

Facts: Albert Siebold, a Baltimore election official, was convicted of stuffing ballot boxes in a federal congressional election under the federal Enforcement Acts of 1870-1871, which made it a criminal offense for state officials to neglect their duties in state or federal elections.

Issue: Does the federal government have the power to enforce federal legislation governing federal elections against state authorities?

Outcome: Upholding Siebold's conviction, the Waite Court stated that a violation of mixed state and federal duties can be punished under federal law.

Vote: 6-2

Participating: Waite, Clifford, Swayne, Miller, Field, Strong, Bradley, Harlan (Hunt not participating)

Opinions: Bradley for the Court; Field, joined by Clifford, dissenting

Significance: Although *Siebold* might have constituted an advance for the Civil War amendments, the Court limited the decision's effect by making its holding applicable only to federal congressional elections and exempting state and local elections from federal power.

STONE V. MISSISSIPPI

Citation: 101 U.S. 814 (1880)
Argued: March 4-5, 1880
Decided: May 10, 1880
Court Below: Mississippi Supreme Court
Basis for Review: *Writ of error
Facts: In 1867 the provisional Reconstruction government of Mississippi granted a corporation, with which John B. Stone was associated, a charter to conduct lotteries for the next 25 years. In 1868, however, Mississippi adopted a new constitution outlawing lotteries. Stone ignored the new constitution, and when the state attorney general obtained an order prohibiting him from continuing his lottery activities, the Mississippi Supreme Court upheld it.
Issue: Does the *Contracts Clause apply equally to public and private contracts?
Outcome: Arguing that the state cannot bargain away its inalienable *police powers, the Waite Court affirmed the lower court's ruling.
Vote: 8-0
Participating: Waite, Clifford, Swayne, Miller, Field, Strong, Bradley, Harlan (Hunt not participating)
Opinion: Waite for the Court
Significance: Cases heard by the Marshall Court resulted in both public and private contracts being declared protected by the constitutional ban against state impairment of contracts. The Waite Court declined to overrule this blanket application, but it narrowed the rule by stating that lotteries — a license rather than a contract granted by the state — could be prohibited as a threat to public morality.

KILBOURN V. THOMPSON

Citation: 103 U.S. 168 (1881)
Argued: January 13-14, 1880

Decided: January 24, 1881
Court Below: District of Columbia Supreme Court
Basis for Review: *Writ of error
Facts: In 1876 the House of Representatives appointed a committee to investigate a real estate company. When Hallett Kilbourn refused to appear before the committee, he was jailed. Kilbourn subsequently sought a writ of *habeas corpus from the District of Columbia Supreme Court, which decided in favor of the committee and John Thompson, the sergeant at arms who had imprisoned Kilbourn for *contempt of Congress.
Issue: What are the limits of congressional investigations?
Outcome: Because the order jailing Kilbourn was issued in pursuit of an unconstitutional goal (Congress can conduct investigations only with regard to future legislation), the lower court's ruling was reversed.
Vote: 7-0
Participating: Waite, Swayne, Miller, Field, Bradley, Harlan, Woods (Clifford and Hunt not participating)
Opinion: Miller for the Court
Significance: This was the first time the Supreme Court exercised its power to review the propriety of congressional investigations. Because the Waite Court viewed the subject of the investigation at issue as a judicial, not a legislative matter, it found that Congress had overreached its authority. Subsequently, the Supreme Court would modify the holding in *Kilbourn* to permit some congressional investigation into the affairs of private citizens, but the basic limitations spelled out in the case remain.

CIVIL RIGHTS CASES (*UNITED STATES V. STANLEY; UNITED STATES V. RYAN; UNITED STATES V. NICHOLS; UNITED STATES V. SINGLETON; ROBINSON V. MEMPHIS & CHARLESTON RAILROAD CO.*)

Citation: 109 U.S. 3 (1883)
Argued: March 29, 1883
Decided: October 15, 1883
Court Below: *Stanley*, United States Circuit Court for the District of Kansas; *Ryan*, United

States Circuit Court for the District of California; *Nichols*, United States Circuit Court for the Western District of Missouri; *Singleton*, United States Circuit Court for the Southern District of New York; *Robinson*, United States Circuit Court for the Western District of Tennessee

Basis for Review: *Stanley*, *Certificate of division of opinion; *Ryan*, *Writ of error; *Nichols*, Certificate of division of opinion; *Singleton*, Certificate of division of opinion; *Robinson*, Writ of error

Facts: All five cases, grouped together for decision, concerned instances of discrimination directed against African Americans by private persons.

Issue: Do the Thirteenth and Fourteenth Amendments, together with the *enabling Civil Rights Act of 1875, give federal government the power to protect African Americans from private, as well as state-sponsored discrimination?

Outcome: The Waite Court majority held that the Fourteenth Amendment prohibits only civil rights violations by states. Furthermore, it said that the Thirteenth Amendment, which merely abolished slavery, does not give Congress power to pass legislation like the 1875 Civil Rights Act, which attempted to bar discrimination against African Americans in public accommodations.

Vote: 8-1

Participating: Waite, Miller, Field, Bradley, Harlan, Woods, Matthews, Gray, Blatchford

Opinions: Bradley for the Court; Harlan dissenting

Significance: The *Civil Rights Cases* set back by generations attempts to combat racial discrimination. By essentially stripping the Civil War amendments of their *original intent, the Waite Court abrogated federal responsibility for policing civil rights to the states, with disastrous results. It was not until Congress passed the 1964 Civil Rights Act that discriminatory acts of private persons in the area of public accommodations were outlawed at the federal level. The 1964 statute's public accommodations provision perhaps owed something to Justice Bradley's majority opinion, which expressly did not rule on the applicability of the *Commerce Clause to congressional legislation in this area. The 1964 act, however, owed more to the spirit of Justice

Harlan's dissent. Harlan, declaring the majority's decision "narrow and artificial," proclaimed that the reach of the Thirteenth Amendment extended to prohibit all "badges of slavery."

*EX PARTE CROW DOG

Citation: 109 U.S. 556 (1883)
Argued: November 20, 1883
Decided: December 17, 1883
Court Below: United States District Court for the Dakota Territory
Basis for Review: Petition for writs of *habeas corpus and *certiorari
Facts: Crow Dog, a Sioux, was tried and convicted in federal territorial court for the murder of another Sioux on Sioux land.
Issue: Do United States courts have *jurisdiction over federal crimes committed by Indians on tribal lands?
Outcome: Ruling that tribal *sovereignty includes exclusive jurisdiction over crimes committed by tribal members — notwithstanding language to the contrary in the Sioux Treaty of 1868 — the Waite Court granted Crow Dog's petition.
Vote: 9-0
Participating: Waite, Miller, Field, Bradley, Harlan, Woods, Matthews, Gray, Blatchford
Opinion: Matthews for the Court
Significance: *Crow Dog* added strength to the late 19th century movement to assimilate the Indian tribes into white society. As a direct result of this case, in 1885 Congress passed a provision making it a federal crime for one Indian to kill another on tribal lands. Despite this legislation, however, *Crow Dog* remains important in its assertion that federal law does not *preempt tribal law unless Congress explicitly indicates so, or the tribe surrenders its authority over a given subject matter.

*EX PARTE YARBROUGH

Citation: 110 U.S. 651 (1884)
Argued: January 23-24, 1884
Decided: March 3, 1884
Court Below: United States Circuit Court for the Northern District of Georgia
Basis for Review: *Writ of certiorari

Facts: Jasper Yarbrough and a band of Ku Klux Klan members were convicted of having beaten and injured an African American man named Barry Saunders in order to prevent him from voting in a federal congressional election.

Issue: Does the federal government have the power to punish interference with exercise of the voting franchise?

Outcome: Stating that sometimes the Fifteenth Amendment, in addition to granting the right to vote, also confers the right to be free of discrimination when voting, the Court upheld Yarbrough's conviction.

Vote: 9-0

Participating: Waite, Miller, Field, Bradley, Harlan, Woods, Matthews, Gray, Blatchford

Opinion: Miller for the Court

Significance: *Yarbrough* marked the single occasion during Reconstruction and the period immediately following it when the Supreme Court upheld the federal government's authority to punish a violation of an individual's voting rights — apparently the violation was simply too egregious to overlook. In a similar case, *James v. Bowman* (1903), however, the Court was able to ignore *Yarbrough*, declaring that the federal government had no power to control private behavior in this area.

HURTADO V. CALIFORNIA

Citation: 110 U.S. 516 (1884)

Argued: January 22-23, 1884

Decided: March 3, 1884

Court Below: California Supreme Court

Basis for Review: *Writ of error

Facts: Based on information supplied by the district attorney, Hurtado was tried and convicted for murder in state court. Hurtado appealed, claiming that the provision in the California constitution permitting prosecution of *felonies on the basis of information given before a *magistrate and without *indictment violated his right to *due process.

Issue: Does the Due Process Clause of the Fourteenth Amendment incorporate the Fifth Amendment's guarantee that a *grand jury indictment will be obtained before the government

prosecutes federal *capital cases, thus making this requirement binding upon the states?

Outcome: Arguing that states are not required to observe any particular procedure in such cases, so long as they observe fundamental principles of justice, the Supreme Court upheld Hurtado's conviction.

Vote: 8-1

Participating: Waite, Miller, Field, Bradley, Harlan, Woods, Matthews, Gray, Blatchford

Opinions: Matthews for the Court; Harlan dissenting

Significance: *Hurtado* provides an exception to the *incorporation doctrine which states that most, but not all of the guarantees embodied in the Bill of Rights are incorporated in the Due Process Clause of the Fourteenth Amendment, thus limiting state and local governments as well as the federal government.

HEAD MONEY CASES (*EDYE V. ROBERTSON; CUNARD STEAM-SHIP CO. V. ROBERTSON*)

Citation: 112 U.S. 580 (1884)

Argued: November 19-20, 1884

Decided: December 8, 1884

Courts Below: *Edye*, United States Circuit Court for the Eastern District of New York; *Cunard*, United States Circuit Court for the Southern District of New York

Basis for Review: *Writs of error

Facts: Before passage of the federal Immigration Act of 1882, individual states regulated entry of immigrants. Concern about the costs associated with supporting immigrants led states to impose head taxes, which were in turn struck down in such decisions as that in the *Passenger Cases* (1849) as an impermissible infringement on congressional *commerce power. The 1882 act imposed a head tax of fifty cents on each immigrant; the proceeds were then distributed to the states for aid to needy immigrants. Shippers challenged the constitutionality of the federal head tax.

Issue: Does the tax imposed by the Immigration Act of 1882 violate the constitutional requirement that all *indirect taxes be applied uniformly throughout the states?

Outcome: Because the head tax was found to be a "mere incident of the regulation of commerce" and not an application of Congress's *taxing power, it was upheld.
Vote: 9-0
Participating: Waite, Miller, Field, Bradley, Harlan, Woods, Matthews, Gray, Blatchford
Opinion: Miller for the Court
Significance: The *Head Money Cases* helped Congress assume greater control over immigration. They also broadened the conception of the taxing power to facilitate execution of other constitutionally imposed powers and responsibilities.

PRESSER V. ILLINOIS

Citation: 116 U.S. 252 (1886)
Argued: November 23-24, 1885
Decided: January 4, 1886
Court Below: Illinois Supreme Court
Basis for Review: *Writ of error
Facts: Herman Presser was convicted of leading armed members of a fraternal organization in a parade in violation of an Illinois statute restricting parading with arms to organized militia.
Issue: Does the Illinois statute violate the Second Amendment's guarantee of the right to keep and bear arms?
Outcome: Reasoning that the Second Amendment only applies to the federal government, the Waite Court upheld Presser's conviction.
Vote: 9-0
Participating: Waite, Miller, Field, Bradley, Harlan, Woods, Matthews, Gray, Blatchford
Opinion: Woods for the Court
Significance: *Presser* is as significant for what it says about the Fourteenth Amendment as about the Second, reflecting the Supreme Court's initial rejection of the use of the former as a means of applying the Bill of Rights to the states. The use of *Presser* as *precedent is questionable, since in modern times most provisions of the Bill of Rights have been applied to the states and few Second Amendment cases have been tried.

BOYD V. UNITED STATES

Citation: 116 U.S. 616 (1886)
Argued: December 11 & 14, 1885

Decided: February 1, 1886
Court Below: United States Circuit Court for the Southern District of New York
Basis for Review: *Writ of error
Facts: The partners of E.A. Boyd & Sons were accused of importing plate glass without paying the duty required under an 1874 customs act. Despite the fact that theirs was a civil proceeding, the United States attorney was able, pursuant to a provision of the act, to obtain a court order for the partners to produce their invoices. They contended that the order violated their Fourth Amendment protection against unreasonable search and seizure, but the circuit court affirmed the partners' convictions for violating the act.
Issue: Does the compelled production of private papers violate the Fourth Amendment prohibition against unreasonable search and seizure, as well as Fifth Amendment protections against self-incrimination?
Outcome: Holding that the act violated both amendments, the Waite Court struck down the lower court's ruling.
Vote: 9-0
Participating: Waite, Miller, Field, Bradley, Harlan, Woods, Matthews, Gray, Blatchford
Opinions: Bradley for the Court; Miller concurring
Significance: *Boyd,* as the first case to appraise the relationship between the Fourth and Fifth Amendments in the context of governmental intrusions into individuals' lives, is a landmark in the line of cases that developed a constitutional right to privacy.

YICK WO V. HOPKINS

Citation: 118 U.S. 356 (1886)
Argued: April 14, 1886
Decided: May 10, 1886
Court Below: California Supreme Court
Basis for Review: *Writ of error
Facts: Yick Wo, a Chinese immigrant who had operated a laundry in San Francisco for 22 years, violated a local ordinance that granted licenses for such businesses in a clearly discriminatory manner. In 1885 the city Board of Supervisors — which had certified Yick Wo's business only the

year before — granted a license to only one Chinese laundry. Yick Wo continued to operate without a license, and he was arrested, found guilty, and fined ten dollars. When he refused to pay the fine, he was jailed and petitioned the California Supreme Court for a writ of *habeas corpus, which was denied.

Issue: Does the San Francisco ordinance violate the Fourteenth Amendment because of the discriminatory results of its implementation?

Outcome: Finding that the ordinance as written depended upon an inordinately broad reading of local *police power used to regulate property, the Waite Court struck down the lower court's ruling.

Vote: 9-0

Participating: Waite, Miller, Field, Bradley, Harlan, Woods, Matthews, Gray, Blatchford

Opinion: Matthews for the Court

Significance: In holding that the Fourteenth Amendment applies to all persons, both citizens and *aliens, Justice Matthews's opinion greatly expanded the amendment's meaning. The *Due Process Clause could now be applied to local, as well as state actions found to be discriminatory. The value of *Yick Wo* as *precedent, however, would not be realized until the Civil Rights movement began in the1950s.

SANTA CLARA COUNTY V. SOUTHERN PACIFIC RAILROAD CO.

Citation: 118 U.S. 394 (1886)

Argued: January 26-29, 1886

Decided: May 10, 1886

Court Below: United States Circuit Court for the District of California

Basis for Review: *Writ of error

Facts: The state of California and several of its counties were attempting to collect taxes from the railroad. The railroad claimed it was exempt from such taxation, and the lower court found in its favor.

Issue: Are such taxes barred by the *Due Process Clause of the Fourteenth Amendment?

Outcome: Narrowly ruling that the taxing statute at issue was invalid because it did not discriminate between different types of property, the Waite Court upheld the California court.

Vote: 9-0

Participating: Waite, Miller, Field, Bradley, Harlan, Woods, Matthews, Gray, Blatchford

Opinions: Harlan for the Court

Significance: *Santa Clara County* is significant not so much for its ruling as for a preliminary statement made by the Chief Justice: "The Court does not wish to hear argument on the question whether the provision in the Fourteenth Amendment to the Constitution, which forbids a State to deny any person within its jurisdiction the equal protection of the laws, applies to these Corporations. We are all of opinion that it does." Thus was resolved the long debate concerning the constitutional status of corporations as "persons." Henceforth, corporations were able to invoke the *Equal Protection and Due Process Clauses with assurance.

WABASH, ST. LOUIS & PACIFIC RAILWAY CO. V. ILLINOIS

Citation: 118 U.S. 557 (1886)

Argued: April 14-15, 1886

Decided: October 25, 1886

Court Below: Illinois Supreme Court

Basis for Review: *Writ of error

Facts: An Illinois statute outlawing railroads from charging more for short than long hauls was upheld in state court.

Issue: Does such state regulation impermissibly burden interstate commerce?

Outcome: Finding that the *Commerce Clause permits "indirect" burdens on interstate commerce, but not such "direct" burdens as the statute imposes, the Waite Court reversed the lower court's ruling.

Vote: 6-3

Participating: Waite, Miller, Field, Bradley, Harlan, Woods, Matthews, Gray, Blatchford

Opinions: Miller for the Court; Bradley, joined by Waite and Gray, dissenting

Significance: Because railroad regulation had been almost exclusively the province of the states up to the time of *Wabash*, the decision created great problems for the federal government. As a direct result of this case, Congress established the Interstate Commerce Commission in 1887, ushering in the modern age of independent federal regulatory agencies. The "direct" versus "indirect" approach to federal and state regulation of commerce was abandoned during the 1930s in favor of a more case-specific approach that balanced one set of interests against the other.

MUGLER V. KANSAS

Citation: 123 U.S. 623 (1887)
Argued: October 11, 1887
Decided: December 5, 1887
Court Below: Kansas Supreme Court
Basis for Review: *Writ of error
Facts: Peter Mugler continued to manufacture beer after Kansas passed a new constitutional provision outlawing the manufacture or sale of intoxicating beverages without a license. For this offense, he was fined and incarcerated, and his brewery was seized by the state. The Kansas Supreme Court upheld his conviction.
Issue: Is the Kansas provision a valid expression of the state's *police powers?
Outcome: Finding the Kansas prohibitionary law permissible as part of the state's duty to protect public health and morality, the Waite Court affirmed the lower court's judgment.
Vote: 9-0
Participating: Waite, Miller, Field, Bradley, Harlan, Woods, Matthews, Gray, Blatchford
Opinions: Harlan for the Court; Field concurring
Significance: While Justice Field agreed with the majority's view that the Kansas law did not violate the *Equal Protection Clause, he argued that seizure of Mugler's brewery and prohibition of the sale of beer he manufactured for export outside the state ran afoul of *due process. The premises of this opinion were accepted after 1890, when the Supreme Court broadened its approach to property rights.

VOTING PATTERNS

As they had on the Chase Court, Justices Samuel F. Miller and Stephen J. Field formed the intellectual nexus of the Waite Court. Justice Waite was an admirable administrator, but an inexperienced jurist, and much of his best work was aided

by the efforts of Justice Joseph P. Bradley, another force on the high bench.

Chief Justice Waite is remembered, in part, as the man who stated once and for all that, for purposes of the Fourteenth Amendment, corporations are "persons." But if Waite is important for his pronouncement, it is Bradley and Field who elaborated on all that it implied. In what was the most significant of the cases decided by the Waite Court, *Munn v. Illinois* (1877), Waite's opinion upheld the right of states to regulate business. The sweeping language of *Munn* would later usher in the modern era of government regulation. At the time, however, Field's dissent, arguing for constitutional protection of certain inalienable rights — the most important of which, for Field, was the right to control property — proved to be more influential. Field's concept, now known as *substantive due process, would become the focus of both the Waite and Fuller Courts, in which conservative majorities employed protection of property — couched in such terms as freedom of contract — as a rationale for removing barriers to enterprise.

Another area in which the Waite Court adopted a conservative philosophy was civil rights. As a corollary of the Court's development of substantive due process out of the *Due Process Clause of the Fourteenth Amendment, the Civil War amendments were stripped of what had been the intent of at least some of those who framed them: to require state and local governments, as well as federal authorities, to honor the guarantees embodied in the Bill of Rights. In the 1883 *Civil Rights Cases*, the Court overturned certain provisions of the 1875 Civil Rights Act aimed at preventing discrimination in public accommodations on grounds that the Fourteenth Amendment addressed only *state action, not the private acts of businesses.

The *Civil Rights Cases* were decided 8 to 1 in favor of overturning the statute. In this, as in other civil rights matters that came before the Waite and Fuller Courts, Justice John Marshall Harlan was often the lone dissenter. Before Harlan's arrival in 1877, the associate justices tended to follow Chief Justice Waite's lead in such cases as *Minor v. Happersett* (1875) (denying female suffrage) and

POLITICAL COMPOSITION
of the Waite Court

Justice & Total Term	Courts Served	Appointing President	Political Party
Morrison R. Waite 1874-1888	Waite	Grant	Republican
Nathan Clifford 1858-1881	Taney Chase Waite	Buchanan	Democrat
Noah H. Swayne 1862-1881	Taney Chase Waite	Lincoln	Republican
Samuel F. Miller 1862-1890	Taney Chase Waite Fuller	Lincoln	Republican
David Davis 1862-1877	Taney Chase Waite	Lincoln	Republican
Stephen J. Field 1863-1897	Taney Chase Waite Fuller	Lincoln	Democrat
William Strong 1870-1880	Chase Waite	Grant	Republican
Joseph P. Bradley 1870-1892	Chase Waite Fuller	Grant	Republican
Ward Hunt 1873-1882	Chase Waite	Grant	Republican
John Marshall Harlan 1877-1911	Waite Fuller White	Hayes	Republican
William B. Woods 1881-1887	Waite	Hayes	Republican
Stanley Matthews 1881-1889	Waite Fuller	Garfield	Republican
Horace Gray 1882-1902	Waite Fuller	Arthur	Republican
Samuel Blatchford 1882-1893	Waite Fuller	Arthur	Republican
Lucius Q. C. Lamar 1888-1893	Waite Fuller	Cleveland	Democrat

United States v. Cruikshank (1876) (finding that interference with the exercise of the franchise by African American voters is not a federal offense), both decided unanimously.

Almost entirely Republican in make up (the nonconformist Field, the all but invisible Clifford, and Lamar, who arrived just months before Waite's passing, were the only exceptions), the Waite Court tended to act in concert in handing down decisions that would foster American economic growth but inhibit the development of individual rights for generations to come.

SPECIAL FEATURES OF THE WAITE COURT

ALTERATIONS OF CUSTOMS

During the 14 years that Morrison Waite oversaw the Supreme Court, he helped to reestablish some of the status it had lost earlier owing to such mis-

steps as the Dred Scott (1857) decision and the overt political maneuverings that characterized the Chase Court. The Court also became more institutionalized during this period. Whereas previously the justices had tended to board together in Washington, D.C., while court was in session, improved transportation after the Civil War — together with the Judiciary Act of 1869, which established a separate *circuit court judiciary — lessened the burden of *circuit riding, enabling the justices to take up residence with their families in the nation's capital.

With the departure of reporter John William Wallace in 1874 (Justices Clifford and Swayne had complained about his editing), and the congressional appropriation that year of funds to publish the Court's opinions under government auspices, the tradition of naming reports after their editors ended. Although the Court continued to have official reporters, reports would henceforth appear under the designation "U.S."

The Fuller Court 1888-1910

BACKGROUND

THE REPUBLICAN INTERVAL AND THE RETURN OF GROVER CLEVELAND

The election of 1888 went to the Republicans, who for the first time since 1875 controlled both houses of Congress and — through their victorious presidential candidate, Benjamin Harrison — the White House. The following four years were essentially a fallow period in American politics, recalled primarily for passage of the Sherman Antitrust Act (which would be largely ignored for the next 20 years), the Sherman Silver Purchase Act (which was repealed three years later), and for the McKinley Tariff (which raised duties on imported goods to the unprecedented level of 49 percent).

This last bit of legislation provided Democrats with the ammunition they needed to secure a landslide victory in the 1890 congressional elections and to restore Grover Cleveland to the presidency in 1892. Decrying the McKinley Tariff as an egregious expression of governmental rapacity, Cleveland again promised reforms. Unfortunately, within two months of his inauguration, the country was plunged into one of the worst depressions it had ever known.

THE PANIC OF 1893

One of the few achievements of Cleveland's second term was maintenance of the gold standard. During the depression of the 1890s farm prices fell dramatically, prompting farmers to demand new forms of "cheap" money that would enable them to sell their crops at higher prices; the theory was that if more dollars were in circulation they would buy less, thus inflating the prices of commodities such as wheat. The country had from the first been theoretically on a bimetallic standard, with banks backing their paper money with either gold or silver. However, in 1873 Congress placed the United States on the gold standard alone, with greenbacks exchangeable for gold, dollar for dollar. After silver coins were taken out of circulation, discoveries of vast silver resources were made in the West, and farmers saw in the combination of lower demand for silver and increased supply a source of cheap money. If the country went back to the bimetallic standard, using the old ratio of 16 ounces of silver to one ounce of gold, the result would have been the inflation they desired.

The Sherman Silver Purchase Act of 1890 was a capitulation to the silver interests — an alliance of farmers and western silver miners — requiring the Treasury to purchase the estimated annual output of the nation's silver mines, paid for with greenbacks. But the Treasury did not have adequate gold reserves to back both its silver and its greenbacks. The resulting run on banks by currency holders anxious to exchange their silver and paper money for gold doubtless contributed to the depression that hit in the spring of 1893. One of Cleveland's first acts upon resuming office was to call Congress into special session to repeal the Silver Purchase Act.

Repeal of the act did not, however, stop the depression. In April of 1894 a band of 400 unemployed workers — led by Ohio businessman

MEMBERS *Of the Court* 1888–1910

(In Order of Seniority)

Melville W. Fuller (Chief Justice)	(1888-1910)
Samuel F. Miller (died)	(1888-1890)
Stephen J. Field (retired)	(1888-1897)
Joseph P. Bradley (died)	(1888-1892)
John Marshall Harlan	(1888-1910)
Stanley Matthews (died)	(1888-1889)
Horace Gray (died)	(1888-1902)
Samuel Blatchford (died)	(1888-1893)
Lucius Q.C. Lamar (died)	(1888-1893)
David J. Brewer (replaced Stanley Matthews)	(1890-1910)
Henry B. Brown (replaced Samuel F. Miller; retired)	(1891-1906)
George Shiras (replaced Joseph P. Bradley; retired)	(1892-1903)
Howell E. Jackson (replaced Lucius Q.C. Lamar; died)	(1893-1895)
Edward D. White (replaced Samuel Blatchford)	(1894-1910)
Rufus W. Peckham (replaced Howell E. Jackson; died)	(1896-1909)
Joseph McKenna (replaced Stephen J. Field)	(1898-1910)
Oliver Wendell Holmes Jr. (replaced Horace Gray)	(1902-1910)
William R. Day (replaced George Shiras)	(1903-1910)
William H. Moody (replaced Henry B. Brown)	(1906-1910)
Horace H. Lurton (replaced Rufus W. Peckham)	(1910-)

"General" Jacob Coxey and known as "Coxey's Army" — descended on Washington, D.C., demanding to be put to work on public projects financed by paper money. No sooner had they been dispersed than Cleveland was confronted with a strike in Chicago by the American Railway Union against the Pullman Palace Car Company, a manufacturer of railroad cars. On the theory that the strike was interfering with interstate commerce, Cleveland's attorney general, Richard Olney, obtained a court *injunction ordering the strikers back to work. When federal troops were sent to enforce the injunction, the strikers exploded into violence, overturning trains and setting railyards on fire. Afterward, the union leader, Eugene V. Debs, was arrested for disobeying a federal court order. He appealed his case all the way to the Supreme Court, contending that an injunction is an inappropriate device to employ against a labor strike. In *In re Debs (1895), the Court found for the government, and until Congress restricted its use 37 years later, the injunction became big business's primary weapon against organized labor.

Cleveland had indebted his administration to the banks and to big business in 1894 by requesting a loan from them to bail the government out of its silver crisis. For the duration of his second term, Cleveland would be disinclined to enforce any business regulation — including the rules of the Interstate Commerce Commission and the Sherman Antitrust Act. This alliance between government and business would prove to be his and his party's undoing.

POPULISM AND THE ELECTION OF 1896

A combination of rising social consciousness and increasing economic oppression led, in 1890, to the formation of the People's Party. Seeking "free silver" (the unlimited coinage of silver at the original ratio of sixteen ounces to one ounce of gold), a graduated income tax, and government ownership of the railroads, the Populists were the first third party to carry a state in a presidential election since the birth of the modern Republican Party in 1856. Initially, they appeared to make an even stronger showing in the 1896 presidential campaign, when Democratic candidate William Jennings Bryan endorsed almost every part of the Populist platform.

Bryan won the Democratic nomination after delivering a rousing speech in favor of free silver in which he proclaimed, "You shall not press down upon the brow of labor this crown of thorns; you shall not crucify mankind upon a cross of gold!" In the end, free silver was the only part of the Populist program that the Democrats adopted. Although Bryan carried the South and much of the Midwest, William McKinley won by a wide margin, ushering in a period of Republican rule (broken only by a brief Democratic revival from 1912 to1920) that was to last until the Great Depression of the 1930s.

MCKINLEY AND AMERICAN IMPERIALISM

Bryan and McKinley were matched again in 1900, and again McKinley won, aided in no small measure by his successful prosecution of one of the most popular military conflicts in the nation's history, the Spanish-American War. War was not officially declared until 1898, but for the previous decade the United States had been rebuilding its navy, primarily as an aid to expansion of overseas trade. The first real test of America's renewed military might came in the aftermath of revolution in Cuba in 1895.

Cuba was then a Spanish colony, but it was commercially dependent upon the United States for the millions of American dollars invested in Cuban sugar and tobacco. This vested interest led to a war of "yellow journalism," in which New York newspapers tried to outdo one another with lurid details of the alleged brutality with which the Spanish put down the Cuban revolt. Public pressure to intervene grew, and in January 1898 McKinley sent the battleship *Maine* on a "courtesy call" to Havana. The next month, the *Maine* exploded in Havana harbor, and although the explosion was probably an accident, it provided the occasion for a declaration of war. On August 12, 1898, 112 days after it began, the conflict was over, with Spain freeing Cuba and ceding control of Puerto Rico to the United States.

The opening engagement of the Spanish-American War, however, took place in another theater. On May 1, 1898, Commander Dewey, in charge of the U.S. Asiatic Squadron, opened fire on the Spanish fleet anchored in Manila Bay, destroying it completely. As a result, the final peace treaty ending the war also ceded two former Spanish colonies — the Philippines (for a payment of $20 million dollars) and Guam (which U.S. naval reinforcements had seized while crossing the Pacific to aid Dewey).

In the aftermath of the Spanish-American War, America annexed two other Pacific posts, Hawaii and Samoa, thus acquiring a series of stepping-stones to China and its vast market for trade. On September 6, 1899, Secretary of State John Hay sent a note to each of the world powers then maintaining a presence in China — Great Britain, France, Germany, Italy, Russia, and Japan — alerting them to America's interest in China and stating his country's desire for an "Open Door" policy permitting equality of commercial access. The next year, when a secret Chinese society known as the Boxers rose up against foreigners in China, American troops joined the international army that formed to protect the Europeans. Shortly thereafter, Secretary Hay sent the second of his Open Door letters, this time stating America's unequivocal right to free trade with China and its commitment to China's territorial and administrative integrity. This was an attempt to prevent the other foreign powers from carving China up into colonial spheres of influence.

American dominance of the Western Hemisphere was cemented in 1903, when President Theodore Roosevelt tacitly approved a Panamanian revolution against Colombia, which subsequently permitted the United States to go ahead with plans to build a canal through the Panamanian isthmus. Like the Philippines in the East, Panama became, in effect, an American protectorate and base for its military and commercial operations.

THEODORE ROOSEVELT AND PROGRESSIVISM

When President McKinley died on September 14, 1901, eight days after being shot by anarchist Leon F. Czolgosz, he was succeeded by his

Melville W. Fuller

vice president, Theodore Roosevelt. Roosevelt had distinguished himself in New York state politics and won a national following during the Spanish-American War for his military exploits as a Rough Rider. Always a maverick, Roosevelt was a deeply conservative man of patrician birth who nonetheless abhorred big business's conspicuous greed and exploitation of working people. As a New York politician he befriended reformers like Jacob Riis. Once in the White House, he energetically embraced many of the aims of the new Progressive ideology.

Progressivism was less an organized social movement than a middle class mentality that arose in reaction to the theories of *laissez faire economics and social Darwinism that had dominated government policy since Reconstruction. Unlike the Populists, Progressives did not seek radical reform of the political system, but rather sought to use government to improve the lives of all Americans. Much of the government intervention they pursued had to do with consumerism;

to that end they promoted, among other things, railroad regulation, pure food and drug laws, and antitrust legislation.

Progressives found an ally in President Roosevelt. Although the Sherman Antitrust Law of 1890 had lain dormant for many years, Roosevelt revived it by going after certain large-scale business combinations and winning major "trust-busting" victories in cases such as *Northern Securities Co. v. United States* (1904) and *Swift & Co. v. United States* (1905). Returned to office in 1904 by the largest popular majority granted any presidential candidate up to that time, Roosevelt pushed pure food and drug legislation through Congress and supported the 1906 Hepburn Act expanding the power of the Interstate Commerce Commission (ICC), which the Supreme Court had rendered all but powerless. After 1906 courts customarily followed the ICC's findings as to railroad rates, and the Hepburn Act became the foundation for railroad regulation in the new century.

PRESIDENT TAFT

Roosevelt declined to run for another term in 1908, instead handpicking William Howard Taft as the Republican nominee. Taft beat the seemingly perennial Democratic candidate, William Jennings Bryan, but he found it difficult to succeed the popular and ebullient Roosevelt. Like Roosevelt, Taft strengthened the Interstate Commerce Commission by urging passage in 1910 of the Mann-Elkins Act, which expanded the ICC's powers to include telephone and telegraph company regulation. He also was resolute in his trust-busting efforts, initiating 65 suits during his four years in office, as compared to the 44 suits prosecuted by Roosevelt during his eight-year tenure as chief executive. Unlike his predecessor, however, Taft failed to galvanize Republicans, instead alienating party progressives with his lukewarm support of tariff and congressional reform. In 1910 Democrats gained control of both houses of Congress, and Teddy Roosevelt returned from safari in Africa to lead a coalition of Republican insurgents in forming a new third political party, the Progressives.

JUDICIAL BIOGRAPHY
Melville Weston Fuller

PERSONAL DATA
Born: February 11, 1833, in Augusta, Maine
Parents: Frederick Augustus Fuller, Catherine Martin Weston Fuller
Higher Education: Bowdoin College (B.A., Phi Beta Kappa, 1853); Harvard Law School, 1854-1855
Bar Admissions: Maine, 1855; Illinois, 1856
Political Party: Democrat
Marriages: June 28, 1858, to Calista Ophelia Reynolds, who bore Fuller two daughters and who died in 1864; May 30, 1866, to Mary Ellen Coolbaugh, who bore Fuller five daughters and one son
Died: July 4, 1910, in Sorrento, Maine

Buried: Graceland Cemetery, Chicago, Illinois

PROFESSIONAL CAREER
Occupations: Lawyer, 1855-1888; Journalist, 1856, early 1880s; Politician, 1856, 1861-1864; Judge, 1888-1910; Diplomat, 1899, 1900-1910
Official Positions: President, Common Council of Augusta, Maine, 1856; City Solicitor, Augusta, 1856; Delegate, Illinois Constitutional Convention, 1861; Member, Illinois House of Representatives, 1863-1864; Chief Justice, United States Supreme Court, 1888-1910; Member, Venezuela-British Guiana Border Commission, 1899; Member, Permanent Court of Arbitration, The Hague, 1900-1910

SUPREME COURT SERVICE
Nominated: April 30, 1888
Nominated By: Grover Cleveland
Confirmed: July 20, 1888
Confirmation Vote: 41-20
Oath Taken: October 8, 1888
Replaced: Chief Justice Morrison R. Waite
Significant Opinions: *United States v. E.C. Knight Co.* (1895); *Pollock v. Farmers' Loan & Trust Co.* (1895); *Loewe v. Lawlor* (1908)
Left Court: Died July 4, 1910
Length of Service: 21 years, 8 months, 26 days
Replacement: Chief Justice Edward Douglass White

FULLER'S EARLY LIFE

Melville Fuller was born into a family of lawyers. At the time of his birth, his father was a lawyer in Augusta, Maine, and his uncle was a lawyer in Bangor, Maine. His paternal grandfather had served as a probate judge in Kennebec County, Maine, and his maternal grandfather sat as chief justice of the Supreme Court of Maine. When Fuller was only two months old, his mother divorced his father, taking her two sons with her to live with her father. When she remarried in 1844, Fuller stayed on with his grandfather.

After graduating from Bowdoin College in 1853, Fuller spent a year reading law with his uncle in Bangor, then attended Harvard Law School for six months, an experience which would later make him the first United States chief justice to have had significant academic legal training. After being admitted to the bar, he clerked briefly in his uncle's law office, but then left to become an editor with the *Augusta Age,* a Democratic newspaper. He entered local politics in 1856, but after a broken marital engagement, Fuller left Maine for the growing Midwestern metropolis of Chicago.

FULLER'S PUBLIC LIFE

Fuller's Chicago law practice grew slowly. As a means of alleviating this situation, Fuller threw himself into Democratic politics, becoming an ardent supporter of Stephen Douglas. He campaigned actively for Douglas in the 1858 Senate race against Abraham Lincoln and again in the 1860 presidential campaign. During the Civil War, Fuller did not see military service, devoting himself instead to becoming one of Illinois's leading Democratic voices. His open criticism of Lincoln's prosecution of the Civil War would later lead to charges that Fuller was a "copperhead" (a Northern Democrat opposed to the war). His views, however, were more a reflection of his dedication to principles of Jeffersonian democracy than an expression of antiwar sentiments. In 1863 he was elected a member of the state house of representatives — the last political office he would hold and the last public service position he would fill until he was nominated to serve on the Supreme Court.

Fuller, whose first wife died in 1864, married the daughter of the president of Chicago's largest bank two years later. His professional outlook improved dramatically when he began representing his father-in-law's bank and other business interests. His practice, which was devoted mainly to real estate and corporate law, led to numerous appearances before the United States Supreme Court.

FULLER AS CHIEF JUSTICE

Fuller, who had never held federal office or served on the bench, was decried by some members of the press as the most obscure man ever appointed chief justice. Although Fuller had proved himself a more than capable lawyer, his appointment to the High Court was largely a matter of luck. When Justice David Davis of Illinois resigned in 1877, he was replaced by John Marshall Harlan of Kentucky, leaving the Seventh *Circuit (Illinois, Indiana, and Wisconsin) unrepresented on the Court for the next 11 years. By this time, Illinois had become second only to New York as a source of Supreme Court litigation, and with a presidential election looming on the horizon, Grover Cleveland heeded advice to look to Illinois for a new chief justice to replace the recently deceased Morrison Waite.

Cleveland's first choice was Illinois Supreme Court Justice John Scholfield, who declined the offer. Cleveland next approached Fuller, to whom he had previously offered positions as chairman of the Civil Service Commission and solicitor general, only to be turned down. Fuller readily accepted this offer, but his confirmation process was far from easy. Republicans, sensing an opportunity for the appointment of one of their own after the upcoming election, stalled the confirmation process by pointing to Fuller's conduct during the Civil War. A pamphlet, titled *The War Record of Melville Fuller,* quickly appeared, accusing the nominee of copperhead leanings. Fuller's endorsement by Robert T. Lincoln, the late president's son, scotched that line of attack. Then others, fearful of Fuller's ties to big business, came forward to accuse the nominee of unethical dealings in legal matters. Such tactics resulted in a two-month delay, after which the nomination emerged from the Senate Judiciary Committee without recommendation. On July 20, 1888, however, Fuller was finally confirmed by a vote of 41 to 20.

Once on the Court, Fuller established himself as an able administrator, if not a brilliant justice. A diminutive person, he was surrounded by other justices who towered over him both physically and mentally. Samuel F. Miller, Stephen J. Field, Joseph P. Bradley, and John Marshall Harlan were all public figures of long standing who expressed strong opinions in memorable fashion. As this old guard changed, the ideological leadership passed to others: Justices David J. Brewer, Rufus W. Peckham and, perhaps most enduringly, Oliver Wendell Holmes Jr.

For his part, Fuller seems to have been comfortable with this state of affairs. Indeed, his most notable characteristic as a justice might be said to have been his steadfast endorsement of the status quo. Under his command, the Supreme Court reached the pinnacle of its conservatism, undermining the states' regulatory authority, enshrining the concept of *substantive due process while mainly ignoring the application of the Fourteenth Amendment to racial discrimination, and upholding freedom of contract at almost any expense. Fuller's own conservatism shows through clearly in the three most significant opinions he wrote for the Court: *United States v. E.C. Knight Co.* (1895), gutting the Sherman Antitrust Act's regulatory authority over business; *Pollock v. Farmers' Loan & Trust Co.* (1895), striking down a federal income tax; and *Loewe v. Lawlor* (1908), employing the Sherman Antitrust Act to defeat labor unions. In all, Fuller authored 840 opinions for the Court and only 30 dissents. He went on record as a dissenter in 150 cases, however, and the fact that many of these cases were among the most publicly visible the Fuller Court heard (for example, *In re Neagle* [1890]) tended to detract from Fuller's authority.

What Fuller lacked in legal stature, however, he more than made up for with his managerial abilities. He was, apparently, a master at leading Court conferences to compromise, and he was ever mindful of bureaucratic niceties, which made for efficient Court operation. While seemingly oblivious to the public uproar caused by the decisions of his Court, Fuller set great store by the dignity of his office, claiming precedence — after only the president and vice president — at all official Washington functions. Towards the end of Fuller's tenure as chief justice, President Cleveland offered him the position of secretary of state and President McKinley asked him to serve on the Spanish-American Peace Commission. Fuller declined both positions because he felt they would detract from the dignity and weight of his office. (He did, however, accept quasi-judicial appointments as an arbitrator for both the Venezuela-British Guiana Border Commission and the Permanent Court of Arbitration in the Hague.)

During Fuller's last years on the bench, the Supreme Court began to moderate its conservative stance. Although he remained in good health, Fuller's own output began to decrease. Newly elected President Theodore Roosevelt, eager to change the Court and to appoint his protege, William Howard Taft as chief justice, either manufactured or manipulated rumors of Fuller's decline. Fuller, however, refused to give in to attempts to force his resignation. He stayed on the job until his death from a sudden heart attack on July 4, 1910, at his summer home in Maine.

ASSOCIATE JUSTICES

For biographies of Associate Justices **Samuel F. Miller** and **Stephen J. Field,** see entries under **THE TANEY COURT.** For a biography of Associate Justice **Joseph P. Bradley,** see the entry under **THE CHASE COURT.** For biographies of Associate Justices **John Marshall Harlan, Stanley Matthews, Horace Gray, Samuel Blatchford,** and **Lucius Q.C. Lamar,** see entries under **THE WAITE COURT.**

DAVID JOSIAH BREWER

PERSONAL DATA
Born: January 20, 1837, in Smyrna, Asia Minor (now Izmir, Turkey)
Parents: Reverend Josiah Brewer, Emilia Field Brewer
Higher Education: Wesleyan University, 1852-1853; Yale University (B.A., with honors, 1856); Albany Law School (LL.B., 1858)
Bar Admissions: New York, 1858; Kansas, 1859
Political Party: Republican
Marriages: October 3, 1861, to Louise R. Landon, who bore Brewer four children and who died in 1898; June 5, 1901, to Emma Miner Mott
Died: March 28, 1910, in Washington, D.C.
Buried: Mount Muncie Cemetery, Leavenworth, Kansas

PROFESSIONAL CAREER
Occupations: Politician, 1859; Lawyer, 1859-1861, 1865-1870; Government Official, 1861-1862, 1865-1870; Judge, 1863-1864, 1870-1910; Diplomat, 1895
Official Positions: Member, School Board of Leavenworth, Kansas, 1859; Commissioner, United States Circuit Court in Leavenworth, 1861-1862; Judge, Leavenworth probate and criminal courts, 1863-1864; District Attorney for Kansas, 1865-1869; City Attorney, Leavenworth, 1869-1870; Associate Justice, Kansas Supreme Court, 1870-1884; Judge, United States Eighth Circuit, 1884-1889; Associate Justice, United States Supreme Court, 1890-1910; President, Venezuela-British Guiana Border Commission, 1895

SUPREME COURT SERVICE
Nominated: December 4, 1889
Nominated By: Benjamin Harrison

Confirmed: December 18, 1889
Confirmation Vote: 53-11
Oath Taken: January 6, 1890
Replaced: Stanley Matthews
Significant Opinions: *Louisville, New Orleans &
Texas Railway Co. v. Mississippi* (1890); **In re Debs*
(1895); *Muller v. Oregon* (1908)
Left Court: Died March 28, 1910
Length of Service: 20 years, 3 months, 10 days
Replacement: Charles E. Hughes

David J. Brewer was born in 1837 in Asia
Minor to the Reverend Josiah Brewer, a
Congregational missionary, and Emilia Field
Brewer, sister of Stephen J. Field, later a justice
of the Supreme Court. Brewer's family returned
the next year to Wethersfield, Connecticut, where
he was raised amidst privilege. After attending
Wesleyan for two years, he transferred to his
father's alma mater, Yale, from which he graduated
with honors in 1856. Brewer read law for a year
in the offices of his uncle David Dudley Field,
after which he attended Albany Law School. He
passed the New York bar in 1858, but the next
year he moved to Leavenworth, Kansas to begin
his professional life.

After working briefly as a notary public and
serving on the local school board, Brewer began
his legal career as an administrator for the United
States circuit court in Leavenworth. He then
served for a time at the local level, first as a probate and criminal court judge, then as a district
attorney and city attorney, before being elevated
to the state supreme court. As a Kansas Supreme
Court justice, Brewer exhibited the conservative
devotion to private property and *laissez faire
constitutionalism that would only grow more pronounced as he advanced in the court system.

President Chester A. Arthur made Brewer a
federal judge on the Eighth Circuit in 1884. He
was serving in that position in 1889 when the
death of Justice Stanley Matthews created a
vacancy on the Supreme Court. Judge Brewer
wrote to President Benjamin Harrison to recommend that it be filled by his friend Henry Billings
Brown, a Michigan district court judge. Brown
would be the next Supreme Court nominee, but

this time Harrison appointed Brewer himself.

Highly productive on the Court, Brewer is
today largely forgotten. In his day, however, he
was one of the pillars of the judicial conservatism
that characterized the Fuller Court. Forming an
ideological alliance first with his uncle, Stephen
J. Field, then with Rufus W. Peckham, Brewer
helped lead his brethren in formulating an
approach to the law that maximized judicial
authority while minimizing state interference
with the economy. He also carried his conservative philosophy to the public as a guest speaker,
a frequent contributor to law journals, and an
author of numerous law books.

Brewer was responsible for such opinions as
*Louisville, New Orleans & Texas Railway Co. v.
Mississippi* (1890), upholding segregated railway
accommodations, and *In re Debs* (1895), in which
the court *injunction found new use as a strike-
breaking tool. And yet, ironically perhaps, his
most lasting legacy to American law is his 1908
opinion in *Muller v. Oregon*, which upheld a
statute restricting the workweek of laundresses.
Brewer's reasoning may have grown out of his
biases about female physical inferiority, but it
established a major *precedent for future workplace litigation.

HENRY BILLINGS BROWN

PERSONAL DATA

Born: March 2, 1836, in South Lee, Massachusetts
Parents: Billings Brown, Mary Tyler Brown
Higher Education: Yale University (B.A., 1856);
Yale Law School, 1858-1859; Harvard Law School,
1859
Bar Admission: Michigan, 1860
Political Party: Republican
Marriages: July 1864 to Caroline Pitts, who died in
1901; June 25, 1904, to Josephine E. Tyler
Died: September 4, 1913, in Bronxville, New York
Buried: Elmwood Cemetery, Detroit, Michigan

PROFESSIONAL CAREER

Occupations: Lawyer, 1860-1875; Government
Official, 1860, 1863-1868; Judge, 1868, 1875-1906;
Educator, ca. 1875-1890

The Fuller Court, 1897. From left: Edward Douglass White, Henry B. Brown, Horace Gray, Stephen J. Field, Melville W. Fuller, John Marshall Harlan, David J. Brewer, George Shiras Jr., Wheeler H. Peckham.

Official Positions: United States Deputy Marshal, 1860; Assistant United States Attorney, 1863-1868; Judge, Michigan Circuit Court for Wayne County, 1868; Judge, United States District Court for the Eastern District of Michigan, 1875-1890; Part-time Lecturer, University of Michigan Law School, ca. 1875-1890; Associate Justice, United States Supreme Court, 1891-1906

SUPREME COURT SERVICE

Nominated: December 23, 1890
Nominated By: Benjamin Harrison
Confirmed: December 29, 1890
Confirmation Vote: Voice vote
Oath Taken: January 5, 1891
Replaced: Samuel F. Miller
Significant Opinions: *Plessy v. Ferguson* (1896); *Holden v. Hardy* (1898); *Downes v. Bidwell* (*Insular Case*) (1901)
Left Court: Retired May 28, 1906
Length of Service: 15 years, 4 months, 23 days
Replacement: William H. Moody

The son of a prosperous New England businessman, Henry B. Brown received his early education in preparatory schools before attending Yale University. After receiving an undergradu-

ate degree from Yale in 1856, he traveled abroad for a year before beginning his legal career. Brown studied first in the offices of an Ellington, Connecticut, attorney, then briefly attended law school at both Yale and Harvard. He continued his training in a Detroit lawyer's office after moving to that city in 1859, finally being admitted to the Michigan bar in 1860.

Brown had sufficient funds to hire a substitute for the military service required during the Civil War. In 1860 he pursued both private practice and a political career. His private practice grew sporadically, and although he received a number of political appointments, his attempts at elective office resulted in failure. His first appointment was as a United States deputy marshall. He was next promoted to assistant U.S. attorney for Wayne County, Michigan, located in the active Great Lakes port, Detroit. It was in this position that Brown began to develop his expertise in *admiralty law. In 1868 he was appointed to fill the unexpired term of a Michigan circuit court judge, but when he tried to regain his seat by election later that year, he was defeated. His attempt to gain the 1872 Republican nomination for the United States Senate also resulted in failure. Brown's appointment as a federal judge in 1875 was a welcome one, and he used his eighteen years on the district court bench to further his reputation as an admiralty law expert through publications, speech-making, and part-time lecturing at the University of Michigan Law School.

For years, Brown had been quietly lobbying for a seat on the High Court, a pursuit that resulted in success when President Harrison nominated him in 1890. His confirmation was unremarkable and, once on the Court, he took care that he remained a centrist. Brown was a social Darwinist and an proponent of *laissez faire, reflecting the philosophic mainstream of his time. In this context, the most infamous opinion he wrote for the Court, *Plessy v. Ferguson* (1896) — a 7 to 1 decision establishing the "separate but equal" doctrine that became the basis for segregationist Jim Crow laws — seems not so much the product of individual bias, but a reflection of the predominating societal mores.

With the exception of *Plessy*, however, Brown has been largely forgotten. Because of his reputation as an expert in technical matters, he was most often assigned cases dealing with admiralty, patent, or bankruptcy issues. Before joining the Fuller Court, Brown suffered an attack of neuritis that blinded him in one eye, a condition that gradually worsened during his 15 years on the high bench and eventually forced his resignation in 1906. He lived on in semi-retirement for seven more years before his death in 1913 at age 77.

GEORGE SHIRAS JR.

PERSONAL DATA

Born: January 26, 1832, in Pittsburgh, Pennsylvania
Parents: George Shiras, Eliza Herron Shiras
Higher Education: Ohio University, 1849-1851; Yale University (B.A., 1853); Yale Law School, 1853-1854
Bar Admission: Pennsylvania, 1855
Political Party: Republican
Marriage: December 31, 1857, to Lillie E. Kennedy, who bore Shiras two sons
Died: August 2, 1924, in Pittsburgh
Buried: Allegheny Cemetery, Pittsburgh

PROFESSIONAL CAREER

Occupations: Lawyer, 1855-1892; Politician, 1888; Judge, 1892-1903
Official Positions: Presidential elector, 1888; Associate Justice, United States Supreme Court, 1892-1903

SUPREME COURT CAREER

Nominated: July 19, 1892
Nominated By: Benjamin Harrison
Confirmed: July 26, 1892
Confirmation Vote: Voice vote
Oath Taken: October 10, 1892
Replaced: Joseph P. Bradley
Significant Opinions: None
Left Court: Retired February 23, 1903
Length of Service: 10 years, 4 months, 13 days
Replacement: William R. Day

George Shiras Jr. was the son of a Pittsburgh brewer who was so successful that he was able to retire early to a farm near the Ohio River, where he raised his three sons. Shiras began his higher education at Ohio University, but transferred after two years to Yale, from which he graduated in 1853. He next enrolled at Yale Law School but did not graduate, completing his legal education through private study in the Pittsburgh offices of Judge Hopewell Hepburn. Shiras opened a practice in Dubuque, Iowa, with one of his brothers, but three years later he returned to Pittsburgh to become Judge Hepburn's law partner.

Shiras did not serve in the Civil War and, except for serving once as a presidential elector, he shunned politics, even refusing the state legislature's offer to nominate him to the United States Senate in 1881. His political independence brought him to the attention of President Harrison, who nominated him for the Supreme Court in 1892, but this same independence made for a difficult confirmation process, when he was opposed by the Pennsylvania Republican machine.

Shiras's output as a Supreme Court justice was moderate: 260 opinions with 14 dissents in ten years. He was moderately conservative in outlook, and he did not always agree with the ultra-conservative majority that dominated the Fuller Court. He is most remembered, possibly inaccurately, as the justice who scuttled progressive tax reform by changing his vote when *Pollock v. Farmers' Loan & Trust Co.* (1895) was reheard. Although his was among the bare five-vote majority that killed the income tax legislation, modern legal scholars believe that the one switched vote that changed the decision from favorable to unfavorable could have belonged to another justice.

Shiras retired from the bench, as he had promised, at the age of 71. He spent the remainder of his life quietly, dying at the age of 92 in Pittsburgh.

HOWELL EDMUNDS JACKSON

PERSONAL DATA
Born: April 8, 1832, in Paris, Tennessee
Parents: Dr. Alexander Jackson, Mary Hurt Jackson
Higher Education: West Tennessee College (B.A., 1849); University of Virginia, 1851-1852; Cumberland University Law School (law degree, 1856)
Bar Admission: Tennessee, 1856
Political Party: Democrat
Marriages: 1859 to Sophia Malloy, who bore Jackson four children, and who died in 1873; April 1874 to Mary E. Harding, who bore Jackson three children
Died: August 8, 1895, in West Meade, Tennessee
Buried: Mount Olivet Cemetery, Nashville, Tennessee

PROFESSIONAL CAREER
Occupations: Lawyer, 1856-1861, 1865-1875, 1877-1880; Government Official, 1861-1865; Politician, 1880-1886; Judge, 1875-1877, 1887-1895
Official Positions: Custodian of Sequestered Property, Confederate States of America, 1861-1865; Judge, Court of Arbitration for Western Tennessee, 1875-1877; Member, Tennessee House of Representatives, 1880-1881; Member, United States Senate, 1881-1886; Judge, United States Sixth Circuit Court of Appeals, 1887-1893; Associate Justice, United States Supreme Court, 1893-1895

SUPREME COURT SERVICE
Nominated: February 2, 1893
Nominated By: Benjamin Harrison
Confirmed: February 18, 1893
Confirmation Vote: Voice vote
Oath Taken: March 4, 1893
Replaced: Lucius Q.C. Lamar
Significant Opinions: None
Left Court: Died August 8, 1895
Length of Service: 2 years, 5 months, 4 days
Replacement: Rufus W. Peckham

Howell E. Jackson was the eldest son of a Virginia physician who migrated to Tennessee in 1830. After the customary primary and secondary schooling, Jackson, at the age of eighteen, received his undergraduate degree from Western Tennessee College. He studied two more years at the University of Virginia, then completed his legal education with a year at Cumberland University, after which he was admitted to the Tennessee bar.

Jackson went into private practice, but his legal partnership was dissolved when Tennessee seceded from the Union. Although personally opposed to secession, Jackson acted as a receiver of sequestered property for the Confederacy during the war. After Appomattox, he resumed private legal practice and switched his political affiliation from the Whigs to the Democrats. Jackson served on the provisional Court of Arbitration for Western Tennessee. When that court was dissolved, he attempted to continue his judicial career by seeking the Democratic nomination for judge of the state supreme court, but he was unsuccessful. In 1880, however, he was elected to the state house, which sent him to the United States Senate the following year.

In the Senate, Jackson formed crucial political relationships with future Presidents Grover Cleveland and Benjamin Harrison. In 1886, at Cleveland's urging, Jackson resigned his Senate seat to take up a federal judgeship. In 1893, after the death of Jackson's fellow southerner, Justice Lucius Q. C. Lamar, President Harrison, a Republican, nominated Jackson to the Supreme Court despite their different political orientations.

Only a year after he assumed his seat on the High Court, Jackson contracted tuberculosis, which curtailed his work — and his presence —

on the bench. He wrote fewer than fifty opinions, of which only four were dissents, and it is estimated that he spent only about fifteen months actually involved with Court activities. In May 1894 he left Washington, D.C., for the West, in search of a cure. In May of the next year, desperately ill, he returned for the second hearing of what was probably the most controversial case of the Fuller era, *Pollock v. Farmers' Loan & Trust Co.* (1895). His vote, it was thought, was sorely needed, as the Court was deadlocked after the first hearing of the case without him. However, Jackson's vote was not decisive. One of the justices who had originally voted in favor of the income tax legislation that was the subject of *Pollock* changed his vote. Nonetheless, Jackson spoke out eloquently in dissent. Less than three months later he succumbed to illness, dying on August 8, 1895.

For a biography of Associate, later Chief Justice **Edward Douglass White,** see entry under **THE WHITE COURT.**

White was President Cleveland's third choice to fill the seat vacated by Samuel Blatchford. Cleveland first tried to replace Blatchford with William B. Hornblower, a New York lawyer nominated on September 19, 1893. The nomination was defeated by Senator David B. Hill, a New York Democratic boss who led a campaign against Hornblower that resulted, on January 15, 1894, in a 30 to 24 vote against him. The next year, when Cleveland offered Hornblower another chance to serve on the Supreme Court, Hornblower declined.

Cleveland's second choice as Blatchford's replacement was Wheeler H. Peckham, another New York political leader and the brother of future Supreme Court Justice Rufus W. Peckham. Wheeler Peckham was formally nominated on January 23, 1894. His nomination, too, was derailed by Senator Hill, who had been on the losing end of a patronage dispute involving Peckham and President Cleveland. Invoking senatorial privilege (a custom allowing a senator to veto a political appointee from his own state and party), Hill precipitated a vote of 41 to 32 against

confirmation on February 16, 1894. The seat finally went to Edward D. White.

RUFUS WHEELER PECKHAM

PERSONAL DATA
Born: November 8, 1838, in Albany, New York
Parents: Rufus Wheeler Peckham, Isabella Lacey Peckham
Higher Education: None
Bar Admission: New York, 1859
Political Party: Democrat
Marriage: November 14, 1866, to Harriette M. Arnold, who bore Peckham two sons
Died: October 24, 1909, in Altamont, New York
Buried: Albany Rural Cemetery, Menands, New York

PROFESSIONAL CAREER
Occupations: Lawyer, 1859-1883; Government Official, 1869-1872, 1881-1883; Politician, ca. 1870s; Judge, 1883-1909
Official Positions: District Attorney, Albany County, New York, 1869-1872; Special Assistant, New York State Attorney General, ca. 1869-1871; Head, Albany County Democratic Committee, ca. mid-1870s; Corporation Counsel, City of Albany, 1881-1883; Associate Justice, New York Supreme Court, 1883-1886; Judge, New York Court of Appeals, 1886-1895; Associate Justice, United States Supreme Court, 1896-1909

SUPREME COURT SERVICE
Nominated: December 3, 1895
Nominated By: Grover Cleveland
Confirmed: December 9, 1895
Confirmation Vote: Voice vote
Oath Taken: January 6, 1896
Replaced: Howell E. Jackson
Significant Opinions: *Allgeyer v. Louisiana* (1897); *Maxwell v. Dow* (1900); *Lochner v. New York* (1905); **Ex parte Young* (1908)
Left Court: Died October 24, 1909
Length of Service: 13 years, 8 months, 18 days
Replacement: Horace H. Lurton

Rufus W. Peckham's father was a lawyer, an Albany County district attorney, a United States congressman, and a judge on both the New York Supreme Court and the state's highest judicial tribunal, the Court of Appeals. It was a career his second son, and namesake, would nearly duplicate.

The younger Rufus Peckham was actually the third lawyer in his immediate family. His older brother, Wheeler, also became a prominent attorney, as well as a force in New York Democratic politics. Wheeler H. Peckham, like his brother, was nominated by President Cleveland for a seat on the Supreme Court. Unfortunately, his nomination — like William B. Hornblower's before him — would be blocked by Senator David B. Hill of New York, who invoked senatorial privilege to bar confirmation and settle a political score with Cleveland. Rufus Peckham's confirmation in 1895 would finally break the patronage imbroglio that had twice prevented Cleveland from appointing a fellow New Yorker to the High Court.

Rufus Peckham received a private education and, after traveling in Europe for a year with his brother, returned to read law in his father's office. Peckham joined his father's firm in 1859, remaining there until he opened his own practice in the mid-1860s. He quickly established himself as a force in local Democratic politics, and his first appointment came in 1869, when he was named Albany County District Attorney, serving at the same time as special assistant to the state attorney general. He went on to serve the city of Albany as its corporation counsel before being elected as a judge, first to the New York Supreme Court, then to the New York Court of Appeals.

As an active member of New York's upstate Democratic faction, Rufus Peckham, like his brother, had long supported Grover Cleveland. Cleveland was able to return the favor by naming Rufus Peckham to the Supreme Court to replace Justice Jackson. Peckham spent almost 14 years on the High Court, during which he wrote 315 opinions, most of which consistently supported the Fuller Court's conservative *laissez faire orientation. Although not known for his inventiveness, Peckham drafted some of the Fuller Court's most influential, if not lasting, opinions.

It was Peckham, for example, who wrote the majority opinion in *Lochner v. New York* (1905), the case that carried freedom of contract to perhaps its utmost extreme. His decisions are best characterized as exemplars of the dominant legal thought of his day. He remained on the Court until he died in 1909. He was a *strict constructionist to the end, despite the fact that by that time the Court, like society at large, had begun a progressive reorientation.

JOSEPH MCKENNA

PERSONAL DATA

Born: August 10, 1843, in Philadelphia, Pennsylvania

Parents: John McKenna, Mary Ann Johnson McKenna

Higher Education: Benicia Collegiate Institute (undergraduate degree, 1865); Columbia University Law School, 1897

Bar Admission: California, 1865

Political Party: Republican

Marriage: June 10, 1869, to Amanda F. Bornemann, who bore McKenna one son and three daughters

Died: November 21, 1926, in Washington, D.C.

Buried: Mount Olivet Cemetery, Washington, D.C.

PROFESSIONAL CAREER

Occupations: Lawyer, 1865-1885, 1897; Government Official, 1866-1870, 1897; Politician, 1875-1892; Judge, 1892-1897, 1898-1925

Official Positions: District Attorney, Solano County, California, 1866-1870; Member for Solano County, California State Assembly, 1875-1876; Member, United States House of Representatives, 1885-1892; Judge, United States Ninth Circuit Court of Appeals, 1892-1897; United States Attorney General, 1897; Associate Justice, United States Supreme Court, 1898-1925

SUPREME COURT SERVICE

Nominated: December 16, 1897

Nominated By: William McKinley

Confirmed: January 21, 1898

Confirmation Vote: Voice vote

Oath Taken: January 26, 1898

Replaced: Stephen J. Field
Significant Opinions: *Williams v. Mississippi* (1898); *Weems v. United States* (1910); *Bunting v. Oregon* (1917)
Left Court: Retired January 5, 1925
Length of Service: 26 years, 11 months, 10 days
Replacement: Harlan F. Stone

Joseph McKenna was the son of Irish immigrants who came to America during the potato famine. His father's Philadelphia bakery languished, in part because of anti-immigrant, anti-Catholic sentiments in the community, and in 1855 the family moved to California. They settled in Benicia, where McKenna, after deciding against the priesthood, studied law at Benicia Collegiate Institute.

McKenna practiced law intermittently, seeing it as merely an avenue into politics. He joined the increasingly powerful California Republicans, becoming acquainted with railroad tycoon Leland Stanford, who later was the state's first Republican governor. In 1866 McKenna was elected a district attorney, and in 1875 a state representative. After failing in his bid for the position of speaker, however, he resigned from the state legislature after one term. Attempts to reach the United States House of Representatives failed twice before he was finally elected in 1885.

In the House, McKenna served on the Ways and Means Committee, becoming a friend of its chairman, William McKinley of Ohio. After McKinley was elected president in 1896, he appointed McKenna first as a judge in the Ninth Circuit Court of Appeals, then as attorney general. McKenna's tenure in the latter position, however, lasted just a few months. When Justice Field was finally persuaded to retire in 1897, McKinley nominated his old friend McKenna to replace his fellow Californian. Although some protested his connections with then Senator Leland Stanford and the railroad interests, McKenna was confirmed after only a short delay.

Commentators are divided as to McKenna's abilities as a Supreme Court justice. He might, as some maintain, have been among the least prepared individuals ever to ascend the High Court

bench; indeed, McKenna himself seems to have felt he lacked adequate preparation. To make up for this deficit in legal education, he studied at Columbia University Law School before assuming his place on the Court. Once on the Court, he wrote 633 opinions, few of which spoke for the majority. While some critics feel that McKenna never developed a coherent legal philosophy or the ability to construct an opinion representing the attitudes of his brethren, others find his style distinctive and clear.

Toward the end of his tenure on the Court, McKenna's mental faculties deteriorated markedly. He tendered his resignation only under considerable pressure from Chief Justice William Howard Taft. He died less than two years later at the age of 83.

OLIVER WENDELL HOLMES JR.

PERSONAL DATA
Born: March 8, 1841, in Boston, Massachusetts
Parents: Oliver Wendell Holmes, Amelia Lee Jackson Holmes
Higher Education: Harvard College (B.A., 1861); Harvard Law School (LL.B., 1866)
Bar Admission: Massachusetts, 1867
Political Party: Republican
Marriage: June 17, 1872, to Fanny Bowdich Dixwell
Died: March 6, 1935, in Washington, D.C.
Buried: Arlington National Cemetery, Arlington, Virginia

PROFESSIONAL CAREER
Occupations: Military Service, 1861-1864; Lawyer, 1867-1882; Educator, 1870-1882; Editor, 1870-1873; Judge, 1882-1932
Official Positions: Instructor, Harvard Law School, 1870-1882; Editor, *American Law Review*, 1870-1873; Professor of Law, Harvard Law School, 1882; Associate Justice, Massachusetts Supreme Court, 1882-1899; Chief Justice, Massachusetts Supreme Court, 1899-1902; Associate Justice, United States Supreme Court, 1902-1932

SUPREME COURT SERVICE
Appointed: August 11, 1902 (recess appointment)

Appointed By: Theodore Roosevelt

Nominated: December 2, 1902

Confirmed: December 2, 1902

Confirmation Vote: Voice vote

Oath Taken: December 8, 1902

Replaced: Horace Gray

Significant Opinions: *Swift & Co. v. United States* (1905); *Lochner v. New York* (dissent) (1905); *Frank v. Mangum* (dissent) (1915); *Hammer v. Dagenhart* (dissent) (1918); *Schenck v. United States* (1919); *Abrams v. United States* (dissent) (1919); *Missouri v. Holland* (1920); *Moore v. Dempsey* (1923); *Gitlow v. New York* (dissent) (1925); *Tyson v. Banton* (dissent) (1927); *Nixon v. Herndon* (1927); *Buck v. Bell* (1927)

Left Court: Retired January 12, 1932

Length of Service: 29 years, 1 month, 4 days

Replacement: Benjamin N. Cardozo

Oliver Wendell Holmes Jr. inherited his father's name and his mother's sensibilities. Although he shared with his father, a Boston physician and man of letters, an aptitude for writing and a marked loquaciousness, Holmes gained from his mother a powerful sense of duty — one mark of which was his attendance at every Supreme Court session for 25 years.

Holmes completed his undergraduate education just as the Civil War began, and he enlisted in the Union army directly. He served with great distinction and was wounded three times before mustering out with the rank of captain, bestowed on him for bravery. Holmes then attended Harvard Law School and made a tour of Europe before passing the bar in 1867. He joined a law firm that year, then briefly gave up practicing law to pursue the life of an independent scholar. Holmes returned almost immediately to the practice of law, but throughout his life he was to devote considerable effort to teaching, editing, and writing.

Holmes's most distinguished literary effort was a series of lectures delivered at the Lowell Institute in Boston in 1880. These were collected and published the next year as *The Common Law*, a volume still heralded as one of the greatest works of American legal scholarship. In it Holmes developed the theory that decisions are based not so much on *precedent and logic as on "felt neces-

sities" reflecting current attitudes. His identification of a new organizing principle for American *jurisprudence — that liability should be based on foreseeable injuries, rather than on the transgressions producing them — greatly influenced *tort and contract law.

Shortly after publication of *The Common Law*, Holmes was appointed to a chair at the Harvard Law School. He taught at Harvard for only one semester before accepting an appointment to the Massachusetts Supreme Court, where he served for 20 years, the last three as chief justice. During those years he wrote over a thousand opinions, many of them concerning labor disputes.

The progressive views Holmes displayed in these opinions were surely one factor that brought him to the attention of Theodore Roosevelt as a replacement for Horace Gray, who left the Fuller Court in 1902. Although Holmes, like many other justices, did not meet some of the expectations of the president who appointed him — criticizing the Sherman Antitrust Act in *Northern Securities Co. v. United States* (1904), for example — in the main he remained a progressive justice throughout his long career on the Court. In cases such as *Lochner v. New York* (1905), in which Holmes penned what is perhaps his best opinion, he objected to the majority's endorsement of an extreme form of freedom of contract and began to earn his reputation as one of the Court's great dissenters, displaying an eloquent pithiness that was his trademark. "The Fourteenth Amendment does not enact Mr. Herbert Spencer's Social Statics," he wrote, indicating that economic principles, such as those enunciated in the 19th century treatise, are not legal ones. Holmes sat on the Supreme Court for nearly 30 years, serving under Chief Justices Fuller, White, Taft, and Hughes, as well as during the administrations of Presidents Roosevelt, Taft, Wilson, Harding, Coolidge, and Hoover. During his time on the Supreme Court, he wrote 873 opinions, more than any justice before him. Although a relatively small proportion of his opinions were dissents, some of them — particularly those concerning *due process and *free speech — have since become *precedents. In his 91st year, after his health had begun to fail, Holmes was finally persuaded by his fellow justices to retire. He died three years later at his home in Washington, D.C., and was buried at Arlington National Cemetery.

WILLIAM RUFUS DAY

PERSONAL DATA

Born: April 17, 1849, in Ravenna, Ohio
Parents: Luther Day, Emily Spalding Day
Higher Education: University of Michigan (B.S., 1870); University of Michigan Law School, 1871-1872
Bar Admission: Ohio, 1872
Political Party: Republican
Marriage: 1875 to Mary Elizabeth Schaefer, who bore Day four sons
Died: July 9, 1923, on Mackinac Island, Michigan
Buried: West Lawn Cemetery, Canton, Ohio

PROFESSIONAL CAREER

Occupations: Lawyer, 1872-1886, 1887-1897; Judge, 1886, 1899-1922; Government Official, 1897-1898; Diplomat, 1899, 1922-1923
Official Positions: Judge, Canton, Ohio Court of Common Pleas, 1886; First Assistant United States Secretary of State, 1897-1898; United States Secretary of State, 1898; Head, United States Delegation, Paris Peace Conference, 1899; Judge, United States Sixth Circuit Court of Appeals, 1899-1903; Associate Justice, United States Supreme Court, 1903-1922; Umpire, Mixed Claims Commission, 1922-1923

SUPREME COURT SERVICE

Nominated: March 2, 1903
Nominated By: Theodore Roosevelt
Confirmed: February 23, 1903
Confirmation Vote: Voice vote
Oath Taken: March 2, 1903
Replaced: George Shiras
Significant Opinions: *Muskrat v. United States* (1911); *Weeks v. United States* (1914); *Buchanan v. Warley* (1917); *Hammer v. Dagenhart* (1918)
Left Court: Retired November 13, 1922
Length of Service: 19 years, 8 months, 11 days
Replacement: Pierce Butler

William R. Day was born to a long line of jurists. His great-grandfather served as chief justice of Connecticut, his grandfather as a member of the Ohio Supreme Court, and his father as chief justice of Ohio. Day read law in his hometown of Ravenna, Ohio, then studied at the University of Michigan Law School for a year before passing the Ohio bar. He then opened a partnership in Canton, Ohio, which soon became the city's most prominent law firm.

At the same time, Day pursued an interest in politics, befriending another Canton attorney with political ambitions, William McKinley. McKinley went on to the federal Congress, then the governor's mansion, and finally the White House. Day at first remained in Canton, where he was elected a judge of the Court of Common Pleas in 1886, a post he resigned after six months because of its poor salary. He was subsequently appointed to the federal bench by President Benjamin Harrison, but declined that post because of poor health. When McKinley became president, he summoned his old friend to Washington to assist Secretary of State John Sherman. Sherman was gradually eased out of the position, however, and Day took his place, assuming command of the Department of State during the crucial months of the Spanish-American War. Day then resigned that post to head the American delegation to the peace conference after the war, where he negotiated the purchase of the Philippines from Spain. He was rewarded by an appointment to the federal bench of the Sixth Circuit Court of Appeals, where he sat with future Supreme Court Justices Horace Lurton and William Howard Taft. After McKinley's assassination in 1901, Day began marking the slain president's birthday with a memorial service. In attendance at the gathering in January 1903 was President Theodore Roosevelt, who made a premature announcement of his intention to name Day to the Supreme Court. Two months later Day was sworn in as an associate justice.

Day acted primarily as a swing vote on the Supreme Court, as his attitudes alternated between the liberal and the moderate ends of the political spectrum. While he endorsed the use of federal regulatory power through the Sherman Antitrust Act, he is perhaps best remembered for his majority opinion in *Hammer v. Dagenhart* (1918), which declared the Federal Child Labor Act unconstitutional on grounds that it trespassed on the states' *police powers. In the main, Day was overshadowed by other great minds, such as Oliver Wendell Holmes Jr. and Louis D. Brandeis, who occupied the bench with him. After Day retired from the Court in November 1922, he served briefly on the Mixed Claims Commission, established to determine claims arising out of World War I. He died in July 1923 on Mackinac Island, Michigan.

WILLIAM HENRY MOODY

PERSONAL DATA

Born: December 23, 1853, in Newbury, Massachusetts
Parents: Henry L. Moody, Melissa A. Emerson Moody
Higher Education: Harvard College (B.A., cum laude, 1876); Harvard University Law School, 1876-1877
Bar Admission: Massachusetts, 1878
Political Party: Republican
Marriage: None
Died: July 2, 1917, in Haverhill, Massachusetts
Buried: Byfield Parish Churchyard, Georgetown, Massachusetts

PROFESSIONAL CAREER

Occupations: Lawyer, 1878-1895, 1904-1906; Government Official, 1888-1895, 1902-1906; Politician, 1895-1902; Judge, 1906-1910
Official Positions: Member, Haverhill, Massachusetts, School Board, 1888; City Solicitor, Haverhill, 1888-1890; District Attorney, Eastern District of Massachusetts, 1890-1895; Member, United States House of Representatives, 1895-1902; United States Secretary of the Navy, 1902-1904; United States Attorney General, 1904-1906; Associate Justice, United States Supreme Court, 1906-1910

SUPREME COURT SERVICE

Nominated: December 3, 1906

Nominated By: Theodore Roosevelt
Confirmed: December 12, 1906
Confirmation Vote: Voice vote
Oath Taken: December 17, 1906
Replaced: Henry B. Brown
Significant Opinion: *Twining v. New Jersey* (1908)
Left Court: Resigned November 20, 1910
Length of Service: 3 years, 11 months, 3 days
Replacement: Willis Van Devanter

William H. Moody made a promising start to his legal career. After graduating from Harvard College and attending Harvard Law School for a year, he read law for 18 months in the offices of the famous Boston lawyer and writer Richard Henry Dana, author of *Two Years Before the Mast* (1840). Although admission to the bar normally required three years' study, Moody was admitted early, owing to the powerful impression he made at his oral examination.

Moody set up in private practice in Haverhill, Massachusetts, where he developed a lucrative corporate practice and a taste for Republican politics. He served in a number of local offices before making a name for himself as the district attorney who unsuccessfully — but brilliantly — prosecuted Lizzy Borden for the axe murder of her parents. During this period he also developed a friendship with rising Republican star Theodore Roosevelt.

When Roosevelt became president, he appointed his friend Moody, then serving in Congress, first as secretary of the navy, then as attorney general. As attorney general, Moody vigorously carried out Roosevelt's trust-busting program, most successfully in *Swift & Co. v. United States* (1905), which he personally argued before the Supreme Court. When Roosevelt nominated Moody to replace retiring Justice Henry B. Brown, the nomination was opposed by senators who feared what they saw as Moody's radical record. After only a short delay, however, Moody was confirmed, and during his time on the Court, he did indeed vote in a consistently liberal manner.

Moody's tenure on the Court, during which he wrote 67 opinions, was cut short by the onset of debilitating rheumatoid arthritis. He was active on the Court for only about two years before his illness forced him to retire to his home in Haverhill. He officially resigned in 1910, after Congress passed legislation enabling him to receive special retirement benefits. He remained an invalid until his death nearly seven years later.

HORACE HARMON LURTON

PERSONAL DATA

Born: February 26, 1844, in Newport, Kentucky
Parents: Dr. Lycurgus Leonidas Lurton, Sarah Ann Harmon Lurton
Higher Education: University of Chicago, 1859-1860; Cumberland University Law School (L.B., 1867)
Bar Admission: Tennessee, 1867
Political Party: Democrat
Marriage: September 1867 to Mary Frances Owen, who bore Lurton two sons and two daughters
Died: July 12, 1914, in Atlantic City, New Jersey
Buried: Greenwood Cemetery, Clarksville, Tennessee

PROFESSIONAL CAREER

Occupations: Military Service, 1861-1865; Lawyer, 1867-1875, 1878-1886; Judge, 1875-1878, 1886-1914; Educator, 1898-1910
Official Positions: Judge, Sixth Chancery Division of Tennessee, 1875-1878; Associate Justice, Tennessee Supreme Court, 1886-1893; Chief Justice, Tennessee Supreme Court, 1893; Judge, United States Sixth Circuit Court of Appeals, 1893-1910; Adjunct Professor of Law, Vanderbilt University, 1898-1905; Dean, Vanderbilt Law School, 1905-1910; Associate Justice, United States Supreme Court, 1910-1914

SUPREME COURT SERVICE

Nominated: December 13, 1909
Nominated By: William Howard Taft
Confirmed: December 20, 1909
Confirmation Vote: Voice vote
Oath Taken: January 3, 1910
Replaced: Rufus W. Peckham
Significant Opinion: *Coyle v. Smith* (1911)
Left Court: Died July 12, 1914
Length of Service: 4 years, 6 months, 9 days
Replacement: James C. McReynolds

Horace H. Lurton was a thoroughgoing southerner, having been born in Kentucky and transplanted at an early age to Clarksville, Tennessee, which would remain his home. He did go north to college, attending the University of Chicago, but leaving before graduating when the Civil War broke out.

Lurton served in the Confederate army with great dedication. He fought bravely and was wounded in 1862. After a brief period of recuperation, Lurton rejoined the Confederate infantry and was captured during Grant's siege of Fort Donelson. He escaped from a prisoner of war camp, joined a band of Confederate guerrillas and was captured again at the battle of Vicksburg. His release from a Union prison was secured by his mother, who traveled to Washington, D.C., to intercede personally with President Lincoln.

Back home, Lurton entered Cumberland University Law School in Lebanon, Tennessee, from which he graduated in 1867. He began practicing law in Clarksville, a pursuit that was interrupted for three years starting in 1875, when he served as a state *equity court chancellor. In 1886 he won election to the Tennessee Supreme Court, becoming its chief justice in 1893. President Grover Cleveland elevated Lurton to the Sixth Circuit Court of Appeals in 1893, where Lurton served alongside William R. Day and William Howard Taft, both of whom also would serve later as Supreme Court justices.

In 1909 when his old friend, Taft by then president, named him to the Supreme Court, Lurton was at the age of 65 the oldest man ever to have been so appointed. In addition, his status as a Southern Democrat and a Confederate veteran made him a surprising choice for the Republican Taft. Upon his confirmation — and as if to confirm his status as a southerner — Lurton took a slow, symbolic train trip through Dixie on his way to assume his new duties in Washington, D.C.

On the Court Lurton failed to distinguish himself, his conservative judicial values and *strict constructionism making him seem almost an anachronism. His service on the high bench was cut short when, toward the end of 1913, he grew ill and was forced to take a leave to recuperate.

He returned to attend the Court's spring 1914 session, but another ostensibly restorative trip to Atlantic City, New Jersey, that summer ended in his death from a heart attack.

SIGNIFICANT CASES

KIDD V. PEARSON

Citation: 128 U.S. 1 (1888)
Argued: April 4, 1888
Decided: October 22, 1888
Court Below: Iowa Supreme Court
Basis for Review: *Writ of error
Facts: An Iowa statute forbade the manufacture of liquor for export outside the state.
Issue: Does the state statute impinge on the federal *commerce power controlling interstate trade?
Outcome: The statute was upheld as a simple exercise of Iowa's *police powers.
Vote: 8-0
Participating: Miller, Field, Bradley, Harlan, Matthews, Gray, Blatchford, Lamar
Opinion: Lamar for the Court
Significance: By drawing a line between manufacture and commerce, ruling that the latter did not begin until the former was completed, the Court was forced to conclude that federal regulatory power did not apply to manufacturing, agriculture, or mining or other extractive activities. Over the years, the holding in *Kidd* has been modified, however, to broaden federal and narrow state regulatory powers. And with regard to state liquor laws, *Kidd* is no longer valid: the federal government can now constitutionally overrule them at any time.

CHAE CHAN PING V. UNITED STATES (THE CHINESE EXCLUSION CASE)

Citation: 130 U.S. 581 (1889)
Argued: March 28, 1889
Decided: May 13, 1889
Court Below: United States Circuit Court for the Northern District of California
Basis for Review: Appeal
Facts: In 1882 Congress barred entry to Chinese laborers under the Chinese Exclusion Act. In 1884 Congress amended the act to allow reentry of Chinese nationals into the United States after travel abroad only on the basis of reentry certificates issued before departure. In 1888 a new statute, the Scott Act, revoked all reentry certificates. Chae Chan Ping, who had been a United States resident for twelve years, but was in China at the time the 1888 statute was enacted, was disallowed reentry despite holding a certificate. Chae Chan Ping applied for a writ of *habeas corpus, which was denied.
Issue: Does Congress have the power retroactively to bar a particular group of *aliens from entry into the United States?
Outcome: In a unanimous decision, the Fuller Court upheld the statute and the denial of a writ of habeas corpus. The power to exclude belongs exclusively to the national government, which may invoke it at any time.
Vote: 8-0
Participating: Fuller, Miller, Field, Bradley, Harlan, Gray, Blatchford, Lamar
Opinion: Field for the Court
Significance: *Chae Chan Ping* was just one of a series of cases concerning Chinese immigration that the Supreme Court heard between 1884 and 1893. During those years, Congress passed a series of increasingly harsh measures designed to exclude Chinese immigrants. After initially fashioning a series of narrow decisions that partially protected Chinese residents and Chinese American citizens, the Court gradually gave in to mounting social pressures — manifested by increasingly arbitrary legislation — to restrict the basic rights of this group.

DE GEOFROY V. RIGGS

Citation: 133 U.S. 258 (1890)
Argued: December 23, 1889
Decided: February 3, 1890
Court Below: District of Columbia Supreme Court
Basis for Review: Appeal
Facts: When T.L. Riggs, an American citizen, died, his heirs were both American and French citizens. Included in the disputed inheritance was property located in Washington, D.C. The lower

court ruled against the French heirs' claim to these lands.

Issue: Can aliens inherit from a U.S. citizen property located in an American territorial *jurisdiction, e.g., the District of Columbia?

Outcome: Finding that a provision of an 1853 treaty between France and the United States permitting French nationals to inherit real estate located in "all states" included that in Washington, D.C., the Fuller Court overturned the lower court's finding.

Vote: 8-0

Participating: Fuller, Miller, Field, Bradley, Harlan, Gray, Blatchford, Lamar

Opinion: Field for the Court

Significance: Although *De Geofroy* primarily affected the right to transfer property and the rights of *aliens in Washington, D.C., it expanded such rights in other U.S. political entities with established governments and clarified them with regard to ambiguities in any state laws. The federal *treaty power, which Justice Field declared was limited only by the Constitution itself, encompassed the power to regulate such inheritances.

LOUISVILLE, NEW ORLEANS & TEXAS RAILWAY CO. V. MISSISSIPPI

Citation: 133 U.S. 587

Argued: January 10, 1890

Decided: March 3, 1890

Court Below: Mississippi Supreme Court

Basis for Review: *Writ of error

Facts: A Mississippi statute required railroads to provide "equal, but separate, accommodation for the white and colored races." Reasoning that the statute only applied to intrastate commerce, the state supreme court upheld it as constitutional.

Issue: Does the statute have a substantial effect on interstate commerce, thereby rendering it an impermissible interference with the federal *commerce power?

Outcome: Accepting the Mississippi court's assertion that the statute would not affect interstate commerce, the Fuller Court upheld the ruling below.

Vote: 7-2

Participating: Fuller, Miller, Field, Bradley, Harlan, Gray, Blatchford, Lamar, Brewer

Opinions: Brewer for the Court; Harlan, joined by Bradley, dissenting

Significance: While the effect on interstate commerce of the statute at issue here was virtually identical to that found unconstitutional in *Hall v. Decuir* (1878), the Fuller Court seemed to find some distinction in the earlier statute's requirement that all parts of vehicles be open to all races. A juxtaposition of the two cases clearly shows the wide latitude states were given to regulate individual rights in the aftermath of the Civil War.

CHICAGO, MILWAUKEE & ST. PAUL RAILWAY CO. V. MINNESOTA (MINNESOTA RATE CASE)

Citation: 134 U.S. 418 (1890)

Argued: January 13-14, 1890

Decided: March 24, 1890

Court Below: Minnesota Supreme Court

Basis for Review: *Writ of error

Facts: An 1887 Minnesota statute created a state commission to set maximum rates for railroads, and the state supreme court upheld the law.

Issue: Does the statute violate the *Due Process Clause of the Fourteenth Amendment by providing for arbitrary confiscation of railroads' property (i.e., profits) without *judicial review?

Outcome: Reasoning that due process requires judicial oversight of administrative agencies, the Fuller Court overruled the state supreme court.

Vote: 6-3

Participating: Fuller, Miller, Field, Bradley, Harlan, Gray, Blatchford, Lamar, Brewer

Opinions: Blatchford for the Court; Miller concurring; Bradley, joined by Gray and Lamar, dissenting

Significance: *Chicago, Milwaukee & St. Paul* effectively negated the *holding of *Munn v. Illinois* (1877), which had upheld the legislature's power to set railroad rates. *Munn* was based on an older view of the balance of power, wherein the Court did not oversee the exercise of discretionary power by other branches. With *Chicago, Milwaukee & St. Paul*, the Supreme Court laid out the modern approach to regulation, whereby the Court is empowered not only to determine whether another branch of government has authority in a given area, but also whether the exercise of that authority is reasonable.

IN RE NEAGLE

Citation: 135 U.S. 1 (1890)
Argued: March 4-5, 1890
Decided: April 14, 1890
Court Below: United States Circuit Court for the Northern District of California
Basis for Review: Appeal
Facts: Justice Field incurred the wrath of his former colleague on the California Supreme Court, David Terry, when as a federal circuit court judge he issued an opinion invalidating Terry's wife's former marriage. When Terry later accosted Field, David Neagle, a federal marshal assigned as Field's bodyguard, killed Terry. Neagle was charged with murder under California law, but he was granted a writ of *habeas corpus by a federal circuit court.
Issue: Can a federal court *preempt state law by making a determination of what constitutes justifiable homicide in order to grant a writ of habeas corpus?
Outcome: The lower court's grant of a writ of habeas corpus was upheld on grounds that federal legislation authorized such a writ if a person is detained in violation of federal law.
Vote: 6-2
Participating: Fuller, Miller, Bradley, Harlan, Gray, Blatchford, Lamar, Brewer (Field *recused)
Opinions: Miller for the Court; Lamar, joined by Fuller, dissenting
Significance: The Fuller Court redefined "law" in the federal legislation to include acts — such as defending a federal official in the line of duty — as well as legislation. The Court minority found this redefinition an impermissible interference with traditional state *jurisdiction over criminal matters.

COUNSELMAN V. HITCHCOCK

Citation: 142 U.S. 547 (1892)
Argued: December 9-10, 1891
Decided: January 11, 1892

Court Below: United States Circuit Court for the Northern District of Illinois
Basis for Review: Appeal
Facts: Charles Counselman, citing his Fifth Amendment right not to be forced to incriminate himself, refused to answer some questions put to him in a *grand jury proceeding. Cited for *contempt of court, he was jailed and sought a writ of *habeas corpus.
Issue: Does the right against self-incrimination protect witnesses in a criminal proceeding as well as the accused?
Outcome: Observing that the federal *immunity statute under which the grand jury sought to force Counselman to testify protected him from use of his testimony as evidence against him, but not from its use to obtain other evidence against him, the Fuller Court struck the statute down. Counselman's writ of habeas corpus was granted.
Vote: 9-0
Participating: Fuller, Field, Bradley, Harlan, Gray, Blatchford, Lamar, Brewer, Brown
Opinion: Blatchford for the Court
Significance: Because the scope of protection afforded by the federal immunity statute at issue in this case was less than that of the Fifth Amendment, the statute offered less than the absolute immunity from prosecution required by the Constitution. While it is still true that only a complete grant of immunity from prosecution for crimes revealed in compelled testimony justifies waiver of the Fifth Amendment, the Court's subsequent holding in *Kastigar v. United States* (1972) modified *Counselman* to the extent that an immunity statute need not protect a witness from prosecution for a crime related to his compelled testimony, if evidence of that crime comes from an independent source.

BUDD V. NEW YORK

Citation: 143 U.S. 517 (1892)
Argued: November 17-18, 1891
Decided: February 29, 1892
Court Below: New York Court of Appeals (as *People v. Budd*)
Basis for Review: *Writ of error

Facts: New York's highest court upheld a state statute regulating rates charged by grain elevators.
Issues: Does the regulation violate the *Due Process Clause of the Fourteenth Amendment? Does it violate the *Commerce Clause of Article I, section 8, of the Constitution?
Outcome: Applying the same reasoning as that of *Munn v. Illinois* (1877), the majority affirmed the lower court decision, adding that because the statute affected only New York, it did not impinge upon the commerce power.
Vote: 5-3
Participating: Fuller, Field, Harlan, Gray, Blatchford, Lamar, Brewer, Brown
Opinions: Blatchford for the Court; Brewer, joined by Field and Brown, dissenting
Significance: In light of the increasing importance of *substantive due process in Supreme Court decisions — and of Blatchford's recent majority opinion upholding the doctrine in *Chicago, Milwaukee & St. Paul Railway Co. v. Minnesota* (1890) — it was doubly surprising that the Court would reaffirm the holding that grain elevators were businesses affecting the public interest and, as such, could be regulated. *Munn* and *Budd* have never been explicitly overruled, but their authority as *precedent has weakened considerably over time.

VIRGINIA V. TENNESSEE

Citation: 148 U.S. 503 (1893)
Argued: March 8-9, 1893
Decided: April 3, 1893
Court Below: None
Basis for Review: *Original Supreme Court jurisdiction
Facts: An 1803 survey set the boundary between Virginia and Tennessee. Virginia sought to have the states' joint recognition of the boundary set aside.
Issue: Does a compact between two states resolving a boundary dispute run afoul of the *Compact Clause of Article I, section 10, of the Constitution, stating that "no state shall, without consent of Congress . . . enter into any agreement or compact with another state"?
Outcome: The unanimous opinion of the Court declared that the Compact Clause does not

require congressional approval of every contract or agreement between states.
Vote: 8-0
Participating: Fuller, Field, Gray, Blatchford, Brewer, Brown Shiras, Jackson (Harlan not participating)
Opinion: Field for the Court
Significance: In finding that only compacts between states that increase state power at the expense of federal authority require formal congressional consent, the Fuller Court at once freed Congress from much nonessential business and gave states considerable latitude in resolving regional disputes. This case remains valid as *precedent.

UNITED STATES V. E.C. KNIGHT CO.

Citation: 156 U.S. 1 (1895)
Argued: October 24, 1894
Decided: January 21, 1895
Court Below: United States Third Circuit Court of Appeals
Basis for Review: Appeal
Facts: The American Sugar Refining Company had, by early 1892, acquired the stock of its largest competitors, thus controlling ninety-five percent of the nation's sugar refining. The federal government brought suit under the newly enacted Sherman Antitrust Act, but the lower court dismissed the government's suit.
Issue: Does Congress have the power to suppress a manufacturing monopoly under the Sherman Act?
Outcome: Stating that Congress lacks the power to regulate manufacturing, which affects interstate commerce only indirectly, the Fuller Court affirmed the lower court's ruling.
Vote: 8-1
Participating: Fuller, Field, Harlan, Gray, Brewer, Brown, Shiras, Jackson, White
Opinions: Fuller for the Court; Harlan dissenting
Significance: In this first interpretation of the Sherman Antitrust Act, the Court limited the statute's effectiveness considerably by distinguishing between the manufacture and the transportation of goods. Because the former could be

said to have only an indirect impact on interstate commerce — even though the products of manufacturing might be destined for interstate transport — its regulation properly belonged to the states. This distinction between direct and indirect effects remained in effect until the 1930s, when the Court adopted a broader view of federal power over commerce that harkened back to the Marshall Court's seminal 1824 decision in *Gibbons v. Ogden*.

POLLOCK V. FARMERS' LOAN & TRUST CO.

First Decision:
Citation: 157 U.S. 429 (1895)
Argued: March 7-13, 1895
Decided: April 8, 1895 (in three parts)
Second Decision:
Citation: 158 U.S. 601 (1895)
Reargued: May 6-8, 1895
Decided: May 20, 1895 (on rehearing)
Court Below: United States Circuit Court for the Southern District of New York
Basis for Review: Appeal
Facts: *Pollock* was a manufactured case that grew out of the Wilson-Gorman Tariff Act of 1894, which levied a two percent tax on yearly incomes exceeding $4,000. Pollock sued to prevent his bank, of which he was a shareholder, from paying the required tax. The Fuller Court first decided the case in three parts, voting: a) against a tax on income from state and municipal bonds; b) against a real estate tax; and c) four to four as to the constitutionality of a general tax on incomes (Justice Jackson was absent due to illness). Dissatisfied with the outcome, the Court voted to rehear the issues concerning the general income tax. Jackson, who was terminally ill, made it to the Court this time to vote in favor of the tax, but in the interim another of the justices changed his vote, invalidating the tax.

Issue: Does a general peacetime tax on incomes violate the constitutional prohibition against *direct taxes?

Outcome: Although the Constitution does not define direct taxes (which must be apportioned, or levied on the states in proportion to their respective populations), and although the

Supreme Court had, in *Springer v. United States* (1881), found a wartime income tax not to be a direct tax, the Fuller Court held the new income tax to be direct. On that basis, the entire tax law was invalidated.

Vote: First decision: a) against a tax on state and municipal bonds, 8-0; b) against a tax on real estate, 6-2; c) as to a general tax on individual and corporate income, 4-4. Second decision: 5-4

Participating: First hearing: Fuller, Field, Harlan, Gray, Brewer, Brown, Shiras, White (Jackson not participating). Second hearing: Fuller, Field, Harlan, Gray, Brewer, Brown, Shiras, Jackson, White

Opinions: First decision: Fuller for the Court; Field concurring; White and Harlan dissenting Second Decision: Fuller for the Court; Harlan, Brown, Jackson, and White dissenting

Significance: *Pollock* was the most controversial decision handed down by the Fuller Court, pitting supporters of private property and *laissez faire against progressive supporters of redistribution of wealth and social reforms. The Sixteenth Amendment, which was ratified in 1913 and authorized Congress to levy a general income tax, directly resulted from *Pollock*, which it overturned. The only part of the *Pollock* decision remaining in the wake of the Sixteenth Amendment was the ban on taxation of income from state and municipal bonds.

*IN RE DEBS

Citation: 158 U.S. 564 (1895)
Argued: March 25-26, 1895
Decided: May 27, 1895
Court Below: United States Circuit Court for the Northern District of Illinois
Basis for Review: Appeal
Facts: Eugene V. Debs, president of the American Railway Union, was one of the leaders of the 1894 Pullman strike. When a federal circuit court issued an *injunction against the strike on grounds that it constituted a restraint of interstate commerce, thus violating the Sherman Antitrust Act, Debs and other union officials continued their strike activities and were arrested and jailed for *contempt of court.

Issue: Can injunctions be used to break up strikes?

Outcome: The Fuller Court unanimously affirmed both the lower court's injunction and Debs's conviction, basing its decision on even broader grounds than those cited by the court below. National *sovereignty, Justice Brewer wrote for the Court, lent federal government the power to remove obstructions to commerce or the mails.

Vote: 9-0

Participating: Fuller, Field, Harlan, Gray, Brewer, Brown, Shiras, Jackson, White

Opinion: Brewer for the Court

Significance: *Debs* marked the first time the injunction was used as a strikebreaking tool, permitting courts to punish strikers not only with criminal penalties, but also by means of *equitable remedies. For the next 30 years, the injunction would remain the corporate weapon of choice in labor disputes.

PLESSY V. FERGUSON

Citation: 163 U.S. 537 (1896)

Argued: April 13, 1896

Decided: May 18, 1896

Court Below: Louisiana Supreme Court

Basis for Review: *Writ of error

Facts: Homer A. Plessy, acting on behalf of the Citizens' Committee to Test the Constitutionality of the Separate Car Act, tested a Louisiana statute requiring "separate but equal" train accommodations for African Americans and whites. Plessy, an African American man who gave the appearance of being white, bought a ticket for a journey entirely within the state to avoid interstate commerce complications. He then refused to move to the "colored only" section of the railroad coach. His arrest and the Louisiana statute were upheld by the state courts.

Issue: Does the "separate but equal" requirement violate Thirteen and Fourteenth Amendment prohibitions against racial discrimination?

Outcome: Reasoning that the Civil War amendments were designed to protect political, rather than social equality, the Fuller Court affirmed the lower court ruling.

Vote: 7-1

Participating: Fuller, Field, Harlan, Gray, Brown, Shiras, White, Peckham (Brewer not participating)

Opinions: Brown for the Court; Harlan dissenting

Significance: While *Pollock* was the Fuller Court's most controversial case, *Plessy* — which was of relatively little significance at the time — has proved to be its most infamous. Justice Harlan's eloquent dissent, with its proclamation that the "Constitution is color-blind, and neither knows nor tolerates classes among citizens," carried little weight. "Separate but equal" remained the law of the land until the landmark decision in *Brown v. Board of Education* (1954).

ALLGEYER V. LOUISIANA

Citation: 165 U.S. 578 (1897)

Argued: Not argued; decided on papers submitted January 6, 1867

Decided: March 1, 1867

Court Below: Louisiana Supreme Court

Basis for Review: *Writ of error

Facts: A Louisiana statute made it illegal for citizens to contract with out-of-state insurance companies, unless those companies met certain preconditions. Allgeyer & Co. entered into a prohibited insurance contract with a New York company and was fined $1,000.

Issue: Does the Louisiana statute violate freedom of contract as protected by the Fourteenth Amendment?

Outcome: Finding the state law unconstitutional because it inhibited the freedom of Louisiana citizens to enter into contracts, the Fuller Court reversed the lower court's ruling.

Vote: 9-0

Participating: Fuller, Field, Harlan, Gray, Brewer, Brown, Shiras, White, Peckham

Opinion: Peckham for the Court

Significance: *Allgeyer* marks the Supreme Court's first recognition of the doctrine of freedom of contract, guaranteed by the *Due Process Clause of the Fourteenth Amendment. The Court would subsequently use this doctrine as a rationale for striking down legislation regulating working conditions, such as maximum hours or minimum wages. The strength of *Allgeyer* as *precedent would remain until the mid-1930s.

CHICAGO, BURLINGTON & QUNICY RAILROAD CO. V. CHICAGO

Citation: 166 U.S. 226 (1897)
Argued: November 6 & 9, 1896
Decided: March 1, 1897
Court Below: Illinois Supreme Court
Basis for Review: *Writ of error
Facts: The Illinois Supreme Court upheld a jury award of one dollar to the Chicago, Burlington & Quincy Railroad Co. when the state opened a road across one of the railroad's tracks, thus obstructing rail traffic.
Issue: Is the state required to pay compensation when *taking private property?
Outcome: Reasoning that the *Due Process Clause of the Fourteenth Amendment requires the state to pay when taking private property for public use, the Fuller Court affirmed the lower court's ruling.
Vote: 7-1
Participating: Field, Harlan, Gray, Brewer, Brown, Shiras, White, Peckham (Fuller not participating)
Opinions: Harlan for the Court; Brewer dissenting
Significance: *Chicago, Burlington & Qunicy Railroad Co.* was one of the first instances in which the Supreme Court used due process to uphold substantive property rights. It was in essence a unanimous decision, as Justice Brewer dissented only in that he found the jury verdict nominal, rather than compensatory.

HOLDEN V. HARDY

Citation: 169 U.S. 366 (1898)
Argued: October 21, 1897
Decided: February 28, 1898
Court Below: Utah Supreme Court
Basis for Review: *Writ of error
Facts: A provision of the Utah state constitution prohibited miners from working more than eight hours per day. Albert F. Holden, a mine operator, began a *habeas corpus proceeding against Harvey Hardy, the sheriff who imprisoned

him for violating the provision. The state supreme court refused to issue the writ and upheld the provision.
Issue: Is freedom of contract subject to state *police powers?
Outcome: *Due process and freedom of contract, as protected by the Fourteenth Amendment, are not without limitations. Citing the state's right to pass laws to protect the welfare of its citizens, the Fuller Court upheld the lower court's ruling.
Vote: 6-2
Participating: Fuller, Harlan, Gray, Brewer, Brown, Shiras, White, Peckham (McKenna not participating)
Opinions: Brown for the Court; Brewer and Peckham dissenting (without written opinions)
Significance: Although *Holden* is important for its recognition of some state regulatory authority, its real significance lies in that fact that it marked the advent of an era of *judicial activism with regard to economic regulation. Just a few years later, in *Lochner v. New York* (1905), the Fuller Court would strike down a state statute limiting bakers' workweeks on grounds that it violated freedom of contract.

SMYTH V. AMES

Citation: 169 U.S. 466 (1898)
Argued: April 5-7, 1897
Decided: March 7, 1898
Court Below: United States Circuit Court for the District of Nebraska
Basis for Review: Appeal
Facts: A federal circuit court struck down a Nebraska statute enacting a railroad rate schedule.
Issue: Who determines what is just compensation for the use of private property in the public service?
Outcome: Reasoning that the state did not provide the railroad with a "fair return" on the "fair value" of its investment, the Fuller Court unanimously upheld the circuit court ruling voiding the Nebraska rate schedule.
Vote: 7-0
Participating: Harlan, Gray, Brewer, Brown, Shiras, White, Peckham (Fuller and McKenna not participating)

Opinion: Harlan for the Court

Significance: *Smyth* is indicative of the Supreme Court's support for *laissez faire economics during the Fuller era. Because states could not be trusted to provide businesses with a fair return, the Fuller Court declared, rate regulation must always be subject to judicial scrutiny. This *precedent remained in effect until *Smyth* was overturned by *Federal Power Commission v. Hope Natural Gas Co.* (1944).

UNITED STATES V. WONG KIM ARK

Citation: 169 U.S. 649 (1898)

Argued: March 5-8, 1897

Decided: March 28, 1898

Court Below: United States District Court for the Northern District of California

Basis for Review: Appeal

Facts: Wong Kim Ark, who was born in San Francisco, California to Chinese parents, was denied reentry to the United States and was detained upon returning from a visit to China. He applied for and was granted a writ of *habeas corpus, a decision the government appealed.

Issue: Does the first clause of the Fourteenth Amendment, providing that "all persons born or naturalized in the United States, and subject to the jurisdiction thereof, are citizens of the United States," apply to persons of Chinese descent?

Outcome: Finding that the Fourteenth Amendment guarantees citizenship to all persons born in the United States, regardless of ethnicity, the Fuller Court affirmed the lower court's ruling.

Vote: 6-2

Participating: Fuller, Harlan, Gray, Brewer, Brown, Shiras, White, Peckham (McKenna not participating)

Opinions: Gray for the Court; Fuller, joined by Harlan, dissenting

Significance: *Wong Kim Ark*, which marked the Supreme Court's first interpretation of the Fourteenth Amendment's *Citizenship Clause, was a significant victory for Chinese Americans during a period of intense xenophobia, which culminated with the passage of the Chinese Exclusion Acts excluding Chinese from the United States.

WILLIAMS V. MISSISSIPPI

Citation: 170 U.S. 213 (1898)

Argued: March 18, 1898

Decided: April 25, 1898

Court Below: Mississippi Supreme Court

Basis for Review: *Writ of error

Facts: Williams, an African American resident of Mississippi, was *indicted for murder by an all-white *grand jury and sentenced to be hanged by an all-white *petit jury. He appealed his sentence on grounds that a Mississippi law imposing literacy and poll tax requirements for voter registration effectively limited the number of blacks qualified to vote. Because only qualified voters could serve on Mississippi juries, Williams maintained that the voter registration law violated his Fourteenth Amendment right to *equal protection, but the state supreme court affirmed the verdict against him.

Issue: Are suffrage provisions, including such requirements as literacy, necessarily violative of equal protection?

Outcome: Because Williams had not shown — as was required by *Yick Wo v. Hopkins* (1886) — that the administration of the Mississippi voting requirements was discriminatory, the Fuller Court unanimously upheld his conviction.

Vote: 9-0

Participating: Fuller, Harlan, Gray, Brewer, Brown, Shiras, White, Peckham, McKenna

Opinion: McKenna for the Court

Significance: The *Williams v. Mississippi* decision allowed other southern states to dictate suffrage requirements that effectively disenfranchised blacks until passage of the Civil Rights Act of 1964 and the Voting Rights Act of 1965.

MAXWELL V. DOW

Citation: 176 U.S. 581 (1900)

Argued: December 4, 1899

Decided: February 26, 1900

Court Below: Utah Supreme Court

Basis for Review: *Writ of error

Facts: Charles L. Maxwell was tried and convicted for robbery before a jury of eight in state court.

Issue: Does trial in state court by a jury of fewer

than the 12 persons required by the Sixth Amendment violate the *privileges and immunities protected by the Fourteenth and Fifteenth Amendments, as well as the right of *due process guaranteed by the former?

Outcome: Stating that trial by a jury of 12 is not among the privileges and immunities accorded United States citizens, the Fuller Court upheld Maxwell's conviction.

Vote: 8-1

Participating: Fuller, Harlan, Gray, Brewer, Brown, Shiras, White, Peckham, McKenna

Opinions: Peckham for the Court; Harlan dissenting

Significance: With *Maxwell*, the Supreme Court continued the process of narrowing the concept of privileges and immunities it had begun with the *Slaughterhouse Cases* in 1873. It is Justice Harlan's dissent, however, that is reflected in modern constitutional decisions. Harlan argued that at a minimum the Privileges and Immunities Clause protects those rights identified in the Bill of Rights, advocating an *incorporation of the first ten amendments into the Fourteenth Amendment, a procedure that the Court would ratify after World War II.

DOWNES V. BIDWELL (INSULAR CASE)

Citation: 182 U.S. 244 (1901)

Argued: January 8-11, 1901

Decided: May 27, 1901

Court Below: United States Circuit Court for the Southern District of New York

Basis for Review: *Writ of error

Facts: *Downes* has come to be regarded as the most significant of 14 cases arising out of United States acquisition of island territories at the end of the Spanish-American War and decided by the Fuller Court between 1901 and 1904. At issue in all of the cases was the status to be accorded these new territories. At issue in *Downes* in particular was a provision of the Foraker Act which imposed a tariff on goods traded between the United States and Puerto Rico — albeit a tariff lower than that applied to other foreign commerce.

Issue: Is congressional power to impose tariffs on trade with newly acquired territories consti-

tutionally limited by the requirement of Article I, section 8, that duties be "uniform throughout the United States"?

Outcome: Stating that the Constitution does not automatically apply to territories, and that for revenue purposes Puerto Rico is not part of the United States, the Fuller Court upheld the Foraker Act.

Vote: 5-4

Participating: Fuller, Harlan, Gray, Brewer, Brown, Shiras, White, Peckham, McKenna

Opinions: Brown for the Court; White, joined by Shiras and McKenna, concurring, Gray concurring; Fuller, joined by Harlan, dissenting; Brewer and Peckham, dissenting; Harlan also dissenting separately

Significance: As a result of the decisions in the early *Insular Cases*, Congress acquired exclusive *jurisdiction over United States territories. Since the Constitution did not "follow the flag," it was up to Congress to determine which parts of the Constitution applied to which territories. Finally, in *Dorr v. United States* (1904), the Court accepted the "incorporation theory" — still in effect — that the Constitution does automatically apply in territories that have been incorporated into the United States by treaty ratification or other act of Congress.

CHAMPION V. AMES (THE LOTTERY CASE)

Citation: 188 U.S. 321 (1903)

Argued: February 27-28, 1901; reargued October 16-17, 1901; reargued December 15-16, 1902

Decided: February 23, 1903

Court Below: United States Circuit Court for the Northern District of Illinois

Basis for Review: Appeal

Facts: Champion was indicted under an 1895 federal statute prohibiting the distribution of lottery tickets through the mail.

Issue: Can Congress use its *commerce power as a *police power?

Outcome: Defining the commerce power broadly, so as to include *jurisdiction over items of such questionable value as lottery tickets, the Fuller Court upheld the statute.

Vote: 5-4
Participating: Fuller, Harlan, Brewer, Brown, Shiras, White, Peckham, McKenna, Holmes
Opinions: Harlan for the Court; Fuller, joined by Brewer, Shiras, and Peckham, dissenting
Significance: *Champion* marks the first recognition of a federal police power, an issue central to the Progressive agenda, with its emphasis on expanding federal authority. By emphasizing the moral aspect of lottery tickets, however, the Court was able to maintain some flexibility that later permitted regrouping when the Progressive movement waned.

NORTHERN SECURITIES CO. V. UNITED STATES

Citation: 193 U.S. 197 (1904)
Argued: December 14-15, 1903
Decided: March 14, 1904
Court Below: United States Circuit Court for the District of Minnesota
Basis for Review: Appeal
Facts: The stock of three major railways, the Northern Pacific, Great Northern, and Burlington Railroads, was held by a massive holding company, Northern Securities. The federal government sought to dissolve Northern Securities under the Sherman Antitrust Act, and a decree was issued ordering a breakup of the trust.
Issue: Does the Sherman Act extend to stock ownership?
Outcome: Finding that the existence of the holding company unreasonably restrained trade by controlling such a quantity of railroad stock, the Fuller Court upheld the decree ordering Northern's dissolution.
Vote: 5-4
Participating: Fuller, Harlan, Brewer, Brown, White, Peckham, McKenna, Holmes, Day
Opinions: Harlan for the Court; Brewer concurring; Holmes, joined by Fuller, White, and Peckham, dissenting; White, joined by Fuller, Peckham, and Holmes, dissenting
Significance: *Northern Securities* represented a change from the Fuller Court's decision in *United States v. E.C. Knight Co.* (1895), which held to a narrow interpretation of the Sherman Act. The

dissenters in *Northern Securities*, arguing that such a broad interpretation as that afforded by Harlan's opinion would unsettle business, ultimately won the day: in *Standard Oil Co. v. United States* (1911), then Chief Justice White convinced a majority of the Court that the Sherman Act should only prohibit unreasonable restraints of trade.

McCRAY V. UNITED STATES

Citation: 195 U.S. 27 (1904)
Argued: December 2, 1903
Decided: May 31, 1904
Court Below: United States District Court for the Southern District of Ohio
Basis for Review: *Writ of error
Facts: An 1886 act of Congress placed an excise tax on oleo-margarine colored yellow to resemble butter. McCray was fined $50 under the act for purchasing colored margarine for resale at the lower tax rate applicable to the uncolored variety.
Issue: Can Congress employ its *taxing power as a regulatory *police power?
Outcome: Arguing that the Court should not interfere with Congress's exercise of its constitutionally mandated powers, the Supreme Court upheld the act, as well as McCray's fine.
Vote: 6-3
Participating: Fuller, Harlan, Brewer, Brown, White, Peckham, McKenna, Holmes, Day`
Opinions: White for the Court; Fuller, Brown, and Peckham dissenting (all without written opinions)
Significance: *McCray* expanded federal police powers by adding the taxing power to the *commerce power, which the Fuller Court had declared the first of Congress's police powers in *Champion v. Ames* (1903). The use of federal taxation as a tool for engineering social welfare increased dramatically with the New Deal in the late 1930s and has since continued.

SWIFT & CO. V. UNITED STATES

Citation: 196 U.S. 375 (1905)
Argued: January 6-9, 1905
Decided: January 30, 1905

Court Below: United States Circuit Court for the Northern District of Illinois
Basis for Review: Appeal
Facts: Meat packers combined to fix the price of livestock and meat in Chicago stockyards and, found to be in violation of the Sherman Antitrust Act, were *enjoined from pursuing such illegal activities in restraint of trade.
Issue: Are business activities taking place solely intrastate within the reach of the federal *commerce power and its regulatory authority over interstate trade?
Outcome: Arguing that interstate commerce incorporates "domestic transactions," a unanimous Court upheld the injunction against the Beef Trust.
Vote: 9-0
Participating: Fuller, Harlan, Brewer, Brown, White, Peckham, McKenna, Holmes, Day
Opinion: Holmes for the Court
Significance: In *Swift*, Justice Holmes introduced the stream of commerce concept, which holds that however intrastate the nature of the discrete acts constituting a type of business, they can in the aggregate make up a current of interstate trade that can be deliberately interrupted. Holmes thus emphasized the importance of intent to antitrust law, an emphasis the Supreme Court would not take full advantage of until the New Deal era in the late 1930s.

LOCHNER V. NEW YORK

Citation: 198 U.S. 45 (1905)
Argued: February 23-24, 1905
Decided: April 17, 1905
Court Below: New York Court of Appeals
Basis for Review: *Writ of error
Facts: Joseph Lochner, owner of a Utica, New York, bakery, was fined $50 for requiring an employee to work more than 60 hours in one week in violation of the 1895 New York Bakeshop Act limiting a baker's hours of labor. Appeals to the *appellate division of the state supreme court and the New York Court of Appeals failed.
Issue: Is the Bakeshop Act a reasonable exercise of New York's *police powers?
Outcome: Declaring the act a violation of *due

process infringing upon the Fourteenth Amendment's guarantee of freedom of contract, the Fuller Court overturned the lower court's decision.
Vote: 5-4
Participating: Fuller, Harlan, Brewer, Brown, White, Peckham, McKenna, Holmes, Day
Opinions: Peckham for the Court; Holmes dissenting, and Harlan, joined by White and Day, dissenting
Significance: *Lochner* represented a watershed for the Fuller Court, pitting the majority conservatives against a progressive minority. Justice Peckham, author of the majority opinion, is today largely forgotten, while his primary antagonist, Justice Holmes, penned a dissent that is probably the most famous ever written. When the majority reasoned that the statute in question was a violation of due process because it interfered with freedom of contract, Holmes responded (referring to the famous economic treatise), "The Fourteenth Amendment does not enact Mr. Herbert Spencer's Social Statics." But because Peckham carried the day, *Lochner* is also remembered as the culmination of the Supreme Court's development of the concept of *substantive due process, elevated here to the status of a fundamental right. By substituting its judgment for that of the state legislature, the conservative Court ushered in an era of nearly unrestrained *judicial activism lasting until the Supreme Court firmly rejected the role of regulatory arbiter in *West Coast Hotel Co. v. Parrish* (1937).

ADAIR V. UNITED STATES

Citation: 208 U.S. 161 (1908)
Argued: October 29-30, 1907
Decided: January 27, 1908
Court Below: United States District Court for the Eastern District of Kentucky
Basis for Review: *Writ of error
Facts: With the Erdman Act of 1898, Congress sought to prevent labor disputes from disrupting interstate commerce by protecting workers from being forced as a condition of employment to sign "yellow dog" contracts, in which they promised not to join labor unions. The act was

challenged by an employer who was convicted for discharging an employee for joining a union after signing such a contract.

Issue: Does Congress have the power to enact legislation, such as the Erdman Act, which inhibits freedom of contract?

Outcome: Reasoning that the act was outside the scope of the *commerce power, as well as an unreasonable invasion of privacy and property rights, the Fuller Court struck it down.

Vote: 6-2

Participating: Fuller, Harlan, Brewer, White, Peckham, McKenna, Holmes, Day (Moody not participating)

Opinions: Harlan for the Court; McKenna and Holmes dissenting

Significance: *Adair* served as *precedent for negation of similar state laws protecting labor unions. Judicial antipathy to the labor movement was not reversed until federal New Deal legislation passed in the 1930s changed government's posture towards labor-management relations.

LOEWE V. LAWLOR (DANBURY HATTERS' CASE)

Citation: 208 U.S. 274 (1908)
Argued: December 4-5, 1907
Decided: February 3, 1908
Court Below: United States Second Circuit Court of Appeals
Basis for Review: *Writ of certiorari
Facts: To facilitate organization of the United Hatters of America at a factory in one state, the American Federation of Labor sponsored secondary boycotts of stores in other states. Loewe, an employer, sued individual members of the hatters' union, including resident agent Martin Lawlor, charging that the union was a combination in restraint of trade.

Issue: Are labor unions subject to suit under the Sherman Antitrust Act?

Outcome: Reasoning that every combination in restraint of trade is illegal, the Court found that the Sherman Act's treble damages clause could be invoked against individual union members.

Vote: 9-0

Participating: Fuller, Harlan, Brewer, White,

Peckham, McKenna, Holmes, Day, Moody

Opinion: Fuller for the Court

Significance: The decision in *Loewe* contrasts markedly with that in *United States v. E.C. Knight Co.* (1895), in which the Supreme Court declared that discrete intrastate acts by the Sugar Trust did not affect interstate commerce and therefore were beyond the reach of the Sherman Act. Congress attempted to correct this judicial imbalance with a provision of the Clayton Antitrust Act of 1914, but express exemption of labor unions from antitrust laws was not provided until the late 1930s.

MULLER V. OREGON

Citation: 208 U.S. 412 (1908)
Argued: January 15, 1908
Decided: February 24, 1908
Court Below: Oregon Supreme Court
Basis for Review: *Writ of error
Facts: A 1903 Oregon statute set the maximum workday for female laundry workers at ten hours. When Curt Muller, a laundry foreman in Portland, Oregon, required Mrs. Elmer Gotcher to work longer then ten hours, he was prosecuted and fined $10 by a local court. On the basis of the Supreme Court's ruling in *Lochner v. New York* (1905), Muller appealed his case to the state supreme court, which upheld the statute.

Issue: Is the Oregon statute an acceptable exercise of the state's *police powers?

Outcome: Reasoning that longer working hours might impair female laundry workers' childbearing abilities, the Fuller Court unanimously affirmed the lower court's ruling upholding the constitutionality of the statute.

Vote: 9-0

Participating: Fuller, Harlan, Brewer, White, Peckham, McKenna, Holmes, Day, Moody

Opinion: Brewer for the Court

Significance: *Muller* is remembered primarily for the introduction of the "Brandeis brief" as an instrument of social reform. Instead of trying to overturn *Lochner*, future Supreme Court Justice Louis D. Brandeis, representing the state, argued not from *precedent, but on the basis of facts and statistics. The innovative strategy proved so effective that subsequent legal arguments on behalf of social reforms, such as in *Brown v. Board of Education* (1954), have adopted it.

EX PARTE YOUNG

Citation: 209 U.S. 123 (1908)
Argued: December 2-3, 1907
Decided: March 23, 1908
Court Below: None; *original Supreme Court jurisdiction invoked
Basis for Review: Petition for writs of *habeas corpus and *certiorari
Facts: A 1907 Minnesota law reduced rates that railroads could charge and imposed heavy fines for failure to comply, provoking railroad shareholders to bring a *derivative suit seeking an *injunction to prevent their companies from complying with and state officers from enforcing the law. A temporary injunction was granted, but Minnesota Attorney General Young violated it by attempting to enforce the new lower rates in court. He was jailed for *contempt and petitioned the Supreme Court for a writ of habeas corpus.
Issue: Do federal courts have the power to enforce an injunction against a state official?
Outcome: Although the Eleventh Amendment restricts federal *jurisdiction in suits against states, when a state official attempts to enforce an unconstitutional statute, he is "stripped of his official or representative character." The Fuller Court refused to grant Young's petition.
Vote: 8-1
Participating: Fuller, Harlan, Brewer, White, Peckham, McKenna, Holmes, Day, Moody
Opinions: Peckham for the Court; Harlan dissenting
Significance: *Ex parte Young*, in which the Supreme Court once again sided with big business, proved to be an unpopular decision. Congress responded with the Three-Judge Panel Act of 1910, which created a special court with the power of direct appeal to the Supreme Court to manage suits for injunctions against state officials. This act was later repealed, but the Court retains — as a necessity of *federalism — the ability to enjoin state officials from violating federal laws.

TWINING V. NEW JERSEY

Citation: 211 U.S. 78 (1908)
Argued: March 19-20, 1908
Decided: November 9, 1908
Court Below: New Jersey Court of Errors and Appeals
Basis for Review: *Writ of error
Facts: A New Jersey judge, as permitted under then existing state law, charged a jury that the failure of defendants Twining and Cornell to testify in their own behalves could be taken into consideration in determining guilt.
Issue: Do the trial judge's instructions violate the Fifth Amendment privilege against *self-incrimination and, if so, does the Fourteenth Amendment extend the privilege to state defendants?
Outcome: Rejecting the argument that the Fourteenth Amendment *incorporates the Bill of Rights, making its provisions applicable to the states, the Fuller Court found the trial judge not to be in error.
Vote: 8-1
Participating: Fuller, Harlan, Brewer, White, Peckham, McKenna, Holmes, Day, Moody
Opinions: Moody for the Court; Harlan dissenting
Significance: The Supreme Court has subsequently ruled that most of the Bill of Rights is incorporated by the Fourteenth Amendment and thus applicable at the state level. *Twining* was explicitly reversed in 1964 by *Malloy v. Hogan*.

WEEMS V. UNITED STATES

Citation: 217 U.S. 349 (1910)
Argued: November 30-December 1, 1909
Decided: May 2, 1910
Court Below: Supreme Court of the Philippines
Basis for Review: *Writ of error
Facts: Weems, an American official residing in the Philippines, was convicted of falsifying documents and sentenced under Philippine law to years of hard labor in chains. He appealed his sentence on grounds that it violated the Eighth Amendment prohibition against cruel and unusual punishment.
Issue: What constitutes cruel and unusual pun-

POLITICAL COMPOSITION
of the Fuller Court

Justice & Total Term	Courts Served	Appointing President	Political Party
Melville W. Fuller 1888-1910	Fuller	Cleveland	Democrat
Samuel F. Miller 1862-1890	Taney Chase Waite Fuller	Lincoln	Republican
Stephen J. Field 1863-1897	Taney Chase Waite Fuller	Lincoln	Democrat
Joseph P. Bradley 1870-1892	Chase Waite Fuller	Grant	Republican
John Marshall Harlan 1877-1911	Waite Fuller White	Hayes	Republican
Stanley Matthews 1881-1889	Waite Fuller	Garfield	Republican
Horace Gray 1882-1902	Waite Fuller	Arthur	Republican
Samuel Blatchford 1882-1893	Waite Fuller	Arthur	Republican
Lucius Q.C. Lamar 1888-1893	Waite Fuller	Cleveland	Democrat
David J. Brewer 1890-1910	Fuller	Harrison	Republican

(Continued on opposite page)

ishment against individuals?

Outcome: Because Philippine law prescribed a punishment disproportionate to his crime, Weems was freed.

Vote: 4-2

Participating: Fuller, Harlan, White, McKenna, Holmes, Day (Lurton not participating)

Opinions: McKenna for the Court; White, joined by Holmes, dissenting

Significance: Using *Weems* as an opportunity to define the protections afforded by the Eighth Amendment, Justice McKenna stated that what is cruel and unusual must be determined by current sensibilities, not by rigid, outmoded legislative formulas, such as those employed in the American territory.

VOTING PATTERNS

The Fuller Court constituted the high-water mark of *laissez faire constitutionalism and, as such, helped generate the Progressive movement as a

POLITICAL COMPOSITION
of the Fuller Court

Justice & Total Term	Courts Served	Appointing President	Political Party
Henry B. Brown 1891-1906	Fuller	Harrison	Republican
George Shiras 1892-1903	Fuller	Harrison	Republican
Howell E. Jackson 1893-1895	Fuller	Harrison	Democrat
Edward D. White 1894-1910 1910-1921	Fuller White	Cleveland Taft	Democrat
Rufus W. Peckham 1896-1909	Fuller	Cleveland	Democrat
Joseph McKenna 1898-1925	Fuller White Taft	McKinley	Republican
Oliver W. Holmes 1902-1932	Fuller White Taft Hughes	T. Roosevelt	Republican
William R. Day 1903-1922	Fuller White Taft	T. Roosevelt	Republican
William H. Moody 1906-1910	Fuller	T. Roosevelt	Republican
Horace Lurton 1910-1914	Fuller White	Taft	Democrat

corrective to the excesses of business practice. While Chief Justice Fuller busied himself with his administrative duties, Justice Field continued to expand on his theory of *substantive due process, supported by his nephew, Justice Brewer. Substantive due process reached the level of orthodoxy during the Fuller Court when it was translated into freedom of contract by Justice Peckham in *Allgeyer v. Louisiana* (1897) and *Lochner v. New York* (1905). However, even though *Allgeyer v. Louisiana* was a unanimous decision, by 1905 some fresh opposition to this extreme conservatism had been introduced into the Court in the person of Justice Holmes.

Holmes was in the tradition of great dissenters on the Court, but he objected to the conservative Court's posture not so much on philosophical grounds but on the grounds of its excessive *judicial activism. Such involvement in governing led, in *United States v. E.C. Knight* (1895) to an 8 to 1 decision (Justice Harlan, another frequent dissenter, was the odd man out) that seriously undercut the effectiveness of the Sherman Antitrust Act.

The majority's determination to maintain the status quo while giving business free rein is no where better illustrated than in the 1895 *Pollock v. Farmers' Loan & Trust Co.*, the Fuller Court's most controversial decision. Striking down a federal income tax as unconstitutional, the majority succumbed to conservative pressure to preserve private property against "communistic" governmental interference — an argument that was the logical end product of substantive due process. As Harlan's impassioned dissent pointed out, such a ruling crippled the power of the federal government. It took a constitutional amendment for Congress to correct the balance of power so seriously upset here by the judicial branch.

As in the Waite Court that preceded it, the Fuller Court's dedication to the interests of business coincided with a deterioration of individual rights. In *In re Debs* (1895), decided only months after *E.C. Knight,* Justice Brewer, writing for a unanimous court, found that the same Sherman Act, so impotent in the face of the monopolies it was meant to regulate, could be used as a strike-breaking tool. In 1896 the Court stripped the Fourteenth Amendment of its guarantee of *equal protection intended to reach African Americans with its infamous *Plessy v. Ferguson* decision, which made "separate but equal" the law of the land for the next half century. Again, Justice Harlan was the only member to dissent.

By the time of Fuller's death, the Court had been almost entirely remade, with only Justice Harlan remaining from the Waite Court. And of those appointed during Fuller's tenure, only McKenna, Holmes, Day, and Lurton would serve with Edward White when he became the next chief justice.

SPECIAL FEATURES OF THE FULLER COURT

THE JUDICIARY ACT OF 1891

The 1891 Judiciary Act did two important things to improve the efficiency of the federal judicial system, as well as the lives of Supreme Court justices: it created a network of intermediate courts of appeal and coincidentally did away with the *circuit riding requirement. The Judiciary Act of 1789, which first established the federal court system, had created district and *circuit trial courts, but except for the limited *appellate powers of the latter, the Supreme Court was the only real avenue of appeal in federal cases. By 1890 the Supreme Court's *docket was considerably overburdened, consisting of 1,816 cases, a nearly sixfold increase since the Civil War. Cases often remained in legal limbo for two or three years before actually being listed for hearing. The establishment of nine federal appellate courts eased this load considerably.

The new circuit courts of appeal did not immediately annul the old circuit courts, although the latter's appellate jurisdiction was abolished; neither did they eliminate all direct appeals to the Supreme Court. The right to appeal to the High Court was maintained in certain federal cases, such as those involving constitutional questions or an amount in controversy exceeding $1,000. The Court also continued to hear appeals from state supreme courts. But by the 1891 term, the Supreme Court docket was reduced to 379 cases.

At the same time, the existence of intermediate appellate courts, each staffed with new judges, did away with any residual need for Supreme Court justices to ride circuit. Consequently, during the Fuller Court the tradition of geographically determined seats on the Court became irrelevant; no longer was there a need, for example, for a native New York justice to service federal appellate courts in that state.

SUBSTANTIVE DUE PROCESS COMES OF AGE

The Fourteenth Amendment, ratified in 1865 in the aftermath of the Civil War, contains, like the Fifth Amendment, a *Due Process Clause. While the Fifth Amendment clause is meant to restrain federal impositions on individual rights, the Fourteenth Amendment imposes these constraints on the states. Prior to adoption of the Fourteenth Amendment, due process had been interpreted primarily in procedural terms, that is, as an assurance of fairness in the means by which the government imposes a burden on the individual.

Modern notions of *substantive due process, concerning actual protections against arbitrary governmental deprivations — primarily of property — rather than the means by which this is accomplished, derive from Justice Field's interpretation of the Fourteenth Amendment in his dissent in the *Slaughterhouse Cases* (1873): "The equality of right, with exemption from all disparaging and partial enactments, in the lawful pursuits of life, throughout the whole country, is the distinguishing privilege of citizens of the United States." Originally a minority view, Field's conception of due process as the freedom to pursue lawful employment — and a fair return on one's investment of time or money — became the centerpiece of the conservative Fuller Court. In cases such as *United States v. E.C. Knight & Co.* (1895), in which the Court denied that the Sherman Antitrust Act applied to manufacturing monopolies, and *In re Debs* (1895), in which it ruled that the Sherman Act could be used as a weapon against labor unions, substantive due process provided the subtext. In *Allgeyer v. Louisiana* (1897) and *Lochner v. New York* (1905), Justice Peckham, the Fuller Court's most conservative member, raised substantive due process to the status of orthodoxy by declaring freedom of contract sacrosanct.

SEPARATE BUT EQUAL

While the majority of the Fuller Court wanted to deny states the ability to regulate business by, for example, setting maximum railroad rates or working hours, it attempted to preserve the federal-state balance of power by ceding another part of the Fourteenth Amendment, the *Equal Protection Clause, to state dominion. In the most egregious example of its *laissez faire orientation, *Plessy v. Ferguson* (1896), the Fuller Court declared that it was no violation of the Fourteenth Amendment for the state to mandate "separate but equal" railroad accommodations for African Americans and whites. The Fourteenth Amendment, it was argued, protected political, not social equality. This de facto sanction of segregation, which the drafters of the Fourteenth Amendment had meant to abrogate, resulted in the proliferation of Jim Crow laws throughout the South.

THE ADVENT OF THE "BRANDEIS BRIEF"

*Briefs, the papers submitted to a court by advocates for each party to a given controversy, customarily present factual background and legal arguments in a fashion that best supports each party's case. Prior to *Muller v. Oregon* (1908), brief writers had relied heavily on pro forma recitation of legal *precedents to make their cases. In *Muller*, however, future Supreme Court Justice Louis D. Brandeis, representing overburdened female laundry workers, argued in favor of a ten-hour workday by devoting the bulk of his brief to statistics and sociological studies demonstrating the detrimental effects of long hours on working women. Brandeis's 112 page brief, which covered the applicable precedents in only two pages, convinced a unanimous Fuller Court to modify its ultraconservative protection of freedom of contract — which it had resoundingly evinced in *Lochner v. New York* (1905) — by upholding the Oregon statute, becoming in the process the model for future attempts to achieve social reform through the courts.

The White Court
1910-1921

BACKGROUND

THE ELECTION OF 1912

The Republicans and their nominee in the 1912 election, President William Howard Taft, were initially challenged by former President Theodore Roosevelt, who, in August 1910, in Osawatomie, Kansas, outlined a progressive program he called the New Nationalism. New Nationalism sought to make the president the steward of the public welfare and, to that end, required a bigger, more bureaucratic federal government to battle special interests and regulate the trusts. Not all Progressives embraced Roosevelt's program, however, and as a result of their lack of unity, Taft was nominated on the first ballot. Roosevelt and his followers then split off, forming the Progressive Party — informally called the Bull Moose Party, after Roosevelt's ebullient declaration that he felt "like a bull moose" when he arrived to accept the Progressive nomination.

The Democrats chose as their candidate a rising star, Woodrow Wilson, who had made a name for himself as a reformer, first as president of Princeton University, then as governor of New Jersey. Wilson brought to the campaign a platform he called the New Freedom, which differed from Roosevelt's New Nationalism chiefly in that while the former advocated breaking up the trusts, the latter wanted to control them.

Taft and Roosevelt effectively split the Republican vote, assuring Wilson of victory. Democrats gained clear majorities in both houses of Congress as well, assuring implementation of the New Freedom.

WILSON'S PROGRESSIVISM

The Democratic platform emphasized the need for tariff and bank reform, and Wilson set to work on these issues immediately upon gaining the White House. A month before his inauguration in March 1913, the Sixteenth Amendment had been ratified, authorizing a federal income tax. With this new source of revenue, Congress was able in October 1913 to institute the first significant reduction in tariff rates since the Civil War. Wilson's campaign promise to reform the banking system was realized with equal dispatch. The Federal Reserve Act was passed in December 1913, establishing a nationwide network of banks from which other, nonmember banks could borrow and which would control the money supply.

Wilson next took on the trusts. His vehicle for doing so was the Clayton antitrust bill, introduced in 1914. The Clayton bill, which enumerated a long list of unfair trade practices, seemed unwieldy and unworkable until Wilson advisor Louis D. Brandeis suggested creation of a federal commission to investigate and suppress illegal trade restraints. The Federal Trade Commission Act, passed in September 1914, and the Clayton Antitrust Act, passed the following month, together held out great hope for American business reform. These hopes were never fully realized. Establishment of the Federal Trade Commission did, however, mark for Wilson the completion of New Freedom's promised reforms.

An asterisk (*) before a word or phrase indicates that a definition will be found in the glossary at the end of this volume.

After initially refusing to entertain issues of women's suffrage, child labor reform, and other social justice issues, Wilson changed his course. With major Republican victories in the 1914 elections and the strong indication that Roosevelt would once again be a candidate in 1916, Wilson took up a number of Progressive causes. He signaled his intentions in January 1916 by naming Louis Brandeis to the Supreme Court. Brandeis, a longtime advocate of reform and a Jew, faced stiff opposition, but eventually he was confirmed. That spring, Wilson helped push through a farm loan bill he had previously opposed, as well as workers' compensation legislation. Perhaps even more significantly, he personally lobbied Congress for passage of a child labor bill. Although in 1918

the Supreme Court would declare it unconstitutional, the 1916 Keating-Owen Child Labor Act, which barred the interstate transportation of goods made with child labor, marked the first time Congress had used its *commerce power to regulate manufacturing.

With the passage during his first term of every major proposal put forward by the Progressives, Wilson was able to deflect attention from Roosevelt and from the eventual Republican candidate in 1916, Charles Evans Hughes, who resigned from the Supreme Court to take up the nomination. It was a close election, but Wilson waged an active campaign, reminding the populace of his progressive reforms and of the fact that he had kept the nation out of the war then raging in Europe. For the first time since Andrew Jackson's long tenure in office, a Democrat won reelection to a second consecutive term in the White House.

WORLD WAR I

Presidents Roosevelt and Taft had instituted a policy of "dollar diplomacy," which promoted investment in the Caribbean and resulted in intervention to protect American interests there. Often this intervention took the form — as it did in Cuba, Nicaragua, Haiti, and Santo Domingo (now the Dominican Republic) — of a military invasion, followed by long years of occupation, during which the United States took control of customs collections and administered national finances.

Woodrow Wilson denounced dollar diplomacy, but he followed his predecessors' lead by meddling in Mexican internal affairs after General Victoriano Huerta hijacked the Mexican presidency in the midst of civil war. On the slightest provocation, Wilson sent in a naval squadron to take on Huerta's troops. Huerta was deposed, and the civil war resumed. When the Mexican revolutionary, Pancho Villa, raided an American border town in order to bring the United States back into the conflict, Wilson accommodated him. American troops occupied northern Mexico but failed to capture Villa. The ill will engendered by this escapade helped draw America into World

MEMBERS Of the Court 1910–1921

(In Order of Seniority)

Edward D. White (Chief Justice)	(1910-1921)
John Marshall Harlan (died)	(1910-1911)
Joseph McKenna	(1910-1921)
Oliver Wendell Holmes	(1910-1921)
William R. Day	(1910-1921)
Horace H. Lurton (died)	(1910-1914)
Charles E. Hughes (resigned)	(1910-1916)
Willis Van Devanter	(1911-1921)
Joseph R. Lamar (died)	(1911-1916)
Mahlon Pitney (replaced John Marshall Harlan)	(1912-1921)
James C. McReynolds (replaced Horace H. Lurton)	(1914-1921)
Louis D. Brandeis (replaced Joseph R. Lamar)	(1916-1921)
John H. Clarke (replaced Charles Evans Hughes)	(1916-1921)

War I when, in February 1917, the British turned over an intercepted German communique offering Mexico a military alliance — and return of the territory it lost to America in 1848 — if the United States entered the war.

President Wilson had long resisted efforts to involve the United States in the calamitous European conflict. Between August 1914, when war broke out, and April 2, 1917, when Wilson asked Congress for a formal declaration of war, America had maintained a neutral posture. Even after the 1915 German U-boat sinking of the British passenger liner *Lusitania*, which resulted in the deaths of 128 Americans, Wilson reacted only with a series of threatening notes. The next year Germany agreed to curtail its submarine warfare, and it was not until German submarines sank several American merchant ships and the U.S. discovered Germany's proposal of a military alliance with Mexico that America entered the war.

Within 15 months, the United States, which instituted a military draft, had deployed a million troops to eastern France, where they played a decisive role in blunting a major German offensive and spearheading a counteroffensive that led to the end of the war. On November 11, 1918, the fighting ended with an armistice, and Wilson began a diplomatic crusade that was intended to bring about "peace without victory," but which ended in his personal defeat.

THE FOURTEEN POINTS AND THE TREATY OF VERSAILLES

Wilson first presented his Fourteen Points, a plan for world peace, before Congress in January 1918. The first five points concerned traditional American goals, such as free trade, freedom of the seas, and reduction of armaments. The next eight points addressed the Allied Powers' plan to divide up the Austro-Hungarian and Ottoman Empires; instead of dividing these lands among the victors, Wilson proposed that they be made into autonomous republics with boundaries determined by language and culture. The fourteenth point introduced Wilson's proposal for a League of Nations, an international alliance whose goal

it would be to insure mutual security.

The Allies, however, had exchanged secret treaties early in the conflict that provided for territorial gains as well as payment of reparations. The Treaty of Versailles that emerged from the negotiations among the Big Four — the United States, Great Britain, France, and Italy — was a compromise between these earlier agreements and Wilson's more generous proposal. The land cessions were generally along the lines of the Fourteen Points, but the other Allies were insistent that Germany be penalized for its aggression. The heavy reparations imposed on the Germans would wreck their economy, ultimately leading to the rise of Adolph Hitler and World War II.

In retrospect, it is clear that Wilson failed to press hard enough on the reparations issue; one reason may be that he was intent on securing agreement to establish the League of Nations. But while the Treaty of Versailles included a provision authorizing the League of Nations, it was this provision that resulted in the Senate's subsequent refusal to ratify the treaty. Wilson had committed a major blunder by failing to include any Republicans or senators in the American peace delegation, and in the aftermath of Versailles, he found few supporters. The Senate stalled the treaty in committee over questions concerning the League of Nations, and Wilson took to the road to drum up public support in a personal crusade to save what he had come to regard as his crowning achievement and the only hope for world peace. After days of whistle-stop appearances and public addresses, Wilson collapsed in Pueblo, Colorado, and returned to Washington only to suffer a debilitating stroke. In the Senate, ratification of the Treaty of Versailles failed for want of a two-thirds majority.

ESPIONAGE AND SEDITION ACTS

During World War I, Congress revived curbs on civil liberties that had not been a feature of the American landscape since the time of John Adams. In fact, the Espionage Act of 1917 and the Sedition Act of 1918 were in some respects more extreme in their prohibitions than the Alien and Sedition Acts of 1798. The Espionage Act, which the Supreme Court upheld in *Schenck v. United States* (1919), provided penalties of up to $10,000 and 20 years in jail for anyone found guilty of aiding the enemy or obstructing the military. It also empowered the postmaster to exclude from the mails any allegedly treasonous material — including, at one time, the *Saturday Evening Post*.

The Sedition Act, an amendment to the Espionage Act, was even more restrictive, making it illegal to inhibit the sale of war bonds or use "disloyal, profane, scurrilous, or abusive language" against the government, the armed forces, the Constitution, or the flag. This measure, which was aimed primarily at Socialist leaders like presidential candidate Eugene V. Debs and Congressman Victor L. Berger, appeared to penalize all criticism of the government. It was nonetheless upheld by the Supreme Court in *Abrams v. United States* (1919).

CONSTITUTIONAL AMENDMENTS

In 1913 two amendments to the Constitution were ratified: the Sixteenth, which authorized Congress to collect a peacetime federal income tax, and the Seventeenth, which altered Article I by changing the indirect method of state legislative selection of United States senators to one of direct popular election. Two more amendments, the Eighteenth and the Nineteenth, ratified in 1919 and 1920, respectively, became law almost as a result of World War I.

The Eighteenth Amendment, which instituted nationwide prohibition, grew out of the temperance movement and had long been associated with feminism, which bore fruit with the ratification of the Nineteenth Amendment granting women the vote. Feminists' advocacy of temperance had, for some time, delayed suffrage because the liquor industry worked against it. With the advent of war, however, the nation needed grain more for food than for manufacture of intoxicating beverages, and passage of the 1917 Lever Act, prohibiting such use of grain, led almost immediately to the Eighteenth Amendment. On October

28, 1919, Congress passed the Volstead Act, *enabling federal enforcement of prohibition.

World War I freed women not just from anti-suffrage liquor lobbyists, but from many of the social and economic constraints that had traditionally militated against female participation in the political process. With so many men called up to battle the Central Powers in Europe, women were able to enter the job force in new capacities, and their new roles contributed to the breakdown of social mores that had previously limited their activities to the domestic realm. While many American women declined to support aspects of the Progressive social revolution, such as contraception, the suffrage movement gained power after 1912. Woodrow Wilson, who initially opposed women's suffrage, was finally forced to yield to its strength, finding the wartime need for national unity a convenient excuse for his reversal.

THE ELECTION OF 1920

Many predicted that once women were granted the vote, they would radically alter the political landscape. This was not to be. The first opportunity for women to exercise their vote came with the presidential election of 1920, when a majority voted for Republican candidate Warren G. Harding.

Harding, who proudly announced that he had no platform and who conducted a "front porch" campaign, swamped the Democratic candidate, James M. Cox, winning 61 percent of the popular vote. It was the most unequal presidential contest since James Monroe won all but one electoral vote in 1820. Harding stood for little other than what he — employing a word he himself coined — called "normalcy." The end of World War I brought temporary peace to Europe, but rising social unrest to America, where four million demobilized men and women reentered the job market simultaneously.

Unemployment and the cost of living soared. A frightened public confused the resulting social tensions in their country with Bolshevik revolutions taking place in other parts of the world, and a Red Scare resulted. Raids in 1919 and 1920,

JUDICIAL BIOGRAPHY
Edward Douglass White

PERSONAL DATA

Born: November 3, 1845, in Lafourche Parish, Louisiana

Parents: Edward Douglass White, Catherine S. Ringgold White

Higher Education: Mount St. Mary's College, 1856; Georgetown College, now Georgetown University, 1857-1861; University of Louisiana, now Tulane University, School of Law, 1866-1868

Bar Admission: Louisiana, 1868

Political Party: Democrat

Marriage: November 1894 to Virginia Montgomery Kent

Died: May 19, 1921, in Washington, D.C.

Buried: Oak Hill Cemetery, Washington, D.C.

PROFESSIONAL CAREER

Occupations: Serviceman, 1861-1865; Lawyer, 1868-1878, 1880-1891; Politician, 1874, 1891-1894; Judge, 1878-1880, 1894-1921

Official Positions: State Senator, Louisiana, 1874; Associate Justice, Louisiana Supreme Court, 1878-1880; Member, United State Senate, 1891-1894; Associate Justice, United States Supreme Court, 1894-1910; Chief Justice, United States Supreme Court, 1910-1921

SUPREME COURT SERVICE

As Associate Justice:

Nominated: February 19, 1894

Nominated By: Grover Cleveland

Confirmed: February 19, 1894

Confirmation Vote: Voice vote

Oath Taken: March 12, 1894

Replaced: Samuel Blatchford

Significant Opinion: *McCray v. United States* (1904)

Left Court: Promoted to chief justice December 18, 1910

Length of Service: 16 years, 9 months, 6 days

Replacement: Joseph R. Lamar

As Chief Justice:

Nominated: December 12, 1910

Nominated By: William Howard Taft

Confirmed: December 12, 1910

Confirmation Vote: Voice vote

Oath Taken: December 19, 1910

Replaced: Melville W. Fuller

Significant Opinions: *Standard Oil v. United States* (1911); *Guinn v. United States* (1915); *Clark Distilling Co. v. Western Maryland Railway Co.* (1917); *Selective Draft Law Cases* (1918)

Left Court: Died May 19, 1921

Length of Service: 10 years, 5 months

Replacement: William Howard Taft

---

organized by Attorney General A. Mitchell Palmer, netted more than five thousand people, many of them aliens suspected of subversive activities. Ultimately over five hundred of these individuals were deported, but the Red Scare quickly expired. Its only immediate legacy was the election of Warren Harding.

WHITE'S EARLY LIFE

Edward D. White was born on a sugar plantation near Thibodaux, Louisiana. His father, a wealthy planter, New Orleans judge, member of the United States House of Representatives, and governor of Louisiana, died when his son and namesake was two years old. White was educated almost entirely in Jesuit institutions. At the age of 11 he was sent by his then remarried mother to attend preparatory school at Mount St. Mary's College in Emmitsburg, Maryland. In 1857 he entered the Jesuits' Georgetown College in Washington, D.C., but his studies were interrupted by the outbreak of the Civil War.

In 1861 the 16-year-old White joined the Confederate army. White saw little action, serving most of the time as an aide-de-camp to various officers. In July 1863, however, he was among those captured by Union forces at Port Hudson, Louisiana, and he was held prisoner for the remainder of the war.

Edward Douglass White

In 1865, having returned home, White studied law in the offices of noted New Orleans attorney Edward Bermudez and, simultaneously, took courses at the University of Louisiana Law School. In 1868 he passed the Louisiana bar and set up a private practice in New Orleans.

WHITE'S PUBLIC LIFE

Almost immediately after passing the bar, White began to pursue politics. He allied himself with the Southern Democratic Redeemers, who sought to oust the Republican carpetbaggers, and became closely associated with Francis T. Nicholls, leader of the Redeemers. Local distaste for Reconstruction ran strong and helped White get elected to the state senate in 1874.

White also benefited from the compromise that settled the 1876 presidential election. Louisiana Democrats pledged their support for Republican Rutherford B. Hayes in exchange for removal of the Radical Republican administration then in control of the state. When Nicholls was subsequently elected governor, he rewarded

White's loyal support with an appointment to the state supreme court. Two years later, however, a Democratic faction opposed to Nicholls took power, replacing him even before his term as governor had expired. Such arbitrary exercise of authority also impacted White when the faction adopted a state constitutional provision setting a minimum age for holders of high office. White was relieved of his judgeship for failure to meet this requirement; he was 33 in 1878.

For the next decade, White associated himself with a succession of influential New Orleans law firms and served as legal advisor to Tulane University, then newly chartered. In 1888 Nicholls regained the governor's office and shortly thereafter named his old friend White to fill a vacancy as junior United States senator from Louisiana. In the Senate, White distinguished himself primarily as a defender of Louisiana sugar interests. As a sugar plantation owner, White was of course demonstrating a considerable conflict of interest, but he seemed unconcerned. Indeed, even after his appointment to the Supreme Court was confirmed in February 1894, he remained for some weeks in the Senate to fight for protection of domestic sugar in the Wilson-Gorman Tariff Act.

White was Grover Cleveland's third nominee to replace Justice Blatchford, who died in July 1893. Conflicts between the president and New York Senator David Hill thwarted confirmation of Cleveland's two earlier attempts to replace Blatchford, a New Yorker, with another native of that state. Finally the president turned in desperation to White, whose status as a southerner might help Cleveland politically. In part because the Senate could not easily reject one of its own members, White was confirmed the very day he was nominated.

White's record on the Fuller Court was inconsistent and undistinguished. While he voted against a state law regulating bakers' working hours in *Lochner v. New York* (1905), White voted to uphold a similar statute limiting laundry workers' hours in *Muller v. Oregon* (1908). But it is worth noting that in both cases he voted with the majority; White's attitude toward cases involving issues of *substantive due process was appar-

The White Court, 1914. From left: William R. Day, Mahlon Pitney, Joseph McKenna, Willis Van Devanter, Edward Douglass White, Joseph R. Lamar, Oliver Wendell Holmes, James C. McReynolds, Charles Evans Hughes

ently no more inconsistent than those of his brethren. Nonetheless, during the nearly 17 years he served as an associate justice, White authored few opinions of lasting significance, and his elevation in 1910 to the chief justiceship — the first such internal promotion in the Court's history — came as something of a surprise.

WHITE AS CHIEF JUSTICE

After the death of Chief Justice Fuller in July 1910, there was some speculation that President Taft would replace him with someone already on the Court. That speculation centered on Charles Evans Hughes, a Taft appointee confirmed in May 1910 who took his seat on the Court the following October. Indeed, upon Hughes's appointment Taft had all but assured him that he would be promoted upon the death of the ailing Chief Justice Fuller. When Fuller died, however, the 53-year-old Taft, who coveted the chief justiceship for himself, passed over the younger Hughes for 65-year-old White. Taft deliberated for months, finally informing White of his decision only after canceling an appointment with Hughes at the last moment.

White's only lasting contribution to American law and society came early in his tenure as chief justice with *Standard Oil v. United States* (1911), in which he persuaded the other members of the Court to ignore strong *precedent and the seemingly plain words of the Sherman Antitrust Act to support the "rule of reason." The act itself outlawed all combinations in restraint of trade, and a string of Supreme Court decisions — culminating in *Northern Securities Co. v. United States* (1904) — militated against interpreting the statute in such a manner as to find monopolistic endeavors "reasonable." White had argued unsuccessfully for 15 years for selective application of the Sherman Act, so his victory in *Standard Oil* was notable. Like his earlier endorsement of the *incorporation doctrine in the *Insular Case, Downes v. Bidwell* (1901) — in which the determination of the degree of constitutional protection accorded American territories was left to the judiciary — White's championing of the "rule of reason" promoted judicial subjectivism. And indeed, subjectivity and unpredictableness seem to have been hallmarks of the White Court. As White grew older, he tended to vote more and more conservatively, and the associate justices who served under him — with the notable exceptions of John Marshall Harlan, Oliver Wendell Holmes, and later, Louis D. Brandeis — tended to defer to his seniority.

With the election of Warren Harding in 1920, Taft's Supreme Court ambitions resurfaced. Shortly after the election, Taft journeyed to the president-elect's home in Marion, Ohio, to make certain that Harding was aware of his desire to be the next chief justice. He made another trip to Washington, D.C., in March 1921 to see White himself and to consult with White's doctor about the chief justice's health. Taft was disappointed to find that, aside from cataract problems, White was in good health and had no plans to resign. Within two months, however, White died, and shortly thereafter Taft gained the position he had so long desired.

ASSOCIATE JUSTICES

For a biography of Associate Justice **John Marshall Harlan,** see the entry under **THE WAITE COURT.** For biographies of Associate Justices **Joseph McKenna, Oliver Wendell Holmes, William R. Day,** and **Horace H. Lurton,** see entries under **THE FULLER COURT.** For a biography of Associate, then Chief Justice **Charles Evans Hughes,** see the entry under **THE HUGHES COURT.**

WILLIS VAN DEVANTER

PERSONAL DATA
Born: April 17, 1859, in Marion, Indiana
Parents: Isaac Van Devanter, Violetta Spencer Van Devanter
Higher Education: Indiana Asbury University, now DePauw University (B.A., 1878); University of Cincinnati Law School (LL.B., 1881)
Bar Admission: Indiana, 1881
Political Party: Republican
Marriage: October 10, 1883, to Dellice Burhans, who bore Van Devanter two children
Died: February 8, 1941, in Washington, D.C.
Buried: Rock Creek Cemetery, Washington, D.C.

PROFESSIONAL CAREER
Occupations: Lawyer, 1881-1888, 1890-1903; Government Official, 1887-1888, 1897-1903; Politician, 1888, 1892-1894, 1896-1900; Judge, 1889-1890, 1903-1937
Official Positions: Member, Wyoming Territorial Statutes Revision Committee, 1886; City Attorney, Cheyenne, Wyoming, 1887-1888; Member, Wyoming Territorial Legislature, 1888; Chief Justice, Wyoming Territorial Supreme Court, 1889-1890; Chairman, Wyoming State Republican Committee, 1892-1894; Member, Republican National Committee, 1896-1900; Assistant United States Attorney General, 1897-1903; Judge, United States Eighth Circuit Court of Appeals, 1903-1910; Associate Justice, United States Supreme Court, 1911-1937

SUPREME COURT SERVICE
Nominated: December 12, 1910
Nominated By: William Howard Taft
Confirmed: December 15, 1910
Confirmation Vote: Voice vote
Oath Taken: January 3, 1911
Replaced: William H. Moody
Significant Opinion: *Dillon v. Gloss* (1921)
Left Court: Retired June 2, 1937
Length of Service: 26 years, 4 months, 30 days
Replacement: Hugo L. Black

On April 17, 1859, Willis Van Devanter was born into a family that had migrated westward nine years earlier. After obtaining an undergraduate degree, then a law degree, Van Devanter joined his father's law practice in Marion, Indiana, for three years before he migrated further west to the Wyoming Territory.

In Cheyenne, Van Devanter devoted himself both to his own law practice and to Republican politics. He helped to revise the territorial statutes, served as city attorney, and was elected to the territorial legislature. When Van Devanter was just 30 years old, President Harrison appointed him chief justice of the territory's highest court. Van Devanter held that post for only one year, resuming private practice in 1890 when Wyoming achieved statehood.

In 1897 Van Devanter's participation in Republican politics led to his appearance on the national scene when President McKinley appointed him an assistant United States attorney general, assigned to the Department of the Interior. In 1903 Van Devanter moved from that position to a federal judgeship when President Theodore Roosevelt appointed him to the Eighth Circuit Court of Appeals.

When President Taft sent Edward D. White's name to the Senate Judiciary Committee for consideration as chief justice, he added to it those of Willis Van Devanter and Joseph R. Lamar, both candidates for associate justice. Van Devanter's nomination was strongly opposed by liberals, as he was widely — and accurately — perceived to be an arch conservative closely allied with the railroads and other interests he had long represented. He was, nonetheless, confirmed in short order.

Van Devanter proved to be one of the foremost conservative intellectual forces on the Court during his 26-year tenure. Always opposed to use of the *commerce power, the *taxing power, and the *Due Process Clause to regulate business, he became during the New Deal Era one of the so-called "Four Horsemen," justices whose disapproval of President Franklin D. Roosevelt's economic and social reforms occasioned comparison with the Four Horsemen of the Apocalypse. (The other three were James C. McReynolds, Pierce Butler, and George Sutherland.) Van Devanter's influence on the Supreme Court was in fact out of proportion to his output, for he wrote few opinions. Instead, he revealed his gifts primarily to his fellow justices in conference, becoming a mainstay for Chief Justices White and Taft. In 1937, after passage of legislation that permitted him to retire with full pay, Van Devanter resigned from the Supreme Court, then under the leadership of Charles Evans Hughes.

JOSEPH RUCKER LAMAR

PERSONAL DATA
Born: October 14, 1857, in Elbert County, Georgia
Parents: James Sanford Lamar, Mary Rucker Lamar
Higher Education: University of Georgia, 1874-1875; Bethany College (B.A., 1877); Washington and Lee University Law School, 1877
Bar Admission: Georgia, 1878
Political Party: Democrat
Marriage: January 13, 1879, to Clarinda Huntington Pendleton, who bore Lamar two sons and one daughter
Died: January 2, 1916, in Washington, D.C.
Buried: Summerville Cemetery, Augusta, Georgia

PROFESSIONAL CAREER
Occupations: Educator, 1878-1879; Lawyer, 1880-1903, 1905-1910; Politician, 1886-1889; Judge, 1903-1905, 1911-1916; Diplomat, 1914
Official Positions: Member for Richmond County, Georgia State Legislature, 1886-1889; Member, Commission to Codify Georgia Laws, 1893; Examiner, Georgia Bar Admissions Committee, ca. late 1890s; Associate Justice, Georgia Supreme Court, 1903-1905; Associate Justice, United States Supreme Court, 1911-1916; Member, Mediation Conference, Niagara Falls, Canada, 1914

SUPREME COURT SERVICE
Nominated: December 12, 1910
Nominated By: William Howard Taft
Confirmed: December 15, 1910
Confirmation Vote: Voice vote
Oath Taken: January 3, 1911
Replaced: Edward D. White
Significant Opinion: *Gompers v. Buck's Stove & Range Co.* (1911)
Left Court: Died January 2, 1916
Length of Service: 4 years, 11 months, 30 days
Replacement: Louis D. Brandeis

Joseph R. Lamar was born to a prominent Georgia family whose illustrious forebears included Mirabeau Buonaparte Lamar, a president of the Republic of Texas, and Lucius Q. C. Lamar, an associate justice of the United States Supreme Court. After his mother died when he was eight, Lamar moved to Augusta, Georgia, with his father, a lawyer who became a minister of the Disciples of Christ church. Owing to his father's influence, Lamar left the University of Georgia for Bethany College, a church-affiliated institution. After graduating from Bethany, however, Lamar followed his father not into the ministry, but into law, which he began practicing (after a year's interlude teaching Latin at Bethany) in 1880.

Lamar pursued Democratic politics, but his real interest lay in the law — particularly the history of Georgia *jurisprudence. While practicing, he also wrote on the evolution of state law and helped to revise the Georgia code. This activity, as well as his service as a state bar examiner and his participation in state politics, led in 1903 to his appointment to the Georgia Supreme Court, but he returned to Augusta before his term had expired.

It was in Augusta that Lamar met President Taft, who was vacationing there in 1909. Much to Lamar's surprise, this brief friendship resulted in his nomination to the United States Supreme Court the following year. Taft, a conservative, apparently felt that Lamar would prove a counterweight to liberals like Justices Harlan and Holmes. Lamar did not disappoint; he almost always voted with the conservative majority on the White Court.

Lamar's Supreme Court career was cut short by his early death at the age of 58. His five-year tenure was apparently too brief for him to have distinguished himself among his brethren, and he is little remembered. He did, however, perform a valuable service toward the end of his life for President Woodrow Wilson, a friend from childhood, by serving on a diplomatic mission concerning Mexico.

MAHLON PITNEY

PERSONAL DATA

Born: February 5, 1858, in Morristown, New Jersey
Parents: Henry Cooper Pitney, Sarah Louisa Halsted Pitney
Higher Education: College of New Jersey, now Princeton University (B.A., 1879; M.A., 1882)
Bar Admission: New Jersey, 1882
Political Party: Republican
Marriage: November 14, 1891, to Florence T. Shelton, who bore Pitney two sons and one daughter
Died: December 9, 1924, in Washington, D.C.
Buried: Evergreen Cemetery, Morristown

PROFESSIONAL CAREER

Occupations: Lawyer, 1882-1895; Politician, 1895-1901; Judge, 1901-1922
Official Positions: Member, United States House of Representatives, 1895-1899; Member, New Jersey Senate, 1899-1901; President, New Jersey Senate, 1901; Associate Justice, New Jersey Supreme Court, 1901-1908; Chancellor of New Jersey, 1908-1912; Associate Justice, United States Supreme Court, 1912-1922

SUPREME COURT SERVICE

Nominated: February 19, 1912
Nominated By: William Howard Taft
Confirmed: March 13, 1912
Confirmation Vote: 50-26
Oath Taken: March 18, 1912
Replaced: John Marshall Harlan
Significant Opinions: *Frank v. Mangum* (1915); *Duplex Printing Press Co. v. Deering* (1921)
Left Court: Resigned December 31, 1922
Length of Service: 10 years, 9 months, 13 days
Replacement: Edward T. Sanford

Mahlon Pitney spent the early part of his life in his father's shadow. Tutored by his father, "a walking encyclopedia of the law," Pitney passed the New Jersey bar in 1882. Although he practiced law for seven years in Dover, New Jersey, Pitney returned to his hometown of Morristown in 1889 to take over the family law practice when his father was named chancellor, New Jersey's highest judicial office.

Pitney did not really break free until he became actively engaged in Republican politics in the 1890s, serving first in the national House of Representatives, then in the state senate. He aspired to become New Jersey's governor but, upon being appointed, like his father before him, as state chancellor, he altered his political ambitions.

As chancellor of his home state, Pitney seemed to have achieved the acme of his career when, in 1912, President Taft nominated him to the Supreme Court after having met him only a week earlier. The two met at a dinner party in Newark, New Jersey, where they discussed the possible nomination of state supreme court associate justice Francis J. Swayze to the federal High Court.

Apparently, Pitney made a powerful impression on the president. He would be the last of Taft's five Supreme Court appointees.

Pitney's nomination was opposed by liberal senators who objected to his anti-labor record. On the Court, he maintained his stance against unions. A proponent of individual liberty, he believed strongly that the freedom to enter into contracts — even so-called "yellow dog" contracts in which one had to promise not to join a union in order to get a job — was an expression of that liberty. His sole pro-organized labor vote came in his dissent in *Truax v. Corrigan* (1921). It seems ironic, therefore, that Pitney's principal contribution to American law was his support for worker's compensation. His advocacy of such legislation was grounded in his promotion of state prerogatives within the federal system, and it was this support that led to his dissent in *Truax*, in which the majority voted against an Arizona statute outlawing the use of labor injunctions.

Pitney worked hard on the Court, writing 274 opinions, 252 of them for the majority. Overwork seems to have contributed to a stroke he suffered in August 1922, which forced him to resign the following December. He died two years later in Washington, D.C.

JAMES CLARK McREYNOLDS

PERSONAL DATA

Born: February 3, 1862, in Elkton, Kentucky
Parents: Dr. John McReynolds, Ellen Reeves McReynolds
Higher Education: Vanderbilt University (B.S., class valedictorian, 1882); University of Virginia Law School (LL.B., 1884)
Bar Admission: Tennessee, 1884
Political Party: Democrat
Marriage: None
Died: August 24, 1946, in Washington, D.C.
Buried: Greenwood Cemetery, Elkton

PROFESSIONAL CAREER

Occupations: Administrator, 1884; Lawyer, 1884-1914; Educator, 1900-1903; Government Official, 1903-1907, 1913-1914; Judge, 1914-1941

Official Positions: Professor of Law, Vanderbilt University, 1900-1903; Assistant United States Attorney, 1903-1907; United States Attorney General, 1913-1914; Associate Justice, United States Supreme Court, 1914-1941

SUPREME COURT SERVICE

Nominated: August 19, 1914
Nominated By: Woodrow Wilson
Confirmed: August 29, 1914
Confirmation Vote: 44-6
Oath Taken: September 5, 1914
Replaced: Horace H. Lurton
Significant Opinions: *Meyer v. Nebraska* (1923); *Pierce v. Society of Sisters* (1925)
Left Court: Retired February 1, 1941
Length of Service: 26 years, 4 months, 27 days
Replacement: James F. Byrnes

James C. McReynolds was raised on a Kentucky plantation under the influence of his mother's strict religious fundamentalism. At Vanderbilt University he proved himself an excellent student of the natural sciences, but after a year of graduate work, he went to the University of Virginia to study law. After serving for a brief period as personal secretary to Senator (and later Supreme Court Justice) Howell E. Jackson, McReynolds began practicing law in Nashville, Tennessee, where he also was appointed a professor of law at Vanderbilt.

McReynolds entered public life in 1886, when he ran for Congress as a "Gold Democrat" with substantial Republican support for his position favoring the gold standard. The arrogant manner that was to afflict him all his life cost him the election, however. Seven years later, despite McReynolds's Democratic affiliation, Republican President Theodore Roosevelt appointed him an assistant attorney general. He made a reputation for himself as a trust-buster, and when he resigned in 1907 to join a prestigious New York law firm, he continued to assist the Justice Department in antitrust matters.

McReynolds's next political appointment came in 1913, when President Woodrow Wilson named him attorney general. McReynolds's haughtiness seems to have caused Wilson a great deal of embarrassment, and in desperation the president nominated him to the Supreme Court to succeed Horace Lurton.

As a member of the Court, McReynolds is most remembered as one of the "Four Horsemen" who opposed President Franklin Roosevelt's reforms in the 1930s (McReynolds voted against more New Deal legislation than any other Supreme Court justice). When, in 1937, the moderates on the Court shifted their allegiance leftward, McReynolds became a bitter dissenter until his retirement in 1941.

LOUIS DEMBITZ BRANDEIS

PERSONAL DATA

Born: November 13, 1856, in Louisville, Kentucky
Parents: Adolph Brandeis, Fredericka Dembitz Brandeis
Higher Education: Annen Real Schule, Germany, 1873-1875; Harvard Law School (LL.B. 1877); Harvard University, 1878-1879
Bar Admission: Massachusetts, 1878
Political Party: Democrat (although officially registered as a Republican)
Marriage: March 23, 1891, to Alice Goldmark, who bore Brandeis two daughters
Died: October 5, 1941, in Washington, D.C.
Buried: Ashes interred in portico of University of Louisville Law School

PROFESSIONAL CAREER:

Occupations: Lawyer, 1878-1916; Social Activist, 1914-1921, 1939-1941; Judge, 1916-1939
Official Positions: Counsel, Public Franchise League and Massachusetts State Board of Trade, 1897-1911; Counsel, New England Policyholders' Protective Committee, 1905; Special Counsel, Wage and Hours Cases in California, Illinois, Ohio, and Oregon, 1907-1914; Counsel, Ballinger-Pinchot Investigation, 1910; Chairman, Arbitration Board, New York Garment Workers' Labor Disputes, 1910-1916; Head, American Zionist Movement, 1914-1921; Associate Justice, United States Supreme Court, 1916-1939

SUPREME COURT SERVICE

Nominated: January 28, 1916

Nominated By: Woodrow Wilson
Confirmed: June 1, 1916
Confirmation Vote: 47-22
Oath Taken: June 5, 1916
Replaced: Joseph R. Lamar
Significant Opinions: *Whitney v. California* (concurrence) (1927); *Olmstead v. United States* (dissent) (1928); *New State Ice Co. v. Liebmann* (dissent) (1932); *Ashwander v. Tennessee Valley Authority* (concurrence) (1936); *Erie Railroad Co. v. Tompkins* (1938)
Left Court: Retired February 13, 1939
Length of Service: 22 years, 8 months, 8 days
Replacement: William O. Douglas

Louis D. Brandeis's parents were Jewish emigrants from Bohemia who had done well in America. His father, a wealthy grain merchant, shut down his business in 1873 and took his family on an extended tour of Europe to escape the ill effects of the depression that began that year. It was during this period that Brandeis attended the Annen Real Schule in Dresden, where he spent two years in preparatory studies. He emerged without a college degree but, nevertheless, enrolled at Harvard Law School at the age of 18, graduating in 1877 with the highest grade average in the school's history.

After staying on for a year of graduate study at Harvard, Brandeis began practicing law in St. Louis, Missouri. He missed Boston, however, and soon returned there to set up a partnership with a former classmate, Samuel D. Warren Jr. At Warren & Brandeis, and its successor firm, Brandeis, Dunbar & Nutter, Brandeis became one of the most sought-after and successful attorneys of his day. At a time when most lawyers in the country were making under $5,000 a year, Brandeis had an annual income that exceeded $50,000.

Brandeis had been raised with a social conscience, however, and he and his wife chose to limit their yearly expenditures to $10,000. At the same time, Brandeis worked to raise money for his alma mater and began to seek out progressive causes. Beginning by fighting corruption in the local transportation system, he went on to battle insurance companies and to set up a system of insurance administered by savings banks — and he did most of this work without charge, one of the first prominent lawyers to undertake such *pro bono activities. This "People's Attorney" was responsible for another first among lawyers when he employed the "Brandeis brief," a largely sociological, rather than strictly legal document, to win a limited work week for female laundry workers in *Muller v, Oregon* (1908).

Brandeis, who helped Woodrow Wilson craft his New Freedom agenda, was rewarded with a Supreme Court nomination in 1916. The nomination encountered fierce resistance, both from anti-Semitic bigots and from political conservatives like former President Taft, who bore a grudge against Brandeis for heading an investigation into the practices of his secretary of the interior, Richard A. Ballinger. After a four-month confirmation battle, Brandeis took his seat on the Court, the first Jew ever to do so.

Not surprisingly, Brandeis had deep differences of opinion with the conservative majorities on the White and Taft Courts. During those years, he frequently found himself writing long dissenting opinions which, like his "Brandeis brief," were meant to educate the justices to the facts behind the reform measures they opposed. During the 1930s, Brandeis customarily voted to uphold progressive New Deal legislation, although doing so violated his principle of *judicial restraint and customary deference to the legislative branch in economic matters. In cases involving free expression or other personal liberties, however, Brandeis exercised no restraint, going so far as to support judicially a right of privacy not found in the Constitution, but which he and Samuel Warren had posited as early as 1890 in a law review article. In this, as in many other areas, Brandeis proved farsighted: the Supreme Court finally accepted the notion of a constitutionally protected right of privacy in 1965 in *Griswold v. Connecticut*.

During his time on the high bench, Brandeis remained politically active, even engaging in some ethically questionable consultations with President Franklin D. Roosevelt. When he retired from the Supreme Court in 1939, he remained involved with social reform, devoting the last two years of his life to the Zionist movement.

JOHN HESSIN CLARKE

PERSONAL DATA
Born: September 18, 1857, in New Lisbon, Ohio
Parents: John Clarke, Melissa Hessin Clarke
Higher Education: Western Reserve University (B.A., Phi Beta Kappa, 1877; M.A. 1880)
Bar Admission: Ohio, 1878 (with honors)
Political Party: Democrat
Marriage: None
Died: March 22, 1945, in San Diego, California
Buried: Lisbon Cemetery, Lisbon, Ohio

PROFESSIONAL CAREER
Occupations: Lawyer, 1878-1914; Journalist, ca. 1880-1897; Judge, 1914-1922; Diplomat, 1922-1930
Official Positions: Judge, United States District Court for the Northern District of Ohio, 1914-1916; Associate Justice, United States Supreme Court, 1916-1922; Head, League of Nations' Non-Partisan Association of the United States, 1922-1930

SUPREME COURT SERVICE
Nominated: July 14, 1916
Nominated By: Woodrow Wilson
Confirmed: July 24, 1916
Confirmation Vote: Voice vote
Oath Taken: August 1, 1916
Replaced: Charles Evans Hughes
Significant Opinion: *Abrams v. United States* (1919)
Left Court: Resigned September 18, 1922
Length of Service: 6 years, 1 month, 17 days
Replacement: George Sutherland

John H. Clarke was the son of Irish Protestant immigrants who settled in Lisbon, Ohio. His father, a lawyer, prepared him for the Ohio bar examination, and after Clarke passed with honors, he joined his father's practice. Two years later, however, he moved to Youngstown, Ohio, where he set up a successful practice and, with the purchase of a half share of the Youngstown *Vindicator,* promoted progressive reform. Other progressive Democrats helped nominate him for various public offices, which he declined. Clarke did, however, run unsuccessfully twice for the United States Senate.

In 1897 Clarke moved to Cleveland to join the firm of William & Cushing, where he became general counsel for the Nickel Plate Railroad. Despite his representation of big business, he continued to speak out in favor of such progressive causes as antitrust legislation and women's suffrage. In 1914 he received his first political appointment when President Wilson made him a federal judge. Two years later, Wilson elevated Clarke to the Supreme Court.

Clarke's nomination to the High Court, like his earlier judicial appointment, proved controversial. He was opposed by many leading conservatives, chief among them former President Taft, who linked him with Louis D. Brandeis and publicly warned of the dangers posed by having two such liberal justices on the nation's highest tribunal. Indeed, Clarke often did side with Brandeis and remained committed to his progressive values. Nonetheless, when Taft later joined the Court as chief justice, his relations with both Brandeis and Clarke were cordial. Justice McReynolds proved another matter. His hostility toward Brandeis was conspicuous, and it spilled over onto Clarke, perhaps even contributing to the latter's resignation after only six years' service.

Clarke's departure — even though it was prompted by a desire to promote the president's plan for a League of Nations — was a disappointment to Wilson, who had appointed Clarke in order to provide a liberal counterweight on the conservative Court. And Clarke, like Wilson, was to be disappointed in the ultimate failure of the League of Nations. His devotion to progressive causes never waned, however. At the age of 80, he emerged from retirement to endorse President Roosevelt's attempt to enlarge the Supreme Court in order to uphold the constitutionality of New Deal legislation.

SIGNIFICANT CASES

MUSKRAT V. UNITED STATES

Citation: 219 U.S. 346 (1911)
Argued: November 30-December 2, 1910

Decided: January 23, 1911
Court Below: United States Court of Claims
Basis for Review: Appeal
Facts: In 1907 Congress passed legislation permitting certain members of the Cherokee Nation, including David Muskrat, to bring suit against the United States in the Court of Claims, with a right of appeal to the Supreme Court. This legislation was designed to test the constitutionality of previous laws concerning Cherokee lands. Congress also paid for the Cherokee's counsel.
Issue: Does this *jurisdictional act violate the constitutional requirement that federal courts hear only real cases and controversies?
Outcome: Calling this a *friendly suit, the Court dismissed it.
Vote: 7-0
Participating: White, Harlan, McKenna, Holmes, Day, Lurton, Hughes (Van Devanter and Lamar not participating)
Opinion: Day for the Court
Significance: Federal jurisdiction, as *Muskrat* demonstrates with the utmost clarity, cannot be invoked for purposes of obtaining a purely *advisory opinion.

STANDARD OIL V. UNITED STATES

Citation: 221 U.S. 1 (1911)
Argued: March 14-16, 1910; reargued January 12-13 & 16-17, 1911
Decided: May 15, 1911
Court Below: United States Circuit Court for the Eastern District of Missouri
Basis for Review: Appeal
Facts: The federal government brought suit under the Sherman Antitrust Act to break up the giant Standard Oil Company. The lower court ordered the company dissolved.
Issue: Does the Sherman Act mandate the breakup of all combinations in restraint of trade?
Outcome: Adopting Chief Justice White's "rule of reason," the Court upheld the lower court, ordering the monopoly broken up.
Vote: 9-0
Participating: White, Harlan, McKenna, Holmes, Day, Lurton, Hughes, Van Devanter, Lamar
Opinions: White for the Court; Harlan concurring

Significance: For the first time, the Supreme Court concluded that the Sherman Act was intended to prohibit only those business combinations that constitute unreasonable restraints of trade. This ruling made judges the ultimate arbiters of which monopolies survived and proved to be highly unpopular, leading to the 1914 Clayton Antitrust Act and the formation of the Federal Trade Commission. Nonetheless, *Standard Oil* provided the Court with a degree of flexibility in deciding subsequent antitrust cases, and the "rule of reason" still applies. [See also p. 201]

GOMPERS V. BUCK'S STOVE & RANGE CO.

Citation: 221 U.S. 418 (1911)
Argued: January 27 & 30, 1911
Decided: May 15, 1911
Court Below: District of Columbia Court of Appeals
Basis for Review: *Writ of certiorari
Facts: The American Federation of Labor (AFL) organized a boycott of Buck's Stove products after workers struck the company. Buck's obtained an *injunction against the boycott, then gained a criminal *contempt citation against AFL leader Samuel Gompers, claiming that the union had violated the injunction by publishing Buck's name in a union paper's list of "unfair" companies.
Issue: Did the AFL violate the terms of the injunction, or was it merely exercising its First Amendment right to *free speech?
Outcome: While ignoring the AFL's free speech argument, the Court dismissed the contempt citation on a technicality, stating that while the union's activities had been criminal, the citation had been for civil contempt, a different offense.
Vote: 9-0
Participating: White, Harlan, McKenna, Holmes, Day, Lurton, Hughes, Van Devanter, Lamar
Opinion: Lamar for the Court
Significance: Although in *Gompers* the White Court gave the appearance of siding with labor, it was a deft and deceptive performance. Lamar's opinion made it clear — in part by citing a string of anti-union opinions — that this Court disapproved of any activity, including mere expression

of ideas, that interfered with property rights.

COYLE V. SMITH

Citation: 221 U.S. 559 (1911)
Argued: April 5-6, 1911
Decided: May 29, 1911
Court Below: Oklahoma Supreme Court
Basis for Review: *Writ of error
Facts: In an act admitting Oklahoma to statehood, Congress stipulated that Guthrie was to be the capital until 1913. After Oklahoma became a state in 1907, the state legislature made Oklahoma City the capital. The action was upheld in state court when the move was challenged.
Issue: Can Congress place conditions on admittance of states that will bind them after they have achieved statehood?
Outcome: Denying congressional authority to impose such restrictions, the White Court upheld the lower court and the action of the Oklahoma legislature.
Vote: 7-2
Participating: White, Harlan, McKenna, Holmes, Day, Lurton, Hughes, Van Devanter, Lamar
Opinions: Lurton for the Court; McKenna and Holmes dissenting (without written opinions)
Significance: Although the Constitution contains no language specifically prohibiting Congress from taking the sort of action at issue in *Coyle*, the Court honored tradition when it held that new states enjoy powers equal to those held by existing states.

WEEKS V. UNITED STATES

Citation: 232 U.S. 383 (1914)
Argued: December 2-3, 1913
Decided: February 24, 1914
Court Below: United States District Court for the Western District of Missouri
Basis for Review: *Writ of error
Facts: On the basis of evidence gathered without a warrant by state officers and a federal marshall, Weeks was convicted of illegally sending lottery tickets through the mails. Weeks petitioned for return of his effects and objected to their introduction as evidence at trial. The lower

court found against him.

Issue: Are federal officers and courts obliged to adhere to the guarantees of the Fourth Amendment's prohibition of unreasonable search and seizure?

Outcome: Observing that Weeks's right to personal liberty and private property had been violated, the White Court reversed the lower court's judgment.

Vote: 9-0

Participating: White, McKenna, Holmes, Day, Lurton, Hughes, Van Devanter, Lamar, Pitney

Opinion: Day for the Court

Significance: *Weeks* originated the federal *exclusionary rule, now fundamental to criminal procedure, which previously had placed the needs of the judicial system above individual rights. The case, however, generated little notice until Prohibition repeatedly raised search and seizure issues.

SHREVEPORT RATE CASES (*HOUSTON, EAST & WEST TEXAS RAILWAY CO. V. UNITED STATES; TEXAS & PACIFIC RAILWAY CO. V. UNITED STATES*)

Citation: 234 U.S. 342 (1914)

Argued: October 28-29, 1913

Decided: June 8, 1914

Courts Below: United States Commerce Court

Basis for Review: Appeal

Facts: Texas railroads discriminated against out-of-state shippers by charging them higher cargo rates than those charged for intrastate shipments traveling an equal distance. The Interstate Commerce Commission (ICC) found that the lower intrastate rates adversely affected interstate commerce.

Issue: Does the ICC have the authority to regulate intrastate rates?

Outcome: Reasoning that intrastate rates can be so interconnected with interstate shipping that regulation of one necessitates regulation of the other, the White Court upheld the ICC finding.

Vote: 7-2

Participating: White, McKenna, Holmes, Day, Lurton, Hughes, Van Devanter, Lamar, Pitney

Opinions: Hughes for the Court; Lurton and Pitney dissenting (without written opinions)

Significance: The *Shreveport Rate Cases*, which for once expanded the authority of the ICC, is one indication that the White Court was not unaffected by the Progressive era's emphasis on federal activism. The "Shreveport Doctrine," permitting regulation of intrastate matters negatively impacting interstate commerce, was later expanded to cover areas other than transportation.

FRANK V. MANGUM

Citation: 237 U.S. 309 (1915)

Argued: February 25-26, 1915

Decided: April 19, 1915

Court Below: United States District Court for the Northern District of Georgia

Basis for Review: Appeal

Facts: Leo Frank, a Northerner and a Jew, was convicted and sentenced to death in state court in Georgia for murdering a 13-year-old female employee of his factory. The atmosphere in the trial court was fraught with violent anti-Semitism. When appeals to higher state courts failed, Frank applied to the federal district court for a writ of *habeas corpus and was rejected.

Issue: Did intimidation of the jury that convicted Frank deprive him of *due process of law?

Outcome: Concluding that review by the highest state court guaranteed due process, the White Court upheld the lower court's ruling.

Vote: 7-2

Participating: White, McKenna, Holmes, Day, Hughes, Van Devanter, Lamar, Pitney, McReynolds

Opinions: Pitney for the Court; Holmes, joined by Hughes, dissenting

Significance: *Frank* was one of the most sensational murder trials of its day and one of the greatest miscarriages of justice in the annals of American law. Frank was most likely innocent. Certainly the Georgia governor believed him to be so when he commuted Frank's sentence to life imprisonment, as a result of which the governor was run out of the state and Frank was lynched. The Supreme Court, which at this phase of its development had no reluctance to employ the Due Process Clause of the Fourteenth Amendment to protect property, was loath to do so to protect individual rights endangered by state criminal proceedings. This attitude toward the Fourteenth Amendment would begin to change with *Moore v. Dempsey* (1923).

GUINN V. UNITED STATES

Citation: 238 U.S. 347 (1915)
Argued: October 17, 1913
Decided: June 21, 1915
Court Below: United States Eighth Circuit Court of Appeals
Basis for Review: *Certification
Facts: Suffrage restriction laws, which attempted to keep African Americans from voting, abounded in the South in the wake of Reconstruction. Many, like Oklahoma's, included a "grandfather clause" intended to encourage poor and illiterate whites to vote. To that end, such clauses permitted anyone to register to vote who, prior to the passage of the Fifteenth Amendment, had been eligible in 1867, or anyone who was a legal descendant of such a man. The Justice Department brought suit to outlaw Oklahoma's law.
Issue: Although Oklahoma's suffrage restriction law does not specifically mention race, does it nonetheless violate the Fifteenth Amendment's enfranchisement of the African American vote?
Outcome: Observing that the Oklahoma law was passed in "direct and positive disregard" of the Fifteenth Amendment, the Court declared it *prima facie unconstitutional.
Vote: 8-0
Participating: White, McKenna, Holmes, Day, Hughes, Van Devanter, Lamar, Pitney (McReynolds *recused)
Opinion: White for the Court
Significance: Although in previous cases, such as *Williams v. Mississippi* (1898), the Supreme Court had declined to throw out racially discriminatory state barriers to voting, *Guinn* was largely a political decision whose outcome was dictated by President Taft's need for African American delegates in order to win renomination in 1912. Furthermore, the Oklahoma statute was a particularly flagrant violation of federal law; whereas grandfather clauses already had lapsed in former Confederate states, Oklahoma's was intended to be permanent.

CLARK DISTILLING CO. V. WESTERN MARYLAND RAILWAY CO.

Citation: 242 U.S. 311 (1917)
Argued: May 10-11, 1915; reargued November 8-9, 1916
Decided: January 8, 1917
Court Below: United States District Court for the District of Maryland
Basis for Review: Appeal
Facts: The Webb-Kenyon Act of 1913 made it illegal to ship intoxicating liquor into a state in violation of state laws. West Virginia obtained an injunction against the Western Maryland Railroad to prevent it from carrying liquor into the state, but Clark Distilling sued the railroad to compel it to accept shipments of liquor for personal use, which was not expressly forbidden by West Virginia.
Issue: Does the Webb-Kenyon Act violate the *Commerce Clause by subjecting goods shipped through interstate commerce to state law prior to their actual arrival in the state?
Outcome: Finding that congressional authority to regulate interstate commerce does extend to prohibiting transport of goods in violation of state law, the Supreme Court upheld the act.
Vote: 7-2
Participating: White, McKenna, Holmes, Day, Van Devanter, Pitney, McReynolds, Brandeis, Clarke
Opinions: White for the Court; McReynolds concurring (without written opinion); Holmes and Van Devanter dissenting (without written opinions)
Significance: The Anti-Saloon League, which agitated for passage of the Webb-Kenyon Act, also defended it before the Supreme Court, as the Justice Department declined to do so. *Clark Distilling*, decided just before the congressional battle over the Eighteenth Amendment, lent strength to those favoring universal prohibition.

BUNTING V. OREGON

Citation: 243 U.S. 426 (1917)
Argued: April 18, 1916; reargued January 9, 1917; reargued January 19, 1917

Decided: April 9, 1917
Court Below: Oregon Supreme Court
Basis for Review: *Writ of error
Facts: A 1913 Oregon law set a maximum ten-hour workday for laborers in mills, factories, and other manufacturing establishments. It also required an employer to pay time and a half for overtime. Bunting, a mill foreman, required an employee to work 13 hours and did not pay the employee overtime. Bunting was convicted of violating state law.
Issue: Does the Oregon statute constitute wage regulation in violation of freedom of contract?
Outcome: Deciding that the time-and-a-half requirement was a penalty designed to discourage overtime, the White Court upheld the statute.
Vote: 5-3
Participating: White, McKenna, Holmes, Day, Van Devanter, Pitney, McReynolds, Clarke (Brandeis *recused)
Opinions: McKenna for the Court; White, Van Devanter, and McReynolds dissenting (without written opinions)
Significance: The statute at issue in *Bunting* was an extension of the one upheld in *Muller v. Oregon* (1908), in which the Court had supported a statute limiting female laundry workers' hours. The White Court did not question that maximum working hours should apply equally to men and women, but it split badly on the issue of overtime payments, which some justices saw as the first step toward a statutorily mandated minimum wage. Brandeis, who had triumphantly represented the state in the earlier case and had already begun work on *Bunting* when he was appointed to the Court, recused himself.

BUCHANAN V. WARLEY

Citation: 245 U.S. 60 (1917)
Argued: April 10-11, 1916; reargued April 27, 1917
Decided: November 5, 1917
Court Below: Kentucky Court of Appeals
Basis for Review: *Writ of error
Facts: A contract for sale of property from a white seller to an African American buyer violated a Louisville, Kentucky, ordinance prohibiting res-

idential integration. The ordinance was challenged in state supreme court, where it was found to be constitutional.
Issue: Does a law requiring residential segregation by race violate the Fourteenth Amendment's *Due Process Clause?
Outcome: Concluding that the ordinance interfered with the rights of both blacks and whites to dispose of their property, the White Court voted unanimously to reverse the lower court's ruling.
Vote: 9-0
Participating: White, McKenna, Holmes, Day, Van Devanter, Pitney, McReynolds, Brandeis, Clarke
Opinion: Day for the Court
Significance: *Buchanan* demonstrates how the sanctity of property rights could be used to convince even a conservative Court that the Fourteenth Amendment secured civil rights. The decision led, nonetheless, to private *restrictive covenants among neighbors which racially limited sales or rentals. The Supreme Court later upheld such covenants in *Corrigan v. Buckley* (1926).

SELECTIVE DRAFT LAW CASES

Citation: 245 U.S. 366 (1918)
Argued: December 13-14, 1917
Decided: January 7, 1918
Courts Below: United States District Court for the District of Minnesota; United States District Court for the Southern District of New York
Bases for Review: *Writs of error
Facts: A number of individuals convicted in lower courts of violating the Selective Service Act of 1917 appealed their convictions to the Supreme Court.
Issue: Does Congress have the authority to draft citizens for military duty?
Outcome: Finding justification for the draft in the *Necessary and Proper Clause of Article I of the Constitution, as well as in Congress's delegated power to raise armies, the White Court unanimously upheld the Selective Service Act.
Vote: 9-0
Participating: White, McKenna, Holmes, Day, Van Devanter, Pitney, McReynolds, Brandeis, Clarke

Opinion: White for the Court

Significance: Although the federal government instituted a draft during the Civil War, a court challenge to its power to do so did not arise until passage of the Selective Service Act of 1917. The Supreme Court saw no logic to arguments that the draft violated the Thirteenth Amendment's ban on involuntary servitude and the First Amendment's protection of free exercise of religion, and it has never questioned this exercise of congressional authority.

HAMMER V. DAGENHART

Citation: 247 U.S. 251 (1918)

Argued: April 15-16, 1918

Decided: June 3, 1918

Court Below: United States District Court for the Western District of North Carolina

Basis for Review: Appeal

Facts: In 1916 Congress passed the Keating-Owen Child Labor Act, which barred goods made with child labor from interstate commerce. Dagenhart, who worked at a cotton mill along with his two minor sons, sued the company, as well as Hammer, the United States attorney for his region, to prevent enforcement of the act. In district court, the act was declared unconstitutional.

Issue: Is the act a proper exercise of federal *police power?

Outcome: Reverting to the distinction between manufacturing and commerce made in *United States v. E.C. Knight* (1895), a divided Court upheld the lower court's ruling, stating that the *Commerce Power can only prohibit interstate transport of goods that are inherently harmful, not the process of their creation.

Vote: 5-4

Participating: White, McKenna, Holmes, Day, Van Devanter, Pitney, McReynolds, Brandeis, Clarke

Opinions: Day for the Court; Holmes, joined by McKenna, Brandeis, and Clarke, dissenting

Significance: While the Keating-Owen Act marked the apogee of progressive federal reforms, *Hammer* was a return to the Court's earlier doctrine of constitutional *laissez faire. In the recent past, in cases like *Champion v. Ames* (1903), the

Supreme Court had expanded the federal police power. However, *Hammer* — which, given its subject matter, seemed an easy case — pushed back the clock. Congress responded by passing new legislation using the *taxing power to regulate child labor, and that too, was struck down in *Bailey v. Drexel Furniture Co.* (1922). Finally, however, the principles enunciated in Justice Holmes's famous dissent, which castigated his fellow justices for their callous disregard for such a profound social evil, were explicitly upheld in *United States v. Darby Lumber Co.* (1941).

SCHENCK V. UNITED STATES

Citation: 249 U.S. 47 (1919)

Argued: January 9-10, 1919

Decided: March 3, 1919

Court Below: United States District Court for the Eastern District of Pennsylvania

Basis for Review: *Writ of error

Facts: Schenck, general secretary of the American Socialist Party, was convicted of violating the 1917 Espionage Act by mailing thousands of antidraft pamphlets to recently conscripted men in Pennsylvania.

Issue: What are the limits, if any, of the First Amendment's guarantees of *freedom of speech and of the press?

Outcome: Reasoning that the right to free speech was never an absolute right, in war or in peace, a unanimous Court upheld the Espionage Act and Schenck's conviction.

Vote: 9-0

Participating: White, McKenna, Holmes, Day, Van Devanter, Pitney, McReynolds, Brandeis, Clarke

Opinion: Holmes for the Court

Significance: In this, the Supreme Court's first consideration of a First Amendment free speech case, Holmes laid out his famous "clear and present danger" test for what constitutes protected political speech, stating that: "Free speech would not protect a man falsely shouting fire in a theatre, and causing a panic." Later in 1919, Holmes would dissent in another free speech case, *Abrams v. United States*, where he refined his definition of clear and present danger to be an immediate evil resulting from specific action. Holmes continued to modify his clear and present danger test in a series of dissents written during the 1920s, and it remains at the core of First Amendment law.

ABRAMS V. UNITED STATES

Citation: 250 U.S. 616 (1919)
Argued: October 21-22, 1919
Decided: November 10, 1919
Court Below: United States District Court for the Southern District of New York
Basis for Review: *Writ of error
Facts: Jacob Abrams, an anarchist Russian immigrant, was convicted under the Sedition Act of 1918 for writing, printing, and distributing two leaflets protesting the presence of American troops in Russia and calling for a general strike to protest this intervention. The district court found Abrams and several of his comrades to be in violation of the act and sentenced them to prison terms ranging from 15 to 20 years.
Issue: What are the boundaries of the "clear and present danger" exception to First Amendment protection of *free speech?
Outcome: Reasoning that the pamphlets, which had been distributed during wartime, constituted an attempt to contravene the war effort, the White Court upheld the convictions.
Vote: 7-2
Participating: White, McKenna, Holmes, Day, Van Devanter, Pitney, McReynolds, Brandeis, Clarke
Opinions: Clarke for the Court; Holmes, joined by Brandeis, dissenting
Significance: Although Justice Clarke's opinion followed the reasoning of Holmes's opinion in *Schenck v. United States* (1919), which first articulated the clear and present danger test, Holmes dissented in this case. "The surreptitious publishing of a silly leaflet by an unknown man" did not for him constitute speech intended to "bring about forthwith certain substantive evils that the United States constitutionally may seek to protect." Here, the danger was not imminent, and the intent was not to cripple the prosecution of the war, but only to stop intervention in Russia. Holmes felt that the draconian Sedition Act was

too encompassing and that, if not curbed, it would inhibit not only free speech but experimentation and the search for truth.

MISSOURI V. HOLLAND

Citation: 252 U.S. 416 (1920)
Argued: March 2, 1920
Decided: April 19, 1920
Court Below: United States District Court for the Western District of Missouri
Basis for Review: Appeal
Facts: Missouri sought to enjoin a federal game warden from enforcing federal regulations designed to facilitate the Migratory Bird Act of 1918, passed in the wake of a treaty the United States signed with Great Britain to protect migratory birds. The lower court denied the injunction and upheld the act.
Issue: In order to implement a treaty, can Congress pass legislation that would otherwise violate state *sovereignty?
Outcome: Because the act was in this case a *"necessary and proper" means of exercising the *treaty power, the White Court upheld it.
Vote: 7-2
Participating: White, McKenna, Holmes, Day, Van Devanter, Pitney, McReynolds, Brandeis, Clarke
Opinions: Holmes for the Court; Van Devanter and Pitney dissenting (without written opinions)
Significance: Migratory birds, the subject of the act, clearly cannot be regulated by the states but can be regulated by means of international agreement. Because the treaty was itself valid, it was the supreme law of the land under Article IV of the Constitution. While the expanded scope of federal authority over interstate and foreign commerce today limits the value of *Missouri v. Holland* as *precedent, it did provide a basis for later cases establishing the supremacy of federal executive agreements and others holding that federal law *preempts state law whenever the latter interferes with foreign affairs.

DUPLEX PRINTING PRESS CO. V. DEERING

Citation: 254 U.S. 443 (1921)
Argued: January 22, 1920

Decided: January 3, 1921
Court Below: United States Second Circuit Court of Appeals
Basis for Review: Appeal
Facts: The 1890 Sherman Antitrust Act prohibited unlawful restraints of interstate commerce, as well as conspiracies to restrain such trade. Federal courts were soon upholding efforts to combat organized labor with *injunctions issued pursuant to the Sherman Act. In response, in 1914 Congress passed the Clayton Act, which was supposed to prohibit the use of antitrust laws to counteract union activity. But in *Deering* a federal court ruled that the secondary boycott of a printing company by a machinist's union that had no direct connection with the printing company constituted an unlawful conspiracy not protected by the Clayton Act, and the court issued an injunction.
Issue: Does the Clayton Act exempt organized labor from antitrust injunctions?
Outcome: Because the Court found the Clayton Act only prohibited the use of injunctions against legal union activities, and because it deemed a secondary boycott an illegal restraint of trade, the injunction was upheld.
Vote: 6-3
Participating: White, McKenna, Holmes, Day, Van Devanter, Pitney, McReynolds, Brandeis, Clarke
Opinions: Pitney for the Court; Brandeis, joined by Holmes and Clarke, dissenting
Significance: For the next decade, the Supreme Court would continue to construe antitrust legislation narrowly, permitting the use of injunctions to battle union collective action. It was only with the passage of the Norris-LaGuardia Act in 1932 that unions were finally exempted from antitrust injunctions.

DILLON V. GLOSS

Citation: 256 U.S. 368 (1921)
Argued: March 22, 1921
Decided: May 16, 1921
Court Below: United States District Court for the Northern District of California
Basis for Review: Appeal

Facts: Dillon was convicted under the Volstead Act, the *enabling legislation that followed passage of the Eighteenth Amendment, of transporting intoxicating liquors in violation of nationwide prohibition. In his defense, he challenged the amendment's internal seven-year ratification deadline.
Issue: Does Congress have the power to set a time within which the states must act on proposed amendments to the Constitution?
Outcome: Finding that Congress has the authority to decide the manner in which states shall ratify amendments, the White Court upheld the amendment and Dillon's conviction.
Vote: 9-0
Participating: White, McKenna, Holmes, Day, Van Devanter, Pitney, McReynolds, Brandeis, Clarke
Opinion: Van Devanter for the Court
Significance: The Eighteenth Amendment was the first to specify a deadline for ratification within its own text. *Dillon* determined that the procedure for ratification was to be left to Congress, an outcome reinforced by *Coleman v. Miller* (1939), which declared ratification to be solely a *political question.

VOTING PATTERNS

The White Court was largely constructed by Republican President William Howard Taft, who appointed six justices, including a chief justice. Whereas presidents customarily name justices from their own parties, Taft appointed three Democrats. These Democrats — White, Lurton, and Lamar — were all southerners who largely shared Taft's values, as did his Republican appointees — Hughes, Van Devanter, and Pitney. Taft, a former solicitor general and federal *circuit court judge, took great care with his appointments, seeking to counterbalance the country's progressive mood and the forces for change represented by the powerful, often unpredictable personages of sitting Justices Harlan and Holmes, frequent dissenters to the *laissez faire philosophy that dominated the predecessor Fuller Court.

Unfortunately for Taft, who had attempted to

POLITICAL COMPOSITION
of the White Court

Justice & Total Term	Courts Served	Appointing President	Political Party
Edward D. White 1894-1910 1910-1921	Fuller White	Cleveland Taft	Democrat
John Marshall Harlan 1877-1911	Waite Fuller White	Hayes	Republican
Joseph McKenna 1898-1925	Fuller White Taft	McKinley	Republican
Oliver W. Holmes 1902-1932	Fuller White Taft Hughes	T. Roosevelt	Republican
William R. Day 1903-1922	Fuller White Taft	T. Roosevelt	Republican
Horace H. Lurton 1910-1914	Fuller White	Taft	Democrat
Charles Evans Hughes 1910-1916 1930-1941	White Hughes	Taft Hoover	Republican
Willis Van Devanter 1911-1937	White Taft Hughes	Taft	Republican
Joseph R. Lamar 1911-1916	White	Taft	Democrat
Mahlon Pitney 1912-1922	White Taft	Taft	Republican
James C. McReynolds 1914-1941	White Taft Hughes	Wilson	Democrat
Louis D. Brandeis 1916-1939	White Taft Hughes	Wilson	Democrat
John H. Clarke 1916-1922	White Taft	Wilson	Democrat

make the Court over in his own image, none of his appointees, with the exception of Van Devanter, had long Court tenures. President Woodrow Wilson added a progressive note with the appointment of three fellow Democrats — McReynolds, Brandeis, and Clarke — during

White's leadership. With the exception of Brandeis, however, Wilson's appointees did little to reorient the conservative Court. McReynolds, who was sent to the Supreme Court because as solicitor general he managed to alienate other members of Wilson's administration, was an arch conservative. Later, along with Van Devanter, McReynolds became a member of a conservative block known as the "Four Horseman" that consistently voted down New Deal legislation. And Clarke, who only sat on the high bench for six years, had too short a tenure to leave any lasting mark on the Court.

Early in Chief Justice White's stewardship, the Court veered away from *laissez faire, seemingly reviving the Sherman Antitrust Act by employing White's "rule of reason" to break up trusts like Standard Oil, which was found to be an unreasonable restraint of trade. But as Justice Harlan pointed out in his concurring opinion in *Standard Oil v. United States* (1911), what the Court had actually done was increase judicial powers of legislation at the expense of Congress by making federal courts the arbiters of reasonableness.

Although the Court took power away from Congress in accepting the rule of reason, it gave some back with the *Shreveport Rate Cases* (1914), which extended the *commerce power to cover regulation of intrastate rail rates. And in *Weeks v. United States* (1914), which introduced the *exclusionary rule, the White Court unanimously decided that an individual's protection against unreasonable search and seizure of private property superseded the judicial system's right to enforce the laws. In two cases handed down in 1917, *Bunting v. Oregon*, a 5 to 3 decision (White, Van Devanter, and McReynolds dissenting; Brandeis recused), and *Buchanan v. Warley*, which was unanimously decided, the White Court interpreted *due process liberally to uphold a maximum hour statute and strike down a racially discriminatory residential ordinance, respectively.

The next year, however, the White Court took a sharp right turn, declaring in a 5 to 4 decision (Holmes, McKenna, Brandeis, and Clarke dissenting) that federal *police powers could not be extended to regulate child labor. *Hammer v. Dagenhart* today stands as one of the Supreme Court's most discredited decisions, but it was not the only one that gave the waning years of the White Court a renewed conservative cast. Justice Holmes, author of a stinging and memorable dissent in *Hammer*, also wrote the opinion in *Schenck v. United States* (1919), in which a unanimous Court at once upheld the Espionage Act of 1917 and ruled that there were limits to the First Amendment. In *Abrams v. United States* (1919), Holmes would modify his stance toward the "clear and present danger" test for determining when the government can constrain *free speech, but he and Brandeis found themselves alone there in dissenting from the White Court's endorsement of the wartime Sedition Act of 1917.

Justice Brandeis, who had been a renowned reformer before he was appointed to the Court, continued his crusade on the high bench. His appointment, however, came rather late in Chief Justice White's term, and the force of Brandeis's intellect and powers of persuasion did not really influence the Court until much later — in fact, many of his ideas, like the right of privacy, were not adopted until years after his death.

In general, the White Court established an inconsistent record, which doubtless had something to do with the nature of its leader. In the *Insular Cases*, which were decided during Melville Fuller's tenure as chief justice, White had advocated the "incorporation theory," which extended constitutional guarantees to American territories only insofar as they were incorporated into the United States by congressional action. In response to the question, "Does the Constitution follow the flag?" White's reply was, "Sometimes." And just as the incorporation concept left it to the judicial branch to decide on a case-by-case basis when constitutional rights and privileges would apply, *judicial subjectivity was the hallmark of White's major contribution to American jurisprudence, the "rule of reason."

White's elevation to chief justice came at a time when the Court was being almost entirely remade, and the turnover in personnel probably added to his prestige and influence with his brethren — as did his status as the first chief justice to be promoted from within. Several of the new associate justices — such as Lamar and Van Devanter — had little prior experience with the major constitutional questions of the day, and as a consequence, they tended to vote with the chief justice. When World War I began, progressivism waned as the nation turned its attention outward. White and his fellow justices, accustomed to inconsistency and largely uncommitted ideologically, slipped back into conservatism.

SPECIAL FEATURES OF THE WHITE COURT

PROMOTION FROM WITHIN

Edward D. White was the first chief justice selected from among associate justices already sitting on the Supreme Court. In the past, presidents had gone outside the Court to find candidates on whom to confer this highly desirable patronage position. Only once before had the chief justiceship been offered to an associate justice. George Washington asked former Associate Justice William Cushing to succeed John Jay (Cushing declined).

William Howard Taft seems to have chosen White as Melville Fuller's successor almost by default. Fuller was in ill health when, on April 22, 1910, Taft offered an associate justiceship to New York Governor Charles Evans Hughes; the offer included an expression of Taft's willingness to promote Hughes from within upon Fuller's death. Hughes accepted promptly, and was confirmed on May 2, 1910. He took his seat on the Court the following October.

When Fuller died on July 4, 1910, Taft passed over the younger Hughes. Taft cherished ambitions of sitting in the chief justice's chair himself someday — a prospect that grew more desirable as hopes for his reelection dimmed. Hughes was a young man, only 48, and Taft himself was 53 — there was a good chance that appointing Hughes chief justice would eliminate Taft's own chances. He looked instead to 65-year-old White, who was already on the Court and who had a claim on the chief justiceship that was clearly superior to Hughes's. Only Harlan had arrived on the Court before White, and although Harlan was interested in succeeding Fuller, Taft said he had no intention of merely making "the position of Chief Justice a blue ribbon for the final years of any member of the Court." Besides, Harlan was too impolitic, too liberal, too old. White was Taft's man.

The Taft Court
1921-1930

BACKGROUND

PRESIDENT HARDING AND THE "OHIO GANG"

Elected by a landslide in 1920, Warren G. Harding is remembered primarily as a figurehead who presided over the most corrupt administration since that of Ulysses S. Grant. Harding made some sound appointments — such as Charles Evans Hughes as secretary of state and Herbert Hoover as secretary of commerce — but in the main his cabinet and the lower ranks of his administration were filled with his friends from Ohio, many of whom indulged in graft. When the dimensions of the scandals finally became apparent to Harding, he left Washington in June 1923 for a speaking tour of the West, hoping to revive his popularity before the next election. The trip only exacerbated Harding's troubles, and he grew increasingly restless and ill. On August 2 Harding died of a stroke in a San Francisco hotel room.

PRESIDENT COOLIDGE AND THE ROARING TWENTIES

Harding was succeeded by his vice president, Calvin Coolidge who, as the Republican candidate in the 1924 election, won a four-year term of his own. *Laissez faire reached its apogee under Coolidge, who stated his philosophy of governing in his typically terse fashion: "The business of America is business." Under Coolidge's determinedly unobtrusive leadership, the country was dominated by corporate executives whom the president accommodated by appointing conservatives favoring business self-regulation over the Federal Trade Commission and by approving higher tariffs to protect American products.

This economic policy resulted in great wealth for some, but left others — most notably, farmers — in distress. While the national income rose by fifty percent between 1921 and 1929, farmers' share of it dropped from sixteen to nine percent owing to overproduction in the aftermath of World War I. Wages of factory workers increased only eight percent during the 1920s, while corporations enriched their shareholders by retaining earnings or paying out larger and larger dividends.

Public interest in stocks skyrocketed, as did the stock market. A general mood of optimism, even recklessness, seized the country, which luxuriated in loosening social mores and bathtub gin. Aviators Charles Lindbergh and Amelia Earhart crossed the Atlantic, and technological innovations such as radio changed the fabric of American life forever.

REACTION

Inevitably, social tensions engendered by economic disparity resulted in retrenchment. In response to the immigration of nearly a million foreigners in 1920, Congress passed a Quota Act in 1921. The racial and ethnic bias behind the move to curb immigration became apparent with the National Origins Act of 1924, which excluded Asians altogether and limited European immigration by nationality. Because the 1924 act based its quotas on the census taken in 1890, when the

---

An asterisk (*) before a word or phrase indicates that a definition will be found in the glossary at the end of this volume.

migration of predominately Roman Catholic and Jewish southern and eastern Europeans had just begun, its effect was undeniably discriminatory. These same groups, together with African Americans, were targeted by a resurgent Ku Klux Klan, which reached the pinnacle of its power in 1924, when membership stood at 4.5 million, and the group controlled several state governments.

Religious fundamentalism also escalated in response to the increased pace of social change. The battle between conservatism and the forces of change was epitomized by the so-called "Scopes Monkey Trial," which took place in the town of Dayton, Tennessee, in July 1925. The trial pitted famous defense attorney Clarence Darrow against a longtime fixture on the American scene, William Jennings Bryan. Darrow represented science instructor Thomas Scopes, who had vio-

lated a state law that prohibited the teaching of evolution. Darrow lost the case, but he subjected Bryan, who testified on behalf of the state as an expert on the Bible, to a withering cross-examination. Shortly after the trial concluded, Bryan died, his end apparently hastened by the rigors of the trial and his public humiliation.

THE ELECTION OF 1928 AND THE CRASH

The schism in American society was again featured in the presidential election of 1928, which pitted Democratic New York Governor Al Smith — urban, Irish, Roman Catholic, and an advocate of repeal of the Eighteenth Amendment — against Republican Herbert Hoover, who represented a more traditional America — rural, Anglo-Saxon, Protestant, and favoring prohibition.

Hoover won by a wide margin, but his popularity was not to last long. The economic downturn that long had been brewing came to a climax on October 24, 1929, when the prolonged bull market on Wall Street came to a dramatic end with a tidal wave of selling. In the ensuing days, banks struggled to hold the market up by buying stocks, but on October 29, "Black Thursday," panic ensued and the market, which had been buoyed up for years by unprecedented speculation, crashed. The "New Era" ushered in by Republican rule was at an end.

TAFT'S EARLY LIFE

William Howard Taft was born into a family of lawyers who devoted much of their lives, as did Taft, to public service. His grandfather, Peter Rawson Taft, served on probate and county courts. His father, Alphonso Taft, was a judge on the Ohio Superior Court before joining President Grant's cabinet. And his brother, Charles Phelps Taft, served one term in the United States House of Representatives.

The law was Taft's first love, and after establishing an impressive undergraduate record at Yale, he immediately entered Cincinnati Law School, working simultaneously as a legal reporter for the Cincinnati *Commercial*. He passed the Ohio bar in 1880 after completing his law degree.

MEMBERS *Of the Court* 1921–1930

(In Order of Seniority)

William Howard Taft (Chief Justice)	(1921-1930)
Joseph McKenna (retired)	(1921-1925)
Oliver Wendell Holmes	(1921-1930)
William R. Day (retired)	(1921-1922)
Willis Van Devanter	(1921-1930)
Mahlon Pitney (resigned)	(1921-1922)
James C. McReynolds	(1921-1930)
Louis D. Brandeis	(1921-1930)
John H. Clarke (resigned)	(1921-1922)
George Sutherland (replaced John H. Clarke)	(1922-1930)
Pierce Butler (replaced William R. Day)	(1923-1930)
Edward T. Sanford (replaced Mahlon Pitney)	(1923-1930)
Harlan F. Stone (replaced Joseph McKenna)	(1925-1930)

JUDICIAL BIOGRAPHY
William Howard Taft

PERSONAL DATA
Born: September 15, 1857, in Cincinnati, Ohio
Parents: Alphonso Taft, Louisa Maria Torrey Taft
Higher Education: Yale University (B.A., salutatorian, 1878); Cincinnati Law School (LL.B., 1880)
Bar Admission: Ohio, 1880
Political Party: Republican
Marriage: June 19, 1886, to Helen Herron, who bore Taft two sons and one daughter
Died: March 8, 1930, in Washington, D.C.
Buried: Arlington National Cemetery, Arlington, Virginia

PROFESSIONAL CAREER
Occupations: Journalist, 1878-1880; Lawyer, 1880-1887, 1890-1891; Government Official: 1881-1883, 1885-1887, 1890-1891, 1900-1908, 1918-1919; Politician, 1909-1913; Judge, 1887-1890, 1892-1900, 1918-1919, 1921-1930; Educator,

1896-1901, 1913-1921; Diplomat,1915
Official Positions: Assistant County Solicitor, Hamilton County, Ohio, 1881-1883; Assistant County Prosector, Hamilton County, 1885-1887; Judge, Superior Court of Ohio, 1887-1890; United States Solicitor General, 1890-1891; Judge, United States Sixth Circuit Court, 1892-1900; Dean and Professor of Property Law, Cincinnati Law School, 1896-1900; Chairman, Philippine Commission, 1900-1901; Governor of the Philippines, 1901-1904; United States Secretary of War, 1904-1908; President of the United States, 1909-1913; Kent Professor of Constitutional Law, Yale Law School, 1913-1921; President, League to Enforce Peace, 1915; Joint Chairman, National War Labor Board, 1918-1919; Chief Justice, United States Supreme Court, 1921-1930

SUPREME COURT SERVICE
Nominated: June 30, 1921
Nominated By: Warren G. Harding
Confirmed: June 30, 1921
Confirmation Vote: Voice vote
Oath Taken: July 11, 1921
Replaced: Chief Justice Edward Douglas White
Significant Opinions: *Truax v. Corrigan* (1921); *Bailey v. Drexel Furniture Co.* (1922); *United States v. Lanza* (1922); *Adkins v. Children's Hospital* (dissent) (1923); *Wolff Packing Co. v. Court of Industrial Relations* (1923); *Carroll v. United States* (1925); *Myers v. United States* (1926); *Olmstead v. United States* (1928)
Left Court: Retired February 3, 1930
Length of Service: 8 years, 6 months, 23 days
Replacement: Chief Justice Charles Evans Hughes

Soon afterward, he became involved in local Republican politics. These dual, and sometimes inimical, attractions to law and politics would characterize his entire life, at times causing him great personal anguish, but helping him to achieve the distinction of being the only person ever to have served as both the nation's chief executive and its chief justice.

TAFT'S PUBLIC LIFE

Initially Taft was able to combine both pursuits, serving first as assistant prosecuting attorney, then as assistant county solicitor for Hamilton County, Ohio. Then, in 1887, at the age of 29, he found what he regarded as his true calling when he was named as the replacement for retiring Ohio Superior Court Judge Judson Harmon. Two years later, he actively lobbied President Benjamin Harrison for a place on the United States Supreme Court. Instead, Harrison offered him the position of solicitor general.

Taft took the post, but he did so largely to appease his politically ambitious wife, the former Helen Herron, whom Taft had married in 1886.

William Howard Taft

Taft's record as solicitor general was a good one — he won 16 of the 18 cases he argued — but he hated the Washington political whirl. A scant two years after his appointment as the lawyer for the executive branch, he resigned to take up a position on the United States Sixth Circuit Court. Taft threw himself into his judicial work and still found time to act as dean and professor of property law at Cincinnati Law School.

In January 1900 Taft was again pulled back into the realm of politics when President McKinley requested that he head a commission to establish civil rule in the new United States territory of the Philippines. Taft would later recall his resignation from the Sixth Circuit as "the hardest thing he ever did," but once again Helen Taft prevailed. Taft joined the commission and ultimately became governor of the Philippines, a position he enjoyed so much that not even President Theodore Roosevelt's 1901 and 1903 offers of a Supreme Court appointment could persuade Taft to come back to Washington. Finally, in February 1904, Roosevelt ordered a reluctant Taft to replace Elihu Root as secretary of war.

By all accounts, Taft served Roosevelt well, helping him win reelection in 1904 and then overseeing the Panama Canal project and investigating revolutionary activity in Cuba. Roosevelt felt so indebted to Taft that he held out the possibility not only of a Supreme Court appointment, but of White House succession. Once again, Helen Taft won the day, and with Roosevelt's backing, Taft became the nation's 27th president in 1909.

Taft's four years as chief executive were anticlimactic and personally unrewarding. In 1910, faced with the prospect of appointing a replacement for Chief Justice Melville Fuller, Taft hedged his bets. He had always coveted the post of chief justice for himself, and in order to preserve his own chances, he chose as Fuller's successor the 65-year-old Associate Justice Edward Douglass White, rather than the front-runner for the position, 48-year-old Associate Justice Charles Evans Hughes. Taft calculated correctly. After losing a half-hearted bid for reelection as president, he retired to academia to teach and to mount a campaign to become the next chief justice. In 1921, upon White's death, President Harding granted Taft his heart's desire. Taft's nomination was confirmed the same day it was put forward, without ever being considered in committee.

TAFT AS CHIEF JUSTICE

Only four senators, all of them of a progressive or radical stripe, voiced opposition to Taft's nomination. And once in office, Taft's judicial philosophy was marked by the conservatism that had given rise to these initial dissents. In his first major opinion for the Court, *Truax v. Corrigan* (1921), he argued against an Arizona statute outlawing court *injunctions of union picketing on the basis that it violated employers' *due process rights. And in *Bailey v. Drexel Furniture Co.* (1922), he wrote the Court's opinion striking down a second congressional attempt to abolish child labor, this time through the *taxing power. (The first federal child labor law, based on the *commerce power, had been similarly overturned in *Hammer v. Dagenhart* [1918].) In *Adkins v. Children's Hospital* (1923), however, Taft found

Members of the Taft Court viewing a model of the proposed Supreme Court building, (ca. 1929).
From left: Louis D Brandeis, Willis Van Devanter, William Howard Taft, Oliver Wendell Holmes,
Pierce Butler, George Sutherland, Harlan Fiske Stone (2 men in the background are unidentified)

himself siding with perennial dissenter (and frequent progressive) Oliver Wendell Holmes against the majority's opposition to a minimum wage law for women and children. He was not always a defender of the *laissez faire dogma that was the hallmark of his age.

Taft's reformist impulses, however, were for the most part directed toward changing the judiciary. Customarily opposed to dissenting opinions (in eight and one-half years, he wrote 249 opinions for the Court, but submitted only four written dissents), Taft had a passion for "massing the Court." In order to achieve such unanimity, he expended considerable effort to assure appointment to the Court of like-minded men. As president, he had successfully appointed six justices (including White's elevation to chief justice), more than any president since Jackson. As chief justice, he continued to deploy his political clout by lobbying for his candidates for judicial appointments both to the High Court and to lower federal courts.

Immediately after assuming the chief justiceship, Taft undertook a campaign of speechmaking and article writing that led in 1922 to passage of a judicial act establishing a national conference of senior federal judges whose goal it was to eliminate administrative defects in the court system. Continuing efforts resulted in passage of the Judiciary Act of 1925, which combated *docket congestion by granting the Supreme Court almost complete discretion over which cases it would hear. A third reform effort, concerning procedural rules, did not pass during Taft's lifetime. But some of his suggested procedural changes, like his vision of a new Supreme Court building, were later realized and have become a valuable part of Taft's legacy to the American legal system.

During Taft's last years as chief justice, his energies began to flag, and he was unable to maintain the kind of unanimity among his brethren that he had achieved earlier. Harlan Fiske Stone, once an ally, began to side more and more with Justices Holmes and Brandeis, whom Taft saw as dangerously liberal. The chief justice became consumed with a desire to preserve the Court's conservative composition. Though gravely ill, he retired barely a month before he died, probably content with the knowledge that President Hoover had passed over one probable successor, Justice Stone, in favor of another, more conservative erstwhile candidate for the post, former Associate Justice Charles Evans Hughes.

Taft resigned as chief justice on February 3, 1930, and died the following March 8. He was interred at Arlington National Cemetery, the first former president to be buried there.

ASSOCIATE JUSTICES

For biographies of Associate Justices **Joseph McKenna, Oliver Wendell Holmes,** and **William R. Day,** see entries under **THE FULLER COURT.** For biographies of Associate Justices **Willis Van Devanter, Mahlon Pitney, James C. McReynolds, Louis D. Brandeis,** and **John H. Clarke,** see entries under **THE WHITE COURT.**

GEORGE SUTHERLAND

PERSONAL DATA
Born: March 15, 1862, in Buckinghamshire, England
Parents: Alexander Sutherland, Frances Slater Sutherland
Higher Education: Brigham Young Academy, now Brigham Young University, 1878-1881; University of Michigan Law School, 1883
Bar Admissions: Michigan and Utah, 1883
Political Party: Republican
Marriage: June 18, 1883, to Rosamund Lee, who bore Sutherland two daughters and one son
Died: July 18, 1942, in Stockbridge, Massachusetts
Buried: Cedar Hill Cemetery, Suitland, Maryland

PROFESSIONAL CAREER
Occupations: Lawyer, 1883-1896, 1903-1904, 1917-1920; Politician, 1896-1903, 1905-1917; Diplomat, 1921-1922; Judge, 1922-1938
Official Positions: State Senator, Utah, 1896-1900; Member, United States House of Representatives, 1901-1903; Member, United States Senate, 1905-1917; Chairman, Advisory Committee to the Washington Conference for the Limitation of Naval Armaments, 1921; United States Counsel, Norway-

United States Arbitration, The Hague, 1921-1922; Associate Justice, United States Supreme Court, 1922-1938

SUPREME COURT SERVICE
Nominated: September 5, 1922
Nominated By : Warren G. Harding
Confirmed: September 5, 1922
Confirmation Vote: Voice vote
Oath Taken: October 2, 1922
Replaced: John H. Clarke
Significant Opinions: *Adkins v. Children's Hospital* (1923); *Massachusetts v. Mellon, Frothingham v. Mellon,* (1923); *Euclid v. Ambler Realty Co.* (1926); *Tyson v. Banton* (1927); *New State Ice Co. v. Liebmann* (1932); *Powell v. Alabama* (1932); *Humphrey's Executor v. United States* (1935); *Grosjean v. American Press Co.* (1936); *Carter v. Carter Coal Co.* (1936); *United States v. Curtiss-Wright Export Corp.* (1936)
Left Court: Retired January 17, 1938
Length of Service: 15 years, 3 months, 15 days
Replacement: Stanley F. Reed

Born in England, George Sutherland immigrated to the United States with his parents when he was less than two years old. His father, a follower of the Mormon faith, settled the family in Utah. Early on, Sutherland's father left the church and went on to pursue a life in the law, a career his son followed.

After attending college in Utah, Sutherland studied briefly at the University of Michigan Law School before joining his father's law practice in Provo, Utah. Sutherland went on to work for another Provo law firm, as well as one in Salt Lake City, before becoming involved in politics, first as a Liberal, then, after Utah achieved statehood, as a member of the newly organized Republican Party. He served in the state senate before going to the United States House of Representatives and Senate.

During his two terms in the U.S. Senate, Sutherland championed many progressive causes, including the Pure Food and Drug Act (1906), the Postal Savings Act (1910), an act providing compensation for workers engaged in interstate commerce (1911-1912), and the Nineteenth

The Taft Court, 1925. From left: James C. McReynolds, Edward T. Sanford, Oliver Wendell Holmes, George Sutherland, William Howard Taft, Pierce Butler, Willis Van Devanter, Harlan Fiske Stone, Louis D. Brandeis

Amendment, granting women the right to vote. He opposed a nearly equal number of such programs, however, including the Federal Reserve Act (1913), the Clayton Antitrust Act (1914), the Federal Trade Commission Act (1914), and the Sixteenth Amendment, imposing a federal income tax. By the time he reached the Court, his views had become more consistently conservative.

In the interim, however, finding himself unable to achieve reelection to the Senate, Sutherland practiced law in Washington, D.C., and made himself useful to the Republican Party. After his former Senate colleague, Warren Harding, won the White House, Sutherland represented the administration as a diplomat before being named as retiring Justice John H. Clarke's replacement.

Writing the majority opinion in *Adkins v. Children's Hospital* (1923), in which the Court struck down a law setting minimum wages for female workers as an unconstitutional interference with freedom of contract, Sutherland quickly established himself as a prominent spokesman for

*laissez faire and property rights. During the 1930s, he became one of the "Four Horsemen" on the high bench who consistently voted against New Deal economic and social reforms. But despite his reputation as one of the Court's leading conservative intellectuals, he was responsible for such opinions as *Powell v. Alabama* (1932), overturning the convictions of the Scottsboro Boys, and *Grosjean v. American Press Co.* (1936), outlawing a state tax on newspapers as *prior restraint.

After Franklin Roosevelt tried to pack the Court in 1937 in order to achieve passage of his New Deal programs, Sutherland resigned, sensing that his legal philosophy was soon to become anachronistic and marginalized.

PIERCE BUTLER

PERSONAL DATA
Born: March 17, 1866, in Northfield, Minnesota
Parents: Patrick Butler, Mary Gaffney Butler

Higher Education: Carleton College (B.A., B.S., 1887)
Bar Admission: Minnesota, 1888
Political Party: Democrat
Marriage: August 25, 1891, to Annie M. Cronin, who bore Butler eight children
Died: November 16, 1939, in Washington, D.C.
Buried: Calvary Cemetery, St. Paul, Minnesota

PROFESSIONAL CAREER

Occupations: Lawyer, 1888-1922; Government Official, 1891-1897; Politician, 1907-1924; Judge, 1922-1939
Official Positions: Assistant County Attorney, Ramsey County, Minnesota, 1891-1893; County Attorney, Ramsey County, 1893-1897; Regent, University of Minnesota, 1907-1924; Associate Justice, United States Supreme Court, 1923-1939

SUPREME COURT SERVICE

Nominated: November 23, 1922 (no action)
Nominated By: Warren G. Harding
Renominated: December 5, 1922
Confirmation: December 21, 1922
Confirmation Vote: 61-8
Oath Taken: January 2, 1923
Replaced: William R. Day
Significant Opinions: Morehead v. New York *ex rel. Tipaldo* (1936); Breedlove v. Suttles (1937)
Left Court: Died November 16, 1939
Length of Service: 16 years, 10 months, 14 days
Replacement: Frank Murphy

Born on a farm near Northfield, Minnesota, Pierce Butler was the sixth of eight children born to Irish immigrants who had fled their homeland during the potato famine of the 1840s. Butler worked at a dairy in order to earn money to attend nearby Carleton College, from which he graduated in 1887 with degrees in both science and the arts. He was admitted to the Minnesota bar in 1888.

Although Butler devoted time to public service in the county attorney's office, most of his efforts went into private practice. In the firm of How, Butler & Mitchell, later Butler, Mitchell & Doherty, Butler made a name for himself defending the railroads against government regulation.

While acting as a regent of the University of Minnesota, he added to his reputation as a railroad advocate by helping to secure dismissal of two professors, one of whom was involved with railroad valuation, while the other supported municipal ownership of street railways.

Butler's conservatism and pro-business stance recommended him to Chief Justice Taft, who lobbied for Butler's appointment by pointing out, in addition, that there was political mileage to be gained by naming another Roman Catholic to the Court to replace the departed Edward D. White. In the Senate, however, Butler's appointment proved problematical. Liberal members vocally opposed the nomination of a man whose whole career seemed to have been devoted to a powerful special interest. At first the Senate simply sat on the nomination, but ultimately Butler was confirmed by a wide margin with only eight senators voting against him.

Once on the Court, Butler lived up to the expectations of both his supporters and his detractors. Although he spoke out against government use of wiretaps in *Olmstead v. United States* (1928), his record on the high bench was one of steady support for *laissez faire and private property. And during the administration of Franklin Roosevelt, he was one of the members of the conservative "Four Horsemen" that consistently voted down New Deal legislation aimed at combating the dire effects of the Great Depression. (The other three were James C. McReynolds, Willis Van Devanter, and George Sutherland.) Butler fought Roosevelt until the end of his life, which came in 1939, while he was still serving on the Court.

EDWARD TERRY SANFORD

PERSONAL DATA

Born: July 23, 1865, in Knoxville, Tennessee
Parents: Edward J. Sanford, Emma Chavannes Sanford
Higher Education: University of Tennessee (B.A., Ph.B., 1883); Harvard University (M.A., 1889); Harvard Law School (LL.B., 1889)

Bar Admission: Tennessee, 1888
Political Party: Republican
Marriage: January 6, 1891, to Lutie Mallory Woodruff, who bore Sanford two daughters
Died: March 8, 1930, in Washington, D.C.
Buried: Greenwood Cemetery, Knoxville

PROFESSIONAL CAREER

Occupations: Lawyer, 1890-1907; Educator, 1898-1907; Government Official, 1906-1907; Judge, 1908-1930
Official Positions: Lecturer in law, University of Tennessee, 1898-1907; Special Assistant to the United States Attorney General, 1906; Assistant United States Attorney General, 1907; Judge, United States District Court for the Eastern and Middle Districts of Tennessee, 1908-1923; Associate Justice, United States Supreme Court, 1923-1930

SUPREME COURT SERVICE

Nominated: January 24, 1923
Nominated By: Warren G. Harding
Confirmed: January 29, 1923
Confirmation Vote: Voice vote
Oath Taken: February 5, 1923
Replaced: Mahlon Pitney
Significant Opinions: Gitlow v. New York (1925); Corrigan v. Buckley (1926); Whitney v. California (1927)
Left Court: Died March 8, 1930
Length of Service: 7 years, 1 month, 3 days
Replacement: Owen J. Roberts

Edward Sanford was born to a wealthy southern Republican family with roots in New England. He studied in both northern and southern schools and completed his broad education with a year's further study in Europe after completing his law degree at Harvard.

Sanford then returned to Knoxville, where he taught law at the University of Tennessee while pursuing private practice. He began his career in federal government in 1906 as one of Theodore Roosevelt's "trust-busters," prosecuting the fertilizer trust for the attorney general. The next year he became an assistant attorney general, and in 1908, Roosevelt named him a federal judge. After World War I, Sanford worked for accep-

tance of the Treaty of Versailles and the League of Nations. Although his efforts were only partially successful, they brought him to the attention of William Howard Taft, who later backed his nomination to the Supreme Court by President Harding.

Although for the most part Sanford followed the chief justice's lead, his most important contribution to American jurisprudence came in a First Amendment case, Gitlow v. New York (1925), in which, writing for the majority, he articulated the *incorporation doctrine making the guarantees of the Bill of Rights applicable at the state level. The Court sustained the conviction of a publisher charged with advocating the violent overthrow of the government, but Gitlow remains a milestone in the evolution of civil liberties. In a remarkable coincidence, Sanford died on the same day Taft died, March 8, 1930.

For a biography of Associate, then Chief Justice **Harlan Fiske Stone,** see the entry under **THE STONE COURT.**

SIGNIFICANT CASES

TRUAX V. CORRIGAN

Citation: 257 U.S. 312 (1921)
Argued: April 29-30, 1920; reargued October 5-6, 1921
Decided: December 19, 1921
Court Below: Arizona Supreme Court
Basis for Review: *Writ of error
Facts: An Arizona statute preventing the issuance of court *injunctions to stop peaceful labor actions was upheld by the state courts but challenged by an Arizona restaurant owner who claimed to have lost 50 percent of his business because of picketing strikers.
Issue: Does the Arizona no-injunction statute violate the Fourteenth Amendment?
Outcome: A majority of the Taft Court overruled the lower court, declaring that because the statute deprived the restaurateur of his property, it violated the *Due Process Clause. And because it

singled out labor disputes for special treatment, it violated the *Equal Protection Clause.

Vote: 5-4

Participating: Taft, McKenna, Holmes, Day, Van Devanter, Pitney, McReynolds, Brandeis, Clarke

Opinions: Taft for the Court; Holmes, Pitney, joined by Clarke, and Brandeis dissenting

Significance: In this case, a bare majority of the justices voted to uphold *laissez faire. It was a bias that would continue to characterize many of the Taft Court decisions, but the reading given the Due Process and Equal Protection Clauses was soon outdated as subsequent Courts upheld anti-injunction laws like that struck down in *Truax*.

BAILEY V. DREXEL FURNITURE CO.

Citation: 259 U.S. 20 (1922)

Argued: March 8, 1922

Decided: May 15, 1922

Court Below: United States District Court for the Western District of North Carolina

Basis for Review: *Writ of error

Facts: After the Court struck down the first federal child labor law in *Hammer v. Dagenhart* in 1918, Congress passed a second such law in 1919 based on Congress's *taxing power, rather than its *commerce power, and imposing a ten percent tax on net profits of companies employing workers under a certain age. The lower court found for Drexel, which sued to recover taxes paid under protest.

Issue: Does this use of the federal taxing power for regulatory purposes impinge on states' control of their internal affairs?

Outcome: Arguing that the Constitution sanctions only such regulatory measures as have incidental effects, the Taft Court invalidated the second child labor act and affirmed the lower court's ruling.

Vote: 8-1

Participating: Taft, McKenna, Holmes, Day, Van Devanter, Pitney, McReynolds, Brandeis, Clarke

Opinions: Taft for the Court; Clarke dissenting (without written opinion)

Significance: Although the White Court had found, in *McCray v. United States* (1904), that the taxing power could be used for regulatory purposes, in *Bailey* the Court argued that the intended use of the power was invalid, because it was penalizing, rather than revenue enhancing. Future exercises of federal *police power were based upon the commerce power.

UNITED STATES V. LANZA

Citation: 260 U.S. 377 (1922)

Argued: November 23, 1922

Decided: December 11, 1922

Court Below: United States District Court for the Western District of Washington

Basis for Review: *Writ of error

Facts: Vito Lanza, a bootlegger, was convicted under Washington law for having manufactured, transported, and possessed intoxicating liquor. The same evidence used to convict him at the state level was used to prosecute him at the federal level for violating the Volstead Act. The federal district court blocked the second prosecution as *double jeopardy, and the Department of Justice appealed to the Supreme Court.

Issue: Where both state and federal *jurisdictions outlaw the same act, do dual prosecutions of the same defendant for the same crime violate the Fifth Amendment's prohibition against double jeopardy?

Outcome: Arguing that both state and federal governments have the power to uphold the public welfare, the Supreme Court overruled the lower court.

Vote: 9-0

Participating: Taft, McKenna, Holmes, Day, Van Devanter, Pitney, McReynolds, Brandeis, Sutherland

Opinion: Taft for the Court

Significance: Clearly seeking to reinforce the recently ratified Eighteenth Amendment, the Taft Court held that the Fifth Amendment only bars repeated federal prosecutions. Because virtually all states had their own prohibition laws, this ruling meant that transgressors could be doubly punished for their offenses.

MOORE V. DEMPSEY

Citation: 261 U.S. 86 (1923)

Argued: January 9, 1923

Decided: February 19, 1923

Court Below: United States District Court for the Eastern District of Arkansas

Basis for Review: Appeal

Facts: In the aftermath of a 1919 racial confrontation in Phillips County, Arkansas, that resulted in the deaths of two hundred African Americans and five whites, six African Americans were given the death sentence after a trial that took place in a mob-dominated atmosphere. The convicts' petitions for writs of *habeas corpus were rejected by the lower federal courts, and the National Association for the Advancement of Colored People (NAACP) sponsored their appeals to the Supreme Court.

Issue: Are the *due process guarantees of the Fourteenth Amendment violated by mob domination of trials at the state level?

Outcome: Writing for the Court, Justice Holmes argued that federal courts are obliged to review convictions obtained at state trials tainted by the threat of mob violence, and ordered that a habeas corpus hearing be held.

Vote: 6-2

Participating: Taft, McKenna, Holmes, Van Devanter, McReynolds, Brandeis, Sutherland, Butler

Opinions: Holmes for the Court; McReynolds, joined by Sutherland, dissenting

Significance: Although the dissenters argued against such federal interference with state jurisdiction, *Moore* marked the beginning of closer federal oversight of state court convictions obtained in violation of constitutional guarantees. *Moore* also marked an advance towards Court adoption of the *incorporation doctrine, which applies the guarantees of the Bill of Rights (in this case, the Sixth Amendment right to a fair trial) to state governments.

ADKINS V. CHILDREN'S HOSPITAL

Citation: 261 U.S. 525 (1923)

Argued: March 14, 1923

Decided: April 9, 1923

Court Below: District of Columbia Court of Appeals

Basis for Review: Appeal

Facts: In 1918 Congress passed legislation setting maximum hours and minimum wages for women working in the District of Columbia.

Issue: Is the federal statute void as a violation of the freedom of contract and therefore of the *Due Process Clause of the Fifth Amendment?

Outcome: Upholding the liberty of contract doctrine the Supreme Court first espoused in the 1890s, a majority of the Taft Court struck the statute down. (It is worth noting that Justice Sutherland, writing for the majority, also pointed to the Nineteenth Amendment — granting women the vote — as further justification for the Court's decision.)

Vote: 5-3

Participating: Taft, McKenna, Holmes, Van Devanter, McReynolds, Sutherland, Butler, Sanford (Brandeis not participating)

Opinions: Sutherland for the Court; Taft, joined by Sanford, dissenting, Holmes dissenting

Significance: *Adkins* was a landmark case in that it applied the freedom of contract doctrine, so long employed in overturning state labor regulations, against federal legislation. Thus it was the Due Process Clause of the Fifth, rather than the Fourteenth Amendment that applied here. The case was a highwater mark of *laissez faire, and it is therefore surprising that the conservative chief justice spoke out against the majority's decision in a passionate dissent. *Adkins* remained in force and was frequently cited as *precedent throughout the next decade, but with the advent of the New Deal, both state and federal governments began to play a more active role in regulating the nation's economy. The case was finally overruled in 1937 by *West Coast Hotel Co. v. Parrish*.

MEYER V. NEBRASKA

Citation: 262 U.S. 390 (1923)

Argued: February 3, 1923

Decided: June 4, 1923

Court Below: Nebraska Supreme Court

Basis for Review: *Writ of error

Facts: Meyer, a parochial school teacher who used a German bible history as a text, was convicted under a Nebraska statute outlawing the teaching of languages other than English to children in grades lower than grade eight. The lower court affirmed his conviction.

Issue: Is the statute a violation of personal liberty protected by the *Due Process Clause of the Fourteenth Amendment?

Outcome: Arguing that individuals have the right to conduct their lives as they see fit, the Taft Court struck down the Nebraska statute and reversed Meyer's conviction.

Vote: 7-2

Participating: Taft, McKenna, Holmes, Van Devanter, McReynolds, Brandeis, Sutherland, Butler, Sanford

Opinions: McReynolds for the Court; Holmes, joined by Sutherland, dissenting (without written opinions)

Significance: *Meyer* marked an advance in the development of the doctrine of *substantive due process, which came in the 1960s to recognize a "social" variation protecting the right of privacy.

MASSACHUSETTS V. MELLON; FROTHINGHAM V. MELLON

Citation: 262 U.S. 447 (1923)
Argued: May 3-4, 1923
Decided: June 4, 1923
Court Below: District of Columbia Court of Appeals
Basis for Review: Appeal
Facts: These cases, which were heard together, both involved challenges — by the state in *Massachusetts* and by an individual taxpayer in *Frothingham* — to a federal grant-in-aid program intended to promote state-sponsored maternity care requiring those states participating to comply with federal regulations and to match federal appropriations.

Issues: Does the federal plan, by requiring compliance with federal regulations, violate state *sovereignty by forcing the states to yield rights reserved to them under the Tenth Amendment? Does the use of federal tax monies to fund the program deprive an individual taxpayer of her property without *due process?

Outcome: Finding that the voluntary nature of the program did not force the states to cede any rights, the Court dismissed *Massachusetts* because it failed to present any case or controversy for the Court

to decide. And because the impact of the program on an individual taxpayer was so minimal as to deprive her of *standing to sue, the Court similarly dismissed *Frothingham* for lack of *jurisdiction.

Vote: 9-0

Participating: Taft, McKenna, Holmes, Van Devanter, McReynolds, Brandeis, Sutherland, Butler, Sanford

Opinion: Sutherland for the Court

Significance: The federal program's *enabling legislation imposed no burdens on the state itself, only requiring its citizens to pay some additional taxes and, as the holding in *Massachusetts* makes clear, the state may not sue to protect citizens from legitimate federal laws. *Massachusetts* remains in force, but the prohibition against taxpayer standing in *Frothingham* was modified in 1968 by *Flast v. Cohen*, which held that under certain circumstances taxpayers can sue in federal court over expenditures made by the national government.

WOLFF PACKING CO. V. COURT OF INDUSTRIAL RELATIONS

Citation: 262 U.S. 522 (1923)
Argued: April 27, 1923
Decided: June 11, 1923
Court Below: Kansas Supreme Court
Basis for Review: *Writ of error
Facts: The 1920 Kansas Industrial Relations Act regulated such industries as food, clothing, and fuel on grounds that they affected a broad public interest.

Issue: Does the state have authority to regulate businesses simply because they are "affected with a public interest"?

Outcome: Arguing that the state cannot arbitrarily sort private businesses into regulated and non-regulated types, the Court struck down the Kansas statute.

Vote: 9-0

Participating: Taft, McKenna, Holmes, Van Devanter, McReynolds, Brandeis, Sutherland, Butler, Sanford

Opinion: Taft for the Court

Significance: Since 1877, when the Court handed down its decision in *Munn v. Illinois*, an increasing number of businesses had been found to be subject to state regulation. With *Wolff*, the Taft Court reversed this trend, stating that only three areas of economic endeavor were subject to state oversight: 1) those carried out under authority of a public grant, such as utilities; 2) those traditionally classified as having a public service orientation, such as public accommodations; and 3) those, such as monopolies, which by definition were immune to rules normally governing businesses.

CARROLL V. UNITED STATES

Citation: 267 U.S. 132 (1925)
Argued: December 4, 1923; reargued March 14, 1924
Decided: March 2, 1925
Court Below: United States District Court for the Western District of Michigan
Basis for Review: *Writ of error
Facts: On the basis of evidence seized from their automobile without a *warrant, George Carroll and John Kiro were convicted under the Volstead Act of illegally transporting liquor. They appealed, arguing that since there had been no basis for their car to be stopped and searched, the evidence so obtained should have been excluded at their trials.
Issue: Does a warrantless search of an automobile violate the Fourth Amendment prohibition against illegal search and seizure?
Outcome: Reasoning that a search of an automobile differs in kind from that of a dwelling, the Taft Court upheld the lower court convictions.
Vote: 7-2
Participating: Taft, Holmes, Van Devanter, McReynolds, Brandeis, Sutherland, Butler, Sanford (McKenna retired January 5, 1925)
Opinions: Taft for the Court; McReynolds, joined by Sutherland, dissenting; (McKenna concurring without written opinion before retirement)
Significance: This extension of the range of acceptable warrantless searches remains valid. The Court continues to recognize a distinction between the privacy interests at stake in a dwelling and those in an automobile — although the exception has not been broadened to cover other types of vehicles.

PIERCE V. SOCIETY OF SISTERS

Citation: 268 U.S. 510 (1925)
Argued: March 16-17, 1925
Decided: June 1, 1925
Court Below: United States District Court for the District of Oregon
Basis for Review: Appeal
Facts: A 1922 Oregon initiative requiring that almost every child between the ages of eight and sixteen attend public school was *enjoined from enforcement by a three-judge panel in federal district court.
Issue: Does the Oregon statute violate the *Due Process Clause of the Fourteenth Amendment?
Outcome: Relying on the interpretation of *substantive due process it enunciated in *Meyer v. Nebraska* (1923), the Taft Court affirmed the lower court ruling.
Vote: 9-0
Participating: Taft, Holmes, Van Devanter, McReynolds, Brandeis, Sutherland, Butler, Sanford, Stone
Opinion: McReynolds for the Court
Significance: The Taft Court, which was marked by its devotion to the protection of property, employed this value in a novel fashion in *Pierce*, finding that such interference with personal liberty as the Oregon initiative would bring about would also interfere with parents' businesses. While recognizing that states have the authority to compel attendance at some schools, the Court held that parents have a constitutional right to choose whether their children attend private or public schools. Although its reliance on substantive due process in reaching this result is no longer esteemed, the case played an important role in the evolution of civil liberties protecting the unwritten right of privacy in cases like *Roe v. Wade* (1973), which used similar reasoning to safeguard a woman's right to abortion.

GITLOW V. NEW YORK

Citation: 268 U.S. 652 (1925)
Argued: April 12, 1923; reargued November 23, 1923
Decided: June 8, 1925

Court Below: New York Supreme Court

Basis for Review: *Writ of error

Facts: Benjamin Gitlow, a member of the Socialist Party, was convicted in state court of violating the New York Criminal Anarchy Law of 1902 by writing, publishing, and distributing a pamphlet urging establishment of socialism through class action.

Issue: Are the *free speech guarantees of the First Amendment binding upon the states?

Outcome: The Taft Court upheld both the New York law and Gitlow's conviction.

Vote: 7-2

Participating: Taft, Holmes, Van Devanter, McReynolds, Brandeis, Sutherland, Butler, Sanford, Stone

Opinions: Sanford for the Court; Holmes, joined by Brandeis, dissenting

Significance: Although Gitlow's conviction stood, the Taft Court accepted the defense counsel's argument to the extent that the majority's opinion in *Gitlow* employed the *Due Process Clause of the Fourteenth Amendment to make the guarantees of the First Amendment binding upon states as well as the federal government. Although no state law was overturned on free speech grounds until *Stromberg v. California* in 1931, *Gitlow* marks the advent of the *incorporation of the First Amendment as a limitation on state authority.

CORRIGAN V. BUCKLEY

Citation: 271 U.S. 323 (1926)

Argued: January 8, 1926

Decided: May 24, 1926

Court Below: District of Columbia Court of Appeals

Basis for Review: Appeal

Facts: In 1921 property owners in the District of Columbia formed a *restrictive covenant intended to prevent sales to African Americans. The lower court upheld enforcement of the act against a white owner who had contracted with an African American buyer.

Issue: Do the Thirteenth, Fourteenth, and Fifteenth Amendments protect citizens from private acts of discrimination?

Outcome: By dismissing the suit for lack of *jurisdiction, the Taft Court in effect affirmed the lower court ruling and upheld the validity of such restrictive covenants.

Vote: 9-0

Participating: Taft, Holmes, Van Devanter, McReynolds, Brandeis, Sutherland, Butler, Sanford, Stone

Opinion: Sanford for the Court

Significance: *Buchanan v. Warley* (1917), outlawing an ordinance requiring residential segregation, had paved the way for housing integration. But with *Corrigan*, the Taft Court effectively closed down this avenue by upholding private contracts such as the restrictive covenant at issue. Only in 1948, with *Shelley v. Kraemer*, did the Supreme Court modify *Corrigan* by making such covenants judicially unenforceable under the *Equal Protection Clause of the Fourteenth Amendment.

MYERS V. UNITED STATES

Citation: 272 U.S. 52 (1926)

Argued: December 5, 1924; reargued April 13-14, 1925

Decided: October 25, 1926

Court Below: United States Court of Claims

Basis for Review: Appeal

Facts: Frank Myers, a postmaster appointed by President Wilson to a four-year term in 1917, but removed from office in 1920, sued for back pay on grounds that the statute creating his position required Senate consent for such removal. The lower court ruled against him.

Issue: Does the statutory requirement of congressional approval impinge on executive authority?

Outcome: The Taft Court denied Myers's appeal and confirmed his removal.

Vote: 6-3

Participating: Taft, Holmes, Van Devanter, McReynolds, Brandeis, Sutherland, Butler, Sanford, Stone

Opinions: Taft for the Court; McReynolds, Brandeis, and Holmes dissenting

Significance: Taft's opinion extended the concept of *separation of powers to its furthest extreme, implying that the president's *removal power was virtually unlimited. This holding, which potentially impaired congressional policy-making, was modified in *Humphrey's Executor v. United States* (1935), in which the Court held that quasi-legislative and quasi-judicial federal appointees can be congressionally protected from arbitrary removal by the executive branch. Only those officials who perform strictly executive functions are still subject to *Myers*.

EUCLID V. AMBLER REALTY CO.

Citation: 272 U.S. 365 (1926)
Argued: January 27, 1926; reargued October 12, 1926
Decided: November 22, 1926
Court Below: United States District Court for the Northern District of Ohio
Basis for Review: Appeal
Facts: Euclid, Ohio, enacted an extensive and restrictive zoning ordinance that included land use, area, and height restrictions. Ambler Realty owned a large parcel of land in the affected area, which it hoped to develop for industrial use. When the zoning ordinance made realization of these plans impossible, Ambler sued in federal district court alleging a government *taking without just compensation, and won an *injunction preventing enforcement of the ordinance.
Issue: Is zoning a proper use of the state *police power?
Outcome: The Taft Court reversed the lower court's ruling, finding zoning to be an acceptable means of regulating private land use.
Vote: 6-3
Participating: Taft, Holmes, Van Devanter, McReynolds, Brandeis, Sutherland, Butler, Sanford, Stone
Opinions: Sutherland for the Court; Van Devanter, McReynolds, and Butler dissenting (without written opinions)
Significance: While in *Euclid* the Court merely recognized the possibility that a particular zoning ordinance might be unconstitutional with regard to a particular parcel of land, this case cleared the way for widespread use of zoning as the accepted means of regulating private land use.

TYSON V. BANTON

Citation: 273 U.S. 418 (1927)
Argued: October 6-7, 1926
Decided: February 28, 1927
Court Below: United States District Court for the Southern District of New York
Basis for Review: Appeal
Facts: A New York statute regulating the resale price of theater tickets was upheld in the lower court.
Issue: Is the statute a violation of freedom of contract?
Outcome: Arguing that a ticket agency was not a business affected with a pubic interest, the Court struck the statute down.
Vote: 5-4
Participating: Taft, Holmes, Van Devanter, McReynolds, Brandeis, Sutherland, Butler, Sanford, Stone
Opinions: Sutherland for the Court; Holmes (joined by Brandeis), Stone (joined by Holmes and Brandeis), and Sanford dissenting
Significance: Writing for a bare majority, Justice Sutherland reflected the extremely narrow interpretation of businesses affected with a public interest — and therefore subject to regulation — outlined by Chief Justice Taft in *Wolff Packing Co. v. Court of Industrial Relations* (1923). The view expressed by Justice Holmes in dissent, that the state has a large role to play in such regulation, would ultimately triumph; however, today state governments systematically regulate economic endeavors, so long as the force of public opinion is with them and they face no constitutional barriers.

NIXON V. HERNDON

Citation: 273 U.S. 536 (1927)
Argued: January 4, 1927
Decided: March 7, 1927
Court Below: United States District Court for the Western District of Texas
Basis for Review: *Writ of error
Facts: After Reconstruction, the Republican Party essentially ceded the South to the Democrats, with the result that the most important south-

ern elections became Democratic primaries. But when African Americans attempted to register, southern states enacted "white primary" laws, such as the Texas statute challenged by Nixon, an African American doctor from El Paso.

Issue: Does the Texas "white primary" law violate the *Equal Protection Clause of the Fourteenth Amendment?

Outcome: A unanimous Court struck down the Texas statute.

Vote: 9-0

Participating: Taft, Holmes, Van Devanter, McReynolds, Brandeis, Sutherland, Butler, Sanford, Stone

Opinion: Holmes for the Court

Significance: Because state "white primary" statutes discriminated solely upon the basis of race, they could be outlawed. But southern states got around the ruling in *Nixon* by putting the onus for excluding African Americans on local Democratic Party organizations, which were essentially transformed into private institutions that could continue to bar African American participation. Not until *Smith v. Allwright* (1944) did the Supreme Court succeed in banishing the all-white southern primary as a violation of the Fifteenth Amendment.

BUCK V. BELL

Citation: 274 U.S. 200 (1927)
Argued: April 22, 1927
Decided: May 2, 1927
Court Below: Virginia Supreme Court
Basis for Review: *Writ of error
Facts: Carrie Buck, an inmate of a Virginia institution for the mentally defective, was the subject of a case intended to test the institution's practice of sterilizing its residents without their consent. Her legal counsel deliberately presented no defense in the lower court, which ordered her sterilization.

Issue: Does involuntary sterilization violate the Fourteenth Amendment's guarantee of *due process?

Outcome: Writing for the Court, Justice Holmes endorsed the current support for eugenics and upheld the lower court ruling.

Vote: 8-1

Participating: Taft, Holmes, Van Devanter, McReynolds, Brandeis, Sutherland, Butler, Sanford, Stone

Opinions: Holmes for the Court; Butler dissenting (without written opinion)

Significance: Holmes's opinion reflected the prejudices of the nation. In the wake of *Buck*, many states passed laws permitting sterilization of the "feeble-minded."

WHITNEY V. CALIFORNIA

Citation: 274 U.S. 357 (1927)
Argued: October 19, 1925; reargued March 18, 1926
Decided: May 26, 1927
Court Below: California Court of Appeals
Basis for Review: *Writ of error
Facts: Charlotte Anna Whitney, a social activist and former member of the Communist Labor Party, was convicted under a 1919 California criminal syndicalism statute. The statute was aimed specifically at the radical syndicalist organization, the Industrial Workers of the World, a union endorsed by the Communist Labor Party.

Issue: Is the California statute a violation of First Amendment guarantees of *free speech and freedom of association?

Outcome: Basing its decision on the state's authority to protect the public from violent political action, the Court upheld the lower court's decision.

Vote: 9-0

Participating: Taft, Holmes, Van Devanter, McReynolds, Brandeis, Sutherland, Butler, Sanford, Stone

Opinions: Sanford for the Court; Brandeis, joined by Holmes, concurring

Significance: Whitney was convicted solely for her one-time, once-removed association with an outlawed organization. As Justice Brandeis's important concurrence pointed out, an elaboration by her attorneys of the "clear and present" danger test for First Amendment protections would have afforded a distinction between Whitney's mere membership in a group and constitutionally unprotected violent action. *Whitney* was later overruled by *Brandenburg v. Ohio* (1969).

POLITICAL COMPOSITION
of the Taft Court

Justice & Total Term	Courts Served	Appointing President	Political Party
William Howard Taft (1921-1930)	Taft	Harding	Republican
Joseph McKenna (1898-1925)	Fuller White Taft	McKinley	Republican
Oliver Wendell Holmes (1903-1932)	Fuller White Taft Hughes	T. Roosevelt	Republican
William R. Day (1903-1922)	Fuller White Taft	T. Roosevelt	Republican
Willis Van Devanter (1911-1937)	White Taft Hughes	Taft	Republican
Mahlon Pitney (1912-1922)	White Taft	Taft	Republican
James C. McReynolds (1914-1941)	White Taft Hughes	Wilson	Democrat
Louis D. Brandeis (1916-1939)	White Taft Hughes	Wilson	Democrat
John H. Clarke (1916-1922)	White Taft	Wilson	Democrat
George Sutherland (1922-1938)	Taft Hughes	Harding	Republican
Pierce Butler (1923-1939)	Taft Hughes	Harding	Democrat
Edward T. Sanford (1923-1930)	Taft Hughes	Harding	Republican
Harlan F. Stone (1925-1941) (1941-1946)	Taft Hughes Stone	Coolidge F D. Roosevelt	Republican Republican

OLMSTEAD V. UNITED STATES

Citation: 277 U.S. 438 (1928)
Argued: February 20-21, 1928
Decided: June 4, 1928
Court Below: United States Ninth Circuit Court of Appeals
Basis for Review: *Writ of certiorari
Facts: Olmstead was convicted of transporting and selling liquor in violation of the National Prohibition Act on the basis of evidence gained through wiretaps.
Issue: Does the use of evidence obtained through illegal wiretaps in a federal criminal prosecution violate the accused's Fourth and Fifth Amendment rights?
Outcome: The lower court's ruling was upheld.
Vote: 5-4
Participating: Taft, Holmes, Van Devanter, McReynolds, Brandeis, Sutherland, Butler, Sanford, Stone
Opinions: Taft for the Court; Brandeis, Holmes, Butler, and Stone dissenting
Significance: Because wiretaps do not involve physical entry onto private property, the Taft Court found that Olmstead's Fourth Amendment guarantee against illegal search and seizure had not been violated. However, the Supreme Court extended the *exclusionary rule to cover wiretaps introduced in federal prosecutions, and with *Katz v. United States* (1967), it overruled *Olmstead* outright.

VOTING PATTERNS

Chief Justice Taft was a great promoter of consensus and, early in his tenure, his congeniality and management skills frequently allowed him to achieve his ambition of "massing the Court." During those early years, he was surrounded by men whose judicial philosophy reflected his own staunch conservatism. He himself appointed Justices Van Devanter and Pitney, and although President Harding had the responsibility of reconstituting the Court shortly after he appointed Taft chief justice, he did so (often with a great deal of assistance from former President Taft) by appointing men who had demonstrated a clear constitu-

tional conservatism. Thus George Sutherland, Pierce Butler, and Edward T. Sanford replaced, respectively, Justices John H. Clarke, William R. Day, and Mahlon Pitney. Taft's one remaining potential problem was Justice Louis D. Brandeis, whose appointment by President Wilson he had bitterly opposed. At first, however, even the liberal Brandeis often went along with Taft's consensus-building — only later would their ideological disparity divide the Court. (In fact, Justice Clarke cited as one reason for his resignation in 1922 the increasing frequency with which Brandeis voted with the majority in cases involving liberal principles, leaving Clarke isolated.)

As chief justice, Taft is remembered most for his effectiveness as an administrator. One of the ways he achieved unanimity — or at least clear majorities — was to reassign opinions if the justices originally given responsibility for them were unable to marshall a high degree of support. Often the energetic chief justice would tackle the most potentially divisive cases himself. Such judicious use of the assignment power may help account for seeming anomalies like *Bailey v. Drexel Furniture Co.* (1922), in which only Justice Clarke dissented (without opinion) from the Court's second invalidation of a federal child labor law. (The first, *Hammer v. Dagenhart* [1918], was decided 5 to 4, with McKenna, Brandeis, Holmes, and Clarke in dissent.) On only one significant occasion during the early years of his chief justiceship, in *Adkins v. Children's Hospital* (1923), did Taft find himself at odds with the conservative majority of his Court. *Adkins* marked the pinnacle of the Taft Court's endorsement of the freedom of contract doctrine, an opinion so extreme that it gave rise to one of the four dissents Taft wrote as chief justice.

In *Adkins*, Taft found himself dissenting along with Justice Holmes. It was a rare pairing. After 1925 — when the chief justice convinced Justice McKenna to step down and encouraged President Coolidge to replace McKenna with Harlan F. Stone — Holmes continued to dissent frequently, but now he regularly was joined by Brandeis and Stone, the latter soon becoming a disappointment to Taft. The battle lines were drawn, and for the remainder of Taft's regime, the progressive threesome consistently arrayed themselves against the champions of private property and *laissez faire.

SPECIAL FEATURES OF THE TAFT COURT

THE JUDICIARY ACT OF 1925

The 1925 Judiciary Act had its origins in a committee, consisting of Justices Day (soon succeeded by Sutherland), McReynolds, and Van Devanter, which Taft set up shortly after he assumed the chief justiceship. This effort to reform the judicial system was, however, largely the result of the chief justice's tireless lobbying, speechmaking, and testifying before Congress.

Taft, a product of the Progressive era, was a proponent of economy and efficiency, and his primary goal was to streamline the Supreme Court's clogged *docket. The 1925 act increased the stature and authority of the Court. It did so in the main by making petitions for *certiorari the primary means of getting a case before the Court and eliminating much of the previously mandatory review of cases from federal appellate and district courts. Thus the makeup of the Court's docket became largely a discretionary matter, and the Court was transformed from a tribunal of last resort to an institution endowed with a power to influence social policy equal to that of the executive and legislative branches.

THE COURT AS LEGISLATURE

Although Taft worked for the empowerment of the judiciary with the 1925 Judicial Act and broadened the authority of the executive with his opinion in *Myers v. United States* (1926), he also presided over a Court that invalidated more pieces of legislation than had been declared unconstitutional in the 50 years prior to his regime. Taft's view — and that of his six-man conservative majority — was that the Supreme Court was the last bastion of the status quo, obliged to protect time-tested values from the experimentation of rash lawmakers.

In the name of *due process and *equal protection, in *Truax v. Corrigan* (1921), the Taft Court annulled such laws as an Arizona statute aimed a protecting strikers from court *injunctions, a goal long shared by many state legislatures and the Congress, which had incorporated a similar prohibition against union-busting use of injunctions into the Clayton Antitrust Act of 1914. The same pro-business agenda fueled the Court's abrogation of a minimum wage law for female workers in *Adkins v. Children's Hospital* (1923), which contradicted, if it did not actually overturn, the Supreme Court's landmark 1908 decision in *Muller v. Oregon*. And with *Wolff Packing Co. v. Court of Industrial Relations* (1923), the Taft Court negated a half-century of regulatory development growing out of *Munn v. Illinois* (1877) by making it virtually impossible for states to regulate private business. This pro-business orientation was born out by *Tyson v. Banton* (1927), where Taft's majority invested a transaction between a theatergoer and a ticket scalper with the dignity of a contractual agreement, granting it protection from state interference. By such means as these, the elected representatives of the people were found incompetent to protect the public interest and the Court accorded the status of what Justice Brandeis called a "super-legislature."

LAW CLERKS

Since 1886 the justices each had been allotted $1,600 per year to pay a secretary or clerk. For most of the justices this meant doing their own research and writing and hiring only stenographers or typists. Justice Horace Gray had begun the practice of hiring promising recent law school graduates as law clerks, a practice his successor on the Massachusetts and later the United States Supreme Court, Oliver Wendell Holmes, continued. By 1922 Congress had provided the justices with funds to hire their own law clerks, and the custom of Gray and Holmes became Court convention. In 1924 Congress made clerks' positions a permanent feature of the Court.

The Hughes Court 1930-1941

BACKGROUND

THE DEPRESSION CONTINUES

In 1930 the number of unemployed stood at four million and 1,352 banks closed their doors, owing to a decrease in the money supply and public runs on bank resources. In 1932 the number of unemployed reached eight million, and 2,294 banks closed. In 1933 the unemployment rate doubled again. President Herbert Hoover proposed a number of government initiatives to counter the precipitous economic decline — among them federal works projects and a Federal Farm Board to buy up surplus production — but his efforts proved to be too little too late.

The Bonus March of 1932 highlighted Hoover's apparent antipathy to public relief and marked the nadir of his administration. In 1925, in an effort to help veterans of World War I, Congress offered them one thousand dollar insurance certificates. The certificates would not mature for 20 years. However, in a 1932 election year ploy, the Democrats proposed legislation that would permit early payment of the certificates as a relief "bonus." Unemployed veterans and their families converged on Washington, D.C., to press for passage of the bill, settling in a tent city along the Potomac River similar to other "Hoovervilles" scattered across the nation.

The Senate rejected the proposed legislation but provided money to send the veterans home. Two thousand of them chose to remain, nonetheless, and Hoover sent in the army to remove them from the nation's capital. In June, cavalry and infantry, armed with bayonets, machine guns, and tanks, and led by Army Chief of Staff Douglas MacArthur, evicted the veterans and burned their tent city to the ground. Their actions were caught on newsreels that later were distributed around the country. The Bonus March spelled the end of Hoover's presidency.

THE ELECTION OF 1932

The Republicans nominated Hoover again in 1932. Sensing that they had an opening for the first time in over a decade, the Democrats nominated New York Governor Franklin Delano Roosevelt. Roosevelt won by a landslide, scoring 457 electoral votes to Hoover's 59.

The Democratic Party, which had also gained control of both houses of Congress, quickly pushed through two constitutional amendments. The Twentieth Amendment moved presidential inaugurations and congressional commencements up to January, thus eliminating lame duck presidents and lame duck congressional sessions, a change made especially urgent by the ongoing Depression. The Twenty-first Amendment ended Prohibition by rescinding the Eighteenth Amendment, the only amendment ever formally repealed. But little, it seemed, could be done to help the economy: in the interim between the presidential election and Roosevelt's inauguration, the banking system virtually shut down.

THE FIRST NEW DEAL

Sensing that the nation had come to a dead end, Roosevelt called for a special session of Congress

---

An asterisk (*) before a word or phrase indicates that a definition will be found in the glossary at the end of this volume.

to convene March 9, five days after he assumed office. This session, which ended June 16 and was later referred to as the "Hundred Days," resulted in legislation affecting banking, industry, agriculture, and unemployment — all of it aimed primarily at national relief and recovery.

From this initial legislative session grew a plethora of "alphabet agencies," including: the Federal Deposit Insurance Corporation (FDIC), which insured private bank deposits up to $5,000 each even if the banks holding them failed; the Civilian Conservation Corps (CCC), which provided public works jobs for unemployed males between the ages of 18 and 25; the Federal Emergency Relief Administration (FERA), which channeled relief grants to state and local authorities; the Agricultural Adjustment Administration (AAA), intended to restore farmers to economic health; the Tennessee Valley Authority (TVA), proposed to achieve regional rehabilitation through rural electrification; the Securities and Exchange Commission (SEC), providing federal oversight of the stock exchanges; and, perhaps most ambitious of all, the National Recovery Administration (NRA), designed as a partnership among government, private enterprise, and labor that would revive business activity.

Most of the New Deal recovery measures were meant to be short-term and self-liquidating, and many of them either did not work or were, like the AAA, declared unconstitutional. Like his predecessor, Roosevelt did not expect the Depression to last long, but he felt that dramatic, innovative measures were needed to restart the economy — doing almost anything was better than doing nothing. When the Depression continued and Roosevelt became the object of Republican criticism, accused of totalitarian leanings, the president shifted leftward, adopting a program for long-term reform that constituted virtually a second New Deal.

THE SECOND NEW DEAL

Roosevelt outlined his plan for the second New Deal in January 1935 as part of his annual message to Congress. It would involve three principal approaches: public relief, labor reform, and social security. To address the first of these, he proposed creation of the Works Progress Administration (WPA), which would oversee a national works program for the unemployed. While most of the jobs thus created involved manual labor, the WPA also employed artists, musicians, actors, and writers. By the time it was officially ended in 1943, the WPA had employed

---

MEMBERS *Of the Court* 1930–1941

(In Order of Seniority)

Charles Evans Hughes (Chief Justice)	(1930-1941)
Oliver Wendell Holmes (retired)	(1930-1932)
Willis Van Devanter (retired)	(1930-1937)
James C. McReynolds (retired)	(1930-1941)
Louis D. Brandeis (retired)	(1930-1939)
George Sutherland (retired)	(1930-1938)
Pierce Butler (died)	(1930-1939)
Edward T. Sanford (died)	(1930)
Harlan F. Stone	(1930-1941)
Owen J. Roberts (replaced Edward T. Sanford)	(1930-1941)
Benjamin N. Cardozo (replaced Oliver Wendell Holmes; died)	(1932-1938)
Hugo L. Black (replaced Willis Van Devanter)	(1937-1941)
Stanley F. Reed (replaced George Sutherland)	(1938-1941)
Felix Frankfurter (replaced Benjamin N. Cardozo)	(1939-1941)
William O. Douglas (replaced Louis D. Brandeis)	(1939-1941)
Frank Murphy (replaced Pierce Butler)	(1940-1941)

8.5 million people — nearly a fifth of the nation's work force — on 1,410,000 different projects, among them highways, dams, bridges, and some memorable art.

Senator Robert Wagner of New York had first proposed legislation favoring organized labor in 1933, but Roosevelt refused to endorse it. In 1935, however, the legislation received the president's blessing, and the Wagner, or National Labor Relations Act, passed both houses of Congress with overwhelming support. Aligning the federal government with labor, the Wagner Act upheld the right of workers to form unions and bargain collectively, while at the same time outlawing unfair practices such as employer dismissal of workers who joined unions. Although later modified to grant employers greater bargaining powers, the Wagner Act remains the cornerstone of United States labor law.

The third goal of the second New Deal was achieved through the Social Security Act, which provided unemployment compensation, old-age and survivors' insurance, old-age pensions, and grants to the states for aid to helpless individuals, such as the destitute blind. Until the end of his life, Roosevelt regarded Social Security as the finest achievement of the New Deal, and it has proved to be his most enduring legacy to the nation.

PACKING THE COURT

Roosevelt won the 1936 presidential election by an even wider margin than the one that had swept him into office four years earlier, carrying all but two states and polling 27.8 million votes to Republican candidate Alfred M. Landon's 16.6 million. Nevertheless, Roosevelt was not without his detractors, some of the most powerful of whom sat on the Supreme Court.

In an effort to counteract the Court's continuing invalidation of New Deal legislation, in February 1937 Roosevelt submitted to Congress a plan to reorganize the judiciary. Dubbed the "court-packing plan," Roosevelt's bill proposed to increase the size of the federal judiciary, thus enabling the president to nominate judges who would uphold the constitutionality of New Deal

legislation. Included was a plan to add one new Supreme Court justice for every sitting justice over the age of 70, up to a maximum of 15, if those over 70 declined to retire. Roosevelt also proposed to add up to 50 judges to all levels of the federal court system, and to send all appeals from lower court constitutional decisions directly to the Supreme Court.

These measures clearly would provide the president with considerable leverage over a supposedly separate and independent judiciary, and it was nearly universally denounced. Nonetheless, Congress began serious consideration of the Judiciary Reorganization Bill, taking the important step of immediately passing a retirement act that would permit Supreme Court justices to retire at full salary. Justice Willis Van Devanter, a New Deal foe, announced his retirement shortly thereafter, opening up one of seven vacancies on the Court that Roosevelt would fill over the next four years. More significantly, largely because of Justice Owen J. Roberts's change of voting posture, the Hughes Court experienced in the spring of 1937 what has come to be known as the "switch in time that saved nine," handing down a series of decisions sustaining important New Deal legislation.

In the end, Roosevelt won the test of wills with the conservatives on the Court, even though his bill went down to defeat. He paid dearly for his victory, however, losing control of the Democratic coalition that had made the New Deal possible. He also lost the faith of a substantial sector of the American public, which had been reminded of the necessity of keeping the Court above the political fray.

PRELUDE TO WAR

The isolationist mood America adopted after World War I continued to dominate the nation throughout the 1920s and 1930s. During this same period, a militant nationalism took hold in Europe, finding its fullest expression in the fascism of Benito Mussolini in Italy and Adolph Hitler in Germany. In 1936 the two dictators formed what they called a "Rome-Berlin Axis" that would dominate the center of Europe, and when civil war broke out in Spain in 1936, both sent aid to a fellow fascist there, General Francisco Franco. Franco's forces ultimately prevailed, and the Spanish Civil War became a rehearsal for the looming global conflict. During the 1930s, Japan, too, had been arming itself for military aggression, first withdrawing from the League of Nations, and in 1937, attacking China. The Sino-Japanese War would eventually merge with the war being waged in Europe, giving rise to World War II.

Britain and France, believing that Hitler sought only to right the inequities of the Versailles Treaty, initially opted for a policy of appeasement, agreeing in September 1938 to cede Hitler control over Czechoslovakia. But less than a year after British Prime Minister Neville Chamberlain announced to the world, "I give you peace in our time," Hitler — after neutralizing the Soviets by signing a nonaggression pact with Joseph Stalin — invaded Poland, whose independence Britain and France were pledged to protect. World War II had begun.

The United States responded to the threat of global war by passing a series of neutrality acts imposing an international arms embargo and prohibiting loans to all combatants. Although Roosevelt had initiated rearmament in 1938 and urged repeal of the embargo in 1939, he was entering an election year during which he would seek an unprecedented third term in office, and he had to match Republican candidate Wendell Wilkie's promises of peace and neutrality.

Roosevelt won the election, again in a landslide. Capitalizing on his renewed mandate, he urged Congress to adopt the Lend Lease Act, which would permit the president, at his discretion, to lend military hardware to countries in need. By this point in the European war, Denmark, Norway, Luxembourg, the Netherlands, Belgium, and France had fallen. Britain remained alone as a bulwark of democracy, but it was running out of arms and funds. But Britain became the first beneficiary of America's new lend-lease policy, and in the summer of 1941, Roosevelt and British Prime Minister Winston Churchill met on an American warship in Argentia Bay, Newfoundland, to draw up a joint statement of principles called the Atlantic Charter. It was only a matter of time before the United States would be forced to enter the war.

HUGHES'S EARLY LIFE

Charles Evans Hughes was the treasured only child of a Baptist minister and a schoolteacher. Raised in an atmosphere of religious fervor and high morality, Hughes received his early education at home. When, at the age of six, the precocious Hughes (who by the age of nine could already read the classics) was sent to public school, he pleaded boredom and within three weeks returned home to study. At the age of 14 he entered Madison College to prepare for the ministry, but after two years, he transferred to Brown University, where he discovered a more liberal atmosphere and a new calling: the law.

Hughes's family was poor and lacked the funds to send him directly to law school, so he spent a year teaching at Delaware Academy in Delhi, New York, reading law part-time. In 1882 he entered Columbia Law School, from which he graduated with highest honors two years later. His performance on the New York bar examination, on which he scored 99.5 out of 100, was equally impressive.

Hughes went directly into private practice with the prestigious firm of Chamberlain, Carter, and Hornblower, with whom he had clerked during law school. While there Hughes met and married Carter's daughter, Antoinette, and soon advanced to partnership.

By all accounts Hughes had a thriving law practice, but at the age of 29, owing to ill health and perhaps boredom, he left to accept a full professorship at Cornell University Law School. Two years later, following what would become a familiar pattern in his life, he bowed to financial pressures and returned to Chamberlain, Carter, and Hornblower. However, for the next 14 years he continued to work part-time as a special lecturer at Cornell and at New York Law School.

HUGHES'S PUBLIC LIFE

In 1905, at the suggestion of Henry W. Taft, brother of then secretary of war William Howard

JUDICIAL BIOGRAPHY
Charles Evans Hughes

PERSONAL DATA
Born: April 11, 1862, in Glens Falls, New York
Parents: Rev. David Charles Hughes, Mary C. Connelly Hughes
Higher Education: Madison College, now Colgate University,1876-1878; Brown University (B.A., Phi Beta Kappa, 1881; M.A. 1884); Columbia University Law School (LL.B., first in class, 1884)
Bar Admission: New York, 1884
Political Party: Republican
Marriage: December 5, 1888, to Antoinette Carter, who bore Hughes one son and three daughters
Died: August 27, 1948, in Osterville, Massachusetts
Buried: The Woodlawn Cemetery, Bronx, New York

PROFESSIONAL CAREER
Occupations: Educator, 1881-1882, 1891-1905; Lawyer, 1884-1891, 1893-1906, 1918-1921, 1925-1926; Government Official, 1905-1906, 1921-1925; Politician, 1906-1910; Judge, 1910-1916, 1926-1941; Diplomat, 1921
Official Positions: Professor of Law, Cornell University Law School, 1891-1893; Special Lecturer, Cornell University Law School & New York Law School, 1893-1905; Special Counsel, New York State Investigative Committees, 1905-1906; Governor, New York, 1906-1910; Associate Justice, United States Supreme Court, 1910-1916; United States Secretary of State, 1921-1925; United States Delegate, Washington Armament Conference, 1921; United States Member, Permanent Court of Arbitration, 1926-1930; Judge, Permanent Court of International Justice, 1928-1930; Chief Justice, United States Supreme Court, 1930-1941

SUPREME COURT SERVICE
As Associate Justice:
Nominated: April 25, 1910
Nominated By: William Howard Taft
Confirmed: May 2, 1910
Confirmation Vote: Voice vote
Oath Taken: October 10, 1910
Replaced: David J. Brewer
Significant Opinion: *Shreveport Rate Cases* (1914)
Left Court: Resigned June 10, 1916
Length of Service: 5 years, 8 months
Replacement: John H. Clarke

As Chief Justice:
Nominated: February 3, 1930
Nominated By: Herbert Hoover
Confirmed: February 13, 1930
Confirmation Vote: 52-26
Oath Taken: February 24, 1930
Replaced: William Howard Taft
Significant Opinions: *Stromberg v. California* (1931); *Near v. Minnesota* (1931); *Home Building & Loan Association v. Blaisdell* (1934); *Panama Refining Co. v. Ryan* (1935); *Gold Clause Cases* (1935); *Norris v. Alabama* (1935); *Schechter Poultry Corp. v. United States* (1935); *Ashwander v. Tennessee Valley Authority* (1936); *Brown v. Mississippi* (1936); *De Jonge v. Oregon* (1937); *West Coast Hotel Co. v. Parrish* (1937); *National Labor Relations Board v. Jones & Laughlin Steel Corp.* (1937); *Lovell v. City of Griffin* (1938); *Missouri *ex rel. Gaines v. Canada* (1938); *Coleman v. Miller* (1939); *Cox v. New Hampshire* (1941)
Left Court: Retired July 1, 1941
Length of Service: 11 years, 4 months, 7 days
Replacement: Harlan Fiske Stone

Taft, Hughes was named special counsel to a New York State ad hoc committee investigating gas and electric rates. In a period of three and one-half months, Hughes participated in 57 public hearings, unearthing a pattern of corruption that resulted in the establishment of a regulatory public service commission. When later that year the state legislature set out to make a similar probe of

Charles Evans Hughes

the insurance industry, Hughes was again named as special counsel and again produced impressive results.

Owing in large part to Hughes's successes on these state-wide committees, President Theodore Roosevelt urged the New York Republican Party to nominate him for the 1906 governor's race. Hughes was elected by a wide margin and again reelected in 1908. Hughes's record as governor was a good one, and when President Taft named him to the federal Supreme Court, the nomination was a popular one. In accepting the nomination, Hughes was humble, publicly disavowing any greater political ambitions. In naming him to the Court in April 1910, Taft had all but promised Hughes that he would be named to replace Chief Justice Melville W. Fuller upon Fuller's death, which seemed imminent. When Fuller died that July, however, Taft turned instead to Associate Justice Edward D. White.

Hughes served ably, if relatively quietly, under Chief Justice White, writing 151 opinions for the Court, many of which promoted social reform. In 1916, however, he resigned to pursue the very political ambitions he had disavowed six years

earlier, becoming the Republican presidential nominee. His campaign was generally negative and lackluster, but he lost to Woodrow Wilson by only a slim margin.

Hughes returned then to private practice as a senior partner at the firm of Hughes, Rounds, Schurman, and Dwight — but not for long. In 1921 he accepted Warren G. Harding's offer to become secretary of state. As secretary of state, Hughes gained Harding's support for the World Court and presided over a highly successful disarmament conference. In 1925, however, suffering from overwork and the need to "recoup his fortune," he followed a by now familiar pattern and resigned to resume the practice of law.

HUGHES AS CHIEF JUSTICE

Despite his return to private life, Hughes kept a high profile, in part through his work as a judge for the Permanent Court of International Justice. His nomination as chief justice on February 3, 1930, by Herbert Hoover did not, however, meet with the same acclaim as had his earlier appointment to the High Court. Hughes's second confirmation process was a rocky one, during which his detractors claimed he would be unable to divorce himself from his long association with the rich and powerful. Nonetheless, he was confirmed by a vote of 52 to 26.

When Hughes assumed control of the Court on February 24, 1930, he was at 67 the oldest man ever to have been chosen as chief justice. The country was in the grip of the Great Depression, and the Hughes Court was confronted with a vast calendar, consisting of many of the most significant cases ever to come before the High Court. Hughes's lifelong habits of commitment and hard work led him to assume a large share of the burden, and during his 11-year tenure as chief justice, he was responsible for 283 opinions of the Court.

Hughes's opinions during this period, like the Court itself, seemed to fall into two categories. On matters of civil liberties and the Bill of Rights, Hughes was an unqualified activist, voting in favor of free speech in *Stromberg v. California* (1931), supporting the rights of the wrongfully accused Scottsboro Boys in *Powell v. Alabama*

(1932), and leading the way, in cases such as *De Jonge v. Oregon* (1937), towards an *incorporation into the Fourteenth Amendment of the guarantees embodied in the Bill of Rights.

In cases like those cited above, Hughes was able to moderate the debate between liberals like Justices Louis D. Brandeis, Harlan F. Stone, Oliver Wendell Holmes and his successor, Benjamin N. Cardozo, and the conservative old-timers who outnumbered them in the early years of the Hughes Court. Regarding economic issues, however, the chief justice was more conflicted. This ambiguity almost certainly contributed to the showdown with Franklin Roosevelt that ensued when the Court ruled against many of the president's New Deal reforms.

Like most of his colleagues, Hughes had been schooled in *laissez faire constitutionalism, a philosophical stance that led him to vote against New Deal legislation such as the National Industrial Recovery Act (in *Schechter Poultry Co. v. United States* [1935]) and the Agriculture Adjustment Act (in *United States v. Butler* [1936]). And yet, even before Roosevelt announced his court-packing plan on February 5, 1937, Hughes, joined by the other swing vote on the Court, Justice Owen J. Roberts, began to foment a constitutional evolution. By such means, the Supreme Court would deemphasize *substantive due process and defer to the will of the people as expressed by the legislative branch. This change was signaled by Hughes's opinion for the Court in *West Coast Hotel Co. v. Parrish* (1937) (although announced on March 29, 1937, it had been decided prior to publication of Roosevelt's Court Reorganization plan), in which the Court upheld a state minimum wage law similar to one it had struck down nine months earlier. The Court's changed orientation was cemented two weeks later with another Hughes opinion, *National Labor Relations Board v. Jones & Laughlin Steel Corp.* (1937), upholding the National Labor Relations Act of 1935.

The Court that Hughes led after 1937 was altogether different from the "first" Hughes Court, both in personnel and in *jurisprudence. The retirement of Willis Van Devanter in 1937 and of

George Sutherland in 1938 broke the conservative voting bloc known as the "Four Horsemen." Addition of liberals Hugo L. Black and William O. Douglas altered the face not just of the Hughes Court, but of several subsequent Courts in which they served. In presiding over both of the Courts that sat during the years 1930-1941 and the national crises they confronted and helped overcome, Hughes exhibited the managerial skills and intellectual flexibility that make for a great chief justice.

On June 2, 1941, at the age of 79, Hughes once again pled ill health in resigning a position. He retired as chief justice on July 1, 1941, but he lived for another seven years, during which he organized his papers for the benefit of those who came after him.

ASSOCIATE JUSTICES

For a biography of Associate Justice **Oliver Wendell Holmes,** see the entry under **THE FULLER COURT.** For biographies of Associate Justices **Willis Van Devanter, James C. McReynolds,** and **Louis D. Brandeis,** see entries under **THE WHITE COURT.** For biographies of Associate Justices **George Sutherland, Pierce Butler,** and **Edward T. Sanford,** see entries under **THE TAFT COURT.** For a biography of Associate, then Chief Justice **Harlan F. Stone,** see the entry under **THE STONE COURT.**

OWEN JOSEPHUS ROBERTS

PERSONAL DATA
Born: May 2, 1875, in Germantown, Pennsylvania
Parents: Josephus Roberts, Emma Laferty Roberts
Higher Education: University of Pennsylvania (B.A., Phi Beta Kappa, 1895; LL.B., cum laude, 1898)
Bar Admission: Pennsylvania, 1898
Political Party: Republican
Marriage: 1904 to Elizabeth Caldwell Rogers, who bore Roberts a daughter
Died: May 17, 1955, in West Vincent Township, Chester County, Pennsylvania

The Hughes Court, 1932. From left: Louis D. Brandeis, Owen J. Roberts, Willis Van Devanter, Pierce Butler, Charles Evans Hughes, Harlan Fiske Stone, James C. McReynolds, Benjamin N. Cardozo, George Sutherland

Buried: St. Andrew's Cemetery, West Vincent Township

PROFESSIONAL CAREER

Occupations: Educator, 1898-1919, 1948-1951; Lawyer, 1898-1930; Government Official, 1901-1904, 1918, 1924-1928, early 1950s; Judge, 1930-1945; Public Official, 1941-1943, 1953-1955

Official Positions: Fellow, University of Pennsylvania, 1898-1900; Lecturer, University of Pennsylvania, 1900-1919; Assistant District Attorney, Philadelphia, 1901-1904; Vice President, Law Academy of Philadelphia, 1903; President, Law Academy of Philadelphia, 1904; Secretary, Law Association of Philadelphia, ca. early 1900s; Special Deputy Attorney General, Eastern District of Pennsylvania, 1918; Special United States Attorney General, 1924-1928; Associate Justice, United States Supreme Court, 1930-1945; Chairman, Pearl Harbor Inquiry Board, 1941-1942; Head, Commission for the Protection and Salvage of Artistic and Historic Monuments in Europe, 1943; Dean, University of Pennsylvania Law School, 1945-1951; Chairman,

Security Board of the Atomic Energy Commission, early 1950s; Chairman, Fund for the Advancement of Education and World Federalism, 1953-1955

SUPREME COURT SERVICE

Nominated: May 9, 1930
Nominated By: Herbert Hoover
Confirmed: May 20, 1930
Confirmation Vote: Voice vote
Oath Taken: June 2, 1930
Replaced: Edward T. Sanford
Significant Opinions: *Nebbia v. New York* (1934); *Grovey v. Townsend* (1935); *United States v. Butler* (1936); *Mulford v. Smith* (1939); *Cantwell v. Connecticut* (1940); *Betts v. Brady* (1942)
Left Court: Resigned July 31, 1945
Length of Service: 15 years, 1 month, 29 days
Replacement: Harold H. Burton

President Hoover's first choice to replace Justice Sanford, who had died, was Judge John J. Parker of the Fourth Circuit Court of Appeals. Nominated on March 21, 1930, Parker was rejected by the Senate on May 7, 1930, by a vote of 41 to 39. His defeat was in large part the result of lobbying on the part of two interest groups, the American Federation of Labor, which opposed a Parker decision upholding "yellow dog" contracts, and the National Association for the Advancement of Colored People, which opposed him on the basis of a 1920 gubernatorial speech in which he denounced African American political participation. After this rejection, and having recently endured a bruising confirmation fight over Chief Justice Hughes, Hoover sought out a popular Court nominee, Owen J. Roberts.

From an early age, Owen J. Roberts exhibited a quiet, scholarly demeanor. His parents sent him to a private academy near his Pennsylvania home for his early education; his higher education all took place at the University of Pennsylvania, where he had such a distinguished career that upon graduating from law school he was named a university fellow.

Roberts's early career was divided between lecturing part-time at the University of Pennsylvania Law School, working in his private law practice, and serving as an assistant district attorney. In 1918, as a special deputy attorney general, he prosecuted several local cases under the Espionage Act. He so distinguished himself that, in 1924, President Calvin Coolidge appointed him one of two U.S. attorneys investigating oil scandals that were a legacy of the Harding administration.

Roberts then returned to his law practice, but his record as a federal prosecutor recommended him as a suitable Supreme Court candidate when President Hoover's nomination of Judge John J. Parker failed. Roberts was easily confirmed, but he played a controversial role upon joining a Court that was dramatically split over the pressing economic and legislative issues of the day. Throughout his tenure, Roberts exhibited no coherent legal philosophy, acting instead as a swing vote — sometimes voting with the conservative bloc of justices, and sometimes with the Court's liberal wing. Criticized for vacillation, Roberts nonetheless played a pivotal role in reorienting the Hughes Court's judicial stance towards the New Deal. The first indication of his softening attitude toward President Roosevelt's agenda

came in *West Coast Hotel Co. v. Parrish* (1937), where his vote favoring a state minimum wage law tipped the balance toward a more restrained judicial approach to legislation. He continued to vote with the majority to sustain major New Deal legislation.

In his later years on the high bench, as the Court turned its attention to civil liberties, Roberts grew more conservative, emphasizing the importance of *precedent and becoming resistant to social change. Even then, however, he remained unpredictable, filing a passionate dissent in *Korematsu v. United States* (1944) excoriating his brethren for violating the rights of Japanese Americans by permitting their internment during World War II.

While a sitting justice, Roberts oversaw the investigation into the Japanese attack on Pearl Harbor and headed a commission for the preservation of historic European monuments threatened by World War II. He resigned from the Court at the age of 70 because of ill health, but remained active in education and public service until his death ten years later.

BENJAMIN NATHAN CARDOZO

PERSONAL DATA
Born: May 24, 1870, in New York, New York
Parents: Albert Cardozo, Rebecca Washington Cardozo
Higher Education: Columbia University (B.A., with honors, 1889; A.M., 1890); Columbia University Law School, 1890-1891
Bar Admission: New York, 1891
Political Party: Democrat
Marriage: None
Died: July 9, 1938, in Port Chester, New York
Buried: Cypress Hills Cemetery, Brooklyn, New York

PROFESSIONAL CAREER
Occupations: Lawyer, 1891-1914; Judge, 1914-1938
Official Positions: Justice, New York Supreme Court, 1914; Judge, New York Court of Appeals, 1914-1926; Chief Judge, New York Court of Appeals, 1926-1932; Associate Justice, United States Supreme Court, 1932-1938

SUPREME COURT SERVICE

Nominated: February 15, 1932
Nominated By: Herbert Hoover
Confirmed: February 24, 1932
Confirmation Vote: Voice Vote
Oath Taken: March 14, 1932
Replaced: Oliver Wendell Holmes
Significant Opinions: *Nixon v. Condon* (1932); *Steward Machine Co. v. Davis* (1937); *Helvering v. Davis* (1937); *Palko v. Connecticut* (1937)
Left Court: Died July 9, 1938
Length of Service: 6 years, 3 months, 25 days
Replacement: Felix Frankfurter

Benjamin Cardozo's ancestors were members of a community of Sephardic Jews established in 1654 in what would later become New York City. His father, a state supreme court judge, was implicated in the Tammany Hall scandals that plagued New York City, and he resigned rather than face impeachment for graft.

Cardozo's own life was considerably more serene. After receiving undergraduate and master's degrees from Columbia University and completing a year of law school at Columbia, he practiced *appellate law for over 20 years with his older brother in New York City. He never married, living with his older sister until she died in 1929. His entire professional life was devoted to the law: from lawyering he moved to adjudicating, and he advanced steadily through the ranks.

Cardozo made much of this externally uneventful life, however, becoming perhaps the most famous *common law judge this country has ever known. Almost single-handedly, he made New York's highest court one of the most respected state courts in the United States. His early writings on the law were compiled and used by other lawyers as handbooks. While on the Court of Appeals, he delivered a series of lectures at Yale University on judicial decision-making that were published in 1921 as *The Nature of the Judicial Process*, which became a classic of its kind. He continued lucidly and eloquently to expound his philosophy of adapting the law to societal change in *The Growth of the Law* (1924) and *The Paradoxes of Legal Science* (1928).

When Justice Oliver Wendell Holmes retired from the Court in 1932, many put Cardozo's name forward as Holmes's replacement. President Hoover, concerned about nominating Cardozo when the Court already included two New Yorkers, one of them a Jew, was unconvinced. Justice Harlan F. Stone, one of the New Yorkers, felt so strongly about the Cardozo nomination that he offered to resign to clear the way. Hoover declined Stone's offer and went with the popular consensus.

Cardozo kept his low profile while serving on the High Court, and he died after serving only six years. Nonetheless, he certainly left his mark. His opinions in *Steward Machine Co. v. Davis* (1937) and *Helvering v. Davis* (1937) upheld the Social Security Act as proper congressional exercises of the *taxing power, and it was his opinion in *Palko v. Connecticut* (1937) that finally made the *incorporation doctrine a matter of settled law. Yet he is most remembered for showing his fellow jurists the means by which traditional principles of law can be adapted to meet current social needs.

HUGO LAFAYETTE BLACK

PERSONAL DATA

Born: February 27, 1886, in Harlan, Alabama
Parents: William L. Black, Martha A. Toland Black
Higher Education: Birmingham Medical College, 1903-1904; University of Alabama Law School (LL.B., with honors, 1906)
Bar Admission: Alabama, 1906
Political Party: Democrat
Marriages: February 1921 to Josephine Foster, who bore Black two sons and a daughter, and who died in 1951; September 11, 1957 to Elizabeth Seay DeMeritte
Died: September 25, 1971, in Washington, D.C.
Buried: Arlington National Cemetery, Arlington, Virginia

PROFESSIONAL CAREER

Occupations: Lawyer, 1906-1910, 1911-1917, 1918-1927; Judge, 1910-1911, 1937-1971; Government Official, 1915-1917; Serviceman, 1917-1918; Politician, 1927-1937
Official Positions: Judge, Birmingham, Alabama,

Police Court, 1910-1911; Solicitor, Jefferson County, Alabama, 1915-1917; Member, United States Senate, 1927-1937; Associate Justice, United States Supreme Court, 1937-1971

SUPREME COURT SERVICE

Nominated: August 12, 1937
Nominated By: Franklin D. Roosevelt
Confirmed: August 17, 1937
Confirmation Vote: 63-16
Oath Taken: August 19, 1937
Replaced: Willis Van Devanter
Significant Opinions: *Johnson v. Zerbst* (1938); *United States v. South-Eastern Underwriters Association* (1944); *Korematsu v. United States* (1944); *United States v. Lovett* (1946); *Everson v. Board of Education of Ewing Township* (1947); *Adamson v. California* (dissent) (1947); *United States v. California* (1947); *Illinois *ex rel. McCollum v. Board of Education* (1948); *Youngstown Sheet & Tube Co. v. Sawyer* (1952); *Engel v. Vitale* (1962); *Gideon v. Wainwright* (1963); *Wesberry v. Sanders* (1964); *Griffin v. County School Board of Prince Edward County* (1964); *Pointer v. Texas* (1965); *Griswold v. Connecticut* (dissent) (1965); *Oregon v. Mitchell, Texas v. Mitchell, United States v. Arizona* (1970); *Younger v. Harris* (1971)
Left Court: Retired September 17, 1971
Length of Service: 34 years, 29 days
Replacement: Lewis F. Powell

Hugo L. Black was the eighth and last child of a poor Alabama farmer who later became a shopkeeper. Although Black's father would gain access to the middle class as a successful small businessman in Ashland, Alabama, and although Black himself attended both medical school and law school, his early experience of being poor and uneducated marked him for life.

Black returned to Ashland after a year at the University of Alabama Law School and set up a law practice. The next year, after his office was destroyed by fire, he moved to Birmingham, Alabama, where he began a new law practice and worked part-time as a police court judge. In his own practice, he specialized in labor and personal injury cases, and in an effort to make contacts in the community, he joined the Ku Klux Klan in 1923. He resigned from the organization three

years later, but his membership would later greatly embarrass him.

Black served as a county solicitor from 1915 to 1917, when he joined the U.S. Army. He did not see action or even leave the country, and after World War I concluded, he returned to his law practice. In 1926 he mounted a campaign for the United States Senate, and although he was derided by some of his fellow Alabamians as a "Bolshevik" because of his prior representation of the United Mine Workers, his election to the Senate was achieved with the help of Klan support.

In the Senate, in order to make up for what he regarded as his poor education, Black began reading history, economics, and the classics at the Library of Congress, a habit he kept up for the rest of his life. He served two terms, achieving high visibility because of his ardent support for the New Deal and chairmanships of committees investigating various industries and lobbying practices. His advocacy of a 30-hour work week was so left-leaning that it alarmed even the president. But when Justice Willis Van Devanter retired in 1937, creating the first opening on the Court in five years, Roosevelt turned to Black.

Black's prior affiliation with the Klan became public knowledge shortly after his confirmation. He confronted the issue head-on, making a public confession over the air waves. Then, in short order, he established one of the most liberal voting records on the Court. Disingenuously referring to himself as a "backward country fellow," Black fought tenaciously for a number of liberal positions, most notably the sanctity of *free speech and *due process. He did this in a deceptively simple fashion, insisting on a literal interpretation of the First Amendment and a construction of the Fourteenth Amendment that was heavily reliant on *original intent (throughout his 34 years on the High Court, he carried a copy of the Constitution in his pocket).

Black contributed as much as any justice to the reorientation of the Court toward civil rights and individual liberties. Toward the end of his career, however, his reading of the Constitution led to a more conservative voting pattern; for example, he

The Hughes Court, 1940. From left: Owen J. Roberts, William O. Douglas, James C. McReynolds, Stanley F. Reed, Charles Evans Hughes, Felix Frankfurter, Harlan Fiske Stone, Frank Murphy, Hugo L. Black

dissented from the majority's endorsement of a right of marital privacy in *Griswold v. Connecticut* (1965). Even here, however, his disagreement seemed based on his *black letter approach to the Constitution, in which he could locate no such right. He retired on September 17, 1971, after suffering a stroke, and died eight days later.

STANLEY FORMAN REED

PERSONAL DATA

Born: December 31, 1884, in Minerva, Kentucky
Parents: Dr. John A. Reed, Frances Forman Reed
Higher Education: Kentucky Wesleyan College (B.A., 1902); Yale University (B.A., 1906); University of Virginia Law School, 1906-1907; Columbia University Law School, 1908-1909; The Sorbonne, Paris, France, 1909-1910
Bar Admission: Kentucky, 1910
Political Party: Democrat
Marriage: May 11, 1908, to Winifred Elgin, who bore Reed two sons
Died: April 2, 1980, in Huntington, New York
Buried: Maysville Cemetery, Maysville, Kentucky

PROFESSIONAL CAREER

Occupations: Lawyer, 1910-1917, 1921-1938, ca. 1957-1960s; Politician, 1912-1916; Serviceman, 1917-1918; Government Official, 1929-1938, 1939-1941, 1957; Judge, 1938-1957
Official Positions: Member, Kentucky General Assembly, 1912-1916; General Counsel, Federal Farm Board, 1929-1932; General Counsel, Reconstruction Finance Corporation, 1932-1935; Special Assistant to the United States Attorney General, 1935; United States Solicitor General, 1935-1938; Associate Justice, United States Supreme Court, 1938-1957; Chairman, Commission on Civil Service Improvement, 1939-1941; Chairman, United States Civil Rights Commission, 1957

SUPREME COURT SERVICE

Nominated: January 15, 1938
Nominated By: Franklin D. Roosevelt
Confirmed: January 25, 1938
Confirmation Vote: Voice Vote
Oath Taken: January 31, 1938
Replaced: George Sutherland
Significant Opinions: *Smith v. Allwright* (1944); *Morgan v. Virginia* (1946); *United Public Workers v. Mitchell* (1947); *Adamson v. California* (1947)

Left Court: Retired February 25, 1957
Length of Service: 19 years, 25 days
Replacement: Charles E. Whittaker

Stanley F. Reed was the only child of a small town Kentucky doctor. Although he began his education in his native state — receiving a bachelor's degree from Kentucky Wesleyan College — he continued to pursue it in several other venues. After earning a second undergraduate degree from Yale, he studied law for a year each at the University of Virginia and Columbia and, after marrying in 1908, combined a prolonged honeymoon in Paris with legal studies at the Sorbonne.

He settled in Mason County, Kentucky, where he opened a solo practice in 1910. Nine years later he joined the firm of Worthinton, Browning and Reed and became active in Democratic politics. He served two years in the state assembly before joining the U.S. Army during World War I. Upon his return, he helped organize the Burley Tobacco Growers' Association and, acting as its counsel, traveled often to Washington, D.C., where he caught the attention of President Hoover. Hoover appointed Reed as general counsel first to the Federal Farm Board, then to the Reconstruction Finance Corporation (RFC).

Reed also met with the approval of Roosevelt, who kept him on at the RFC, then appointed him as a special assistant to the attorney general with the task of arguing the government's case for eliminating the gold standard before the Supreme Court in the *Gold Clause Cases* (1935). After winning these, Reed was appointed solicitor general, in which position he won Court approval for the Tennessee Valley Authority, but failed to do so for the National Industrial Recovery Act and the Agricultural Adjustment Act. Despite Reed's mixed success, Roosevelt named him to fill a Court vacancy.

Reed's Supreme Court record reveals him to be liberal on economic issues but more conservative towards social ones. He wrote 228 opinions for the Court, 21 concurrences and 79 dissents, usually upholding congressional power exercised under the *Commerce Clause, but, with the notable excep-

tion of freedom of expression, often rejecting expansion of civil liberties.

Reed retired from the Court in 1957 because of ill health. In retirement, he remained active in the law, however, arguing 35 cases before the Court of Claims and 25 before the Court of Appeals in the District of Columbia. He died in 1980 at the age of 95.

FELIX FRANKFURTER

PERSONAL DATA
Born: November 15, 1882, in Vienna, Austria
Parents: Leopold Frankfurter, Emma Winter Frankfurter
Higher Education: College of the City of New York (B.A., 1902); Harvard Law School (LL.B., first in class, 1906)
Bar Admission: New York, 1905
Political Party: Democrat
Marriage: December 20, 1919, to Marion A. Denman
Died: February 21, 1965, in Washington, D.C.
Buried: Mount Auburn Cemetery, Cambridge, Massachusetts

PROFESSIONAL CAREER
Occupations: Lawyer, 1905-1913; Educator, 1913-1939; Government Official, 1906-1913, 1917-1918; Judge, 1939-1962
Official Positions: Assistant United States Attorney, Southern District of New York, 1906-1909; Law Officer, Bureau of Insular Affairs, United States Department of War, 1910-1913; Professor, Harvard Law School, 1913-1939; Secretary and Counsel, Mediation Commission on Labor Problems, 1917-1918; Chairman, War Labor Policies Board, 1918; Associate Justice, United States Supreme Court, 1939-1962

SUPREME COURT SERVICE
Nomination: January 5, 1939
Nominated By: Franklin D. Roosevelt
Confirmation: January 17, 1939
Confirmation Vote: Voice vote
Oath Taken: January 30, 1939
Replaced: Benjamin N. Cardozo
Significant Opinions: *Minersville School District v.*

Gobitis (1940); *Colegrove v. Green* (1946); *Wolf v. Colorado* (1949); *Rochin v. California* (1952); *Ullman v. United States* (1956); *Mallory v. United States* (1957); *Gomillion v. Lightfoot* (1960); *Communist Party v. Subversive Activities Control Board* (1961)
Left Court: Retired August 28, 1962
Length of Service: 23 years, 6 months, 29 days
Replacement: Arthur J. Goldberg

Felix Frankfurter was born in Vienna, Austria, and emigrated to the United States with his family when he was 12. The Frankfurters settled on the lower east side of Manhattan. Frankfurter obtained all of his undergraduate education in New York City. He attended Harvard Law School, where he performed brilliantly. He then returned to New York, working only briefly in private practice before being recruited for the U.S. Attorney's office by Henry L. Stimson.

When Stimson went to Washington, D.C., as President Taft's secretary of war, Frankfurter followed his mentor. Frankfurter served in a variety of government positions before being offered a place on the Harvard Law School faculty in 1913. Although he would take great pleasure in teaching at Harvard for the next 26 years, Frankfurter continued his involvement with public service. He declined a nomination to the Massachusetts Supreme Court in 1932 as well as President Franklin Roosevelt's offer in 1933 of the solicitor general's position. He seemed to prefer a more informal, behind the scenes role, serving as an advisor to FDR, as well as to the National Association for the Advancement of Colored People, the anarchists Nicola Sacco and Bartolomeo Vanzetti, and the National Consumers' League. He also established the American Civil Liberties Union and *The New Republic* magazine, and participated in the International Zionist Organization.

Frankfurter developed a close friendship with President Roosevelt, and the future justice and his proteges became prime movers in formulating and implementing the New Deal. For this reason, and because of Frankfurter's libertarian history, it was expected that once Roosevelt placed him on the Supreme Court, Frankfurter would continue on a progressive track, following the same path taken by Justice Oliver Wendell Holmes, whom Frankfurter regarded as his legal forbear. But although the Court became increasingly liberal during the years Frankfurter was a member, it was Justice Hugo L. Black, not Frankfurter, who shepherded this leftward movement. Black and Frankfurter in fact became intellectual adversaries, with Frankfurter developing into the leading conservative on the Court, especially during the years it was led by Chief Justices Fred M. Vinson and Earl Warren.

On the Court Frankfurter did, however, exhibit the same qualities that made him a great law teacher. At times these attributes — his tendency to lecture his brethren during judicial conferences, for example — were not well received. But Frankfurter viewed the High Court as a tutor to the lower courts, and he felt that the Court should take on only those cases that were truly *ripe and would illustrate significant points of law, which were then to be set forth in a balanced, restrained manner. He was ideologically opposed to the kind of commitment to abstract principles and political outcomes that motivated his rival, Justice Black.

Toward the end of Frankfurter's tenure, he and Justice Black reconciled, in part because of the latter's own drift toward a more conservative orientation. In 1962, after suffering a debilitating stroke, Frankfurter retired. He died two and a half years later, at the age of 82.

WILLIAM ORVILLE DOUGLAS

PERSONAL DATA
Born: October 16, 1898, in Maine, Minnesota
Parents: William Douglas, Julia F. Bickford Douglas
Higher Education: Whitman College (B.A., Phi Beta Kappa, 1920); Columbia University Law School (LL.B., second in class, 1925)
Bar Admission: New York, 1925
Political Party: Democrat
Marriages: August 16, 1923, to Mildred Riddle, who bore Douglas a son and a daughter, and whom Douglas divorced in 1954; December 14, 1954, to

Mercedes Hester, whom Douglas divorced in 1963; August 1963 to Joan Martin, whom Douglas divorced in 1966; July 1966 to Cathleen Heffernan
Died: January 19, 1980, in Washington, D.C.
Buried: Arlington National Cemetery, Arlington, Virginia

PROFESSIONAL CAREER

Occupations: Serviceman, 1918; Educator, 1920-1922, 1927-1934; Lawyer, 1925-1927; Government Official, 1936-1939; Judge, 1939-1975
Official Positions: Professor, Columbia Law School, 1927-1929; Professor, Yale Law School, 1929-1934; Member, Securities and Exchange Commission, 1936-1937; Chairman, Securities and Exchange Commission, 1937-1939; Associate Justice, United States Supreme Court, 1939-1975

SUPREME COURT SERVICE

Nominated: March 20, 1939
Nominated By: Franklin D. Roosevelt
Confirmed: April 4, 1939
Confirmation Vote: 62-4
Oath Taken: April 17, 1939
Replaced: Louis D. Brandeis
Significant Opinions: *Skinner v. Oklahoma* (1942); *Murdock v. Pennsylvania* (1943); *Ballard v. United States* (1946); *Terminiello v. Chicago* (1949); *Zorach v. Clauson* (1952); *Kent v. Dulles* (1958); *Lassiter v. Northampton County Board of Elections* (1959); *Gray v. Sanders* (1963); *Griffin v. California* (1965); *Griswold v. Connecticut* (1965); *Harper v. Virginia Board of Elections* (1966); *Elfbrandt v. Russell* (1966); *Argersinger v. Hamlin* (1972)
Left Court: Retired November 12, 1975
Length of Service: 36 years, 6 months, 26 days
Replacement: John Paul Stevens

William Orville Douglas was born at the turn of the century in northern Minnesota. In early childhood, he moved with his family to the vicinity of Yakima, Washington, because of his father's poor health. Unfortunately, Douglas's father, a Presbyterian missionary, died when Douglas was six years old, leaving his family penniless. Douglas himself suffered from polio as a child but, taking Theodore Roosevelt's outdoor gospel to heart, he began a regimen of strenuous outdoor exercise

that he would follow for the remainder of his life.

Douglas worked his way through Whitman College, located in nearby Walla Walla, Washington. He then served in the Army and taught school for two years in order to save enough money to go east to continue his education. When he traveled to New York to attend Columbia Law School, he did so by hopping a freight train and by hitchhiking. At Columbia, he again worked his way through school, graduating near the top of his class despite working as a tutor nearly full time.

Another recent law graduate got the clerkship with Justice Harlan F. Stone that Douglas coveted, so he settled for a job with a Wall Street law firm. Douglas's misgivings about taking this position proved well-founded. After two years, he left what is now Cravath, Swaine & Moore and returned to Yakima. A year later he accepted a job teaching law at Columbia. He then moved to Yale two years later after a rift with the new Columbia dean. Douglas flourished at Yale, specializing in corporate law and becoming one of the law school's youngest professors to hold an endowed chair.

However, Douglas soon became restive and went to Washington, D.C., to work on the New Deal as first a member, then chairman of the Securities and Exchange Commission. He became part of Roosevelt's inner circle, and when Justice Louis D. Brandeis retired, the president confidently nominated his companion to take Brandeis's place. Douglas was confirmed easily and, at the age of 40, became the youngest appointee to the High Court since Joseph Story took his seat 128 years earlier at age 32.

Roosevelt nominated Douglas in large part because of the latter's ultra-liberal political orientation. Once on the bench, Douglas quickly became Justice Hugo L. Black's closest ally in upholding the constitutionality of the New Deal and of the civil rights legislation which later came before the Court. Even so, Douglas's most significant contribution as a justice arguably came in a series of opinions concerning business regulation that he wrote in the 1940s. In the later years of Black's tenure, the views of the two justices diverged, Black's outlook growing more conservative while Douglas maintained a mainly liberal course. Douglas never seemed concerned about standing alone in dissent; indeed, in his later years he cultivated the image of a maverick, both on the Court and in his personal life.

In the 1950s he divorced his wife of 29 years and married three more times in quick succession. His fourth marriage, which occurred when he was 67, was to 22-year-old Cathleen Heffernan. Unlike most modern justices, he dabbled in politics and was often mentioned as a possible vice presidential candidate in the 1940s. When his political ambitions came to an end, he embarked on a series of highly visible world travels to promote his many books on travel, other cultures, and the environment. His nonconformist behavior — which included taking some egregious stances on the Court, where he also was accused of writing sloppy opinions — led to two attempts to impeach him, first in 1953, after he granted Julius and Ethel Rosenberg a stay of execution, and again in 1970. The latter attempt, based on allegations of ethical violations, was the more serious one, but Douglas defended himself ably, and eight months after House Minority Leader Gerald R. Ford called for his impeachment, it was rejected by a House judiciary subcommittee.

In December 1974 Douglas suffered a paralyzing stroke that kept him away from Court for most of the remainder of that term. When he returned the following October, he was still disabled, and in November 1975, he retired as the longest-serving Supreme Court justice in history.

WILLIAM FRANCIS MURPHY

PERSONAL DATA

Born: April 13, 1890, in Sand Beach, now Harbor Beach, Michigan
Parents: John T. Murphy, Mary Brennan Murphy
Higher Education: University of Michigan (B.A., 1912; LL.B., 1914); Lincoln's Inn, London, England, 1919; Trinity College, Dublin, Ireland, 1919
Bar Admission: Michigan, 1914
Political Party: Democrat

Marriage: None
Died: July 19, 1949, in Detroit, Michigan
Buried: Our Lady of Lake Huron Cemetery, Harbor Beach

PROFESSIONAL CAREER

Occupations: Lawyer, 1914-1917, 1919-1923, 1939-1940; Educator, 1914-1917; Serviceman, 1917-1918, 1942; Judge, 1923-1930, 1940-1949; Government Official, 1919-1920, 1939-1940; Politician, 1930-1933, 1937-1940; Diplomat, 1933-1936
Official Positions: Chief Assistant Attorney General, Eastern District of Michigan, 1919-1920; Judge, Recorder's Court, Detroit, Michigan, 1923-1930; Mayor, City of Detroit, 1930-1933; Governor General, the Philippine Islands, 1933-1935; United States High Commissioner, the Philippines, 1935-1936; Governor, Michigan, 1937-1939; United States Attorney General, 1939-1940; Associate Justice, United States Supreme Court, 1940-1949

SUPREME COURT SERVICE

Nominated: January 4, 1940
Nominated By: Franklin D. Roosevelt
Confirmed: January 16, 1940
Confirmation Vote: Voice vote
Oath Taken: January 18, 1940
Replaced: Pierce Butler
Significant Opinions: *Thornhill v. Alabama* (1940); *Chaplinsky v. New Hampshire* (1942)
Left Court: Died July 19, 1949
Length of Service: 9 years, 6 months, 1 day
Replacement: Tom C. Clark

Frank Murphy was born into an Irish Catholic family that filled him, from an early age, with idealism and religious fervor. He followed his father into the law, graduating from the University of Michigan Law School in 1914. He then practiced law for three years with a Detroit, Michigan, firm, and at the same time taught law at night school.

When World War I came, Murphy joined the Army and served with the American Expeditionary Force in France, as well as in Germany with the Army of Occupation. After the war ended, he stayed on in Europe for a time to study law at Lincoln's Inn in London, England, and at Trinity

College in Dublin, Ireland. He then returned to Detroit to resume his legal career, this time with the government. He served first as an assistant attorney general before becoming a judge for Detroit's Recorder's Court, the city's highest criminal tribunal. While on the court, he established a progressive record which led, in 1930, to his election as mayor.

Murphy's strong support of Franklin Roosevelt in the 1932 presidential campaign led to his appointment the next year as the last governor general of the Philippines. In 1935, when the Philippines won commonwealth status, Murphy became its first United States high commissioner. In the Philippines, as in his native Detroit, he embraced New Deal reforms, enacting such legislation as maximum hour and minimum wage laws. In 1937 his liberalism swept him into office as governor of Michigan, but his refusal to call in troops to deal with a sit-down strike of automotive workers in 1938 cost him reelection the next year.

Murphy was anxious to be involved in America's mobilization for World War II, and he lobbied Roosevelt to be appointed secretary of war. Instead, Roosevelt made him U.S. attorney general, then in 1940, an associate justice of the Supreme Court. Murphy accepted the advancement reluctantly, privately expressing doubts about his fitness for the Court and publicly continuing his support of the war effort by serving as an infantry officer during Court recesses.

On the high bench, Murphy demonstrated a penchant for exercising "justice tempered by Murphy," delivering moralizing opinions and bending the law to achieve what he saw as the right result — invariably, one that hewed to a liberal path. He was criticized for judging with his heart rather than his head, and under Chief Justice Harlan F. Stone, who distrusted his abilities, was seldom given responsibility for important cases. Nonetheless, in cases like *Korematsu v. United States* (1944), where he dissented from what he labeled the "legalization of racism," Murphy established a record favoring civil rights which later was vindicated by the Court.

SIGNIFICANT CASES

STROMBERG V. CALIFORNIA

Citation: 283 U.S. 359 (1931)
Argued: April 15, 1931
Decided: May 18, 1931
Court Below: California District Court of Appeals
Basis for Review: Appeal
Facts: Yetta Stromberg, a teacher at a summer youth camp, was convicted under a previously unenforced California statute prohibiting public displays of red flags on grounds that such demonstrations constituted opposition to the government and induced sedition.
Issue: Does the California Red Flag Law prohibit symbolic speech and therefore violate the First Amendment's guarantee of *freedom of speech?
Outcome: The Hughes Court voted to overturn Stromberg's conviction, and in 1933 California repealed the statute in question.
Vote: 7-2
Participating: Hughes, Holmes, Van Devanter, McReynolds, Brandeis, Sutherland, Butler, Stone, Roberts
Opinions: Hughes for the Court; McReynolds and Butler dissenting
Significance: The Hughes opinion did not directly address the First Amendment issue raised by *Stromberg*, *holding instead that the California statute was impermissibly vague and violated liberties protected by the Fourteenth Amendment. Nonetheless, this case was important to the development of First Amendment law, in that it was the first to apply Fourteenth Amendment sanctions to state curbs on the First Amendment.

NEAR V. MINNESOTA

Citation: 283 U.S. 697 (1931)
Argued: January 30, 1930
Decided: June 1, 1931
Court Below: Minnesota Supreme Court
Basis for Review: Appeal
Facts: The 1925 Minnesota Public Nuisance Abatement Law, also known as the Minnesota Gag Law, permitted judges to stop publication of newspapers deemed obscene, malicious, or defam-

atory. The Gag Law was first used to stop publication of the *Saturday Press*, a weekly muckraking newspaper, whose publisher was J.M. Near.
Issue: Does the First Amendment prohibition against *prior restraint apply at the state level?
Outcome: The Gag Law was struck down.
Vote: 5-4
Participating: Hughes, Holmes, Van Devanter, McReynolds, Brandeis, Sutherland, Butler, Stone, Roberts
Opinions: Hughes for the Court; Butler, joined by Van Devanter, McReynolds, and Sutherland, dissenting
Significance: *Near* nationalized freedom of the press by making it clear that the *Due Process Clause of the Fourteenth Amendment made the constitutional interdiction against prior restraint, the very heart of the First Amendment, applicable to the states.

NIXON V. CONDON

Citation: 286 U.S. 73 (1932)
Argued: January 7, 1932; reargued March 15, 1932
Decided: May 2, 1932
Court Below: United States Fifth Circuit Court of Appeals
Basis for Review: *Writ of certiorari
Facts: The Democratic Party dominated the South after Reconstruction and tried to disenfranchise African American voters by barring them from participating in primary elections, a practice the Supreme Court outlawed in *Nixon v. Herndon* (1927). Texas attempted to get around this prohibition by permitting state party executive committees to decide upon voter qualifications. Nixon, an African American, was denied a primary ballot under this arrangement, and he sued.
Issue: Was the Democratic committee a private entity that could determine its own membership, or was it acting under color of state authority in excluding African Americans from primaries?
Outcome: Justice Cardozo, in his first opinion for the Court, declared that the Democratic committee was acting under the authority of the state and therefore violated the Fourteenth Amendment.
Vote: 5-4

Participating: Hughes, Van Devanter, McReynolds, Brandeis, Sutherland, Butler, Stone, Roberts, Cardozo
Opinions: Cardozo for the Court; McReynolds, joined by Van Devanter, Sutherland, and Butler, dissenting
Significance: Cardozo's opinion, finding that the power to determine member qualifications belonged to the state party convention, which had not delegated this power to its executive, left Texas with an opening. The state next repealed all primary election statutes, thus allowing state party conventions to exclude African Americans, a practice that was not repudiated until *Smith v. Allwright* (1944).

NEW STATE ICE CO. V. LIEBMANN

Citation: 285 U.S. 262 (1932)
Argued: February 19, 1932
Decided: March 21, 1932
Court Below: United States Tenth Circuit Court of Appeals
Basis for Review: Appeal
Facts: To prevent Liebmann from selling ice, New State Ice Company brought suit against him under an Oklahoma statute that granted licenses for the manufacture and sale of ice only upon a showing of necessity.
Issue: Does the license requirement violate the *Due Process Clause of the Fourteenth Amendment by, in effect, prohibiting entrepreneurial efforts?
Outcome: Reasoning that a state may not regulate any business it arbitrarily declares affected with a public use, the Court struck down the Oklahoma statute.
Vote: 6-2
Participating: Hughes, Van Devanter, McReynolds, Brandeis, Sutherland, Butler, Stone, Roberts (Cardozo not participating)
Opinions: Sutherland for the Court; Brandeis, joined by Stone, dissenting
Significance: *New State Ice* is remembered most for Justice Brandeis's dissent, in which he argued that eliminating harmful competition was a matter for the legislature, a view subsequently adopted by the Court in decisions granting the legislature

broad powers to regulate business. *New State Ice* has not, however, been expressly overruled.

POWELL V. ALABAMA

Citation: 287 U.S. 45 (1932)
Argued: October 10, 1932
Decided: November 7, 1932
Court Below: Alabama Supreme Court
Basis for Review: *Writ of certiorari
Facts: Powell was one of nine African American youths accused of raping two white women in this, the first of the *Scottsboro Boys* cases. All nine were quickly *indicted, and eight were sentenced to death in a one-day trial, during which they were effectively without legal representation. One youth was released because of a hung jury.
Issue: Does the *Due Process Clause of the Fourteenth Amendment require the state to appoint lawyers for indigent criminal defendants?
Outcome: Finding that due process mandates appointment of counsel in state criminal cases and that failure to do so would result in an unfair trial, the Supreme Court reversed the convictions.
Vote: 7-2
Participating: Hughes, Van Devanter, McReynolds, Brandeis, Sutherland, Butler, Stone, Roberts, Cardozo
Opinions: Sutherland for the Court; Butler, joined by McReynolds, dissenting
Significance: Alabama retried and reconvicted one of the Scottsboro defendants, a result the Supreme Court reversed in *Norris v. Alabama* in 1935 because African Americans had been barred from the jury. In *Powell*, the Court did not rule that the Sixth Amendment requirement that counsel be appointed for all indigent criminal defendants in *capital cases applied in state courts. In 1963, however, with *Gideon v. Wainwright*, the Court *incorporated the Sixth Amendment *Assistance of Counsel Clause into the Fourteenth Amendment, thus requiring states to appoint counsel for all indigent defendants facing serious criminal charges, whether capital or noncapital.

NEBBIA V. NEW YORK

Citation: 291 U.S. 502 (1934)
Argued: December 4-5, 1933

Decided: March 5, 1934
Court Below: County Court of Monroe County, New York
Basis for Review: Appeal
Facts: Following New Deal reforms aimed at combatting the Depression at the federal level, New York passed the Milk Control Act of 1933, fixing milk prices in an effort to aid small retailers. Leo Nebbia, a grocer, was convicted under the statute for selling a quart of milk for a price exceeding the legal maximum.
Issue: Is the milk industry, which is not one traditionally affected with a public interest, subject to state regulation?
Outcome: Abandoning the *substantive due process argument that the Fourteenth Amendment gives the state authority to regulate only businesses affected with a public interest, the Hughes Court declared the New York law valid and upheld Nebbia's conviction.
Vote: 5-4
Participating: Hughes, Van Devanter, McReynolds, Brandeis, Sutherland, Butler, Stone, Roberts, Cardozo
Opinions: Roberts for the Court; McReynolds, joined by Van Devanter, Sutherland, and Butler, dissenting
Significance: *Nebbia* ended a long line of decisions, starting with *Munn v. Illinois* (1877), in which the Court distinguished public from private enterprise in ruling on the constitutionality of regulatory legislation. Now the Court ruled that a state could regulate any business, so long as the legislation it enacted was reasonable and designed to promote the public welfare.

HOME BUILDING & LOAN ASSOCIATION V. BLAISDELL

Citation: 290 U.S. 398 (1934)
Argued: November 8-9, 1933
Decided: June 8, 1934
Court Below: Minnesota Supreme Court
Basis for Review: Appeal
Facts: The 1933 Minnesota Mortgage Moratorium Law was a New Deal-inspired emergency measure intended to provide relief from foreclosures

during the Depression. The Blaisdells, who had purchased a home and lot from the Home Building and Loan Association, cited the law in an attempt to extend their mortgage redemption period. The association appealed a state district court ruling in the Blaisdells' favor, which was affirmed by the state supreme court.

Issue: Does the Minnesota law violate the *Contracts Clause of Article I of the Constitution barring state action that impairs the obligation of contracts?

Outcome: Stating that the Contracts Clause is not absolute and that states have the power to safeguard the welfare of their citizens, the Court upheld the statute.

Vote: 5-4

Participating: Hughes, Van Devanter, McReynolds, Brandeis, Sutherland, Butler, Stone, Roberts, Cardozo

Opinions: Hughes for the Court; Sutherland, joined by Van Devanter, McReynolds, and Butler, dissenting

Significance: *Blaisdell* is important not only because it struck directly at the heart of the *laissez faire philosophy that had dominated the Court for so long, but also because it vividly illustrated the schism in the Hughes Court, which was divided between the old "Four Horsemen" — Van Devanter, McReynolds, Sutherland, and Butler — who voted as a bloc against nearly all New Deal legislation, and the newer, more liberal members of the Court, who supported Roosevelt. The case also demonstrated the importance of swing votes on the Court, with Hughes and Roberts holding the balance of power.

PANAMA REFINING CO. V. RYAN

Citation: 293 U.S. 388 (1935)
Argued: December 10-11, 1934
Decided: January 7, 1935
Court Below: United States Fifth Circuit Court of Appeals
Basis for Review: *Writ of certiorari
Facts: After oil prices collapsed during the Depression, Congress tried to buoy them up by limiting production in a provision of the National Industrial Recovery Act of 1934 (NIRA) autho-

rizing the president to prohibit interstate shipment of "hot oil" produced in excess of state quotas.

Issue: Is the hot oil provision a violation of the *separation of powers?

Outcome: Finding the provision an unconstitutional delegation to the president of legislative powers, the Court struck it down.

Vote: 8-1

Participating: Hughes, Van Devanter, McReynolds, Brandeis, Sutherland, Butler, Stone, Roberts, Cardozo

Opinions: Hughes for the Court; Cardozo dissenting

Significance: In *Nebbia v. New York* and *Home Building & Loan Association v. Blaisdell*, both decided in 1934, the Court indicated its support for state legislation intended to relieve economic pressures brought on by the Depression. With *Panama Refining*, the Court had its first opportunity to rule on the constitutionality of federal New Deal legislation. The 8 to 1 vote against the hot oil provision came as a surprise, not only because of *Nebbia* and *Blaisdell*, but also because the Court had never before found that Congress had violated the separation of powers doctrine by delegating some of its powers to the president. *Panama Refining* was the first of a series of decisions striking down New Deal legislation which ultimately resulted in President Roosevelt's court-packing plan. It was followed quickly by *Schechter Poultry Corp. v. United States* (1935), which struck down another section of NIRA on the same grounds; neither case has been overruled.

GOLD CLAUSE CASES (NORMAN V. BALTIMORE & OHIO RAILROAD CO.; NORTZ V. UNITED STATES; PERRY V. UNITED STATES)

Citations: *Norman*, 294 U.S. 240 (1935); *Nortz*, 294 U.S. 317 (1935); *Perry*, 294 U.S. 330 (1935)
Argued: January 8-10, 1935 (*Norman*); January 10, 1935 (*Nortz*); January 10-11, 1935 (*Perry*)
Decided: February 18, 1935
Courts Below: New York Supreme Court (*Norman*); United States Court of Claims (*Nortz*, *Perry*)

Bases for Review: *Writ of certiorari (*Norman*);
*Certification (*Nortz, Perry*)
Facts: In 1933, in an attempt to conserve gold
resources and inflate currency values to alleviate
the Depression, Congress passed a resolution
invalidating clauses in private and public con-
tracts requiring payment in gold.
Issue: Does the action constitute a breach of the
obligation of contract and a deprivation of property without *due process?
Outcome: The Hughes Court upheld Congress's
authority over monetary policy and denied all
three claims.
Vote: (In each case) 5-4
Participating: Hughes, Van Devanter, McReynolds,
Brandeis, Sutherland, Butler, Stone, Roberts,
Cardozo
Opinions: (In each case) Hughes for the Court;
McReynolds, joined by Van Devanter, Sutherland,
and Butler, dissenting (without written opinions
in *Nortz* and *Perry*)
Significance: The *Gold Clause Cases* were decided
on a strictly pragmatic basis — as indeed they
had to be, for allowing enforcement of gold clauses
in contracts would have depressed the nation's
economy further. Such clauses in private contracts were deemed to be merely agreements for
payment in money, and although such clauses in
government bonds could not be abrogated, the
Court permitted holders of such bonds to recover
only nominal damages.

GROVEY V. TOWNSEND

Citation: 295 U.S. 45 (1935)
Argued: March 11, 1935
Decided: April 1, 1935
Court Below: Justice Court, Harris County, Texas
Basis for Review: *Writ of certiorari
Facts: Texas's practice of excluding African
Americans from Democratic primaries was out-
lawed in *Nixon v. Herndon* (1927). When the Texas
legislature countered by authorizing the
Democratic executive committee to exclude
African Americans from primaries, in *Nixon v.
Condon* (1932) that practice also was ruled uncon-
stitutional. After the Texas Democratic convention
limited membership to whites only, R.R. Grovey,

an African American Texan, sued.
Issue: Does the exclusion of African Americans
from the party's convention constitute discrimi-
natory *state action in violation of the Fourteenth
Amendment?
Outcome: Because the Texas Democratic Party
was a voluntary association, a unanimous Court
upheld the practice as a strictly private exercise.
Vote: 9-0
Participating: Hughes, Van Devanter, McReynolds,
Brandeis, Sutherland, Butler, Stone, Roberts,
Cardozo
Opinion: Roberts for the Court
Significance: The Hughes Court reached this
result in *Grovey* while at the same time acknowledging that the state in fact regulated primaries
in a variety of other ways. The contradictions of
its ruling here were definitively overruled in *Smith
v. Allwright* (1944).

NORRIS V. ALABAMA

Citation: 294 U.S. 587 (1935)
Argued: February 15-18, 1935
Decided: April 1, 1935
Court Below: Alabama Supreme Court
Basis for Review: *Writ of certiorari
Facts: In *Powell v. Alabama* (1932), the Hughes
Court had reversed the convictions of eight
African American youths for raping two white
women because the defendants had lacked ade-
quate representation at trial. In the second
Scottsboro Boys case, when the state of Alabama
retried them, one defendant, Norris, was recon-
victed. He appealed this decision on grounds that
African Americans had been systematically
excluded from the *grand jury that *indicted him
and the *petit jury that tried him.
Issue: Does the exclusion of African Americans
from juries violate the *Equal Protection Clause
of the Fourteenth Amendment?
Outcome: The Court reversed Norris's convic-
tion on grounds that it violated the Equal
Protection Clause.
Vote: 8-0
Participating: Hughes, Van Devanter, Brandeis,
Sutherland, Butler, Stone, Roberts, Cardozo
(McReynolds not participating)

Opinion: Hughes for the Court
Significance: Both *Scottsboro Boys* Cases marked important steps in reclaiming the *original intent of the drafters of the Fourteenth Amendment.

HUMPHREY'S EXECUTOR V. UNITED STATES

Citation: 295 U.S. 602 (1935)
Argued: May 1, 1935
Decided: May 27, 1935
Court Below: United States Court of Claims
Basis for Review: *Certification
Facts: When William E. Humphrey, a conservative political appointee, died while contesting his removal by President Roosevelt from the Federal Trade Commission, his estate carried on the suit.
Issue: Is the president's *removal power unlimited?
Outcome: Finding that the removal power can be exercised only for cause, the Hughes Court found for the estate.
Vote: 9-0
Participating: Hughes, Van Devanter, McReynolds, Brandeis, Sutherland, Butler, Stone, Roberts, Cardozo
Opinions: Sutherland for the Court; McReynolds concurring (without written opinion)
Significance: *Humphrey's Executor* marked a retreat from the Taft Court's endorsement in *Myers v. United States* (1926) of virtually unfettered presidential removal powers. Here the Court found the unqualified exercise of such authority violated the *separation of powers. This reversal, with its implication that Roosevelt had willfully violated the Constitution, contributed to the president's determination to pack the Court with his own nominees. While many other decisions hostile to Roosevelt were quickly reversed, *Humphrey's Executor* never has been and was, in fact, expanded upon in *Weiner v. United States* (1958).

SCHECHTER POULTRY CORP. V. UNITED STATES

Citation: 295 U.S. 495 (1935)
Argued: May 2-3, 1935
Decided: May 27, 1935
Court Below: United States Second Circuit Court of Appeals
Basis for Review: *Writ of certiorari
Facts: The National Industrial Recovery Act (NIRA) of 1933 was the most significant piece of legislation passed during the first New Deal. It attempted to combat the national economic emergency mainly through fair competition codes drawn up by industry groups. Some Brooklyn slaughterhouses, including Schechter, were found guilty of violating these codes.
Issues: Does the national emergency justify enactment of NIRA? Does NIRA represent an excessive delegation of legislative power? Does NIRA violate the *commerce power?
Outcome: The Hughes Court voted unanimously to strike NIRA down as unconstitutional.
Vote: 9-0
Participating: Hughes, Van Devanter, McReynolds, Brandeis, Sutherland, Butler, Stone, Roberts, Cardozo
Opinions: Hughes for the Court; Cardozo, joined by Stone, concurring
Significance: Although a year earlier in *Home Building & Loan Association v. Blaisdell* (1934) the Court had found other New Deal legislation justified by the Depression, now Hughes's opinion declared that "extraordinary conditions do not create or enlarge constitutional power." In particular, the Court found that Congress had unconstitutionally delegated legislative power by allowing industry groups to draft the codes that were the subject of NIRA, an error compounded by President Roosevelt's cooperation. Furthermore, the poultry code at issue regulated essentially intrastate commerce only, and Congress was not justified in using its commerce power to intervene. *Schechter* killed what essentially was unworkable legislation, but it also helped give rise, two years later, to Roosevelt's court-packing plan.

UNITED STATES V. BUTLER

Citation: 297 U.S. 1 (1936)
Argued: December 9-10, 1935
Decided: January 6, 1936
Court Below: United States First Circuit Court of Appeals
Basis for Review: *Writ of certiorari

Facts: The Agricultural Adjustment Act (AAA) of 1933, a central piece of New Deal legislation, attempted to raise farm prices by paying farmers to reduce their production. Funds for these payments were to come from taxes levied on commodities processors. Butler, a processor, refused to pay these taxes, and a decision in his favor was upheld in the circuit court of appeals.

Issue: Does the AAA impinge on the powers reserved to the states in the Tenth Amendment?

Outcome: Reasoning that agricultural regulation was properly within the purview of the states, Roberts, for the Court, upheld the lower court's ruling.

Vote: 6-3

Participating: Hughes, Van Devanter, McReynolds, Brandeis, Sutherland, Butler, Stone, Roberts, Cardozo

Opinions: Roberts for the Court; Stone, joined by Brandeis and Cardozo, dissenting

Significance: Although it was the first case to test Congress's power to spend for the general welfare — a power Justice Roberts's opinion upheld — *Butler* has been largely discredited. The agricultural program at issue in *Butler* was later reenacted under the *commerce power, rather than — as with the AAA — under the *taxing power, and upheld in *Mulford v. Smith* (1939) and *Wickard v. Filburn* (1942). Today *Butler* is remembered primarily for Justice Stone's dissent, in which he decried the majority's lack of *judicial restraint in repeatedly striking down New Deal legislation.

GROSJEAN V. AMERICAN PRESS CO.

Citation: 297 U.S. 233 (1936)
Argued: January 13-14, 1936
Decided: February 10, 1936
Court Below: United States District Court for the Eastern District of Louisiana
Basis for Review: Appeal
Facts: Louisiana imposed an advertising sales license tax on all newspapers operating within the state that had a circulation of more than 20,000 per week. Of the 163 newspapers in Louisiana, only 13 fit this description, and of those, 12 opposed the policies of Governor Huey Long.

Issue: Does the Louisiana tax impinge on freedom of the press?

Outcome: The tax was unanimously struck down.

Vote: 9-0

Participating: Hughes, Van Devanter, McReynolds, Brandeis, Sutherland, Butler, Stone, Roberts, Cardozo

Opinion: Sutherland for the Court

Significance: The Supreme Court held, both before and after *Grosjean*, that nondiscriminatory taxes on newspapers are constitutional. The real issue in this case was the state's attempt at *prior restraint of criticism of its policies.

ASHWANDER V. TENNESSEE VALLEY AUTHORITY

Citation: 297 U.S. 288 (1936)
Argued: December 19-20, 1935
Decided: February 17, 1936
Court Below: United States Fifth Circuit Court of Appeals
Basis for Review: *Writ of certiorari
Facts: Minority shareholders in a utility company challenged the company's purchase of electricity from the Tennessee Valley Authority (TVA).

Issues: Did Congress exceed its authority in creating the TVA? Can the TVA legitimately sell the electrical power that is a byproduct of its dam construction projects?

Outcome: Reasoning that the TVA's dam construction fell within the parameters of national defense and that the Constitution grants the federal government power to sell property that legitimately belongs to it, the Court disallowed the shareholders' suit and, by implication, upheld the legislation establishing the TVA.

Vote: 8-1

Participating: Hughes, Van Devanter, McReynolds, Brandeis, Sutherland, Butler, Stone, Roberts, Cardozo

Opinions: Hughes for the Court; Brandeis, joined by Stone, Roberts, and Cardozo, concurring; McReynolds dissenting

Significance: In his concurring opinion, Justice Brandeis argued that the Court never should have heard this case, as it was essentially a shareholders' internal dispute and did not in fact concern any constitutional questions. Today *Ashwander* is recalled primarily for Brandeis's "Ashwander rules," which provide guidelines for circumventing overly broad constitutional interpretations.

BROWN V. MISSISSIPPI

Citation: 297 U.S. 278 (1936)
Argued: January 10, 1936
Decided: February 17, 1936
Court Below: Mississippi Supreme Court
Basis for Review: *Writ of certiorari
Facts: Coerced confessions were used to convict three African American tenant farmers for the murder of a white planter. The Mississippi Supreme Court upheld the convictions.
Issue: Is the use of a person's coerced confession as evidence at his trial a violation of *due process?
Outcome: The Hughes Court unanimously reversed the court below.
Vote: 9-0
Participating: Hughes, Van Devanter, McReynolds, Brandeis, Sutherland, Butler, Stone, Roberts, Cardozo
Opinion: Hughes for the Court
Significance: Although the Hughes Court held that the *Self-Incrimination Clause of the Fifth Amendment does not apply in state courts, it nevertheless found that criminal convictions based on coerced confessions violate the right to a fair trial. *Brown* was the first in a line of Supreme Court cases concerning coerced confessions of criminal defendants that culminated in *Miranda v. Arizona* (1966).

CARTER V. CARTER COAL CO.

Citation: 298 U.S. 238 (1936)
Argued: March 11-12, 1936
Decided: March 18, 1936
Court Below: United States Court of Appeals for the District of Columbia
Basis for Review: *Writ of certiorari
Facts: The Bituminous Coal Conservation Act of 1935, a New Deal attempt to stem industry overproduction and to provide miners with collective bargaining rights, was challenged in a shareholder's suit.
Issue: Does the *Commerce Clause grant

Congress authority to regulate commercial activities and labor relations, or is the coal act an intrusion on powers the Tenth Amendment reserves to the states?
Outcome: A divided Court, with the chief justice writing a separate but concurring opinion, found the act unconstitutional.
Vote: 6-3
Participating: Hughes, Van Devanter, McReynolds, Brandeis, Sutherland, Butler, Stone, Roberts, Cardozo
Opinions: Sutherland for the Court; Hughes concurring; Cardozo, joined by Brandeis and Stone, dissenting
Significance: Justice Sutherland's opinion for the Court used the old direct-indirect test in determining that because coal mining was production, having no direct effect on commerce, Congress could not employ its commerce power to regulate the industry. The industry and its labor relations were thus under control of the states. *Carter*, however, marked the last time the Tenth Amendment was used to override the Commerce Clause. The next year, in *National Labor Relations Board v. Jones & Laughlin Steel Corp.* (1937), the Court reversed its position, and the commerce power became the basis for the second New Deal.

MOREHEAD V. NEW YORK *EX REL. TIPALDO

Citation: 298 U.S. 587 (1936)
Argued: April 28-29, 1936
Decided: June 1, 1936
Court Below: New York Supreme Court
Basis for Review: *Writ of certiorari
Facts: New York State passed a minimum wage law covering women and children.
Issue: Is the minimum wage law a violation of the Fourteenth Amendment's *Due Process Clause?
Outcome: By a narrow majority, the Court found the law unconstitutional.
Vote: 5-4
Participating: Hughes, Van Devanter, McReynolds, Brandeis, Sutherland, Butler, Stone, Roberts, Cardozo
Opinions: Butler for the Court; Hughes, joined by Brandeis, Stone, and Cardozo, dissenting, and

Stone, joined by Brandeis and Cardozo, dissenting
Significance: In *Morehead,* the conservative old majority on the Court harked back to *laissez faire, declaring all minimum wage laws impermissible interferences with contracts. When the Hughes Court changed its overall posture toward *state action the next year, *West Coast Hotel Co. v. Parrish* (1937) would overrule this unpopular decision.

UNITED STATES V. CURTISS-WRIGHT EXPORT CORP.

Citation: 299 U.S. 304 (1936)
Argued: November 19-20, 1936
Decided: December 21, 1936
Court Below: United States District Court for the Southern District of New York
Basis for Review: Appeal
Facts: By joint resolution, Congress granted the president the right to prohibit arms sales to warring nations, specifically Bolivia and Paraguay. President Roosevelt imposed such an embargo, and when Curtiss-Wright was indicted for violating it, the company challenged the constitutionality of Congress's resolution.
Issue: Is the resolution an unconstitutional delegation of legislative powers to the executive branch?
Outcome: Finding that the president's authority in foreign affairs is plenary and not dependant upon congressional action, the Court upheld the resolution and the embargo.
Vote: 7-1
Participating: Hughes, Van Devanter, McReynolds, Brandeis, Sutherland, Butler, Roberts, Cardozo (Stone not participating)
Opinions: Sutherland for the Court; McReynolds dissenting (without written opinion)
Significance: *Curtiss-Wright* was one of the most significant decisions handed down by the Hughes Court. In contrast to the majority of cases concerning conflicts between the executive and legislative branches, this case did not involve *political questions which the Court declined to address. Instead, Justice Sutherland's opinion employed broad language regarding executive power and privilege in the arena of foreign affairs

that has been used to justify many presidential actions, from Roosevelt's prosecution of World War II to other presidents' prosecution of the Vietnam War.

DE JONGE V. OREGON

Citation: 299 U.S. 353 (1937)
Argued: December 9, 1936
Decided: January 4, 1937
Court Below: Oregon Supreme Court
Basis for Review: Appeal
Facts: Dirk De Jonge was convicted under Oregon's criminal syndicalism law for having participated in a meeting organized by the Communist Party to protest persecution of striking longshoremen, although at the meeting no one advocated overthrowing the government or any other unlawful activity.
Issue: Does the Oregon statute violate the right of peaceable assembly protected by the First Amendment?
Outcome: Finding the right of assembly to be as important as that of free press and free speech, the Court struck down the Washington law.
Vote: 8-0
Participating: Hughes, Van Devanter, McReynolds, Brandeis, Sutherland, Butler, Roberts, Cardozo (Stone not participating)
Opinion: Hughes for the Court
Significance: *De Jonge* marked the first time that the freedom to assemble peaceably was made applicable to the states by means of the *Due Process Clause of the Fourteenth Amendment.

WEST COAST HOTEL CO. V. PARRISH

Citation: 300 U.S. 379 (1937)
Argued: December 16-17, 1936
Decided: March 29, 1937
Court Below: Washington Supreme Court
Basis for Review: Appeal
Facts: Ellie Parrish, a hotel worker, sued under a Washington state minimum wage law for women to recover the difference between what she had been paid and the legal minimum.
Issue: Does such legislation violate freedom of contract and thus *due process?
Outcome: Finding that states have the power to

enact such legislation, so long as it is not arbitrary, the Court upheld the Washington law by one vote.

Vote: 5-4

Participating: Hughes, Van Devanter, McReynolds, Brandeis, Sutherland, Butler, Stone, Roberts, Cardozo

Opinions: Hughes for the Court; Sutherland, joined by Van Devanter, McReynolds, and Butler, dissenting

Significance: Overturning *Adkins v. Children's Hospital* (1923) and the previous year's *Morehead v. New York *ex rel. Tipaldo* (1936), *Parrish* signaled the end of the dominance of *substantive due process over the Court's attitude towards government regulation of contracts. Hughes's opinion unequivocally stated, "The Constitution does not speak of freedom of contract." *Parrish* also marked a turning point in the Court's attitude towards the New Deal. Although Justice Roberts was accused of succumbing to the pressure of Roosevelt's court-packing plan and switching sides in the debate over minimum wage laws, in fact his vote was cast before the announcement of the president's strategy for changing the makeup of the Court.

NATIONAL LABOR RELATIONS BOARD V. JONES & LAUGHLIN STEEL CORP.

Citation: 301 U.S. 1 (1937)

Argued: February 10-11, 1937

Decided: April 12, 1937

Court Below: United States Fifth Circuit Court of Appeals

Basis for Review: *Writ of certiorari

Facts: The National Labor Relations Act (NLRA), passed by Congress in 1935, guaranteed workers the right to organize and bargain collectively in businesses operating in or affecting interstate commerce. The NLRA was invoked at Jones & Laughlin Steel Corporation's Aliquippa, Pennsylvania, plant where a labor dispute threatened to close down production.

Issue: What is the extent of Congress's power to regulate commerce?

Outcome: Construing the *Commerce Clause broadly, the Court found that Congress can reg-

ulate interstate commerce not only directly, but also by regulating industries that operate locally and affect interstate commerce only indirectly. In addition, the Court upheld government protection of workers' rights to organize unions.

Vote: 5-4

Participating: Hughes, Van Devanter, McReynolds, Brandeis, Sutherland, Butler, Stone, Roberts, Cardozo

Opinions: Hughes for the Court; McReynolds, joined by Van Devanter, Sutherland, and Butler, dissenting

Significance: *Jones & Laughlin* was one of five cases decided on April 12, 1937, in which Justices Hughes and Roberts exchanged their previously narrow interpretation of the Commerce Clause for a broader one, thus enabling a majority of the Hughes Court to uphold the NLRA and, in doing so, to forestall Roosevelt's court-packing plan. This decision contradicted other recent ones, such as *Schechter Poultry Corp. v. United States* (1935) and *Carter v. Carter Coal Co.* (1936), in which the Court had adhered to the traditional view that the *Due Process Clause of the Fifth Amendment protects freedom of contract from government interference, and signaled the Court's new willingness to uphold legislation permitting federal control of the economy.

STEWARD MACHINE CO. V. DAVIS

Citation: 301 U.S. 548 (1937)

Argued: April 8-9, 1937

Decided: May 24, 1937

Court Below: United States Fifth Circuit Court of Appeals

Basis for Review: *Writ of certiorari

Facts: Under the Social Security Act of 1935, employers were given a tax credit in return for payroll taxes used to fund unemployment compensation and old-age benefits. Steward Machine sued Harwell G. Davis, the Alabama state tax collector, for a refund of taxes the company had paid in accordance with the act.

Issue: Is the payroll tax used to fund unemployment benefits a proper exercise of Congress's *taxing and spending power?

Outcome: The unemployment feature of the

Social Security Act was upheld.

Vote: 5-4

Participating: Hughes, Van Devanter, McReynolds, Brandeis, Sutherland, Butler, Stone, Roberts, Cardozo

Opinions: Cardozo for the Court; McReynolds, Sutherland, joined by Van Devanter, and Butler, dissenting

Significance: In this case and its companion, *Helvering v. Davis* (1937), the Hughes Court upheld the totality of the Social Security Act and, in effect, endorsed the use of the taxing power as a means of achieving social change.

HELVERING V. DAVIS

Citation: 301 U.S. 619 (1937)

Argued: May 5, 1937

Decided: May 24, 1937

Court Below: United States First Circuit Court of Appeals

Basis for Review: *Writ of certiorari

Facts: The Social Security Act of 1935 levied payroll taxes — which were offset by tax credits — on employers in order to fund old-age benefits for retired workers. The act was challenged by a shareholder in an attempt to prevent his company from collecting such taxes.

Issue: Is the use of the *taxing power to fund old-age benefits a constitutional exercise of congressional authority?

Outcome: The Court upheld the old-age benefit provisions of the Social Security Act.

Vote: 7-2

Participating: Hughes, Van Devanter, McReynolds, Brandeis, Sutherland, Butler, Stone, Roberts, Cardozo

Opinions: Cardozo for the Court; Butler and McReynolds dissenting (without written opinions)

Significance: In this and a companion case, *Steward Machine Co. v. Davis* (1937), the Hughes Court upheld the constitutionality of the Social Security Act, the centerpiece of the New Deal's social reform program. Days before the Court handed down the decision in *Helvering v. Davis*, Justice Van Devanter told the president of his intention to resign. Roosevelt, who could now make his own appointment to the Court, was thus

enabled to pursue his second New Deal agenda with confidence.

BREEDLOVE V. SUTTLES

Citation: 302 U.S. 277 (1937)

Argued: November 16-17, 1937

Decided: December 6, 1937

Court Below: Georgia Supreme Court

Basis for Review: Appeal

Facts: A white male citizen of Georgia brought suit to strike down a state poll tax which exempted all those under the age of 21 and over the age of 60, blind individuals, and women. His challenge was dismissed in the lower courts.

Issue: Does the poll tax violate the Fourteenth Amendment guarantee of *equal protection and the Nineteenth Amendment's prohibition against discrimination in voting based on gender?

Outcome: Reasoning that the Equal Protection Clause does not guarantee absolute equality, the Court unanimously upheld the Georgia tax.

Vote: 9-0

Participating: Hughes, McReynolds, Brandeis, Sutherland, Butler, Stone, Roberts, Cardozo, Black

Opinion: Butler for the Court

Significance: The appeal to the Nineteenth Amendment in this case was rejected; the Court reasoned that invalidating the Georgia law *enabling the poll tax would have placed impermissible curbs on the state's own *taxing power.

PALKO V. CONNECTICUT

Citation: 302 U.S. 319 (1937)

Argued: November 12, 1937

Decided: December 6, 1937

Court Below: Connecticut Supreme Court

Basis for Review: Appeal

Facts: Palko was tried in a Connecticut court for first-degree murder, but a jury found him guilty of murder in the second degree and sentenced him to life imprisonment. When the prosecution appealed this verdict, Palko was subjected to a new trial, where he was found guilty of the greater offense and sentenced to death.

Issue: Did the Connecticut law permitting the state to appeal verdicts in certain criminal cases subject defendants like Palko to *double jeopardy in violation of the Fifth and Fourteenth Amendments' *due process guarantees?

Outcome: Finding that not all parts of the Bill of Rights apply to the states, the Court upheld the Connecticut law.

Vote: 8-1

Participating: Hughes, McReynolds, Brandeis, Sutherland, Butler, Stone, Roberts, Cardozo, Black

Opinions: Cardozo for the Court; Butler dissenting (without written opinion)

Significance: While *Palko* subscribed to a doctrine later espoused by Justice Frankfurter as the "fundamental fairness" test, the alternative *incorporation doctrine, making the guarantees of the Bill of Rights applicable to the states through the Due Process Clause of the Fourteenth Amendment, ultimately won. Not only were guarantees like *freedom of speech and the right to counsel made applicable at the state level, but in 1969 *Benton v. Maryland* overruled *Palko*, adding double jeopardy to the list of provisions incorporated into the Fourteenth Amendment.

LOVELL V. CITY OF GRIFFIN

Citation: 303 U.S. 444 (1938)
Argued: February 4, 1938
Decided: March 28, 1938
Court Below: Georgia Court of Appeals
Basis for Review: Appeal
Facts: Alma Lovell, a Jehovah's Witness, was found guilty of violating a city ordinance requiring written permission from the city manager in order to distribute circulars, magazines, pamphlets, or handbills on the street.
Issue: Does the city ordinance violate the First Amendment?
Outcome: Finding the ordinance an impermissible *prior restraint and a violation of freedom of the press, the Court struck it down.
Vote: 8-0
Participating: Hughes, McReynolds, Brandeis, Butler, Stone, Roberts, Black, Reed (Cardozo not participating)
Opinion: Hughes for the Court
Significance: Until the Court definitively ruled,

in *Everson v. Board of Education of Ewing Township* (1947), that the Fourteenth Amendment *incorporates both the religious *Establishment Clause and *Free Speech Clause of the First Amendment, making them applicable to the states, religious cases were often treated like free speech cases. The opinion in *Lovell* did not even refer to Alma Lovell's religious affiliation, the factor she relied upon in her defense.

ERIE RAILROAD CO. V. TOMPKINS

Citation: 304 U.S. 64 (1938)
Argued: January 31, 1938
Decided: April 25, 1938
Court Below: United States Second Circuit Court of Appeals
Basis for Review: *Writ of certiorari
Facts: Harry J. Tompkins, a Pennsylvania citizen, sued the railroad for personal injuries he sustained. The federal district court found for him on the basis of "general law," rather than Pennsylvania law, under which he might have lost and which the railroad insisted was appropriate.
Issue: Should the doctrine of *Swift v. Tyson* (1842), recognizing a federal general *common law, be overturned?
Outcome: Declaring that "there is no federal general common law," Justice Brandeis, writing for the Court, overturned *Swift*.
Vote: 8-0
Participating: Hughes, McReynolds, Brandeis, Butler, Stone, Roberts, Black, Reed (Cardozo not participating)
Opinions: Brandeis for the Court; Butler, joined by McReynolds, and Reed, concurring
Significance: The Judiciary Act of 1789 provides that, "the laws of the several states... shall be regarded as rules of decision in trials at common law" in federal courts. In *Swift v. Tyson* (1842), Justice Joseph Story interpreted this passage so as to exclude contractual and other commercial disputes, thereby acknowledging a body of federal *common law governing commerce. After the Civil War, the power of the federal judiciary expanded and the Supreme Court put increasing emphasis on *substantive due process and freedom of contract, with the result that states were

deprived of their regulatory powers. Justice Brandeis took the unprecedented step here of holding *Swift* unconstitutional because it impinged upon rights reserved to the states under the Tenth Amendment. The same day, however, Brandeis also indicated that although federal general common law did not exist, federal common law does exist with regard to certain specialized areas of law. The debate about the existence and extent of federal common law continues.

JOHNSON V. ZERBST

Citation: 304 U.S. 458 (1938)
Argued: April 4, 1938
Decided: May 23, 1938
Court Below: United States Fifth Circuit Court of Appeals
Basis for Review: *Writ of certiorari
Facts: Johnson, who was indigent, was without benefit of counsel when convicted in federal court of *feloniously passing counterfeit money. While imprisoned, he petitioned the federal district court for a writ of *habeas corpus and was denied, a ruling upheld in the *appellate court.
Issue: Are federal courts required to assign counsel to indigent defendants in criminal cases?
Outcome: Finding that under the Sixth Amendment an accused person cannot be deprived of his life or liberty unless he or she is assisted at trial by counsel, or waives the right to counsel, the Supreme Court overruled the court of appeals.
Vote: 6-2
Participating: Hughes, McReynolds, Brandeis, Butler, Stone, Roberts, Black, Reed (Cardozo not participating)
Opinions: Black for the Court; Reed concurring (without written opinion); McReynolds and Butler dissenting (without written opinions)
Significance: In *Johnson*, the Supreme Court used the Sixth Amendment to impose a higher standard on federal courts than it had imposed on state courts six years earlier in *Powell v. Alabama* (1932) on the basis of *due process as outlined in the Fourteenth Amendment. While in the earlier case the Court held that counsel must be appointed for all indigent defendants in *capital cases, the Court ruled in *Johnson* that such

appointments must be made in all criminal cases tried in federal courts.

MISSOURI *EX REL. GAINES V. CANADA

Citation: 305 U.S. 337 (1938)
Argued: November 9, 1938
Decided: December 12, 1938
Court Below: Missouri Supreme Court
Basis for Review: *Writ of certiorari
Facts: In a *test case managed by the National Association for the Advancement of Colored People (NAACP), Lloyd L. Gaines, an African American resident of Missouri, applied for admission to the state's all-white law school. His rejection was upheld by the state courts on grounds that Missouri had offered to pay his tuition at an out-of-state school and had plans to create an in-state law school for African Americans. The NAACP applied to the United States Supreme Court for a writ of *mandamus to compel Missouri to admit Gaines.
Issue: Did Missouri violate the *Equal Protection Clause of the Fourteenth Amendment?
Outcome: Reasoning that neither of Missouri's alternate plans met the "separate but equal" test, the Court ordered the state law school to admit Gaines.
Vote: 6-2
Participating: Hughes, McReynolds, Brandeis, Butler, Stone, Roberts, Black, Reed
Opinions: Hughes for the Court; McReynolds, joined by Butler, dissenting
Significance: Ever since the 1896 decision in *Plessy v. Ferguson*, the Court had adhered to the "separate but equal" standard for determining what types of segregation were legal. The *Gaines* case was a turning point in the reevaluation of *Plessy* that culminated in 1954 in *Brown v. Board of Education*, which outlawed segregated schooling and fueled the civil rights revolution of the 1950s and 1960s.

GRAVES V. NEW YORK *EX REL. O'KEEFE

Citation: 306 U.S. 466 (1939)
Argued: March 6, 1939
Decided: March 27, 1939
Court Below: New York Supreme Court
Basis for Review: *Writ of certiorari

Facts: The state of New York imposed an income tax on a state resident employed by the Federal Home Owners Corporation, which appealed the tax on grounds of *intergovernmental immunity.
Issue: Are the incomes of state and federal employees immune to taxes imposed by the non-employing government entity?
Outcome: Finding that nothing in the Constitution grants such immunities, the Court upheld the tax.
Vote: 6-2
Participating: Hughes, McReynolds, Butler, Stone, Roberts, Black, Reed, Frankfurter
Opinions: Stone for the Court; Hughes (without written opinion) and Frankfurter concurring; Butler and McReynolds dissenting (without written opinions)
Significance: Overruling *Dobbins v. Erie County* (1842) and *Collector v. Day* (1871), *Graves* did away with most intergovernmental tax immunities.

MULFORD V. SMITH

Citation: 307 U.S. 38 (1939)
Argued: March 8, 1939
Decided: April 17, 1939
Court Below: United States District Court for the Middle District of Georgia
Basis for Review: Appeal
Facts: The constitutionality of a tobacco quota imposed by the second Agricultural Adjustment Act (1938) was challenged by Mulford, a tobacco producer who had been penalized for overproduction.
Issue: Does Congress have the power to limit production of certain agricultural products?
Outcome: Reasoning that the *Commerce Clause gives Congress authority to limit amounts of any commodity shipped through interstate commerce, the Court upheld the second Agricultural Adjustment Act.
Vote: 6-2
Participating: Hughes, McReynolds, Butler, Stone, Roberts, Black, Reed, Frankfurter
Opinions: Roberts for the Court; Butler, joined by McReynolds, dissenting
Significance: Justice Roberts, the author of the opinion in *United States v. Butler* (1936), the decision striking down the first Agricultural

Adjustment Act, also wrote the opinion here. Although the cases were decided on different grounds (the *taxing power had been at issue in *Butler*), there can be no better illustration than *Mulford* of the complete turnabout in the Hughes Court's attitude towards the New Deal and the necessity of Roosevelt's economic reforms.

COLEMAN V. MILLER

Citation: 307 U.S. 433 (1939)
Argued: October 10, 1938; reargued April 17-18, 1939
Decided: June 5, 1939
Court Below: Kansas Supreme Court
Basis for Review: *Writ of certiorari
Facts: Kansas ratified the proposed Child Labor Amendment to the Constitution 13 years after Congress introduced it without imposing a time limit for ratification. The state already had rejected the amendment once before.
Issues: What is a reasonable time within which constitutional amendments must be ratified by the states? Can a state ratify an amendment it has previously rejected?
Outcome: Finding these issues to be *political questions for Congress to decide, the Court affirmed the lower court's denial of a writ of *mandamus, which had been sought to prevent ratification of the amendment.
Vote: 7-2
Participating: Hughes, McReynolds, Butler, Stone, Roberts, Black, Reed, Frankfurter, Douglas
Opinions: Hughes for the Court; Black, joined by Roberts, Frankfurter, and Douglas, and Frankfurter, joined by Roberts, Black, and Douglas, concurring; Butler, joined by McReynolds, dissenting
Significance: In *Dillon v. Gloss* (1921), the Court had ruled that although ratification deadlines should be set by Congress, they must be contemporaneous throughout the states. *Coleman* broadened this holding by making ratification wholly a political question subject to determination by Congress alone.

HAGUE V. CONGRESS FOR INDUSTRIAL ORGANIZATIONS

Citation: 307 U.S. 496 (1939)

Argued: February 27-28, 1939
Decided: June 5, 1939
Court Below: United States Third Circuit Court of Appeals
Basis for Review: *Writ of certiorari
Facts: Mayor Frank Hague of Jersey City, New Jersey, employed a city ordinance requiring permits for public meetings and public distribution of literature primarily to prohibit union activities. The Congress of Industrial Organizations obtained an *injunction ordering the city to stop interfering with union meetings.
Issue: To what extent can the state control public gatherings?
Outcome: In a *plurality opinion, the Court upheld the injunction, declaring that the ordinance violated the rights of peaceable assembly and *free speech.
Vote: 5-2
Participating: Hughes, McReynolds, Butler, Stone, Roberts, Black, Reed (Frankfurter and Douglas not participating)
Opinions: No opinion of the Court; Butler delivered the Court's judgment; Roberts, joined by Black, Stone, joined by Reed, and Hughes, concurring; McReynolds and Butler dissenting
Significance: Although the justices disagreed as to their reasons for doing so, a majority found that although the state can regulate public meetings, it cannot arbitrarily prohibit them. While Roberts found access to public places a First Amendment right that is a privilege of citizens, Stone found such access to be a personal liberty protected by the *Due Process Clause of the Fourteenth Amendment. The second, broader view, extending the right of peaceable assembly and free speech to all persons, was later adopted by the Court.

THORNHILL V. ALABAMA

Citation: 310 U.S. 88 (1940)
Argued: February 29, 1940
Decided: April 22, 1940
Court Below: Alabama Court of Appeals
Basis for Review: *Writ of certiorari
Facts: An Alabama statute prohibited all forms of picketing.

Issue: Is peaceful picketing protected by the *Free Speech Clause of the First Amendment?
Outcome: Because the statute did not attempt to specify which elements of picketing it aimed to regulate, the Court struck it down.
Vote: 8-1
Participating: Hughes, McReynolds, Stone, Roberts, Black, Reed, Frankfurter, Douglas, Murphy
Opinions: Murphy for the Court; McReynolds dissenting (without written opinion)
Significance: While Justice Murphy's opinion recognized that the First Amendment does not guarantee an unconditional right to picket, it also acknowledged that some of the second New Deal's reforms affected organized labor. While *Thornhill* would be used to regulate picketing that disrupted the smooth functioning of society, it also legitimized peaceful picketing's function as a tool to educate the public about important economic matters.

CANTWELL V. CONNECTICUT

Citation: 310 U.S. 296 (1940)
Argued: March 29, 1940
Decided: May 20, 1940
Court Below: Connecticut Supreme Court
Basis for Review: *Writ of certiorari
Facts: A Jehovah's Witness who was canvasing door-to-door was convicted of violating a Connecticut law requiring prior approval of such activities from the secretary of public welfare.
Issue: Does the state law violate the First Amendment's guarantee of the free exercise of religion?
Outcome: Because the statute failed to specify time, place, and manner restrictions, the conviction was overturned.
Vote: 9-0
Participating: Hughes, McReynolds, Stone, Roberts, Black, Reed, Frankfurter, Douglas, Murphy
Opinion: Roberts for the Court
Significance: *Cantwell* was the Court's first decision directly addressing the *Free Exercise Clause of the First Amendment.

MINERSVILLE SCHOOL DISTRICT V. GOBITIS

Citation: 310 U.S. 586 (1940)
Argued: April 25, 1940
Decided: June 3, 1940
Court Below: United States Third Circuit Court of Appeals
Basis for Review: *Writ of certiorari
Facts: A child, who was also a Jehovah's Witness, was expelled from school for refusing on religious grounds to salute the American flag and therefore violating state law.
Issue: Was the expulsion a violation of the *Free Exercise Clause of the First Amendment?
Outcome: Stating that the "felt necessities" of society are superior to the individual's religious conscience, Justice Frankfurter's opinion for the Court upheld the statute and the expulsion.
Vote: 8-1
Participating: Hughes, McReynolds, Stone, Roberts, Black, Reed, Frankfurter, Douglas, Murphy
Opinions: Frankfurter for the Court; McReynolds concurring (without written opinion); Stone dissenting
Significance: Tensions associated with the onset of World War II are clearly evident in this, the first "flag salute" case. Three years later, the Court would cite First Amendment concerns when reversing *Gobitis* in *West Virginia State Board of Education v. Barnette* (1943).

UNITED STATES V. DARBY

Citation: 312 U.S. 100 (1941)
Argued: December 19-20, 1940
Decided: February 3, 1941
Court Below: United States District Court for the Southern District of Georgia
Basis for Review: Appeal
Facts: The Fair Labor Standards Act of 1938, which stipulated maximum hours and minimum wages for employees of businesses engaged in interstate commerce, was the last major piece of New Deal legislation. Its constitutionality was tested in this case, involving a Georgia lumber processor, who was indicted for violating the act.

Issue: Does Congress have authority under the *Commerce Clause to regulate hours and wages?
Outcome: The Hughes Court unanimously upheld the act.
Vote: 8-0
Participating: Hughes, Stone, Roberts, Black, Reed, Frankfurter, Douglas, Murphy
Opinion: Stone for the Court
Significance: In *Hammer v. Dagenhart* (1918), the Supreme Court had rejected the Federal Child Labor Act of 1916 on grounds that its prohibition against interstate transport of items produced with child labor interfered with powers reserved to the states under the Tenth Amendment. In *Darby* Justice Stone, referring to Justice Oliver Wendell Holmes's dissent in the earlier case, specifically overruled *Hammer*. The Fair Labor Standards Act contained ambiguities that fostered a debate about its applicability to state workers and led to the resurrection of *Hammer v. Dagenhart* in *National League of Cities v. Usery* (1976). *Usery* was in turn reversed in 1985 by *Garcia v. San Antonio Metropolitan Transit Authority*.

COX V. NEW HAMPSHIRE

Citation: 312 U.S. 569 (1941)
Argued: March 7, 1941
Decided: March 31, 1941
Court Below: New Hampshire Supreme Court
Basis for Review: Appeal
Facts: In the 1930s the Jehovah's Witnesses began a campaign to test the constitutionality of various statutes and ordinances they felt denied them religious freedom. Cox, a leader of the group, argued that an unlicensed single-file march of Witnesses through the streets carrying placards did not violate a Manchester, New Hampshire, ordinance requiring parade groups to obtain a license and pay a fee in advance.
Issue: Does the ordinance violate rights of *free speech, assembly, and worship protected at the state level by the Fourteenth Amendment?
Outcome: Calling the ordinance a reasonable exercise of the state's *police power, the Court unanimously upheld it.
Vote: 8-0
Participating: Hughes, Stone, Roberts, Black,

Reed, Frankfurter, Douglas, Murphy
Opinion: Hughes for the Court
Significance: *Cox* was the first in a long line of cases in which the Court upheld government's right to impose reasonable place, time, and manner restrictions on speech, so long as such restrictions are not discriminatorily imposed.

UNITED STATES V. CLASSIC

Citation: 313 U.S. 299 (1941)
Argued: April 7, 1941
Decided: May 26, 1941
Court Below: United States District Court for the Eastern District of Louisiana
Basis for Review: Appeal
Facts: The new Civil Rights Division of the Justice Department brought this *test case against Louisiana electoral commissioners, charging they deliberately altered and miscounted ballots in a congressional primary, thus violating the federal Criminal Code passed by Congress.
Issue: Does Congress have authority under Article I of the Constitution to regulate primary elections and to protect them from private as well as state interference?
Outcome: A bare majority of the Court found that the officials could be held accountable under the code.
Vote: 4-3
Participating: Stone, Roberts, Black, Reed, Frankfurter, Douglas, Murphy (Hughes not participating)
Opinions: Stone for the Court; Douglas, joined by Black and Murphy, dissenting
Significance: *Classic* explicitly overruled *Newberry v. United States* (1921), in which the Court found that Congress could regulate only general elections, not primaries. It also implicitly overruled *Grovey v. Townsend* (1935), in which a state Democratic Party convention's exclusion of African Americans from primary elections was found to be an exercise of private, not *state action.

VOTING PATTERNS

Chief Justice Hughes is generally perceived to have presided over two entirely different Courts.

The first one, which lasted from 1930 until 1937, was made up almost entirely of justices who had served on the ultra-conservative Taft Court. The only exceptions were the Republican Owen J. Roberts, who replaced Edward T. Sanford during the first year of Hughes's tenure, and the Democrat Benjamin N. Cardozo, who arrived in 1932 to take Justice Holmes's place and who assumed his predecessor's progressive role on the Court. Still, in some early decisions of the Hughes Court, such as *Nebbia v. New York* and *Home Building & Loan Association v. Blaisdell*, both decided early in 1934, the Court indicated that it was prepared to abandon its old *laissez faire orientation and support New Deal legislation.

Soon, however, it became apparent that Hughes and Roberts were swing votes, not committed members of the liberal bloc consisting of Brandeis, Stone, and Cardozo. Over the next three years Justice Roberts, in particular, consistently voted with the Court's hard line "Four Horsemen" — Van Devanter, McReynolds, Sutherland, and Butler — to strike down one piece of New Deal legislation after another. While the Roosevelt administration lost 12 decisions on New Deal measures between 1934 and 1936, it won just one in the October 1934 term — the *Gold Clause Cases* (1935), in which Hughes voted with the liberal bloc — and one in the spring of 1936, *Ashwander v. Tennessee Valley Authority*.

After a landslide victory in 1936 gave Roosevelt his second term, he announced his judicial reform proposal on February 5, 1937. The unveiling of this court-packing plan marked a watershed in the history of the Court and, in particular, a turning point for the Hughes Court. Starting with *West Coast Hotel Co. v. Parrish*, decided March 29, 1937, the Court upheld the constitutionality of every New Deal law that came before it.

While the decision in *Parrish* was not announced until after Roosevelt had made public his plan to reconfigure the Court, in fact the justices already had voted on the case in conference about a month before Roosevelt presented his plan to Congress. While the threat presented by this plan may have had something to do with Hughes's and Roberts's reorientation, it seems

POLITICAL COMPOSITION
of the Hughes Court

Justice & Total Term	Courts Served	Appointing President	Political Party
Charles Evans Hughes (1910-1916) (as Chief Justice, 1930-1941)	White Hughes	Taft Hoover	Republican
Oliver Wendell Holmes (1902-1932)	Fuller White Taft Hughes	T. Roosevelt	Republican
Willis Van Devanter (1911-1937)	White Taft Hughes	Taft	Republican
James C. McReynolds (1914-1941)	White Taft Hughes	Wilson	Democrat
Louis D. Brandeis (1916-1939)	White Taft Hughes	Wilson	Democrat
George Sutherland (1922-1938)	Taft Hughes	Harding	Republican
Pierce Butler (1923-1939)	Taft Hughes	Harding	Democrat
Edward T. Sanford (1923-1930)	Taft Hughes	Harding	Republican
Harlan F. Stone (1925-1941) (1941-1946)	Taft Hughes Stone	Coolidge F. D. Roosevelt	Republican Democrat

(Continued on opposite page)

clear that they already had begun to recognize the necessity of jettisoning an outdated judicial philosophy for the good of the country.

The "Four Horsemen," in contrast, never altered their opposition to the New Deal. They did, however, take advantage of the Supreme Court Retirement Act, passed March 1, 1937, permitting them to retire at the age of 70 at full salary. In May 1937 Justice Van Devanter informed the president of his intention to retire at the end of the Court term, thus giving Roosevelt the opportunity to make his first Supreme Court appointment and solidify support for the New Deal. Justice

Sutherland's retirement followed Van Devanter's seven months later, and in November 1939, Justice Butler died. The last holdout was McReynolds, who retired only five months before the chief justice and who continued his opposition to Roosevelt's policies, voting against more New Deal legislation than any of his colleagues.

Although the "second" Hughes Court came into existence even before any personnel changes occurred, Roosevelt did, in fact, have the opportunity to reshape the Court by appointing five new justices. These new members helped validate the second New Deal, but most of their

POLITICAL COMPOSITION
of the Hughes Court

Justice & Total Term	Courts Served	Appointing President	Political Party
Owen J. Roberts (1930-1945)	Hughes Stone	Hoover	Republican
Benjamin N. Cardozo (1932-1938)	Hughes	Hoover	Democrat
Hugo L. Black (1937-1971)	Hughes Stone Vinson Warren Burger	F. D. Roosevelt	Democrat
Stanley F. Reed (1938-1957)	Hughes Stone Vinson Warren	F. D. Roosevelt	Democrat
Felix Frankfurter (1939-1962)	Hughes Stone Vinson Warren	F. D. Roosevelt	Democrat
William O. Douglas (1939-1975)	Hughes Stone Vinson Warren Burger	F. D. Roosevelt	Democrat
Frank Murphy (1940-1949)	Hughes Stone Vinson	F. D. Roosevelt	Democrat

groundbreaking work would take place under subsequent chief justices. Still, as early as 1937, Van Devanter's replacement, Hugo Black, indicated his support for *incorporation of the Bill of Rights into the Fourteenth Amendment by voting with the majority in *Palko v. Connecticut*.

Black's opinion for the Court in *Johnson v. Zerbst* (1938), with its emphasis on the Sixth Amendment right to counsel, was another harbinger of his future leadership of the *due process revolution that was about to take place on the Court. By ceding control of economic matters to the other branches of government and returning to an expanded view of Congress's powers under the *Commerce Clause, the Court made space on its calendar for a new agenda emphasizing individual liberties. Black's campaign for full incorporation of the Bill of Rights would receive strong support from Roosevelt appointees William O. Douglas and Frank Murphy and opposition from the formerly ardent New Dealer, Felix Frankfurter. Roosevelt's other appointee to the Hughes Court, Stanley F. Reed, was perhaps even more conservative than Frankfurter on social issues. However, surrounded by some of the greatest figures ever to serve on the Supreme Court,

Reed, best known for his inclination towards *judicial restraint, left little impression.

SPECIAL FEATURES OF THE HUGHES COURT

A HOME OF THEIR OWN

A new Supreme Court building was begun in 1925 at Chief Justice William Howard Taft's behest. When the October 1935 term opened, it did so in a building dedicated solely to the Supreme Court and worthy of the Court's august stature. Situated across from the Capitol, it was modeled after a Greek temple, and had the words "Equal Justice Under Law" inscribed over the front entrance. However, while one of the most compelling arguments for creating a separate building to house the Court was the lack of office space in the old Senate chamber it had occupied, most of the justices refused to occupy their spacious new suites, preferring to continue working at home, as was their custom. As a result, Hugo Black, the first new appointee to the Hughes Court, got his pick of chambers. He chose a desirable corner suite, which he continued to occupy until his death 34 years later.

VOTING BLOCS AND SWING VOTES

Although the tradition of unanimity had been steadily dissipating since it was initiated by Chief Justice John Marshall, dependable voting alliances and determinative swing votes were largely unknown prior to the Hughes Court. Four of the holdovers from the conservative Taft Court — Justices Van Devanter, McReynolds, Sutherland, and Butler — were so cohesive in their opposition to New Deal reforms that they became known collectively as the "Four Horsemen," after the Four Horsemen of the Apocalypse that brought destruction to the land in the last book of the Bible. Arrayed against these four was a minority of three liberals, Justices Holmes (soon replaced by the even more liberal Cardozo), Brandeis, and Stone. Deciding votes belonged with the chief justice and Justice Roberts, both of whom were as apt (before 1937) to "swing" their vote to the conservative bloc as to the liberal side of the Court.

Justice Roberts was the one member of the Hughes Court who can most appropriately be labeled a swing vote, for at the crucial moment when the Court was faced with President Roosevelt's threat to reconstitute it, it was he who reversed his position on minimum wage laws, thereby creating a "second" Hughes Court. Previously, it was Roberts's vote that had consistently helped the conservatives on the Court strike down New Deal legislation in 5 to 4 decisions. After *West Coast Hotel Co. v. Parrish* (1937), he would consistently uphold New Deal measures, many of them essentially identical to ones he previously had voted against.

The Stone Court 1941-1946

BACKGROUND

WORLD WAR II

In July 1941, after the Japanese had conquered most of Indochina, America responded by freezing Japanese assets located in the United States, ending export to Japan of vital materials such as oil, and closing the Panama Canal to Japanese shipping. Japan in turn offered to with-

draw from Indochina if the United States would drop its embargo and recognize Japanese *sovereignty over the considerable lands it now controlled in China. President Roosevelt's reaction was swift and uncompromising: adhering to America's longstanding Open Door policy toward China, he demanded that Japan withdraw from that country altogether.

In October 1941 the moderate Japanese premier, Prince Konoye, was replaced by the militant General Tojo, who swiftly issued orders for the Japanese fleet to attack Pearl Harbor in Hawaii, where the American Pacific fleet (except for its aircraft carriers) lay at anchor. On December 7, which Roosevelt called a "day that will live in infamy," the Japanese attacked, destroying 18 warships, 180 aircraft, and killing 2,043 Americans. The next day Congress declared war on Japan. Owing to the 1940 Tripartite Pact pledging Japan, Germany, and Italy to mutual defense against attack from the United States, America was now at war with all three countries.

On New Year's Day, 1942, the United States joined Great Britain and the Soviet Union in a "Grand Alliance," agreeing to concentrate its initial efforts on Germany, which simultaneously was bombing Britain and threatening to capture Moscow.[†] Too weak at the time to mount an invasion of Europe, the Allies staged a holding action against the Japanese in the Pacific, while fighting General Erwin Rommel in North Africa, where the Nazis were menacing the Suez Canal. Joseph Stalin pleaded for the opening of a second front to save the Soviet Union, but President Roosevelt and British Prime Minister Winston

---

MEMBERS Of the Court 1941–1946 (In Order of Seniority)	
Harlan F. Stone (Chief Justice)	(1941-1946)
Owen J. Roberts (resigned)	(1941-1945)
Hugo L. Black	(1941-1946)
Stanley F. Reed	(1941-1946)
Felix Frankfurter	(1941-1946)
William O. Douglas	(1941-1946)
Frank Murphy	(1941-1946)
James F. Byrnes (resigned)	(1941-1942)
Robert H. Jackson (replaced Harlan F.Stone as associate justice)	(1941-1946)
Wiley B. Rutledge (replaced James F. Byrnes)	(1943-1946)
Harold H. Burton (replaced Owen J. Roberts)	(1945-1946)

An asterisk (*) before a word or phrase indicates that a definition will be found in the glossary at the end of this volume.

[†] As early as 1942 Germany had begun its campaign to exterminate the Jews of Europe, but the Nazi "final solution" was not the Allies' primary reason for focusing on Germany at this point in the war.

Churchill, meeting in Casablanca in 1943, decided instead to use American troops deployed in North Africa to invade Italy and reclaim it from the Nazis.

The slow conquest of Italy throughout the latter half of 1943 was but a prelude to the Allied invasion at Normandy, France, which was being masterminded by General Dwight D. Eisenhower. On June 6, 1944, the largest invasion force ever assembled landed on the beaches of northern France and quickly reclaimed the whole country from the Nazis. The Allied forces swept on through Europe, meeting serious resistance only once, at the Battle of the Bulge, where the Nazis staged a final assault in December 1944. On April 30, 1945, Adolph Hitler committed suicide in his Berlin bunker, and on May 8 Germany formally surrendered.

Victory in the Pacific came later. By June 1945 American naval forces had penetrated all of Japan's external defenses and were preparing to invade the Japanese islands themselves. The new Japanese government, appointed by the emperor in the spring of 1945 and ordered to end the war, was engaged in an internal struggle with the Japanese military and failed to make its intentions clear. Meanwhile, Harry S. Truman had replaced President Roosevelt after Roosevelt died on April 12, 1945, less than three months into his fourth term. Truman was notified that a team of scientists had succeeded in exploding an atomic bomb in the New Mexico desert. To end the war with Japan, Truman ordered that the bomb be dropped, first on Hiroshima on August 6, 1945, then on Nagasaki three days later. On September 2, Japan formally surrendered. The Allies had achieved their aim of unconditional surrender.

THE YALTA CONFERENCE AND THE COMMENCEMENT OF THE COLD WAR

The pivotal wartime conference among the Allies occurred at the Crimean resort of Yalta in February 1945. By this time, Stalin had taken over the Baltic States and, against express British and American wishes, set up a Communist regime in Poland. While Churchill and Roosevelt regarded Poland as a bulwark against Soviet

aggression, Stalin steadfastly insisted on setting up a postwar system of "balance-of-power" diplomacy, wherein the great powers would dominate separate regions of the world. Fearful that Germany would rise again, Stalin also got the Allies to agree to the dismemberment of that country. The Eastern Bloc of Communist states was born.

For their part, Roosevelt and Churchill were counting on the U.S.S.R. to help win the war still raging against Japan. Stalin agreed to enter that conflict three months after Germany surrendered. He also agreed that the Soviet Union would participate in a postwar international organization, to be called the United Nations, modeled on the ill-fated League of Nations. But by the end of 1945, it was clear that the Grand Alliance was no more. Stalin was consolidating his stranglehold on Eastern Europe, while at the same time threatening Turkey, Greece, and Iran and aiding the Chinese Communist insurgents. On March 5, 1946, at Westminster College in Fulton, Missouri, former Prime Minister Churchill delivered a speech that laid out the boundaries of the new postwar world: "from Stettin on the Baltic to Trieste on the Adriatic, an iron curtain has descended across the Continent." Describing Churchill's speech as a "call to war," Stalin responded by withdrawing from the World Bank and the International Monetary Fund, opening salvos in what would become the Cold War.

STONE'S EARLY LIFE

Harlan F. Stone was the son of a New Hampshire farmer. He seemed destined to follow his father in his choice of occupation until an accidental assault on a college chaplain during a melée caused Stone to be expelled from Massachusetts Agricultural College. He went on to graduate Phi Beta Kappa from Amherst College, where he gave early evidence of his judicial temperament by writing an opinion overruling a faculty decision to expel one of his fellow students. Deciding to pursue a career in law, Stone set about determining how a poor farmer's son could afford such an education. Exhibiting the Yankee virtues of

JUDICIAL BIOGRAPHY
Harlan Fiske Stone

PERSONAL DATA
Born: October 11, 1872, in Chesterfield, New Hampshire
Parents: Frederick Lawson Stone, Ann Sophia Butler Stone
Higher Education: Amherst College (B.A., Phi Beta Kappa, 1894; M.A., 1897); Columbia University Law School (LL.B., 1898)
Bar Admission: New York, 1898
Political Party: Republican
Marriage: September 7, 1899, to Agnes Harvey, who bore Stone two sons
Died: April 22, 1946, in Washington, D.C.
Buried: Rock Creek Cemetary, Washington, D.C.

PROFESSIONAL CAREER
Occupations: Educator, 1894-1895, 1898-1923; Lawyer, 1899-1925; Government Official, 1924-1925; Judge, 1925-1946

Official Positions: Professor, Columbia University Law School, 1898-1910; Dean, Columbia University Law School, 1910-1923; United States Attorney General, 1924-1925; Associate Justice, United States Supreme Court, 1925-1941; Chief Justice, United States Supreme Court, 1941-1946

SUPREME COURT SERVICE
As Associate Justice:
Nominated: January 5, 1925
Nominated By: Calvin Coolidge
Confirmed: February 5, 1925
Confirmation Vote: 71-6
Oath Taken: March 2, 1925
Replaced: Joseph McKenna
Significant Opinions: *United States v. Butler* (dissent) (1936); *Graves v. New York *ex rel. O'Keefe* (1939); *United States v. Darby* (1941); *United States v.*

Classic (1941)
Left Court: Promoted to Chief Justice July 2, 1941
Length of Service: 16 years, 4 months
Replacement: Robert H. Jackson

As Chief Justice:
Nominated: June 12, 1941
Nominated By: Franklin D. Roosevelt
Confirmed: June 27, 1941
Confirmation Vote: Voice vote
Oath Taken: July 3, 1941
Replaced: Charles Evans Hughes
Significant Opinions: *Ex parte Quirin* (1942); *Hirabayashi v. United States* (1943); *Yakus v. United States* (1944)
Left Court: Died April 22, 1946
Length of Service: 4 years, 9 months, 19 days
Replacement: Fred M. Vinson

---

hard work and independence, Stone found work teaching high school chemistry, a job that provided him with the funds to attend Columbia University Law School, from which he graduated in 1898.

Shortly thereafter, Stone accepted a position on the faculty of Columbia University Law School. The following year, he took up a position practicing law with the New York firm of Sullivan & Cromwell, thus beginning a dual career that would last for the next 25 years. He reached the pinnacle of his academic calling in 1910, when he was named dean of Columbia Law School, a position he would hold for the next 13 years. His career in private practice culminated in

his being made head of the litigation department at Sullivan & Cromwell in 1923.

STONE'S PUBLIC LIFE

So influential were Stone's reformist legal writings that when President Calvin Coolidge needed someone to straighten out the mess left at the Justice Department by the scandals of Warren Harding's administration, he appointed Stone attorney general. Stone previously had served as counsel to J.P. Morgan, and some feared that he had a pro-business orientation that would inhibit his work at the Justice Department. However, upon his appointment, Stone began a major reorganization of the department. Only one year after

Harlan Fiske Stone

Stone assumed this position, however, Coolidge elevated him to the Supreme Court. Reservations about his ties to Wall Street remained, and Stone suggested that he address these concerns directly by answering in person questions put to him by the Senate Judiciary Committee, thus setting the pattern for the current confirmation process. He was confirmed by a vote of 61 to 6.

Until President Franklin D. Roosevelt attempted to pack the Court with supporters of the New Deal in 1937 — engendering a revolution in the Court's orientation — Stone, as an associate justice, customarily found himself in agreement with Justices Oliver Wendell Holmes and Louis D. Brandeis (and later, Benjamin Cardozo), dissenting from the conservative majorities on the Taft and Hughes Courts. In opinions such as his dissent in *United States v. Butler* (1936), Stone spoke out strongly against what he regarded as the Court's interference with the legislative process and its attitude that it was "the only agency of government that must be assumed to have capacity to govern." During

the early years of Roosevelt's administration, Stone was the one who voted most often to uphold New Deal legislation, which would become law after the president's court-packing plan reversed the attitudes of swing voters on the Hughes Court.

Stone's career as an associate justice is also notable for his opinion in *United States v. Carolene Products Co.* (1938), an otherwise obscure case remembered only for a footnote in which he suggested that civil rights matters, unlike economic issues, merited special judicial latitude. Having articulated the so-called preferred freedoms doctrine, under which those rights embodied in the Bill of Rights — the First Amendment in particular — were accorded special treatment, Stone became the lone dissenter in *Minersville School District v. Gobitis* (1940), in which the Court upheld the expulsion from school of a Jehovah's Witness child who refused to participate in the daily flag salute ceremony. Later, however, Stone would oppose the agendas of civil rights activists such as Justices Hugo Black and William O. Douglas, which gained ascendancy after *laissez faire was displaced as the Court's preoccupation in 1937.

STONE AS CHIEF JUSTICE

Stone's elevation to the chief justiceship, after beginning as the most junior justice and sitting consecutively in every seat on the Court — literally rising through the ranks in a way no other chief justice has — was heralded by his brethren. After Edward D. White, Stone was only the second member of the Court to be promoted internally to the lead position.[†] And again after White, Stone was only the second chief justice to be appointed by a president from the opposing party.

Another of Stone's distinctions as chief justice is that he is the only one to have served in two earlier Courts. Unfortunately, however, Stone lacked the leadership abilities that both William Howard Taft and Charles Evans Hughes had abundantly displayed. Instead of Taft's political machinations in massing the Court and Hughes's firm grip on the proceedings at judicial conferences, Stone's approach to consensus-building consisted

---

[†] Stone's predecessor, Charles Evans Hughes, had left the Court to pursue the presidency before returning as chief justice.

of a lengthy, laborious airing of all views. As a consequence, the Stone Court is remembered as one of the most frequently divided, most publicly quarrelsome in history.

Stone's tenure as chief justice was the shortest since Oliver Ellsworth's resignation ended his tenure in 1800. However, in the scant four years and nine months that Stone served as chief justice, he did act as midwife to the Court's new focus on individual rights. Just as, when he was an associate justice, he had objected to the *laissez faire excesses of the conservative "Four Horsemen," as chief justice he opposed what he viewed as the interjection of political bias into the civil liberties issues that seemed to dominate the docket. But in the landmark *free speech case *West Virginia State Board of Education v. Barnette* (1943), he saw his dissent in *Gobitis* become law. As was his custom in cases where his earlier minority views were adopted by the majority, Stone assigned the opinion to another justice, in this case Robert Jackson.

Stone's exit from the Court was dramatic. On April 22, 1946, while reading a dissent from the bench in a naturalization case, *Girouard v. United States*, he faltered. He was then helped from the bench and died later that day of a cerebral hemorrhage.

ASSOCIATE JUSTICE

For biographies of Associate Justices **Owen J. Roberts, Hugo L. Black, Stanley F. Reed, Felix Frankfurter, William O. Douglas,** and **Frank Murphy,** see entries under **THE HUGHES COURT.**

JAMES FRANCIS BYRNES

PERSONAL DATA

Born: May 2, 1879, in Charleston, South Carolina
Parents: James F. Byrnes, Elizabeth E. McSweeney Byrnes
Higher Education: None
Bar Admission: South Carolina, 1903
Political Party: Democrat
Marriage: May 2, 1906, to Maude Busch

Died: April 9, 1972, in Columbia, South Carolina
Buried: Trinity Cathedral Graveyard, Columbia

PROFESSIONAL CAREER

Occupations: Court Reporter, 1900-1908; Journalist, early 1900s; Lawyer, 1903-1910, 1925-1930, 1947-1951; Government Official, 1908-1910, 1942-1947; Politician, 1911-1925, 1931-1941, 1951-1955; Judge, 1941-1942
Official Positions: Court Reporter, Second Circuit, South Carolina, 1900-1908; Editor, Aiken, South Carolina *Journal and Review*, early 1900s; Solicitor, Second Circuit, South Carolina, 1908-1910; Member, United States House of Representatives, 1911-1925; Member, United States Senate, 1931-1941; Associate Justice, United States Supreme Court, 1941-1942; Director, Office of Economic Stabilization, 1942-1943; Director, Office of War Mobilization and Reconversion, 1943-1945; United States Secretary of State, 1945-1947; Governor, South Carolina, 1951-1955

SUPREME COURT SERVICE

Nominated: June 12, 1941
Nominated By: Franklin D. Roosevelt
Confirmed: June 12, 1941
Confirmation Vote: Voice vote
Oath Taken: July 8, 1941
Replaced: James C. McReynolds
Significant Opinion: *Edwards v. California* (1941)
Left Court: Resigned October 3, 1942
Length of Service: 1 year, 2 months, 25 days
Replacement: Wiley B. Rutledge

James F. Byrnes was the son of Irish immigrants who settled in Charleston, South Carolina. His father died before Byrnes was born, and his mother worked as a dressmaker to support the family. Byrnes had to leave school at the age of 14 and never acquired a formal education. Instead, he read law in his spare time while working in Aiken, South Carolina, as a court stenographer and reporter for the state's Second Circuit. In 1903 he passed the state bar and acquired the local newspaper, where he became editor.

Shortly thereafter, Byrnes went into politics, first serving as solicitor (district attorney) for the Second Circuit, then serving for two terms in

*The Stone Court, 1943. From left: Stanley F. Reed, Robert H. Jackson, Owen J. Roberts,
William O. Douglas, Harlan Fiske Stone, Frank Murphy, Hugo L. Black, Wiley B. Rutledge,
Felix Frankfurter*

the United States House of Representatives. He
lost a race for the U.S. Senate in 1924, but a
second try in 1930 proved successful. During his
decade as a senator, Byrnes was an ardent supporter of the New Deal and a close advisor to
President Roosevelt. During the crisis occasioned
by Roosevelt's 1937 insightful plan, Byrnes's
advice was especially helpful: cognizant of the
coming Court realignment, Byrnes counseled the
president to wait, rather than to push for passage of his plan.

So important was Byrnes to Roosevelt that in
1940 there was speculation that he would be
named the president's running mate. Instead,
Roosevelt named him as James McReynolds's
replacement on the Court — even though the
announcement of the nomination was delayed
six months while Byrnes continued to act as a
presidential aide.

Byrnes's Supreme Court career was brief, lasting just over a year, during which he wrote only
16 majority opinions and no concurrences or dis-

sents. He was restive the entire 14 months, anxious to serve his country more directly during
wartime.

Even after assuming the bench, Byrnes continued to serve Roosevelt by preparing and promoting emergency war legislation. Finally,
Roosevelt requested that Byrnes step down in
order to help with the war effort. Immediately
after his resignation, he was appointed head of
the Economic Stabilization Board. The next year
he was appointed director of the War Mobilization
Board, where he became known as Roosevelt's
"assistant president." After Roosevelt's death,
Byrnes stayed on at Harry Truman's request as
secretary of state, but after two years he resigned
to return to South Carolina.

Byrnes practiced law again briefly, but in 1950
he reentered the political arena, easily winning
the governorship of his home state. He served
five years as a relatively progressive Southern
governor, supporting separate but equal educational facilities, but also working for legislative

suppression of the Ku Klux Klan. Pleading ill health, he resigned in 1955 but lived on another 17 years, during which he chronicled his eventful past in an autobiography titled *All in One Lifetime* (1958).

ROBERT HOUGHWOUT JACKSON

PERSONAL DATA

Born: February 13, 1892, in Spring Creek, Pennsylvania
Parents: William Eldred Jackson, Angelina Houghwout Jackson
Higher Education: Albany Law School, 1912
Bar Admission: New York, 1913
Political Party: Democrat
Marriage: April 24, 1916, to Irene Gerhardt, who bore Jackson one daughter and one son
Died: October 9, 1954, in Washington, D.C.
Buried: Maple Grove Cemetery, Frewsburg, New York

PROFESSIONAL CAREER

Occupations: Politician, 1912-1913; Lawyer, 1914-1941, 1945-1946; Government Official, 1920s, 1934-1941; Judge, 1941-1954
Official Positions: Democratic State Committeeman, New York, 1912-1913; President, Bar Association of Jamestown, New York, 1924; Corporation Counsel, Jamestown, New York, ca. 1920s; General Counsel, Internal Revenue Bureau, 1934-1936; Special Counsel, Securities and Exchange Commission, 1935; Assistant United States Attorney General, 1936-1938; United States Solicitor General, 1938-1939; United States Attorney General, 1940-1941; Associate Justice, United States Supreme Court, 1941-1954; Chief United States Prosecutor, Nuremberg War Crimes Trials, 1945-1946

SUPREME COURT SERVICE

Nominated: June 12, 1941
Nominated By: Franklin D. Roosevelt
Confirmed: July 7, 1941
Confirmation Vote: Voice vote
Oath Taken: July 11, 1941
Replaced: Harlan F. Stone
Significant Opinions: *Edwards v. California* (concur-

rence) (1941); *Wickard v. Filburn* (1942); *West Virginia State Board of Education v. Barnette* (1943); *Youngstown Sheet & Tube Co. v. Sawyer* (concurrence) (1952)
Left Court: Died October 9, 1954
Length of Service: 13 years, 2 months, 28 days
Replacement: John Marshall Harlan II

Robert H. Jackson was the descendant of farmers who settled in eastern Pennsylvania in the 18th century. When he was five, Jackson's family moved to Frewsburg in upstate New York, where his father soon owned a hotel and livery stable. Although he attended one year at Albany Law School, Jackson was the last Supreme Court justice to have prepared for the bar by reading law on his own.

Before actually beginning to practice law, Jackson entered public life as a state Democratic committeeman. He did not care much for politics, but this venture did introduce him to Franklin D. Roosevelt, a contact that would prove important for Jackson's future. An informal but vital relationship formed between the two while Roosevelt was serving as governor of New York from 1928 to 1932. When Roosevelt ran for president in 1932, Jackson campaigned actively for him, and after Roosevelt was established in Washington, D.C., he invited Jackson to join his administration. Jackson acted informally as a Roosevelt advisor while serving in a variety of roles, first in the Treasury Department and then at the Justice Department. In 1941 Roosevelt nominated Harlan F. Stone to succeed retiring Chief Justice Charles E. Hughes and replaced Stone with Jackson.

Roosevelt clearly expected that while on the Court Jackson would align himself with New Deal liberals such as William O. Douglas. Instead, Jackson's judicial stance came to resemble most closely that of Felix Frankfurter, another Roosevelt appointee whose conservative orientation on the Court came as a surprise. While he did support New Deal legislation in cases like *Wickard v. Filburn* (1942), and write convincingly about First Amendment freedoms in cases like *West Virginia State Board of Education v. Barnette* (1943), Jackson tempered his liberalism in the wake of World War II.

One experience that doubtless helped to reshape Jackson's judicial philosophy was his service in 1945 and 1946 as the chief United States prosecutor at the Nuremberg war crimes tribunals, a role he took on at President Truman's request. At Nuremberg he developed the theory that because they had planned and carried out an aggressive and destructive war, the Nazi leaders could be tried for crimes against humanity. The theory was a reflection of his new thinking about the need for order in society, and with it he gained criminal convictions of the Nazis.

Jackson returned to the Court in the fall of 1946 after Chief Justice Stone's death. His name and that of Hugo Black were being circulated as possible candidates to head the next Court. It was reported that two justices threatened to resign if Jackson was appointed, and Jackson made the public controversy worse by releasing a letter addressed to the president in which he reproached Justice Black for not *recusing himself from a case argued by Black's former law partner. Ultimately, both Jackson and Black threatened to leave if the other was appointed, and President Truman turned to an outsider, Fred M. Vinson. Jackson continued to serve on the Court until his death in 1954.

WILEY BLOUNT RUTLEDGE JR.

PERSONAL DATA

Born: July 20, 1894, in Cloverport, Kentucky
Parents: Wiley Blount Rutledge, Mary Lou Wigginton Rutledge
Higher Education: Maryville College, Tennessee, 1910-1912; University of Wisconsin (B.A., 1914); Indiana Law School, 1914-1915; University of Colorado Law School (LL.B. 1922)
Bar Admission: Colorado, 1922
Political Party: Democrat
Marriage: August 28, 1917, to Annabel Person, who bore Rutledge two daughters and one son
Died: September 10, 1949 in York, Maine
Buried: Green Mountain Cemetery, Boulder, Colorado

PROFESSIONAL CAREER

Occupations: Educator, 1914-1915, 1917-1922, 1924-1939; Lawyer, 1922-1924; Judge, 1939-1949
Official Positions: Associate Professor, University of Colorado Law School, 1924-1926; Professor, Washington University Law School, 1926-1930; Dean, University of Colorado Law School, 1930-1935; Dean, State University of Iowa Law School, 1935-1939; Judge, United States Court of Appeals for the District of Columbia, 1939-1943; Associate Justice, United States Supreme Court, 1943-1949

SUPREME COURT SERVICE

Nominated: January 11, 1943
Nominated By: Franklin D. Roosevelt
Confirmed: February 8, 1943
Confirmation Vote: Voice vote
Oath Taken: February 15, 1943
Replaced: James F. Byrnes
Significant Opinions: None
Left Court: Died September 10, 1949
Length of Service: 6 years, 6 months, 26 days
Replacement: Sherman Minton

Because his father was an itinerant Baptist minister and his mother a tubercular in search of health, as a child Wiley Rutledge moved constantly with his family. When he was nine, his mother died, and his father moved the family to Maryville, Tennessee, where Rutledge began his college education in 1910. In his junior year he transferred from Maryville College to the University of Wisconsin, from which he graduated with a B.A. degree in 1914.

Rutledge took a job teaching high school while he attended Indiana Law School in the evenings. In 1915, however, he was diagnosed as suffering from tuberculosis and entered a sanatorium in Asheville, North Carolina. While at the sanatorium, he married Annabel Person, whom he had known at Maryville College. The couple then moved to New Mexico for reasons of Rutledge's health, and in Albuquerque he again took up high school teaching. He later continued his recuperation in Boulder, Colorado. He graduated with a law degree from the University of Colorado in 1922, seven years after he began his legal studies.

Rutledge joined a Boulder firm, where he practiced law for two years before returning to the academy. From 1924 to 1930, he taught law, first at the University of Colorado, then at Washington University in St. Louis, Missouri. In 1930 he became an administrator, serving as dean first at the University of Colorado and then at the State University of Iowa. Throughout the 1930s Rutledge was an outspoken critic of the Supreme Court's failure to support New Deal reforms, and when President Roosevelt introduced his court-packing plan in 1937, Rutledge supported it enthusiastically. This backing made him the subject of much public criticism, but it also brought him, in 1939, a presidential appointment to the prestigious District of Columbia Court of Appeals.

When Roosevelt elevated him to the Supreme Court in 1943, Rutledge was again criticized, this time for insufficient legal qualifications. As a liberal, a New Dealer, an academic, and a westerner, Rutledge, however, met the president's political requirements in light of the upcoming presidential election, and on February 15, 1943, he became Roosevelt's eighth and final Supreme Court appointee (excepting Roosevelt's elevation of Harlan F. Stone to chief justice).

On the Court, Rutledge quickly aligned himself with the liberal voting bloc consisting of Justices Hugo Black, William O. Douglas, and Frank Murphy. During his six years of service he wrote 171 opinions, including concurrences and dissents, the most significant of which concerned civil liberties, as well as more specialized matters such as administrative law, procedure, labor law, and taxation. He died in 1949, still a member of the Court.

HAROLD HITZ BURTON

PERSONAL DATA

Born: June 22, 1888, in Jamaica Plain, Massachusetts
Parents: Alfred E. Burton, Gertrude Hitz Burton
Higher Education: Bowdoin College (B.A. summa cum laude, 1909); Harvard Law School (LL.B., 1912)
Bar Admissions: Ohio, 1912; Utah, 1914
Political Party: Republican
Marriage: June 15, 1912, to Selma Florence Smith,

who bore Burton two daughters and two sons
Died: October 28, 1964, in Washington, D.C.
Buried: Highland Park Cemetery, Cleveland, Ohio

PROFESSIONAL CAREER

Occupations: Lawyer, 1912-1914, 1917, 1919-1934; Businessman, 1914-1916; Serviceman, 1917-1918; Politician, 1929-1932, 1935-1945; Judge, 1945-1958
Official Positions: Member, Ohio House of Representatives, 1929; Director of Law, Cleveland, Ohio, 1929-1932; Acting Mayor, Cleveland, 1931-1932; Mayor, Cleveland, 1935-1941; Member, United States Senate, 1941-1945; Associate Justice, United States Supreme Court, 1945-1958

SUPREME COURT SERVICE

Nominated: September 18, 1945
Nominated By: Harry S. Truman
Confirmed: September 19, 1945
Confirmation Vote: Voice vote
Oath Taken: October 1, 1945
Replaced: Owen J. Roberts
Significant Opinion: *Joint Anti-Fascist Refugee Committee v. McGrath* (1951)
Left Court: Retired October 13, 1958
Length of Service: 13 years, 12 days
Replacement: Potter Stewart

After an accomplished, but unremarkable, education on the East Coast, where he grew up, Harold Burton decided after passing the bar in 1912 that his prospects for setting up a legal practice would be better in the West. That year he moved to Cleveland, Ohio, with his new wife.

In Cleveland, Burton did indeed prosper, developing his own successful law practice. From 1914 to 1917, he worked for two utility companies, one in Utah and one in Idaho. When the United States entered World War I, he interrupted his progress to enter the Army, where he rose to the rank of captain and received a Purple Heart.

After the war, Burton returned to Cleveland, where he entered politics, first as a member of the state legislature, then as the chief legal officer and acting mayor of Cleveland. In 1935, running on an anti-corruption platform, he was elected mayor in his own right. Reelected twice by the largest majorities in the city's history, he resigned in 1941 to take a seat in the United States Senate.

In the Senate, Burton supported the United Nations, sponsoring a resolution urging United States participation in the international body. He also worked closely with future President Harry Truman's committee investigating fraudulent wartime defense contracts. After Truman became president and Justice Roberts resigned, the Democratic Truman came under heavy pressure to nominate someone from the Republican Party to the Court, where Chief Justice Stone was the only sitting Republican. Truman turned to a known quantity, Harold Burton.

Burton was not as loyal as Truman might have expected him to be, voting against the administration in such cases as *Youngstown Sheet & Tube Co. v. Sawyer* (1952) on grounds that the president had exceeded his constitutional authority in seizing private steel mills. For the most part, Burton hewed to a moderate course, liberal on social matters and conservative on economic ones. Like most of Truman's other appointees, he tended to vote with the bloc led by Felix Frankfurter, who advocated *judicial restraint and eschewed, for the most part, special treatment of civil liberties issues. Never an intellectual leader of the Court, Burton was nevertheless one of its hardest working members. His diligence and attention to detail made him popular with his fellow justices and their clerks who, in 1954, voted Burton their choice to preside should they ever be on trial.

After Earl Warren assumed the chief justiceship and the Court's orientation grew increasingly more liberal, Burton became a member of a dissenting minority. In 1958, suffering the debilitating effects of Parkinson's disease, Justice Burton retired. He died six years later.

SIGNIFICANT CASES

EDWARDS V. CALIFORNIA

Citation: 314 U.S. 160 (1941)
Argued: April 28, 1941; reargued October 21, 1941
Decided: November 24, 1941

Court Below: California Superior Court for Yuba County
Basis for Review: Appeal
Facts: The so-called California "Okie Law," passed during the Depression when many poor Oklahoma residents were displaced from the dust bowl, prohibited anyone from bringing into the state any nonresident individual who was indigent.
Issue: Does the California statute violate a constitutionally protected right to travel?
Outcome: The Stone Court found that transportation of persons constituted commerce within the meaning of the *Commerce Clause and that the statute constituted an impermissible interference with interstate commerce.
Vote: 9-0
Participating: Stone, Roberts, Black, Reed, Frankfurter, Douglas, Murphy, Byrnes, Jackson
Opinions: Byrnes for the Court; Douglas, joined by Black and Murphy, and Jackson, concurring
Significance: *Edwards* would have a two-fold effect on the evolution of civil rights law. First, it strengthened the constitutional right to travel, which would later be the basis for several landmark civil rights cases. Second, Justice Jackson's concurrence, arguing that the possession of property cannot be a precondition to a person's rights as a citizen, prefigured subsequent Court decisions outlawing statutes that discriminated against the poor.

CHAPLINSKY V. NEW HAMPSHIRE

Citation: 315 U.S. 568 (1942)
Argued: February 5, 1942
Decided: March 9, 1942
Court Below: New Hampshire Supreme Court
Basis for Review: Appeal
Facts: Chaplinsky's distribution of Jehovah's Witnesses pamphlets was interrupted by a city marshal, whom Chaplinsky called a "racketeer" and a "Fascist." Chaplinsky was then convicted under a state law prohibiting the use of offensive and derisive speech in public.
Issue: Does the statute's prohibition of certain types of public speech run afoul of First Amendment guarantees?
Outcome: Reasoning that the Constitution does

not protect certain "well-defined and narrowly limited" types of speech, the Court upheld the statute and Chaplinsky's conviction.

Vote: 9-0

Participating: Stone, Roberts, Black, Reed, Frankfurter, Douglas, Murphy, Byrnes, Jackson

Opinion: Murphy for the Court

Significance: *Chaplinsky* introduced a two-tiered theory of the First Amendment that placed "fighting words," such as those used by Chaplinsky, as well as lewd, obscene, profane, and libelous language — types of speech ostensibly lacking any redeeming social value — outside the protection of the First Amendment. Although the decision has not been overruled, it has been considerably weakened by subsequent cases, some of which found constitutional protection even for verbal assaults on police officers. *Chaplinsky* is in fact the last Supreme Court case upholding a conviction for the use of fighting words against a public official.

BETTS V. BRADY

Citation: 316 U.S. 455 (1942)

Argued: April 13-14, 1942

Decided: June 1, 1942

Court Below: Maryland Court of Appeals

Basis for Review: *Writ of certiorari

Facts: *Indicted for robbery, the indigent Betts asked that the court appoint counsel to represent him at trial. His request was refused, and he represented himself, only to be convicted. His petitions for *habeas corpus were refused by the lower courts.

Issue: Does the state court's refusal to appoint counsel in noncapital *felony cases violate Sixth Amendment rights *incorporated into the Fourteenth Amendment?

Outcome: Distinguishing Betts's case from that of the defendants in the first of the *Scottsboro Boys* cases, *Powell v. Alabama* (1932), which involved a *capital offense, the Court declined to extend the right of legal counsel here.

Vote: 6-3

Participating: Stone, Roberts, Black, Reed, Frankfurter, Douglas, Murphy, Byrnes, Jackson

Opinions: Roberts for the Court; Black, joined by Douglas and Murphy, dissenting

Significance: *Betts* would ultimately be overruled by *Gideon v. Wainwright* (1963), which adopted the minority view expressed here that the constitutional right to counsel in noncapital felony cases should apply in both federal and state court.

SKINNER V. OKLAHOMA

Citation: 316 U.S. 535 (1942)

Argued: May 6, 1942

Decided: June 1, 1942

Court Below: Oklahoma Supreme Court

Basis for Review: *Writ of certiorari

Facts: Skinner, who had been convicted once for stealing chickens and twice for armed robbery, was ordered sterilized under the Oklahoma Criminal Sterilization Act.

Issue: Does the Oklahoma statute violate the *Equal Protection Clause of the Fourteenth Amendment?

Outcome: Finding that the Oklahoma law distinguished among categories of individuals convicted for the same crime, the Court struck down the Oklahoma statute.

Vote: 9-0

Participating: Stone, Roberts, Black, Reed, Frankfurter, Douglas, Murphy, Byrnes, Jackson

Opinions: Douglas for the Court; Stone and Jackson concurring

Significance: Although it did not outlaw all sterilization laws, the Court held that when fundamental rights such as procreation are at stake, the state may intervene only when *strict scrutiny of those affected revealed no discrimination. The Oklahoma law, based on a eugenics theory positing the inheritability of criminal tendencies, was invalidated because it exempted repeat offenders convicted of embezzlement or various political crimes. Justice Douglas reasoned that there was no *rational basis to conclude that while a predisposition to rob could be handed down, the tendency to embezzle could not.

*EX PARTE QUIRIN

Citation: 317 U.S. 1 (1942)

Argued: July 29-30, 1942

Decided: July 31, 1942, *per curiam

Opinion Filed: October 29, 1942

Court Below: United States Court of Appeals for the District of Columbia

Basis for Review: *Writ of certiorari

Facts: In a special session called in July 1942, the Court summarily rejected petitions for *habeas corpus filed by eight Nazi saboteurs, arrested in the United States and convicted in a military tribunal for violating the uncodified international law of war. Six of those convicted were executed shortly thereafter, and several months later the Court issued its full opinion.

Issues: Does the president have authority to set up special military commissions to try war crimes? Are convictions handed down by such commissions subject to *judicial review?

Outcome: Although it found that military commissions are subject to judicial review, the Court upheld the saboteurs' convictions on grounds that the commission, which was properly authorized by the president's powers as commander in chief, congressional legislation, and the international *common law of war, acted within its *jurisdiction in handing down the convictions.

Vote: 8-0

Participating: Stone, Roberts, Black, Reed, Frankfurter, Douglas, Byrnes, Jackson (Murphy not participating)

Opinion: Stone for the Court

Significance: *Quirin* established the power of civil courts to review the findings of military tribunals. In it the Court distinguished *Ex parte Milligan* (1866), in which military trials in time of war were barred where civil courts were operating, on grounds that the accused anti-war conspirator Milligan was not an enemy agent.

WICKARD V. FILBURN

Citation: 317 U.S. 111 (1942)

Argued: May 4, 1942; reargued October 13, 1942

Decided: November 9, 1942

Court Below: United States District Court for the Southern District of Ohio

Basis for Review: Appeal

Facts: Roscoe C. Filburn, an Ohio farmer, was fined for producing, but not marketing, more wheat than was permitted under the Agricultural Adjustment Act of 1938 (AAA).

Issue: Should the act apply to wheat that does not leave the farm and therefore has no direct impact on interstate commerce?

Outcome: While Filburn exceeded the federal quota by only 239 bushels, he was among the multitude of producers who grew wheat for their own consumption, thereby contributing to the depression of farm prices. Finding that such excess production could be regulated under the *Commerce Clause, the Court upheld the AAA and Filburn's fine.

Vote: 8-0

Participating: Stone, Roberts, Black, Reed, Frankfurter, Douglas, Murphy, Jackson

Opinion: Jackson for the Court

Significance: *Wickard* was the highwater mark of the Court's extension of regulatory power under the Commerce Clause. Whereas some earlier Supreme Court decisions had declined to extend such power to production, and others disallowed regulation of intrastate commerce that did not directly burden interstate commerce, *Wickard* stands for the proposition that economic realities, not abstractions, should determine the reach of the commerce power.

MURDOCK V. PENNSYLVANIA

Citation: 319 U.S. 105 (1943)

Argued: March 10-11, 1943

Decided: May 3, 1943

Court Below: Pennsylvania Superior Court

Basis for Review: *Writ of certiorari

Facts: Murdock and others were cited for violating a city ordinance imposing a license fee on Jehovah's Witnesses who solicit door-to-door. Their convictions were affirmed by the state superior court.

Issue: Does the license fee violate First Amendment protection of the *free exercise of religion?

Outcome: Declaring that the ordinance "restrains in advance those constitutional liberties of press and religion and inevitably tends to suppress their exercise," the Court struck it down.

Vote: 5-4

Participating: Stone, Roberts, Black, Reed,

Frankfurter, Douglas, Murphy, Jackson, Rutledge
Opinions: Douglas for the Court; Reed, joined by Roberts, Frankfurter, and Jackson, and Frankfurter, joined by Jackson and Roberts, dissenting
Significance: By one vote the Court overruled its decision handed down just the previous year in *Jones v. Opelika,* in which the application of a similar license fee to Jehovah's Witnesses was upheld. *Murdock* came early in the Court's postwar expansion of "preferred liberties" protected by the First Amendment, and Douglas's references to *prior restraint indicate that the Court's attitude toward freedom of religion had not yet evolved to the point where it could be readily distinguished from *freedom of speech and freedom of the press.

WEST VIRGINIA STATE BOARD OF EDUCATION V. BARNETTE

Citation: 319 U.S. 624 (1943)
Argued: March 11, 1943
Decided: June 14, 1943
Court Below: United States District Court for the Southern District of West Virginia
Basis for Review: Appeal
Facts: In 1940, in *Minersville School District v. Gobitis,* the Supreme Court had found constitutional a law requiring that schoolchildren participate in a daily flag salute ceremony. The decision proved highly unpopular, and when Walter Barnette and other Jehovah's Witnesses brought suit to overturn it, the lower court found in their favor.
Issue: Does a law mandating participation in a flag salute ceremony, which violates the tenets of some religions, violate the First Amendment's protection of freedom of religion?
Outcome: Reasoning that the flag salute constitutes a form of speech which the government cannot compel its citizens to engage in, the Court overturned both the West Virginia statute and its previous ruling in *Gobitis.*
Vote: 6-3
Participating: Stone, Roberts, Black, Reed, Frankfurter, Douglas, Murphy, Jackson, Rutledge
Opinions: Jackson for the Court; Black, joined by Douglas, and Murphy, concurring; Frankfurter,

Roberts, and Reed dissenting (Reed without written opinion)
Significance: Patriotism, inflamed by the outbreak of World War II, clearly played a part in determining the outcome in *Gobitis.* By 1943 the composition of the Court had changed, owing to Roosevelt's appointments. Chief Justice Stone's lonely dissent in the earlier case now became the majority opinion. Justice Jackson, whom Stone assigned to write the opinion in *Barnette,* penned a statement about individual liberty which — although it relied on the *Free Speech Clause, rather than the *Free Exercise of the First Amendment for its rationale — remains one of the Court's most compelling arguments for religious freedom.

HIRABAYASHI V. UNITED STATES

Citation: 320 U.S. 81 (1943)
Argued: May 10-11, 1943
Decided: June 21, 1943
Court Below: United States Ninth Circuit Court of Appeals
Basis for Review: *Certification
Facts: Gordon Hirabayashi, an American-born citizen of Japanese ancestry living in the state of Washington, deliberately violated a curfew and a reporting requirement that had been placed on West Coast Japanese Americans. He was convicted on both counts and sentenced to concurrent three-month sentences.
Issue: Do the curfew and reporting requirements discriminate solely on the basis of race and thus violate the Fifth Amendment?
Outcome: Reasoning that the curfew was justified by the government's necessity to wage war successfully, the Court upheld Hirabyashi's conviction for violating that order. (Because Hirabayashi's sentences were to run concurrently, the Court did not consider the constitutionality of the reporting requirement.)
Vote: 9-0
Participating: Stone, Roberts, Black, Reed, Frankfurter, Douglas, Murphy, Jackson, Rutledge
Opinions: Stone for the Court; Douglas, Murphy, and Rutledge concurring
Significance: *Hirabayashi,* together with

Korematsu v. United States, decided the next year, marked the high point of wartime patriotic fervor and a low point in constitutional jurisprudence, in which severe infringements of civil liberties — based on race alone — were justified in the name of self-defense.

YAKUS V. UNITED STATES

Citation: 321 U.S. 414 (1944)
Argued: January 7, 1944
Decided: March 27, 1944
Court Below: United States First Circuit Court of Appeals
Basis for Review: *Writ of certiorari
Facts: The Emergency Price Control Act of 1942, a measure intended to hold down wartime inflation, was enforceable by the federal courts. However, by its terms, the rules promulgated by its regulatory body, the Office of Price Administration (OPA), were not *judicially reviewable. Albert Yakus, a Massachusetts meat dealer convicted of having violated the price limits on beef, challenged the jurisdiction of the OPA.
Issue: Does the act constitute an unconstitutional delegation of power to the executive branch?
Outcome: Finding that Congress had the power to extend such lawmaking authority to an administrative agency, and that review of regulations by the OPA and its special tribunal satisfied the demands of *due process, the Court upheld Yakus's conviction.
Vote: 6-3
Participating: Stone, Roberts, Black, Reed, Frankfurter, Douglas, Murphy, Jackson, Rutledge
Opinions: Stone for the Court; Rutledge, joined by Murphy, and Roberts, dissenting (Roberts without written opinion)
Significance: Wartime necessity — in particular, the president's need to control allocation of resources — rather than a constitutionally sanctioned delegation of authority, explain the outcome of *Yakus*, in which the administration was given unprecedented power over private property.

SMITH V. ALLWRIGHT

Citation: 321 U.S. 649 (1944)
Argued: November 10-12, 1943; reargued January 12, 1944
Decided: April 3, 1944
Court Below: United States Fifth Circuit Court of Appeals
Basis for Review: *Writ of certiorari
Facts: Since Reconstruction, the Texas Democratic Party had used a variety of means to exclude African American citizens from voting in primary elections. A series of Supreme Court cases had found most of these means unconstitutional, and in *United States v. Classic* (1941), the Court held that Congress could regulate primary as well as general elections for federal office. The National Association for the Advancement of Colored People then backed Smith in his suit alleging that because of his race he had been denied a ballot in a primary election by Texas Democratic Party officials.
Issue: Do actions of a political party to bar African Americans from voting in primary elections that include candidates for federal office constitute *state action violating the Fifteenth Amendment's ban on discrimination in voting procedures?
Outcome: Reasoning that because party primaries are a part of state election procedures, they are not purely private in nature, the Court overruled its decision in *Grovey v. Townsend* (1935), which held such primaries to be beyond the reach of the Constitution.
Vote: 8-1
Participating: Stone, Roberts, Black, Reed, Frankfurter, Douglas, Murphy, Jackson, Rutledge
Opinions: Reed for the Court; Frankfurter concurring (without written opinion); Roberts dissenting
Significance: With *Allwright*, the Court originated the "public function" concept stipulating that certain government-related activities, such as elections, are inherently state action and therefore subject to constitutional limitations. This concept was the foundation of later civil rights advances in such areas as school desegregation and *reapportionment of political districts. Discrimination in voting procedures continued, taking such forms as literacy tests and poll taxes,

but even these barriers were overcome with the passage of various civil rights acts in the 1950s and 1960s, together with the Voting Rights Act of 1965 and ratification in 1964 of the Twenty-Fourth Amendment, which abolished poll taxes.

UNITED STATES V. SOUTH-EASTERN UNDERWRITERS ASSOCIATION

Citation: 322 U.S. 533 (1944)
Argued: January 11, 1944
Decided: June 5, 1944
Court Below: United States District Court for the Northern District of Georgia
Basis for Review: Appeal
Facts: The Justice Department sued the South-Eastern Underwriters Association, charging it with fixing the prices of premiums for fire insurance in violation of the Sherman Antitrust Act.
Issue: Do insurance policies issued to out-of-state holders constitute interstate commerce subject to federal regulation?
Outcome: Overruling a long line of cases holding that purely financial and contractual transactions like insurance are not commerce, the Court declared South-Eastern's actions subject to the Sherman Act.
Vote: 4-3
Participating: Stone, Black, Frankfurter, Douglas, Murphy, Jackson, Rutledge (Roberts and Reed not participating)
Opinions: Black for the Court; Stone and Frankfurter dissenting; Jackson dissenting in part
Significance: By the time that *South-Eastern Underwriters* overruled *Paul v. Virginia* (1869), state regulation of insurance was so entrenched that Congress responded by immediately passing the McCarran Act, explicitly granting states authority over the insurance industry.

KOREMATSU V. UNITED STATES

Citation: 323 U.S. 214 (1944)
Argued: October 11-12, 1944
Decided: December 18, 1944
Court Below: United States Ninth Circuit Court of Appeals
Basis for Review: *Writ of certiorari
Facts: After the attack on Pearl Harbor, the military ordered Japanese Americans away from the West Coast and, in addition, prevented them from relocating. In effect, the orders forced the majority of this segment of American society to report to assembly centers, from which they were then shipped to government internment camps set up away from the West Coast. Fred Korematsu, an American-born descendant of Japanese immigrants, disobeyed the orders by moving from the San Francisco Bay area to a nearby town, changing his name, and undergoing facial surgery in order to make the claim that he was Mexican American. He was arrested, convicted, paroled, and sent to a relocation camp in Utah.
Issue: Are the orders regarding Japanese Americans justified by wartime military necessity?
Outcome: Although Justice Black did not address the constitutionality of the relocation camps, his majority opinion upheld the military orders to be valid exercises of the war powers granted Congress and the president.
Vote: 6-3
Participating: Stone, Roberts, Black, Reed, Frankfurter, Douglas, Murphy, Jackson, Rutledge
Opinions: Black for the Court; Frankfurter concurring; Roberts, Murphy, and Jackson dissenting
Significance: *Korematsu* is remembered in part for Justice Black's statement that, "all legal restrictions which curtail the rights of a single racial group are immediately suspect." Still, it is the only case in Supreme Court history in which the Court, applying a "rigid scrutiny" test to a restriction based solely on race, upheld a restriction on civil liberties. In more recent times, *Korematsu* has been roundly denounced, though never overruled. In 1980 Congress authorized payments of $20,000 each to survivors of the internment camps.

MORGAN V. VIRGINIA

Citation: 328 U.S. 373 (1946)
Argued: March 27, 1946
Decided: June 3, 1946
Court Below: Virginia Supreme Court
Basis for Review: Appeal
Facts: When Irene Morgan, an African American woman, boarded a bus in Gloucester City, Virginia,

that was en route to Baltimore, Maryland, she was ordered to sit at the back of the bus, as Virginia law required. She refused, after which she was arrested, convicted, and fined ten dollars. The Virginia Supreme Court upheld her conviction.

Issue: Does the Virginia law requiring segregation of riders on interstate transport inhibit interstate commerce?

Outcome: Because it forced passengers on interstate transport constantly to reconfigure themselves in order to conform to the laws of various states, the statute constituted an impermissible burden on interstate commerce and was struck down.

Vote: 6-1

Participating: Black, Reed, Frankfurter, Douglas, Murphy, Rutledge, Burton (Jackson not participating)

Opinions: Reed for the Court; Rutledge, Black, and Frankfurter concurring (Rutledge without written opinion); Burton dissenting

Significance: *Morgan* was one of a series of cases brought by the National Association for the Advancement of Colored People (NAACP) after World War II challenging racial segregation in the South. Although segregation on buses certainly continued after *Morgan*, the case effectively overruled *Louisville, New Orleans & Texas Railway Co. v. Mississippi* (1890) and was an important step towards the NAACP's culminating victory in *Brown v. Board of Education* (1954).

UNITED STATES V. LOVETT

Citation: 328 U.S. 303 (1946)
Argued: May 3-6, 1946
Decided: June 3, 1946
Court Below: United States Court of Claims
Basis for Review: *Writ of certiorari
Facts: Because they had been found to be disloyal to the nation, Lovett and two other federal employees were specifically left out of a salary appropriations act passed by Congress.
Issue: Was the act an impermissible *bill of attainder prohibited by Article I of the Constitution?
Outcome: The act was struck down.
Vote: 7-0
Participating: Black, Reed, Frankfurter, Douglas,

Murphy, Rutledge, Burton (Jackson not participating)
Opinion: Black for the Court; Frankfurter, joined by Reed, concurring
Significance: A reflection of the mounting anti-Communist hysteria that characterized the late 1940s, *Lovett* marks one of only four times the Court has struck down statutes as bills of attainder, two of them dating from Reconstruction and one from around the same time as *Lovett*. While anti-Communist feelings raged on, the legacy of abuses surrounding the Revolutionary War, when American colonists were subjected to retroactive British legislation, provoked even stronger reactions. No further attempts were made to single out individuals in punitive laws.

COLEGROVE V. GREEN

Citation: 328 U.S. 549 (1946)
Argued: March 7 & 8, 1946
Decided: June 10, 1946
Court Below: Unitred States District Court for the Northern District of Illinois
Basis for Review: Appeal
Facts: Kenneth W. Colegrove sued Dwight H. Green, a member of the Primary Certifying Board of the State of Illinois, challenging the equality of congressional election districts, which had not been redrawn since 1901. The district court dismissed his case.
Issue: Are election districts subject to judicial *reapportionment?
Outcome: Declaring such issues to be *political questions to be resolved by state legislatures under congressional supervision, the Court affirmed the lower court's dismissal.
Vote: 4-3
Participating: Black, Reed, Frankfurter, Douglas, Murphy, Rutledge, Burton (Jackson not participating)
Opinions: Frankfurter for the court; Rutledge concurring; Black, joined by Douglas and Murphy, dissenting
Significance: *Colegrove* would be overruled by the Warren Court's momentous 1962 decision in *Baker v. Carr,* in which the court declared that *apportionment issues are subject to the

POLITICAL COMPOSITION
of the Stone Court

Justice & Total Term	Courts Served	Appointing President	Political Party
Harlan F. Stone (1925-1941) (As Chief Justice, 1941-1946)	Taft Hughes Stone	Coolidge F. D. Roosevelt	Republican
Owen J. Roberts (1930-1945)	Hughes Stone	Hoover	Republican
Hugo L. Black (1937-1971)	Hughes Stone Vinson Warren Burger	F. D. Roosevelt	Democrat
Stanley F. Reed (1938-1957)	Hughes Stone Vinson Warren	F. D. Roosevelt	Democrat
Felix Frankfurter (1939-1962)	Hughes Stone Vinson Warren	F. D. Roosevelt	Democrat
William O. Douglas (1939-1975)	Hughes Stone Vinson Warren Burger	F. D. Roosevelt	Democrat
Frank Murphy (1940-1949)	Hughes Stone Vinson	F. D. Roosevelt	Democrat
James F. Byrnes (1941-1942)	Stone	F. D. Roosevelt	Democrat
Robert H. Jackson (1941-1954)	Stone Vinson Warren	F. D. Roosevelt	Democrat
Wiley B. Rutledge (1943-1949)	Stone Vinson	F. D. Roosevelt	Democrat
Harold H. Burton (1945-1958)	Stone Vinson Warren	Truman	Republican

Fourteenth Amendment's *Equal Protection Clause and which began a reapportionment revolution overseen by the federal judiciary.

VOTING PATTERNS

Owing to the chief justice's management style — or lack of one — the Stone Court was one of the most contentious in Supreme Court history. Unlike his predecessor, Charles Evans Hughes, who had maintained a firm control over assertive and potentially antagonistic egos such as Justice Black's and Justice Frankfurter's, Stone permitted every man to have his full say. Consequently, judicial conferences to discuss and decide cases were interminable under Stone, and what should have been a homogenous group — mostly Democratic and almost entirely appointed by Franklin D. Roosevelt — frequently disintegrated into quarrelsomeness.

While the old rivalry between New Dealers and the conservative "Four Horsemen" was gone, the Stone Court did include two ideological camps, with the liberal wing led by Black and the conservatives led by Frankfurter. Because the liberals — Black, Douglas, Murphy, and Rutledge — could usually be counted on to vote together, the Stone Court continued the development of the *incorporation doctrine begun during Hughes's tenure, making the Bill of Rights applicable at the state level and fueling the expansion of civil liberties. Voting alliances typical of this development can be seen in *West Virginia State Board of Education v. Barnette* (1943), which overruled *Minersville School District v. Gobitis*, decided just three years earlier. Stone, the only dissenter in the earlier case, now was joined by Black, Douglas, Murphy, Jackson, and Rutledge in rejecting, on *free speech grounds, a law requiring Jehovah's Witness children to participate in school flag salute ceremonies.

Nonetheless, World War II overshadowed all else during the six years of the Stone Court, and patriotic feelings often made for strange bedfellows. Perhaps the strangest voting lineup occurred in *Korematsu v. United States* (1944), the case that legitimized concentration camps for Japanese Americans on U.S. soil. *Korematsu* was written by the then arch civil libertarian, Hugo Black. The majority also included Black's customary liberal voting partners Douglas and Rutledge, as well as the more moderate Justices Stone and Reed. Justice Frankfurter wrote a separate concurring opinion. Among the usual leftwing bloc, only Murphy spoke up in dissent, as did the usually more conservative Roberts and Jackson — the latter objecting not so much to the clear racial bias of the military orders resulting in the incarcerations as to the potential damage to constitutional *jurisprudence. In *Korematsu*, as in many other cases the Court decided between 1941 and 1946, *judicial activism took a back seat to endorsement of displays of executive power, perhaps in part because of a habit of backing Roosevelt's radical attempts to rescue the nation from the Depression, now transformed into a recognition of military necessity.

SPECIAL FEATURES OF THE STONE COURT

JACKSON V. BLACK

Disagreements between justices, though certainly not unheard of, are normally confined to the exceedingly secretive judicial conference room. In the waning days of the Stone Court, however, an ideological dispute developed into personal antagonism that was placed on public display.

In 1944 the Court was divided over whether the Fair Labor Standards Act of 1938, regulating minimum wages and maximum hours, should apply to the mining industry. Initially, a majority of the Court sided with the employer in *Jewell Ridge Coal Corp. v. Local No. 6167, United Mine Workers of America* (1945). Jackson was assigned to write the opinion of the Court. But Justice Reed changed sides, and the deciding vote rested with Black, whose former law partner represented the union. Despite Jackson's insistence, Black refused to *recuse himself from the case, and the new majority opinion was written by Justice Murphy.

Jackson retaliated by writing a dissenting opinion quoting remarks Black had made earlier while serving in the Senate which now apparently contradicted the outcome in *Jewell Ridge*. His enmity towards Black became overt, however, after Chief Justice Stone died while still serving on the Court. At the time, Jackson was in Nuremberg, Germany, acting as the United States prosecutor at the war crimes trial, and Black had temporarily assumed the chief justice's duties. Jackson, before whom Roosevelt had dangled the chief justiceship when appointing him in 1941, was convinced that Black was now trying to outmaneuver him. He reacted by sending a letter to Congress reiterating the controversy surrounding the *Jewell Ridge* case and by airing his brief against Black at a press conference. The controversy made headlines, and although Jackson and Black resumed an outwardly cordial relationship, their antagonism had at least temporarily dispelled the aura of impartiality that surrounded the Supreme Court. The effect on Jackson was more long-lived, undermining his effectiveness for the remainder of his time on the Court.

The Vinson Court 1946-1953

BACKGROUND

THE TRUMAN DOCTRINE AND THE MARSHALL PLAN

I n the months after the close of World War II, with Europe in ruins the Soviet Union began threatening Greece and Turkey. In February 1947 President Truman consulted with congressional leaders about the possibility of providing aid to Greece and Turkey. On March 12,

MEMBERS Of the Court 1946–1953

(In Order of Seniority)

Fred M. Vinson (Chief Justice)	(1946-1953)
Hugo L. Black	(1946-1953)
Stanley F. Reed	(1946-1953)
Felix Frankfurter	(1946-1953)
William O. Douglas	(1946-1953)
Frank Murphy (died)	(1946-1949)
Robert H. Jackson	(1946-1953)
Wiley B. Rutledge (died)	(1946-1949)
Harold H. Burton	(1946-1953)
Tom C. Clark (replaced Frank Murphy)	(1949-1953)
Sherman Minton (replaced Wiley B. Rutledge)	(1949-1953)

1947, he addressed a joint session of Congress where, before the media, he announced what would become the Truman Doctrine: "I believe that it must be the policy of the United States to support free peoples who are resisting attempted subjugation by armed minorities or by outside pressures." For the first time in its history, America would provide substantial foreign economic aid in time of peace.

With Communist parties winning some elections in France and Italy, it soon became apparent that an extension of this aid to the rest of Europe was inevitable. In a speech that June, Secretary of State George Marshall announced a proposed enlargement. The plan to rebuild Europe was offered to all its nations and was contingent upon them working together to formulate a coordinated relief program. When Britain and France objected to a Soviet proposal that each country draw up its own agenda, the U.S.S.R. withdrew from the plan.

A by-product of the Soviet withdrawal was the ease with which the Truman administration achieved congressional approval for its plan. As the president observed, the Truman Doctrine and the Marshall Plan were "two halves of the same walnut." Passage of the latter was clearly linked to Truman's — and America's — perception that the Communists were menacing Western Europe, and Soviet participation in any effort to rebuild economic stability there would almost certainly have doomed the Marshall Plan. Ultimately, $17 billion was appropriated and distributed among 16 Western European nations between 1948 and 1952.

An asterisk (*) before a word or phrase indicates that a definition will be found in the glossary at the end of this volume.

THE COLD WAR CONTINUES

The Truman administration adopted toward the Soviets what State Department expert George Kennan outlined in an influential 1947 article in *Foreign Affairs* magazine as a policy of containment. In the 1946 off-year elections, Republicans had gained control of Congress for the first time in 15 years and wasted no time before attacking the Democratic Truman administration for being soft on Communism. Soviet actions in Europe continued to fuel Republican charges. In August 1947 Soviet agents orchestrated the Hungarian elections to insure installation of a Communist government there. The following February, the Soviet mission to Czechoslovakia forced the resignation of the non-Communist premier and installed a puppet government of the U.S.S.R. And in June, the Soviets imposed an embargo on all traffic between Berlin, surrounded by the Soviet-controlled German zone, and the other German occupation zones controlled by the United States, Britain, and France.

Truman met this first cold war showdown not with force, but with the Berlin Airlift, which lasted from June 1948 to May 1949. At its height, the Airlift flew 13,000 tons of food, clothing, and fuel daily into the city from airfields in western Germany. Out of this success grew the North Atlantic Treaty Organization, a military alliance including the U.S., Canada, and ten Western European nations, as well as Truman's upset victory over Republican Thomas E. Dewey in the 1948 presidential election.

A NEW RED SCARE

Domestically, Truman countered charges of weakness in the face of the Communist threat by instituting a plan to root out internal subversion, ordering investigations of federal officeholders and authorizing the attorney general to create a list of subversive organizations. The Justice Department also obtained indictments in 1948 of members of the Central Committee of the American Communist Party, charging them under the Smith Act with conspiracy to overthrow the government. Although passed in 1940, the Smith Act, also known as the Alien Registration Act, had gone largely unenforced during World War II, when the Soviet Union was America's ally. Now, in the intense atmosphere of the cold war, Truman was able to employ the act as both a propaganda tool against the U.S.S.R. and a political weapon against domestic Communism.

Congress answered with a House Un-American Activities Committee (HUAC) investigation of Hollywood, which resulted in the incarceration for *contempt of Congress of ten individuals who refused to testify before the committee. Over three hundred others, blacklisted by studio executives as Communist sympathizers, were unable to find work in Hollywood for over a decade. In the summer of 1948, HUAC gained worldwide attention after Whittaker Chambers, an editor at *Time* magazine and a self-proclaimed former Soviet spy, testified that Alger Hiss, head of the Carnegie Endowment for Peace and a former State Department official, once had passed secret government documents to him. Owing in part to the efforts of Representative Richard M. Nixon, Hiss was ultimately tried, convicted of perjury, and sentenced to five years in prison.

Although the Palmer Raids of 1919 turned up no evidence of a Communist conspiracy in the U.S. following the Bolshevik Revolution, during the cold war spying on behalf of the Soviets did occur in the United States. Julius and Ethel Rosenberg, for example, were executed for atomic espionage in 1953 after British physicist Klaus Fuchs revealed that an international Communist spy ring had infiltrated the U.S. nuclear installation at Los Alamos, New Mexico. Soviet espionage was not, however, as pervasive as the American public was led to believe. The individual perhaps most responsible for intensifying the nation's concern about Communism was Wisconsin's Republican Senator Joseph McCarthy who, two days after the Fuchs admissions were made public, claimed that he had an extensive list of Communists who worked for the State Department. Over the next four years McCarthy's charges grew more and more outrageous, as he took on Secretaries of State George Marshall and

Fred M. Vinson

Dean Acheson, the Democratic Party, and even the U.S. Army. The hysteria he promoted probably would have faded sooner had it not been for the Communist victory in China and the ensuing Korean War.

THE FALL OF CHINA AND THE KOREAN WAR

In the years immediately following World War II, the Truman administration's focus was trained on Europe. Little attention was paid to the civil war raging in China between the Nationalist forces led by Chiang Kai-shek and the Communists, headed by Mao Tse-tung. When the Communists routed the Nationalists and Mao proclaimed the People's Republic of China in October 1949, America was taken aback. After a half century of defending an Open Door policy toward China, the United States felt it had a proprietary stake there, and strong bonds existed between the Nationalists and many congressional leaders. Under political pressure from the China lobby, the Truman administration refused to recognize Mao's government, with the result that in February 1950, the People's Republic threw its lot in with the Soviets, signing a treaty in Moscow.

The significance of the Sino-Soviet Pact became apparent almost immediately. On June 25, 1950, North Korean troops — probably on orders from Moscow, and certainly with support from the Soviets, who had created the North Korean government — invaded South Korea. Intelligence already had alerted the Truman administration to the probability of the attack, and the U.S. responded swiftly. On the same day the North Koreans crossed the border into South Korea, the United Nations Security Council (without the participation of the Soviet Union, then boycotting the U.N. for its failure to recognize the People's Republic of China) approved a resolution, prepared by the State Department, granting the United States broad powers in combating North Korean aggression. General Douglas MacArthur, overseeing the installation of a democratic postwar government in Japan, was then ordered to send American troops to Korea.

American forces, joined by troops from other United Nations member countries, pushed the North Koreans back across the 38th parallel, then proceeded, despite warnings from the Chinese, to attempt conquest of the entire Korean peninsula. As U.N. forces approached the Chinese border, they were attacked by masses of Chinese troops, who moved the line of battle back, once again, to the 38th parallel. There it remained for the next two and one-half years, while the terms of an armistice were negotiated. A truce, but not an actual peace treaty, signed in July 1953 recognized the reality of the stalemate by formalizing the opponents' positions as the border between the two Koreas.

THE ELECTION OF 1952

In 1951 the states ratified the Twenty-second Amendment, limiting presidents to two elected terms. The amendment also limited to one elected term presidents who had served in that office more than two years of the remaining term of the previously elected president. President Truman, who had served out most of Roosevelt's fourth term after Roosevelt died in 1945, and then had gone on to win the presidency in his own right in 1948, was exempted from the provisions of the

JUDICIAL BIOGRAPHY
Frederick Moore Vinson

PERSONAL DATA
Born: January 22, 1890, in Louisa, Kentucky
Parents: James Vinson, Virginia Ferguson Vinson
Higher Education: Centre College (B.A., 1909; LL.B., 1911)
Bar Admission: Kentucky, 1911
Political Party: Democrat
Marriage: January 24, 1923, to Roberta Dixson, who bore Vinson two sons
Died: September 8, 1953, in Washington, D.C.
Buried: Pinehill Cemetary, Louisa

PROFESSIONAL CAREER
Occupations: Lawyer, 1911-1924, 1929-1931; Government Official: ca. 1920, 1923-1924, 1943-1946; Politician, 1924-1929, 1931-1938; Judge, 1938-1943, 1946-1953
Official Positions: City Attorney, Louisa, Kentucky, ca. 1920; Kentucky Commonwealth Attorney, 32d Judicial District, 1923-1924; Member, United States House of Representatives, 1924-1929, 1931-1938; Judge, United States Court of Appeals for the District of Columbia, 1938-1943; Director, Office of Economic Stabilization, 1943-1945; Federal Loan Administrator, 1945; Director, Office of War Mobilization and Reconversion, 1945; Secretary, Department of the Treasury, 1945-1946; Chief Justice, United States Supreme Court, 1946-1953

SUPREME COURT CAREER
Nominated: June 6, 1946
Nominated By: Harry S. Truman
Confirmed: June 20, 1946
Confirmation Vote: Voice vote
Oath Taken: June 24, 1946
Replaced: Chief Justice Harlan F. Stone
Significant Opinions: *United States v. United Mine Workers* (1947); *Shelley v. Kraemer* (1948); *American Communications Association v. Douds* (1950); *Sweatt v. Painter* (1950); *McLaurin v. Oklahoma State Regents for Higher Education* (1950); *Kunz v. New York* (1951); *Feiner v. New York* (1951); *Dennis v. United States* (1951); *Rosenberg v. United States* (1953)
Left Court: Died September 8, 1953
Length of Service: 7 years, 2 months, 15 days
Replacement: Chief Justice Earl Warren

new amendment, but Truman declined to run. In April 1951 Truman had relieved General MacArthur of his command after the latter publicly sided with the Republicans against the Truman administration's decision to wage only a limited war against the Chinese in Korea. Outrage over the president's treatment of the American war hero, together with the public's continuing discomfort about the cold war, contributed to a deterioration of support for Truman's administration.

Instead, the nation turned to another war hero, Dwight D. Eisenhower, who chose as his running mate a leading anti-Communist, Richard M. Nixon, and who handily won both the Republican nomination and the election. In his inauguration address, Eisenhower painted the world in black and white terms and, over the next six years, his administration followed the hawkish philosophy of his secretary of state, John Foster Dulles: what had been a policy of containment toward the Soviets became one of brinkmanship.

VINSON'S EARLY LIFE

Fred M. Vinson was born into a poor family in Louisa, Kentucky, where his father worked as the local jail keeper. Vinson attended Centre College in Danville, Kentucky, where he excelled at sports and attained the best academic record in the history of the school. Going on to obtain a law degree at Centre, he then passed the state bar and, at the age of 21, began to practice law in his home town.

VINSON'S PUBLIC LIFE

Almost immediately, Vinson became interested in politics. Starting at the local level, he served briefly as city attorney for Louisa, then as district attorney for Kentucky's 32d judicial district. In 1923 he was elected to federal office as a Democrat, serving in the House of Representatives until 1929. He was defeated for reelection in the 1928 Republican landslide, but in 1931 he returned to Congress, where he served eight more years. During this period he became an important member of the influential House Ways and Means Committee, an outspoken supporter of President Franklin D. Roosevelt, and a friend of then Senator Harry S. Truman.

Roosevelt, grateful for Vinson's backing of his 1937 court-packing plan and his help in developing several New Deal programs, appointed him in 1938 to the prestigious federal Court of Appeals for the District of Columbia. On the bench, Vinson continued to back the administration, and in 1943, Roosevelt made him part of the administration. Starting as director of the Office of Economic Stabilization, Vinson became, in rapid succession, the Federal Loan Administrator, the head of the Office of War Mobilization and Reconversion, and finally, in 1945, President Truman's secretary of the Treasury.

VINSON AS CHIEF JUSTICE

So impressed was Truman with Vinson's administrative ability that upon the death of Chief Justice Harlan F. Stone in 1946, the president turned to Vinson as the best antidote to the internecine warfare over succession that had developed among the associate justices. But if Truman held Vinson in high esteem, Vinson's brethren on the Court did not. The new chief justice was regarded by his associate justices as deficient in both education and experience — and he was considered lazy to boot. Criticized for having only a superficial grasp of issues that presented themselves at judicial conferences, he was also said to do his writing "with his hands in his pockets," letting his clerks do most of the work.

Vinson, for his part, felt that overwork contributed to some justices' early deaths, and to combat the Court's increasingly heavy workload, he appointed additional clerks and cut the *docket back to mid-19th-century proportions. Where the Hughes Court had decided about two hundred cases per year, the Vinson Court averaged half that many. Critics contended that many significant issues went unaddressed, but the narrowed scope of review exercised by the Court under Vinson reflected its leader's conditioned support for strong government and limited conception of the Court's role. In Vinson's view, the Supreme Court should defer to the executive and legislative branches, deciding only cases of the utmost constitutional and national importance. Vinson remained true to this concept — and to the president who appointed him — throughout his tenure, voting against the majority in *Youngstown Sheet & Tube Co. v. Sawyer* (1952), which held that the president did not have inherent authority to seize private steel mills in order to forestall a labor strike during the Korean War.

One measure of Vinson's failings as a leader and unifier of the Court is, indeed, the number of dissents he filed. Vinson averaged 13 dissents per term, in comparison with Chief Justice Charles Evans Hughes's average of two. Prior to 1937, when the Hughes Court — owing in part to the threat posed by Roosevelt's court-packing plan — changed its posture halfway through Hughes's tenure, the Supreme Court had historically decided the vast majority of its cases (usually 85 percent) unanimously. During Vinson's first term only 36 percent of the Court's decisions were unanimous, and the number continued to drop until it reached a record low of 19 percent in 1952.

After 1949, however, Vinson's attitudes gained ascendancy, mostly because of personnel changes, rather than his own persuasiveness. That year liberal Justices Frank Murphy and Wiley B. Rutledge died and were replaced by Truman appointees Tom C. Clark and Sherman Minton, who shared the chief justice's notions of *judicial restraint. Even then, however, the role of intellectual leader passed from Hugo Black to Felix

Frankfurter, bypassing Vinson.

In one area of law, however, Vinson did help move the Court forward. Generally conservative on economic and civil liberties issues, Vinson was a progressive when it came to race relations, and he assigned himself opinions in many of the significant cases in this area that came before the Court between 1946 and 1953. In *Shelley v. Kraemer* (1948), for example, he declared for a unanimous Court that judicial enforcement of discriminatory *restrictive covenants was unconstitutional. And in two important cases handed down in 1950, *Sweatt v. Painter* and *McLaurin v. Oklahoma State Regents for Higher Education*, he edged the Court toward overturning the "separate but equal" doctrine of *Plessy v. Ferguson* (1896). Such cases as these paved the way for the landmark case, *Brown v. Board of Education* (1954), which was first argued in December 1952, but which, owing to internal divisions in the Vinson Court, was decided only after the Supreme Court had gained a new leader.

Truman, who had wanted to send Vinson to Moscow in 1948 to help ease the tensions of the cold war, reconfirmed his confidence in Vinson's capabilities in 1952, urging the chief justice to replace him as president. Vinson, however, declined to reenter the political arena. The next year he died suddenly of a heart attack, just months after the Eisenhower administration was installed in the White House.

ASSOCIATE JUSTICES

For biographies of Associate Justices **Hugo L. Black, Stanley F. Reed, Felix Frankfurter, William O. Douglas,** and **Frank Murphy,** see entries under **THE HUGHES COURT.** For biographies of Associate Justices **Robert H. Jackson, Wiley B. Rutledge,** and **Harold H. Burton,** see entries under **THE STONE COURT.**

TOM CAMPBELL CLARK

PERSONAL DATA

Born: September 23, 1899, in Dallas, Texas
Parents: William H. Clark, Jennie Falls Clark

Higher Education: Virginia Military Academy, 1917-1918; University of Texas (B.A., 1921; LL.B., 1922)
Bar Admission: Texas, 1922
Political Party: Democrat
Marriage: November 8, 1924, to Mary Jane Ramsey, who bore Clark one daughter and two sons
Died: June 13, 1977, in New York, New York
Buried: Restland Memorial Park, Dallas

PROFESSIONAL CAREER

Occupations: Serviceman, 1918; Lawyer, 1922-1949; Government Official, 1927-1932, 1937-1949; Judge, 1949-1977; Judicial Activist, ca. 1960-1970
Official Positions: Civil District Attorney, Dallas County, Texas, 1927-1932; Special Assistant, United States Department of Justice, 1937-1943; Assistant United States Attorney General, 1943-1945; United States Attorney General, 1945-1949; Associate Justice, United States Supreme Court, 1949-1967; Judge, Various Circuits of the United States Court of Appeals, 1967-1977; Director, Federal Judicial Center, 1968-1970

SUPREME COURT SERVICE

Nominated: August 2, 1949
Nominated By: Harry S. Truman
Confirmed: August 18, 1949
Confirmation Vote: 73-8
Oath Taken: August 24, 1949
Replaced: Frank Murphy
Significant Opinions: *Slochower v. Board of Education of New York* (1956); *Mapp v. Ohio* (1961); *Ker v. California* (1963); *Abington School District v. Schempp* (1963); *Heart of Atlanta Motel, Inc. v. United States* (1964); *Katzenbach v. McClung* (1964); *Sheppard v. Maxwell* (1966)
Left Court: Retired June 12, 1967
Length of Service: 17 years, 9 months, 19 days
Replaced By: Thurgood Marshall

Tom Clark was the son of a prominent Dallas lawyer active in Democratic politics. After brief service in the military and graduation from the University of Texas Law School, Clark, together with his brother, went to work at his father's law firm. His father's connections, as well as his own marriage in 1924 to the daughter of a Texas Supreme Court justice, and his friendship with

The Vinson Court, 1950. From left; Felix Frankfurter, Tom C. Clark, Hugo L. Black, Robert H. Jackson, Fred M. Vinson, Harold H. Burton, Stanley F. Reed, Sherman Minton, William O. Douglas

Tom Connolly, a powerful Texas congressman, helped Clark enter politics in 1929 as a civil district attorney for Dallas County.

After a brief hiatus, during which he returned to private practice, Clark reentered the political arena, this time joining the Roosevelt administration in 1937 as a special assistant in the Justice Department. Part of his job at the Justice Department during World War II was to assist in the relocation of Japanese Americans to internment camps and to investigate fraudulent war claims against the government, an assignment that put him in contact with then Senator Harry S. Truman. In 1943 he was promoted to assistant attorney general and was placed in charge of the Anti-Trust Division. He was then placed in charge of the Criminal Division. The next year he helped Truman secure the vice presidential nomination, and when Truman became president upon Roosevelt's death in 1945, Clark was promoted to attorney general.

As attorney general, Clark distinguished himself as an anti-Communist, promoting loyalty programs, drafting a list of subversive organizations, and prosecuting the American Communist Party. Such activities helped to combat allegations that the Truman administration was soft on Communism and, perhaps, helped Truman win his surprising upset victory over Thomas E. Dewey in 1948.

Truman rewarded Clark with an appointment to the Supreme Court after Justice Frank Murphy's death in 1949. Then Clark's hardline anti-Communist stance became a temporary liability, allowing liberal opponents to hold up his confirmation during three days of debate in the Senate. Afterward, however, he was confirmed by a vote of 73 to 8.

Once on the Court, Clark retained his interest in national security, often voting with the Vinson Court's conservative bloc. Under the more activist Earl Warren, he moved further to the right. Yet Clark is perhaps best characterized as an independent, first demonstrating his autonomy by voting against President Truman in the *Steel Seizure Case* in 1952, and later authoring such important cases as *Mapp v. Ohio* (1961), which established the *exclusionary rule for evidence obtained through unreasonable search and seizure, and *Abington School District v. Schempp* (1963), which outlawed religious practices in public schools.

Equally important is Clark's legacy as a judicial reformer. In 1967, after President Lyndon Johnson appointed Clark's son, Ramsey, as attorney general, Clark retired from the Court in order to avoid conflicts of interest. Even before leaving, he had begun a nationwide program to improve judicial efficiency, and in 1968 he helped found the Federal Judicial Center, where he served as the first director. From 1967 until his death ten years later, Clark also served by special arrangement on various federal *appellate courts as part of a plan to reduce their *dockets, a practice continued by other retired Supreme Court justices.

SHERMAN MINTON

PERSONAL DATA

Born: October 20, 1890, in Georgetown, Indiana
Parents: John Evan Minton, Emma Lyvers Minton
Higher Education: Indiana University (LL.B., first in class, 1915); Yale University (LL.M., 1917)
Bar Admission: Indiana, 1915
Political Party: Democrat
Marriage: August 11, 1917, to Gertrude Gurtz, who bore Minton two sons and one daughter
Died: April 9, 1965, in New Albany, Indiana
Buried: Holy Trinity Catholic Cemetery, New Albany

PROFESSIONAL CAREER

Occupations: Serviceman, 1917-1918; Lawyer, 1918-1935; Government Official, 1933-1934, 1941; Politician, 1935-1941; Judge, 1941-1956
Official Positions: State Public Counselor, Indiana, 1933-1934; Member, United States Senate, 1935-1941; Presidential Administrative Assistant, 1941; Judge, United States Seventh Circuit Court of

Appeals, 1941-1949; Associate Justice, United States Supreme Court, 1949-1956

SUPREME COURT SERVICE

Nominated: September 15, 1949
Nominated By: Harry S. Truman
Confirmed: October 4, 1949
Confirmation Vote: 48-16
Oath Taken: October 12, 1949
Replaced: Wiley B. Rutledge
Significant Opinions: None
Left Court: Retired October 15, 1956
Length of Service: 7 years, 3 days
Replaced By: William J. Brennan Jr.

Born on a farm in rural Indiana, Sherman Minton attended Indiana University, where he excelled in both athletics and academics, graduating at the top of his class in the university law college. His achievements won him a scholarship to attend Yale University for a year of graduate legal studies.

After practicing law quietly for several years, Minton was appointed counselor for the Indiana Public Service Commission by a former Indiana University classmate, Governor Paul V. McNutt. Together, Minton and McNutt helped to implement a statewide version of President Roosevelt's New Deal, which helped Indiana through the Depression. Growing public recognition won Minton a Senate seat in 1935. In the Senate, Minton rose to the rank of assistant Democratic whip, supporting Roosevelt's legislative agenda and court-packing plan and becoming a fast friend of then Senator Harry S. Truman.

A Republican sweep of Indiana in the wake of native son Wendell Wilkie's presidential bid resulted in Minton's loss of his Senate seat in 1940. In 1941 Minton was planning to return to private practice in Indiana when President Roosevelt summoned him to the White House to act as his administrative assistant in charge of coordinating military agencies. That same year Roosevelt named Minton to a vacancy on the Seventh Circuit Court of Appeals.

Minton seemed to have a gift for friendship, which paid off once again when Truman nominated him in 1949 to succeed Wiley B. Rutledge on the Supreme Court. Minton took an unusual attitude toward the confirmation process, declining to testify before the Senate Judiciary Committee on grounds that to do so would be inappropriate for a sitting federal judge. Although Senate Republicans attempted to have his nomination recommitted, Minton was confirmed by a vote of 48 to 16.

On the Court Minton evinced the support for strong government he had espoused as a New Dealer. In the cold war era this made him a conservative on the Vinson Court, where he consistently voted with the bloc consisting of Justices Reed, Frankfurter, and Jackson, together with the other Truman appointees, Vinson, Burton, and Clark. Minton, perhaps less resourceful than many of his brethren, not only consistently favored the government's efforts to suppress dissent during the era of anti-Communist hysteria, but was also one of only three members of the Court to dissent from the majority's invalidation of Truman's seizure of the steel industry in *Youngstown Sheet & Tube Co. v. Sawyer* (1952). Afflicted for many years with pernicious anemia, Minton retired from the Court in 1956. He died eight years later.

SIGNIFICANT CASES

BALLARD V. UNITED STATES

Citation: 329 U.S. 187 (1946)
Argued: October 5, 1946
Decided: December 9, 1946
Court Below: United States Ninth Circuit Court of Appeals
Basis for Review: *Writ of certiorari
Facts: Edna W. Ballard was convicted of mail fraud in federal court in California after a trial before a jury consisting solely of men. Although California considered women eligible as jurors, in fact they were never called. Federal law at the time required federal courts to follow the practice of the states in which they were located.
Issue: Does the jury selection process followed by federal courts in California violate the aim of federal court statutes of having accused persons

tried by a representative cross-section of their communities?
Outcome: Reasoning that because California law considered women eligible jurors, they were a part of the community from which federal courts sitting in that state should draw its juries, the Court reversed Ballard's conviction.
Vote: 5-4
Participating: Vinson, Black, Reed, Frankfurter, Douglas, Murphy, Jackson, Rutledge, Burton
Opinions: Douglas for the Court; Jackson concurring in the result; Frankfurter, joined by Vinson, Jackson, and Burton, dissenting
Significance: Although *Ballard* turned on the Court's interpretation of federal statutes, it paved the way for the Supreme Court's decision in *Taylor v. Louisiana* (1975) that the Sixth Amendment requires juries in federal criminal trials to be truly representative of the accused individuals' communities.

EVERSON V. BOARD OF EDUCATION OF EWING TOWNSHIP

Citation: 330 U.S. 1 (1947)
Argued: November 20, 1946
Decided: February 10, 1947
Court Below: New Jersey Court of Appeals
Basis for Review: Appeal
Facts: A New Jersey statute authorized reimbursement by school boards of parents' costs of transporting their children to schools, including parochial schools. As a taxpayer involuntarily obliged to support the reimbursements, Arch Everson challenged the law.
Issue: Does the New Jersey statute violate the *Establishment Clause of the First Amendment mandating separation of church and state?
Outcome: Reasoning that the statute benefitted parents, not church-affiliated schools, the Court upheld its constitutionality.
Vote: 5-4
Participating: Vinson, Black, Reed, Frankfurter, Douglas, Murphy, Jackson, Rutledge, Burton
Opinions: Black for the Court; Jackson, joined by Frankfurter, dissenting; and Rutledge, joined by Jackson and Burton, dissenting
Significance: *Everson* was the first case in which

the Court found that the Fourteenth Amendment made the religion clauses of the First Amendment applicable at the state level. Although finding that New Jersey had not breached the separation between church and state, Justice Black's opinion went to great lengths to explain the tradition and reasoning behind the constitutional ban on government support of religion.

UNITED PUBLIC WORKERS V. MITCHELL

Citation: 330 U.S. 75 (1947)
Argued: December 3, 1945; reargued October 17, 1946
Decided: February 10, 1947
Court Below: United States District Court for the District of Columbia
Basis for Review: Appeal
Facts: The 1940 Hatch Act barred executive branch employees from taking part in most political activities. Some of those affected asked the Supreme Court for a *declaratory judgment ruling the act unconstitutional.
Issue: Do the restrictions of the Hatch Act violate First Amendment *free speech guarantees?
Outcome: Balancing free speech rights against the government's interest in maintaining an atmosphere of impartiality, the Court upheld the Hatch Act.
Vote: 4-3
Participating: Vinson, Black, Reed, Frankfurter, Douglas, Rutledge, Burton (Murphy and Jackson not participating)
Opinions: Reed for the Court; Rutledge dissenting in part (without written opinion); Frankfurter concurring; Black dissenting; Douglas dissenting in part
Significance: While accepting that free speech rights are fundamental, Justice Reed's opinion for the Court nonetheless declared that they are not absolute, but subject to tests balancing them against other, competing interests.

UNITED STATES V. UNITED MINE WORKERS

Citation: 330 U.S. 258 (1947)
Argued: January 14, 1947
Decided: March 6, 1947

Court Below: United States Court of Appeals for the District of Columbia
Basis for Review: *Writ of certiorari
Facts: Proclaiming the necessity of continued coal production during the postwar transition period, President Truman took control of the nation's coal mines on May 21, 1946, after the United Mine Workers went on strike to protest a breakdown in contract negotiations. When the union refused to go back to work, the government obtained an *injunction prohibiting the work stoppage. When even this tactic failed, the union was declared in *contempt of court and fined, as was its leader, John L. Lewis.
Issue: Does the Norris-LaGuardia Act of 1932 prevent federal courts from enjoining labor strikes?
Outcome: Finding that the act does not pertain to situations where the government is the employer, the Court upheld the convictions and fines against Lewis and his union.
Vote: 7-2
Participating: Vinson, Black, Reed, Frankfurter, Douglas, Murphy, Jackson, Rutledge, Burton
Opinions: Vinson for the Court; Jackson (without written opinion) and Frankfurter concurring in the outcome; Black and Douglas concurring in part and dissenting in part; Murphy dissenting; and Rutledge, joined by Murphy, dissenting
Significance: This decision, which met with wide public acceptance, resulted in the passage in 1947 of the Taft-Hartley Act, reducing the latitude granted labor during the New Deal era.

ADAMSON V. CALIFORNIA

Citation: 332 U.S. 46 (1947)
Argued: January 15-16, 1947
Decided: June 23, 1947
Court Below: California Supreme Court
Basis for Review: Appeal
Facts: The prosecutor in a California state criminal trial of Adamson for murder in the first degree drew the jury's attention to the fact the defendant refused to testify.
Issue: Do such actions on the part of a state prosecutor violate the defendant's right not to incriminate himself, which is guaranteed by the Fifth Amendment?

Outcome: The conviction was upheld because, the Court reasoned, the Fourteenth Amendment does not make all rights embodied in the Bill of Rights applicable to the states, but only those "implicit in the concept of ordered liberty," as stated in *Palko v. Connecticut* (1937).

Vote: 5-4

Participating: Vinson, Black, Reed, Frankfurter, Douglas, Murphy, Jackson, Rutledge, Burton

Opinions: Reed for the Court; Frankfurter concurring; Murphy, joined by Rutledge, dissenting; and Black, joined by Douglas, dissenting

Significance: Justice Black's dissent argued for "total incorporation" of the Bill of Rights into the Fourteenth Amendment. The Court rejected this theory, and continues to do so, preferring instead to follow a philosophy of selective *incorporation of the first ten amendments. Nonetheless, the Court overruled *Adamson* in 1965 with *Griffin v. California*, and made nearly all of the Bill of Rights applicable to the states.

UNITED STATES V. CALIFORNIA

Citation: 332 U.S. 19 (1947)

Argued: March 13-14, 1947

Decided: June 23, 1947

Court Below: None

Basis for Review: *Original Supreme Court jurisdiction

Facts: The federal government sued California over ownership rights to tidelands adjacent to the state's coast and over the oil and gas deposits located there.

Issue: Do the states, as inheritors of claims originally laid by the 13 colonies, properly own their own coastal waters?

Outcome: Stating that the federal government had always owned these areas, even if it had never attempted to control them, the Court ruled against the state.

Vote: 6-2

Participating: Vinson, Black, Reed, Frankfurter, Douglas, Murphy, Rutledge, Burton (Jackson not participating)

Opinions: Black for the Court; Frankfurter and Reed dissenting

Significance: After the Court upheld this ruling in two subsequent cases, Congress passed the Submerged Lands Act in 1953, ceding control of the property at issue to the states.

ILLINOIS *EX REL. MCCOLLUM V. BOARD OF EDUCATION

Citation: 333 U.S. 203 (1948)

Argued: December 8, 1947

Decided: March 8, 1948

Court Below: Illinois Supreme Court

Basis for Review: Appeal

Facts: The Illinois Board of Education permitted students to receive religious instruction for 30 to 45 minutes per week. Instructors in such programs were not paid with public funds, and while students enrolled in the programs were required to attend, those who were not enrolled went elsewhere in the school.

Issue: Do the Illinois programs constitute state aid to religion in violation of the First Amendment?

Outcome: The Court declared that the state could not permit such programs to take place within school buildings.

Vote: 8-1

Participating: Vinson, Black, Reed, Frankfurter, Douglas, Murphy, Jackson, Rutledge, Burton

Opinions: Black for the Court; Jackson concurring; Reed dissenting

Significance: By coming out strongly against what Justice Reed called incidental aid to religion in this, one of the first decisions regarding the *Establishment Clause, the Court indicated that it regarded the barrier between church and state to be nearly impenetrable. This view was later modified by *Zorach v. Clausen* (1952).

SHELLEY V. KRAEMER

Citation: 334 U.S. 1 (1948)

Argued: January 15-16, 1948

Decided: May 3, 1948

Court Below: Missouri Supreme Court

Basis for Review: *Writ of certiorari

Facts: Kraemer sued Shelley to enforce a *restrictive covenant against property ownership or occupancy by African Americans. A judgment for the defendant was reversed in the state supreme court.

Issues: Does enforcement by state courts of restrictive covenants violate the *Equal Protection Clause of the Fourteenth Amendment? Does such enforcement by federal courts violate the *Due Process Clause of the Fifth Amendment?

Outcome: Labeling them purely private actions, the Court did not prohibit creation of such agreements, but it did rule out their judicial enforcement as impermissible *state action.

Vote: 6-0

Participating: Vinson, Black, Frankfurter, Douglas, Murphy, Burton (Reed, Jackson, and Rutledge not participating)

Opinion: Vinson for the Court

Significance: Although *Shelley* has frequently been criticized for displaying faulty logic (the point at which private action becomes attributed to the state was inadequately explained) and has seldom been cited as *precedent in subsequent civil right cases, its impact on the development of the civil rights struggle is undeniable. Restrictive racial covenants, which arose in the wake of the Supreme Court's ban on race-based zoning in *Buchanan v. Warley* (1917) and which were sanctioned by the Court in *Corrigan v. Buckley* (1926), were gaining in popularity. *Shelley* succeeded in making this form of segregation unenforceable in the courts.

TERMINIELLO V. CHICAGO

Citation: 337 U.S. 1 (1949)
Argued: February 1, 1949
Decided: May 16, 1949
Court Below: Illinois Supreme Court
Basis for Review: *Writ of certiorari
Facts: While Terminiello addressed a sympathetic audience inside a meeting hall, a hostile crowd, calling him an anti-Semite, gathered outside. Terminiello was himself arrested and convicted of breaching the peace. Illinois state courts upheld the conviction on grounds that Terminiello had used "fighting words" designed to provoke conflict.

Issue: Did Terminiello's use of inflammatory language constitute a clear and present danger justifying curtailment of his First Amendment right of *free speech?

Outcome: Finding that the trial court's defini-

tion of breach of peace was so broad as to include speech clearly protected by the First Amendment, the Court reversed Terminiello's conviction.

Vote: 5-4

Participating: Vinson, Black, Reed, Frankfurter, Douglas, Murphy, Jackson, Rutledge, Burton

Opinions: Douglas for the Court; Frankfurter, dissenting; Vinson, joined by Jackson and Burton, dissenting; and Jackson, joined by Burton, dissenting

Significance: Douglas's opinion was criticized for failing to address the constitutionality of political speech that is deliberately imbued with emotional and inflammatory rhetoric.

WOLF V. COLORADO

Citation: 338 U.S. 25 (1949)
Argued: October 19, 1948
Decided: June 27, 1949
Court Below: Colorado Supreme Court
Basis for Review: *Writ of certiorari
Facts: The Colorado Supreme Court affirmed Wolf's conviction for conspiracy to commit abortion, despite the claim that the evidence used against him was obtained through unreasonable search and seizure.

Issue: Is the Fourth Amendment's prohibition against unreasonable search and seizure *incorporated into the Fourteenth Amendment and therefore applicable to the states?

Outcome: The Court did find the Fourth Amendment applicable at the state level, but it declined to overturn Wolf's conviction, ruling that state judges are not obliged to disregard evidence produced by illegal searches.

Vote: 6-3

Participating: Vinson, Black, Reed, Frankfurter, Douglas, Murphy, Jackson, Rutledge, Burton

Opinions: Frankfurter for the Court; Black concurring; Rutledge, joined by Murphy, dissenting; Murphy, joined by Rutledge, dissenting; Douglas dissenting

Significance: The *exclusionary rule first outlined and applied at the federal level in *Weeks v. United States* (1914), would not be strictly applied to the states until *Wolf* was overruled by *Mapp v. Ohio* (1961).

AMERICAN COMMUNICATIONS ASSOCIATION V. DOUDS

Citation: 339 U.S. 382 (1950)
Argued: October 10-11, 1949
Decided: May 8, 1950
Court Below: United States District Court for the Southern District of New York
Basis for Review: *Writ of certiorari
Facts: Officers of the union challenged a requirement of the 1947 Taft-Hartley Act that union officials affirm in writing that they were not members or supporters of the Communist Party.
Issue: Does the Taft-Hartley requirement violate First Amendment protections of political speech?
Outcome: Basing its decision on Congress's *commerce power, the Court found that the nation's interest in preventing the political strikes it presumed Communists would wage outweighed the curtailment of union leaders' First Amendment rights.
Vote: 5-1
Participating: Vinson, Black, Reed, Frankfurter, Jackson, Burton (Douglas, Clark, and Minton not participating)
Opinions: Vinson for the Court; Frankfurter concurring in part; Jackson concurring and dissenting; Black dissenting
Significance: A remnant of the anti-Communist reaction of the cold war era, *Douds* has not been overturned, but its value as legal *precedent has been undermined by subsequent cases overturning the section of the Taft-Hartley Act at issue in the case.

SWEATT V. PAINTER

Citation: 339 U.S. 629 (1950)
Argued: April 4, 1950
Decided: June 5, 1950
Court Below: Texas Court of Civil Appeals
Basis for Review: *Writ of certiorari
Facts: Herman Marion Sweatt, an African American resident of Houston, was denied admission to the University of Texas Law School because of his race. In an effort to comply with *Missouri *ex rel. Gaines v. Canada* (1938), the state then attempted to set up a separate law school for African Americans.
Issue: Does the *Equal Protection Clause of the Fourteenth Amendment require Texas to admit Sweatt to its previously all-white state law school?
Outcome: Finding that the state could not possibly create a new law school for African Americans equal to the existing law school attended by white students, the Court found Texas in violation of the "separate but equal" standard established in *Plessy v. Ferguson* (1896).
Vote: 9-0
Participating: Vinson, Black, Reed, Frankfurter, Douglas, Jackson, Burton, Clark, Minton
Opinion: Vinson for the Court
Significance: While still adhering to the separate but equal doctrine of *Plessy*, the Court made it clear in *Sweatt* that this was an unobtainable standard in the field of education. Four years later, the Court would broaden this holding in *Brown v. Board of Education*, spelling the end of segregation.

MCLAURIN V. OKLAHOMA STATE REGENTS FOR HIGHER EDUCATION

Citation: 339 U.S. 637 (1950)
Argued: April 3-4, 1950
Decided: June 5, 1950
Court Below: United States District Court for the Western District of Oklahoma
Basis for Review: Appeal
Facts: George W. McLaurin, an African American and an Oklahoma citizen, applied for admission to the all-white graduate school of the state university in Norman, Oklahoma. After he was denied admission because of his race, he sought relief in federal district court, which ordered Oklahoma to admit him. Because the university required segregated instruction, however, McLaurin was forced to sit apart in all school facilities, including the library and the cafeteria. He returned to federal court, where it was held that the conditions of his education did not deny him *equal protection under the law, and eventually he appealed to the Supreme Court.
Issue: Does the state, in its separate treatment of McLaurin, violate the Fourteenth Amendment's

Equal Protection Clause?

Outcome: The Court ordered the university to end its de facto segregation of McLaurin from the rest of the student body.

Vote: 9-0

Participating: Vinson, Black, Reed, Frankfurter, Douglas, Jackson, Burton, Clark, Minton

Opinion: Vinson for the Court

Significance: Decided the same day as *Sweatt v. Painter, McLaurin* broadened the ruling in that case by declaring unequivocally that *McLaurin* must not only be admitted to the formerly all-white state university, but that once there he "must receive the same treatment at the hands of the state as students of other races."

KUNZ V. NEW YORK

Citation: 340 U.S. 290 (1951)

Argued: October 17, 1950

Decided: January 15, 1951

Court Below: New York Court of Appeals

Basis for Review: Appeal

Facts: Carl J. Kunz, a Baptist minister, was convicted of having violated a New York City ordinance requiring a police permit before religious observances could be performed on the street. Although the ordinance itself specified no requirements, Kunz had twice been denied permits after being accused of attacking Catholics and Jews while operating under a previous permit. His conviction was upheld twice in New York courts.

Issue: Does the ordinance constitute a *prior restraint on the *free exercise of religion in violation of the First Amendment?

Outcome: Because the ordinance provided no standards for issuing or denying permits, the Court found it unconstitutional.

Vote: 8-1

Participating: Vinson, Black, Reed, Frankfurter, Douglas, Jackson, Burton, Clark, Minton

Opinions: Vinson for the Court; Black and Frankfurter concurring in the result (without written opinions); Jackson dissenting

Significance: *Kunz* introduced the principle that the state must carefully outline any restrictions it puts on free expression and that these restrictions must be strictly circumscribed.

FEINER V. NEW YORK

Citation: 340 U.S. 315 (1951)

Argued: October 17, 1950

Decided: January 15, 1951

Court Below: New York Court of Appeals

Basis for Review: *Writ of certiorari

Facts: After refusing police requests to stop his street corner diatribe attacking President Truman and urging African Americans in the audience to take up arms, Irving Feiner was arrested and convicted of disturbing the peace under a New York statute prohibiting the use of offensive or threatening language. The arresting officer pointed to the unruliness of the crowd that had gathered around Feiner as justification for his arrest.

Issue: Did the New York ordinance violate *free speech rights guaranteed by the First Amendment?

Outcome: Stating that Feiner's arrest was necessary to maintain public order, the Court upheld the statute and Feiner's conviction.

Vote: 6-3

Participating: Vinson, Black, Reed, Frankfurter, Douglas, Jackson, Burton, Clark, Minton

Opinions: Vinson for the Court; Frankfurter concurring (without written opinion); Black, and Douglas, joined by Minton, dissenting

Significance: Decided the same day as *Kunz v. New York, Feiner* is more representative of the Vinson Court's usual deference to strong government. Taken together, the two cases may indicate some preliminary attempt to distinguish the First Amendment's protection of *free exercise of religion from that extended to free speech.

DENNIS V. UNITED STATES

Citation: 341 U.S. 494 (1951)

Argued: December 4, 1950

Decided: June 4, 1951

Court Below: United States Second Circuit Court of Appeals

Basis for Review: *Writ of certiorari

Facts: Eleven members of the board of the American Communist Party were convicted under the Smith Act (1940) for conspiring to overthrow the government. Their convictions were upheld

in the *appellate court despite indications of judicial bias and prosecutorial misconduct at the trial. The Supreme Court granted certiorari only with regard to the constitutionality of the Smith Act.
Issue: Do the Smith Act's prohibitions against advocating the overthrow of the government violate First Amendment *free speech rights?
Outcome: Modifying the traditional "clear and present danger" test as the basis for exceptions to the First Amendment to one of "grave and probable danger," Chief Justice Vinson's majority opinion upheld the act and the convictions.
Vote: 6-2
Participating: Vinson, Reed, Black, Frankfurter, Douglas, Jackson, Burton, Minton (Clark not participating)
Opinions: Vinson for the Court; Frankfurter and Jackson concurring; Black and Douglas dissenting
Significance: The new standard created by Vinson was considerably less protective of speech than was Justice Oliver Wendell Holmes's "clear and present danger" test. Vinson's substitution aroused considerable discomfort among the other justices — even those who agreed with his pro-government orientation. And indeed, the Department of Justice used *Dennis* as the basis for a frontal assault on the Communist Party. Over the next six years, nearly 150 people were indicted for violations of the Smith Act. The indictments did not cease until the Court reversed itself in 1957 with *Yates v. United States*.

JOINT ANTI-FASCIST REFUGEE COMMITTEE V. MCGRATH

Citation: 341 U.S. 123 (1951)
Argued: October 11, 1950
Decided: April 30, 1951
Court Below: United States Court of Appeals for the District of Columbia Circuit
Basis for Review: *Writ of certiorari
Facts: Under executive order, Attorney General Tom C. Clark (his successor, J. Howard McGrath, was the party eventually sued) drew up a list of allegedly subversive organizations. Those listed were afforded no avenue of appeal, and the list was extensively used to persecute them. Three organizations listed, among them the Joint Anti-Fascist Refugee Committee, sued to be removed from the list. After the district court's dismissal of their complaint was upheld by a federal *appellate court, they appealed to the Supreme Court.
Issue: Does the attorney general have constitutional authority to create such a list?
Outcome: Finding the manner in which the list was created unconstitutional, the Vinson Court reversed the lower court's ruling and *remanded both cases to the district court.
Vote: 5-3
Participating: Vinson, Black, Reed, Frankfurter, Douglas, Jackson, Burton, Minton (Clark not participating)
Opinions: Burton for the Court; Black, Frankfurter, Douglas, and Jackson concurring; Reed, joined by Vinson and Minton, dissenting
Significance: The *holding in *McGrath* is surprising, both because of the Vinson Court's customarily conservative stance and because of the period during which the case was decided. However, because each member of the majority wrote his own opinion, the Court's ruling lacked real force.

ROCHIN V. CALIFORNIA

Citation: 342 U.S. 165 (1952)
Argued: October 16, 1951
Decided: January 2, 1952
Court Below: California Supreme Court
Basis for Review: *Writ of certiorari
Facts: Rochin was convicted of drug possession in a California court on the basis of evidence obtained when his stomach was pumped against his will. The state supreme court refused to review his case after he lost on appeal.
Issue: Does involuntary stomach pumping to obtain evidence constitute unreasonable search and seizure in violation of the *Due Process Clause of the Fourteenth Amendment?
Outcome: The Court found that the police officers who ordered Rochin's involuntary procedure had violated his constitutional rights.
Vote: 8-0
Participating: Vinson, Black, Reed, Frankfurter, Douglas, Jackson, Burton, Clark (Minton not participating)

Opinions: Frankfurter for the Court; Black and Douglas concurring

Significance: While Frankfurter based his majority opinion on the Fourteenth Amendment, because Rochin was forced to incriminate himself, Black and Douglas in concurrence argued for a Fifth Amendment justification for the outcome of the case. These distinctions, however, became immaterial in the wake of *Mapp v. Ohio* (1961), which established that the *exclusionary rule governing admission of evidence applied to the states, and *Malloy v. Hogan* (1964), which *incorporated the Fifth Amendment into the Fourteenth.

ZORACH V. CLAUSON

Citation: 343 U.S. 306 (1952)

Argued: January 31, 1951 & February 1, 1952

Decided: April 28, 1952

Court Below: New York Court of Appeals

Basis for Review: Appeal

Facts: New York City sponsored a program of "released time," during which public school students were permitted time off during the school week to attend religious instruction held away from the school premises.

Issue: Does the New York program violate the *Establishment Clause of the First Amendment separating church and state?

Outcome: Emphasizing the importance of fulfilling children's religious needs, the Court upheld the program.

Vote: 6-3

Participating: Vinson, Black, Reed, Frankfurter, Douglas, Jackson, Burton, Clark, Minton

Opinions: Douglas for the Court; Black, Frankfurter, and Jackson dissenting

Significance: Douglas's opinion distinguished New York's program from the one struck down in *Illinois *ex rel. McCollum v. Board of Education* (1948) by pointing to the fact that religious instruction in the former took place on school property. Black, Frankfurter, and Jackson, all of whom had written opinions supporting the outcome in the earlier case, disdained this logic. Douglas, too, would later come to disavow the result in *Zorach*, although it has been cited to support subsequent instances of state accommodation of religion.

YOUNGSTOWN SHEET & TUBE CO. V. SAWYER (STEEL SEIZURE CASE)

Citation: 343 U.S. 579 (1952)

Argued: May 12-13, 1952

Decided: June 2, 1952

Court Below: United States Court of Appeals for the District of Columbia Circuit

Basis for Review: *Writ of certiorari

Facts: President Truman, in order to ward off a potential strike and citing the economic necessity of continued steel production during the Korean War, ordered Secretary of Commerce Charles Sawyer to seize the nation's steel mills and continue operating them under government authority. After the fact, the administration notified Congress, which took no action. The steel company, seeking a *declaratory judgment against Sawyer, was granted a temporary *injunction.

Issue: Did Truman's seizure of the mills exceed the executive authority invested in the presidency by Article I of the Constitution?

Outcome: Based on its determination that such a seizure was a legislative task, the Court ruled against Truman's actions.

Vote: 6-3

Participating: Vinson, Black, Reed, Frankfurter, Douglas, Jackson, Burton, Clark, Minton

Opinions: Black for the Court; Jackson, Clark, Douglas, and Frankfurter concurring; Vinson, joined by Reed, dissenting; and Minton dissenting

Significance: The lasting importance of the *Steel Seizure Case* is its role in upholding the balance of power between the two political branches of government. It has been subsequently cited as authority for disallowing claims of inherent presidential authority regarding such matters as national security and executive privilege.

TERRY V. ADAMS

Citation: 345 U.S. 461 (1953)

Argued: January 16, 1953

Decided: May 4, 1953

Court Below: United States Fifth Circuit Court of Appeals

Basis for Review: *Writ of certiorari

Facts: Starting in 1889 the all-white Jaybird Democratic Association of Fort Bend County, Texas, a voluntary association, held primary elections to select candidates for county office. Although the Jaybird primaries had no official approval, their candidates invariably won in the official elections.

Issue: Do the Jaybird primaries, by excluding blacks, violate the Fifteenth Amendment?

Outcome: Declaring the Jaybird primaries an integral part of the election process, the Court ruled them unconstitutional.

Vote: 8-1

Participating: Vinson, Black, Reed, Frankfurter, Douglas, Jackson, Burton, Clark, Minton

Opinions: No opinion of the Court; Black, joined by Douglas and Burton, announced the Court's judgment; Frankfurter concurring, and Clark, joined by Vinson, Reed, and Jackson, concurring; Minton dissenting

Significance: *Terry* was the last of the series of "white primary" cases, starting with *Nixon v. Herndon* (1927), brought against Texas Democrats. Cumulatively, these cases provided authority for the Voting Rights Act of 1965, granting the federal government authority to enforce voting rights directly and uniformly throughout the states.

ROSENBERG V. UNITED STATES

Citation: 346 U.S. 273 (1953)

Argued: June 18, 1953

Decided: June 19, 1953

Court Below: United States Second Circuit Court of Appeals

Basis for Review: Application for *stay of execution

Facts: Julius and Ethel Rosenberg were convicted under the Espionage Act of 1917 for conspiring to pass atomic secrets to the Soviet Union. Their death sentence was affirmed by the *appellate court, and a petition for *certiorari was turned down by the Supreme Court. Supporters then filed an application for a stay of execution with the Court, arguing that the death sentence was improper because certain aspects of the Espionage

Act had been superseded by the Atomic Energy Act of 1946. Reasoning that the legal question was a substantial one, Justice Douglas granted a stay. The Court met in special session to consider the issue.

Issue: Is there a conflict between the two acts and, if so, which one applies to the Rosenbergs' sentencing?

Outcome: Concluding that the Rosenbergs had been properly sentenced, the Court lifted the stay.

Vote: 6-3

Participating: Vinson, Black, Reed, Frankfurter, Douglas, Jackson, Burton, Clark, Minton

Opinions: Vinson for the Court; Black, Douglas, and Frankfurter dissenting

Significance: The Rosenbergs were executed the day this decision was handed down. Their case was one of the most controversial ones to arise in the intense atmosphere that characterized the early years of the cold war, and its merits are still debated. Douglas's decision to grant their stay of execution resulted in the first of two drives — both unsuccessful — to impeach him.

VOTING PATTERNS

President Truman appointed his friend Fred Vinson as chief justice in hopes that Vinson could smooth over the ideological and personal controversies that had left the Stone Court badly damaged both internally and in the public's perception. But the Court that Vinson inherited was still divided into the same ideological voting blocs that had dominated the Stone Court. Initially, the liberal bloc that Justice Black led — which included Douglas, Murphy, and Rutledge — tended to be more cohesive and therefore was dominant over the conservatives, guided by Frankfurter. Jackson often voted with Frankfurter, but the other conservative members of the early Vinson Court — Reed, Burton, and the chief justice himself — were less reliable, at times failing to adhere to the philosophy of *judicial restraint Frankfurter religiously espoused. Political affiliation seemed to have no bearing on these groupings: all but Burton were Democrats, and six of them had been

POLITICAL COMPOSITION
of the Vinson Court

Justice & Total Term	Courts Served	Appointing President	Political Party
Fred M. Vinson (1946-1953)	Vinson	Truman	Democrat
Hugo L. Black (1937-1971)	Hughes Stone Vinson Warren Burger	F. D. Roosevelt	Democrat
Stanley F. Reed (1938-1957)	Hughes Stone Vinson Warren	F. D. Roosevelt	Democrat
Felix Frankfurter (1939-1962)	Hughes Stone Vinson Warren	F. D. Roosevelt	Democrat
William O. Douglas (1939-1975)	Hughes Stone Vinson Warren Burger	F. D. Roosevelt	Democrat
Frank Murphy (1940-1949)	Hughes Stone Vinson	F. D. Roosevelt	Democrat
Robert H. Jackson (1941-1954)	Stone Vinson Warren	F. D. Roosevelt	Democrat
Wiley B. Rutledge (1943-1949)	Stone Vinson	F. D. Roosevelt	Democrat
Harold H. Burton (1945-1958)	Stone Vinson Warren	Truman	Republican
Tom C. Clark (1949-1967)	Vinson Warren	Truman	Democrat
Sherman Minton (1949-1956)	Vinson Warren	Truman	Democrat

appointed by Franklin Roosevelt.

In 1949, however, with the deaths of Justices Murphy and Rutledge, and the addition of Justices Clark and Minton, the balance on the Vinson Court shifted abruptly, as judicial restraint assumed dominance over *judicial activism. Vinson, always a believer in strong central government and in the strong president who had appointed him, was joined by the other Truman appointees, Burton, Clark, and Minton. Vinson failed, however, to exercise adequate leadership. Now Frankfurter, whose views seemingly resembled those of the chief justice and were usually diametrically opposed to those of Black, frequently voted with his ideological adversary.

As a result, the number of dissents that the Vinson Court delivered prior to 1949 — many of them Vinson's own — multiplied, rather than decreased. Unanimous decisions, which constituted a historically low 36 percent of those decisions announced in the October 1946 term, decreased steadily, reaching a record low of 19 percent by 1952. By this, and other measures, Vinson is often judged to have been the least effective of all Supreme Court chief justices.

SPECIAL FEATURES OF THE VINSON COURT

A MULTIPLICITY OF OPINIONS

Unanimous opinions were the rule from the time of Chief Justice John Marshall up to the watershed separating the Hughes Court into two distinct entities — the 1937 court-packing crisis that marked the beginning of a splintering of the Court that persists today. While the tradition of Court dissent is a long and honored one, *plurality opinions — those announcing the judgment of the Court but failing to achieve majority assent — came into their own during the Vinson years. Not only did Justice Frankfurter give free rein during this postwar period to his tendency to write long disquisitions in the form of concurrences, but members' opinions expressing partial agreement and partial disagreement became commonplace. This formal expression of the Vinson Court's internal turbulence only seems to have further fragmented and undermined the Court's authority, continuing a process begun under Chief Justice Stone. By 1953 the Supreme Court was sorely in need of a strong leader.

The Warren Court 1953-1969

BACKGROUND

THE DOMINO PRINCIPLE

The domino principle was born of America's involvement with Vietnam. The war in Vietnam, originally a French colonial war, became a legacy to the United States on April 7, 1954, when at a press conference President Dwight D. Eisenhower referred to Southeast Asia as a row of dominos, placed on end. If the first one fell to international Communism, the rest "would go over very quickly."

Direct involvement of U.S. troops in Vietnam was still a way off, however. Eisenhower turned a deaf ear to French cries for help, and in Geneva that July France signed agreements with the Vietnamese that divided the country at the 17th parallel, leaving the North to the Communist Viet Minh. Eisenhower then committed the United States to financial aid for the South.

Eisenhower's first genuine face-off with Communists came in January 1955 when, in response to Nationalist bombing of mainland Chinese ports, the Chinese Communists began shelling Quemoy and Matsu, two islands in the Formosa Straits still occupied by Nationalist forces. Eisenhower, citing the domino principle, asked Congress for authority to defend the islands, and Secretary of State John Foster Dulles began internal discussions about the possibility of a limited nuclear war.

The Chinese backed down, but the prospect of nuclear warfare led Eisenhower to the conclusion that the United States needed to reach an accommodation with at least the Soviets. A summit conference in Geneva in July 1955 did not achieve substantive results, but it did succeed in easing tensions between the Soviets and the Americans in what was now called the "Third World," consisting of underdeveloped, ostensibly nonaligned nations, many of them former European colonies in Africa and Asia.

The first test of this new rapprochement came when Arab Nationalist and Egyptian President Gamal Abdul Nasser, after having expelled the British from his country, proposed damming the Nile River. When his request for a facilitating loan from the World Bank was turned down, largely because of a veto from Dulles, Nasser seized control of the vital Suez Canal from the British in July 1956. The crisis was resolved on October 29 when the Israelis, with British and French backing, destroyed Nasser's army and occupied the Sinai Peninsula. However, when it was revealed that the air strike was primarily aimed at ousting Nasser, and because it had been undertaken without their consent, the U.S. and the U.S.S.R. together backed a United Nations-sponsored resolution condemning France and Britain, which resulted in their withdrawal.

In the aftermath of the Suez debacle, Nasser informally allied himself with the Soviets, and Eisenhower secured congressional authority to intervene militarily in the Middle East whenever a nation in that region, threatened by "international communism," requested U.S. aid. Nonetheless, neither the Soviet crushing of the Hungarian Revolution in November 1956, nor the invocation of the so-called Eisenhower Doctrine in 1958 — permitting the U.S. to send marines into Lebanon to counter threats to the government there from Arab nationalists — resulted in an immediate reescalation of the cold war.

MEMBERS *Of the Court* 1953–1969

(In Order of Seniority)

Earl Warren (Chief Justice)	(1953-1969)
Hugo L. Black	(1953-1969)
Stanley F. Reed (retired)	(1953-1957)
Felix Frankfurter (retired)	(1953-1962)
William O. Douglas	(1953-1969)
Robert H. Jackson (died)	(1953-1954)
Harold H. Burton (retired)	(1953-1958)
Tom C. Clark (retired)	(1953-1967)
Sherman Minton (retired)	(1953-1956)
John M. Harlan II (replaced Robert H. Jackson)	(1955-1969)
William J. Brennan Jr. (replaced Sherman Minton)	(1956-1969)
Charles E. Whittaker (replaced Stanley F. Reed; retired)	(1957-1962)
Potter Stewart (replaced Harold H. Burton)	(1958-1969)
Byron R. White (replaced Charles E. Whittaker)	(1962-1969)
Arthur J. Goldberg (replaced Felix Frankfurter; resigned)	(1962-1965)
Abe Fortas (replaced Arthur J. Goldberg; resigned)	(1965-1969)
Thurgood Marshall (replaced Tom C. Clark)	(1967-1969)

SPUTNIK AND OTHER COLD WAR TECHNOLOGY

In the 1956 election Eisenhower ran once more against Democratic presidential candidate Adlai Stevenson, and once again Eisenhower won — this time by an even wider margin than in 1952. The cold war rivalry that had contributed to Eisenhower's victory was soon intensified, however, by news of a new front opening up in space. In October 1957 the Soviets announced that they had launched an artificial satellite into earth's orbit. The American public was stunned. The Eisenhower administration responded to this evidence of Soviet technical achievement by focusing on its military implications for the arms race with the U.S.S.R., a race that would continue until the end of the cold war more than 30 years later.

In January 1959 Fidel Castro triumphed over the right-wing Cuban dictator, Fulgencio Batista, and commenced a program of agrarian reform that confiscated American property. After the Eisenhower administration cut off aid in retaliation, Castro began selling sugar to the Soviet Union in exchange for economic and military assistance. The United States eventually severed diplomatic relations with Cuba in January 1961. This establishment of a Soviet beachhead in the western hemisphere was followed by the May 5, 1960, downing of a U-2 high altitude American spy plane inside Soviet territory. A previously planned summit conference in Paris went forward but ended in disarray.

KENNEDY AND THE NEW FRONTIER

Eisenhower, whose last years in office were undermined not only by poor relations with the Soviets, but by his own poor health, was supplanted in 1961 by the Democratic candidate, John F. Kennedy.[†] The seemingly vigorous (it was later revealed that Kennedy suffered from a usually fatal disease of the adrenal glands), 43-year-old Kennedy presented a vivid contrast with the grandfatherly Eisenhower, but in fact Kennedy's initial political positions differed little from his predecessor's. Shortly after assuming office, Kennedy discovered that the so-called missile gap

---

[†] Because of the heart attacks Eisenhower suffered while in office and the assassination of his successor, Kennedy, the need for a constitutional procedure for replacing disabled presidents was underscored. The Twenty-fifth Amendment, ratified February 10, 1967, provided the means for a vice president to assume the presidency and in turn appoint a new vice president. The first use of the amendment came in October 1973, when bribery charges forced the resignation of Vice President Spiro T. Agnew. To succeed Agnew, President Richard M. Nixon appointed Republican Congressman Gerald R. Ford, minority

between the U.S.S.R. and the U.S., for which he had blamed the Eisenhower administration during his campaign, never had existed. He prevented this information from being made public, however, and gained additional congressional appropriations to continue the arms buildup. After the Soviets and East Germans constructed the Berlin Wall in 1961 in an attempt to stem the exodus of refugees from East to West, Kennedy traveled to Berlin to make a speech reaffirming Western rights in that city. Standing in front of the wall, he declared defiantly, "Ich bin ein Berliner." And when Soviet Premier Khrushchev declared that the U.S.S.R. was ending a three-year moratorium on nuclear testing, Kennedy responded that the U.S. had no choice but to do the same.

The Kennedy administration's policy toward Cuba was equally assertive. On April 17, 1961, the Central Intelligence Agency sponsored a badly bungled attempt to invade Cuba at the Bay of Pigs. And on October 22, 1962, Kennedy went before the cameras to inform the American public that he was prepared to go to war to prevent the Soviets from placing intermediate-range missiles at launching sites in Cuba. It was the most dangerous moment of the cold war, but ultimately the Soviets backed down, turning their missile-carrying vessels around in the middle of the Atlantic and even recommending a nuclear test-ban treaty.

Kennedy's domestic agenda, which was billed as the New Frontier, called for federal aid to higher education, manpower training programs, subsidized health care, and a Peace Corps. Only the last of these programs received congressional approval — and then, only because a plan to provide educators and technicians to Third World countries was viewed as a means of combating international Communism. Kennedy's initially cautious approach toward the civil rights struggle at home seemed to be evolving toward a more activist agenda when he was assassinated on November 22, 1963.

JOHNSON AND THE GREAT SOCIETY

Kennedy's vice president, Lyndon B. Johnson, assumed the presidency under a cloud of uncertainty. Kennedy's suspected assassin, Lee Harvey Oswald, a former Marine with Communist ties, was fatally shot by Jack Ruby, a Dallas nightclub owner with underworld connections, before Oswald could be brought to trial. Ruby's own murder conviction was reversed on appeal, and he died before he could be retried. A commission, headed by Chief Justice Earl Warren, was assigned the task of investigating the circumstances surrounding the Kennedy assassination, and although the Warren Report declared Oswald to be the lone assassin, conspiracy theories persisted.[†]

Johnson, a former Senate majority leader and a force within the Democratic Party since the days of Franklin Roosevelt, sought to replicate the social reforms of the New Deal with a program he called the Great Society. To New Frontier legislative proposals for a civil rights act, medicare, and such community development strategies as Headstart (a training program for impoverished preschoolers) Johnson added a "war on poverty," aimed at combating such problems as illiteracy, pollution, and urban blight. In the 1964 presidential election his Republican counterpart, Barry Goldwater, called not just for defeat of Johnson's agenda, but a rollback of many New Deal reforms. Goldwater's resounding defeat assured public support for continued implementation of the Great Society.

THE CIVIL RIGHTS MOVEMENT

The return of African American veterans — whose units had been desegregated by President Truman in 1948 — from the Korean War helped fuel mounting pressures for increased civil rights. *Brown v. Board of Education*, decided by the Supreme Court in 1954, made it clear that segregation was no longer the law of the land — not just in education, but in all areas of American public life. *Brown II*, handed down the next year, outlined the means by which school desegregation was to take place, with "all deliberate speed." This ambivalent phrase afforded latitude for foot-dragging. The recalcitrant attitudes of certain southern states, as well as the apathy of federal government officials, gave birth to the civil rights movement.

---

leader in the House of Representatives. When the Watergate scandal forced Nixon himself to resign in August 1974, Ford assumed the presidency and appointed Nelson A. Rockefeller as vice president.

[†] A new inquiry into Kennedy's assassination was undertaken in 1976 by the House of Representatives Select Committee on Assassinations, which concluded that the circumstances of Kennedy's death did not rule out the possibility of conspiratorial action.

Initially the civil rights movement adopted a philosophy of nonviolence. The 1955-1956 Montgomery, Alabama, bus boycott, initiated by Rosa Parks's refusal to sit in the back of a city bus and led by the Reverend Martin Luther King Jr., resulted in a lawsuit and the city's eventual capitulation to integrated public transportation. Continued nonviolent action by King's Southern Christian Leadership Conference helped promote the 1957 civil rights Act, legislation aimed at protecting voting rights. This act represented the first federal civil rights law since Reconstruction.

Violent reaction to the civil rights movement began with attempts to integrate public education. In 1956 Arkansas Governor Orval Faubus mobilized the National Guard to prevent African American students from entering Little Rock's Central High School. Eisenhower could not overlook this challenge to federal authority. He in turn federalized the National Guard in order to combat rioting and insure the African American students' entry. In 1962 a federal court ordered the University of Mississippi to admit African American veteran James Meredith. Meredith did enroll, but he did so with an escort of federal marshals and only after two people had been killed and 375 injured. The Kennedy administration responded with civil rights legislation aimed at furthering school desegregation and preventing voting rights violations.

After King carried his civil rights crusade to Birmingham, Alabama, where he and his followers were met with fire hoses and police attack dogs, and after National Association for the Advancement of Colored People official Medgar Evers was assassinated in Mississippi, Kennedy proposed a new civil rights act, this one prohibiting segregation in all public accommodations. More social action followed, some nonviolent — such as King's August 1963 march on Washington — and some violent — such as the murder in Mississippi that same summer of five student voter registration workers. Ultimately, the demonstrations and sacrifices led to adoption of three significant pieces of legislation, the 1964 Civil Rights Act, aimed broadly at eliminating legally sanctioned discrimination in such areas as public accommodations and employment, and the more narrowly drawn 1965 Voting Rights Act and 1968 Fair Housing Act.

THE VIETNAM WAR AND SOCIAL UNREST

As Johnson's attention shifted from prosecuting the war on poverty to prosecuting the war in Vietnam, the social fabric of the nation began to unravel. While Kennedy added Special Forces units to the military advisors Eisenhower had sent to prop up the corrupt regime of Ngo Dinh Diem in South Vietnam, it was Johnson who exponentially increased American involvement in Southeast Asia. In August 1964, in response to North Vietnamese attacks on U.S. ships in the Gulf of Tonkin, Johnson won congressional support for a resolution permitting "the President, as Commander-in-Chief, to take all necessary measures to repel any armed attack against the forces of the United States and to prevent further aggression." While initially he used this unprecedented grant of executive power in a limited way, by 1967 over 500,000 American troops were fighting in Vietnam in an undeclared war.

The Tet Offensive in January 1968, during which North Vietnamese forces penetrated deep into South Vietnam, resulted in a call for 200,000 more American troops. It proved to be a turning point in the war. Student protests in the U.S. and expressions of antiwar sentiments by powerful individuals such as Senator J. William Fulbright succeeded in turning public sentiment against Johnson. In the March 1968 New Hampshire presidential primary, antiwar Democratic challenger, Minnesota Senator Eugene McCarthy, a write-in anti-war candidate, polled 42 percent of the vote to Johnson's 49 percent. Another Democratic challenger, New York Senator Robert Kennedy, then entered the race, and on March 31 Johnson announced his withdrawal as a presidential candidate.

The remainder of 1968 was a calendar of catastrophes. In the wake of Martin Luther King Jr.'s assassination on April 4, African Americans rioted in the streets of numerous cities, reenacting the expressions of civic unrest and social dislocation that had erupted in the Los Angeles

JUDICIAL BIOGRAPHY

PERSONAL DATA

Born: March 19, 1891, in Los Angeles, California

Parents: Methias Warren, Chrystal Hernlund Warren

Higher Education: University of California (B.A., 1912; J. D. 1914)

Bar Admission: California, 1914

Political Party: Republican

Marriage: October 14, 1925, to Nina Palmquist Meyers, who bore Warren two sons and three daughters; Warren adopted a third son from his wife's previous marriage

Died: July 9, 1974, in Washington, D.C.

Buried: Arlington National Cemetery, Arlington, Virginia

PROFESSIONAL CAREER

Occupations: Lawyer, 1914-1917, 1918-1943; Serviceman, 1917-1918; Government Official, 1919-1943, 1963-1964; Politician, 1943-1953; Judge,

1953-1969

Official Positions: Deputy City Attorney, Oakland, California, 1919-1920; Deputy Assistant District Attorney, Alameda County, California, 1920-1923; Chief Deputy District Attorney, Alameda County, 1923-1925; District Attorney, Alameda County, 1925-1939; Attorney General, California, 1939-1943; Governor, California, 1943-1953; Chief Justice, United States Supreme Court, 1953-1969; Chairman, commission to investigate the assassination of President John F. Kennedy, 1963-1964

SUPREME COURT SERVICE

Appointed: October 2, 1953 (recess appointment)

Appointed By: Dwight D. Eisenhower

Oath Taken: October 5, 1953

Nominated: January 11, 1954

Confirmed: March 1, 1954

Confirmation Vote: Voice vote

Oath Retaken: March 2, 1954

Replaced: Chief Justice Fred M. Vinson

Significant Opinions: *Brown v. Board of Education* (1954); *Brown v. Board of Education II* (1955); *Pennsylvania v. Nelson* (1956); *Watkins v. United States* (1957); *Trop v. Dulles* (1958); *Reynolds v. Sims* (1964); *South Carolina v. Katzenbach* (1966); *Miranda v. Arizona* (1966); *Klopfer v. North Carolina* (1967); *Loving v. Virginia* (1967); *United States v. Robel* (1967); *United States v. O'Brien* (1968); *Flast v. Cohen* (1968); *Terry v. Ohio* (1968); *Powell v. McCormack* (1969)

Left Court: Retired June 23, 1969

Length of Service: 15 years, 8 months, 18 days

Replacement: Chief Justice Warren E. Burger

---

neighborhood of Watts in 1965, and in Atlanta, Chicago, Cleveland, and Detroit in 1967. Two months later, on June 4, 1968, Robert Kennedy was assassinated while campaigning in Los Angeles, and in August the Democratic National Convention in Chicago took place amidst a street brawl between antiwar demonstrators and the police.

Out of the upheaval arose a new social consciousness. The Civil Rights Act of 1964 provided new economic opportunities for racial and ethnic minorities and for women, who had begun to organize a movement for gender equality. But the turbulent 1960s also gave rise to a conservative "silent majority" which, in 1968, elected Republican candidate Richard M. Nixon as the nation's 37th president.

WARREN'S EARLY LIFE

Earl Warren's parents were born in Scandinavia and emigrated to the United States as children. After they married, the family settled in Bakersfield, California, where Warren's father worked as a mechanic for the Southern Pacific Railroad. (In 1938 his father was bludgeoned to

Earl Warren

death, a murder that was never solved.) Warren knew poverty and hardship growing up. As a young man he, too, performed manual labor for the railroad. He worked his way through the University of California at Berkeley where, in 1912, he was one of the first students from his high school to receive a bachelor's degree and where, in 1914, he received his law degree. He worked briefly for an oil company and for a law firm, and in 1917 he enlisted in the Army in hopes of seeing action abroad in World War I. Instead, he was stationed in training camps in the U.S. and discharged a year later.

WARREN'S PUBLIC LIFE

After his demobilization, Warren went immediately into public life, first working as a legislative and municipal aide in Oakland, California, then joining the Alameda County district attorney's office. There he rose through the ranks until, in 1925, he himself became the district attorney, a position he held for the next 13 years. As a prosecutor he was known for his toughness, but

also for his fair-mindedness, and in 1931 a survey found him to be "the best district attorney in the United States."

As district attorney, Warren was responsible for sending a city manager and several councilmen to jail for graft and for uncovering a fraudulent waste management scheme. His reputation for incorruptibility helped him win election in 1938 as state attorney general. (He won three primaries, for although he was registered as a Republican, he cross-filed with the Democratic and Progressive Parties as well.) He served only one term in the office of state attorney general, a period remembered primarily for his enforcement, in the aftermath of Pearl Harbor, of the evacuation and internment of Japanese Americans living on the West Coast.

In 1942 he garnered 57.1 percent of the popular vote in the California gubernatorial election, trouncing the incumbent. He was a popular governor and was reelected in 1946 (when he won both the Republican and Democratic nominations) and in 1950, becoming the first chief executive of the state to be elected three times. Although he had begun to shows signs of liberalism — in 1945 he proposed a state program of prepaid medical insurance — Warren remained a favorite of conservative Republicans, who saw him as destined for national office. In 1944 newspaper magnate William Randolph Hearst promoted Warren as a possible Republican presidential candidate, and in 1948 he was Thomas Dewey's running mate. In 1952 Warren was a serious presidential contender, but he threw his support to Dwight D. Eisenhower, helping Eisenhower win the nomination and securing an important political favor for himself.

Eisenhower promised Warren the first vacancy on the Supreme Court. In the interim, he offered Warren the solicitor general's position, which Warren had already accepted when, on September 8, 1953, Chief Justice Fred Vinson died unexpectedly. When Eisenhower was slow to honor his earlier promise, Warren was quick to remind him of it. Although he may have had doubts about Warren's commitment to a conservative agenda, publicly the president stated that he had chosen

Warren as the next chief justice because of the governor's "integrity, honesty, middle-of-the-road philosophy." Later, Eisenhower would call his appointment of Warren "the biggest damn-fool mistake I ever made."

WARREN AS CHIEF JUSTICE

A recess appointment, Warren joined the Court on opening day of the 1953 term. Lacking familiarity with Court procedures, he initially let Senior Associate Justice Hugo Black lead judicial conferences. Within weeks, however, Warren asserted his leadership and, in short order, he demonstrated a gift for managing the Court second only to that of the great John Marshall.

One of the most pressing items on the Court's *docket was *Brown v. Board of Education*. First argued in 1952 during Chief Justice Vinson's tenure, *Brown* remained undecided primarily because of an ideological split in the Court between those supporting the *due process revolution being led by Justice Black, and the faction led by Felix Frankfurter, which favored *judicial restraint and opposed overturning the "separate but equal" doctrine enshrined in *Plessy v. Ferguson* (1896). At the first judicial conference following reargument of the case on the issue of the applicability of the Fourteenth Amendment's *Equal Protection Clause, Warren straightforwardly announced his view of the case: racial segregation could be upheld only if one accepted the premise of racial inequality, and he did not. Nonetheless, mindful of the deep divisions with the Court and of the implications for the nation of whatever decision it reached, Warren did not push aggressively for adoption of his views. Eventually all but Stanley Reed came to agree with the chief justice, and even he, in the end, capitulated to Warren's desire for unanimity. The chief justice himself wrote the opinion of the Court, displaying the straightforwardness, concern for justice — and lack of concern for legal scholarship — that would become hallmarks of his future opinions.

Brown is possibly the most important American case to be decided in the 20th century. It also proved to be an accurate forecast of the Court's direction for the next 15 years: under Warren, the justices hastened the process of reorientation from property rights to individual rights begun under Chief Justices Stone and Vinson, becoming the most activist Court in the nation's history. Still, it was not immediately clear that Warren would take that direction himself. Lacking Justice Black's unwavering commitment to the rights embodied in the first ten amendments of the Constitution — and Black's strict adherence to the letter of that law — Warren gave some early indications that he could approve just as readily of Frankfurter's conservative philosophy. But with the appointment in 1956 of Frankfurter's former law student, William J. Brennan Jr., Warren found his truest ally and someone who could help him articulate the legal bases of his preoccupation with fundamental fairness in American society.

Warren addressed this concern in such ground breaking opinions as *Reynolds v. Sims* (1964), requiring legislative *reapportionment to insure observance of the principle of "one person, one vote," and *Miranda v. Arizona* (1966), which mandated that persons accused of crimes be officially informed of their rights. Cases such as these set the tone for the entire Court — which under Warren came to see itself as a vigorous participant in the process of governing — and alienated conservatives to the extent that the chief justice's public appearances were sometimes boycotted, while an informal, unorganized movement to impeach him occasionally percolated up through the public consciousness.

A week after John F. Kennedy's assassination in November 1963, President Johnson requested that Warren head a commission consisting of past and current members of all three branches of government whose goal it was to conduct an investigation into the circumstances of Kennedy's death. Although he yielded to the president's wishes, the chief justice disliked the assignment, fearing that it tended to undermine the *separation of powers. He was equally unhappy with the outcome of the investigation, which made a finding — based on less than complete evidence and since then frequently challenged — that the assassination did not involve a conspiracy.

In June 1968 Warren informed President Johnson of his intent to retire, but he agreed not to do so until his successor had been confirmed. When Johnson's nomination of Associate Justice Abe Fortas for chief justice was derailed that October by allegations of financial impropriety brought by Republicans, Warren stayed on until the new Republican president, Richard M. Nixon, could replace him with another chief justice. In his last term, however, Warren delivered a final opinion affirming the power of the Court, *Powell v. McCormack* (1969), in which he declared that Congress's refusal to seat duly elected Representative Adam Clayton Powell was unconstitutional.

Warren officially stepped down one week later, on June 23, 1969, the same day he administered the oath of office to his replacement, Warren Burger. He spent his remaining five years writing his memoirs and making the rounds of the speakers' circuit, addressing problems of law and public policy. He also maintained his interest in the Court, opposing a proposal to introduce an intermediate federal *appellate court, which he felt would undermine the Supreme Court's *jurisdiction. He died of congestive heart failure on July 9, 1974.

ASSOCIATE JUSTICES

For biographies of Associate Justices **Hugo L. Black, Stanley F. Reed, Felix Frankfurter,** and **William O. Douglas,** see entries under **THE HUGHES COURT.** For biographies of Associate Justices **Robert H. Jackson** and **Harold H. Burton,** see entries under **THE STONE COURT.** For biographies of Associate Justices **Tom C. Clark** and **Sherman Minton,** see entries under **THE VINSON COURT.**

JOHN MARSHALL HARLAN II

PERSONAL DATA

Born: May 20, 1899, in Chicago, Illinois
Parents: John Maynard Harlan, Elizabeth Flagg Harlan

Higher Education: Princeton University (B.A., 1920); Balliol College, Oxford University (Rhodes Scholar, B.A. in jurisprudence, 1923); New York Law School (LL.B., 1925)
Bar Admission: New York, 1925
Political Party: Republican
Marriage: November 10, 1928, to Ethel Andrews, who bore Harlan a daughter
Died: December 29, 1971, in Washington, D.C.
Buried: Emmanuel Church Cemetery, Weston, Connecticut

PROFESSIONAL CAREER

Occupations: Lawyer, 1925-1943, 1945-1953; Government Official, 1925-1930, 1951-1953; Serviceman, 1943-1945; Judge, 1954-1971
Official Positions: Assistant United States Attorney, Southern District of New York, 1925-1927; Special Assistant Attorney General, New York State, 1928-1930; Chief Counsel, New York State Crime Commission, 1951-1953; Director, New York City Legal Aid Society, early 1950s; Chairman, Committee on Ethics and Committee on the Judiciary, and Vice President, Association of the Bar of the City of New York, early 1950s; Judge, United States Second Circuit Court of Appeals, 1954-1955; Associate Justice, United States Supreme Court, 1955-1971

SUPREME COURT SERVICE

Nominated: November 9, 1954 (no action)
Nominated By: Dwight D. Eisenhower
Renominated: January 10, 1955
Confirmed: March 16, 1955
Confirmation Vote: 71-11
Oath Taken: March 28, 1955
Replaced: Robert H. Jackson
Significant Opinions: *Yates v. United States* (1957); *National Association for the Advancement of Colored People v. Alabama *ex rel. Patterson* (1958); *Barenblatt v. United States* (1959); *Hoyt v. Florida* (1961); *Scales v. United States, Noto v. United States* (1961); *Katz v. United States* (concurrence) (1967); *Cohen v. California* (1971)
Left Court: Retired September 23, 1971
Length of Service: 16 years, 5 months, 26 days
Replacement: William H. Rehnquist

The Warren Court, 1954. From left: Felix Frankfurter, Tom C. Clark, Hugo L. Black, Robert H. Jackson, Earl Warren, Harold H. Burton, Stanley F. Reed, Sherman Minton, William O. Douglas

John Marshall Harlan II, who went by John M. Harlan to distinguish himself from the illustrious grandfather [See biography p. 140] for whom he was named, had the distinction of being the only descendant of a Supreme Court justice to become a justice himself. Harlan's father was a prominent Chicago lawyer active in Republican politics whose wealth and social connections contributed to his son's patrician background. Harlan, too, had a blue chip education, receiving his first degree from Princeton University, and going on to Oxford University in England as a Rhodes Scholar. Although Harlan received an English degree in *jurisprudence, it was not considered adequate preparation to practice law in the United States. On the advice of his mentor at Root, Clark, Buckner & Howland, the New York law firm that hired him upon his return, Harlan simultaneously worked and took a law degree at New York Law School, completing a two-year program in half the time.

Harlan's professional mentor was Emory Buckner, the firm's chief litigator, who had a penchant for public service. When he became U.S.

attorney for the Southern District of New York in 1925, Buckner took his protege with him. At the U.S. Attorney's office, Harlan was given responsibility for enforcing prohibition laws. When Buckner became a state prosecutor in 1927 at the request of New York Governor Al Smith, Harlan again went with him and was responsible for the conviction of the Queens borough president on graft charges. Harlan's public spirit also propelled him into the armed forces during World War II. His service on a panel providing technical advice to Allied bombing operations won him a U.S. Legion of Merit as well as a Croix de Guerre from France and Belgium. After the war, Harlan returned to private practice, making another foray into public service in 1951, when he became chief counsel of the New York State Crime Commission.

In the latter role, Harlan came to know New York Governor Thomas E. Dewey and his associate, Herbert Brownell. When Brownell became President Eisenhower's attorney general, he recommended Harlan's appointment to fill a vacancy on the federal Second Circuit Court of Appeals.

Harlan, who had had a brilliant career as a litigator, heeded Brownell's advice that the Eisenhower administration would require that future Supreme Court nominees have prior judicial experience. He was quickly confirmed as a federal judge and had served only eight months when Justice Robert H. Jackson died suddenly on October 9, 1954. Eisenhower named Harlan as his replacement. Harlan's confirmation was delayed for nearly five months while segregationist senators, hoping to derail implementation of the Warren Court's school integration order in *Brown v. Board of Education* (1954) by denying the Court full membership, debated the nominee's ostensibly "internationalist" leanings, which they claimed might lead to surrender of United States *sovereignty. Finally, following his renomination, Harlan was confirmed by a vote of 71 to 11.

On the Court, Harlan immediately allied himself with Justice Felix Frankfurter, adopting the latter's posture of *judicial restraint and favoring *federalism and government claims of national security. On the activist Warren Court, he became, like his grandfather before him, a great dissenter. But whereas the first Justice Harlan had been a maverick remembered primarily for his solo dissent in *Plessy v. Ferguson* (1896), the decision which established segregation as the law of the land, John M. Harlan opposed the Warren Court's adoption of a "one person, one vote" principle requiring state legislative *reapportionment. In contrast to Justice Hugo Black's absolutist approach to the Bill of Rights, Harlan favored a policy of "fundamental fairness," which allowed states more latitude in enforcing individual rights.

But Harlan also could adopt quite liberal positions, endorsing a right to marital privacy as outlined in Justice William O. Douglas's opinion for the Court in *Griswold v. Connecticut* (1965). His own majority opinion in *Cohen v. California* (1971) expanded constitutional protections for provocative and offensive speech by upholding the right of an antiwar protestor to wear a jacket emblazoned with an obscene denunciation of the Vietnam War.

Harlan was one of the hardest working members of the Warren Court, averaging 43 opinions per term from 1963 to 1967, when his eyesight began to fail. During his last six years as a justice, he was functionally blind, but he continued to carry his share of the responsibility for opinion writing. In September 1971, after cancer of the spine was diagnosed, he retired, dying three months later.

WILLIAM JOSEPH BRENNAN JR.

PERSONAL DATA
Born: April 25, 1906, in Newark, New Jersey
Parents: William J. Brennan, Agnes McDermott Brennan
Higher Education: Wharton School of Finance, University of Pennsylvania (B.S., with honors, 1928); Harvard Law School (LL.B., 1931)
Bar Admission: New Jersey, 1931
Political Party: Democrat
Marriages: May 5, 1928, to Marjorie Leonard, who bore Brennan two sons and a daughter and who died in 1982; 1983 to Mary Fowler

PROFESSIONAL CAREER
Occupations: Lawyer, 1931-1942, 1946-1949; Serviceman, 1942-1946; Judge, 1949-1990
Official Positions: Judge, New Jersey Superior Court, 1949-1950; Judge, New Jersey Superior Court, Appellate Division, 1950-1952; Associate Justice, New Jersey Supreme Court, 1952-1956; Associate Justice, United States Supreme Court, 1956-1990

SUPREME COURT SERVICE
Appointed: October 15, 1956 (recess appointment)
Appointed By: Dwight D. Eisenhower
Oath Taken: October 16, 1956
Nominated: January 14, 1957
Confirmation: March 19, 1957
Confirmation Vote: Voice vote
Oath Retaken: March 22, 1957
Replaced: Sherman Minton
Significant Opinions: *Roth v. United States, Alberts v. California* (1957); *Baker v. Carr* (1962); *National Association for the Advancement of Colored People v. Button* (1963); *Fay v. Noia* (1963); *New York Times*

The Warren Court, 1960–1961. From left: William O. Douglas, Charles Evans Whittaker, Hugo L. Black, John M. Harlan II, Earl Warren, William J. Brennan Jr., Felix Frankfurter, Potter Stewart, Tom C. Clark

Co. v. Sullivan (1964); Malloy v. Hogan (1964); Dombrowski v. Pfister (1965); Albertson v. Subversive Activities Control Board (1965); Keyishian v. Board of Regents (1967); United States v. Wade (1967); Green v. County School Board of New Kent County (1968); Shapiro v. Thompson (1969); Goldberg v. Kelly (1970); *In re Winship (1970); Eisenstadt v. Baird (1972); Frontiero v. Richardson (1973); Keyes v. Denver School District No. 1 (1973); Craig v. Boren (1976); Nixon v. Administrator of General Services (1977); Orr v. Orr (1979); United Steelworkers of America v. Weber (1979); Plyler v. Doe (1982); Roberts v. United States Jaycees (1984); Local 28 of the Sheet Metals Workers' International Association v. Equal Employment Opportunity Commission (1986); Johnson v. Santa Clara County (1987); Texas v. Johnson (1989); United States v. Eichman (1990); Metro Broadcasting, Inc. v. Federal Communications Commission (1990)
Left Court: Retired July 20, 1990
Length of Service: 33 years, 9 months, 4 days
Replacement: David H. Souter

William J. Brennan was born into a working class family headed by Irish immigrants who had come to America in the 1890s. His father worked as a coal stoker at a brewery until he became a leader of the local union and finally a member of the Newark, New Jersey, Board of Commissioners. The younger Brennen shared his father's social philosophy, though not his taste for politics. After excelling in the business curriculum at the Wharton School, he entered Harvard Law School, where he financed his legal education through a combination of scholarships and odd jobs.

After graduating with an LL.B. in 1931, Brennan joined the prominent Newark firm of Pitney, Hardin and Skinner, where he developed a specialty in labor law. When the United States entered World War II, Brennan joined the Army, rising to the rank of colonel and receiving the Legion of Merit as a result of his efforts to resolve labor disputes arising from the wartime conversion of private businesses. When the war ended, he returned to private practice and began a campaign to reform the New Jersey court system. His activism brought him to the attention of Governor Alfred Driscoll, who in 1949 appointed Brennan to the state superior court. Within three years,

Brennan advanced to the superior court's *appellate division and then to the bench of the New Jersey Supreme Court, where he became Chief Justice Arthur Vanderbilt's closest associate.

When Justice Sherman Minton retired on the eve of the 1956 election, President Eisenhower, seeing a political advantage in demonstrating bipartisanship, appointed Brennan — an apparently safely inactive Democrat — as Minton's replacement. The only voice raised against Brennan during his confirmation by a reconvened Senate was that of Senator Joseph McCarthy, who presumably objected to the public manner in which Brennan had compared the senator's tactics for ferreting out Communists with the Salem witch trials.

Brennan quickly joined forces with the liberal voting bloc on the Warren Court and, as he had done on the New Jersey Supreme Court, became the chief justice's right-hand man. Warren and Brennan began to meet before the weekly judicial conferences to plan their strategy for convincing a majority of the justices to endorse their views on the cases under consideration. Warren valued Brennan greatly, not just for his articulateness and ability to parse a legal argument, but for the genial (some said manipulative) nature that enabled him to accommodate the concerns of his brethren. During the years of the Warren Court, Brennan was responsible for writing some of the Court's most influential opinions, including *Baker v. Carr* (1962), the "one person, one vote" decision Warren termed the most important of his time on the Court.

During the subsequent tenures of Chief Justices Warren Burger and William Rehnquist, the Court adopted a more conservative tone, and Brennan often found himself in the minority. Although he seldom wrote dissenting opinions between 1956 and 1969 (one year, in fact, he wrote none), after 1969 the number rose considerably, reaching as high as 122 in 1972. Still, he continued to provide leadership on such important issues as *equal protection, particularly in the area of gender discrimination and affirmative action, and with regard to First Amendment freedoms. In his final term on the Court, Brennan authored the opinion in *United States v. Eichman* (1990), which declared that burning an American flag constituted constitutionally protected symbolic speech and added to the legacy of landmark Brennan opinions, such as *New York Times Co. v. Sullivan* (1964), which increased the bounds of free expression. He retired on July 20, 1990, because of declining health.

CHARLES EVANS WHITTAKER

PERSONAL DATA
Born: February 22, 1901, in Troy, Kansas
Parents: Charles Whittaker, Ida Miller Whittaker
Higher Education: University of Kansas City Law School (LL.B., 1924)
Bar Admission: Missouri, 1923
Political Party: Republican
Marriage: July 7, 1928, to Winifred R. Pugh, who bore Whittaker three sons
Died: November 26, 1973, in Kansas City, Missouri
Buried: Calvary Cemetery, Kansas City

PROFESSIONAL CAREER
Occupations: Lawyer, 1923-1954, 1965-1966; Judge, 1954-1962
Official Positions: President, Missouri Bar Association, 1953-1954; Judge, United States District Court for the Western District of Missouri, 1954-1956; Judge, United States Eighth Circuit Court of Appeals, 1956-1957; Associate Justice, United States Supreme Court, 1957-1962

SUPREME COURT SERVICE
Nominated: March 2, 1957
Nominated By: Dwight D. Eisenhower
Confirmed: March 19, 1957
Confirmation Vote: Voice vote
Oath Taken: March 25, 1957
Replaced: Stanley F. Reed
Significant Opinions: None
Left Court: Retired April 1, 1962
Length of Service: 5 years, 7 days
Replacement: Byron R. White

Charles Whittaker was born on his father's farm near Troy, Kansas, where he attended high school until he was 16, when he quit school after his mother died. He worked on the farm for the next three years until he left for Kansas City, Missouri, determined to go to law school. He was admitted to Kansas City School of Law on the condition that he simultaneously complete his high school curriculum. He did so, at the same time taking law classes at night and working during the day as an office boy for the law firm of Watson, Gage & Ess. In 1923, a year before receiving his law degree, he passed the Missouri bar.

Whittaker went to work for Watson, Gage, concentrating at first on litigation, then on corporate practice. One of his clients in the 1950s was the *Kansas City Star*, owned by Roy Roberts. Roberts, a personal friend of Dwight D. Eisenhower, was impressed with Whittaker's legal talents, and when Whittaker asked Roberts to recommend him to fill a vacancy on the federal district court for western Missouri, Roberts did so gladly. On July 5, 1954, Whittaker assumed a seat on the bench.

When a seat on the Eighth Circuit Court of Appeals came open in December 1955, Eisenhower, who had a strong preference for elevating sitting federal judges, again turned to Whittaker. Whittaker assumed his new duties the following June, but *appellate work did not suit him as well as presiding over trials. This predilection was brought even more to the fore nine months later when Eisenhower named Whittaker as Justice Stanley F. Reed's replacement on the Supreme Court.

On the early Warren Court, Whittaker frequently acted as a swing vote, sometimes siding with the liberal bloc consisting of the chief justice and Associate Justices Hugo L. Black, William O. Douglas, and William J. Brennan, and sometimes with the conservatives, Justices Felix Frankfurter, Harold Burton, Tom C. Clark, and John M. Harlan. Over time, he came to vote more consistently with the conservatives, although he himself was not responsible for any major opinions. Beset with a perfectionism born of a sense of inferior preparation and an inability to delegate, Whittaker worked himself into a nervous breakdown and on March 6, 1962, five years after assuming the high bench, he entered Walter Reed

Hospital, where his doctors recommended that he retire. He did so on March 29, making his retirement effective three days later.

After his retirement from the Court, Whittaker became an arbitrator for General Motors and accepted a Senate commission to draft a senatorial code of ethics, but he never resumed full-time legal practice and, unlike other retired justices, he did not engage in public service. He died on November 26, 1973, of a ruptured abdominal aneurysm.

POTTER STEWART

PERSONAL DATA

Born: January 23, 1915, in Jackson, Michigan
Parents: James Garfield Stewart, Harriet L. Potter Stewart
Higher Education: Yale University (B.A., cum laude, Phi Beta Kappa, 1937); Cambridge University, England, 1937-1938; Yale University Law School (LL.B.., with honors, Order of the Coif, 1941)
Bar Admissions: Ohio, 1942; New York, 1942
Political Party: Republican
Marriage: April 24, 1943, to Mary Ann Bertles, who bore Stewart two sons and a daughter
Died: December 7, 1985, in Hanover, New Hampshire
Buried: Arlington National Cemetery, Arlington, Virginia

PROFESSIONAL CAREER

Occupations: Lawyer, 1942, 1945-1950; Serviceman, 1942-1945; Politician, 1950-1953; Judge, 1954-1985
Official Positions: Member, Cincinnati, Ohio, City Council, 1950-1953; Vice Mayor, Cincinnati, 1952-1953; Judge, United States Sixth Circuit Court of Appeals, 1954-1958; Associate Justice, United States Supreme Court, 1958-1981

SUPREME COURT SERVICE

Appointed: October 14, 1958 (recess appointment)
Appointed By: Dwight D. Eisenhower
Oath Taken: October 14, 1958
Nominated: January 17, 1959
Confirmed: May 5, 1959
Confirmation Vote: 70-17

The Warren Court, 1968. From left: John M. Harlan II, Abe Fortas, Hugo L. Black, Potter Stewart, Earl Warren, Byron R. White, William O. Douglas, Thurgood Marshall, William J. Brennan Jr.

Oath Retaken: May 15, 1959

Replaced: Harold H. Burton

Significant Opinions: *Robinson v. California* (1962); *Edwards v. South Carolina* (1963); *Massiah v. United States* (1964); *Katz v. United States* (1967); *Jones v. Alfred H. Mayer Co.* (1968); *Chimel v. California* (1969); *Albermarle Paper Co. v. Moody* (1975); *Runyon v. McCrary* (1976); *Gregg v. Georgia* (1976); *Woodson v. North Carolina* (1976); *Mobile v. Bolden* (1980); *Harris v. McRae* (1980)

Left Court: Retired July 3, 1981

Length of Service: 22 years, 8 months, 19 days

Replacement: Sandra Day O'Connor

Potter Stewart was born into a socially prominent and politically active Cincinnati, Ohio, family. His father, a well known trial attorney, served several terms on the city council, then was mayor of Cincinnati for nine years before becoming a justice of the Ohio Supreme Court. Stewart was privileged to receive an excellent education, first at the University School in Cincinnati and at Hotchkiss School in Connecticut, then at Yale University. Upon graduating with honors from Yale in 1937, he was

awarded a fellowship to study at Cambridge University for a year, after which he returned to Yale to attend law school.

In 1941 Stewart graduated from Yale Law School, again with honors, and just had begun practicing with a New York law firm when the Japanese attacked Pearl Harbor. He then joined the Navy, receiving three battle stars for his service on fuel transports in the Atlantic and the Mediterranean. Stewart was discharged in 1945 as a lieutenant. He returned to his New York law firm for a brief time, but then moved back to Cincinnati, where he joined another firm and quickly gained a reputation as an outstanding litigator. Law led him to politics, and he was elected to the Cincinnati City Council in 1949 and 1951, also serving as vice mayor for a term.

Although he returned to private practice in 1953, Stewart's participation in Republican politics, particularly in the 1948 and 1952 presidential campaigns, led to his appointment in 1954 by President Eisenhower to the Sixth Circuit Court of Appeals. There Stewart established himself as one of the leaders of the federal bench, and when Justice Harold Burton retired from the Supreme

Court in 1958, Eisenhower named Stewart as a recess replacement. Stewart's confirmation hearings the following spring were delayed by southern senators who sought to undo, or at least delay, enforcement of the Court's integration orders growing out of *Brown v. Board of Education* (1954). On May 5, however, the Senate voted overwhelmingly to confirm Stewart. He was, at the age of 43, the youngest justice on the Warren Court and the second youngest justice (after William O. Douglas) to be appointed since the Civil War.

Stewart was a nonaligned swing vote throughout his career on the Court, during both Earl Warren's liberal regime and Warren Burger's more conservative one. Perhaps no clearer illustration of Stewart's significance as an independent exists than his opinion for the majority in *Gregg v. Georgia* (1976), in which the Court affirmed the constitutionality of the death penalty four years after Stewart had joined a 5 to 4 majority striking it down as cruel and unusual punishment in *Furman v. Georgia* (1972). *Gregg*, where a procedural change in Georgia's method of imposing *capital punishment produced the change in Stewart's posture, illustrates another of his salient attributes: his predilection for deciding cases on the narrowest possible grounds. Such an approach to decisions, he felt, permitted government flexibility in addressing social problems. His most significant contribution to constitutional *jurisprudence, *Jones v. Alfred H. Mayer Co.* (1968), greatly expanded the scope of civil rights legislation by allowing government, for the first time, to combat private discrimination. In cases such as *Katz v. United States* (1967), Stewart's opinions for the Court considerably restricted the scope of permissible search and seizure.

During his nearly 23 years on the Court, Stewart wrote over six hundred opinions, many of them concurrences designed to spell out with precision the reasoning behind his positions. His commitment to the Supreme Court was profound, but as Earl Warren approached retirement, Stewart quietly removed himself from consideration for elevation to chief justice by meeting privately with President Nixon. In 1981, at the relatively young age of 66, Stewart retired, and over the next four years served on selected federal appellate courts and on an international arbitration commission. He died on December 7, 1985, following a stroke.

BYRON RAYMOND WHITE

PERSONAL DATE
Born: June 8, 1917, in Fort Collins, Colorado
Parents: Alpha Albert White, Maude Burger White
Higher Education: University of Colorado (B.A., valedictorian, Phi Beta Kappa, 1938); Oxford University, England, Rhodes Scholar, 1939; Yale University Law School (LL.B., magna cum laude, Order of the Coif, 1946)
Bar Admission: Colorado, 1947
Political Party: Democrat
Marriage: 1946 to Marion Stearns, who bore White a son and a daughter

PROFESSIONAL CAREER
Occupations: Professional Athlete, 1938, 1940-1941; Serviceman, 1942-1946; Lawyer, 1946-1962; Government Official, 1961-1962; Judge, 1962-1993
Official Positions: Law Clerk to Chief Justice Fred Vinson, United States Supreme Court, 1946-1947; Chairman, Citizens for Kennedy, 1960; United States Deputy Attorney General, 1961-1962; Associate Justice, United States Supreme Court, 1962-1993

SUPREME COURT SERVICE
Nominated: April 3, 1962
Nominated By: John F. Kennedy
Confirmed: April 11, 1962
Confirmation Vote: Voice vote
Oath Taken: April 16, 1962
Replaced: Charles E. Whittaker
Significant Opinions: *Duncan v. Louisiana* (1968); *Williams v. Florida* (1970); *Johnson v. Louisiana, Apodaca v. Oregon* (1972); *Branzburg v. Hayes,* **In re Pappas, United States v. Caldwell* (1972); *Taylor v. Louisiana* (1975); *Washington v. Davis* (1976); *United Jewish Organizations of Williamsburgh, Inc. v. Carey* (1977); *Coker v. Georgia* (1977); *Zurcher v. The Stanford Daily* (1978); *Butz v. Economou* (1978); *Grove City College v. Bell* (1984); *United States v. Leon* (1984); *Bowers v. Hardwick* (1986); *Club*

Association v. City of New York (1988); *Ward's Cove Packing Co. v. Atonio* (1989); *Missouri v. Jenkins* (1990); *United States v. Fordice* (1992)
Left Court: Retired July 1, 1993
Length of Service: 31 years, 2 months, 15 days
Replaced By: Ruth Bader Ginsburg

Although Byron White's father served as mayor of Wellington, the small northern Colorado town where his family lived, the Whites were not a particularly prosperous family. As a youth, White excelled at academics and at the same time performed manual labor, working in the beet fields and on the railroad, to help support the family. At the University of Colorado, which he attended on scholarship, White continued to pursue both his intellectual and his physical development, being named a football All American in 1937 (he was named to the Collegiate Hall of Fame in 1954) and graduating first in his class the next year. He was awarded a prestigious Rhodes Scholarship, but he delayed taking it up for a term while he played professional football with the Pittsburgh Steelers, where as a running back he led the league in rushing and was the highest-paid player in the nation.

White went to Oxford University in January 1939, but with the outbreak of World War II that September he returned home along with other American students. He then entered Yale Law School while simultaneously playing professional football on weekends with the Detroit Lions during the 1940 and 1941 seasons. When the United States entered the war, so did White, enlisting in the Navy and serving as an intelligence officer in the Pacific until he was discharged as a lieutenant with a Bronze Star in 1946. He then returned to Yale Law School, from which he graduated with honors the same year.

After clerking for Chief Justice Vinson (White is one of only four future justices to have clerked at the Supreme Court), White took a position with a Denver law firm, where he devoted himself to general practice and developed a taste for politics. During the 1960 presidential contest, he organized Colorado Democrats behind candidate John F. Kennedy. He was asked by the future president's brother, Robert F. Kennedy, to head

Citizens for Kennedy, a nonpartisan group intended to attract uncommitted voters. After John F. Kennedy won the election, he appointed White as his brother Robert's deputy attorney general. In that position, which White held for a year, he was responsible for vetting the selection of nominees for lower federal court appointments and overseeing the enforcement of civil rights.

Upon Justice Charles E. Whittaker's retirement from the Court in April 1962, President Kennedy turned to White who, although he had never held elective office or served on the bench, seemed dedicated to Kennedy's New Frontier agenda. White took his seat on April 16 and, contrary to expectation, did not align himself with the liberal voting bloc headed by Chief Justice Earl Warren. With the replacement of Justice Felix Frankfurter that fall by Arthur J. Goldberg, the conservatives lost their long-time leader and the liberal bloc gained a solid majority. White responded by moving to the center, where his voting record and independence came to resemble Justice Potter Stewart's.

Although White was a consistent supporter of the Civil Rights Act of 1964 and the Voting Rights Act of 1965, he objected to what he viewed as the Court's fashioning of new individual rights. In *Roe v. Wade* (1973), he was one of only two dissenters, delivering a powerful rebuke to the majority for exercising "raw judicial power" in overturning statutes outlawing abortion based on a right of privacy that he found nowhere in the Constitution. And in 1986 he wrote the opinion for the Court in *Bowers v. Hardwick*, which upheld state antisodomy laws in the face of constitutional challenges once again based on privacy. In the area of Fourth Amendment and Eighth Amendment litigation, White repeatedly demonstrated disapproval for expansion of criminal rights; like Justice Stewart, he voted in favor of the death penalty, which the Court upheld in *Gregg v. Georgia* (1976) four years after striking it down in *Furman v. Georgia* (1972).

White retired from the Court at the end of the 1992 term, after spending more than three decades as a pragmatic, nondoctrinaire interpreter of the Constitution.

ARTHUR JOSEPH GOLDBERG

PERSONAL DATA

Born: August 8, 1908, in Chicago, Illinois
Parents: Joseph Goldberg, Rebecca Perlstein Goldberg
Higher Education: Crane Junior College, 1924-1925; DePaul University, 1924-1926; Northwestern University (B.S.L., first in class, 1929); Northwestern University Law School (J.D., summa cum laude, 1930)
Bar Admission: Illinois, 1929
Political Party: Democrat
Marriage: July 18, 1931, to Dorothy Kurgans, who bore Goldberg a daughter and a son
Died: January 19, 1990, in Washington, D.C.
Buried: Arlington National Cemetery, Arlington, Virginia

PROFESSIONAL CAREER

Occupations: Lawyer, 1929-1942, 1944-1961, 1968-1990; Serviceman, 1942-1944; Educator, 1945-1948, ca. 1970-1990; Government Official, 1961-1962; Judge, 1962-1965; Diplomat, 1965-1968, 1977-1978
Official Positions: United States Secretary of Labor, 1961-1962; Associate Justice, United States Supreme Court, 1962-1965; United States Ambassador, United Nations, 1965-1968; United States Ambassador-at-Large, 1977-1978

SUPREME COURT SERVICE

Nominated: August 31, 1962
Nominated By: John F. Kennedy
Confirmed: September 25, 1962
Confirmation Vote: Voice vote
Oath Taken: October 1, 1962
Replaced: Felix Frankfurter
Significant Opinions: *Murphy v. Waterfront Commission of New York* (1964); *Aptheker v. Secretary of State* (1964); *Escobedo v. Illinois* (1964)
Left Court: Resigned July 25, 1965
Length of Service: 2 years, 9 months, 24 days
Replacement: Abe Fortas

Arthur J. Goldberg's biography fits the archetype of the American success story. The youngest of eight children of poor Russian Jewish immigrants, he held odd jobs in his youth to help support his family, but he still managed to complete high school by the age of 15. He then began studying a college curriculum at Crane Junior College by day and DePaul University at night. At Northwestern University, where he transferred a year later, he graduated first in his class and received an honors law degree.

Having passed the Illinois bar at the age of 20, a year before receiving his law degree, Goldberg clerked for the Chicago law firm of Pritzker and Pritzker before opening his own practice. Except for the war years, during which he served in military intelligence investigating labor sabotage, he practiced law until 1961. He devoted himself to labor law, in 1948 becoming general counsel to the United Steelworkers of America and to the Congress of Industrial Organizations (CIO). He helped engineer the 1955 merger of the CIO and American Federation of Labor (AFL), and he remained as special counsel to the AFL-CIO until 1961.

Goldberg helped organize labor support for John F. Kennedy's successful 1960 bid for the presidency, and Kennedy rewarded Goldberg by naming him secretary of labor in 1961. The next year, after the retirement of Justice Felix Frankfurter, Goldberg was nominated to succeed him on the so-called "Jewish seat" on the Supreme Court (Justice Benjamin N. Cardozo had preceded Frankfurter). Goldberg immediately became Chief Justice Earl Warren's close friend and close ally, adding a crucial fifth vote to the liberal bloc that also included Justices Hugo L. Black, William O. Douglas, and William J. Brennan Jr. Goldberg's tenure on the Court lasted less than three years, but in that time he was responsible for a number of opinions that advanced individual liberties, such as *Escobedo v. Illinois* (1964), which overturned Escobedo's criminal conviction because he had been refused benefit of counsel during police interrogation.

In 1965, under pressure from President Lyndon B. Johnson, Goldberg reluctantly resigned from the Court to become U.S. ambassador to the United Nations. Goldberg did not find his new position congenial, and his frequent disagreements with Johnson over prosecution of the Vietnam War contributed to his resignation in

1968. Afterward, Goldberg resumed practicing law in New York City, and ran unsuccessfully for governor of New York against incumbent Nelson A. Rockefeller in 1970. He continued to practice law, and began lecturing on law and diplomacy at various universities. From 1977 to 1978 he served under President Jimmy Carter as ambassador-at-large, and in 1978 Carter awarded him the Presidential Medal of Freedom.

ABE FORTAS

PERSONAL DATA

Born: June 19, 1910, in Memphis, Tennessee
Parents: William Fortas, Ray Berson Fortas
Higher Education: Southwestern College (B.A., first in class, 1930); Yale University Law School (LL.B., second in class, Order of the Coif, 1933)
Bar Admissions: Connecticut, 1934; District of Columbia, 1945
Political Party: Democrat
Marriage: July 9, 1935, to Carolyn Eugenia Agger
Died: April 5, 1982, in Washington, D.C.
Buried: Cremated, no interment

PROFESSIONAL CAREER

Occupations: Educator, 1933-1939; Lawyer, 1934-1941, 1946-1965, 1969-1982; Government Official, 1934-1946; Judge, 1965-1969
Official Positions: Professor, Yale Law School, 1933-1939; Assistant Director, Corporate Reorganization Study, Securities and Exchange Commission, 1934-1937; Assistant Director, Public Utilities Division, Securities and Exchange Commission, 1938-1939; General Counsel, Public Works Administration, 1939-1940; Counsel, Bituminous Coal Division, 1939-1941; Director, Division of Power, Department of the Interior, 1941-1942; Undersecretary, Department of the Interior, 1942-1946; Associate Justice, United States Supreme Court, 1965-1969; Board Member, Kennedy Center for the Performing Arts, ca. 1970s; Board Member, Carnegie Hall International, ca. 1970s

SUPREME COURT SERVICE

As Associate Justice:
Nominated: July 28, 1965

Nominated By: Lyndon B. Johnson
Confirmed: August 11, 1965
Confirmation Vote: Voice vote
Oath Taken: October 4, 1965
Replaced: Arthur J. Goldberg
Significant Opinions: *In re Gault* (1967); *Tinker v. Des Moines Independent Community School District* (1969)
Left Court: Resigned May 14, 1969
Length of Service: 3 years, 7 months, 10 days
Replacement: Harry A. Blackmun
As Chief Justice:
Nominated: June 26, 1968
Nominated By: Lyndon B. Johnson
Nomination Withdrawn: October 4, 1968

As the son of an Orthodox Jewish cabinetmaker who emigrated from England, Abe Fortas began life modestly. He was academically gifted, however, and earned a scholarship to attend Southwestern College in his hometown, Memphis, Tennessee, from which he graduated first in his class in 1930. At Yale Law School he did nearly as well, graduating second in his class and becoming a protégé of then Professor William O. Douglas. Upon graduation, Fortas was offered a faculty position at Yale, and with the encouragement and assistance of New Dealer Douglas, Fortas simultaneously began working for the administration of Franklin D. Roosevelt.

Fortas first worked part time at the Agricultural Adjustment Administration, but in 1934 Douglas secured a position for him at the Securities and Exchange Commission. In 1939 Fortas quit teaching altogether and went to work for the Public Works Administration (PWA) as general counsel, transferring a few months later to the Bituminous Coal division when he realized the PWA would soon be dismantled. He continued to rise in the New Deal administration, finally becoming chief assistant to Secretary of the Interior Harold Ickes.

In 1946, at the end of the New Deal era, Fortas left government service to join in setting up Porter, Arnold & Fortas, a law firm specializing in representation of corporate clients. A number of the lawyers at the firm — Fortas among them — also engaged in *pro bono litigation involving civil rights. Among others, Fortas defended Owen Lattimore, a foreign policy expert targeted by Joseph McCarthy's anti-Communist crusade. And Fortas represented *appellants in a number of important cases concerning individual liberties, including *Durham v. United States* (1954), a District of Columbia Circuit Court case that liberalized the insanity defense, and *Gideon v. Wainwright* (1963), in which the Supreme Court extended the right to counsel to all criminal defendants in state courts.

Fortas also represented Lyndon Johnson in the latter's fight to save his narrow election victory in the 1948 Texas Democratic senatorial primary. From that time forward, Fortas and Johnson remained friends, and after Johnson reached the White House, Fortas was one of his closest advisors. Fortas enjoyed the ability to contribute informally to the administration while retaining his lucrative legal practice, and he refused Johnson's 1964 offer to make him attorney general. The next year, however, Johnson pressured Arthur Goldberg to step down from the Supreme Court, and without first obtaining Fortas's permission, nominated him as Goldberg's replacement.

Fortas was easily confirmed as associate justice, and over the next three years, like his predecessor, he voted with the Warren Court's liberal bloc, paying special attention, in opinions like that in *In re Gault* (1967), to the rights of juveniles. In 1968, after Chief Justice Warren informed the president of his wish to retire, Johnson attempted to elevate Fortas to the chief justiceship. By this point, however, Johnson was a lame-duck president, having announced his decision not to seek reelection, and Republicans, seeing an opportunity to have the next chief justice appointed by a president from their own party, filibustered the nomination. Many, including some sitting justices, were distressed by the presidential advisory role Fortas had continued to play even after joining the Court, and charges of cronyism were compounded by allegations of financial impropriety. Finally, Fortas requested that Johnson withdraw his nomination.

Fortas continued to serve on the Court, but a year later *Life* magazine disclosed that in 1966

Justice Fortas had accepted, then returned, $20,000 from a charitable foundation set up by one of his former clients, who at the time of the payment was under investigation for stock manipulation. On May 14, 1969, Fortas resigned, three days after a member of the House announced that he had prepared articles of impeachment against the justice and one day after the House Judiciary Committee began preliminary investigations into Fortas's financial dealings. When his old firm refused to take him back, he started a new one in Washington, D.C., again combining corporate and pro bono work. In 1982 he appeared once more before the Supreme Court as an advocate for Puerto Rico. Two weeks later he was dead of a heart attack.

THURGOOD MARSHALL

PERSONAL DATA
Born: July 2, 1908, in Baltimore, Maryland
Parents: William Canfield Marshall, Norma Arica Williams Marshall
Higher Education: Lincoln University (B.A., cum laude, 1930); Howard University Law School (LL.B., first in class, 1933)
Bar Admission: Maryland, 1933
Political Party: Democrat
Marriages: September 4, 1929, to Vivian Burey, who died on February 11, 1955; December 17, 1955 to Cecilia Suyat, who bore Marshall two sons
Died: January 24, 1993, in Washington, D.C.
Buried: Arlington National Cemetery, Arlington, Virginia

PROFESSIONAL CAREER
Occupations: Lawyer, 1933-1961, 1965-1967; Judge, 1961-1965, 1967-1991; Government Official, 1965-1967
Official Positions: Assistant Special Counsel, National Association for the Advancement of Colored People (NAACP), 1936-1938; Special Counsel, NAACP, 1938-1939; Director-Counsel, NAACP Legal Defense and Education Fund, Inc., 1939-1961; Judge, United States Second Circuit Court of Appeals, 1961-1965; United States Solicitor

General, 1965-1967; Associate Justice, United States Supreme Court, 1967-1991

SUPREME COURT SERVICE
Nominated: June 13, 1967
Nominated By: Lyndon B. Johnson
Confirmed: August 30, 1967
Confirmation Vote: 69-11
Oath Taken: October 2, 1967
Replaced: Tom C. Clark
Significant Opinion: *Benton v. Maryland* (1969)
Left Court: Retired June 27, 1991
Length of Service: 23 years, 8 months, 25 days
Replacement: Clarence Thomas

Thurgood (born Thoroughgood) Marshall, the first African American to serve on the nation's highest court, was named for his grandfather, a freed slave. Marshall's father was a club steward and his mother a schoolteacher. As an undergraduate, Marshall attended all-black Lincoln University in Pennsylvania, from which he graduated with honors in 1930. His demonstrated debating skills led him to decide on law school, and he briefly considered applying to his own state university, the University of Maryland, but gave up on the idea because the school only admitted white students. Instead, Marshall settled on all-black Howard University, from which he graduated in 1933 first in his class, despite having to commute to Washington, D.C., from his parents' home in Baltimore and despite having to work part time while pursuing his legal studies.

Howard University proved to be a fortuitous choice for Marshall, who made a vivid impression on law school Dean Charles Houston. In 1936, three years after Marshall had opened his own law practice in Baltimore, Houston was working as special counsel for the National Association for the Advancement of Colored People (NAACP), and he invited Marshall to act as his assistant. Using a strategy Marshall had already found effective in convincing the courts that a separate law school for African Americans at the University of Maryland was unequal to that attended by white students, Houston and Marshall won a major victory in the Supreme Court with *Missouri *ex rel. Gaines v. Canada* (1938). It was

only the first of 29 Supreme Court triumphs Marshall was responsible for, first in his capacity as special counsel of the NAACP, then as director of the NAACP Legal Defense and Education Fund, an organization set up to provide free legal representation to indigent African Americans who had discrimination complaints. These triumphs culminated in 1954 with the group of cases known as *Brown v. Board of Education*, in which Marshall used sociological data to convince the Court that the "separate but equal" doctrine was inherently unconstitutional.

In September 1961 President John F. Kennedy nominated Marshall to serve on the Second Circuit Court of Appeals, but Marshall served eleven months before he was finally confirmed in the wake of a prolonged attack by several southern senators. Marshall's record as a judge was as notable as it had been when he served as an advocate. In four years on the federal bench, none of his 98 opinions for the majority was overturned by the Supreme Court. In 1965 Kennedy named Marshall as the nation's first African American solicitor general, and again Marshall acquitted himself with singular distinction, winning 14 of the 19 cases he argued before the Supreme Court.

When Justice Tom C. Clark retired in 1967, President Lyndon B. Johnson decided that the time was right for the Court to receive its first African American member. Marshall had an impressive record, but he was obliged once again to undergo extensive questioning prior to his confirmation. Finally he was approved by a vote of 69 to 11.

Marshall joined the Warren Court in its waning days, and he not surprisingly became a member of the liberal voting bloc led by the chief justice. It is telling that the most important majority opinion Marshall wrote during his nearly 24 years on the Court, *Benton v. Maryland* (1969), which extended protection against *double jeopardy to state criminal defendants, was written in the last year of Earl Warren's tenure. After Warren Burger, and then William Rehnquist, assumed leadership of the Court, it took on a more conservative tone, and Marshall found himself frequently cast in the role of passionate dissenter.

After the Court reversed its position on the death penalty, legalizing it again in *Gregg v. Georgia* (1976), Marshall and the like-minded Justice William J. Brennan Jr. made it a practice to dissent in every case in which the death penalty was upheld by the Court.

Marshall had hoped to serve long enough to see his successor appointed by a Democratic president, but deteriorating health led him to resign in June 1991 while Republican President George Bush was still in office. Marshall continued to serve on selected federal *appellate courts until he died 19 months later.

SIGNIFICANT CASES

BROWN V. BOARD OF EDUCATION

Citation: 347 U.S. 483 (1954) (*Brown I*); 349 U.S. 294 (1955) (*Brown II*)
Argued: December 9, 1952; reargued December 7-9, 1953 (*Brown I*); reargued concerning implementation of desegregation, April 11-14, 1955 (*Brown II*)
Decided: May 17, 1954 (*Brown I*); May 31, 1955 (*Brown II*)
Courts Below: United States District Courts for the District of Kansas, the Eastern District of South Carolina, the Eastern District of Virginia, and the Delaware Supreme Court
Bases for Review: Appeals
Facts: *Brown* actually consisted of several cases, originating in Kansas, Delaware, Virginia, South Carolina, and the District of Columbia (the D.C. case was eventually decided separately on different grounds), tried together because of their commonality of issues. The titular case was brought by Oliver Brown, an African American Kansan, on behalf of his then seven-year-old daughter, Linda, who was not permitted to enroll in the school nearest her home because of state-mandated segregation.

The National Association for the Advancement of Colored People (NAACP) had, since the 1930s, brought a number of cases involving segregation before the Court in an effort to overturn the "separate but equal" doctrine of

Plessy v. Ferguson (1896), adopted throughout much of the nation and applied to all manner of public accommodations. Starting with *Missouri *ex rel. Gaines v. Canada* (1938), which outlawed Missouri's scheme of protecting its segregated schools by providing tuition assistance to prospective African American law students who agreed to attend out-of-state schools, the NAACP had gradually chipped away at the underlying legal rationale of *Plessy*: that the requirements of the Fourteenth Amendment's *Equal Protection Clause could be met with separate but equal accommodations for African Americans and whites. With acknowledgment, in cases such as *McLaurin v. Oklahoma State Regents for Higher Education* (1950) and *Sweatt v. Painter* (1950), that segregation caused intangible but real harm to African American citizens, the Supreme Court paved the way for *Brown*.

Yet, given the difficulty of dismantling the apparatus of Jim Crow laws, Chief Justice Fred Vinson, who had written the unanimous opinions in *McLaurin* and *Sweatt*, hesitated to endorse the NAACP's argument — buttressed by sociological data — that because it is harmful to African American children, separate but equal schooling violates the Fourteenth Amendment and is inherently unconstitutional. A divided Court decided to request reargument, but to delay it for a year. In the interim Vinson died.

Brown was one of the first issues Earl Warren had to confront when he became chief justice, and he did not shirk his responsibility. By separating the constitutional decision regarding segregated schooling from that concerning implementation of integration, he was able to convince every justice — even Robert H. Jackson, who had prepared a separate concurring opinion, and Stanley F. Reed, who had consistently voiced his intention to dissent — to sign onto his opinion and to make the Court's decision unanimous. (Because the rationale for integration in the District of Columbia could be found in the Fifth Amendment's *Due Process Clause, rather than the Fourteenth Amendment, which applies only to states, the Court's opinion in that case was issued separately as *Bolling v. Sharpe* [1954].) A second opinion in *Brown* (*Brown II*),handed down a year later, ordered the states to integrate their schools with "all deliberate speed," and placed the onus for enforcement on lower federal courts.

Issue: Does segregated schooling in state public school systems violate the Fourteenth Amendment's guarantee of *equal protection?

Outcome: Declaring that, "in the field of public education, the doctrine of 'separate but equal' has no place," Warren's opinion for the Court held that "[s]eparate educational facilities are inherently unequal," and overruled *Plessy v. Ferguson* in the area of public accommodations.

Vote: 9-0 (*Brown I*); 9-0 (*Brown II*)

Participating: Warren, Black, Reed, Frankfurter, Douglas, Jackson, Burton, Clark, Minton (*Brown I*); Warren, Black, Reed, Frankfurter, Douglas, Burton, Clark, Minton, Harlan (*Brown II*)

Opinion: Warren for the Court (*Brown I & II*)

Significance: Perhaps no case has had as great an impact on society as *Brown*. After the Court outlawed segregated schooling, it was inevitable that this ruling would be extended to other public accommodations. Over the next four years, the Court issued *per curiam opinions citing Brown as *precedent for invalidating segregated state parks, beaches, bathhouses, golf courses, and public transportation. Brown arguably provided impetus for the movement in Congress that resulted in the Civil Rights Act of 1964 and the Voting Rights Act of 1965 and, in the Court itself, for decisions that expanded the definition of civil rights to include enhanced First Amendment rights and rights accorded criminal defendants in state courts.

ULLMAN V. UNITED STATES

Citation: 350 U.S. 422 (1956)
Argued: December 6, 1955
Decided: March 26, 1956
Court Below: United States Second Circuit Court of Appeals
Basis for Review: *Writ of certiorari
Facts: Ullman was ordered under the Immunity Act of 1950 to testify before a *grand jury investigating threats to the national security. The act, which prohibited a witness from refusing to testify on grounds of self-incrimination, provided only *transactional immunity, prohibiting prosecution of the witness for criminal acts revealed in the course of the compelled testimony. Arguing that his testimony might cost him his job or result in social opprobrium, Ullman refused to testify and was given a five-month prison sentence for *contempt of court.

Issue: Does the Immunity Act of 1950 violate the Fifth Amendment privilege against self-incrimination?

Outcome: The Court upheld the Immunity Act.

Vote: 7-2

Participating: Warren, Black, Reed, Frankfurter, Douglas, Burton, Clark, Minton, Harlan

Opinions: Frankfurter for the Court; Reed concurring in part and dissenting in part (without written opinion); Douglas, joined by Black, dissenting

Significance: Because the Fifth Amendment only provides protection against compelled testimony that might result in criminal prosecution, not the kind of harm Ullman cited, the privilege against self-incrimination had no application in the context of the Immunity Act.

PENNSYLVANIA V. NELSON

Citation: 350 U.S. 497 (1956)
Argued: November 15-16, 1955
Decided: April 2, 1956
Court Below: Pennsylvania Supreme Court
Basis for Review: *Writ of certiorari
Facts: Steven Nelson, a Communist Party leader, was convicted in Pennsylvania state court of violating a state law proscribing *seditious libel. His conviction was reversed in the Pennsylvania Supreme Court, and the state appealed.

Issue: Does federal legislation, such as the 1940 Smith Act, which outlaws threats to the federal government, *preempt state statutes against the same activities, despite the fact that Congress has not expressly occupied the field governing such offenses?

Outcome: The Supreme Court found the Pennsylvania antisedition law, and other similar state laws, unconstitutional, and upheld the lower court's reversal of Nelson's conviction.

Vote: 6-3

Participating: Warren, Black, Reed, Frankfurter, Douglas, Burton, Clark, Minton, Harlan

Opinions: Warren for the Court; Reed, joined by Burton and Minton, dissenting

Significance: The *Nelson* decision proved to be anathema to the cold war mentality dominating Congress at the time it was handed down. A movement to pass legislation to overturn *Nelson* ultimately failed, however, because it was part of a broader legislation that aimed at ending implied preemption of all state laws that impinged on federal *jurisdiction, a proposal Congress found unpalatable.

SLOCHOWER V. BOARD OF EDUCATION OF NEW YORK

Citation: 350 U.S. 551 (1956)

Argued: October 19, 1955

Decided: April 9, 1956

Court Below: New York Court of Appeals

Basis for Review: Appeal

Facts: Harry Slochower, a tenured professor at Brooklyn College in New York, invoked his Fifth Amendment privilege against self-incrimination when testifying before the Senate Subcommittee on Internal Security, which was investigating subversion among educators. Citing a provision of the municipal charter, which prohibited invoking the Fifth Amendment with regard to testimony about official conduct, the New York City Board of Education terminated Slochower without first affording him the customary hearing.

Issue: Does the city charter provision violate the Fourteenth Amendment's guarantee of *due process under law?

Outcome: The provision was found unconstitutional.

Vote: 5-4

Participating: Warren, Black, Reed, Frankfurter, Douglas, Burton, Clark, Minton, Harlan

Opinions: Clark for the Court; Reed, joined by Burton, dissenting; and Minton and Harlan dissenting

Significance: The provision, which made the Fifth Amendment privilege equivalent to a confession of guilt, was clearly unconstitutional.

Without further investigation into Slochower's fitness, his dismissal was clearly unwarranted. Yet the fierce patriotism and suspicion bred by the cold war produced a close vote.

WATKINS V. UNITED STATES

Citation: 354 U.S. 178 (1957)

Argued: March 7, 1957

Decided: June 17, 1957

Court Below: United States Court of Appeals for the District of Columbia Circuit

Basis for Review: *Writ of certiorari

Facts: John T. Watkins, a union official, was called to testify before the House Un-American Activities Committee. He agreed to testify about his own affiliation with the Communist Party and about others he knew to be members of the party, but he refused to answer questions about individuals who might have been associated with it. He was convicted for *contempt of Congress.

Issue: Does Congress have unlimited power to investigate the private lives of individuals?

Outcome: Finding that the committee failed to limit its questions to the subject of the investigation, the Court set aside Watkins's conviction.

Vote: 6-1

Participating: Warren, Black, Frankfurter, Douglas, Clark, Harlan, Brennan (Burton and Whittaker not participating)

Opinions: Warren for the Court; Frankfurter concurring; Clark dissenting

Significance: *Watkins,* which held that the scope of congressional investigations is limited by their pertinence to the legislative function, is also significant for the general limits it placed on congressional power. Congress is not empowered to enforce the law, a function of the executive branch, or to try individuals, a function of the judiciary. Furthermore, the guarantees of the Bill of Rights limit the extent to which Congress may invade the private lives of individual citizens.

YATES V. UNITED STATES

Citation: 354 U.S. 298 (1957)

Argued: October 8-9, 1956

Decided: June 17, 1957

Court Below: United States Ninth Circuit Court of Appeals

Basis for Review: *Writ of certiorari

Facts: Fourteen alleged leaders of the Communist Party were convicted under the Smith Act of conspiring to organize party members to advocate the violent overthrow of the United States Government.

Issue: Does the Smith Act prohibit such abstract and hypothetical subversion?

Outcome: Finding that the statute prohibited only active planning and engagement in overthrowing the government, the Court struck down the convictions of five *appellants on grounds of insufficient evidence and *remanded the other nine cases for retrial.

Vote: 6-1

Participating: Warren, Black, Frankfurter, Douglas, Burton, Clark, Harlan (Brennan and Whittaker not participating)

Opinions: Harlan for the Court; Burton concurring; Black, joined by Douglas, concurring in part; Clark dissenting

Significance: The ruling in *Yates* curtailed the kind of sweeping government power to prosecute alleged subversion that had followed in the wake of *Dennis v. United States* (1951), in which the Court upheld the convictions of 11 defendants under the Smith Act for actually planning future subversion. Although the Court took considerable pains to distinguish its holding in *Yates* from that in *Dennis*, the distinction now made between advocacy of action and advocacy of doctrine made enforcement of the Smith Act far more difficult, and in fact no further charges were brought under its conspiracy provisions.

MALLORY V. UNITED STATES

Citation: 354 U.S. 449 (1957)

Argued: April 1, 1957

Decided: June 24, 1957

Court Below: United States District Court for the District of Columbia

Basis for Review: *Writ of certiorari

Facts: Andrew Mallory, a criminal suspect, was interrogated by police without being informed of his constitutional rights and endured a prolonged period of detainment before being brought before a court, where he was convicted and sentenced to death.

Issue: What are the constitutional limits to prolonged, unfocused police interrogations?

Outcome: Reasoning that the police should have probable cause before making an arrest, Justice Frankfurter, for the Court, reversed the conviction.

Vote: 9-0

Participating: Warren, Black, Frankfurter, Douglas, Burton, Clark, Harlan, Brennan, Whittaker

Opinion: Frankfurter for the Court

Significance: *Mallory*, together with the earlier *McNabb v. United States* (1943), in which incriminating statements made by an illegally detained defendant were ruled inadmissible in federal court, resulted in the so-called McNabb-Mallory rule, used by the Supreme Court to overturn state criminal convictions obtained in violation of a defendant's Fourteenth Amendment *due process rights. The *Mallory* ruling provoked considerable outrage, and the Court turned instead, in *Miranda v. Arizona* (1966), to a defendant's right to counsel and the privilege against self-incrimination to deal with the matter of inadmissible confessions. The McNabb-Mallory rule, which was not a constitutional precept, but a Court-formulated rule of evidence, was curtailed by federal legislation passed in 1968.

ROTH V. UNITED STATES; ALBERTS V. CALIFORNIA

Citation: 354 U.S. 476 (1957)

Argued: April 22, 1957

Decided: June 24, 1957

Courts Below: United States Second Circuit Court of Appeals (*Roth*); California Superior Court, Los Angeles County (*Alberts*)

Bases for Review: *Writ of certiorari (*Roth*); Appeal (*Alberts*)

Facts: Both defendants were convicted for violating statutes (one federal, the other state) prohibiting the production, mailing, or publishing of obscene or indecent materials.

Issues: Is publication of obscene material protected by the First Amendment? What constitutes obscenity?

Outcome: Reaffirming the *common law view that obscenity is not protected by the First Amendment, the Court upheld both federal and state antiobscenity laws.

Vote: 6-3 (*Roth*); 7-2 (*Alberts*)

Participating: Warren, Black, Frankfurter, Douglas, Burton, Clark, Harlan, Brennan, Whittaker

Opinions: Brennan for the Court; Warren concurring; Harlan dissenting in *Roth* only; Douglas, joined by Black, dissenting

Significance: *Roth* is important because in it the Court offered its first definition of obscenity, described in First Amendment terms. Although the Court accepted the long-standing common law view that obscenity is not protected, it did so in First Amendment terms, likening obscene matter to certain types of speech or conduct, such as perjury, which conveys no ideas and is "utterly without redeeming social importance." Justice Brennan's opinion defined obscenity as material, which, taken as a whole, appeals only to the prurient interest of the average person. This definition would be revised in *Miller v. California* (1973).

TROP V. DULLES

Citation: 356 U.S. 86 (1958)

Argued: May 2, 1957; reargued October 28-29, 1957

Decided: March 31, 1958

Court Below: United States Second Circuit Court of Appeals

Basis for Review: *Writ of certiorari

Facts: Albert A. Trop was found guilty of desertion during wartime and deprived of his American citizenship.

Issue: Is expatriation or denaturalization permissible punishment for wartime desertion?

Outcome: Arguing that denaturalization constitutes cruel and unusual punishment in violation of the Eighth Amendment, Chief Justice Warren's opinion for a *plurality of the Court reversed the decision below, *remanding the case for further hearings.

Vote: 5-4

Participating: Warren, Black, Frankfurter, Douglas, Burton, Clark, Harlan, Brennan, Whittaker

Opinions: Warren, joined by Black, Douglas, and Whittaker, for the plurality; Black, joined by Douglas, concurring; Brennan concurring; Frankfurter, joined by Burton, Clark, and Harlan, dissenting

Significance: The chief justice's Eighth Amendment argument convinced only a plurality of the Court (Brennan concurred on other grounds), but it later became the foundation for constitutional rulings regarding the death penalty, such as in *Gregg v. Georgia* (1976).

KENT V. DULLES

Citation: 357 U.S. 116 (1958)

Argued: April 10, 1958

Decided: June 16, 1958

Court Below: United States Court of Appeals for the District of Columbia Circuit

Basis for Review: *Writ of certiorari

Facts: The State Department denied Rockwell Kent a passport on the basis of the department's stated policy not to provide passports to Communists or others whose travel abroad might be against U.S. interests.

Issue: Does the State Department policy contravene the right to travel and the First Amendment right of free association?

Outcome: Deciding the case on statutory, rather than constitutional grounds, the Court ruled that the State Department was not empowered by Congress to withhold passports on the basis of individuals' beliefs or associations.

Vote: 5-4

Participating: Warren, Black, Frankfurter, Douglas, Burton, Clark, Harlan, Brennan, Whittaker

Opinions: Douglas for the Court; Clark, joined by Burton, Harlan, and Whittaker, dissenting

Significance: In *dicta Douglas acknowledged that the right to travel is protected by the *Due Process Clause of the Fifth Amendment, with the result that the Court recognized a constitutionally protected right to travel abroad.

NATIONAL ASSOCIATION FOR THE
ADVANCEMENT OF COLORED PEOPLE V.
ALABAMA *EX REL. PATTERSON

Citation: 357 U.S. 449 (1958)
Argued: January 15, 1958
Decided: June 30, 1958
Court Below: Alabama Supreme Court
Basis for Review: *Writ of certiorari
Facts: When the state of Alabama attempted legally to expel the National Association for the Advancement of Colored People (NAACP), the trial court requested that the association produce a number of documents, including its membership roster. The NAACP refused this last order and was found in *contempt and fined $100,000.
Issue: Did the Court's order violate the NAACP's right of association guaranteed by the First Amendment?
Outcome: A unanimous Court found for the NAACP.
Vote: 9-0
Participating: Warren, Black, Frankfurter, Douglas, Burton, Clark, Harlan, Brennan, Whittaker
Opinion: Harlan for the Court
Significance: This case is significant for its validation of two "new" First Amendment rights, which the Court found to be implicit in the amendment. In addition to the right to associate freely, *Alabama ex rel. Patterson* stands for the proposition that the right of free association includes a right of privacy. Permitting the NAACP to assert the rights of its members as a defense, the Court concluded that the individuals who make up the organization have a right to associate lawfully with whomever they choose without having their lives subjected to government scrutiny.

COOPER V. AARON

Citation: 358 U.S. 1 (1958)
Argued: August 28 and September 11, 1958
Decided: September 12, 1958 (*per curiam); September 29, 1958 (full opinion)
Court Below: United States Eighth Circuit Court of Appeals

Basis for Review: *Writ of certiorari
Facts: After *Brown v. Board of Education II* (1955) ordered public schools to integrate with "all deliberate speed," without providing an enforcement mechanism, Arkansas Governor Orval Faubus called in the state National Guard to prevent the entrance of nine African American students into Little Rock Central High School in September 1957. The governor backed off, but a riotous crowd prevented the students from entering. The next day, President Dwight D. Eisenhower sent federal troops to enforce the Court's desegregation order. Because of the turmoil, at the end of the school year the district court granted the Little Rock school board a 30-month extension of the deadline for implementing its desegregation plan. The National Association for the Advancement of Colored People appealed the federal court's extension to the Supreme Court. The Court met in special session during the summer of 1958 to hear the case.
Issues: Does postponement of integration owing to racial unrest violate the African American students rights? Are the governor and legislature of a state bound by decisions of the Supreme Court such as *Brown*?
Outcome: Holding that any postponement violated the students' right of *equal protection and that by virtue of the *Supremacy Clause, state executives and legislators are obliged to uphold Supreme Court decisions, the Court affirmed the *appellate court's reversal of the extension.
Vote: 9-0
Participating: Warren, Black, Frankfurter, Douglas, Burton, Clark, Harlan, Brennan, Whittaker
Opinion: One opinion of the Court, signed by all members
Significance: *Cooper* was the first — but not the last — serious attempt to challenge the *Brown* decision. It would take years of pressure by civil rights activists before Congress provided a mechanism to enforce desegregation. The Civil Rights Act of 1964 cited the *Brown* decision and gave the attorney general authority to intervene directly to compel states to comply with the Supreme Court ruling.

BARENBLATT V. UNITED STATES

Citation: 360 U.S. 109 (1959)
Argued: November 18, 1958
Decided: June 8, 1959
Court Below: United States Court of Appeals for the District of Columbia Circuit
Basis for Review: *Writ of certiorari
Facts: Barenblatt, called before the House Committee on Un-American Activities to testify about participation in a Communist organization at the University of Michigan, refused to comply. He was convicted of *contempt of Congress.
Issue: Are the First Amendment rights of a congressional witness subject to limitation?
Outcome: Using a balancing of interests, in which the government's interest in self-preservation outweighed a witness's right to such things as free association, the Court upheld Barenblatt's conviction.
Vote: 5-4
Participating: Warren, Black, Frankfurter, Douglas, Clark, Harlan, Brennan, Whittaker, Stewart
Opinions: Harlan for the Court; Black, joined by Warren and Douglas, dissenting; Brennan dissenting
Significance: Apparently in response to the congressional backlash that followed the 1957 decision in *Watkins v. United States* to limit the scope of congressional investigations, a majority of the Court retreated from this prior *holding, now permitting inquiry into political beliefs and associations and ignoring First Amendment concerns.

LASSITER V. NORTHAMPTON COUNTY BOARD OF ELECTIONS

Citation: 360 U.S. 45 (1959)
Argued: May 18-19, 1959
Decided: June 8, 1959
Court Below: North Carolina Supreme Court
Basis for Review: Appeal
Facts: An African American citizen of North Carolina challenged the state requirement that all citizens must be able to read and write a section of the state constitution in English in order to vote.

Issue: Does the North Carolina literacy requirement violate the *Equal Protection Clause of the Fourteenth Amendment by discriminating among potential voters?
Outcome: Finding that states have broad powers to set voting prerequisites, so long as they are not discriminatory, the Court upheld the South Carolina literacy requirement.
Vote: 9-0
Participating: Warren, Black, Frankfurter, Douglas, Clark, Harlan, Brennan, Whittaker, Stewart
Opinion: Douglas for the Court
Significance: When the Voting Rights Act was instituted in 1965, it temporarily suspended all requirements for voting, including literacy tests. In cases decided after passage of the act, such as *South Carolina v. Katzenbach* (1966) and *Katzenbach v. Morgan* (1966), the Court ruled against literacy tests, and subsequent amendments to the Voting Rights Act prohibited them altogether.

GOMILLION V. LIGHTFOOT

Citation: 364 U.S. 339 (1960)
Argued: October 18-19, 1960
Decided: November 14, 1960
Court Below: United States Fifth Circuit Court of Appeals
Basis for Review: *Writ of certiorari
Facts: African American voters challenged redrawing the boundaries of Tuskegee, Alabama, to exclude all but a handful of African Americans, but no whites. Their complaint was dismissed in federal district court, and the dismissal was affirmed upon appeal.
Issue: Is the legislative redistricting plan a violation of the Fifteenth Amendment's guarantee of the right to vote?
Outcome: The Supreme Court unanimously reversed the lower court.
Vote: 9-0
Participating: Warren. Black, Frankfurter, Douglas, Clark, Harlan, Brennan, Whittaker, Stewart
Opinion: Frankfurter for the Court; Douglas concurring (without written opinion), Whittaker concurring

Significance: Justice Frankfurter essentially reversed the views he had expressed 14 years earlier in *Colegrove v. Green* (1946) by resting his decision on the Fifteenth, rather than the Fourteenth Amendment. By making redistricting a subject for judicial consideration, rather than the *political question it previously had been, the Court opened itself to further challenges to legislative *apportionment. Shortly after handing down the decision in *Gomillion*, the Court indicated its intention to hear *Baker v. Carr* (1962), the case that would inaugurate the reapportionment revolution.

COMMUNIST PARTY V. SUBVERSIVE ACTIVITIES CONTROL BOARD

Citation: 367 U.S. 1 (1961)
Argued: October 11-12, 1960
Decided: June 5, 1961
Court Below: United States Court of Appeals for the District of Columbia Circuit
Basis for Review: *Writ of certiorari
Facts: The Subversive Activities Control Board (SACB), the enforcement mechanism for the 1950 Internal Security Act (the McCarran Act), ordered the Community Party to register with the attorney general. The party refused to do so because members of registered organizations were subject to such penalties as denials of passports and of employment in the defense industry. Eleven years of litigation followed, finally arriving at the Court with this case.
Issue: Are the registration provisions of the McCarran Act unconstitutional as *bills of attainder or violations of First Amendment guarantees?
Outcome: Although it did not address the constitutionality of the penalties for failure to register, the Court generally upheld the registration requirement.
Vote: 5-4
Participating: Warren, Black, Frankfurter, Douglas, Clark, Harlan, Brennan, Whittaker, Stewart
Opinions: Frankfurter for the Court; Warren, Black, and Douglas dissenting; Brennan, joined by Warren, dissenting

Significance: The Warren Court subsequently found most of the sanctions connected with the McCarran Act unconstitutional. In 1964, in *Aptheker v. Secretary of State*, passport denial was found to be a violation of the right to travel. In 1965, in *Albertson v. SACB*, compelled registration of members was ruled a violation of the Fifth Amendment. And in 1967, in *United States v. Robel*, the Court ended the ban on registered members working in defense plants. Finally, in 1973, the SACB was allowed to expire for lack of appropriation.

SCALES V. UNITED STATES; NOTO V. UNITED STATES

Citation: 367 U.S. 203 (1961) (*Scales*); 367 U.S. 290 (1961) (*Noto*)
Argued: Reargued October 10, 1960 (*Scales*); October 10-11, 1960 (*Noto*)
Decided: June 5, 1961
Courts Below: United States Fourth Circuit Court of Appeals (*Scales*); United States Second Circuit Court of Appeals (*Noto*)
Bases for Review: *Writs of certiorari
Facts: In both cases the *appellant was a member of the Communist Party convicted under the Smith Act.
Issue: Does the membership clause of the Smith Act, which requires proof of "active" membership in a subversive organization in order to convict, violate the *Due Process Clause of the Fifth Amendment or First Amendment guarantees of *freedom of speech and association?
Outcome: While a bare majority of the Court upheld Scales's conviction, by unanimous vote the justices overturned Noto's.
Vote: 5-4 (*Scales*); 9-0 (*Noto*)
Participating: Warren, Black, Frankfurter, Douglas, Clark, Harlan, Brennan, Whittaker, Stewart
Opinions: *Scales:* Harlan for the Court; Black and Douglas dissenting; Brennan, joined by Warren and Douglas, dissenting. *Noto:* Harlan for the Court; Brennan, Warren (without written opinion), Black, and Douglas concurring
Significance: While the Court found that the

level of Scales's involvement with the Communist Party included planning to overthrow the government, the party's advocacy of violence could not, without more evidence, be imputed to persons, like Noto, who were merely party members.

MAPP V. OHIO

Citation: 367 U.S. 643 (1961)
Argued: March 29, 1961
Decided: June 19, 1961
Court Below: Ohio Supreme Court
Basis for Review: Appeal
Facts: Police officers claiming they had a *warrant, although they did not, broke into Dollree Mapp's home in Cleveland, Ohio. While they did not find what they allegedly were seeking, their search turned up several allegedly obscene books and pictures. Mapp was convicted of possession of obscene materials, and her conviction was upheld in the Ohio Supreme Court on the basis of *Wolf v. Colorado* (1949), in which the Supreme Court held that the *exclusionary rule did not apply to state criminal prosecutions.
Issue: Does the Fourteenth Amendment *incorporate the Fourth Amendment's prohibition against illegal search and seizure, making it applicable to the states?
Outcome: A majority of the Court reversed Mapp's conviction and overruled *Wolf*, although only a four-member *plurality agreed with the Fourth Amendment rationale, Justice Black finding that incorporation was mandated by a combination of the Fourth and the Fifth Amendments. (Justice Stewart wrote separately, voting to reverse the judgment below, but refusing to join the opinion of the Court because he felt the issue of the exclusionary rule had not been properly *briefed).
Vote: 5-3-1
Participating: Warren, Black, Frankfurter, Douglas, Clark, Harlan, Brennan, Whittaker, Stewart
Opinions: Clark for the Court; Black and Douglas concurring; Harlan, joined by Frankfurter and Whittaker, dissenting; Stewart writing separately
Significance: After *Mapp*, the Fourth

Amendment was fully incorporated into the Fourteenth Amendment, requiring state police officials to follow Fourth Amendment guidelines during searches and state courts to honor the exclusionary rule in criminal prosecutions.

HOYT V. FLORIDA

Citation: 368 U.S. 57 (1961)
Argued: October 19, 1961
Decided: November 20, 1961
Court Below: Florida Supreme Court
Basis for Review: Appeal
Facts: Gwendolyn Hoyt murdered her husband when, during a quarrel about his adultery, he refused her offer of forgiveness. An all-male jury — the product of a Florida law providing that women could be included on jury lists only at their own request — convicted Hoyt of second degree murder. She appealed her sentence, claiming that female jurors would have better understood her plight.
Issue: Does the Florida statute deprive female criminal defendants of *equal protection under the law?
Outcome: Because it found that Florida did not apply its jury statute arbitrarily and allowed women to serve if they so chose, the Court upheld the law and Hoyt's conviction.
Vote: 9-0
Participating: Warren, Black, Frankfurter, Douglas, Clark, Harlan, Brennan, Whittaker, Stewart
Opinions: Harlan for the Court; Warren, joined by Black and Douglas, concurring
Significance: The decision in *Hoyt* overlooked the Court's earlier ruling, in *Ballard v. United States* (1946), that juries need to represent a cross-section of the defendant's community. Yet *Hoyt* was not rejected until nearly 30 years later, in *Taylor v. Louisiana* (1975).

BAKER V. CARR

Citation: 369 U.S. 186 (1962)
Argued: April 19-20, 1961; reargued October 9, 1961
Decided: March 26, 1962
Court Below: United States District Court for the

Middle District of Tennessee

Basis for Review: Appeal

Facts: A number of residents of Memphis, Nashville, and Knoxville, Tennessee, brought suit against Joe C. Carr, the Tennessee secretary of state, to overturn the state's existing electoral districts for the General Assembly, contending that it violated the *equal protection clause of the Fourteenth Amendment. The legislative district had not been reapportioned since 1901, and since then a considerable population shift from rural to urban areas had occurred. The state courts had refused to intervene. The federal court dismissed their complaint, finding that it lacked *jurisdiction and that the issue itself was a *political question not subject to judicial decision.

Issue: Are constitutional challenges to malapportionment of legislative districts open to adjudication in federal courts?

Outcome: Finding that the *Equal Protection Clause of the Fourteenth Amendment justified intervention by federal courts, the Court *remanded the case to the lower court for decision.

Vote: 6-2

Participating: Warren, Black, Frankfurter, Douglas, Clark, Harlan, Brennan, Stewart (Whittaker not participating)

Opinions: Brennan for the Court; Douglas, Clark, and Stewart concurring; Frankfurter, joined by Harlan, dissenting; and Harlan, joined by Frankfurter, dissenting

Significance: Chief Justice Warren called this case "the most vital decision" made during his tenure. Although *Baker v. Carr* did not establish the principle of "one person, one vote" — that occurred a year later in *Gray v. Sanders* — it opened federal courts to urban voters seeking equal representation. In one year 36 states were involved in reapportionment battles. The standard of reapportionment applied here, a "rationality test," soon became "one person, one vote," but it was further refined to require strict mathematical equality in federal congressional districts, while state legislatures were allowed more latitude in determining voting districts.

ENGLE V. VITALE

Citation: 370 U.S. 421 (1962)

Argued: April 3, 1962

Decided: June 25, 1962

Court Below: New York Court of Appeals

Basis for Review: *Writ of certiorari

Facts: Adoption by schools of a voluntary nondenominational prayer recommended by the New York State Board of Regents was challenged by the parents of ten students and the American Civil Liberties Union.

Issue: Does official state sanction of any religious utterance, even if it is nondenominational and only voluntarily recited, violate the First Amendment prohibition against state establishment of religion?

Outcome: The prayer was found to be unconstitutional.

Vote: 6-1

Participating: Warren, Black, Douglas, Clark, Harlan, Brennan, Stewart (Frankfurter and White not participating)

Opinions: Black for the Court; Douglas concurring; Stewart dissenting

Significance: While previous rulings on the constitutionality of prayer in public school in cases such as *Illinois *ex rel. McCollum v. Board of Education* (1948) and *Zorach v. Clauson* (1952) varied in their reading of how high the wall separating church and state should be, *Engel* made it clear that the Constitution does not permit public schools to sponsor religious activities.

ROBINSON V. CALIFORNIA

Citation: 370 U.S. 660 (1962)

Argued: April 17, 1962

Decided: June 25, 1962

Court Below: Los Angeles County Superior Court

Basis for Review: Appeal

Facts: Laurence Robinson was convicted under a California law making it a crime to be a drug addict and was sentenced to 90 days in jail.

Issue: Does the California law constitute cruel and unusual punishment prohibited by the Eighth Amendment and in violation of the Fourteenth

Amendment?

Outcome: The statute, which did not require proof of drug purchases, possession, or use, was ruled unconstitutional, and Robinson's conviction was reversed.

Vote: 6-2

Participating: Warren, Black, Douglas, Clark, Harlan, Brennan, Stewart, White (Frankfurter not participating)

Opinions: Stewart for the Court; Douglas concurring; White and Clark dissenting

Significance: The Supreme Court finding in *Robinson* that addiction is an illness rather than a crime has proven to be highly controversial. Indeed, the Court itself did not follow its own *precedent in *Powell v. Texas* (1968), where it upheld criminal conviction of a chronic alcoholic. Still, *Robinson* remains important for *incorporating the *Cruel and Unusual Punishment Clause of the Eighth Amendment into the Fourteenth Amendment, making it applicable to the states.

NATIONAL ASSOCIATION FOR THE ADVANCEMENT OF COLORED PEOPLE V. BUTTON

Citation: 371 U.S. 415 (1963)

Argued: November 8, 1961; reargued October 9, 1962

Decided: January 14, 1963

Court Below: Virginia Supreme Court

Basis for Review: *Writ of certiorari

Facts: A Virginia statute outlawing solicitation of cases by attorneys representing organizations that have no pecuniary interest in the outcome was challenged by the National Association for the Advancement of Colored People (NAACP).

Issue: Does the Virginia statute violate First Amendment protection of *free speech and association?

Outcome: Holding that group litigation, such as the racial discrimination suits brought by the NAACP, is protected by the First Amendment, the Court struck down the Virginia statute.

Vote: 6-3

Participating: Warren, Black, Douglas, Clark, Harlan, Brennan, Stewart, White, Goldberg

Opinions: Brennan for the Court; White concurring in part and dissenting in part; Harlan, joined by Clark and Stewart, dissenting

Significance: Stating that "the First Amendment . . . protects vigorous advocacy, certainly of lawful ends, against government intrusion," Brennan's opinion for the Court was a landmark for special interest groups which sought to utilize the courts to help achieve political ends. As the Court noted, sponsored litigation like *Button* was often the only means available to certain groups seeking solutions for problems long overlooked by legislators. Decisions of the Warren Court such as *Brown v. Board of Education* (1954) — which was sponsored by the NAACP — energized the whole Civil Rights movement and prompted passage of the Civil Rights Act of 1964 and the Voting Rights Act of 1965.

EDWARDS V. SOUTH CAROLINA

Citation: 372 U.S. 229 (1963)

Argued: December 13, 1962

Decided: February 25, 1963

Court Below: South Carolina Supreme Court

Basis for Review: *Writ of certiorari

Facts: Approximately two hundred fifty African American students marched peaceably to the state capitol in Columbia, South Carolina, where with placards they protested racial discrimination. Although a crowd of onlookers gathered, it too was peaceful. Nonetheless, the students were arrested and convicted of breach of peace.

Issue: Does the South Carolina breach of peace statute violate First Amendment guarantees of *free speech?

Outcome: Citing the student protest as a classic exercise of First Amendment privileges, the Court struck down the state law and reversed the students' convictions.

Vote: 8-1

Participating: Warren, Black, Douglas, Clark, Harlan, Brennan, Stewart, White, Goldberg

Opinions: Stewart for the Court; Clark dissenting

Significance: *Edwards* established the principle that the Fourteenth Amendment, which *incorporates the First Amendment, prohibits states from outlawing the expression of views deemed unacceptable, so long as they are expressed in a proper time, place, and manner.

FAY V. NOIA

Citation: 372 U.S. 391 (1963)
Argued: January 7-8, 1963
Decided: March 18, 1963
Court Below: United States Second Circuit Court of Appeals
Basis for Review: *Writ of certiorari
Facts: Noia was convicted in state court in New York of *felony murder on the basis of a confession, which in the case of two of his cohorts had been coerced. Noia failed to appeal his conviction to the state *appellate court in time, and now he applied to the federal courts for a writ of *habeas corpus. While the district court denied his request on grounds that he had not, as required, exhausted his state remedies, the court of appeals found that special circumstances excused Noia from this requirement.
Issue: May a state prisoner challenge his incarceration by seeking a federal writ of habeas corpus, even though he has not appealed his conviction through the state judiciary?
Outcome: Finding that Noia's procedural fault in letting too much time elapse before seeking review of his case in state court did not constitute a waiver of his right to seek federal relief, the Supreme Court upheld the federal appellate ruling.
Vote: 6-3
Participating: Warren, Black, Douglas, Clark, Harlan, Brennan, Stewart, White, Goldberg
Opinions: Brennan for the Court; Harlan, joined by Clark and Stewart, dissenting
Significance: The Judiciary Act of 1867 made a federal writ of habeas corpus available to state prisoners who alleged that their incarceration was the result of a violation of their federal rights. *Fay* expanded that right by making it clear that there were exceptions to the prerequisite that state prisoners must see their appeals all the way through the state system before seeking federal relief. In addition, in *dicta, the Court ruled that another prerequisite, petitioning the Supreme Court for *certiorari, no longer was considered a

state remedy in this context and no longer was necessary.

GIDEON V. WAINWRIGHT

Citation: 372 U.S. 335 (1963)
Argued: January 15, 1963
Decided: March 18, 1963
Court Below: Florida Supreme Court
Basis for Review: *Writ of certiorari
Facts: Clarence Earl Gideon was tried in a Florida state court for breaking and entering a pool hall with intent to commit a robbery. Under Florida law, this combination of offenses constituted a *felony. Gideon, who was indigent, was denied benefit of counsel. He defended himself, but he was convicted and sentenced to five years in prison. While incarcerated, he appealed directly and personally to the Supreme Court for redress.
Issue: Does the Sixth Amendment, as applied to the states through the Fourteenth Amendment, mandate appointment of counsel to all indigent criminal defendants charged in state court with serious offenses?
Outcome: A unanimous Court ruled that the state must appoint counsel in all such circumstances, and ordered that Gideon be retried.
Vote: 9-0
Participating: Warren, Black, Douglas, Clark, Harlan, Brennan, Stewart, White, Goldberg
Opinions: Black for the Court; Douglas, Clark, and Harlan concurring
Significance: In *Betts v. Brady* (1942), the Supreme Court held that the state need only appoint counsel to indigent criminal defendants under special circumstances. Since 1950, however, the Court had never upheld the state in cases concerning denial of representation and had been looking to overturn *Betts*. *Gideon* not only explicitly overruled *Betts*, but contributed enormously to the *due process revolution going on in the Warren Court. Later, in *Argersinger v. Hamlin* (1972), the Court made it clear that the *Gideon* ruling applied not only to alleged felons, but also to state *misdemeanor defendants faced with the prospect of incarceration. In addition, *Gideon* has given rise to cases in which it is argued that the right to counsel implies a right to effec-

tive counsel, and to other cases in which the juncture at which such appointments are made is the central issue.

GRAY V. SANDERS

Citation: 372 U.S. 368 (1963)
Argued: January 17, 1963
Decided: March 18, 1963
Court Below: United States District Court for the Northern District of Georgia
Basis for Review: Appeal
Facts: The Georgia county unit system of determining the outcome of state and federal congressional primary elections heavily favored rural voters, so that winners of the popular vote frequently lost elections. The federal district court found this system to be unconstitutional.
Issue: Does the Georgia election system violate the *Equal Protection Clause of the Fourteenth Amendment?
Outcome: The Warren Court upheld the lower court's invalidation of the Georgia system.
Vote: 8-1
Participating: Warren, Black, Douglas, Clark, Harlan, Brennan, Stewart, White, Goldberg
Opinions: Douglas for the Court; Stewart, joined by Clark, concurring; Harlan dissenting
Significance: Elaborating on its holding in *Baker v. Carr* (1962), the Warren Court set the stage for a series of cases resulting in legislative *reapportionment. Writing for the Court, Justice Douglas declared, "The conception of political equality... can only mean one thing — one person, one vote."

KER V. CALIFORNIA

Citation: 374 U.S. 23 (1963)
Argued: December 11, 1962
Decided: June 10, 1963
Court Below: California Second District Court of Appeal
Basis for Review: *Writ of certiorari
Facts: California police, without a search *warrant and using a passkey, entered George and Diane Ker's apartment, where they seized marijuana later used to convict the couple.
Issue: Are state officials held to the same Fourth Amendment standard of what constitutes rea-

sonable search and seizure applied to federal officials?
Outcome: Although eight of the justices found that states are held to the same standard as the federal government, four of them agreed that the warrantless search at issue here met that standard. Together with Justice Harlan, who disagreed with them on the constitutional issue, they voted to uphold the convictions.
Vote: 5-4
Participating: Warren, Black, Douglas, Clark, Harlan, Brennan, Stewart, White, Goldberg
Opinions: Clark for the Court; Brennan, joined by Warren, Douglas, and Goldberg, dissenting in part; Harlan concurring in the result
Significance: *Ker* is significant for making the *exclusionary rule binding upon the states. The finding that a warrantless search of a residence is legitimate, however, was implicitly overruled by subsequent decisions such as *Payton v. New York* (1980).

ABINGTON SCHOOL DISTRICT V. SCHEMPP

Citation: 374 U.S. 203 (1963)
Argued: February 27-28, 1963
Decided: June 17, 1963
Court Below: United States District Court for the Eastern District of Pennsylvania
Basis for Review: Appeal
Facts: The Schempps, whose case was sponsored by the American Civil Liberties Union, objected to a Pennsylvania statute mandating that Bible verses be read at the commencement of every school day in public schools.
Issue: Does the Pennsylvania law run afoul of the First Amendment's prohibition against state-sponsored religious activities?
Outcome: Reaffirming its *holding of a year earlier in *Engel v. Vitale*, the Court struck down the Pennsylvania law.
Vote: 8-1
Participating: Warren, Black, Douglas, Clark, Harlan, Brennan, Stewart, White, Goldberg
Opinions: Clark for the Court; Douglas and Brennan concurring; Goldberg, joined by Harlan, concurring; Stewart dissenting
Significance: The 1962 decision in *Engel v. Vitale*

had provoked great public outrage, even generating a multitude of proposals for constitutional amendments to reverse it. The Court's reaction was to restate the Constitution's clear ban on state establishment of religion. This time, however, the justices offered a standard for determining when legislation might breach the wall separating church and state: such laws should have "a secular legislative purpose and a primary effect that neither advances nor inhibits religion."

WESBERRY V. SANDERS

Citation: 376 U.S. 1 (1964)
Argued: November 18-19, 1963
Decided: February 17, 1964
Court Below: United States District Court for the Northern District of Georgia
Basis for Review: Appeal
Facts: Voters in Georgia's Fifth Congressional District, which contained at least twice as many voters as other congressional districts in the state, filed a *class action suit to prevent the state from conducting further elections until the district could be redrawn. The district court dismissed their complaint on grounds that it concerned a *political question not subject to judicial resolution.
Issue: Does the Georgia *apportionment violate Article I, section 2, of the Constitution, which provides that federal representatives are to be chosen by "the People of the several states," and the Fourteenth Amendment requirement that "Representatives shall be apportioned among the several states according to their respective populations"?
Outcome: The Georgia apportionment statute was found to be unconstitutional.
Vote: 7-2
Participating: Warren, Black, Douglas, Clark, Harlan, Brennan, Stewart, White, Goldberg
Opinions: Black for the Court; Clark concurring in part and dissenting in part; Harlan dissenting
Significance: The landmark case of *Baker v. Carr* (1962) held only that federal courts could rule on apportionment questions. With *Wesberry*, the reapportionment revolution became a reality.

States were now required to draw congressional districts so that they were as equal as possible in the number of voters each included, thus making each person's vote as weighty as the next.

NEW YORK TIMES CO. V. SULLIVAN

Citation: 376 U.S. 254 (1964)
Argued: January 6-7, 1964
Decided: March 6, 1964
Court Below: Alabama Supreme Court
Basis for Review: *Writ of certiorari
Facts: Four African American clergymen, associated with an organization called the Committee to Defend Martin Luther King and the Struggle for the South, and *The New York Times* were sued by Montgomery, Alabama, City Commissioner L.B. Sullivan over an advertisement carried in the newspaper. Sullivan claimed that the ad, which called for support of the Civil Rights movement and criticized Montgomery and other southern locales, not only contained a number of minor factual discrepancies but also libeled him. The trial court, which was instructed that the ad constituted *per se libel, found for Sullivan, awarding him $500,000 in damages against each defendant. The Alabama Supreme Court affirmed this verdict.
Issue: To what extent do First Amendment protections of *freedom of speech and of the press limit damage awards in libel suits brought by public officials?
Outcome: The Court overturned the award, holding that public officials may not recover damage awards for publication of defamatory falsehoods connected with their official conduct, unless they can prove such statements result from "actual malice," that is, they are "made with . . . knowledge that [they are] false or with reckless disregard of whether [they are] false or not."
Vote: 9-0
Participating: Warren, Black, Douglas, Clark, Harlan, Brennan, Stewart, White, Goldberg
Opinions: Brennan for the Court; Black, joined by Douglas concurring; and Goldberg, joined by Douglas, concurring
Significance: *The New York Times* case, which removed libelous statements from the universe

of unprotected speech (which includes other categories such as perjury and obscenity), was one of the most important of all First Amendment decisions. As Justice Brennan's opinion pointed out, the inherent difficulty with leaving arguably defamatory, possibly false criticisms of public officials unprotected is the chilling effect thus produced on the very type of expression the First Amendment was intended to safeguard. *New York Times* was subsequently expanded in cases such as *Curtis Publishing Co. v. Butts* (1967) to include allegedly libelous falsehoods directed at "public figures" such as film stars and athletes who, though not public officials, are well known to the public. This expansion was modified, however, in *Gertz v. Robert Welch, Inc.* (1974), which held that the actual malice standard does not apply to private individuals, even when they are associated with matters of public concern.

MASSIAH V. UNITED STATES

Citation: 377 U.S. 201 (1964)
Argued: March 3, 1964
Decided: May 18, 1964
Court Below: United States Second Circuit Court of Appeals
Basis for Review: *Writ of certiorari
Facts: After he had been *indicted for and pleaded not guilty to federal narcotics charges, Winston Massiah was released on bail. One of his codefendants, who had also pleaded not guilty and been released on bail, inveigled Massiah into discussing the case in the codefendant's car. Unbeknownst to Massiah, his codefendant, to whom he made several incriminating statements, had become an agent of the government and had wired his car with a radio transmitter.
Issue: Can Massiah's unwitting statements be used against him in court?
Outcome: Finding that the government's deliberate attempts to elicit information from Massiah outside the presence of his counsel constituted a violation of the Sixth Amendment, the Court ruled inadmissible Massiah's statements concerning the charges then pending against him.
Vote: 6-3

Participating: Warren, Black, Douglas, Clark, Harlan, Brennan, Stewart, White, Goldberg
Opinions: Stewart for the Court; White, joined by Clark and Harlan, dissenting
Significance: *Massiah* and the later *Miranda v. Arizona* (1966) marked radical changes in criminal procedure. But while the expansion of criminal rights under the later case was based on the Fifth Amendment privilege against self-incrimination, the outcome of *Massiah* hinged on the fact that the government approached the defendant after proceedings had begun and the Sixth Amendment right to counsel had been activated. Subsequent cases have limited the *Massiah* doctrine by allowing admission of incriminating statements gathered by a government "passive" informant who merely absorbs information, rather than actively draws the defendant out.

GRIFFIN V. COUNTY SCHOOL BOARD OF PRINCE EDWARD COUNTY

Citation: 377 U.S. 218 (1964)
Argued: March 30, 1964
Decided: May 25, 1964
Court Below: United States Fourth Circuit Court of Appeals
Basis for Review: *Writ of certiorari
Facts: Rather than comply with the desegregation order of *Brown v. Board of Education II* (1955), the school board of Prince Edward County, Virginia, in line with state law, closed public schools and provided tuition grants and tax credits to all-white private schools.
Issue: Does the closing of all public schools to prevent integration violate the *Equal Protection Clause of the Fourteenth Amendment?
Outcome: The Court found that the federal district court overseeing compliance with *Brown II* had authority over the board's taxing and spending powers, and could thus *enjoin financial aid to private schools. It was also within the district court's power, in the majority's view, to order public schools to reopen (Justices Tom C. Clark and John M. Harlan noted their disagreement with this last point).
Vote: 9-0

Participating: Warren, Black, Douglas, Clark, Harlan, Brennan, Stewart, White, Goldberg
Opinions: Black for the Court; Clark concurring and Harlan concurring (without written opinion)
Significance: School boards across the country heard the impatience in Justice Black's declaration that the "time for mere 'deliberate speed' has run out." After *Griffin*, school boards began serious efforts to desegregate the public schools.

MALLOY V. HOGAN

Citation: 378 U.S. 1 (1964)
Argued: March 5, 1964
Decided: June 15, 1964
Court Below: Connecticut Supreme Court
Basis for Review: *Writ of certiorari
Facts: Malloy's guilty plea to unlawful gambling charges in state court resulted in a one-year prison term. After serving 90 days, however, he was released and placed on two years of probation. During this time, he was called to testify before a state committee investigating gambling, but pleading the Fifth Amendment, he refused to answer questions concerning his previous conviction and was found in *contempt and placed back in jail until he agreed to testify. The state courts had refused his petitions for *habeas corpus.
Issue: Is the Fifth Amendment privilege against self-incrimination applicable to the states?
Outcome: Finding that the *Due Process Clause of the Fourteenth Amendment *incorporates this privilege, the Court reversed the court below.
Vote: 5-4
Participating: Warren, Black, Douglas, Clark, Harlan, Brennan, Stewart, White, Goldberg
Opinions: Brennan for the Court; Douglas concurring (without written opinion); Harlan, joined by Clark dissenting; and White, joined by Stewart, dissenting
Significance: *Malloy* overturned the traditional view that the Fourteenth Amendment's Due Process Clause only required the states to exhibit fundamental fairness towards criminal defendants and did not require adoption of the privilege against self-incrimination. The decision also overruled *Twining v. New Jersey* (1908) and *Adamson v. California* (1947), henceforth placing on the

state the burden of producing evidence against criminal defendants who do not testify willingly at their own trials.

MURPHY V. WATERFRONT COMMISSION OF NEW YORK

Citation: 378 U.S. 52 (1964)
Argued: March 5, 1964
Decided: June 15, 1964
Court Below: New Jersey Supreme Court
Basis for Review: *Writ of certiorari
Facts: The petitioners in *Murphy* were *subpoenaed to testify before the New York Waterfront Commission. When they refused to answer certain questions, citing self-incrimination, they were granted *immunity from prosecution in New York and New Jersey, but they still refused to answer on grounds that such testimony might incriminate them under federal law.
Issue: Can the state compel a witness to testify under an immunity statute when his testimony might prove incriminating in a federal prosecution?
Outcome: The outcome of *Malloy v. Hogan* (1964), decided the same day, also was determinative of the outcome in this case. The Court found that compelled incriminating testimony obtained by either state or federal authorities is inadmissible in courts of either *jurisdiction.
Vote: 9-0
Participating: Warren, Black, Douglas, Clark, Harlan, Brennan, Stewart, White, Goldberg
Opinion: Goldberg for the Court; Harlan, joined by Clark, concurring
Significance: *Murphy* made it clear that immunity granted in one jurisdiction had to be broad enough to include all jurisdictions. This so-called "use" immunity nullifies any subsequent proceeding in another jurisdiction in which the defendant's earlier testimony is used against him, unless the proceeding results from evidence obtained entirely independently of the earlier proceeding.

REYNOLDS V. SIMS

Citation: 377 U.S. 533 (1964)
Argued: November 13, 1963

Decided: June 15, 1964

Court Below: United States District Court for the Middle District of Alabama

Basis for Review: Appeal

Facts: Much litigation followed the Court's decision in *Baker v. Carr* (1962) to the effect that federal courts were able to rule on the relative sizes of legislative districts. The Court decided six separate *reapportionment cases from six different states — collectively known as the *Reapportionment Cases* — on June 16, 1964, but delivered its rationale in connection with *Reynolds*, the case from Alabama. *Reynolds* originated in a state where voter distribution was especially lopsided and had produced the first judicially ordered redistricting plan in the nation, which was promptly appealed to the Supreme Court.

Issue: Does the Fourteenth Amendment's requirement that "Representatives shall be apportioned among the several states according to their respective populations" require application of the "one person, one vote" principle to state legislatures?

Outcome: The Court held that the Fourteenth Amendment, applicable to states only, dictates that representation in both houses of state legislatures be based on population.

Vote: 8-1

Participating: Warren, Black, Douglas, Clark, Harlan, Brennan, Stewart, White, Goldberg

Opinions: Warren for the Court; Clark and Stewart concurring; Harlan dissenting

Significance: The results of *Reynolds* were extraordinarily far-reaching. Because the Court rejected the argument that state legislatures could be modeled along the same lines as the federal Congress, in which the size of one house — the Senate — was not determined by population, at least one-half of most state legislatures were now rendered unconstitutional. Within two years, virtually all states had redrawn their legislative districts, putting into practice the principle of equal representation. This case also led to expanded suffrage in the District of Columbia in 1961, when the Twenty-third Amendment granted eligible residents of D.C. the right to vote in presidential elections.

APTHEKER V. SECRETARY OF STATE

Citation: 378 U.S. 500 (1964)

Argued: April 21, 1964

Decided: June 22, 1964

Court Below: United States District Court for the District of Columbia

Basis for Review: Appeal

Facts: Two prominent members of the American Communist Party were denied passports under the Internal Security Act of 1950 (the McCarran Act).

Issue: Does the McCarran Act unconstitutionally interfere with the right to travel?

Outcome: Finding the language of the act too broad because it failed to distinguish between actual subversives and passive, "unknowing" members of the party, the Court struck down the provision in question.

Vote: 6-3

Participating: Warren, Black, Douglas, Clark, Harlan, Brennan, Stewart, White, Goldberg

Opinions: Goldberg for the Court; Black and Douglas concurring; Clark, joined by Harlan, dissenting; White dissenting in part

Significance: Although the Court had ruled in *Kent v. Dulles* (1958) that international travel was protected by the Fifth Amendment, the legislative authority overturned there rested on a policy developed during the cold war under the Passport Act of 1926. In *Aptheker* the government relied on the McCarran Act, which had been upheld in *Communist Party v. Subversive Activities Control Board* (1961). Now this cold war prohibition on travel by alleged Communists was similarly found unconstitutional.

ESCOBEDO V. ILLINOIS

Citation: 378 U.S. 478 (1964)

Argued: April 29, 1964

Decided: June 22, 1964

Court Below: Illinois Supreme Court

Basis for Review: *Writ of certiorari

Facts: Danny Escobedo was detained by police on suspicion of murder. The police continually ignored his requests to speak with his lawyer, who was at the police station. During interrogation, Escobedo admitted to committing the crime. His conviction was first reversed by the Illinois Supreme Court, but then, after a retrial, reinstated on grounds that the right to counsel does not attach until a criminal suspect is formally *indicted.

Issue: At what point in criminal proceedings does the Sixth Amendment right to counsel become operative?

Outcome: Escobedo's conviction and confession were thrown out.

Vote: 5-4

Participating: Warren, Black, Douglas, Clark, Harlan, Brennan, Stewart, White, Goldberg

Opinions: Goldberg for the Court; White, joined by Clark and Stewart, dissenting, and Harlan dissenting

Significance: In *Massiah v. United States* (1964), the Court overturned a criminal conviction because the defendant's damning admissions were obtained at a point when he was without benefit of counsel after the commencement of adversarial proceedings. *Escobedo* clearly went beyond this, because Escobedo's confession was obtained during police interrogation. Nonetheless, Justice Goldberg's opinion for the Court was less than clear about when the right to counsel attaches. The issue was clarified two years later in *Miranda v. Arizona* (1966), in which the Warren Court's expansion of criminals' rights and tightening of standards for admissibility of coerced confessions was explained in terms of the Fifth Amendment privilege against self-incrimination.

HEART OF ATLANTA MOTEL, INC. V. UNITED STATES

Citation: 379 U.S. 241 (1964)
Argued: October 5, 1964
Decided: December 14, 1964
Court Below: United States District Court for the Northern District of Georgia
Basis for Review: Appeal
Facts: The Heart of Atlanta Motel, which catered to transient out-of-state clients, refused to accommodate African American patrons. The federal district court, relying on the public accommodations section of the Civil Rights Act of 1964, permanently *enjoined the motel from such racial discrimination.

Issue: Can federal antidiscrimination legislation laws be enforced against privately owned public accommodations?

Outcome: Citing Congress's powers under the *Commerce Clause to regulate intrastate facilities that affect interstate commerce, the Court unanimously affirmed the district court's decision.

Vote: 9-0

Participating: Warren, Black, Douglas, Clark, Harlan, Brennan, Stewart, White, Goldberg

Opinions: Clark for the Court; Black, Douglas, and Goldberg concurring

Significance: Effectively overruling the *Civil Rights Cases* (1883), *Heart of Atlanta* was an important endorsement of the Civil Rights Act of 1964, as well as Congress's broad *police powers under the Commerce Clause.

KATZENBACH V. MCCLUNG

Citation: 379 U.S. 294 (1964)
Argued: October 5, 1964
Decided: December 14, 1964
Court Below: United States District Court for the Northern District of Alabama
Basis for Review: Appeal
Facts: Ollie's Barbeque, a small restaurant located in Birmingham, Alabama, had a policy of refusing to serve African Americans.

Issue: Can small-scale private racial discrimination in public accommodations be regulated by Congress?

Outcome: The Court held that because some of the food served in the restaurant originated out of state, the *Commerce Clause empowered Congress to proscribe segregation at Ollie's.

Vote: 9-0

Participating: Warren, Black, Douglas, Clark, Harlan, Brennan, Stewart, White, Goldberg

Opinions: Clark for the Court; Black, Douglas, and Goldberg concurring

Significance: Because racial segregation continued to dog the nation and Congress had not yet conclusively acted to counter it, the Court employed an extraordinarily expansive interpretation of the commerce power as a solution. *Katzenbach*, which remains as *precedent and stands for the proposition that Congress needs only a *"rational basis" for connecting local economic activity with interstate commerce to justify regulation, demonstrates the flexibility and far-reaching nature of this constitutional grant of authority.

POINTER V. TEXAS

Citation: 380 U.S. 400 (1965)
Argued: March 15, 1965
Decided: April 5, 1965
Court Below: Texas Court of Criminal Appeals
Basis for Review: *Writ of certiorari
Facts: Pointer, a criminal defendant, was convicted largely on the basis of the state trial court's admission of transcribed testimony taken at an earlier proceeding at which Pointer had been present, but was not represented by counsel.
Issue: Is the Sixth Amendment guarantee of the right of the accused to confront and cross-examine witnesses against him applicable in state criminal proceedings?
Outcome: Citing the *Due Process Clause of the Fourteenth Amendment, the Court held that this privilege does apply to the states and reversed Pointer's conviction, *remanding his case for further hearings.
Vote: 9-0
Participating: Warren, Black, Douglas, Clark, Harlan, Brennan, Stewart, White, Goldberg
Opinions: Black for the Court; Harlan, Stewart, and Goldberg concurring
Significance: Although most states had long recognized the right of confrontation, *Pointer* is important because it emphasized that the standards for applying this right were to be uniform: although Pointer was present at the proceeding where the determinative testimony was given, his right to cross-examination by counsel had been thwarted.

DOMBROWSKI V. PFISTER

Citation: 380 U.S. 479 (1965)
Argued: January 25, 1965
Decided: April 26, 1965
Court Below: United States District Court for the Eastern District of Louisiana
Basis for Review: Appeal

Facts: Dombrowski, an official of the Southern Conference Educational Fund, sought to *enjoin the governor, police, and a state antisubversive committee from enforcing Louisiana's subversion statutes. Dombrowski claimed that constant harassment by the state was endangering his organization's First Amendment rights, but the federal district court dismissed his complaint on grounds that the *abstention doctrine permitted state courts to interpret state laws that conformed to the Constitution.
Issue: Must federal courts refrain from ruling on the constitutionality of state criminal statutes when the person challenging them has not exhausted all available state procedures?
Outcome: Finding that the Louisiana statutes violated the First Amendment, the Supreme Court reversed the lower court.
Vote: 5-2
Participating: Warren, Douglas, Clark, Harlan, Brennan, White, Goldberg (Black and Stewart not participating)
Opinions: Brennan for the Court; Harlan, joined by Clark, dissenting
Significance: Brennan's opinion for the Court stressed that the chilling effect of the Louisiana statutes on free expression was so great that it justified federal intervention, despite the federal practice of not interfering with state criminal prosecutions. Subsequently, many cases were filed in federal courts by those attempting to circumvent state criminal prosecutions, but the Court ended this practice with its decision in *Younger v. Harris* (1971).

GRIFFIN V. CALIFORNIA

Citation: 380 U.S. 609 (1965)
Argued: March 9, 1965
Decided: April 28, 1965
Court Below: California Supreme Court
Basis for Review: *Writ of certiorari
Facts: Griffin was convicted of first degree murder after failing to testify on the issue of his guilt. He did testify at a separate penalty hearing, where both the prosecutor and the judge's jury instructions referred unfavorably to his earlier failure to testify. He was sentenced to death.

Issue: Does a state violate the Fifth Amendment privilege against self-incrimination when a judge or prosecutor comments unfavorably on a criminal defendant's failure to testify on his own behalf?
Outcome: Griffith's conviction and sentence were reversed.
Vote: 6-2
Participating: Black, Douglas, Clark, Harlan, Brennan, Stewart, White, Goldberg (Warren not participating)
Opinions: Douglas for the Court; Harlan, concurring; Stewart, joined by White, dissenting
Significance: Overruling *Adamson v. California* (1947), *Griffin* underscores the importance of the presumption of innocence in the American criminal justice system. As Justice Douglas's opinion for the Court states, defendants should not be forced to pay a price for refusing to speak.

GRISWOLD V. CONNECTICUT

Citation: 381 U.S. 479 (1965)
Argued: March 29, 1965
Decided: June 7, 1965
Court Below: Connecticut Supreme Court
Basis for Review: Appeal
Facts: Griswold and Buxton, the executive and medical directors of the Planned Parenthood League of Connecticut, were convicted under an 1879 state statute prohibiting the use of contraceptives as well as distribution of information and advice on contraception to married couples.
Issues: Do Griswold and Buxton have *standing to sue? Does the Connecticut statute violate the rights of married persons?
Outcome: The Court found that Griswold and Buxton had *standing to raise the issue of the constitutional rights of those with whom they had professional relationships, and it struck the statute down as violative of such persons' constitutional right to privacy.
Vote: 7-2
Participating: Warren, Black, Douglas, Clark, Harlan, Brennan, Stewart, White, Goldberg
Opinions: Douglas for the Court; Goldberg, joined by Warren and Brennan, concurring; Harlan and White concurring; Black, joined by Stewart, dissenting

Significance: *Griswold* is significant primarily for two reasons. First, by granting full constitutional protection to a right of privacy, the decision amplified the increased scrutiny the Court had been giving since 1937 to laws hindering fundamental personal rights. Second, by providing ample justification for the protection of this "new" right, *enumerated nowhere in the Constitution, the decision sparked a profound debate about the nature of constitutional decision-making. Because of his unwavering support for the expansion of individual rights, Justice Hugo L. Black's dissenting opinion might at first seem surprising. Justice Black felt, however, that in protecting a right without a constitutional identity, the Warren Court was repeating the error made by those justices who, at the turn of the century, imposed their personal biases on society by endorsing *substantive due process. But to William O. Douglas, writing for the majority, "specific guarantees . . . have penumbras, formed by emanations from those guarantees that help give them life and substance," in this instance the First, Third, Fourth, Fifth, and Ninth Amendments. The right of privacy reached its apogee in 1973 with *Roe v. Wade*, where it was used to protect a woman's right to abortion. But as the Court has subsequently trimmed back this protection and refused to extend the right of privacy to homosexuals, the future of this implicit right has become uncertain.

ALBERTSON V. SUBVERSIVE ACTIVITIES CONTROL BOARD

Citation: 382 U.S. 70 (1965)
Argued: October 18, 1965
Decided: November 15, 1965
Court Below: United States Court of Appeals for the District of Columbia Circuit
Basis for Review: *Writ of certiorari
Facts: Albertson and other leaders of the Communist Party refused to register with the attorney general as required by the Internal Security Act of 1950 (the McCarran Act).
Issue: Does the registration requirement violate the Fifth Amendment privilege against self-incrimination?

Outcome: The Court found that although registration itself was purportedly not grounds for prosecution, it might be used as evidence in some future criminal action. The justices voted unanimously to strike down this provision of the McCarran Act.

Vote: 8-0

Participating: Warren, Black, Douglas, Clark, Harlan, Brennan, Stewart, Fortas (White not participating)

Opinions: Brennan for the Court; Black concurring (without written opinion)

Significance: Although the Court previously had upheld the registration requirement of the act in *Communist Party v. Subversive Activities Control Board* (1961), decisions on the sanctions connected with failing to register were delayed until properly brought before the Court. One by one, they too were struck down, and the board was allowed to die in 1973 for lack of appropriation.

SOUTH CAROLINA V. KATZENBACH

Citation: 383 U.S. 301 (1966)

Argued: January 17-18, 1966

Decided: March 7, 1966

Court Below: None

Basis for Review: *Original Supreme Court jurisdiction

Facts: South Carolina challenged the application and validity of the Voting Rights Act of 1965.

Issue: Is the act a proper exercise of congressional power under the Fifteenth Amendment's ban on racial discrimination in voting?

Outcome: Constitutional authorization for the act, as well as its various enforcement provisions, were upheld.

Vote: 8-1

Participating: Warren, Black, Douglas, Clark, Harlan, Brennan, Stewart, White, Fortas

Opinions: Warren for the Court; Black concurring in part and dissenting in part

Significance: Warren's opinion stressed the traditional latitude given Congress in its role as legislature: legitimate constitutional goals may be pursued by all appropriate means. This reasoning, applied to enforce the Fifteenth Amendment,

proved to be a powerful *precedent for enforcing the other Civil War Amendments in *Katzenbach v. Morgan* (1966) and *Jones v. Alfred H. Mayer Co.* (1968).

HARPER V. VIRGINIA STATE BOARD OF ELECTIONS

Citation: 383 U.S. 663 (1966)

Argued: January 25-26, 1966

Decided: March 24, 1966

Court Below: United States District Court for the Eastern District of Virginia

Basis for Review: Appeal

Facts: In 1964 the states ratified the Twenty-fourth Amendment, prohibiting the use of poll taxes as a condition to voting in federal elections. This case challenged the Virginia $1.50 annual poll tax levied as a requirement for voting in state elections. The federal district court, following *Breedlove v. Suttles* (1937), dismissed the *complaint.

Issue: Do state poll taxes violate the *Equal Protection Clause of the Fourteenth Amendment?

Outcome: The Court found that such fees as the Virginia poll tax were unconstitutional, partially overruling *Breedlove*.

Vote: 6-3

Participating: Warren, Black, Douglas, Clark, Harlan, Brennan, Stewart, White, Fortas

Opinions: Douglas for the Court; Black dissenting; and Harlan, joined by Stewart, dissenting

Significance: By holding that all voters must have equal access to state elections, Harper advanced the logic of *Reynolds v. Sims* (1964).

ELFBRANDT V. RUSSELL

Citation: 384 U.S. 11 (1966)

Argued: February 24, 1966

Decided: April 18, 1966

Court Below: Arizona Supreme Court

Basis for Review: *Writ of certiorari

Facts: In connection with a loyalty oath required of all Arizona state employees, a teacher objected to the legislature's use of the oath to prohibit membership in the Communist Party or any other organization planning the violent overthrow of the government. Violators could be fired or prosecuted for perjury. After the state supreme court upheld the oath, the Warren Court *remanded the case for reconsideration. The Arizona Supreme Court upheld the oath once more.

Issue: Does the Arizona loyalty oath, as interpreted by the state legislature, impinge on freedom of association as guaranteed by the First and Fourteenth Amendments?

Outcome: Finding that the legislative gloss on the Arizona statute failed to discriminate between those who join a suspect organization to further its illegal ends and those who do so with lawful goals in mind, the Court declared that the loyalty oath was unconstitutional.

Vote: 5-4

Participating: Warren, Black, Douglas, Clark, Harlan, Brennan, Stewart, White, Fortas

Opinions: Douglas for the Court; White, joined by Clark, dissenting; and Harlan and Stewart dissenting

Significance: Although the Court had earlier struck down state loyalty oaths that punished employees who were aware of a suspect organization's unlawful goals when they joined, *Elfbrandt* narrowed this rule by making only those employees who join with the specific intention of furthering such goals subject to punishment.

SHEPPARD V. MAXWELL

Citation: 384 U.S. 333 (1966)
Argued: February 28, 1966
Decided: June 6, 1966
Court Below: United States Sixth Circuit Court of Appeals
Basis for Review: *Writ of certiorari
Facts: In a case that aroused considerable public interest and garnered much media attention, Dr. Sam Sheppard was convicted of having murdered his wife. After serving several years of his sentence, Sheppard sought a writ of *habeas corpus.
Issue: Does extensive prejudicial publicity of a criminal trial jeopardize the defendant's Sixth Amendment right to *due process?
Outcome: Because the judge failed to make efforts to minimize the effect of publicity on the trial, the Supreme Court reversed Sheppard's conviction.

Vote: 8-1
Participating: Warren, Black, Douglas, Clark, Harlan, Brennan, Stewart, White, Fortas
Opinions: Clark for the Court; Black dissenting (without written opinion)
Significance: While the Court had customarily given the media relatively free rein, this latitude was counterbalanced in *Sheppard* by the expansion of rights accorded criminal defendants under the Warren Court.

MIRANDA V. ARIZONA

Citation: 384 U.S. 436 (1966)
Argued: February 28 and March 1-2, 1966
Decided: June 13, 1966
Court Below: Arizona Supreme Court
Basis for Review: *Writ of certiorari
Facts: Ernesto Miranda, who was at the time a 23-year-old indigent with an eighth-grade education, was apprehended on suspicion of committing a rape-kidnapping. When the police first began to interrogate him, he denied guilt, but after two hours of questioning, the police obtained a confession that became the basis for Miranda's conviction in state court.
Issue: Did the police interrogation procedure Miranda was subjected to, without benefit of counsel, violate his Fifth Amendment privilege against self-incrimination?
Outcome: The Warren Court ruled that Miranda's confession was inadmissible as evidence against him, holding that: a) the Fifth Amendment is applicable to police interrogations; b) unless the detainee is provided with protective mechanisms to dispel the coercive atmosphere of interrogations, confessions obtained in such settings are inadmissible; and c) such procedures should consist, at a minimum, of four warnings delivered to detainees. These warning are: 1) you have the right to remain silent; 2) anything you say can and will be used against you; 3) you have the right to talk to a lawyer before being questioned and to have him present when you are being questioned; and 4) if you cannot afford a lawyer, one will be provided for you before any questioning if you so desire.
Vote: 5-4
Participating: Warren, Black, Douglas, Clark,

Harlan, Brennan. Stewart, White, Fortas

Opinions: Warren for the Court; Clark dissenting; Harlan, joined by Stewart and White, dissenting; and White, joined by Harlan and Stewart, dissenting

Significance: For many, *Miranda* marked the apogee of the revolution in criminal procedure brought about by the Warren Court. But although use of the now-familiar "Miranda warnings" has proven not to interfere significantly with law enforcement, and although detainees have continued to make incriminating remarks, the decision has been widely criticized. In 1974 Justice William H. Rehnquist, writing for the majority in *Michigan v. Tucker,* declared that the Miranda warnings themselves were not required by the Constitution, and subsequent decisions have gone even further in undermining the constitutional basis for *Miranda.*

KEYISHIAN V. BOARD OF REGENTS

Citation: 385 U.S. 589 (1967)
Argued: November 17, 1966
Decided: January 23, 1967
Court Below: United States District Court for the Western District of New York
Basis for Review: Appeal
Facts: The New York Board of Regents created a list of banned organizations, including the Communist Party. Teachers and professors employed in state educational institutions could be decertified if found guilty of "treasonable or seditious acts," or merely for belonging to any listed group.
Issue: Are the New York statutes and administrative rules designed to prevent employment of subversive educators constitutional?
Outcome: Finding the statutes and rules vague and uncertain, the Court struck them down.
Vote: 5-4
Participating: Warren, Black, Douglas, Clark, Harlan, Brennan, Stewart, White, Fortas
Opinions: Brennan for the Court; Clark, joined by Harlan, dissenting, Stewart and White dissenting
Significance: In addition to striking a blow for educational freedom, *Keyishian* did away with one

of the most pernicious legacies of the McCarthy era, which had given the state power to require surrender of constitutional rights as a condition of employment.

KLOPFER V. NORTH CAROLINA

Citation: 386 U.S. 213 (1967)
Argued: December 8, 1966
Decided: March 13, 1967
Court Below: North Carolina Supreme Court
Basis for Review: *Writ of certiorari
Facts: Klopfer's first trial ended in a *mistrial. The state prosecutor reinstituted the charges against him, but declined to proceed, delaying Klopfer's second trial indefinitely.
Issue: Is the Sixth Amendment guarantee of a speedy trial applicable at the state level?
Outcome: The Court found that the same standards for a speedy trial apply at both the state and federal levels.
Vote: 9-0
Participating: Warren, Black, Douglas, Clark, Harlan, Brennan, Stewart, White, Fortas
Opinions: Warren for the Court; Stewart concurring (without written opinion) and Harlan concurring
Significance: *Klopfer* was the Supreme Court's first thorough exploration of the constitutional right to a speedy trial, and it found that although Klopfer was neither in custody nor under any constraints, the anxiety and embarrassment produced by his pending prosecution violated his rights. In subsequent tests of this right, however, the Court usually has found for the prosecution.

*IN RE GAULT

Citation: 387 U.S. 1 (1967)
Argued: December 6, 1966
Decided: May 15, 1967
Court Below: Arizona Supreme Court
Basis for Review: Appeal
Facts: Fifteen-year-old Gerald Gault was committed to the Arizona State Industrial School until he reached the age of majority. He had been found guilty of making an obscene telephone call while on probation for another charge, an offense which, had he been an adult, would have resulted

in a maximum of a $50 fine or two months in jail. What is more, he was judged guilty without being accorded *due process, and was adjudged without benefit of counsel, without any opportunity to cross-examine his accuser, and without any protection against self-incrimination. He was committed primarily on the basis of damaging remarks he himself made.

Issue: Are juvenile offenders owed the same due process accorded adults accused of criminal offenses?

Outcome: Justice Abe Fortas, writing for the majority, extended to juvenile defendants most of the rights accorded adult criminal defendants under the Fourteenth Amendment.

Vote: 8-1

Participating: Warren, Black, Douglas, Clark, Harlan, Brennan, Stewart, White, Fortas

Opinions: Fortas for the Court; Black and White concurring; Harlan concurring in part and dissenting in part; Stewart dissenting

Significance: In re Gault overturned many of the distinctions that had divided juvenile from adult prosecutions for over half a century. While many of these paternalistic notions were acceptable in theory, in reality they robbed juvenile offenders of fundamental rights such as the right to counsel and the privilege against self-incrimination, rights restored with this landmark decision.

LOVING V. VIRGINIA

Citation: 388 U.S. 1 (1967)
Argued: April 10, 1967
Decided: June 12, 1967
Court Below: Virginia Supreme Court
Basis for Review: Appeal
Facts: Loving, a white man married to an African American woman, challenged the antimiscegenation law of Virginia, one of 16 states still honoring such statutes.

Issue: Do state laws against interracial marriage violate the *Equal Protection Clause of the Fourteenth Amendment?

Outcome: A unanimous Court struck the statute down as an invidious racial classification.

Vote: 9-0

Participating: Warren, Black, Douglas, Clark, Harlan, Brennan, Stewart, White, Fortas

Opinions: Warren for the Court; Stewart concurring

Significance: This case marked the first time the Court called classification by race "inherently suspect," justifiable only by a showing of *compelling state interest.

UNITED STATES V. WADE

Citation: 388 U.S. 218 (1967)
Argued: February 16, 1967
Decided: June 12, 1967
Court Below: United States Fifth Circuit Court of Appeals
Basis for Review: *Writ of certiorari
Facts: Wade, who had been indicted for robbery, was placed in a lineup without notification to his attorney. All participants in the lineup were obliged to wear a mask and say, "Put the money in the bag."

Issues: Were the conditions of the lineup such that it violated the Fifth Amendment privilege against self-incrimination? Does a criminal suspect have a Sixth Amendment right to counsel during a police lineup?

Outcome: Although it did not find that the conditions of the lineup constituted compelled self-incrimination, the Court held that lineups constitute a critical stage of criminal prosecutions, warranting the presence of counsel. Wade's conviction was vacated and his case *remanded for further hearings.

Vote: 5-4

Participating: Warren, Black, Douglas, Clark, Harlan, Brennan, Stewart, White, Fortas

Opinions: Brennan for the Court; Douglas dissenting from the first part of the *holding; Clark concurring; Black dissenting from the first part of the holding and voting to uphold the conviction; White, joined by Harlan and Stewart, dissenting from the second part of the holding and voting to uphold the conviction; Fortas, joined by Warren and Douglas, dissenting from the first part of the holding and voting to reverse the conviction

Significance: Given the fractured nature of the vote in Wade, it is perhaps not surprising that the decision has been steadily eroded by subsequent Supreme Court decisions and by Congress itself. The Crime Control and Safe Streets Act of 1968 permitted admission of lineup evidence in federal court even when it had been obtained in the absence of counsel.

UNITED STATES V. ROBEL

Citation: 389 U.S. 258 (1967)
Argued: November 14, 1966; reargued October 9, 1967
Decided: December 11, 1967
Court Below: United States District Court for the Western District of Washington
Basis for Review: Appeal
Facts: Robel, a member of the Communist Party, was employed by a shipyard engaged in defense work. He was indicted for violating the Subversive Activities Control Act of 1950, which prohibited members of listed subversive organizations from working in the defense industry.
Issue: Does the section of the act prohibiting employment by members of listed organizations violate the First Amendment right to free association?
Outcome: Finding that the section attributed guilt solely on the basis of association, the Court struck it down.
Vote: 6-2
Participating: Warren, Black, Douglas, Harlan, Brennan, Stewart, White, Fortas (Marshall not participating)
Opinions: Warren for the Court; Brennan concurring; White, joined by Harlan, dissenting
Significance: *Robel* was one in a series of Warren Court decisions that found various provisions of the Subversive Activities Control Act unconstitutional primarily because the act failed to discriminate between active and passive membership in proscribed organizations. The act was finally allowed to die in 1973 for lack of appropriation.

KATZ V. UNITED STATES

Citation: 389 U.S. 347 (1967)
Argued: October 17, 1967
Decided: December 18, 1967
Court Below: United States Ninth Circuit Court of Appeals
Basis for Review: *Writ of certiorari

Facts: Katz was convicted of using interstate wire transmissions for purposes of wagering largely on the basis of information he gave over a public telephone which he habitually used and which the government had tapped by attaching an external listening device to the phone booth. The lower court found that because the phone booth had not been physically invaded, this investigative method did not constitute a "search."
Issue: Does electronic eavesdropping constitute a search subject to the Fourth Amendment's *warrant and *probable cause provisions?
Outcome: Finding that the government had violated Katz's privacy, the Court held that the electronic surveillance technique used by federal agents constituted an illegal search and seizure in violation of Katz's Fourth Amendment rights.
Vote: 7-1
Participating: Warren, Black, Douglas, Harlan, Brennan, Stewart, White, Fortas (Marshall not participating)
Opinions: Stewart for the Court; Douglas, joined by Brennan, concurring; Harlan and White concurring; Black dissenting
Significance: Katz substituted a "reasonable expectation of privacy" test for the physical intrusion test the Court previously had used to determine when a search was unconstitutional. Justice Harlan's concurrence later was used by lower courts and the Supreme Court itself to parse the meaning of *Katz:* "there is a twofold requirement, first that a person have exhibited an actual (subjective) expectation of privacy and, second, that the expectation be one that society is prepared to recognize as 'reasonable.'" There were problems with this formulation, however, as Harlan himself later recognized, stating in *United States v. White* (1971) that an evaluation of a questionable search must of necessity "transcend the search for subjective expectations."

DUNCAN V. LOUISIANA

Citation: 391 U.S. 145 (1968)
Argued: January 17, 1968
Decided: May 20, 1968
Court Below: Louisiana Supreme Court
Basis for Review: Appeal

Facts: In a nonjury trial, Duncan was convicted in Louisiana state court of *misdemeanor battery, for which the maximum sentence was two years in prison and a $300 fine. Although Louisiana law provided for jury trials only in cases involving capital crimes or those carrying sentences involving hard labor, and Duncan's sentence was 60 days in jail and a $150 fine, he appealed his conviction to the Supreme Court.

Issue: Does the *Due Process Clause of the Fourteenth Amendment *incorporate the right to trial by jury in all cases concerning serious criminal offenses?

Outcome: Finding that the alleged crime in Duncan's case was not a petty one, the Court reversed his conviction and upheld his right to a jury trial.

Vote: 7-2

Participating: Warren, Black, Douglas, Harlan, Brennan, Stewart, White, Fortas, Marshall

Opinions: White for the Court; Fortas concurring; and Black, joined by Douglas, concurring; Harlan, joined by Stewart, dissenting

Significance: With *Duncan*, the right to a jury trial for virtually all prosecutions for serious criminal offenses became fundamental at both the federal and state levels.

GREEN V. COUNTY SCHOOL BOARD OF NEW KENT COUNTY

Citation: 391 U.S. 430 (1968)
Argued: April 3, 1968
Decided: May 27, 1968
Court Below: United States Fourth Circuit Court of Appeals
Basis for Review: *Writ of certiorari
Facts: As a means of avoiding — or at least slowing — compliance with the school desegregation order of *Brown v. Board of Education II* (1955), New Kent County, Virginia, instituted a freedom-of-choice plan allowing pupils in its residentially integrated district to attend either of two schools, one formerly all-white, the other formerly all-black. After three years, the population of both schools remained largely unchanged, and African American students brought suit.

Issue: Does a "freedom-of-choice" plan comply

with the mandate of *Brown II*?

Outcome: Striking down the existing plan, the Court ordered the New Kent County School Board to come up with a new plan that promised prompt remediation.

Vote: 9-0

Participating: Warren, Black, Douglas, Harlan, Brennan, Stewart, White, Fortas, Marshall

Opinion: Brennan for the Court

Significance: While some states initially interpreted *Brown II* to require that they merely do away with race-based school assignment, *Green* made it clear that the purpose of both *Brown* decisions was not just to undo overt legal impediments to school integration, but also to correct the effects of segregation. Under *Green*, the only means of meeting this objective was to promote numerical racial equality in schools through such means as busing.

UNITED STATES V. O'BRIEN

Citation: 391 U.S. 367 (1968)
Argued: January 24, 1968
Decided: May 27, 1968
Court Below: United States First Circuit Court of Appeals
Basis for Review: *Writ of certiorari
Facts: O'Brien burned his draft card on the steps of the South Boston Courthouse to demonstrate his opposition to the war in Vietnam. He was convicted under a federal statute prohibiting the destruction of draft cards.

Issue: Is the federal statute an unconstitutional impairment of *freedom of speech?

Outcome: The Court upheld the statute and O'Brien's conviction.

Vote: 7-1

Participating: Warren, Black, Douglas, Harlan, Brennan, Stewart, White, Fortas (Marshall not participating)

Opinions: Warren for the court; Harlan concurring; Douglas dissenting

Significance: In *O'Brien*, the Court detailed a new test for determining when government regulation of symbolic speech is justified: the government interest being protected must be an important one, unrelated to suppression of speech, and the regulation must be no more restrictive than necessary to protect that interest. Later, the test was also applied to cases concerning regulations restricting the time, place, or manner of various types of speech.

FLAST V. COHEN

Citation: 392 U.S. 83 (1968)
Argued: March 12, 1968
Decided: June 10, 1968
Court Below: United States District Court for the Southern District of New York
Basis for Review: Appeal
Facts: A taxpayer challenge to use of federal funds to pay for the teaching of secular subjects in private religious schools was dismissed for lack of *standing under *Frothingham v. Mellon* (1923), which had essentially done away with taxpayer suits.
Issue: Does a federal taxpayer have standing to challenge federal taxing and spending programs?
Outcome: Reversing the lower court and modifying *Frothingham*, the Court held that in certain circumstances such cases may go forward.
Vote: 8-1
Participating: Warren, Black, Douglas, Harlan, Brennan, Stewart, White, Fortas, Marshall
Opinions: Warren for the Court; Douglas, Stewart, and Fortas concurring; Harlan dissenting
Significance: In keeping with its philosophy of making federal courts accessible to the public, the Warren Court held that taxpayer suits are valid if they do not challenge merely "incidental" expenditures in connection with the exercise of Congress's enumerated powers, and if the taxpayer can demonstrate that the challenged expenditures are prohibited by the *Taxing and Spending Clause of Article I of the Constitution. Later, the Burger Court would curtail this *holding in such cases as *Valley Forge Christian College v. Americans United for Separation of Church and State* (1982).

TERRY V. OHIO

Citation: 392 U.S. 1 (1968)
Argued: December 12, 1967
Decided: June 10, 1968

Court Below: Ohio Supreme Court
Basis for Review: *Writ of certiorari
Facts: Terry was convicted of carrying a concealed weapon after a policeman, observing Terry's participation in what he thought was a prelude to robbery, stopped him and frisked him.
Issue: Do "stop and frisk" police procedures violate the Fourth Amendment's prohibition against illegal searches and seizures?
Outcome: The Court upheld the validity of "stop and frisk," as well as Terry's conviction.
Vote: 8-1
Participating: Warren, Black, Douglas, Harlan, Brennan, Stewart, White, Fortas, Marshall
Opinions: Warren for the Court; Harlan concurring (without written opinion); Harlan and White concurring; Douglas dissenting
Significance: The Court concluded that "stop and frisk" does not require *probable cause and a *warrant because, although the law enforcement objective in patting a person down in search of a concealed weapon is obviously great, the invasion of privacy involved in the procedure is minimal.

JONES V. ALFRED H. MAYER CO.

Citation: 392 U.S. 409 (1968)
Argued: April 1-2, 1968
Decided: June 17, 1968
Court Below: United States Eighth Circuit Court of Appeals
Basis for Review: *Writ of certiorari
Facts: Jones, who charged that private individuals refused to sell him a home because he was African American, brought suit under a provision of the Civil Rights Act of 1866.
Issue: Does the statute prohibit racial discrimination practiced by private persons?
Outcome: The Court held that the Thirteenth Amendment outlaws both state and private racial discrimination in residential sales and rentals.
Vote: 7-2
Participating: Warren, Black, Douglas, Harlan, Brennan, Stewart, White, Fortas, Marshall
Opinions: Stewart for the Court; Douglas concurring; Harlan, joined by White, dissenting
Significance: Whereas the *Civil Rights Cases*

(1883) held that the Thirteenth Amendment's empowerment of Congress to outlaw incidents and badges of slavery did not reach private acts of racial discrimination, the Warren Court interpreted this power far more broadly. Together with *Runyon v. McCrary* (1976), which prohibited private discrimination in contracts, *Jones* gave the federal government great latitude in regulating previously restricted areas. The Rehnquist Court cut back on this power in *Patterson v. McLean Credit Union* (1989) by holding that federal legislation cannot reach postcontractual conduct, a finding Congress in turn overruled in the Civil Rights Act of 1991.

TINKER V. DES MOINES INDEPENDENT COMMUNITY SCHOOL DISTRICT

Citation: 393 U.S. 503 (1969)
Argued: November 12, 1968
Decided: February 24, 1969
Court Below: United States Eighth Circuit Court of Appeals
Basis for Review: *Writ of certiorari
Facts: Des Moines, Iowa, high school and junior high school students who wore black armbands to school to protest the war in Vietnam were suspended pursuant to a regulation passed two days prior to their actions.
Issue: Does the First Amendment protect this nondisruptive form of social protest?
Outcome: Stating that the students' symbolic wearing of black armbands was "akin to pure speech," the Court struck down the school regulation.
Vote: 7-2
Participating: Warren, Black, Douglas, Harlan, Brennan, Stewart, White, Fortas, Marshall
Opinions: Fortas for the Court; Stewart and White concurring; Black and Harlan dissenting
Significance: Justice Fortas's opinion for the Court found two primary reasons for upholding the students' symbolic speech: 1) it was not disruptive of regular school activities; and 2) the school district had permitted other types of symbolic speech, such as the wearing of campaign buttons. Suppression of peaceful war protest was clearly discriminatory and impermissible.

SHAPIRO V. THOMPSON

Citation: 394 U.S. 618 (1969)
Argued: April 29, 1968; reargued October 23-24, 1968
Decided: April 21, 1969
Court Below: United States District Court for the District of Connecticut
Basis for Review: Appeal
Facts: Vivian Thompson was a 19-year-old single mother who was denied welfare benefits because she had not yet resided in Connecticut for one year when she applied. Her case was heard with two others, testing similar welfare residency requirements in Pennsylvania and the District of Columbia. In all three cases, lower courts found against the states.
Outcome: Stressing that the right to travel is fundamental, the Supreme Court upheld the lower federal courts.
Vote: 6-3
Participating: Warren, Black, Douglas, Harlan, Brennan, Stewart, White, Fortas, Marshall
Opinions: Brennan for the Court; Stewart concurring; Warren, joined by Black, dissenting; and Harlan dissenting
Significance: Because the right to travel was deemed "fundamental," any state restriction of this right was subject to *strict scrutiny as to whether the state had a *compelling interest in maintaining the restraint or could accomplish its aims by some less restrictive means. The Court could find nothing to justify the residency requirements here, and its ruling set a *precedent for subsequent attacks on other residency requirements limiting access to such things as voting and professional licensing.

POWELL V. MCCORMACK

Citation: 395 U.S. 486 (1969)
Argued: April 21, 1969
Decided: June 16, 1969
Court Below: United States District Court for the District of Columbia
Basis for Review: *Writ of certiorari
Facts: Adam Clayton Powell Jr., was reelected in 1966 to represent the same New York City dis-

trict he had served in the House since 1944. Allegedly owing to Powell's financial improprieties, the House voted to exclude him and declare his seat vacant. Powell then sought a *declaratory judgment in federal court that would reinstate him and refund his back pay.

Issue: Is Congress's decision to exclude one of its own members a nonjusticiable *political question?

Outcome: While the Court found that Powell's suit against members of Congress could not go forward, it ruled that the suit could proceed against House employees.

Vote: 7-1

Participating: Warren, Black, Douglas, Harlan, Brennan, Stewart, White, Marshall

Opinions: Warren for the Court; Douglas concurring; Stewart dissenting

Significance: Congress, the Court found, only had authority under Article I, section 2, of the Constitution to judge a member's constitutional qualifications. Since Powell met these qualifications, any congressional attempt to exclude him for other reasons was impermissible. While his suit was pending, Powell again was reelected. This time he was allowed to take his seat, but he was fined $25,000 and deprived of a House chairmanship.

BENTON V. MARYLAND

Citation: 395 U.S. 784 (1969)

Argued: December 12, 1968; reargued March 24, 1969

Decided: June 23, 1969

Court Below: Maryland Court of Special Appeals

Basis for Review: *Writ of certiorari

Facts: John Dalmer Benton was convicted of burglary and acquitted of a larceny charge. He appealed and was ordered retried, whereupon he was convicted for both burglary and larceny.

Issue: Does the *Due Process Clause of the Fourteenth Amendment *incorporate the Fifth Amendment prohibition against *double jeopardy, thus making it applicable to the states?

Outcome: Finding that the interdiction against double jeopardy is fundamental to American justice, the Court held that states must honor it.

Vote: 6-2

Participating: Warren, Black, Douglas, Harlan,

Brennan, Stewart, White, Marshall

Opinions: Marshall for the Court; White concurring; Harlan, joined by Stewart, dissenting

Significance: In *Palko v. Connecticut* (1937), the Court ruled that states were obliged to honor only those Bill of Rights guarantees "implicit in the concept of ordered liberty," and that the double jeopardy bar was not among them. In *Benton*, however, the Warren Court partially overruled the earlier decision, declaring that the prohibition had been a part of American *jurisprudence since its inception.

CHIMEL V. CALIFORNIA

Citation: 395 U.S. 752 (1969)

Argued: March 27, 1969

Decided: June 23, 1969

Court Below: California Supreme Court

Basis for Review: *Writ of certiorari

Facts: Chimel, who was suspected of having committed a burglary a month earlier, was arrested in his home, where the police at the same time conducted a *warrantless search.

Issue: What is the permissible extent of a warrantless search of a criminal arrestee?

Outcome: The Court held that police may search only the person of an arrested criminal suspect and the area "within his immediate control."

Vote: 6-2

Participating: Warren, Black, Douglas, Harlan, Brennan, Stewart, White, Marshall

Opinions: Stewart for the Court; Harlan concurring; White, joined by Black, dissenting

Significance: *Chimel* modified the earlier rule that had been applied in such situations. The rule limited a search not by area, but only by the nature of what was sought. The rationale behind this modification is that on those occasions when arrests happen too swiftly for police to obtain a warrant in advance, the goal of the search should be limited to locating a weapon and preventing destruction of evidence.

VOTING PATTERNS

It is perhaps not surprising that the Warren Court, remembered for its *judicial activism and pro-

POLITICAL COMPOSITION
of the Warren Court

Justice & Total Term	Courts Served	Appointing President	Political Party
Earl Warren (1953-1969)	Warren	Eisenhower	Republican
Hugo L. Black (1937-1971)	Hughes Stone Vinson Warren Burger	F. D. Roosevelt	Democrat
Stanley F. Reed (1938-1957)	Hughes Stone Vinson Warren	F. D. Roosevelt	Democrat
Felix Frankfurter (1939-1962)	Hughes Stone Vinson Warren	F. D. Roosevelt	Democrat
William O. Douglas (1939-1975)	Hughes Stone Vinson Warren Burger	F. D. Roosevelt	Democrat
Robert H. Jackson (1941-1954)	Stone Vinson Warren	F. D. Roosevelt	Democrat
Harold H. Burton (1945-1958)	Stone Vinson Warren	Truman	Republican

(Continued on opposite page)

motion of liberal causes, was dominated by Democrats. What is surprising is that from 1953 to 1969, the Court was led by a Republican. Although Chief Justice Earl Warren did not have the most liberal record on the Court when it came to civil liberties — Douglas surpassed him in this area, in part because of Warren's discomfort about endorsing First Amendment claims involving sexual matters — Warren set the tone for what transpired during his 15-year tenure. And in 1962, after the retirement of Felix Frankfurter — long the Court's chief advocate of *judicial restraint — the liberal voting bloc of Warren, Hugo Black,

William O. Douglas, and William J. Brennan received a solid majority with the addition of Arthur Goldberg, whose voting record on civil liberties duplicated Douglas's.

After 1962 the liberal wing of the Warren Court remained dominant, as Goldberg was replaced by the liberal Abe Fortas and the equally liberal Thurgood Marshall succeeded Tom C. Clark, whose record reflected his caution on civil liberties issues (albeit a less restrained attitude towards changing the economic status quo). In contrast, after 1963 Justice Black, the original leader of the *due process revolution and a First

POLITICAL COMPOSITION
of the Warren Court

Justice & Total Term	Courts Served	Appointing President	Political Party
Tom C. Clark (1949-1967)	Vinson Warren	Truman	Democrat
Sherman Minton (1949-1956)	Vinson Warren	Truman	Democrat
John M. Harlan II (1955-1971)	Warren Burger	Eisenhower	
William J. Brennan Jr. (1956-1990)	Warren Burger Rehnquist	Eisenhower	Democrat
Charles E. Whittaker (1957-1962)	Warren	Eisenhower	Republican
Potter Stewart (1958-1981)	Warren Burger	Eisenhower	Republican
Byron R. White (1962-1993)	Warren Burger Rehnquist	Kennedy	Democrat
Arthur J. Goldberg (1962-1965)	Warren	Kennedy	Democrat
Abe Fortas (1965-1969)	Warren	Johnson	Democrat
Thurgood Marshall (1967-1991)	Warren Burger Rehnquist	Johnson	Democrat

Amendment absolutist, became markedly more conservative in his voting habits. Whereas a decade earlier, during the 1953 term, Black had supported the liberal position in 100 percent of the civil rights and First Amendment cases that came before the Court, in 1963 his comparative figures in these categories were 85.5 percent and 88.9 percent, respectively, and over the next six years they continued to decline, reaching 54.5 percent and 80 percent in the 1968 term.

The more conservative group of voters during the Warren years, consisting first of Justices Stanley Reed, Felix Frankfurter, Harold Burton, Tom Clark, and Sherman Minton, decreased over time to a minority, eventually consisting of Clark, Harlan, Stewart, and White. (Justice Robert Jackson, who served only one year under Warren, also tended to vote as a moderate conservative, as did Justice Charles Whittaker, who replaced Reed in 1957 and served on the Court only five years.) And of Clark, Harlan, Stewart, and White, only Harlan can accurately be characterized as a conservative in the Frankfurter mold (the two agreed on more than 80 percent of the cases they participated in together). The other three justices were centrists with no set agenda.

Justice Clark, who had begun his tenure on the high bench as a conservative, evolved into a true independent. Stewart, who initially served as a swing vote when the Warren Court was still evenly divided, remained a centrist as the Court moved leftward. And White, too, tended to vote pragmatically, developing no set voting pattern except in the area of criminal justice, where he consistently opposed the Warren Court's efforts to expand defendants' rights.

SPECIAL FEATURES OF THE WARREN COURT

THE SUPREME COURT AS AN INSTRUMENT OF SOCIAL CHANGE

Under Earl Warren's leadership, the Court had a more profound effect on the social and political life of the nation than it had had at any time since that of Chief Justice John Marshall in the early 19th century. After decades of upholding property rights, the Court now emphasized individual rights, and decisions such as those mandating school desegregation (*Brown v. Board of Education [1954]*), higher standards for convicting cold war "subversives" (*Yates v. United States [1957]*), legislative *reapportionment (*Baker v. Carr [1962], Reynolds v. Sims [1964]*), and greater *due process for criminal suspects (*Miranda v. Arizona [1966]*), provoked strong public and legislative resistance — as well as a number of abortive attempts to impeach Warren himself.

To be sure, Warren presided over the Court at a time of enormous societal upheaval, but Warren and his justices demonstrated singular courage and creativity in meeting such challenges as the Civil Rights movement. Perhaps the best demonstration of the Warren Court's adaptability can be found in *Brown*, the one Supreme Court case that arguably has had more wide-ranging and long-lasting effects than any other. In footnote 11 of *Brown*, Warren, writing for the Court, cited as authority for overturning the "separate but equal" doctrine, not legal *precedent, but seven works by social scientists demonstrating the deleterious effects of segregation. The significance of

the footnote has been overemphasized by critics of the decision, but its presence is nonetheless telling, indicating the Warren Court's willingness to try new approaches to cure society's ills.

NEW RIGHTS

Among the Warren Court's innovations in constitutional *jurisprudence was the recognition of new individual rights. Foremost among these is the right of privacy, a right only implicitly guaranteed by the Bill of Rights but explicitly recognized by the court in *Griswold v. Connecticut* (1965). While acknowledging the seeming silence of the Constitution on the subject of privacy, Justice William O. Douglas based his opinion for the Court in *Griswold* on the notion that the central purpose of the nation's foundation document was to "create zones of privacy" protecting the individual from government interference. In this mode of thinking Douglas resembled the chief justice, whose activist approach to constitutional *jurisprudence owed little to legal *precedent and much to fundamental notions of fairness.

Another Warren Court innovation, freedom of association, an offshoot of the freedom of assembly protected by the First Amendment, can be traced more directly to the Bill of Rights. In a number of cold war era cases, such as *Yates v. United States* (1957), the Warren Court upheld the right of individuals to associate freely and struck down government attempts to root out allegedly subversive activity. And in *National Association for the Advancement of Colored People v. Alabama *ex rel Patterson* (1958), the Court upheld the right of organizations pursuing legitimate ends to be free of government harassment.

DIVERSITY

It is altogether fitting that Thurgood Marshall, who led the winning legal team in *Brown v. Board of Education* (1954), the case that effectively outlawed segregation, should have been the first African American appointed to the Court. As President Johnson said in appointing Marshall, the grandson of a freed slave for whom the justice was named, it was "the right thing to do, the right time to do it, the right man and the right place."

Marshall's appointment ended the tradition of an all-white Supreme Court and paved the way for later introduction of female appointees Sandra Day O'Connor and Ruth Bader Ginsburg. At the same time, Marshall's selection seems to have created a new tradition, that of an African American seat, to which Clarence Thomas succeeded in 1991.

The Burger Court 1969-1986

BACKGROUND

DÉTENTE

President Richard M. Nixon and his secretary of state, Henry Kissinger, significantly modified America's cold war attitude towards the Communist world. After 1969 brinkmanship became détente, as the United States began to differentiate among, and negotiate with, Communist regimes.

Nixon took his first step to establish this new agenda in August 1969, when he visited Romania, demonstrating his willingness to capitalize on the Soviet satellite's nationalist leanings. Nixon's biggest coup came in February 1972, when he took advantage of the Sino-Soviet split by visiting China as part of his administration's effort to normalize relations between the United States and the Peoples' Republic.

Four months later, in June 1972, Nixon took the next logical step, visiting the Soviet Union to sign the first formal treaty growing out of the Strategic Arms Limitations Talks (SALT). The signing did not end the arms race, but it signaled a thaw in U.S.-U.S.S.R. relations.

"PEACE WITH HONOR" IN VIETNAM

Nixon had been elected, in part, on a promise to end U.S. involvement in Vietnam. Shortly after taking office, he announced a policy of "Vietnamization," which amounted to gradual American withdrawal, and over the next four years the number of U.S. troops in Vietnam declined from 475,000 to 23,000.

However, when the North Vietnamese responded to the implementation of this policy by stepping up their attacks on South Vietnam, Nixon began secretly bombing North Vietnamese supply routes in Laos and Cambodia. News of these attacks on allegedly neutral nations provoked antiwar protests on American college campuses, which reached fever pitch after the United States and South Vietnam invaded Cambodia. In April 1970 four students were killed by National Guard troops attempting to quell a demonstration at Kent State University in Ohio.

A continuation of the bombing raids did, however, achieve the objective of bringing the North Vietnamese to the bargaining table. On January 8, 1973, the parties reached a formal agreement, permitting the United States to attain what it labeled "peace with honor" — essentially, little more than a brief interval to permit the Americans to withdraw completely. Within two years, the Communists had taken over all of Vietnam.

WATERGATE

Nixon had been angered by leaks to the press about the supposedly secret attacks on Cambodia, and he ordered the Federal Bureau of Investigation (FBI) to investigate the leaks. The White House also assembled a special force called The Plumbers, who were called on to investigate the source of leaks from within the government. Daniel Ellsberg, a former Pentagon employee turned antiwar activist, was among The Plumbers' first targets. Ellsberg had handed over a set of classified government documents concerning the Vietnam War to the news media, which in turn

An asterisk (*) before a word or phrase indicates that a definition will be found in the glossary at the end of this volume.

published them as the *Pentagon Papers* after winning a victory in the Supreme Court in *New York Times Co. v. United States* (1971). The Plumbers then broke into the offices of Ellsberg's psychiatrist in an effort to obtain information that might discredit him. An attempt to prosecute Ellsberg for theft of government property and violation of the Espionage Act was dismissed in 1973 when it was revealed that the evidence against him had been illegally obtained.

The Plumbers' next escapade was even more badly bungled. Now allied with the Committee for the Reelection of the President (CREEP), they were responsible for the June 17, 1972, break-in at Democratic Party Headquarters, located in the Watergate complex in Washington, D.C. The burglars were apprehended, but both CREEP and

MEMBERS *Of the Court* 1969–1986

(In Order of Seniority)

Warren Burger (Chief Justice)	(1969-1986)
Hugo L. Black (retired)	(1969-1971)
William O. Douglas (retired)	(1969-1975)
John M. Harlan II (retired)	(1969-1971)
William J. Brennan Jr.	(1969-1986)
Potter Stewart (retired)	(1969-1981)
Byron R. White	(1969-1986)
Thurgood Marshall	(1969-1986)
Harry A. Blackmun	(1970-1986)
Lewis F. Powell Jr. (replaced Hugo L. Black)	(1972-1986)
William H. Rehnquist (replaced John M. Harlan II)	(1972-1986)
John Paul Stevens (replaced William O. Douglas)	(1975-1986)
Sandra Day O'Connor (replaced Potter Stewart)	(1981-1986)

the White House denied any involvement. Nixon went on to swamp Democratic candidate George McGovern in the 1972 presidential election.

At The Plumbers' burglary trial the next year, however, it quickly became apparent that the Nixon administration had been involved in the Watergate debacle — if not in the break-in itself, certainly in the cover-up that followed. A special Senate investigative committee uncovered evidence that conversations in the Oval Office had been secretly recorded on tapes held by the White House. Nixon at first refused to surrender the tapes, claiming executive privilege. After the Supreme Court ordered him to turn over the tapes in *United States v. Nixon* (1974), a "smoking gun" among the tapes linked the president with a conspiracy to prevent investigation of the burglary. On August 9, 1974, under threat of impeachment, Nixon resigned, the first president in American history ever to do so.

PRESIDENT FORD

On October 10, 1973, in the middle of the Watergate crisis, Nixon's vice president, Spiro T. Agnew, charged with tax evasion (allegations that Agnew had accepted bribes while governor of Maryland were dropped as part of a plea bargain), was also forced to resign. Under the provisions of the Twenty-fifth Amendment, ratified just six years earlier, Nixon nominated House Minority Leader Gerald R. Ford as vice president. After confirmation by both houses of Congress, Ford took the vice presidential oath of office on December 6, 1973. Nine months later, on August 9, 1974, Ford was sworn in as the nation's 38th, and only unelected president.

THE ELECTION OF 1976 AND THE DEMOCRATIC INTERVAL

One month after he became president, Ford granted Richard Nixon a full pardon for any crimes Nixon might have committed while in office. Over the next two years, as the United States and the rest of the world suffered through a recession exacerbated by the manipulation of oil prices by the petroleum cartel, the Organization of Petroleum Exporting Countries (OPEC), Ford did little. It was, however, the Nixon pardon and its Watergate baggage that doomed Ford's chances for election in 1976. Instead, Jimmy Carter, a former Georgia governor, won the White House.

Carter's presidency, too, was dogged by inflation and lack of economic growth. Unable to solve the nation's domestic woes, in time-honored fashion Carter turned his attention to foreign policy. Picking up where Nixon and Kissinger left off, Carter signed the SALT II arms limitation treaty with the Soviets and established formal diplomatic relations with China. The greatest triumph of his four years in office occurred in March 1979 when Carter brokered a peace treaty between Egypt and Israel.

Foreign affairs also proved to be Carter's undoing. Since 1953, when a coup abetted by the Central Intelligence Agency helped restore the Shah of Iran's family to power, the Shah had been a close ally of the U.S. By 1979, however, the Shah's unpopularity in his own country forced him into exile in America. Enraged, Iranian Islamic militants stormed the U.S. embassy in Teheran, taking 50 embassy employees hostage. Six months later, in April 1980, Carter tried a desperate attempt to rescue them, but the mission failed miserably. The hostages were held prisoner in the embassy for 15 months, the remainder of Carter's term of office.

THE REAGAN REVOLUTION

In the election of 1980, Republican candidate Ronald Reagan took 489 electoral votes to Carter's 49. Armed with this electoral mandate, Reagan began the biggest peacetime arms buildup in the history of the nation. A longtime anti-Communist, Reagan resuscitated the confrontational rhetoric of the cold war, supporting anti-Soviet guerrillas in the civil war in Afghanistan. The Reagan administration's focus, however, was on a civil war being waged closer to home, in El Salvador. Claiming that the leftist rebels in El Salvador were being supplied with arms by the Communist Sandanistas who had assumed power in neighboring Nicaragua, Secretary of State Alexander Haig invoked the domino theory as justification for U.S. intervention.

At the same time Congress approved Reagan's vast military expenditures, it also passed his budget, which called for the biggest tax cuts in history. In order to finance this two-pronged plan to stimulate economic growth, the government began incurring record deficits. The economy did recover for a time, and this improvement, together with a renewed sense of national pride born of the administration's aggressive foreign policy, contributed to Reagan's carrying every state but one in the 1984 presidential election.

During Reagan's second term, after the establishment of a moderate government in El Salvador, the U.S. government turned its attention to Nicaragua, where the Sandanista regime had forged a strong alliance with the Soviets. To counteract the Sandanistas, the administration looked for ways to support the indigenous Nicaraguan rebels, called Contras. This effort was blocked in Congress in 1984 by the Boland Amendment, which restricted assistance to the Contras to humanitarian aid. The next year, all aid was cut off.

Colonel Oliver North, an official with the National Security Council, a White House policy-making entity, then sought surreptitious means of funneling assistance to the Contras. Early in 1984 the Reagan administration had effectively withdrawn from the Middle East after nearly three hundred U.S. Marines were killed trying to keep peace in Lebanon. Seeking to reassert American influence in the region, in 1985 Reagan approved limited arms sales to Iran, then engaged in a war with Iraq. The sales were kept secret, however, for in the wake of the hostage crisis, the administration had been urging the rest of the world not to trade with Iran. Colonel North soon used inflated profits from these secret arms sales to fund the National Security Council's equally secret support of the Contras. It was only a matter of time until the Iran-Contra affair was made public and the Reagan administration became embroiled in a scandal of major proportions.

THE FORTAS CONTROVERSY

Earl Warren first announced his intention of resigning in June 1968, and to replace him

President Lyndon Johnson proposed to elevate sitting Justice Abe Fortas, whom Johnson had named to the Court in 1965. By then, however, Johnson was a lame duck, having already announced his intention not to seek reelection. He was powerless to combat charges of cronyism and financial impropriety that Republican senators raised during Fortas's confirmation hearings. After asking Johnson to withdraw his nomination as chief justice, Fortas resigned a year later from the Court altogether, dogged by allegations of graft. Warren honored his promise to Johnson to stay on until his successor could be confirmed, and it was left to the new president, Richard Nixon, to chose his own candidate, Warren Burger.

BURGER'S EARLY LIFE

Warren Burger is acknowledged to be a self-made man. Born into a working class family, the fourth of seven children, he contributed to the family finances from an early age, harvesting tomatoes, delivering newspapers, and picking up odd jobs such as making theater backdrops. A good student, he won a scholarship to Princeton University, but because it was not generous enough to sustain him, he was forced to turn it down. Instead, he attended college part time in the evenings, working days as an accountant for an insurance company. After two years of night classes at the University of Minnesota and four years at St. Paul College of Law, he emerged with an honors degree in law. The partners at the St. Paul law firm of Boyesen, Otis & Faricy were impressed with Burger's industry, and they offered him a job. Burger worked there from 1931 to 1953, specializing in corporate, real estate, and probate law. In addition, in 1931 he accepted an adjunct appointment at St. Paul College of Law, where he continued to teach contract law for the next 17 years.

BURGER'S PUBLIC LIFE

Burger quickly became active in civic affairs, serving as president of St. Paul's Junior Chamber of Commerce, leading a campaign to reform the police department, and assisting in local efforts to aid Japanese Americans displaced by World War II. Involvement in state politics was a logical next step, and in the late 1930s, Burger joined in an effort to revive the Republican Party in Minnesota, backing Harold Stassen's successful 1938 gubernatorial campaign.

Stassen's unsuccessful bids for the presidential nomination in 1948 and 1952 provided Burger's introduction to national politics. In the second election, Burger played an important role in delivering Stassen's votes to Dwight D. Eisenhower, helping Eisenhower secure a majority of Republican votes and, ultimately, the White House. The next year, Burger's efforts were repaid with an appointment as assistant attorney general in the Claims Division (later, the Civil Division), charged initially with prosecuting postwar government restitution claims. Later, his duties changed, and he was responsible for arguing the government's case in the Supreme Court against John F. Peters, a part-time federal employee dismissed on charges of disloyalty. The solicitor general, Simon Sobeloff, had found the case so distasteful that he refused to sign the government's *brief. For voluntarily assuming the unpleasant job, Burger was denounced by liberals, but Eisenhower remembered him in 1955 when a vacancy appeared on the federal Court of Appeals for the District of Columbia Circuit, one of the nation's most prestigious benches.

On the D.C. Circuit Court of Appeals, Burger quickly aligned himself with the conservative wing, becoming especially visible in his opposition to what he viewed as the Warren Court's leniency towards criminal defendants. His concurring opinion in *Blocker v. United States*, which the D.C. Circuit Court decided in 1961, criticized the liberalization of the insanity defense available to criminal defendants. And Burger was even more critical of the Supreme Court's decision in *Miranda v. Arizona* (1966), which held that police must provide criminal suspects with information about their rights before questioning them.

During his tenure as a federal *appellate judge, Burger turned increasingly to *extrajudicial means

JUDICIAL BIOGRAPHY
Warren Earl Burger

PERSONAL DATA

Born: September 17, 1907, in St. Paul, Minnesota

Parents: Charles J. Burger, Katharine Schnittger Burger

Higher Education: University of Minnesota, 1925-1927; St. Paul College of Law, later William Mitchell College of Law (LL.B., magna cum laude, 1931)

Bar Admission: Minnesota, 1931

Political Party: Republican

Marriage: November 8, 1933, to Elvera Stromberg, who bore Burger a son and a daughter

Died: June 25, 1995 in Washington, D.C.

Buried: Arlington National Cemetary, Arlington, Virginia

PROFESSIONAL CAREER

Occupations: Accountant, 1925-1931; Educator, 1931-1948; Lawyer, 1931-1956; Government Official, 1953-1956; Judge, 1956-1986

Official Positions: Adjunct Professor of Contracts, St. Paul College of Law, 1931-1948; United States Assistant Attorney General, Justice Department Claims Division, 1953-1956; Judge, United States Court of Appeals for the District of Columbia Circuit, 1956-1969; Chief Justice, United States Supreme Court, 1969-1986; Chairman, National Gallery of Art Board, ca. 1970s–mid-1980s; Chancellor, Smithsonian Institution, ca. 1970s–mid-1980s; Chairman, Bicentennial Commission, 1986-ca. 1991

SUPREME COURT SERVICE

Nominated: May 21, 1969

Nominated By: Richard M. Nixon

Confirmed: June 9, 1969

Confirmation Vote: 74-3

Oath Taken: June 23, 1969

Replaced: Chief Justice Earl Warren

Significant Opinions: *Harris v. New York* (1971); *Griggs v. Duke Power Co.* (1971); *Swann v. Charlotte-Mecklenburg Board of Education* (1971); *Lemon v. Kurtzman* (1971); *Reed v. Reed* (1971); *Wisconsin v. Yoder* (1972); *Miller v. California* (1973); *Miami Herald Publishing Co. v. Tornillo* (1974); *United States v. Nixon* (1974); *Milliken v. Bradley* (1974); *Nebraska Press Association v. Stuart* (1976); *Hutchinson v. Proxmire* (1979); *Fullilove v. Klutznick* (1980); *Richmond Newspapers, Inc. v. Virginia* (1980); *Immigration and Naturalization Service v. Chadha* (1983); *Lynch v. Donnelly* (1984); *Bowsher v. Synar* (1986)

Left Court: Retired September 26, 1986

Length of Service: 17 years, 3 months, 3 days

Replacement: Chief Justice William H. Rehnquist

of conveying his conservative views on criminal matters. For example, he used a May 1961 speech at Duke University as an occasion to criticize the modern insanity defense. He also became a public advocate for judicial reform, urging adoption of administrative means of streamlining federal *dockets. Indeed, for Burger the two concerns were linked: expanded constitutional protections for criminal defendants contributed in large part to the inefficiency of a system where it sometimes took as long as five years to bring a case to trial, and where *habeas corpus petitions and other appellate procedures permitted a single

defendant to make multiple court appearances.

For a time Burger co-chaired the American Bar Association project on Minimum Standards for Criminal Justice, and helped establish the Appellate Judges' Seminar at New York University. He wrote articles and lectured, declaring in a widely-publicized speech before the 1967 graduating class at Rippon College that the court system was "not working" for "decent people," who experience "a suppressed rage, frustration and bitterness," while criminals "feel that they can 'get by' with anything." His activity had every appearance of a political campaign.

Warren E. Burger

As it happened, the 1968 Republican presidential candidate, Richard M. Nixon, was himself campaigning on a law and order platform. Because of the debacle surrounding the abortive Abe Fortas nomination, it was obvious that the winner of the election would be in a position to appoint the next chief justice, and one of Nixon's principal campaign promises was to find a conservative, *strict constructionist successor to Earl Warren — preferably a sitting federal judge. Burger, by then a favorite of conservatives in Congress and in the media, was Nixon's choice.

BURGER AS CHIEF JUSTICE

As chief justice, Burger continued his program of judicial reform. In the Court itself, he introduced technological advances such as word processors and copying machines. Lawyers seeking admission to the Supreme Court bar could do so by mail, rather than in person. Oral arguments before the Court, previously limited to two hours, were cut in half. The justices themselves summarized, rather than read their opinions from the bench.

In the federal court system, Burger made similar headway. Although he did not succeed in convincing Congress of the need to establish a national court of appeals to lighten the Supreme Court's burden, he spearheaded the establishment in 1970 of the Institute for Court Management, responsible for training non-judicial court administrators. In the following decade, dispositions of federal district and appellate cases increased by more than 30 percent. Burger's proposal for limiting federal juries in civil cases to six persons was adopted in many *jurisdictions, and he convinced the Federal Bureau of Prisons to take steps to monitor prisoner grievances as a means of cutting down on habeas corpus petitions.

Burger's reforms also reached state courts, many of which adopted his proposal for cooperative councils that would eliminate the need for parallel state and federal trials in some mass *tort cases. Correspondingly, he urged membership in the recently established National Center for State Courts, where state judiciaries could pool their experiences.

Like one of his predecessors, William Howard Taft, Burger was a committed and accomplished court reformer. Unfortunately, he lacked Taft's talent for bringing the Court together. Multiple opinions on individual cases, a relative rarity during Warren's tenure, proliferated once again. Burger himself dissented more frequently from the majority than any chief justice except Harlan F. Stone. And Burger did not increase his stature among his brethen by frequently engaging in the practice of vote switching so as to control opinion writing assignments.

Contrary to the expectations of some, the Burger Court consolidated, rather than cut back on, the expansion of individual liberties that had taken place during the Warren years. With *Roe v. Wade* (1973), the Burger Court even augmented this expansion by elaborating a right that had been little recognized, the right of privacy. Burger himself lent new meaning to the truism that Supreme Court justices often disappoint the presidents who appoint them when he wrote the opinion for the Court in *United States v. Nixon* (1974), the decision that led directly to Nixon's resignation under threat of *impeachment.

Throughout his tenure, Burger devoted considerable effort to extrajudicial activities, not just to court reform, but to the arts. While he was chief justice, he also served as chairman of the board for the National Gallery of Art and as chancellor of the Smithsonian Institution. He took personal responsibility for redecorating the Court cafeteria and redesigning the Court bench. He had an aptitude and a lifelong interest in sculpting. When he was 15, he sculpted a head of Benjamin Franklin, which was reproduced in 1987 so that copies could be sold to support the bicentennial celebration of the Constitution. The year before, Burger accepted President Ronald Reagan's request that he head the Commission for the Bicentennial, retiring from the Court on September 26, 1986. He died on June 25, 1995, of heart failure.

ASSOCIATE JUSTICES

For biographies of Associate Justices **Hugo L. Black** and **William O. Douglas,** see entries under **THE HUGHES COURT.** For biographies of Associate Justices **John M. Harlan II, William J. Brennan Jr., Potter Stewart, Byron R. White,** and **Thurgood Marshall,** see entries under **THE WARREN COURT.**

HARRY ANDREW BLACKMUN

PERSONAL DATA

Born: November 12, 1908, in Nashville, Illinois
Parents: Corwin Blackmun, Theo Reuter Blackmun
Higher Education: Harvard College (B.A., summa cum laude in mathematics, Phi Beta Kappa, 1929); Harvard Law School (LL.B., 1932)
Bar Admission: Minnesota, 1932
Political Party: Republican
Marriage: June 21, 1941, to Dorothy E. Clark, who bore Blackmun three daughters

PROFESSIONAL CAREER

Occupations: Law Clerk, 1932-1933; Lawyer, 1932-1959; Educator, 1935-1941, 1945-1947; Judge, 1959-1994

Official Positions: Law Clerk, United States Eighth Circuit Court of Appeals, 1932-1933; Instructor, Mitchell College of Law, 1935-1941; Instructor, University of Minnesota Law School, 1945-1947; Judge, United States Eighth Circuit Court of Appeals, 1959-1970; Associate Justice, United States Supreme Court, 1970-1994

SUPREME COURT SERVICE

Nominated: April 15, 1970
Nominated By: Richard M. Nixon
Confirmed: May 12, 1970
Confirmation Vote: 94-0
Oath Taken: June 9, 1970
Replaced: Abe Fortas
Significant Opinions: Graham v. Richardson (1971); McKeiver v. Pennsylvania (1971); Roe v. Wade (1973); Bigelow v. Virginia (1975); Bates v. State Bar of Virginia (1977); Ballew v. Georgia (1978); Garcia v. San Antonio Metropolitan Transit Authority (1985); Bowers v. Hardwick (dissent) (1986); Thornburgh v. American College of Obstetricians and Gynecologists (1986); Mistretta v. United States (1989); Allegheny County v. ACLU Greater Pittsburgh Chapter (1989); Pacific Mutual Life Insurance Co. v. Haslip (1991); California v. Acevedo (1991); J.E.B. v. Alabama *ex rel. T.B. (1994); International Union, United Mine Workers v. Bagwell (1994)
Left Court: Retired June 30, 1994
Length of Service: 24 years, 21 days
Replacement: Stephen G. Breyer

Although Justice Blackmun often referred to himself humorously as the "third man" chosen to fill Abe Fortas's seat on the Court, he can more accurately be called the fourth man. On June 26, 1968, when President Lyndon Johnson attempted to elevate Fortas to the chief justiceship to succeed Earl Warren, Johnson at the same time nominated Homer Thornberry, a federal *appellate judge, to replace Fortas as an associate justice. When controversy forced Fortas to withdraw his nomination as chief justice early the following October, he resumed his place as associate justice, thus obliging Thornberry to withdraw, too.

Although continuing scandal eventually forced Fortas to resign from the Court altogether, he did not do so until May 1969, after Richard M. Nixon had

The Burger Court, 1972. From left: Potter Stewart, Lewis F. Powell Jr., William O. Douglas, Thurgood Marshall, Warren E. Burger, Harry A. Blackmun, William J. Brennan Jr., William H. Rehnquist, Byron R. White

assumed the presidency. Nixon, who had made conservative reform of the Supreme Court an election issue, named two unsuccessful candidates to succeed Fortas before arriving at Blackmun. On August 18, 1969, he nominated Clement Haynsworth Jr., chief judge of the Fourth Circuit Court of Appeals. On November 21, 1969, the Senate rejected Haynsworth by a vote of 55 to 45, largely because of allegations of ethical improprieties and Haynsworth's inadequate support for civil rights and organized labor. Nixon then nominated G. Harrold Carswell, a judge on the Fifth Circuit Court of Appeals, on January 19, 1970. On April 8, 1970, the Senate rejected Carswell by a vote of 51 to 45, following fierce opposition based on Carswell's poor record as a district judge and his suspected racism. Observing that the Senate seemed unwilling to confirm a conservative southerner to the Court, Nixon then adopted Chief Justice Burger's suggestion, nominating Burger's old friend from Minnesota, Harry Blackmun.

Born in Illinois, Harry A. Blackmun moved at an early age with his family to St. Paul, Minnesota, where his father worked as a small grocery and hardware store owner. Blackmun's family was of modest means, and he was fortunate to receive a tuition scholarship to Harvard College from the Harvard Club of Minnesota. Even so, he worked at a variety of odd jobs to help put himself through college and, following his graduation summa cum laude in mathematics, through Harvard Law School, where one of his professors was future Supreme Court Justice Felix Frankfurter.

After law school, Blackmun returned to Minnesota to clerk for a year for Judge John Sanborn on the Eighth Circuit Court of Appeals. In 1933 he joined the Minneapolis firm of Dorsey, Coleman, Barker, Scott and Barber, where he specialized in taxation, estate law, and civil litigation, while at the same time teaching tax and property law part time at the St. Paul College of Law and the University of Minnesota Law School. In 1950 Blackmun, who earlier had considered a career in medicine, became resident counsel at the Mayo Clinic in Rochester, Minnesota. He later described his tenure there as the happiest decade of his life.

In 1959 President Dwight D. Eisenhower chose Blackmun to succeed his former mentor, Judge Sanborn, on the Eighth Circuit Court of Appeals.

As a federal *appellate judge, Blackmun established a reputation as a conservative, and it was this reputation, as well as the recommendation of Chief Justice Burger, his friend since grade school, that led President Nixon to nominate him to the Supreme Court in 1970. One month later, the Senate — grateful, no doubt, finally to be considering an uncontroversial candidate — unanimously confirmed the low-key, little known midwesterner.

Initially, Blackmun and the conservative Burger were paired in the popular conscience and referred to as the "Minnesota Twins." And indeed, during Blackmun's first term on the Court, the two voted together nearly 90 percent of the time. Over time, however, they diverged, both personally and judicially. By the middle of the 1980s, Blackmun had formed a liberal voting bloc with Justices William J. Brennan and Thurgood Marshall. His transformation really began more than a decade earlier, however, with his majority opinion in the landmark *Roe v. Wade* (1973) case, which upheld a woman's right to abortion. He was also responsible for a trio of breakthrough First Amendment opinions, *Bigelow v. Virginia* (1975), *Virginia State Board of Pharmacy v. Virginia Citizens Consumer Council* (1976), and *Bates v. State Bar of Arizona* (1977), which afforded protection to *commercial speech. He remained conservative longer in his attitude toward criminal justice, but by the end of his judicial career personal doubts about the death penalty received professional expression when he announced in *Collins v. Collins* (1994) that he had concluded that the death penalty was unconstitutional. During the near quarter century he served on an increasingly conservative Court, Blackmun evolved in a contrary direction, and while he never abandoned his modest demeanor, he became ever more outspoken about his concern that the nation's supreme judicial tribunal was drifting too far to the right.

LEWIS FRANKLIN POWELL JR.

PERSONAL DATA

Born: November 19, 1907, in Suffolk, Virginia

Parents: Lewis F. Powell, Mary Gwathmey Powell
Higher Education: Washington and Lee University (B.S., first in class, Phi Beta Kappa, 1929); Washington and Lee University Law School (LL.B., 1931); Harvard Law School (LL.M., 1932)
Bar Admission: Virginia, 1933
Political Party: Democrat
Marriage: May 2, 1936, to Josephine M. Rucker, who bore Powell three daughters and a son

PROFESSIONAL CAREER

Occupations: Lawyer, 1933-1942, 1946-1972; Serviceman, 1942-1946; Public Official, 1952-1972; Judge, 1972-1987
Official Positions: President, School Board of Richmond, Virginia, 1952-1961; Member, Virginia State Board of Education, 1961-1968; President, American Bar Association, 1964-1965; Member, Presidential Crime Commission, 1966; President, Virginia State Board of Education, 1968-1969; President, American College of Trial Lawyers, 1968-1969; President, American Bar Foundation, 1969-1971; Member, Virginia Constitutional Revision Committee, late 1960s; Member, Board of Trustees of Washington and Lee University, 1970-1972; Associate Justice, United States Supreme Court, 1972-1987; Also, at various times prior to 1972: President, Richmond Family Services Society; Member, Richmond City Manager Charter Reform Commission; Member, National Advisory Committee on Legal Services to the Poor; Vice President, National Legal Aid and Defender Society; and Chairman or President of the Richmond Citizens Association, the Colonial Williamsburg Foundation, and the Virginia State Library Board

SUPREME COURT SERVICE

Nominated: October 22, 1971
Nominated By: Richard M. Nixon
Confirmed: December 6, 1971
Confirmation Vote: 89-1
Oath Taken: January 7, 1972
Replaced: Hugo L. Black
Significant Opinions: *Kastigar v. United States* (1972); *United States v. United States District Court* (1972); *San Antonio Independent School District v. Rodriguez* (1973); *Gertz v. Robert Welch, Inc.* (1974); *Stone v. Powell* (1976); *Arlington Heights v. Metropolitan Housing*

Development Corp. (1977); *Regents of the University of California v. Bakke* (1978); *Akron v. Akron Center for Reproductive Health, Inc.* (1983); *Batson v. Kentucky* (1986); *McClesky v. Kemp* (1987)

Left Court: Retired June 26, 1987
Length of Service: 15 years, 5 months, 19 days
Replacement: Anthony M. Kennedy

Lewis F. Powell was born into an old Virginia family that traced its roots in the state back to the Jamestown Colony. He grew up in Richmond, where he spent most of the remainder of his life, and attended Washington and Lee University in Lexington, Virginia. At Washington and Lee he obtained first an undergraduate degree, then — in two rather than the customary three years — a law degree. He then obtained a master of laws degree from Harvard, writing a thesis on administrative law and studying under Felix Frankfurter, who would shortly thereafter be named a justice of the Supreme Court.

After completing his formal education, Powell returned to Richmond, where he joined the law firm of Christian, Barton, and Parker. That association lasted only two years, however, as Powell soon joined Hunton, Williams, Anderson, Gay, and Moore, the Richmond firm he was to remain with until he joined the Supreme Court. His career at Hunton, Williams was interrupted by World War II. Although Powell was exempt from the draft, he enlisted in the Army Air Corps, joining its intelligence unit. During his military service he rose to the rank of colonel and garnered such decorations as the Legion of Merit and the Bronze Star.

Rejoining Hunton, Williams after the war, Powell focused on corporate law, advising a number of major companies as counsel and as a director. At the same time, he became involved in local government, serving on a number of civic advisory boards and, as president of the city school board, helping Richmond comply with the Supreme Court's desegregation order in *Brown v. Board of Education II* (1955). During the 1960s, he became active on a national level, advising presidential commissions and leading professional organizations. Before joining the Supreme Court,

he also played a prominent role in professional organizations, serving as president of the American Bar Association and the American College of Trial Lawyers.

In naming Powell to the Court in 1971, President Nixon was fulfilling his goal of appointing a conservative southerner to the nation's highest tribunal, an aim that had been frustrated by his failed attempts to replace Abe Fortas first with Clement Haynsworth, then Harrold Carswell, the year before. Citing advanced age, Powell previously had resisted Nixon's request that he allow his name to be put before the Senate Judiciary Committee, but on January 7, 1972, after having been confirmed by a virtually unanimous full Senate, he became, at the age of 64, the second oldest junior associate justice in Supreme Court history.

Powell was also one of only a handful of justices to come to the Court directly from private practice. He carried with him a pragmatic, lawyerly approach to the law that led him to conform to *precedents even when he did not agree with them and contributed to his status as a centrist who often acted as the swing vote on a Court divided between activist holdovers from the Warren years and more conservative recent appointees. He is perhaps best remembered for his opinion for the Court in *Regents of the University of California v. Bakke* (1978), which with its careful distinctions and cautious endorsement of the principle of affirmative action clearly reflects Powell's four decades of practical legal experience. Powell, who agreed with aspects of both *pluralities' opinions, cast the deciding vote in *Bakke*. His own opinion, though joined by no other justice, remains an authoritative pronouncement on affirmative action as it applies to public education.

After retiring from the Court in 1987, Powell continued to serve occasionally on federal *appellate courts, focusing on the Fourth Circuit Court of Appeals in his hometown, Richmond.

For a biography of Associate, later Chief Justice **William H. Rehnquist,** see the entry under **THE REHNQUIST COURT.**

JOHN PAUL STEVENS

PERSONAL DATA

Born: April 20, 1920, in Chicago, Illinois
Parents: Ernest James Stevens, Elizabeth Street Stevens
Higher Education: University of Chicago (BA., Phi Beta Kappa, 1941); Northwestern University School of Law (J.D., magna cum laude, first in class, 1947)
Bar Admission: Illinois, 1949
Political Party: Republican
Marriages: 1942 to Elizabeth Jane Sheeren, who bore Stevens one son and three daughters, and who was divorced from Stevens in 1979; 1980 to Maryan Mulholland Simon

PROFESSIONAL CAREER

Occupations: Serviceman, 1942-1945; Law Clerk, 1947-1948; Lawyer, 1949-1970; Government Official, 1951, 1953-1955, 1969; Educator, 1952-1956; Judge, 1970-present
Official Positions: Law Clerk to Justice Wiley B. Rutledge, United States Supreme Court, 1947-1948; Associate Counsel, subcommittee for the study of monopoly power, United States House Judiciary Committee, 1951; Adjunct Professor, Northwestern University School of Law, 1952-1954; Member, Attorney General's National Committee to Study Antitrust Laws, 1953-1955; Adjunct Professor, University of Chicago Law School, 1955-1956; General Counsel, Illinois commission investigating state supreme court justices, 1969; Judge, United States Seventh Circuit Court of Appeals, 1970-1975; Associate Justice, United States Supreme Court, 1975-

SUPREME COURT SERVICE

Nominated: November 28, 1975
Nominated By: Gerald R. Ford
Confirmed: December 17, 1975
Confirmation Vote: 98-0
Oath Taken: December 19, 1975
Replaced: William O. Douglas
Significant Opinions: *Young v. American Mini Theatres, Inc.* (1976); *Payton v. New York* (1980); *United States v. Ross* (1982); *Wallace v. Jaffree* (1985); *Hodgson v. Minnesota* (1990); *Cipollone v. Liggett Group, Inc.* (1992); *Honda Motor Co. v. Oberg* (1994); *U.S. Term Limits, Inc. v. Thornton* (1995)

John Paul Stevens was born into a wealthy Chicago family whose residence abutted the University of Chicago campus. Stevens attended high school at the university's laboratory school, and he went on to obtain an undergraduate degree in English at the university. World War II intervened before he could choose a career path, and he spent the war years working for Naval intelligence in Washington, D.C. In 1945 he returned to Chicago to attend law school at Northwestern University, from which he graduated in 1947 with the highest marks in the history of the law school.

After receiving his J.D., Stevens clerked for a year for Supreme Court Justice Wiley B. Rutledge before joining a prominent law firm specializing in antitrust law. Stevens became an expert in the field, founding his own firm in 1951 and serving on two federal antitrust investigatory committees. In 1970 President Richard M. Nixon appointed him to the Seventh Circuit Court of Appeals.

Although he was registered as a Republican, Stevens was by no means politically doctrinaire, as his five-year tenure on the federal appeals bench demonstrated. It was his moderation and very lack of strong ideological identification that made him stand out on the list of eleven candidates President Gerald Ford considered in 1975 as a replacement for retiring Justice William O. Douglas. In the aftermath of the Watergate scandal, Ford wanted his first (and, as it turned out, only) appointment to the Supreme Court to be a political moderate whose integrity would help restore public confidence in government. When Attorney General Edward Levi took the unprecedented action of circulating a limited list of potential Court candidates among members of the American Bar Association, Stevens received their unqualified endorsement. This support clearly helped to make Stevens President Ford's choice.

On the Court, Stevens has fully met these expectations, remaining firmly in the center of the Court and adapting easily to its transition from a civil rights orientation to a more conservative agenda. Like his predecessor, Justice Douglas, Stevens is a true maverick, who frequently expresses himself in separate concurring or dissenting opinions. In his first full term, 1976-1977, he wrote more concurrences and dissents than any other justice, setting a precedent he has continued to follow throughout most Court terms. Unlike Douglas, however, he has been as likely to vote with the conservative bloc, represented by justices like Warren Burger and William Rehnquist, as with the liberal bloc represented by Justices William J. Brennan and Thurgood Marshall. His independence, which has at times been criticized for atomizing an already sharply divided Court, remains his most pronounced characteristic.

SANDRA DAY O'CONNOR

PERSONAL DATA
Born: March 26, 1930, in El Paso, Texas
Parents: Harry A. Day, Ada Mae Wilkey Day
Higher Education: Stanford University (B.A., magna cum laude, 1950); Stanford University Law School (LL.B., with high honors, Order of the Coif, 1952)
Bar Admissions: California, 1952; Arizona, 1957
Political Party: Republican
Marriage: December 20, 1952, to John J. O'Connor III, with whom she has had three sons

PROFESSIONAL CAREER
Occupations: Lawyer, 1952-1957, 1958-1960, 1965-1969; Government Official, 1952-1953, ca. 1960-1969; Politician, early 1960s-1975; Judge, 1974-present
Official Positions: Deputy County Attorney, San Mateo, California, 1952-1953; Member, County Board of Adjustments and Appeals, Maricopa County, Arizona, ca. 1960-1965; Republican County Precinct Officer, 1960-1965; Republican District Chairman, 1965; Member, Governor's Committee on Marriage and Family (Arizona), 1965; Assistant Attorney General, Arizona, 1965-1969; Member, Arizona State Senate, 1969-1975; Majority Leader, Arizona State Senate, 1972-1974; Co-chair, Arizona committee to reelect Richard Nixon, 1972; Judge, Maricopa County Superior Court, 1974-1979; Judge, Arizona Court of Appeals, 1979-1981; Associate Justice, United States Supreme Court, 1981-

SUPREME COURT SERVICE
Nominated: July 7, 1981
Nominated By: Ronald Reagan

Confirmed: September 21, 1981
Confirmation Vote: 99-0
Oath Taken: September 25, 1981
Replaced: Potter Stewart
Significant Opinions: *Mississippi University for Women v. Hogan* (1982); *Akron v. Akron Center for Reproductive Health, Inc.* (dissent) (1983); *Lynch v. Donnelly* (concurrence) (1984); *Hawaii Housing Authority v. Midkiff* (1984); *Richmond v. J. A. Croson Co.* (1989); *Penry v. Lynaugh* (1989); *Maryland v. Craig* (1990); *Simon & Schuster v. Crime Victims Board* (1992); *Hudson v. McMillian* (1992); *New York v. United States* (1992); *Planned Parenthood of Pennsylvania v. Casey* (1992); *Shaw v. Reno* (1993); *Harris v. Alabama* (1995); *Adarand Constructors, Inc. v. Pena* (1995)

Sandra Day O'Connor spent her early youth on her parents 198,000 acre ranch in an isolated part of southeastern Arizona. When time came for her to enter school, she began spending nine months every year with her maternal grandmother in El Paso, Texas. After graduating from high school at the age of 16, she went to Stanford University, where she received an undergraduate degree in economics and then went on to graduate third in her law school class (future Justice William H. Rehnquist took first place).

Despite her superior academic record, O'Connor was unable to find a job practicing law in the private sector because of gender bias, so she worked for a year as a deputy county attorney while her husband finished his law degree at Stanford. In 1953 the couple left for Frankfurt, Germany, where John O'Connor was a member of the U.S. Army Judge Advocate General Corps and where O'Connor worked for the Army as a civilian attorney. In 1957 they returned to the United States, settling in Maricopa County, Arizona, and with the exception of a two-year stint practicing law in her own firm, O'Connor devoted the next seven years to a combination of raising a family and civic and political volunteer work.

In 1965 O'Connor resumed full-time employment as assistant state attorney general. Four years later the governor appointed her to complete the unexpired term of a departing state senator. She won reelection to the state senate twice in her own right, in 1972 becoming senate majority leader, the first woman in the country to hold this office. And in 1974, with election to Maricopa County Superior Court, O'Connor began the judicial career that culminated in her appointment in 1981 as the first female Supreme Court justice.

O'Connor had been active in Republican politics since her return from overseas, and her support for Ronald Reagan's 1976 presidential bid undoubtedly contributed to his settling on her when it came time to fulfill his campaign promise to name a woman to the nation's highest court. In addition, during her service in all three branches of state government, O'Connor had demonstrated a commitment to conservatism that comported with Reagan's own political ideology. Indeed, during the early years of her tenure on the Court, O'Connor was popularly paired with the clearly conservative Justice Rehnquist as the "Arizona Twins," and the two frequently voted together on close cases. Subsequently, O'Connor has continued to vote consistently with the conservatives on the Court, often adding her own, narrower concurring opinions. She has been responsible for significant decisions on religious freedom, such as *Lynch v. Donnelly* (1984), in which she proposed a new, more lenient test for the constitutionality of regulations that has since been adopted by a majority of the Court. Correspondingly, her test for affirmative action programs, requiring *strict scrutiny of remedial needs, first advanced in a series of individual opinions, was adopted by a majority of the Court in *Richmond v. J.A. Croson Co.* (1989). On some issues — most notably, abortion — she seems to be emerging as a swing vote. Characteristically, although she has declined to overrule *Roe v. Wade* (1973) outright, she has continued to support state regulations restricting the scope of that decision.

SIGNIFICANT CASES

*IN RE WINSHIP

Citation: 397 U.S. 358 (1970)
Argued: January 20, 1970

Decided: March 31, 1970
Court Below: New York Court of Appeals
Basis for Review: Appeal
Facts: A 12-year-old boy was committed to training school in New York State. The same act that put him there, if committed by an adult, would have constituted larceny requiring the state to prove its case against the defendant "beyond a reasonable doubt." At the time, however, applicable New York law stipulated that detention of juveniles could follow a determination of guilt by a "preponderance of the evidence."
Issue: Does *due process under the Fourteenth Amendment require states to apply the same standard of proof in criminal proceedings against both adult and juvenile offenders?
Outcome: The New York rule, and the boy's sentence, were reversed.
Vote: 5-3
Participating: Burger, Black, Douglas, Harlan, Brennan, Stewart, White, Marshall
Opinions: Brennan for the Court; Harlan concurring; Burger, joined by Stewart, dissenting; and Black dissenting
Significance: In this case the Court tried to bring the states in line with the standards for juvenile procedure it had delineated in *In re Gault* (1967). In holding that the reasonable doubt standard should apply to juvenile criminal defendants, however, Justice Brennan had to reach beyond the Constitution for a rationale, citing *common law and custom. While this explanation also holds true for application of reasonable doubt to adult offenders, its extra-Constitutional foundation later provided the Court with a justification for reining in due process guarantees for minors. In *McKeiver v. Pennsylvania* (1971), juveniles were denied the right to a trial by jury.

GOLDBERG V. KELLY

Citation: 397 U.S. 254 (1970)
Argued: October 13, 1969
Decided: March 23, 1970
Court Below: United States District Court for the Southern District of New York
Basis for Review: Appeal
Facts: John Kelly, and other New York City wel-

fare recipients, filed suit against the city commissioner of social services when their benefits were terminated. In accordance with applicable regulations, they had received a seven-day notice of termination of benefits and the right to file a letter of protest, but they were denied a hearing prior to the cut-off date.

Issue: Does *due process under the Fourteenth Amendment require that a welfare recipient be afforded a hearing before termination of public assistance?

Outcome: Finding the New York procedures constitutionally inadequate, the Court ruled in favor of the welfare recipients.

Vote: 5-3

Participating: Burger, Black, Douglas, Harlan, Brennan, Stewart, White, Marshall

Opinions: Brennan for the Court; Black, Burger, and Stewart dissenting

Significance: Welfare recipients are entitled to a pre-termination hearing before an impartial adjudicator, the Court stated, because their benefits not only promote the general welfare, but "are a matter of statutory entitlement for persons qualified to receive them." Thus the notion of entitlements as constitutionally protected property rights was introduced into American *jurisprudence.

WILLIAMS V. FLORIDA

Citation: 399 U.S. 78 (1970)

Argued: March 4, 1970

Decided: June 22, 1970

Court Below: Florida Third District Court of Appeal

Basis for Review: *Writ of certiorari

Facts: Williams was tried and convicted of committing a *felony by a jury of six persons, as permitted under state law.

Issue: Does a jury of fewer than the traditional 12 deprive an individual of his Sixth Amendment right to trial by jury?

Outcome: Calling the 12-person jury merely an "historical accident," the Court upheld the use of six-person juries in *noncapital state cases, as well as Williams's conviction.

Vote: 7-1

Participating: Burger, Black, Douglas, Harlan,

Brennan, Stewart, White, Marshall (Blackmun not participating)

Opinions: White for the Court; Burger, Harlan, and Stone concurring; Black, joined by Douglas, concurring in part and dissenting in part; Marshall dissenting

Significance: Given that the Court had extended the right to trial by jury to state defendants only two years before, in *Duncan v. Louisiana* (1968), the outcome in *Williams* took many observers by surprise. The Burger Court remained committed to smaller juries, however, and in *Colegrove v. Battin* (1973), approved six-person juries for civil cases tried in federal courts.

OREGON V. MITCHELL; UNITED STATES V. IDAHO; TEXAS V. MITCHELL; UNITED STATES V. ARIZONA

Citation: 400 U.S. 112 (1970)

Argued: October 19, 1970

Decided: December 21, 1970

Courts Below: None

Bases for Review: *Original Supreme Court jurisdiction

Facts: Amendments passed in 1970 to the 1965 Voting Rights Act stipulated that states could not prohibit persons 18 years of age and older from voting in any local, state, or federal election.

Issue: Does the Fifteenth Amendment accord Congress the authority to lower the minimum voting age nationwide?

Outcome: A sharply divided Court ruled that Congress could set the voting age at 18 for federal, but not state and local elections.

Vote: 5-4

Participating: Burger, Black, Douglas, Harlan, Brennan, Stewart, White, Marshall, Blackmun

Opinions: Black for the *plurality; Douglas, Harlan, Brennan, White, and Marshall concurring in part and dissenting in part; and Stewart, joined by Blackmun, concurring in part and dissenting in part

Significance: The other justices, four of whom agreed with Black and four of whom found that Congress had no authority to lower the voting age for state elections, filed five separate opinions in the case. Responding to the confusion that followed release of the decision and anticipating complications in the upcoming 1972 elections, Congress proposed the Twenty-sixth Amendment on March 23, 1971. The amendment, which constitutionalized the intent of the Voting Rights Act additions, was ratified within 107 days, more quickly than any preceding constitutional amendment had ever been approved by the states.

YOUNGER V. HARRIS

Citation: 401 U.S. 37 (1971)
Argued: April 1, 1969; reargued April 26 and November 16, 1970
Decided: February 23, 1971
Court Below: United States District Court for the Central District of California
Basis for Review: Appeal
Facts: Harris, who was *indicted in California court for violating a state criminal syndicalism act, applied to federal court for an *injunction prohibiting his prosecution. Based on *Brandenburg v. Ohio* (1969), in which the Supreme Court found another identical state law unconstitutional, the federal court granted the injunction.
Issue: Do federal courts have the right to intervene in state court proceedings?
Outcome: The Supreme Court reversed the order of the court below and lifted the injunction, permitting the prosecution to go forward.
Vote: 8-1
Participating: Burger, Black, Douglas, Harlan, Brennan, Stewart, White, Marshall, Blackmun
Opinions: Black for the Court; Brennan, joined by White and Marshall, concurring; Stewart, joined by Harlan, concurring; Douglas dissenting
Significance: Basing his opinion for the Court on the tenets of *federalism, Justice Black wrote that, absent a showing of irreparable harm to the defendant if the proceeding should go forward, federal judges should not interfere with state court proceedings. Black acknowledged that First Amendment concerns at issue in *Brandenburg* were also present here, but found that the chilling effect on *free speech generated by Harris's prosecution could not justify federal intervention.

HARRIS V. NEW YORK

Citation: 401 U.S. 222 (1971)
Argued: December 17, 1970
Decided: February 24, 1971
Court Below: New York Court of Appeals
Basis for Review: *Writ of certiorari
Facts: Harris, who testified in his own defense that a bag he sold to an undercover agent did not contain narcotics, had provided police with a different statement during his interrogation. Because he had been questioned without having been given his Miranda warnings, Harris now asserted that his prior voluntary statement could not be used against him in court.
Issue: Can voluntary statements provided by criminal suspects to police absent Miranda warnings be used by the prosecution at trial?
Outcome: The Court found that although such statements cannot be used as evidence per se, if the defendant takes the stand they can be cited for purposes of *impeachment.
Vote: 5-4
Participating: Burger, Black, Douglas, Harlan, Brennan, Stewart, White, Marshall, Blackmun
Opinions: Burger for the Court; Black dissenting (without written opinion), and Brennan, joined by Douglas and Marshall, dissenting
Significance: Burger, whom President Nixon had appointed to the Court in large measure because of his opposition to *Miranda v. Arizona* (1966), reasoned that the earlier case did not explicitly rule out use of uncounseled statements like Harris's for every purpose at the time of trial. *Harris* was the first case to limit the far-reaching effects of the *Miranda* decision.

GRIGGS V. DUKE POWER CO.

Citation: 401 U.S. 424 (1971)
Argued: December 14, 1970
Decided: March 8, 1971
Court Below: United States Fourth Circuit Court of Appeals
Basis for Review: *Writ of certiorari
Facts: African American employees of Duke Power Co. brought suit under Title VII of the Civil Rights Act of 1964, alleging that they had

been discriminated against in the company's hiring and promotion policies. Prior to passage of the act, these policies had been blatantly racist; more recently instituted criteria included a high school education and certain minimum scores on aptitude tests. The lower court found that the company's earlier policies were beyond the reach of Title VII and that the newer ones did not violate federal law because they were not intentionally discriminatory.

Issue: Do job requirements which are not on their face discriminatory violate Title VII?

Outcome: Holding that intent or discriminatory purpose is irrelevant, the Burger Court reversed the lower court's ruling.

Vote: 8-0

Participating: Burger, Black, Douglas, Harlan, Stewart, White, Marshall, Blackmun (Brennan not participating)

Opinion: Burger for the Court

Significance: *Griggs* is the most significant case on employment discrimination the Court has ever decided. Hiring and promotion requirements, the Court declared, must be strictly job related. Furthermore, no matter how seemingly neutral such requirements are, if they *disparately impact any group protected by the act, they are per se illegal. While the *burden of proof (which *Griggs* places squarely on the employer) as to the discriminatory effect of various employment practices has shifted back and forth between defendants and plaintiffs, the essential tenets of *Griggs* remain in effect.

SWANN V. CHARLOTTE-MECKLENBURG BOARD OF EDUCATION

Citation: 402 U.S. 1 (1971)
Argued: October 12, 1970
Decided: April 20, 1971
Court Below: United States Fourth Circuit Court of Appeals
Basis for Review: *Writ of certiorari
Facts: Plaintiff Swann brought suit in federal court to force the Charlotte, North Carolina, school district to do more to comply with the Supreme Court's desegregation order in *Green v. County School Board of New Kent County* (1968). Fifteen years after *Brown v. Board of Education II* (1955),

over half of the African American students, who constituted approximately 29 percent of the students in the school district, were still attending schools without any white students. The district court ordered implementation of a large-scale busing program.

Issue: What court-ordered methods are permissible for achieving school desegregation?

Outcome: The Supreme Court upheld the lower court's plan.

Vote: 9-0

Participating: Burger, Black, Douglas, Harlan, Brennan, Stewart, White, Marshall, Blackmun

Opinion: Burger for the Court

Significance: *Swann* was the Court's lengthiest treatment to date of the issues raised by *Brown II*. It is remembered primarily for its approval of busing and mathematical racial equations as techniques for achieving school desegregation. While keeping faith with the Warren Court, however, Chief Justice Burger added two provisos: 1) the scope of the court-ordered remedy was to be based on the extent of the violations; and 2) once a school district reached an undefined "unity," the court's *jurisdiction over it ended.

COHEN V. CALIFORNIA

Citation: 403 U.S. 15 (1971)
Argued: February 22, 1971
Decided: June 7, 1971
Court Below: California Court of Appeal
Basis for Review: Appeal
Facts: Paul Robert Cohen, who wore a jacket emblazoned with vulgarly phrased antiwar sentiments in a Los Angeles courthouse, was convicted under a California statute prohibiting disturbances of the peace by offensive conduct.

Issue: Does Cohen's conduct constitute political "speech" protected by the First Amendment?

Outcome: The Court struck down the California law and reversed Cohen's conviction.

Vote: 5-4

Participating: Burger, Black, Douglas, Harlan, Brennan, Stewart, White, Marshall, Blackmun

Opinions: Harlan for the Court; Blackmun, joined by Burger and Black, and in part by White, dissenting

Significance: The Court found that the state cannot objectively distinguish vulgar from non-vulgar political speech, and it provided protection for possibly offensive speech which does not constitute "fighting words" directed at an individual or group and meant as an incitement.

GRAHAM V. RICHARDSON

Citation: 403 U.S. 365 (1971)
Argued: March 22, 1971
Decided: June 14, 1971
Court Below: United States District Court for the District of Arizona
Basis for Review: Appeal
Facts: Carmen Richardson, a Mexican citizen admitted to the United States legally, was denied welfare benefits on the basis of Arizona regulations stipulating that an individual must be a resident of, or have citizenship in the U.S. for 15 years or more in order to receive public assistance.
Issue: Do such state regulations violate the *Equal Protection Clause of the Fourteenth Amendment?
Outcome: Finding that *alienage is a "suspect" classification requiring the Court to employ *strict scrutiny in determining the constitutionality of its use in legislation, the Court struck down the Arizona regulations.
Vote: 9-0
Participating: Burger, Black, Douglas, Harlan, Brennan, Stewart, White, Marshall, Blackmun
Opinions: Blackmun for the Court; Harlan concurring (without written opinion)
Significance: In *Graham*, the Court offered an alternate rationale for its decision: because the federal government, not the states, is given the constitutional power to admit aliens, Arizona's regulations could be said to violate the *Supremacy Clause. Subsequent decisions have indicated that this alternative method for determining the validity of alienage classifications could lead to more latitude in the Court's attitude toward them.

MCKEIVER V. PENNSYLVANIA

Citation: 403 U.S. 528 (1971)
Argued: December 9-10, 1970

Decided: June 21, 1971
Courts Below: Pennsylvania Supreme Court; North Carolina Supreme Court
Bases for Review: Appeal (Pennsylvania cases); *Writs of certiorari (North Carolina cases)
Facts: *McKeiver* consolidated several juvenile cases being prosecuted in Pennsylvania and North Carolina.
Issue: Does the *Due Process Clause of the Fourteenth Amendment require states to extend the right to trial by jury to juvenile defendants?
Outcome: The Court ruled that the Sixth Amendment right to trial by jury does not apply to juveniles being tried in state proceedings.
Vote: 6-3
Participating: Burger, Black, Douglas, Harlan, Brennan, Stewart, White, Marshall, Blackmun
Opinions: Blackmun announced the judgment of the Court; White concurring; Brennan concurring in part and dissenting in part; Harlan concurring; Douglas, joined by Black and Marshall, dissenting
Significance: Reading the recent *precedent *In re Winship* (1970) narrowly, Justice Blackmun declared for the Court that due process required only "fundamental fairness" in juvenile proceedings. Because the presence of a jury might interfere with the flexibility that characterizes such proceedings, it was unnecessary. States are free to provide juries at juvenile trials but none does so.

LEMON V. KURTZMAN

Citation: 403 U.S. 602 (1971)
Argued: March 3, 1971
Decided: June 28, 1971
Court Below: United States District Court for the District of Pennsylvania
Basis for Review: Appeal
Facts: At issue in this case (and two others decided concurrently) were challenges to Rhode Island and Pennsylvania laws permitting direct payments by the state to teachers of secular subjects in parochial schools.
Issue: Do these laws violate the First Amendment, which mandates separation of church and state?
Outcome: The Court struck both laws down.

Vote: 8-0
Participating: Burger, Black, Douglas, Harlan, Brennan, Stewart, White, Blackmun (Marshall not participating in the *Lemon* case)
Opinions: Burger for the Court; Douglas, joined by Black and Marshall, concurring; Brennan and White concurring in part and dissenting in part
Significance: To previously established requirements that laws such as those under consideration in *Lemon* be intended to effect a secular purpose and have a primary effect that neither advances nor inhibits religion, this case added a third element: laws must not foster excessive government entanglement with religion. The laws at issue both failed this third prong of the "Lemon test" because they would require prolonged government surveillance in order to insure that secular subjects taught in religious schools remained entirely secular.

NEW YORK TIMES CO. V. UNITED STATES

Citation: 403 U.S. 713 (1971)
Argued: June 26, 1971
Decided: June 30, 1971
Court Below: United States Second Circuit Court of Appeals
Basis for Review: *Writ of certiorari
Facts: Daniel Ellsberg, a former State Department employee and antiwar activist, surreptitiously acquired copies of the *Pentagon Papers*, a set of classified documents concerning government plans for the Vietnam War which had been prepared during the Johnson administration. Ellsberg leaked the document to the press, and on June 13, 1971, *The New York Times* began printing excerpts. Other newspapers followed suit. On June 15 the administration of Richard M. Nixon obtained a temporary federal court *injunction preventing further publication. Three days later the same court declined to grant the government a permanent injunction, but continued to prevent publication while the administration appealed to the Supreme Court. The Court met on June 25 to consider an expedited appeal.
Issue: Do government arguments that publication would endanger lives and the attempt to secure a peaceful end to the war justify *prior restraint?

Outcome: In a *per curiam opinion, the Court rejected the government's request for a permanent order barring further publication of the *Pentagon Papers*.
Vote: 6-3
Participating: Burger, Black, Douglas, Harlan, Brennan, Stewart, White, Marshall, Blackmun
Opinions: Black, Douglas, Brennan, Stewart, White, and Marshall, concurring separately; Harlan, joined by Burger and Blackmun, dissenting
Significance: The dissenters all objected to the hurried nature of the decision, which in itself contributed to the fragmentation of the Court's opinions. A majority of the justices agreed, however, that the government had not been able to override the "heavy presumption against [the] constitutional validity" of prior restraint on the press. The so-called "Pentagon Papers Case" increased the power of the media and added to the animus between it and government. A case against Ellsberg was subsequently dropped, owing to the government's illegal methods of gathering evidence against him.

REED V. REED

Citation: 404 U.S. 71 (1971)
Argued: October 19, 1971
Decided: November 22, 1971
Court Below: Idaho Supreme Court
Basis for Review: Appeal
Facts: Sally Reed sued her husband, Cecil, from whom she was separated, for the right to administer the estate of their dead son. Applicable state law favored males over females as executors.
Issue: Does the state law violate the Fourteenth Amendment guarantee of *equal protection under the law?
Outcome: The Court struck down the state law.
Vote: 7-0
Participating: Burger, Douglas, Brennan, Stewart, White, Marshall, Blackmun
Opinion: Burger for the Court
Significance: Observing that gender discrimination is "the very kind of arbitrary legislative choice forbidden by the Equal Protection Clause," the Court countermanded a long history of deny-

ing women their constitutional rights. *Reed*, the first Supreme Court case to *hold against gender discrimination on Fourteenth Amendment grounds, was frequently cited over the next decade as *precedent for striking down other statutes exhibiting gender bias.

EISENSTADT V. BAIRD

Citation: 405 U.S. 438 (1972)
Argued: November 17-18, 1971
Decided: March 22, 1972
Court Below: United States First Circuit Court of Appeals
Basis for Review: Appeal
Facts: After a lecture on birth control, William Baird, who was neither a physician nor a pharmacist, gave one of the women in the audience a non-prescription contraceptive. He was convicted under a Massachusetts law prohibiting distribution of contraceptives to anyone other than married couples by anyone other than a doctor or pharmacist.
Issue: Does the Massachusetts law violate the *Equal Protection Clause of the Fourteen Amendment by distinguishing between married and unmarried individuals?
Outcome: The Massachusetts statute was held unconstitutional.
Vote: 6-1
Participating: Burger, Douglas, Brennan, Stewart, White, Marshall, Blackmun (Powell and Rehnquist not participating)
Opinions: Brennan for the Court; Douglas concurring; White, joined by Blackmun, concurring; Burger dissenting
Significance: *Eisenstadt* enlarged on the holding of *Griswold v. Connecticut* (1965), in which the Court first ruled that a state law banning the use of contraceptives by married couples violated a constitutional right of privacy.

WISCONSIN V. YODER

Citation: 406 U.S. 205 (1972)
Argued: December 8, 1971
Decided: May 15, 1972
Court Below: Wisconsin Supreme Court
Basis for Review: *Writ of certiorari

Facts: Jonas Yoder, a member of the Conservative Amish Mennonite Church, challenged a state law requiring his children to attend high school.
Issue: Does the Wisconsin compulsory school attendance statute violate the Amish parents' right to *free exercise of religion under the First Amendment?
Outcome: Balancing the state's interest in educating its citizens against the Amish parents' interest in bringing their children up within the framework of their faith, the Court exempted high school-aged Amish children from the Wisconsin law.
Vote: 6-1
Participating: Burger, Douglas, Brennan, Stewart, White, Marshall, Blackmun (Powell and Rehnquist not participating)
Opinions: Burger for the Court; Stewart, joined by Brennan, concurring; White, joined by Brennan and Stewart, concurring; Douglas dissenting in part
Significance: The value of *Yoder* as *precedent is questionable, for as Burger's opinion for the Court makes clear, the *holding in the case was exceedingly narrow. The opinion repeatedly stresses the distinctiveness and traditional self-sufficiency of the Amish, even going so far as to state that few other groups would be able to tilt the balance against the state's interest in universal education.

JOHNSON V. LOUISIANA; APODACA V. OREGON

Citations: 406 U.S. 356 (1972) (*Johnson*); 406 U.S. 404 (1972) (*Apodaca*)
Argued: March 1, 1971; reargued January 10, 1972
Decided: May 22, 1972
Courts Below: Louisiana Supreme Court (*Johnson*); Oregon Court of Appeals (*Apodaca*)
Bases for Review: Appeal (*Johnson*); *Writ of certiorari (*Apodaca*)
Facts: Both cases involved challenges to convictions in state court by juries voting less than unanimously in *noncapital criminal trials.
Issue: Do the Fourteenth Amendment's *Due Process and *Equal Protection Clauses compel state courts, like their federal counterparts, to

require jury unanimity to convict in noncapital criminal trials?

Outcome: Finding that not all elements of the Sixth Amendment, concerning criminal prosecutions, had been *incorporated into the Fourteenth Amendment, the Court held that states can employ nonunanimous juries in trials of noncapital offenses.

Vote: 5-4 (in both cases)

Participating: Burger, Douglas, Brennan, Stewart, White, Marshall, Blackmun, Powell, Rehnquist

Opinions: *Johnson:* White for the Court; Blackmun and Powell concurring; Stewart, joined by Brennan and Marshall, dissenting; Douglas, joined by Brennan and Marshall, dissenting; Brennan, joined by Marshall, dissenting, and Marshall, joined by Brennan, dissenting. *Apodaca:* White for a *plurality of the Court; Blackmun concurring; Powell concurring in the judgment; Stewart, joined by Brennan and Marshall, dissenting; Douglas, joined by Brennan and Marshall, dissenting; Brennan, joined by Marshall, dissenting; and Marshall, joined by Brennan, dissenting

Significance: Although *Johnson* and *Apodaca* remain in force, few states have adopted the rule of permitting nonunanimous verdicts in criminal trials.

KASTIGAR V. UNITED STATES

Citation: 406 U.S. 441 (1972)
Argued: January 11, 1972
Decided: May 22, 1972
Court Below: United States Ninth Circuit Court of Appeals
Basis for Review: *Writ of certiorari
Facts: Kastigar challenged the immunity provisions of the 1970 Organized Crime Control Act, which granted potential witnesses at *grand jury proceedings only *use immunity, preventing use of such testimony as evidence against the witness in any subsequent criminal proceeding.
Issue: Can witnesses be forced to give grand jury testimony under a grant of use immunity?
Outcome: The Court found that use immunity was sufficient to prevent violation of a witness's Fifth Amendment guarantee against self-incrimi-

nation.
Vote: 5-2
Participating: Burger, Douglas, Stewart, White, Marshall, Blackmun, Powell (Brennan and Rehnquist not participating)
Opinions: Powell for the Court; Douglas and Marshall dissenting
Significance: Kastigar argued for so-called transactional immunity, which prevents subsequent prosecution for any offenses related to the witness's testimony. The Court, however, ruled that the government's authority to compel testimony is only limited by the Fifth Amendment, and that use immunity is sufficient to protect the rights at issue.

ARGERSINGER V. HAMLIN

Citation: 407 U.S. 25 (1972)
Argued: December 6, 1971; reargued February 28, 1972
Decided: June 12, 1972
Court Below: Florida Supreme Court
Basis for Review: *Writ of certiorari
Facts: Argersinger was convicted in state court of carrying a concealed weapon. He was indigent and unrepresented by counsel when the court sentenced him to spend 90 days in jail. His application to the Florida Supreme Court for a writ of *habeas corpus was rejected.
Issue: Do state defendants facing possible jail sentences have a Sixth Amendment right to counsel?
Outcome: A unanimous Supreme Court reversed the court below, releasing Argersinger.
Vote: 9-0
Participating: Burger, Douglas, Brennan, Stewart, White, Marshall, Blackmun, Powell, Rehnquist
Opinions: Douglas for the Court; Burger concurring; Brennan, joined by Douglas and Stewart, concurring; and Powell, joined by Rehnquist, concurring
Significance: *Argersinger* extended *Gideon v. Wainwright* (1963), in which the Court held that indigents charged with serious crimes in state court must be granted state-appointed counsel. In *Scott v. Illinois* (1979), however, the Court limited the implication in *Argersinger* that all indigent state defendants must be appointed counsel

when accused of crimes where imprisonment is a possible punishment.

MOOSE LODGE V. IRVIS

Citation: 407 U.S. 163 (1972)
Argued: February 28, 1972
Decided: June 12, 1972
Court Below: United States District Court for the Middle District of Pennsylvania
Basis for Review: Appeal
Facts: Irvis, an African American, was denied service as a guest at a Moose Lodge in Harrisburg, Pennsylvania. On grounds that the state liquor licensing authority was involved with the lodge insofar as it had granted the lodge a license, Irvis was able to gain an *injunction requiring the licensing authority to suspend its grant to the lodge until its discriminatory practices ended.
Issue: Does Pennsylvania's involvement with the lodge rise to the level of rendering the lodge's conduct discriminatory *state action violating *equal protection under the Fourteenth Amendment?
Outcome: Because the state was not involved in any effort to enforce the lodge's discriminatory policies, the Court held that the law could not reach what amounted to essentially private racial discrimination.
Vote: 6-3
Participating: Burger, Douglas, Brennan, Stewart, White, Marshall, Blackmun, Powell, Rehnquist
Opinions: Rehnquist for the Court; Douglas, joined by Marshall, dissenting; and Brennan, joined by Marshall, dissenting
Significance: *Moose Lodge* ended the extension of the *state action principle, permitting court intervention in cases where private discrimination is practiced with at least some government involvement, a process that began with *Shelley v. Kraemer* in 1948.

UNITED STATES V. UNITED STATES DISTRICT COURT

Citation: 407 U.S. 297 (1972)
Argued: February 24, 1972
Decided: June 19, 1972

Court Below: United States Sixth Circuit Court of Appeals
Basis for Review: *Writ of certiorari
Facts: On the basis of evidence obtained through government wiretaps placed without *warrants, three defendants were charged with conspiracy to destroy government property. In response to a federal district court order to reveal the source of the government's evidence, Attorney General John Mitchell responded with an *affidavit claiming that national security mandated placement of the wiretaps on executive authority alone.
Issue: Does Article II of the Constitution empower the president to authorize electronic surveillance in the name of national security?
Outcome: A unanimous Court rejected the administration's claim.
Vote: 8-0
Participating: Burger, Douglas, Brennan, Stewart, White, Marshall, Blackmun, Powell (Rehnquist not participating)
Opinions: Powell for the Court; Burger concurring (without written opinion); and Douglas and White concurring
Significance: The Supreme Court reasoned that the government's interpretation of Article II allowed for abuse not only of Fourth Amendment search and seizure protections, but of the First Amendment. Electronic surveillance authorized only by the president was likely to be trained on those groups opposed to the administration then in power. The Court's reasoning was sound: two days before the opinion in this case was handed down, White House "Plumbers" were caught attempting to bug Democratic National Headquarters in the Watergate complex in Washington, D.C.

BRANZBURG V. HAYES; *IN RE PAPPAS; UNITED STATES V. CALDWELL

Citation: 408 U.S. 665 (1972)
Argued: February 22-23, 1972
Decided: June 29, 1972
Courts Below: Kentucky Court of Appeals (*Branzburg*); Massachusetts Supreme Court (*Pappas*); United States Ninth Circuit Court of Appeals (*Caldwell*)

Bases for Review: *Writs of certiorari

Facts: Paul Branzburg, Paul Pappas, and Earl Caldwell were all journalists who refused to provide *grand juries with information gleaned from confidential sources.

Issue: Does the First Amendment protect the press with a special *immunity from testifying before a grand jury?

Outcome: A divided Court declined to extend an exemption to the news media.

Vote: 5-4

Participating: Burger, Douglas, Brennan, Stewart, White, Marshall, Blackmun, Powell, Rehnquist

Opinions: White for the Court; Powell concurring; Douglas dissenting; and Stewart, joined by Brennan and Marshall, dissenting

Significance: Lively public debate in the aftermath of *Branzburg* prompted a number of states to create or modify press shield statutes. The federal government, however, has declined to follow suit.

FURMAN V. GEORGIA

Citation: 408 U.S. 238 (1972)

Argued: January 17, 1972

Decided: June 29, 1972

Court Below: Georgia Supreme Court

Basis for Review: *Writ of certiorari

Facts: Furman was convicted of murder and sentenced to death in Georgia. Two other defendants in the case had received the death sentence for rape convictions in Texas. All three petitioners were African American.

Issue: Does the death penalty constitute *cruel and unusual punishment in violation of the Eighth Amendment?

Outcome: Finding that state procedures for imposing the death penalty were ambiguous and arbitrary, the Court nullified death penalty statutes in all 39 states then authorizing this ultimate form of punishment.

Vote: 5-4

Participating: Burger, Douglas, Brennan, Stewart, White, Marshall, Blackmun, Powell, Rehnquist

Opinions: *Per curiam: Douglas, Brennan, Stewart, White, and Marshall concurring separately; Burger, Blackmun, Powell, and Rehnquist

dissenting jointly and separately

Significance: Only two of those justices contributing to the Court's per curiam decision, Brennan and Marshall, found the death penalty to be cruel and unusual per se. Because the Court was fractured and deeply divided on the issue, states were able to remedy defects of vagueness and ambiguity in their death penalty statutes, thus permitting the Court to reverse its opinion on the punishment in *Gregg v. Georgia* (1976).

ROE V. WADE

Citation: 410 U.S. 113 (1973)

Argued: December 13, 1971; reargued October 11, 1972

Decided: January 22, 1973

Court Below: United States Fifth Circuit Court of Appeals (appeal held in abeyance pending U.S. Supreme Court decision)

Basis for Review: Appeal

Facts: Norma McCorvey, a pregnant, unmarried Texan, challenged her state's abortion ban under the pseudonym "Jane Roe." The lower court declared the law unconstitutional. Responsibility for writing the Supreme Court's opinion was given to Justice Blackmun, who initially drafted an opinion outlawing the Texas statute because of its vagueness. When it became apparent that Blackmun's first draft opinion failed to convince a majority of his fellow justices, the case was set for reargument, after which Blackmun reemerged with a second opinion based on the right of privacy.

Issue: Can states constitutionally outlaw abortion?

Outcome: Finding a) that there is a "fundamental right" to abortion grounded in the right of privacy; and b) that states can only limit fundamental rights if there is a "compelling state interest" in doing so, the Court upheld a woman's right to abortion.

Vote: 7-2

Participating: Burger, Douglas, Brennan, Stewart, White, Marshall, Blackmun, Powell, Rehnquist

Opinions: Blackmun for the Court; Burger, Douglas, and Stewart concurring; White, joined by Rehnquist, dissenting; and Rehnquist dissenting

Significance: *Roe v. Wade* is undoubtedly the

most controversial Supreme Court decision of recent times. Many critics of Blackmun's opinion found it fundamentally flawed because it relied on the discredited doctrine of *substantive due process for its justification of the right to privacy. In their view a better approach — particularly because of the burgeoning women's movement, then pursuing ratification of the Equal Rights Amendment to the Constitution (which ultimately died in 1982) — was an analysis based on gender discrimination barred by the *Equal Protection Clause of the Fourteenth Amendment.

Laypersons responded by making Roe a political cause célèbre. On the right, the "right to life" movement gained strong support among Republicans, and when Ronald Reagan was elected president in 1980, his administration made federal judicial appointments —including those to the Supreme Court — contingent upon opposition to *Roe.* Because Blackmun's opinion left room for some state regulation of abortion during the second trimester of a pregnancy and great latitude for limitation during the third trimester, the right to life movement also succeeded in pressuring some state legislatures into passing laws aimed at restricting abortion as much as possible.

A number of these statutes passed constitutional muster in the Supreme Court, and supporters of *Roe,* faced with the prospect that the Court might overrule it, rallied to defeat the nomination of Reagan's conservative candidate to replace the retiring Justice Powell, Robert Bork. Subsequent Court appointments, as well as state and federal elections, have been colored by the continuing abortion debate.

MAHAN V. HOWELL

Citation: 410 U.S. 315 (1973)
Argued: December 12, 1972
Decided: February 21, 1973
Court Below: United States District Court for the Eastern District of Virginia
Basis for Review: Appeal
Facts: A 1971 Virginia legislative districting plan, which created districts that varied from one another in population by as much as 16 percent,

but which conformed with city and county boundaries, was struck down in federal district court.
Issue: Must state legislative districts be strictly equal in population size?
Outcome: Reaffirming its earlier *dicta in *Reynolds v. Sims* (1964) indicating that while federal congressional districts must be equal, the standard for state legislative districts is less rigid, the Court upheld the Virginia plan.
Vote: 5-3
Participating: Burger, Douglas, Brennan, Stewart, White, Marshall, Blackmun, Rehnquist (Powell not participating)
Opinions: Rehnquist for the Court; Brennan, joined by Douglas, dissenting; and Marshall dissenting
Significance: *Mahan* was one of four cases handed down in 1972 that addressed the question of how much variance is permitted in legislative redistricting. In *Gaffney v. Cummings* and *White v. Register,* the Court ruled against smaller population variances than those in the Virginia plan because Connecticut and Texas failed to provide rationales for them. And in *White v. Weiser,* the Court confirmed that there is little flexibility in determining federal congressional districts.

SAN ANTONIO INDEPENDENT SCHOOL DISTRICT V. RODRIGUEZ

Citation: 411 U.S. 1 (1973)
Argued: October 12, 1972
Decided: March 21, 1973
Court Below: United States District Court for the Western District of Texas
Basis for Review: Appeal
Facts: Demetrio Rodriguez, together with other parents living in one of San Antonio's poorer districts, filed a *class action suit challenging the state's practice of appropriating only minimal funds for public education. School boards increased their budgets with local property taxes, with the effect that those students living in areas where property values were low received an education backed by few financial resources. The federal district court, applying *strict scrutiny to the Texas plan, which resulted in different classes of students distinguished by wealth, held it to be

unconstitutional.

Issue: Do public school financing plans that depend upon local property taxes violate the *Equal Protection Clause of the Fourteenth Amendment?

Outcome: Holding that education is not a fundamental right guaranteed by the Constitution, the Supreme Court reversed the court below.

Vote: 5-4

Participating: Burger, Douglas, Brennan, Stewart, White, Marshall, Blackmun, Powell, Rehnquist

Opinions: Powell for the Court; Stewart concurring; Brennan dissenting; White, joined by Douglas and Brennan, dissenting; and Marshall, joined by Douglas, dissenting

Significance: A majority of the Court did not find wealth to be a constitutionally *suspect classification and therefore employed only the *rational basis test (the most lenient standard) in evaluating the Texas plan. Observing that the state did not deprive any student of an education, the Court reasoned that the use of property taxes to enhance school district budgets furthered Texas's legitimate interest in promoting local participation in public education. Seventeen years later, however, the Texas Supreme Court ordered an overhaul of the state school financing program to equalize expenditures in order to bring the program in line with the stricter requirements of the state constitution.

FRONTIERO V. RICHARDSON

Citation: 411 U.S. 677 (1973)
Argued: January 17, 1973
Decided: May 14, 1973
Court Below: United States District Court for the Middle District of Alabama
Basis for Review: Appeal
Facts: Air Force Lieutenant Sharron Frontiero challenged a federal law granting supplemental monetary benefits to married servicemen. Married women serving in the military were only granted these benefits if they could prove that they funded more than 50 percent of their husband's expenses.
Issues: Does the federal law violate equal protection under the *Due Process Clause of the Fifth Amendment? Is gender, like race, a consti-

tutionally *suspect classification, requiring a showing of *compelling state interest to justify any law based on gender discrimination?

Outcome: Justice Brennan, writing for a *plurality of the Court, struck the law down.

Vote: 8-1

Participating: Burger, Douglas, Brennan, Stewart, White, Marshall, Blackmun, Powell, Rehnquist

Opinions: Brennan for the plurality; Stewart concurring; Powell, joined by Burger and Blackmun, concurring; Rehnquist dissenting

Significance: The justices once again sidestepped the issue of whether or not gender is a suspect classification, first raised — but left unanswered — in *Reed v. Reed* (1971). While Justice Brennan found such classifications "inherently invidious," Justice Powell felt that the Court should wait for the outcome of the Equal Rights Amendment ratification process, then underway. Although the justices agreed that Frontiero had a claim against the government, the issue of how to judge gender discrimination would have to wait until *Craig v. Boren* was handed down in 1976.

KEYES V. DENVER SCHOOL DISTRICT NO. 1

Citation: 413 U.S. 189 (1973)
Argued: October 12, 1972
Decided: June 21, 1973
Court Below: United States Tenth Circuit Court of Appeals
Basis for Review: *Writ of certiorari
Facts: Public schools in Denver, Colorado School District No. 1 had been segregated racially and ethnically not by law, but by various school policies and practices.
Issue: Are public school districts that include schools that are racially segregated not as a result of law, but as a result of school board policies, obliged to desegregate?
Outcome: The Court held that such school districts must desegregate.
Vote: 7-1
Participating: Burger, Douglas, Brennan, Stewart, Marshall, Blackmun, Powell, Rehnquist (White not participating)
Opinions: Brennan for the Court; Burger concurring (without written opinion); Douglas con-

curring; Powell concurring in part and dissenting in part; Rehnquist dissenting

Significance: This was the first time the Court held that northern schools, never segregated by law, must nonetheless desegregate if school board policies had caused them to be racially segregated.

MILLER V. CALIFORNIA

Citation: 413 U.S. 15 (1973)
Argued: January 18-19, 1972; reargued November 7, 1972
Decided: June 21, 1973
Court Below: California Superior Court
Basis for Review: Appeal
Facts: Miller was convicted of having mailed obscene material in violation of California law.
Issue: Do states have the power to regulate obscene materials without violating First Amendment protections of *free speech?
Outcome: The Court, agreeing on the first definition of obscenity since *Roth v. United States* (1957), afforded the states some latitude in regulating allegedly obscene material.
Vote: 5-4
Participating: Burger, Douglas, Brennan, Stewart, White, Marshall, Blackmun, Powell, Rehnquist
Opinions: Burger for the Court; Douglas dissenting; and Brennan, joined by Stewart and Marshall, dissenting
Significance: According to Justice Burger's opinion for the Court, materials were obscene if "(a) the average person, applying contemporary community standards, would find that the work, taken as a whole, appeals to the prurient interest; (b) the work depicts or describes, in a patently offensive way, sexual conduct specifically defined by the applicable state law; and (c) the work, taken as a whole, lacks serious literary, artistic, political, or scientific value." While *Miller* appeared to grant localities considerable latitude in determining their own community standards, subsequent Supreme Court opinions made it clear that broad departures from the norm would not be tolerated. Furthermore, a nationwide standard would be used to judge whether a work met requirement (c). In a companion case decided the same day, *Paris Adult Theatre v. Slaton*, the Court reaffirmed

Roth's holding that obscenity is not protected by the First Amendment.

EDELMAN V. JORDAN

Citation: 415 U.S. 651 (1974)
Argued: December 12, 1973
Decided: March 25, 1974
Court Below: United States Seventh Circuit Court of Appeals
Basis for Review: *Writ of certiorari
Facts: John Jordan initiated a *class action against Illinois state officials, charging that they were administering federal aid belatedly, in violation of government regulations.
Issue: To what extent are there exceptions to the Eleventh Amendment's grant of immunity to states from suits brought in federal court without their permission?
Outcome: The Court held that Illinois's participation in federal programs did not constitute a waiver of Eleventh Amendment rights, and that although there are exceptions to the amendment that permit federal courts to issue *injunctions against future enforcement of laws, these courts cannot order remedies for past damages.
Vote: 5-4
Participating: Burger, Douglas, Brennan, Stewart, White, Marshall, Blackmun, Powell, Rehnquist
Opinions: Rehnquist for the Court; Douglas and Brennan dissenting; and Marshall, joined by Blackmun, dissenting
Significance: Eleventh Amendment immunity has been eroded since *Edelman* by decisions holding that states can be sued in federal court for violations of the Fourteenth Amendment and the *Commerce Clause.

GERTZ V. ROBERT WELCH, INC.

Citation: 418 U.S. 323 (1974)
Argued: November 14, 1973
Decided: June 25, 1974
Court Below: United States Seventh Circuit Court of Appeals
Basis for Review: *Writ of certiorari
Facts: Elmer Gertz was an attorney representing plaintiffs suing a police officer for civil damages connected with the officer's earlier conviction

for murder. A publication of the right-wing John Birch Society accused Gertz of having framed the policeman for the murder conviction. The publication also called Gertz a criminal and a "Leninist." Gertz lost his suit for defamation in the lower federal court, and his appeal to the circuit court also was unsuccessful.

Issue: What is the extent of the "actual malice" standard, required in *New York Times Co. v. Sullivan* (1964) to prove defamation of public officials?

Outcome: The Court held that the need to prove "actual malice" applies only to public officials and public figures, not to private plaintiffs such as Gertz. But the Court also held that private plaintiffs cannot recover punitive damages in the absence of a showing of actual malice on the part of defendants.

Vote: 5-4

Participating: Burger, Douglas, Brennan, Stewart, White, Marshall, Blackmun, Powell, Rehnquist

Opinions: Powell for the Court; Blackmun concurring; Burger, Douglas, Brennan, and White dissenting

Significance: Eleven years later, in *Dun & Bradstreet, Inc. v. Greenmoss Builders* (1985), the Burger Court restricted the application of the *Gertz* standard to private plaintiffs involved in matters of public concern. Other private plaintiffs seeking redress for defamation would do so under *common law rules.

MIAMI HERALD PUBLISHING CO. TORNILLO

Citation: 418 U.S. 241 (1974)
Argued: April 17, 1974
Decided: June 25, 1974
Court Below: Florida Supreme Court
Basis for Review: Appeal
Facts: In response to negative editorials in the *Miami Herald*, state legislative candidate Pat Tornillo demanded that, in accordance with the Florida "right to reply" statute, the paper print his responses to its criticisms. After the lower court declared the law unconstitutional, the Florida Supreme Court upheld it on appeal.
Issue: Does the "right to reply" law violate First

Amendment guarantees of press freedom?
Outcome: A unanimous Court struck the statute down.
Vote: 9-0
Participating: Burger, Douglas, Brennan, Stewart, White, Marshall, Blackmun, Powell, Rehnquist
Opinions: Burger for the Court; Brennan, joined by Rehnquist, concurring; and White concurring
Significance: *Tornillo* underscored the distinction made by the Court between print and broadcast media. In *Red Lion Broadcasting Co. v. Federal Communications Commission* (1969), the Court had upheld the federal "fairness doctrine," requiring that air time be set aside for responses to personal or political attacks, on grounds that access to the airwaves was limited in ways that access to print media is not.

UNITED STATES V. NIXON

Citation: 418 U.S. 683 (1974)
Argued: July 8, 1974
Decided: July 24, 1974
Court Below: United States District Court for the District of Columbia
Basis for Review: *Writ of certiorari (before judgment rendered in court below)
Facts: After the 1972 discovery of the break-in at Democratic National Headquarters in the Watergate complex in Washington, D.C., President Nixon and Attorney General Elliott Richardson appointed Archibald Cox to act as special prosecutor to investigate the case. When congressional hearings uncovered the fact that Nixon had tape recorded conversations held in his office, Cox asked the White House to hand over the tapes. When Cox refused Nixon's demand that he discontinue these requests, Nixon ordered the attorney general to fire Cox. Both Richardson and his deputy resigned rather than carry out the president's order, which finally was executed by Solicitor General Robert Bork (serving as acting attorney general). A second special prosecutor, Leon Jaworski, was quickly appointed, and he obtained a federal district court *subpoena for the tapes. The White House countered with claims of *executive privilege and *separation of powers, declaring that because the special pros-

ecutor was a member of the executive branch, federal courts had no authority to intervene.

Issue: What is the nature of presidential immunity?

Outcome: Rejecting the separation of powers argument on grounds that the special prosecutor was ultimately answerable to the federal courts, the Supreme Court held that executive privilege does not shield the president from demands for evidence in a criminal proceeding.

Vote: 8-0

Participating: Burger, Douglas, Brennan, Stewart, White, Marshall, Blackmun, Powell (Rehnquist not participating)

Opinion: Burger for the Court

Significance: In addition to being a landmark case that established the conditional nature of executive privilege, *United States v. Nixon* also acted as an historical watershed. The tapes turned over to the special prosecutor contained proof that Nixon knew of the attempt to cover up the Watergate fiasco and thus was guilty of obstruction of justice. Less than three weeks later, Nixon resigned, becoming the only president in United States history to do so.

MILLIKEN V. BRADLEY

Citation: 418 U.S. 717 (1974)
Argued: February 27, 1974
Decided: July 25, 1974
Court Below: United States Sixth Circuit Court of Appeals
Basis for Review: *Writ of certiorari
Facts: Plaintiffs sponsored by the National Association for the Advancement of Colored People (NAACP) sued Michigan Governor Milliken in an attempt to rectify the racial imbalance in the Detroit public school district caused by white flight to the city suburbs. A federal district court found that the Detroit school district had followed racially discriminatory policies and ordered a busing plan remedy that included some suburban schools. The ruling was affirmed by the *appellate court.

Issue: What are the limits to remedies intended to reverse school segregation?

Outcome: Finding that only those school dis-

tricts actually responsible for segregation could be ordered to participate in desegregation plans, the Court overturned the ruling below.

Vote: 5-4

Participating: Burger, Douglas, Brennan, Stewart, White, Marshall, Blackmun, Powell, Rehnquist

Opinions: Burger for the Court; Stewart concurring; Douglas dissenting; White, joined by Douglas, Brennan, and Marshall, dissenting; and Marshall, joined by Douglas, Brennan, and White, dissenting

Significance: *Milliken* ended 20 years of NAACP success in fighting school segregation. For the first time, the Court rejected an NAACP-sponsored desegregation plan, instead establishing a limit to court-ordered remedies to segregation.

JACKSON V. METROPOLITAN EDISON CO.

Citation: 419 U.S. 345 (1974)
Argued: October 15, 1974
Decided: December 23, 1974
Court Below: United States Third Circuit Court of Appeals
Basis for Review: *Writ of certiorari
Facts: Jackson, a resident of York, Pennsylvania, brought suit against Metropolitan Edison, a private utility company, claiming that when the company turned off her service without providing her an opportunity for a hearing, it violated *due process.

Issue: At what point does a privately owned entity become so public in nature that it is bound by the *state action doctrine of the Fourteenth Amendment's Due Process Clause?

Outcome: The Court ruled that Metropolitan Edison was not bound by the Due Process Clause.

Vote: 6-3

Participating: Burger, Douglas, Brennan, Stewart, White, Marshall, Blackmun, Powell, Rehnquist

Opinions: Rehnquist for the Court; Douglas, Brennan, and Marshall dissenting

Significance: *Jackson*, although it remains in force, served to further the confusion surrounding the state action doctrine. Privately owned utility companies, as subsequent state regulatory legislation implies, are quasi-public entities subject to governmental restrictions.

TAYLOR V. LOUISIANA

Citation: 419 U.S. 522 (1975)
Argued: October 16, 1974
Decided: January 21, 1975
Court Below: Louisiana Supreme Court
Basis for Review: Appeal
Facts: Taylor challenged his conviction for aggravated kidnapping by an all-male jury that was the product of Louisiana's voluntary jury service policy.
Issue: Does an all-male jury violate the Sixth Amendment right in criminal trials to a jury consisting of a representative cross-section of the community?
Outcome: Finding that women cannot be systematically excluded or granted exemptions from jury duty if the result is all-male panels, the Court struck down the Louisiana policy and *remanded Taylor's case for further consideration.
Vote: 8-1
Participating: Burger, Douglas, Brennan, Stewart, White, Marshall, Blackmun, Powell, Rehnquist
Opinions: White for the Court; Burger concurring; Rehnquist dissenting
Significance: *Taylor* effectively overruled *Hoyt v. Florida* (1961), in which the Court ruled against a female defendant's claim that a similar Florida provision violated her right to *equal protection by allowing her to be convicted by an all-male jury.

BIGELOW V. VIRGINIA

Citation: 421 U.S. 809 (1975)
Argued: December 18, 1974
Decided: June 16, 1975
Court Below: Virginia Supreme Court
Basis for Review: Appeal
Facts: Jeffrey C. Bigelow, editor of the Charlottesville *Virginia Weekly*, was prosecuted by the state for publishing an advertisement for a New York organization that assisted women in obtaining abortions. His challenge to the Virginia statute making it a *misdemeanor to publish anything that would "encourage or prompt the procuring of abortion" was rejected by the state supreme court, which found that Bigelow lacked

*standing to mount a court challenge because of the commercial nature of the material at issue.
Issue: Does the First Amendment protect publication of *commercial speech?
Outcome: Finding that the advertisement contained truthful information about a matter of considerable public interest, the Court granted it First Amendment protection.
Vote: 7-2
Participating: Burger, Douglas, Brennan, Stewart, White, Marshall, Blackmun, Powell, Rehnquist
Opinions: Blackmun for the Court; Rehnquist, joined by White, dissenting
Significance: Although the Court previously had held that commercial speech lacked sufficient content to be accorded First Amendment protection, the connection between the *Virginia Weekly* advertisement and the recent landmark decision in *Roe v. Wade* (1973) was enough to prompt the Court to review its *precedents. One year later, with *Virginia State Board of Pharmacy v. Virginia Citizens Consumer Council* (1976), the Court would grant commercial speech some constitutional protection, adding to the burgeoning of First Amendment freedoms.

ALBEMARLE PAPER CO. V. MOODY

Citation: 422 U.S. 405 (1975)
Argued: April 14, 1975
Decided: June 25, 1975
Court Below: United States Fourth Circuit Court of Appeals
Basis for Review: *Writ of certiorari
Facts: African American employees of Albemarle's Roanoke Rapids, North Carolina, mill brought suit charging that the company's seniority system and preemployment examinations perpetuated the racial segregation that existed prior to passage of Title VII in 1965, which outlawed employment discrimination. The lower court found that the plaintiffs were locked into lower-paying jobs, but declined to order payment of back pay or *enjoin the preemployment testing program.
Issue: Is back pay an appropriate remedy for violations of Title VII, even when there is no evidence that the employer purposely adopted discriminatory policies?

Outcome: The Supreme Court ruled that the district court should have enjoined the preemployment exams, which were insufficiently job related, and awarded back pay to the employees adversely affected by the company's hiring and promotion policies.

Vote: 7-1

Participating: Burger, Douglas, Brennan, Stewart, White, Marshall, Blackmun, Rehnquist (Powell not participating)

Opinions: Stewart for the Court; Marshall, Rehnquist, and Blackmun concurring; Burger concurring in part and dissenting in part

Significance: In ruling that back pay was the appropriate remedy for violations of Title VII, which is intended to rectify damage done to victims of unlawful discrimination, the Burger Court established one of the major remedies available under this federal legislation.

BUCKLEY V. VALEO

Citation: 424 U.S. 1 (1976)
Argued: November 10, 1975
Decided: January 30, 1976
Court Below: United States District Court for the District of Columbia
Basis for Review: Appeal
Facts: Various political candidates challenged the 1974 amendments to the Federal Election Campaign Act (FECA) and the Revenue Act of 1971, seeking to prevent the amendments from going into effect prior to the 1976 elections.
Issues: Does the provision of FECA permitting Congress to appoint a majority of members to the Federal Election Commission (FEC) violate the *separation of powers doctrine? Do FECA's restrictions on private campaign contributions and expenditures violate the First Amendment? Do FECA provisions regarding public campaign financing violate either the First Amendment or the Fifth Amendment's *Due Process Clause?
Outcome: The Court found as follows: 1) only the president has the power to appoint officers to administrative bodies such as the FEC; 2) while contribution limits are constitutional (although indirect contributions to political campaigns not tied to a candidate or a campaign committee

remain unrestricted), those on expenditures violate First Amendment protection of political expression (although a presidential candidate must agree voluntarily to set a limit on expenditures as a condition to receiving public funding); and 3) provisions for public financing are a valid exercise of Congress's power to spend to promote the general welfare.

Vote: 8-0

Participating: Burger, Brennan, Stewart, White, Marshall, Blackmun, Powell, Rehnquist (Stevens not participating)

Opinion: Unsigned *per curiam opinion (all members joined Part One of the opinion; votes on other parts varied)

Significance: By extensively reshaping federal legislation concerning election financing, *Buckley* greatly affected the way political campaigns are run. Perhaps the most significant change wrought by the decision was the finding that there should be no restrictions on expenditures by individuals and groups helping candidates, so long as these monies are "independent" of the candidates and of official campaign committees. In the wake of *Buckley*, so-called political action committees advancing various political agenda proliferated.

WASHINGTON V. DAVIS

Citation: 426 U.S. 229 (1976)
Argued: March 1, 1976
Decided: June 7, 1976
Court Below: United States Court of Appeals for the District of Columbia Circuit
Basis for Review: *Writ of certiorari
Facts: African American members of and unsuccessful applicants to the Washington, D.C., Metropolitan Police Department sued the department for discriminatory hiring and promotion policies. In particular, they cited a written test which a disproportionately high number of African Americans failed. The district court found for the police department, but the *appellate court, relying on *Griggs v. Duke Power Co.* (1971), reversed, finding the *disparate impact of the test to be evidence of employment discrimination.
Issue: Do federal job qualification tests which minorities fail in disproportionate numbers vio-

late the *Due Process Clause of the Fifth Amendment?

Outcome: Finding that disparate impact alone is insufficient evidence of racial discrimination, the Burger Court reversed the court below.

Vote: 7-2

Participating: Burger, Brennan, Stewart, White, Marshall, Blackmun, Powell, Rehnquist, Stevens

Opinions: White for the Court; Stevens concurring; Brennan, joined by Marshall, dissenting

Significance: Justice White, speaking for the Court, stated unequivocally that some evidence of discriminatory intent must be present in order for such tests to be found unconstitutional. What constituted such evidence, however, was far from clear. While his opinion stated that discriminatory intent could be inferred from a totality of circumstances, the test for it was left indeterminate until *Personnel Administrator v. Feeney* (1979), which clarified the test so that it advantaged employers.

YOUNG V. AMERICAN MINI THEATRES, INC.

Citation: 427 U.S. 50 (1976)
Argued: March 24, 1976
Decided: June 24, 1976
Court Below: United States Sixth Circuit Court of Appeals
Basis for Review: *Writ of certiorari
Facts: American Mini Theatres challenged a Detroit, Michigan, zoning ordinance which attempted to prevent concentration of sexually oriented but legal businesses in certain locations. The ordinance did not require an official determination that the material disseminated by these establishments was legally obscene before the businesses could be prohibited.
Issue: Does the ordinance violate First Amendment guarantees of *free speech?
Outcome: Finding that some degree of regulation of sexually explicit, but not obscene material, was permissible, the Court upheld the ordinance.
Vote: 5-4
Participating: Burger, Brennan, Stewart, White, Marshall, Blackmun, Powell, Rehnquist, Stevens
Opinions: Stevens for a *plurality of the Court;

Powell concurring; Stewart, joined by Brennan, Marshall, and Blackmun, dissenting; and Blackmun, joined by Brennan, Stewart, and Marshall, dissenting
Significance: *Young* ushered in a new era of First Amendment rulings in which the Court, led by Justice Stevens, began to make distinctions among forms of protected speech, permitting varying degrees of restriction to be imposed on expression deemed offensive.

NATIONAL LEAGUE OF CITIES V. USERY

Citation: 426 U.S. 833 (1976)
Argued: April 16, 1975; reargued March 2, 1976
Decided: June 24, 1976
Court Below: United States District Court for the District of Columbia
Basis for Review: Appeal
Facts: The National League of Cities challenged 1974 amendments to the federal Fair Labor Standards Act which extended federal minimum wage and maximum hour standards to state and local government.
Issue: Do the amendments violate the Tenth Amendment's reservation of *unenumerated powers to the states?
Outcome: Finding that Congress had exceeded its authority to regulate interstate commerce and violated state *sovereignty, the Court struck the provisions down as unconstitutional.
Vote: 5-4
Participating: Burger, Brennan, Stewart, White, Marshall, Blackmun, Powell, Rehnquist, Stevens
Opinions: Rehnquist for the Court; Blackmun concurring; Brennan, joined by White and Marshall, dissenting; and Stevens dissenting
Significance: For the first time since the New Deal era, the Supreme Court voted in such a way as to uphold *federalism. Justice Rehnquist's test for what constituted areas not subject to federal regulation — including "functions essential to separate and independent existence" and "traditional aspects of state sovereignty" — proved unworkable, however. In 1985 the Court overruled *Usery* with *Garcia v. San Antonio Metropolitan Transit Authority*.

RUNYON V. MCCRARY

Citation: 427 U.S. 160 (1976)
Argued: April 26, 1976
Decided: June 25, 1976
Court Below: United States Fourth Circuit Court of Appeals
Basis for Review: *Writ of certiorari
Facts: Parents of African American children brought suit against private schools in Virginia that had denied their children admission. The circuit court upheld a decision for the parents in district court.
Issue: Does section 1981 of the Civil Rights Act of 1866 prohibit private schools from denying admission to African Americans?
Outcome: The Court upheld section 1981 and enjoined the schools from discriminating on the basis of race.
Vote: 7-2
Participating: Burger, Brennan, Stewart, White, Marshall, Blackmun, Powell, Rehnquist, Stevens
Opinions: Stewart for the Court; Powell and Stevens concurring; White, joined by Rehnquist, dissenting
Significance: *Jones v. Alfred H. Mayer Co.* (1968) had upheld another provision of the 1866 Civil Rights Act, prohibiting racial discrimination in housing. With *Runyon*, the Court broadened its earlier holding to imply that section 1981 applied to all contracts. This seeming breadth caused the Court to narrow, if not outright overrule *Runyon* in *Patterson v. McLean Credit Union* (1989), but the Civil Rights Act of 1991 in turn overruled *Patterson*.

NEBRASKA PRESS ASSOCIATION V. STUART

Citation: 427 U.S. 539 (1976)
Argued: April 19, 1976
Decided: June 30, 1976
Court Below: Nebraska Supreme Court
Basis for Review: *Writ of certiorari
Facts: Members of the press sued Stuart, a judge of the district court trying the case of a defendant accused of murdering six in a small Nebraska town. Judge Stuart imposed a gag order, upheld in state supreme court, that prohibited publication of certain evidence presented at the trial.
Issue: Do First Amendment concerns override the Sixth Amendment guarantee of a fair trial with regard to a court-ordered press gag order?
Outcome: Stressing the traditional bias against *prior restraint, the Court unanimously struck down the gag order.
Vote: 9-0
Participating: Burger, Brennan, Stewart, White, Marshall, Blackmun, Powell, Rehnquist, Stevens
Opinions: Burger for the Court; White and Powell concurring; Brennan, joined by Stewart and Marshall, concurring; and Stevens concurring
Significance: Most judges, the Court found, can find less extreme means of insuring a fair trial than the gag order; furthermore, press reports themselves often insure against miscarriages of justice.

GREGG V. GEORGIA

Citation: 428 U.S. 153 (1976)
Argued: March 31, 1976
Decided: July 2, 1976
Court Below: Georgia Supreme Court
Basis for Review: *Writ of certiorari
Facts: Gregg was convicted in Georgia of armed robbery and murder. He was given the death sentence under a new state procedure that took into account aggravating and mitigating circumstances and provided for mandatory review in the state supreme court.
Issue: Does the death penalty, imposed with safeguards as in the Georgia procedure, violate the Eighth Amendment's prohibition of *cruel and unusual punishment?
Outcome: A *plurality of the Court upheld the death penalty as imposed by Georgia.
Vote: 7-2
Participating: Burger, Brennan, Stewart, White, Marshall, Blackmun, Powell, Rehnquist, Stevens
Opinions: Stewart, joined by Powell and Stevens, announced the decision; White, Burger, Rehnquist, and Blackmun concurrung; Brennan and Marshall dissenting
Significance: Owing in part to changes in personnel, the Court in *Gregg* reversed the ban on

capital punishment announced in *Furman v. Georgia* (1972). Death penalty procedures such as those in Georgia circumvented the arbitrariness and prejudice that characterized earlier capital punishment proceedings. The Georgia procedure included such safeguards as a bifurcated trial that separately examined the evidence and imposed the penalty, specific fact finding by the sentencing body, and state supreme court review to insure such things as the proportionality of the sentence to the crime. Even these precautions, as the Court acknowledged, cannot prevent abuses — as the steady stream of death penalty cases still reviewed by the High Court attests.

WOODSON V. NORTH CAROLINA

Citation: 428 U.S. 280 (1976)
Argued: March 31, 1976
Decided: July 2, 1976
Court Below: North Carolina Supreme Court
Basis for Review: *Writ of certiorari
Facts: Woodson, an accomplice to a robbery and murder, was convicted of first-degree murder, which in North Carolina carried a mandatory death sentence. His sentence was upheld in the state supreme court.
Issue: Do mandatory death penalty statutes violate the Eighth Amendment's ban on *cruel and unusual punishment?
Outcome: The Court reversed the lower court's endorsement of the mandatory death sentence.
Vote: 5-4
Participating: Burger, Brennan, Stewart, White, Marshall, Blackmun, Powell, Rehnquist, Stevens
Opinions: Stewart for the Court; Brennan and Marshall concurring; White, joined by Burger and Rehnquist, dissenting; Blackmun and Rehnquist dissenting
Significance: In *Woodson*, decided the same day as *Gregg v. Georgia*, the Court ruled mandatory death sentences unconstitutional because they fail to take into account individual circumstances surrounding the crime.

STONE V. POWELL

Citation: 428 U.S. 465 (1976)
Argued: February 24, 1976

Decided: July 6, 1976
Court Below: United States Ninth Circuit Court of Appeals
Basis for Review: *Writ of certiorari
Facts: Lloyd Charles Powell, a state prisoner, alleged that illegally obtained evidence had been used to convict him and petitioned a federal court for a writ of *habeas corpus under Title 28, a federal law permitting prisoners to challenge the constitutionality of their convictions.
Issue: Does the federal statute permit federal review of issues already decided by state courts?
Outcome: The Court exempted Fourth Amendment search and seizure concerns already decided by state courts from Title 28's habeas corpus grant.
Vote: 6-3
Participating: Burger, Brennan, Stewart, White, Marshall, Blackmun, Powell, Rehnquist, Stevens
Opinions: Powell for the Court; Burger concurring; Brennan, joined by Marshall, dissenting; and White dissenting
Significance: Despite concerns that *Stone* would be used to decimate federal grants of habeas corpus to state prisoners, the Court has not added other grounds as exceptions to Title 28.

CRAIG V. BOREN

Citation: 429 U.S. 190 (1976)
Argued: October 5, 1976
Decided: December 20, 1976
Court Below: United States District Court for the Western District of Oklahoma
Basis for Review: Appeal
Facts: Two underage Oklahoma men, Mark Walker and Curtis Craig, together with female beer vendor Carolyn Whitener, challenged a state law making it legal for females to purchase 3.2 percent beer when they reached the age of 18, while men had to be 21 to enjoy the same privilege.
Issue: Do gender-based classifications such as the Oklahoma beer law violate the *Equal Protection Clause of the Fourteenth Amendment?
Outcome: Finding that the state's statistical evidence, presented to justify the gender discrimination inherent in the statute, did not substantially advance Oklahoma's purpose of preventing traffic

accidents, the Court struck down the liquor law.
Vote: 7-2
Participating: Burger, Brennan, Stewart, White, Marshall, Blackmun, Powell, Rehnquist, Stevens
Opinions: Brennan for the Court; Blackmun, Powell, Stevens, and Stewart concurring; Blackmun concurring in part; Burger and Rehnquist dissenting
Significance: In *Craig*, the Court announced that gender classifications in legislation would henceforth have to meet the highest standard, *strict scrutiny, in order to pass constitutional muster; that is, they must be substantially related to an important government objective.

ARLINGTON HEIGHTS V. METROPOLITAN HOUSING DEVELOPMENT CORP.

Citation: 429 U.S. 252 (1977)
Argued: October 13, 1976
Decided: January 11, 1977
Court Below: United States Seventh Circuit Court of Appeals
Basis for Review: *Writ of certiorari
Facts: The development corporation proposed to build racially integrated low- and moderate-income housing in the Chicago suburb of Arlington Heights, but the Arlington Heights board turned down the corporation's zoning petition.
Issue: Does the board's ruling violate the Fourteenth Amendment by discriminating on account of race?
Outcome: Finding that there had been no showing of discriminatory intent, the Court upheld the board's ruling.
Vote: 7-1
Participating: Burger, Brennan, Stewart, White, Marshall, Blackmun, Powell, Rehnquist (Stevens not participating)
Opinions: Powell for the Court; Marshall, joined by Brennan, concurring in part and dissenting in part; White dissenting
Significance: *Arlington Heights* affirmed the Court's holding in *Washington v. Davis* (1976) that *disparate impact is not enough to show constitutionally impermissible racial discrimination, seemingly increasing the obstructions to challenging prejudice in federal court.

UNITED JEWISH ORGANIZATIONS OF WILLIAMSBURGH, INC. V. CAREY

Citation: 430 U.S. 144 (1977)
Argued: October 6, 1976
Decided: March 1, 1977
Court Below: United States Second Circuit Court of Appeals
Basis for Review: *Writ of certiorari
Facts: Under the Voting Rights Act of 1965, New York was obliged to obtain the attorney general's approval for a legislative redistricting plan. The attorney general rejected the plan with respect to one district, which contained virtually an entire community of Hasidic Jews and relatively few African American voters. New York then proposed to divide the Hasidic community between two districts, but the community brought suit seeking to *enjoin the division.
Issue: Do racial criteria used in legislative *reapportionment violate Fourteenth and Fifteenth Amendment prohibitions on racial discrimination?
Outcome: The Court found New York's plan to be constitutional under the Voting Rights Act.
Vote: 7-1
Participating: Burger, Brennan, Stewart, White, Blackmun, Powell, Rehnquist, Stevens (Marshall not participating)
Opinions: White for the Court; Brennan concurring; Stewart, joined by Powell, concurring; Burger dissenting
Significance: The Court's holding emphasized that the use of racial quotas to establish African American majority voting districts — even at the cost of diluting the Hasidic vote — does not automatically violate the Fourteenth and Fifteenth Amendments. Furthermore, employment of such racial criteria may be necessary to rectify past discrimination.

BATES V. STATE BAR OF ARIZONA

Citation: 433 U.S. 350 (1977)
Argued: January 18, 1977
Decided: June 27, 1977
Court Below: Arizona Supreme Court
Basis for Review: Appeal

Facts: Two attorneys, John Bates and Van O'Steen, challenging a state prohibition on advertising by lawyers, placed a newspaper advertisement stressing the reasonableness of their fees. The state bar association recommended that their licenses be suspended, but the state supreme court censured them instead.

Issue: Do state rules barring attorney advertising constitute restraints of trade in violation of the Sherman Antitrust Act? Alternatively, do they violate First Amendment *free speech rights?

Outcome: Rejecting the antitrust argument, the Court nevertheless found for the defendants on First Amendment grounds.

Vote: 5-4

Participating: Burger, Brennan, Stewart, White, Marshall, Blackmun, Powell, Rehnquist, Stevens

Opinions: Blackmun for the Court; Burger dissenting; Powell, joined by Stewart, dissenting; and Rehnquist dissenting

Significance: *Bates* added to the development of the *commercial speech doctrine by emphasizing the public's right to know about legal fees. In the aftermath of the decision, competition among attorneys increased and fees decreased, although the Court did place some limits on *Bates* with *Ohralik v. Ohio State Bar Association* (1978), which barred in-person attorney solicitation.

NIXON V. ADMINISTRATOR OF GENERAL SERVICES

Citation: 433 U.S. 425 (1977)
Argued: April 20, 1977
Decided: June 28, 1977
Court Below: United States District Court for the District of Columbia
Basis for Review: Appeal
Facts: By agreement with the General Services Administration (GSA), reached subsequent to his resignation from the presidency, Richard Nixon vested partial control over his papers and tape recordings (some of which were relevant to the Watergate break-in cover-up) in the GSA for a period of three years, after which he would regain full control. Congress passed the Presidential Recordings and Materials Act in 1976 to prevent this transfer of authority over

historically significant documents, and Nixon challenged the act the day after it was signed into law. Both the district court and the court of appeals upheld the act over Nixon's claims that it violated the *separation of powers, as well as his right to privacy, and — because former presidents had retained control over their papers — that it was a *bill of attainder.

Issue: Does the act violate the doctrine of separation of powers or Nixon's right to privacy, or operate as an unconstitutional bill of attainder?

Outcome: Justice Brennan, speaking for the Court, rejected all of Nixon's arguments and upheld the act.

Vote: 7-2

Participating: Burger, Brennan, Stewart, White, Marshall, Blackmun, Powell, Rehnquist, Stevens

Opinions: Brennan for the Court; White, Stevens, Blackmun, and Powell concurring; Burger and Rehnquist dissenting

Significance: The GSA argued that because President Jimmy Carter had signed the bill into law, Nixon had no right to assert *executive privilege. Brennan rejected this argument, but his opinion once again demonstrated to Nixon that presidential immunity is qualified.

COKER V. GEORGIA

Citation: 433 U.S. 584 (1977)
Argued: March 28, 1977
Decided: June 29, 1977
Court Below: Georgia Supreme Court
Basis for Review: *Writ of certiorari
Facts: Jailed for convictions on charges of murder, rape, kidnapping, and aggravated assault, Coker escaped and committed armed robbery and rape. Following the guidelines of *Gregg v. Georgia* (1976), the jury in a bifurcated trial found that Coker's record constituted aggravating circumstances and sentenced him to death for rape. His sentence was upheld by the state supreme court.

Issue: Does imposing the death penalty for a rape conviction violate the Eighth Amendment's ban on cruel and unusual punishment?

Outcome: Finding the penalty disproportionate to the crime, the Supreme Court reversed Coker's death sentence and *remanded his case for further hearings.

Vote: 7-2

Participating: Burger, Brennan, Stewart, White, Marshall, Blackmun, Powell, Rehnquist, Stevens

Opinions: White for a *plurality of the Court; Brennan, Powell, and Marshall concurring; Burger, joined by Rehnquist, dissenting

Significance: Georgia was the only state to impose *capital punishment for the rape of an adult and, Justice White repeatedly emphasized, death is a suitable punishment only for murder.

BALLEW V. GEORGIA

Citation: 435 U.S. 223 (1978)

Argued: November 1, 1977

Decided: March 21, 1978

Court Below: Georgia Supreme Court

Basis for Review: *Writ of certiorari

Facts: In accordance with state law, Ballew was tried and convicted of a *misdemeanor offense by a jury of five. His appeal, based on Sixth and Fourteenth Amendment challenges, was rejected in the state courts.

Issue: What is the minimum size required for state juries sitting in criminal trials?

Outcome: Finding that a minimum of six jurors is required to meet Sixth Amendment fair trial guarantees, the Court reversed Ballew's sentence and *remanded his case for further proceedings.

Vote: 9-0

Participating: Burger, Brennan, Stewart, White, Marshall, Blackmun, Powell, Rehnquist, Stevens

Opinions: Blackmun for the Court; Stevens and White concurring; Powell, joined by Burger and Rehnquist, concurring; Brennan, joined by Stewart and Marshall, concurring in part in a separate opinion

Significance: In *Williams v. Florida* (1970), the Court held that a six-person state criminal jury is permissible, but did not stipulate whether or not a smaller jury was constitutionally permissible. More confusion resulted from decisions in *Johnson v. Louisiana* (1972) and *Apodaca v. Oregon* (1972), holding nonunanimous jury verdicts acceptable in state criminal trials. After *Ballew* the rule was clear: six-person juries are the acceptable minimum in federal civil trials and in both civil and criminal trials in state courts.

ZURCHER V. THE STANFORD DAILY

Citation: 436 U.S. 547 (1978)

Argued: January 17, 1978

Decided: May 31, 1978

Court Below: United States Ninth Circuit Court of Appeals

Basis for Review: *Writ of certiorari

Facts: Following a violent confrontation between police and Stanford University demonstrators, *The Stanford Daily* published a photograph of the confrontation. Armed with a search *warrant, police subsequently searched the newspaper's offices, and although they found no other photographs of the incident, they read some of the paper's confidential files. The paper's suit against the police charged them with violations of First Amendment press freedoms and Fourth Amendment search and seizure provisions. The district court found that a *subpoena, rather than a search warrant, was the appropriate authorization for a search of press offices, and this ruling was upheld in federal *appellate court.

Issue: Do the First and Fourth Amendments mandate that a subpoena, rather than a warrant, be obtained prior to a police search of press offices?

Outcome: Finding that nothing in the Fourth Amendment accorded the press special treatment, the Supreme Court reversed the ruling below.

Vote: 5-3

Participating: Burger, Stewart, White, Marshall, Blackmun, Powell, Rehnquist, Stevens (Brennan not participating)

Opinions: White for the Court; Powell concurring; Stewart, joined by Marshall, dissenting; and Stevens dissenting

Significance: *Zurcher* caused considerable consternation among the media, resulting in passage of the federal Privacy Protection Act of 1980, which limited the use of warrants in police searches of news organizations.

REGENTS OF THE UNIVERSITY OF CALIFORNIA V. BAKKE

Citation: 438 U.S. 265 (1978)

Argued: October 12, 1977

Decided: June 28, 1978

Court Below: California Supreme Court
Basis for Review: *Writ of certiorari
Facts: The University of California Medical School at Davis admitted 100 students every year. Eighty-four of these places were filled in the usual competitive fashion, but the remainder were set aside for minority applicants only. After having been twice rejected by the medical school despite his high test scores and excellent academic record, Allen Bakke, a white applicant, sued, charging that the special admissions program violated his right to *equal protection under the Fourteenth Amendment as well as Title VI of the Civil Rights Act of 1964, which prohibits racial preferences in programs receiving federal funds. The state courts found that the admissions program was constitutionally impermissible.
Issue: Are affirmative action programs like the medical school's permissible under the Fourteenth Amendment and Title VI?
Outcome: Based on the medical school's violation of Title VI, it was ordered that Bakke be admitted.
Vote: 5-4
Participating: Burger, Brennan, Stewart, White, Marshall, Blackmun, Powell, Rehnquist, Stevens
Opinions: Powell for the *plurality; Brennan, Marshall, and Blackmun concurring in the judgment and dissenting in part; White, Marshall, and Blackmun filed separate opinions; Stevens, joined by Burger, Stewart, and Rehnquist, concurring in the judgment in part and dissenting in part
Significance: While the Court held that a state university may take race into consideration as part of its admissions process, it did so without addressing the constitutionality of affirmative action. The Court was initially divided equally, with half its members arguing that Bakke must be admitted because the medical school's exclusionary admissions process clearly violated Title VI. The other half argued that there was no essential difference between the statute and the Equal Protection Clause and that, consequently, such affirmative action as the school was undertaking was acceptable. Justice Powell cast the deciding vote, agreeing that Bakke should be admitted, but also upholding race-conscious admissions policies

at state educational facilities, so long as they are not "fixed quotas." Far from being a definitive statement on affirmative action, *Bakke* only provided guidelines for state educational facilities. It must be noted, however, that owing to recent policy changes by the Board of Regents of the University of California, as well as the Rehnquist Court's contraction of affirmative action in such cases as *Richmond v. J.A. Croson Co.* (1989) and *Adarand Constructors, Inc. v. Pena* (1995), the future status of *Bakke* is far from certain.

BUTZ V. ECONOMOU

Citation: 438 U.S. 478 (1978)
Argued: November 7, 1977
Decided: June 29, 1978
Court Below: United States Second Circuit Court of Appeals
Basis for Review: *Writ of certiorari
Facts: Secretary of Agriculture Earl Butz filed a claim against Economou, a commodities dealer. After successfully countering this claim, Economou in turn sued Butz, claiming that the Department of Agriculture had sought to punish him for publicly criticizing the department's policies. The department asserted absolute *immunity from suit, but although the trial court dismissed Economou's suit, on appeal it was reinstated on grounds that federal officials are only entitled to qualified immunity.
Issue: Are federal officials immune from suits based on their performance of their official duties?
Outcome: The Court denied that Butz had absolute immunity but *remanded the case for further proceedings to determine if his and certain other officials' actions were subject to qualified immunity.
Vote: 5-4
Participating: Burger, Brennan, Stewart, White, Marshall, Blackmun, Powell, Rehnquist, Stevens
Opinions: White for the Court; Rehnquist, joined by Burger, Stewart, and Stevens, concurring in part and dissenting in part
Significance: Justice White's opinion for the Court stated that executive officials like Butz do not enjoy the same measure of immunity as do members of the judiciary or members of the exec-

utive branch who function in judicial roles. Customarily, executive officials are only covered by "qualified good-faith immunity," which does not include official acts committed in bad faith. This distinction was later clarified in *Harlow v. Fitzgerald* (1982), in which the Court stated that executive immunity was only at risk if no reasonable decision maker would consider a given action on the part of a member of the executive branch to be lawful.

ORR V. ORR

Citation: 440 U.S. 268 (1979)
Argued: November 27, 1978
Decided: March 5, 1979
Court Below: Alabama Supreme Court
Basis for Review: Appeal
Facts: Mr. Orr, who was divorced, challenged an Alabama law that permitted alimony orders against men only.
Issue: Does the gender classification of the alimony statute violate the *Equal Protection Clause of the Fourteenth Amendment?
Outcome: The Court struck down the Alabama alimony law.
Vote: 6-3
Participating: Burger, Brennan, Stewart, White, Marshall, Blackmun, Powell, Rehnquist, Stevens
Opinions: Brennan for the Court; Blackmun and Stevens concurring; Powell dissenting; and Rehnquist, joined by Burger, dissenting
Significance: A majority of the Court agreed that the *strict scrutiny used in *Craig v. Boren* (1976) to appraise laws based on gender classification invalidated the statute at issue here because it was not "substantially related" to important government goals. Since the primary purpose of alimony is to provide support for needy former spouses, hearings leading to alimony orders could determine which spouse required continuing support. Therefore, a gender-neutral law was sufficient.

HUTCHINSON V. PROXMIRE

Citation: 443 U.S. 111 (1979)
Argued: April 17, 1979
Decided: June 26, 1979
Court Below: United States Seventh Circuit Court of Appeals
Basis for Review: *Writ of certiorari
Facts: Senator William Proxmire gave his annual "Golden Fleece" award for wasteful government expenditures to agencies supporting Dr. Ronald Hutchinson's research into aggression. Proxmire announced his award on the floor of the Senate, but he also discussed it in interviews and issued a press release about it. Hutchinson sued, charging defamation. The district court granted *summary judgment to Proxmire, a judgment affirmed on appeal.
Issue: Does the *Speech and Debate Clause of Article I of the Constitution provide *immunity to members of Congress for acts not a part of essential Congressional concerns?
Outcome: Construing the Speech and Debate Clause narrowly, the Court found for Hutchinson.
Vote: 8-1
Participating: Burger, Brennan, Stewart, White, Marshall, Blackmun, Powell, Rehnquist, Stevens
Opinions: Burger for the Court; Stewart concurring in part and dissenting in part; Brennan dissenting
Significance: *Hutchinson* also affirmed the definition of a public figure that the Court had outlined in *New York Times v. Sullivan* (1964): if a private individual is thrust into the light of public scrutiny and does not seek it himself, he is not subject to the higher "actual malice" standard of proof applied to public figures seeking damages for defamation.

UNITED STEELWORKERS OF AMERICA V. WEBER

Citation: 443 U.S. 193 (1979)
Argued: March 28, 1979
Decided: June 27, 1979
Court Below: United States Fifth Circuit Court of Appeals
Basis for Review: *Writ of certiorari
Facts: A collective bargaining agreement between the union and Kaiser Aluminum reserved 50 percent of the company's openings in a special training program for whites and based admission on seniority. The program grew out of a settlement

of employment discrimination claims and was meant to rectify historical bias against minorities. Weber, a white employee at Kaiser's Gramercy, Louisiana, plant, had more seniority than some African Americans admitted to the program but less than any of the whites admitted. He sued, charging that the program violated Title VII of the Civil Rights Act of 1964, which outlawed racial discrimination in employment.

Issue: Can employers adopt race-conscious affirmative action programs without violating Title VII?

Outcome: Noting that Title VII does not outlaw all preferential treatment based on race, the Court ruled against Weber's claim.

Vote: 5-2

Participating: Burger, Brennan, Stewart, White, Marshall, Blackmun, Rehnquist (Powell and Stevens not participating)

Opinions: Brennan for the Court; Blackmun concurring; Rehnquist, joined by Burger, dissenting

Significance: *Weber* marked the first time the Court addressed the issue of affirmative action in employment. Although the Court did not create a bright line between acceptable and unacceptable practices, it noted that Title VII does allow employers sole discretion in voluntarily adopting plans aimed at righting long-standing racial imbalances.

PAYTON V. NEW YORK

Citation: 445 U.S. 573 (1980)

Argued: March 26, 1979; reargued October 9, 1979

Decided: April 15, 1980

Court Below: New York Court of Appeals

Basis for Review: Appeal

Facts: Theodore Payton was convicted of a *felony after having been arrested by police who, in accordance with New York law, entered his residence with *probable cause, but without his permission and without a *warrant.

Issue: Does the Fourth Amendment require that a warrant be obtained prior to police entry onto private premises for purposes of making an arrest?

Outcome: Noting that a warrant is a prerequisite for police searches of private premises, the Court held that warrants are also necessary for entry to facilitate an arrest.

Vote: 6-3

Participating: Burger, Brennan, Stewart, White, Marshall, Blackmun, Powell, Rehnquist, Stevens

Opinions: Stevens for the Court; Blackmun concurring; White, joined by Burger and Rehnquist, dissenting; and Rehnquist dissenting

Significance: *Payton* required only an arrest warrant, but in *Steagald v. United States* (1981) the Court ruled that if the entry onto private property was made in order to arrest a guest, a search warrant was necessary to protect the property owner.

MOBILE V. BOLDEN

Citation: 446 U.S. 55 (1980)

Argued: March 19, 1979; reargued October 29, 1979

Decided: April 22, 1980

Court Below: United States Fifth Circuit Court of Appeals

Basis for Review: Appeal

Facts: African American residents of Mobile, Alabama, brought suit alleging that the historically all-white city commission violated the Fourteenth and Fifteenth Amendments, as well as the Voting Rights Act of 1965.

Issue: Is *state action that is neutral on its face impermissible?

Outcome: Stating that a demonstration of discriminatory intent was required in order to overturn the outcome of elections to which African Americans had equal access, the Court found no constitutional infringement.

Vote: 6-3

Participating: Burger, Brennan, Stewart, White, Marshall, Blackmun, Powell, Rehnquist, Stevens

Opinions: Stewart for the Court; Blackmun and Stevens concurring; White, Brennan, and Marshall dissenting

Significance: As a result of the public furor that greeted *Bolden* and its emphasis on the significance of discriminatory intent, in 1982 Congress incorporated a modified effects test into the Voting Rights Act.

HARRIS V. MCRAE

Citation: 448 U.S. 297 (1980)
Argued: April 21, 1980
Decided: June 30, 1980
Court Below: United States District Court for the Eastern District of New York
Basis for Review: Appeal
Facts: Cora McRae brought a *class action against Secretary of Health and Human Services Patricia Harris to *enjoin enforcement of the Hyde Amendment, limiting Medicaid reimbursement for abortions.
Issues: Does the Hyde Amendment violate the Fifth Amendment's *due process guarantee? Are states obliged to fund medically necessary abortions despite the Hyde Amendment?
Outcome: The Court upheld the amendment, also holding that states are not obliged to make up abortion funds withheld from the federal program.
Vote: 5-4
Participating: Burger, Brennan, Stewart, White, Marshall, Blackmun, Powell, Rehnquist, Stevens
Opinions: Stewart for the Court; White concurring; Brennan, joined by Marshall and Blackmun, dissenting; and Marshall, Blackmun, and Stevens dissenting
Significance: A majority of the Burger Court as it was now constituted interpreted *Roe v. Wade* (1973) to mean that although a woman's right to abortion was protected, government did not have to fund her choice to undergo the procedure.

FULLILOVE V. KLUTZNICK

Citation: 448 U.S. 448 (1980)
Argued: November 27, 1979
Decided: July 2, 1980
Court Below: United States Second Circuit Court of Appeals
Basis for Review: *Writ of certiorari
Facts: Nonminority contractors challenged the 10 percent "set-aside" provision of the Public Works Employment Act of 1977, which explicitly reserved federally funded projects for businesses owned by minorities. The district court's dismissal

of the suit was affirmed on appeal.
Issue: Does the set-aside provision violate the Fifth Amendment's *due process guarantee?
Outcome: Relying on Congress's constitutional authority to control government expenditures, the Court upheld the set-asides.
Vote: 6-3
Participating: Burger, Brennan, Stewart, White, Marshall, Blackmun, Powell, Rehnquist, Stevens
Opinions: Burger for the *plurality; Powell concurring; Marshall, joined by Brennan, concurring; Blackmun concurring; Stewart, joined by Rehnquist, dissenting; and Stevens dissenting
Significance: Minority set-aside programs flourished after *Fullilove*, but although federal programs were upheld, in *Richmond v. J.A. Croson Co.* (1989) the Court struck down similar racial preferences at the state and local levels.

RICHMOND NEWSPAPERS, INC. V. VIRGINIA

Citation: 448 U.S. 555 (1980)
Argued: February 19, 1980
Decided: July 2, 1980
Court Below: Virginia Supreme Court
Basis for Review: *Writ of certiorari
Facts: This case grew out of a murder trial that had been tried three times before in Virginia state court, once resulting in a reversal on appeal and twice ending in *mistrials. Fearing that pretrial publicity endangered his case, the defendant asked that the press be excluded from this fourth trial, and the court, relying on Virginia law, issued an order barring the media. Richmond Newspapers, Inc. suing for access, failed to overturn the exclusion order.
Issue: Do the First and Fourteenth Amendments guarantee the press and public a right of access to criminal trials?
Outcome: In six different opinions, a majority of the Court upheld the right of press and public to attend criminal trials.
Vote: 7-1
Participating: Burger, Brennan, Stewart, White, Marshall, Blackmun, Rehnquist, Stevens (Powell not participating)
Opinions: Burger for the *plurality; White and Stevens concurring; Brennan joined by Marshall,

concurring; and Stewart and Blackmun concurring; Rehnquist dissenting

Significance: *Richmond Newspapers, Inc.* ended a decade of confusion about whether or not the press has a First Amendment right of access to criminal trials. It left open, however, the question of access to pretrial hearings, government proceedings, and civil trials. *Press-Enterprise Co. v. Superior Court* (1986) answered the question affirmatively for pretrial hearings, but the issue of media access to the other two venues remains open.

ROSTKER V. GOLDBERG

Citation: 453 U.S. 57 (1981)
Argued: March 24, 1981
Decided: June 25, 1981
Court Below: United States District Court for the Eastern District of Pennsylvania
Basis for Review: Appeal
Facts: In 1971 Goldberg and several other men facing the prospect of being drafted for military service in Vietnam challenged the government's policy of conscripting men only. After the war ended, the case lay dormant until Congress revived the draft in 1980. Three days before the new draft provisions were to go into effect, a specially convened three-judge district court panel *enjoined the government from reinstituting conscription. Rostker, chairman of the Selective Service Commission, then requested that the Supreme Court *stay the injunction pending its appeal. The stay was granted, and registration commenced while the parties pursued their case.
Issue: Does a males-only draft violate the *Due Process Clause of the Fifth Amendment?
Outcome: Finding that the exclusion of women from the draft fulfilled an "important government interest" — i.e., military flexibility, which would be hindered by conscription of noncombatant females — the Court upheld the Military Selective Service Act's exclusion of women.
Vote: 6-3
Participating: Burger, Brennan, Stewart, White, Marshall, Blackmun, Powell, Rehnquist, Stevens
Opinions: Rehnquist for the Court; White, joined by Brennan, dissenting; and Marshall, joined by Brennan, dissenting

Significance: The dissenters, like the Court majority, did not question the exclusion of women from combat. Instead, they argued that registration does not necessitate service in combat and therefore should apply equally to men and women.

DAMES & MOORE V. REGAN

Citation: 453 U.S. 654 (1981)
Argued: June 24, 1981
Decided: July 2, 1981
Court Below: United States Ninth Circuit Court of Appeals
Basis for Review: *Writ of certiorari
Facts: In January 1981 President Jimmy Carter, in order to obtain release of hostages being held in the American embassy in Teheran, issued executive orders suspending all legal actions against Iran by U.S. nationals and attachments of Iranian property by U.S. courts. Such claims were to be transferred to an independent arbitration tribunal. Dames & Moore, which had obtained a judgment against Iran in federal court, then sued Ronald Reagan's secretary of the Treasury, Donald T. Regan, to prevent execution of the executive orders.
Issue: Does the president have the authority to make foreign policy decisions in the absence of congressional authorization?
Outcome: Relying on a theory of implied power, rather than explicit statutory authority, the Court upheld the executive orders.
Vote: 9-0
Participating: Burger, Brennan, Stewart, White, Marshall, Blackmun, Powell, Rehnquist, Stevens
Opinions: Rehnquist for the Court; Stevens concurring in part; Powell concurring and dissenting in part
Significance: *Dames & Moore* broadened the president's authority in the field of foreign relations to include methods that almost certainly would be unacceptable in domestic affairs.

UNITED STATES V. ROSS

Citation: 456 U.S. 798 (1982)
Argued: March 1, 1982
Decided: June 1, 1982
Court Below: United States Court of Appeals for the District of Columbia Circuit

Basis for Review: *Writ of certiorari

Facts: Acting on a tip that someone was selling drugs out of his car, District of Columbia police, without a *warrant, twice searched the trunk of the suspect's car. Heroin and cash discovered in the trunk were used to convict Ross.

Issue: Does the exception to the Fourth Amendment permitting warrantless searches of automobiles also extend to containers in the automobiles?

Outcome: The Court held that warrantless searches of such containers were permissible so long as police have *probable cause to conduct the searches.

Vote: 6-3

Participating: Burger, Brennan, White, Marshall, Blackmun, Powell, Rehnquist, Stevens, O'Connor

Opinions: Stevens for the Court; Blackmun concurring; White dissenting; and Marshall, joined by Brennan, dissenting

Significance: Under *Ross*, probable cause, the same minimal standard used to obtain a search warrant, is determined not by a court, but by the police themselves.

PLYLER V. DOE

Citation: 457 U.S. 202 (1982)

Argued: December 1, 1981

Decided: June 15, 1982

Court Below: United States Fifth Circuit Court of Appeals

Basis for Review: Appeal

Facts: Texas's denial of free public education to children of undocumented aliens living in the state was challenged in a *class action filed on behalf of certain school-aged children of Mexican descent living in Smith County, Texas.

Issue: Does the state's refusal to provide an education to illegal alien children violate the *Equal Protection Clause of the Fourteenth Amendment?

Outcome: Holding that the guarantees of the Fourteenth Amendment extend to every person residing within the state's boundaries, regardless of their status, the Court ruled against Texas.

Vote: 5-4

Participating: Burger, Brennan, White, Marshall,

Blackmun, Powell, Rehnquist, Stevens, O'Connor

Opinions: Brennan for the Court; Marshall, Blackmun, and Powell concurring; Burger, joined by White, Rehnquist, and O'Connor, dissenting

Significance: *Plyler* continues to be a controversial decision, and given that the Court found that education is not a fundamental right, challenges to the decision seem probable.

MISSISSIPPI UNIVERSITY FOR WOMEN V. HOGAN

Citation: 458 U.S. 718 (1982)

Argued: March 22, 1982

Decided: July 1, 1982

Court Below: United States Fifth Circuit Court of Appeals

Basis for Review: *Writ of certiorari

Facts: Hogan, a male Mississippian, challenged the state-supported university's policy of admitting only women.

Issue: Does an educational institution receiving state funding violate *equal protection under the Fourteenth Amendment if it fails to admit both male and female applicants?

Outcome: Applying *intermediate scrutiny, Justice O'Connor, in her first opinion for the Court, reasoned that the university's policy was not justified as compensation for past discrimination against women and ruled its admissions policy unconstitutional.

Vote: 5-4

Participating: Burger, Brennan, White, Marshall, Blackmun, Powell, Rehnquist, Stevens, O'Connor

Opinions: O'Connor for the Court; Burger and Blackmun dissenting; and Powell, joined by Rehnquist, dissenting

Significance: *Hogan* effectively marked the end of state-supported colleges for women.

AKRON V. AKRON CENTER FOR REPRODUCTIVE HEALTH, INC.

Citation: 462 U.S. 416 (1983)

Argued: November 30, 1982

Decided: June 15, 1983

Court Below: United States Sixth Circuit Court of Appeals

Basis for Review: *Writ of certiorari

Facts: Akron, Ohio, placed a number of restrictions on abortions performed in the city: second-trimester abortions could not be performed in clinics, only in hospitals; physicians were required to provide detailed information about abortions prior to obtaining consent forms; and a 24-hour waiting period was imposed between the time the consent was signed and the abortion performed.

Issue: Do such restrictions violate the right to privacy as defined in *Roe v. Wade* (1973)?

Outcome: The Court struck down the restrictions as an attempt to hinder access to abortion.

Vote: 6-3

Participating: Burger, Brennan, White, Marshall, Blackmun, Powell, Rehnquist, Stevens, O'Connor

Opinions: Powell for the Court; O'Connor, joined by White and Rehnquist, dissenting

Significance: In her first major abortion opinion, Justice O'Connor, a possible swing vote on the issue, seemed to signal disaffection with *Roe v. Wade*, calling its trimester distinctions unworkable. She has continued to voice similar complaints, but has thus far declined to argue for the outright abolition of abortion.

IMMIGRATION AND NATURALIZATION SERVICE V. CHADHA

Citation: 462 U.S. 919 (1983)

Argued: February 22, 1982; reargued December 7, 1982

Decided: June 23, 1983

Court Below: United States Ninth Circuit Court of Appeals

Basis for Review: *Writ of certiorari

Facts: British passport holder Jagdish Rai Chadha, a Kenyan born of Indian parents, came to the United States on a student visa. When his visa expired, neither Kenya nor Britain would permit his return, so he applied for permanent residence status in the U.S. The Immigration and Naturalization Service (INS) granted him residence status, but two years later the House of Representatives used the so-called "legislative veto" to block the INS ruling. Facing deportation, Chadha challenged the congressional action.

Issue: Does the legislative veto, intended to give Congress a measure of control over administrative agencies' rule-making power, violate the constitutional *separation of powers?

Outcome: The Court struck down the legislative veto.

Vote: 7-2

Participating: Burger, Brennan, White, Marshall, Blackmun, Powell, Rehnquist, Stevens, O'Connor

Opinions: Burger for the Court; Powell concurring; Rehnquist, joined by White, dissenting

Significance: Because the legislative veto had been incorporated into more than two hundred laws enacted since 1932, the Court overturned more legislation with *Chadha* than it had over the course of its entire history.

GROVE CITY COLLEGE V. BELL

Citation: 465 U.S. 555 (1984)

Argued: November 29, 1983

Decided: February 28, 1984

Court Below: United States Third Circuit Court of Appeals

Basis for Review: *Writ of certiorari

Facts: Grove City College was accused of discriminating against women. Some of the students received federal educational grants under Title IX of the Education Amendments of 1972. Although the college received no other federal funds, the Carter administration's Department of Education, under Terrel H. Bell, attempted to force it to comply fully with Title IX by terminating student financial assistance. The college and four of its students brought suit.

Issue: Does Title IX, which bars gender discrimination in any "program or activity" receiving federal aid, apply to an entire educational institution, or only to those areas actually receiving aid?

Outcome: The Court upheld only a limited cutoff of funding to the college under the theory that only those programs receiving aid need comply with Title IX.

Vote: 7-2

Participating: Burger, Brennan, White, Marshall, Blackmun, Powell, Rehnquist, Stevens, O'Connor

Opinions: White for the Court; Powell, joined by Burger and O'Connor, concurring; Stevens concurring; Brennan, joined by Marshall, concurring in part and dissenting in part

Significance: Negative public reaction to *Grove City* resulted in passage in 1987, over President Ronald Reagan's veto, of the Civil Rights Restoration Act, which overturned the decision and made Title IX applicable to any educational institution which receives any federal funds.

LYNCH V. DONNELLY

Citation: 465 U.S. 668 (1984)
Argued: October 4, 1983
Decided: March 5, 1984
Court Below: United States First Circuit Court of Appeals
Basis for Review: *Writ of certiorari
Facts: Pawtucket, Rhode Island, annually erected in a shopping mall a Christmas display that included secular items as well as a creche.
Issue: Does the display violate the separation of church and state requirement of the First Amendment's *Establishment Clause?
Outcome: By one vote, the Court rejected the constitutional attack on the Christmas display.
Vote: 5-4
Participating: Burger, Brennan, White, Marshall, Blackmun, Powell, Rehnquist, Stevens, O'Connor
Opinions: Burger for the Court; O'Connor concurring; Brennan, joined by Marshall, Blackmun, and Stevens, dissenting; and Blackmun, joined by Stevens, dissenting
Significance: Justice O'Connor provided the fifth vote to uphold the constitutionality of the Christmas display, as well as a new standard for determining when the state has violated the Establishment Clause. Her assertion that the distinction turned on whether or not the state intended to endorse religion seems to have been adopted by the majority in *Allegheny County v. ACLU Greater Pittsburgh Chapter* (1989), in which the display of a creche in a public building was ruled impermissible.

HAWAII HOUSING AUTHORITY V. MIDKIFF

Citation: 467 U.S. 229 (1984)
Argued: March 26, 1984
Decided: May 30, 1984

Court Below: United States Ninth Circuit Court of Appeals
Basis for Review: Appeal
Facts: Midkiff, a Hawaiian landowner, challenged a state statute that attempted to disperse the long-standing concentration of property control by giving lessees the power to invoke *eminent domain and to purchase the land they leased.
Issue: Is the Hawaii statute a violation of the Fifth Amendment requirement that any government *taking of property must be for "public use"?
Outcome: Stating that it is the purpose of the taking, rather than the subsequent use of the property that matters, the Court upheld the statute.
Vote: 8-0
Participating: Burger, Brennan, White, Blackmun, Powell, Rehnquist, Stevens, O'Connor (Marshall not participating)
Opinion: O'Connor for the Court
Significance: The Court found that the state's power to condemn property is as extensive as its *police powers, and that there need only be a rational relationship between the taking and some purpose that would benefit the public.

ROBERTS V. UNITED STATES JAYCEES

Citation: 468 U.S. 609 (1984)
Argued: April 18, 1984
Decided: July 3, 1984
Court Below: United States Eighth Circuit Court of Appeals
Basis for Review: Appeal
Facts: The United States Jaycees brought suit against the acting commissioner of the Minnesota Department of Human Rights, challenging a state law forbidding sex discrimination in public accommodations.
Issue: Does the Minnesota Human Rights Act, in requiring the state Junior Chamber of Commerce to admit female members, violate the First and Fourteenth Amendments' guarantees of freedom of association?
Outcome: Citing the encompassing, nonexclusive nature of the group, the Court ruled against the Jaycees.
Vote: 7-0
Participating: Brennan, White, Marshall, Powell,

Rehnquist, Stevens, O'Connor (Burger and Blackmun not participating)

Opinions: Brennan for the Court; Rehnquist concurring (without written opinion), and O'Connor concurring

Significance: Justice Brennan's opinion for the Court stated that freedom of association is not absolute, but can be overridden by a *compelling state interest — here Minnesota's interest in outlawing gender discrimination.

UNITED STATES V. LEON

Citation: 468 U.S. 897 (1984)

Argued: January 17, 1984

Decided: July 5, 1984

Court Below: United States Ninth Circuit Court of Appeals

Basis for Review: *Writ of certiorari

Facts: Drugs and other evidence obtained with an apparently valid search *warrant were used to *indict Leon. Although the police had acted in good faith, the warrant was found to have been invalid.

Issue: Is evidence obtained pursuant to a later invalidated search warrant still subject to the Fourth Amendment's *exclusionary rule?

Outcome: The Court upheld the use of such evidence at trial.

Vote: 6-3

Participating: Burger, Brennan, White, Marshall, Blackmun, Powell, Rehnquist, Stevens, O'Connor

Opinions: White for the Court; Blackmun concurring; Brennan, joined by Marshall, dissenting; and Stevens dissenting

Significance: Warren Burger had been appointed chief justice largely because of his outspoken opposition to the exclusionary rule, which he and other critics felt impeded police and coddled criminals. *Leon* is significant because it was the first exception to the rule the Court had ever endorsed, but it was not the broad "good faith exception" applicable to the majority of searches — usually conducted without a warrant — critics had hoped for.

GARCIA V. SAN ANTONIO METROPOLITAN TRANSIT AUTHORITY

Citation: 469 U.S. 528 (1985)

Argued: March 19, 1984; reargued October 1, 1984

Decided: February 19, 1985

Court Below: United States District Court for the Western District of Texas

Basis for Review: Appeal

Facts: The transit authority brought suit seeking a *declaratory judgment exempting it from federal minimum wage provisions.

Issue: Does federal regulation of a municipal transportation system, through application of the Fair Labor Standards Act, violate state *sovereignty and the Tenth Amendment?

Outcome: Overruling *National League of Cities v. Usery* (1976), which had restricted Congress's power to regulate wages and hours of state and city employees, the Court upheld the Fair Labor Standards Act.

Vote: 5-4

Participating: Burger, Brennan, White, Marshall, Blackmun, Powell, Rehnquist, Stevens, O'Connor

Opinions: Blackmun for the Court; Powell, joined by Burger, Rehnquist, and O'Connor, dissenting; Rehnquist dissenting; and O'Connor, joined by Powell and Rehnquist, dissenting

Significance: Reasoning that the framers of the Constitution relied on Congress to protect states' interest in the federal system, Justice Blackmun's opinion for the Court insulated Congress's exercise of the *commerce power from attacks based on *federalism.

WALLACE V. JAFFREE

Citation: 472 U.S. 38 (1985)

Argued: December 4, 1984

Decided: June 4, 1985

Court Below: United States Eleventh Circuit Court of Appeals

Basis for Review: Appeal

Facts: Ishmael Jaffree, a resident of Mobile, Alabama, and a parent of three minor children, challenged a state law which, as enacted in 1978, authorized a minute of silent "meditation" in the public schools. In 1981 this act was amended to provide a minute of silence for "meditation or silent prayer." It was changed again in 1982 to permit teachers to lead those students who wished to participate in a prayer to "Almighty God." Only the 1981 version was at issue in the case.

Issue: Can public schools provide students with a minute of silence each day for the purpose of "meditation or prayer"?

Outcome: Citing its own earlier *precedents banning school prayer on First Amendment grounds, the Court struck down the Alabama statute.

Vote: 6-3

Participating: Burger, Brennan, White, Marshall, Blackmun, Powell, Rehnquist, Stevens, O'Connor

Opinions: Stevens for the Court; Powell concurring; O'Connor concurring in the judgment; Burger, White, and Rehnquist dissenting

Significance: Continuing public resistance to the doctrine of separation of church and state and the Reagan administration's support for school prayer led various states to pass legislation that would reintroduce prayer into the public schools. While remaining firm in its opposition to such statutes as Alabama's — where the legislative history made it clear that the state's intent was to endorse religion — the Court left an opening for an undefined, uncommitted moment of silence in the schools.

BATSON V. KENTUCKY

Citation: 476 U.S. 79 (1986)

Argued: December 12, 1985

Decided: April 30, 1986

Court Below: Kentucky Supreme Court

Basis for Review: *Writ of certiorari

Facts: Batson, an African American, was tried for a *felony by a jury that contained no African Americans (the prosecution used its *peremptory challenges to remove all four potential African American jurors from the panel). Batson's appeal of his subsequent conviction was denied.

Issue: Does the removal of all African American potential jurors from a jury panel violate a defendant's right to a fair trial under the Sixth Amendment and his right to *equal protection under the Fourteenth Amendment?

Outcome: The Court found for Batson, substantially restricting the use of prosecutors' peremptory challenges.

Vote: 7-2

Participating: Burger, Brennan, White, Marshall, Blackmun, Powell, Rehnquist, Stevens, O'Connor

Opinions: Powell for the Court; White concurring; Stevens, joined by Brennan, concurring; and O'Connor concurring; Burger, joined by Rehnquist, dissenting; and Rehnquist, joined by Burger, dissenting

Significance: The *Batson* principle has been extended in subsequent cases: in *Edmonson v. Leesville Concrete* (1991), exclusion of potential jurors from a civil case because of race was ruled impermissible, and in *Powers v. Ohio* (1991), the Court held that white defendants convicted by a jury from which African Americans have been excluded are entitled to new trials.

THORNBURGH V. AMERICAN COLLEGE OF OBSTETRICIANS AND GYNECOLOGISTS

Citation: 476 U.S. 747 (1986)

Argued: November 5, 1985

Decided: June 11, 1986

Court Below: United States Third Circuit Court of Appeals

Basis for Review: Appeal

Facts: Pennsylvania instituted regulations requiring that women seeking abortions be given detailed abortion information in advance, that abortion providers keep especially detailed records, and that after a certain point in pregnancies, special care be taken to protect fetuses in procedures that were to be overseen by second physicians.

Issue: Are the Pennsylvania regulations an overly burdensome encumbrance on the right to abortion?

Outcome: Finding the regulations in reality an attempt to discourage abortion, the Court overruled them.

Vote: 5-4

Participating: Burger, Brennan, White, Marshall, Blackmun, Powell, Rehnquist, Stevens, O'Connor

Opinions: Blackmun for the Court; Stevens concurring; Burger dissenting; White, joined by Rehnquist, dissenting; and O'Connor, joined by Rehnquist, dissenting

Significance: Although Justice Blackmun's opinion expressed dismay over states' continuing attempts to roll back *Roe v. Wade* (1973), *Thornburgh* marked the last time a clear majority of the Court supported a woman's right to abortion. Burger and White in dissent both argued that the case should be overruled. Three years after *Thornburgh*, however, the Court upheld a substantial attack on abortion in *Webster v. Reproductive Services* (1989).

BOWERS V. HARDWICK

Citation: 478 U.S. 186 (1986)
Argued: March 31, 1986
Decided: June 30, 1986
Court Below: United States Eleventh Circuit Court of Appeals
Basis for Review: *Writ of certiorari
Facts: Michael Hardwick, a gay man living in Atlanta, Georgia, was arrested for engaging in consensual homosexual sex in his own bedroom. Although the local district attorney did not prosecute Hardwick, he declined to drop sodomy charges against him. Hardwick then challenged the constitutionality of the Georgia antisodomy statute, naming the state attorney general, Michael Bowers, as defendant. The district court granted Bowers's motion to dismiss the suit, but the *appellate court reversed this ruling.
Issue: Does the right of privacy protect consensual sexual acts between persons of the same sex?
Outcome: The Supreme Court affirmed the ruling below and upheld the Georgia statute.
Vote: 5-4
Participating: Burger, Brennan, White, Marshall, Blackmun, Powell, Rehnquist, Stevens, O'Connor
Opinions: White for the Court; Burger and Powell concurring; Blackmun, joined by Brennan, Marshall, and Stevens, dissenting; and Stevens, joined by Brennan and Marshall, dissenting
Significance: Writing for the Court, Justice White declared that the earlier decisions of the Court regarding the right to privacy were limited to issues surrounding marriage, procreation, and the family. Homosexual activity bore "no connection" to these *precedents, he declared. In an angry dissent, Justice Blackmun denied that the issue in *Bowers* was the right to homosexual sex, declaring that it concerned the "right to be let

alone." Justice Powell, who provided the majority's fifth vote, had initially voted to strike the statute down, but because Hardwick had not been prosecuted and no Eighth Amendment cruel and unusual punishment issue was present, he changed his vote. Powell would later publicly declare his vote switch a mistake.

LOCAL 28 OF THE SHEET METAL WORKERS' INTERNATIONAL ASSOCIATION V. EQUAL EMPLOYMENT OPPORTUNITY COMMISSION

Citation: 478 U.S. 421 (1986)
Argued: February 25, 1986
Decided: July 2, 1986
Court Below: United States Second Circuit Court of Appeals
Basis for Review: *Writ of certiorari
Facts: The union was found guilty of violating Title VII of the Civil Rights Acts of 1964 for employing racially discriminatory admissions practices. A federal court ordered the union to establish a recruitment goal for nonwhite members, and the union appealed.
Issue: Do court-ordered quotas for minority membership in labor unions violate Title VII, which prohibits racial discrimination?
Outcome: The Court upheld the quotas.
Vote: 6-3
Participating: Burger, Brennan, White, Marshall, Blackmun, Powell, Rehnquist, Stevens, O'Connor
Opinions: Brennan for the *plurality; Powell concurring; O'Connor concurring in part and dissenting in part; White dissenting; and Rehnquist, joined by Burger, dissenting
Significance: The Court upheld affirmative action as an appropriate remedy for discrimination in union membership and thus for employment discrimination under Title VII.

BOWSHER V. SYNAR

Citation: 478 U.S. 714 (1986)
Argued: April 23, 1986
Decided: July 7, 1986
Court Below: United States District Court for the District of Columbia
Basis for Review: Appeal

POLITICAL COMPOSITION
of the Burger Court

Justice & Total Term	Courts Served	Appointing President	Political Party
Warren E. Burger (1969-1986)	Burger	Nixon	Republican
Hugo L. Black (1937-1971)	Hughes Stone Vinson Warren Burger	F. D. Roosevelt	Democrat
William O. Douglas (1939-1975)	Hughes Stone Vinson Warren Burger	F. D. Roosevelt	Democrat
John M. Harlan II (1955-1971)	Warren Burger	Eisenhower	Republican
William J. Brennan Jr. (1956-1990)	Warren Burger Rehnquist	Eisenhower	Democrat
Potter Stewart (1958-1981)	Warren Burger	Eisenhower	Republican
Byron R. White (1962-1993)	Warren Burger Rehnquist	Kennedy	Democrat
Thurgood Marshall (1967-1991)	Warren Burger Rehnquist	Johnson	Democrat
Harry A. Blackmun (1970-1994)	Burger Rehnquist	Nixon	Republican
Lewis F. Powell Jr. (1972-1987)	Burger Rehnquist	Nixon	Democrat
William H. Rehnquist (1972-1986) (1986-)	Burger Rehnquist	Nixon Reagan	Republican
John Paul Sevens (1975-)	Burger Rehnquist	Ford	Republican
Sandra Day O'Connor (1981-)	Burger Rehnquist	Reagan	Republican

Facts: The Balanced Budget and Emergency Deficit Reduction Plan of 1985 gave the comptroller general, a legislative branch employee, the power to specify budget cuts if Congress was unable to agree on them.

Issue: Does vesting authority in the controller general to make cuts in the federal budget, an executive branch function, violate the principle of *separation of powers?

Outcome: The Court struck down the contested provision of the act.

Vote: 7-2

Participating: Burger, Brennan, White, Marshall, Blackmun, Powell, Rehnquist, Stevens, O'Connor

Opinions: Burger for the Court; Stevens, joined by Marshall, concurring; White and Blackmun dissenting

Significance: *Bowsher* gave the Court an opportunity to define further the roles played by the executive and legislative branches of government. Legislative action, the Court said, involves adoption of general legal standards, while an executive action is performed in accord with specific statutes.

VOTING PATTERNS

President Richard Nixon, who campaigned in 1968 on a promise to curtail what he regarded as the liberal, activist excesses of the Warren Court, did manage to appoint four new justices during his first term, including a new chief justice. And although two of Nixon's appointees, Justice William H. Rehnquist and Chief Justice Warren Burger, frequently voted to undo Warren Court *precedents, the others, Justices Harry A. Blackmun and Louis F. Powell, joined the solid center that was the locus of power during the Burger years.

Liberal holdovers from the Warren era, William O. Douglas, William J. Brennan, and Thurgood Marshall, remained liberal. But Douglas retired midway through Burger's tenure, while Brennan and Marshall came to occupy the left wing of the Court. The latter two, indeed, exhibited nearly identical voting patterns during the 1969-1986 period, but the effect of their pairing

was often canceled out by that of Burger and Rehnquist. Justices Hugo L. Black and John M. Harlan continued along the more conservative course they had pursued during the Warren years (Black's conservatism having developed only toward the end of that period), but their judicial philosophies were not as right-leaning as those espoused by Chief Justice Burger, and they did not contribute to any intended rollback of recent precedents. The remaining veterans of the Warren Court, Potter Stewart and Byron White, remained in place, helping to make up the Burger Court's moderate core.

Justice John Paul Stevens, who replaced Douglas in 1975, had, like his predecessor, a penchant for solo dissent, but unlike Douglas's voting record, Stevens's put him statistically at the center of the Burger Court, disagreeing approximately one-third of the time with Brennan on the left and one-third of the time with Rehnquist on the right.

The net result of these personnel changes was that although many significant decisions handed down during Earl Warren's time as chief justice were limited during Burger's tenure, no landmark case decided by the Warren Court was overturned by its successor. Indeed, the Burger Court extended some important Warren Court innovations, most notably, perhaps, the right of privacy, which Douglas outlined in *Griswold v. Connecticut* (1965) and Blackmun then elaborated into a woman's right to abortion in *Roe v. Wade* (1973). And under Warren Burger, the Supreme Court also endorsed some newly asserted rights, such as gender equality (see, for example, *Craig v. Boren* [1976]) and affirmative action (as in *Fullilove v. Klutznick* [1980]). Another measure of the Court's continuing commitment to *judicial activism under Warren Burger was the number of laws it invalidated, which far outstripped the Warren Court's record.

The only justice sitting on the Burger Court who consistently declined to vote in favor of overturning legislation was William Rehnquist, whose devotion to conservatism and *judicial restraint earned him the moniker "Mr. Right." After Sandra Day O'Connor replaced Potter

Stewart in 1981, Rehnquist became the ideological leader of the Court. O'Connor, appointed by President Ronald Reagan, was herself a committed conservative, and although she did not always join with her "Arizona Twin," Rehnquist, she was less likely than her predecessor to serve as a swing vote. Five-to-four decisions — a common occurrence throughout the Burger years — began to favor Rehnquist's *jurisprudence rather than Brennan's. The counterrevolution, which had been hibernating for more than a decade, had found its chief.

SPECIAL FEATURES OF THE BURGER COURT

JUDICIAL REVIEW REVISITED

United States v. Nixon (1974), in which the Burger Court forced the president of the United States to act against his own interests and ultimately to resign, certainly stands for the proposition that the Supreme Court is the ultimate arbiter of constitutionality. It also marked a turning point in the Court's status vis-a-vis the other branches of government. In the wake of Franklin D. Roosevelt's 1937 court-packing plan, the Supreme Court had retreated from its imperious refusal to endorse New Deal legislation and its role as what Justice Louis D. Brandeis called a "super-legislature." In the intervening years, the Court did not cease to exercise its power of *judicial review, but during the Burger era, this authority gained added significance because of the number of important cases concerning *separation of powers that came before the Court. The Court reasserted its dominance in *United States v. Nixon*, and in such decisions as *Immigration and Naturalization Service v. Chadha* (1983), which invalidated the legislative veto, and *Bowsher v. Synar* (1986), finding the Gramm-Rudman-Hollings budget law unconstitutional because it granted executive functions to an administrator controlled by Congress.

THE FIRST FEMALE JUSTICE

One year before the 1981 appointment of Sandra Day O'Connor, the Court, anticipating just such an eventuality, dropped its practice of designating an opinion's author as "Mr. Justice _____." The increased visibility of women in all areas of public life and the social and political ferment caused by the women's movement prompted Ronald Reagan to promise, as part of his 1980 presidential campaign, to nominate a woman to the Supreme Court. Six months into his first term, he was given an opportunity to fulfill that promise when Justice Potter Stewart retired. Stewart's replacement, Justice O'Connor, was not only the first female justice to sit on the Court, she was also the only member of the Burger Court to have been elected to public office and to have served in all three branches of government.

The Rehnquist Court 1986-

BACKGROUND

THE ELECTION OF 1988, THE WAR ON DRUGS

Despite a stock market crash on October 19, 1987, which saw the Dow Jones Industrial Average plummet an unprecedented 508.32 points in one day, and despite the ballooning federal deficit, which had nearly tripled during the eight years of the Reagan administration, Ronald Reagan's vice president, George Bush, won the 1988 presidential election. In the final months of the campaign, Bush was able to surge ahead of his Democratic opponent, Massachusetts Governor Michael Dukakis, in part by attacking a Massachusetts prison furlough program and Dukakis's veto of a state law requiring school-children to recite the Pledge of Allegiance.

Toward the end of 1989, the administration launched a sudden invasion of Panama to over-throw the government and arrest Panamanian leader General Manuel Noriega, accused of cor-ruption and drug dealing. Other government offensives in the war on drugs — such as the $65 million the United States offered Columbia to help it combat its cocaine cartel — were also directed abroad. At home, Bush continued to deny accusations of complicity in the Iran-Contra scandal, as various other members of the Reagan administration were charged for their involvement.

THE END OF THE COLD WAR, THE WAR IN THE PERSIAN GULF

Soviet Premier Mikhail Gobachev had been vig-orously pursuing détente with the West and inter-nal restructuring in the U.S.S.R. for several years by the time the Berlin Wall — for 27 years a sym-bol of Communist suppression and a divided Europe — fell November 9, 1989. With the end of the cold war, the Soviet Union began to break apart, the Eastern Bloc began to reorganize itself, and the United States began to consider what to do with its supposed "peace dividend," resulting from nuclear disarmament and the reduction of conventional weapons and forces.

Before the Bush administration could capi-talize on this economic windfall, however, it was obliged to deploy troops to Saudi Arabia in response to Iraq's August 2, 1990, invasion of neighboring Kuwait. By December, the United States had approximately 300,000 troops sta-tioned in the Persian Gulf as part of a multina-tional effort now aimed not only at pushing Iraq out of Kuwait, but at freeing foreign hostages held in Iraq and Kuwait, toppling Iraqi strongman Saddam Hussein, destroying Iraq's capacity to manufacture nuclear weapons, and protecting the international oil supply.

Ultimately, the U.S. deployed 450,000 troops to the Gulf — by far the largest contingent — of which 148 were killed in the few months of fight-ing it took to defeat Iraq. In the end, Saddam

Hussein remained in power. Nonetheless, the major goals of the allies had been achieved in a swift and brilliant military campaign orchestrated by the U.S. The wounds left by the Vietnam War were at least partially healed as the nation basked in its military victory in what the majority of the population seemed to agree was a just cause.

THE PRESIDENTIAL ELECTION OF 1992,
THE MIDTERM ELECTIONS OF 1994

In the spring of 1991, in the aftermath of the Gulf War, President Bush enjoyed an approval rating of 90 percent, a figure none of his predecessors had

achieved. By November, however, this rating had dropped to below 50 percent, as America's attention refocused on domestic problems. The economy remained mired in recession, and Democrats found that they had an issue that would give them an opportunity to capture the White House for the first time since Jimmy Carter's election in 1976. Democratic Arkansas Governor Bill Clinton, campaigning as the candidate of change, won the election by 43 percent to Bush's 38 percent, with 19 percent of the vote going to independent candidate Ross Perot. At the age of 43, Clinton became the youngest man to assume the presidency since John Kennedy took office more than 30 years earlier.

This endorsement of Clinton and the Democrats proved short-lived, however. In November 1994 Americans, dissatisfied with Clinton's wavering leadership and with the gridlock that seemed to prevent passage of significant legislation, resoundingly deprived Democrats of the control they had exercised over Congress for 40 years.[†] Republican majorities were elected to both the House of Representatives and the Senate, and, in addition, Republicans supplanted Democrats in many state governments.

THE HOMEFRONT

Meanwhile, the nation was shocked repeatedly by episodes of violence, generated both by internal strife and by foreign terrorists. In May 1992, after an all-white jury acquitted four policemen whose beating of an African American man, Rodney King, had been caught on videotape, riots erupted in Los Angeles. Before the riots were quelled several days later, dozens of people had been killed and damage to property was in the millions. In February 1993 followers of a radical Egyptian Muslim cleric bombed the World Trade Center in New York City, killing six. Between March 1993 and December 1995 scores of abortion clinics were targets of violence, while six clinic doctors and staffers were killed by abortion foes. A 51-day siege by the Federal Bureau of Alcohol, Tobacco, and Firearms at a Waco, Texas, compound occupied by an obscure religious cult resulted in 1993 in the shooting of several federal

MEMBERS *Of the Court* 1986 –

(In Order of Seniority)

William H. Rehnquist *(Chief Justice)*	(1986-)
William J. Brennan Jr. *(retired)*	(1986-1990)
Byron R. White *(retired)*	(1986-1993)
Thurgood Marshall *(retired)*	(1986-1991)
Harry A. Blackmun *(retired)*	(1986-1994)
Lewis F. Powell, Jr. *(retired)*	(1986-1987)
John Paul Stevens	(1986-)
Sandra Day O'Connor	(1986-)
Antonin Scalia *(replaced William H. Rehnquist as associate justice)*	(1986-)
Anthony M. Kennedy *(replaced Lewis F. Powell Jr.)*	(1988-)
David H. Souter *(replaced William J. Brennan Jr.)*	(1990-)
Clarence Thomas *(replaced Thurgood Marshall)*	(1991-)
Ruth Bader Ginsburg *(replaced Byron R. White)*	(1993-)
Stephen G. Breyer *(replaced Harry A. Blackmun)*	(1994-)

[†] In the late 1980s and early 1990s, strong public resentment of Congress may have contributed to adoption of the Twenty-seventh Amendment, making congressional pay raises effective only after an intervening election of representatives. The amendment, ratified May 7, 1992, was first proposed by James Madison in 1787.

JUDICIAL BIOGRAPHY
William Hubbs Rehnquist

PERSONAL DATA

Born: October 1, 1924, in Milwaukee, Wisconsin
Parents: William B. Rehnquist, Margery Peck Rehnquist
Higher Education: Stanford University (B.A., with great distinction, Phi Beta Kappa, 1948; M.A., 1948); Harvard University (M.A., 1950); Stanford University Law School (LL.B., first in class, 1952)
Bar Admission: Arizona, 1953
Political Party: Republican
Marriage: August 29, 1953, to Natalie Cornell, who bore Rehnquist a son and two daughters and who died in October 1991

PROFESSIONAL CAREER

Occupations: Serviceman, 1943-1946; Law Clerk, 1952-1953; Lawyer, 1953-1971; Government Official, 1969-1971; Judge, 1971-
Official Positions: Law Clerk to Justice Robert H. Jackson, United States Supreme Court, 1952-1953; Assistant United States Attorney General, Office of Legal Counsel, 1969-1971; Associate Justice, United States Supreme Court, 1971-1986; Chief Justice, United States Supreme Court, 1986-

SUPREME COURT SERVICE

As Associate Justice:
Nominated: October 22, 1971
Nominated By: Richard M. Nixon
Confirmed: December 10, 1971
Confirmation Vote: 68-26
Oath Taken: January 7, 1972
Replaced: John M. Harlan II
Significant Opinions: *Moose Lodge v. Irvis* (1972); *Mahan v. Howell* (1973); *Edelman v. Jordan* (1974); *Jackson v. Metropolitan Edison Co.* (1974); *National League of Cities v. Usery* (1976); *Rostker v. Goldberg* (1981); *Dames & Moore v. Regan* (1981)
Left Court: Promoted to chief justice September 26, 1986
Length of Service: 14 years, 8 months, 19 days
Replacement: Antonin Scalia

As Chief Justice:
Nominated: June 17, 1986
Nominated By: Ronald Reagan
Confirmed: September 17, 1986
Confirmation Vote: 65-33
Oath Taken: September 26, 1986
Replaced: Warren E. Burger
Significant Opinions: *First English Evangelical Lutheran Church of Glendale v. County of Los Angeles* (1987); *Morrison v. Olson* (1988); *Martin v. Wilks* (1989); *Webster v. Reproductive Health Services* (1989); *Cruzan v. Director, Missouri Department of Health* (1990); *Rust v. Sullivan* (1991); *Barnes v. Glen Theatre, Inc.* (1991); *Payne v. Tennessee* (1991); *International Society for Krishna Consciousness, Inc. v. Lee* (1992); *Nixon v. United States* (1993); *National Organization for Women, Inc. v. Scheidler* (1994); *United States v. Lopez* (1995); *Missouri v. Jenkins* (1995)

---

agents, as well as a conflagration that killed some 75 cult members. Although the fire that consumed the compound apparently was set by cult members, federal officials were blamed for ineptitude. The April 1995 bombing of an Oklahoma City federal office building — possibly committed in retaliation for the Waco incident — killed at least 168.

In June 1994 former football player O.J. Simpson was accused of brutally murdering his former wife, Nicole Brown Simpson, and a male acquaintance, Ronald Goldman. For some nine months America trained its attention on Simpson's Los Angeles trial, which ended in his acquittal in October 1995. The trial, which was broadcast on nationwide television, was widely followed by the public and covered exhaustively in the media, which speculated that the nation's fascination was a reflection of its obsession with race matters (Simpson is African American, while the murder victims were white). As a by-product of this close scrutiny, much of the nation received an unprece-

William H. Rehnquist

dented education in the workings of the American legal system. However, there was widespread anger and astonishment among white Americans at the not guilty verdict reached by the predominantly African American jury.

REHNQUIST'S EARLY LIFE

William H. Rehnquist, the son of a paper salesman, grew up in a politically conservative household in the Milwaukee suburb of Shorewood, Wisconsin. During World War II he served with the Army Air Corps in North Africa as a weather observer, reaching the rank of sergeant. After the war ended he attended Stanford University, where he received both a bachelor's degree and a master's degree in political science. He next took a second master's in government at Harvard before returning to Stanford to study law. In 1952 he graduated first in a class that also included future Supreme Court Justice Sandra Day O'Connor. Rehnquist then clerked for Justice Robert H. Jackson before moving to Phoenix, Arizona, where he practiced law at various firms before forming his own partnership with a friend.

REHNQUIST'S PUBLIC LIFE

From the start, Rehnquist was active in conservative Republican politics, which had found a firm base in Phoenix. He became an official of the Republican Party there, as well as an outspoken opponent of the Warren Court's liberalism and of local measures to integrate public accommodations and institute school busing. While campaigning for Republican presidential candidate Barry Goldwater in 1964, Rehnquist became acquainted with another local Republican activist, Richard Kleindienst. After Kleindienst joined President Richard Nixon's administration as deputy attorney general, he was instrumental in securing Rehnquist's appointment as head of the Justice Department's Office of Legal Counsel.

As assistant attorney general, Rehnquist proved to be one of the Nixon administration's most articulate spokesmen, testifying before numerous congressional committees in support of *warrantless executive branch wiretapping, the president's war powers, preventive detention, and abolition of the *exclusionary rule. It was also Rehnquist's job to screen potential Supreme Court nominees, and in 1971, he became a nominee himself when Nixon appointed him to replace Justice John M. Harlan.

Resistance in the Senate to Rehnquist's nomination was fierce, owing to his consistent record of dedication to conservatism. Opponents focused on a memorandum he had written in 1952, while serving as Justice Robert H. Jackson's clerk, on the upcoming *Brown v. Board of Education* (1954). Rehnquist claimed that the memo, which stated, "I think *Plessy v. Ferguson* was right and should be re-affirmed," was meant to reflect Jackson's thinking on the case, not his own. Despite the controversy generated by the memo's endorsement of a discredited, segregationist judicial philosophy, Rehnquist was confirmed by the Senate by a vote of 68 to 26.

As an associate justice, Rehnquist remained true to his conservative precepts, and during his early years on the Burger Court he was often the only dissenter, endorsing such principles as *states' rights, which many of his brethren believed to be retrograde. Unquestionably the Burger Court's most conservative member, he was dubbed "Mr. Right." But Rehnquist also continued to exhibit the articulateness and persuasiveness that had marked his earlier public life, and he was assigned responsibility for writing some of the Burger Court's most significant opinions.

Then, in the 1975 term, the political orientation of the Court began to change, and Rehnquist came into his own with *National League of Cities v. Usery* (1976), which limited Congress's power to regulate state employees' wages and hours. *National League of Cities* was overruled in 1985 by one vote in *Garcia v. San Antonio Metropolitan Transit Authority*, but by the end of Chief Justice Warren Burger's tenure in 1986, Rehnquist was nonetheless the undisputed intellectual leader of the Court. His appointment as Burger's successor by the equally conservative Republican Ronald Reagan seemed almost inevitable. Once again, his nomination met with resistance in the Senate — where the debate about his *Brown* memo was revived, together with allegations concerning harassment of African American voters when he served as a Republican Party official in Phoenix — but three months after he was nominated, he was once again confirmed by a vote of 65 to 33, if by a somewhat narrower margin than before.

REHNQUIST AS CHIEF JUSTICE

As chief justice, Rehnquist — who has said that he models himself after the highly effective Chief Justice Charles Evans Hughes — has received high praise for his abilities as an administrator. Even those justices who disagree with his politics have commended his consistency and directedness. The commitment to counteract what he sees as the liberal excesses of the Warren Court remains as strong today as it was when he first entered public life. He continues to espouse positions he took early in his judicial career: enlargement of police power, support for the death penalty, protection of private property, restriction of the rights of criminal defendants, opposition to abortion, and affirmative action.

The decisions of the Court led by Chief Justice Rehnquist have generally reflected his conservative agenda. *Richmond v. J. A. Croson Co.* (1989), for which Justice Sandra Day O'Connor wrote the opinion of the Court, raised the standard for determining the constitutionality of affirmative action programs. Although it was later overturned by the 1991 Civil Rights Act, *Ward's Cove Packing Co. v. Atonio* (1989), for which Justice Byron White wrote the opinion of the Court, placed the burden of proving employment discrimination on plaintiffs. And while the Court thus far has declined to overrule the landmark 1973 case validating a woman's right to abortion, *Roe v. Wade*, it came close to doing so in 1989 with *Webster v. Reproductive Health Services*, for which Rehnquist himself wrote the opinion adopted by a *plurality of the court.

With the retirements of Justices William H. Brennan and Thurgood Marshall in 1990 and 1991, respectively, and their replacement with Justices David Souter and Clarence Thomas, Rehnquist seems to have gained a conservative majority on the Court. Since then the Court has succeeded in limiting some of the most significant Warren Court decisions liberalizing criminal procedure, cases such as *Mapp v. Ohio* (1961), *Gideon v. Wainwright* (1963), and *Miranda v. Arizona* (1966). And with *United States v. Lopez* (1995), for which Rehnquist wrote the majority opinion, the Supreme Court struck down a federal law written under authority of the *Commerce Clause. The last time that happened was during the early New Deal era, when the Court was led by Rehnquist's exemplar, Chief Justice Hughes. But whereas the Hughes Court underwent a conversion from *judicial activism to *judicial restraint, Rehnquist seems determined to lead his brethren in the long-delayed counterrevolution that was to have taken place under Warren Burger.

ASSOCIATE JUSTICES

For biographies of Associate Justices **William J. Brennan Jr., Byron R. White,** and **Thurgood Marshall,** see entries under **THE WARREN**

COURT. For biographies of Associate Justices **Harry A. Blackmun, Lewis F. Powell Jr., John Paul Stevens,** and **Sandra Day O'Connor,** see entries under **THE BURGER COURT.**

ANTONIN SCALIA

PERSONAL DATA

Born: March 11, 1936, in Trenton, New Jersey
Parents: Eugene S. Scalia, Catherine Panaro Scalia
Higher Education: Georgetown University (B.A., summa cum laude, class valedictorian, 1957); University of Fribourg, Switzerland, 1957; Harvard Law School (LL.B., magna cum laude, 1960)
Bar Admissions: Ohio, 1962; Virginia, 1970
Political Party: Republican
Marriage: September 1960, to Maureen McCarthy, who has borne Scalia nine children

PROFESSIONAL CAREER

Occupations: Lawyer, 1961-1967, 1971-1972, 1974-1977; Educator, 1967-1971, 1977-1982; Government Official, 1971-1977; Judge, 1982-
Official Positions: Professor of Law, University of Virginia, 1967-1971; General Counsel, White House Office of Telecommunications Policy, 1971-1972; Chairman, Administrative Conference of the United States, 1972-1974; Assistant Attorney General, Office of Legal Counsel, 1974-1977; Professor, Georgetown University Law Center, 1977; Professor of Law, University of Chicago, 1977-1982; Chairman, American Bar Association, Section on Administrative Law, 1981-1982; Chairman, American Bar Association, Conference of Section Chairs, 1981-1982; Judge, United States Court of Appeals for the District of Columbia Circuit, 1982-1986; Associate Justice, United States Supreme Court, 1986-

SUPREME COURT SERVICE

Nominated: June 17, 1986
Nominated By: Ronald Reagan
Confirmed: September 17, 1986
Confirmation Vote: 98-0
Oath Taken: September 26, 1986
Replaced: William H. Rehnquist
Significant Opinions: *Stanford v. Kentucky* (1989); *R.A.V. v. St. Paul* (1992); *St. Mary's Honor Center v. Hicks* (1993); *Veronia School District v. Acton* (1995); *Capitol Square Review Board v. Pinette* (1995)

Antonin Scalia, the first Supreme Court justice of Italian ancestry, was born to a father who immigrated from Sicily and a mother who was herself the child of Italian immigrants. Scalia's family was academically oriented — his mother was a schoolteacher and his father a professor of Romance languages — and he distinguished himself throughout his academic career. After graduating first in his class at Georgetown University and receiving an honors degree from Harvard Law School, he spent a year traveling and studying in Europe as a Sheldon Fellow of Harvard University.

Scalia spent six years practicing law with the prominent Cleveland, Ohio, firm of Jones, Day, Cockley, and Reavis, but then he returned to the academy, assuming the position of professor of law at the University of Virginia. In 1971 he embarked on a successful career in government, joining the Nixon administration as general counsel to the Office of Telecommunications and moving on to chair the Administrative Conference of the United States, an independent agency set up to monitor and improve the administrative process in federal government. From 1974 to 1977 he served the administration of Gerald Ford as assistant attorney general for the Office of Legal Counsel, the same position William Rehnquist had held before his own appointment to the Supreme Court.

Scalia, however, returned once more to academia before assuming the bench, teaching law at Georgetown, at the University of Chicago and, as a visiting professor, at Stanford University. In 1982 Ronald Reagan appointed him to the United States Court of Appeals for the District of Columbia Circuit, where Scalia began to expound on his belief in the *separation of powers and in *strict construction of the Constitution. Four years later, when Reagan promoted him to the Supreme Court, Scalia used his confirmation hearings to reiterate his view that the system of checks and balances was the most important concept contained in the Constitution.

Scalia was nominated the same day Justice Rehnquist's name was sent to the Senate Judiciary Committee as Reagan's candidate to succeed Chief Justice Burger, but despite Scalia's own blunt conservatism, his appointment, unlike Rehnquist's, met with no resistance. He was confirmed by a vote of 98 to 0 and, together, with Rehnquist, took his oath of office on September 26, 1986.

Scalia is the first academic since Felix Frankfurter to be appointed to the High Court. Expectations were that his fierce intellect would make him a leader among his brethren, but apparently because of his dogmatic inflexibility — and because of Rehnquist's own strong leadership and advocacy of conservative causes — Scalia's influence has remained marginal, his *jurisprudence the most conservative espoused by any member of the conservative Rehnquist Court.

ANTHONY McLEOD KENNEDY

PERSONAL DATA

Born: July 23, 1936, in Sacramento, California
Parents: Anthony Kennedy, Gladys McLeod Kennedy
Higher Education: Stanford University (B.A., Phi Beta Kappa, 1958); London School of Economics, 1957-1958; Harvard Law School (LL.B., cum laude, 1961)
Bar Admission: California, 1961
Political Party: Republican
Marriage: 1963 to Mary Davis, who has borne Kennedy two sons and a daughter

PROFESSIONAL CAREER

Occupations: Serviceman, 1961; Lawyer, 1961-1975; Educator, 1965-1988; Judge, 1975-
Official Positions: Lecturer in Law, University of the Pacific, 1965-1988; Judge, United States Ninth Circuit Court of Appeals, 1975-1988; Associate Justice, United States Supreme Court, 1988-

SUPREME COURT SERVICE

Nominated: November 24, 1987
Nominated By: Ronald Reagan
Confirmed: February 3, 1988
Confirmation Vote: 97-0
Oath Taken: February 18, 1988
Replaced: Lewis F. Powell Jr.
Significant Opinions: *National Treasury Employees Union v. Von Raab, Skinner v. Railway Labor Executives' Association* (1989); *Patterson v. McLean Credit Union* (1989); *Masson v. New Yorker Magazine, Inc.* (1991); *Freeman v. Pitts* (1992); *Planned Parenthood of Pennsylvania v. Casey* (1992); *United States v. James Daniel Good Real Property* (1993); *McKennon v. Nashville Banner Publishing Co.* (1995); *Miller v. Abrams* (1995); *Rosenberger v. University of Virginia* (1995)

When Lewis F. Powell Jr. retired from the Court in 1987, Ronald Reagan first tried to replace him, on July 1, 1987, with Robert H. Bork, a judge on the United States Court of Appeals for the District of Columbia Circuit. Liberals saw this vacancy as crucial because of the increasing conservatism of the Court and the pivotal role played by swing vote Justice Powell, and they strongly opposed Bork's appointment because of his well-known hostility to liberal causes. After a lengthy, highly publicized confirmation battle, Bork's nomination was defeated on October 23, 1987, by a vote of 58 to 42.

Reagan was prepared next to choose his old California colleague, Anthony Kennedy, but Bork supporters intervened, proposing that he nominate Douglas Ginsburg, a former official in the Reagan administration then serving, like Bork, on the D.C. Circuit Court of Appeals. Appointed on October 29, 1987, Ginsburg withdrew his nomination nine days later in the wake of allegations of former conflicts of interest and his admission of having smoked marijuana while teaching at Harvard Law School some years earlier. Kennedy again rose to the top of Reagan's short list.

Anthony Kennedy was born and raised in California's state capital, Sacramento, where both his parents were involved in state politics. His mother was a leader in local civic affairs, while his father was a lawyer and lobbyist in the state legislature. Kennedy grew up knowing many prominent state politicians, including Governor Earl Warren, who would go on to become chief justice of the Supreme Court.

After spending the final year of his undergraduate education studying at the London School of Economics before graduating from Stanford, he went on to receive an honors law degree from Harvard before joining the San Francisco firm of Thelen, Marrin, Johnson, and Bridges in 1961. During his first year there, he took a leave of absence to go on active duty with the Army National Guard, and in 1963, after his father's death, Kennedy returned to Sacramento to take over his father's law practice.

For the next dozen years, aside from teaching constitutional law part-time at McGeorge School of Law at the University of the Pacific (he continued to teach part-time until his elevation to the Supreme Court), Kennedy devoted himself to Evans, Jackson, and Kennedy. In addition to legal work, Kennedy continued his father's lobbying activities. He got to know Ronald Reagan after the latter was elected governor in 1966, and he was responsible for developing and promoting legislation intended to limit permanently the state's taxing and spending powers. Although Kennedy's proposal was defeated, it paved the way for Proposition 13, which later succeeded in limiting state taxation.

When an opening occurred on the U.S. Ninth Circuit Court of Appeals in 1974, Reagan, by then a considerable power on the national scene, persuaded President Gerald Ford to appoint Kennedy. Kennedy served on the circuit court for 12 years, compiling a solid conservative record, before then President Reagan appointed him to the Supreme Court in 1987. Although he was clearly a conservative, Kennedy unlike Bork, was perceived as flexible and pragmatic, and he was easily confirmed.

On the Court, Kennedy has been closely aligned with Chief Justice William Rehnquist, who has frequently assigned him responsibility for writing opinions in major cases. Although he has followed the Court's conservative trend, particularly with regard to criminal procedure, he also joined with Justice William Brennan to uphold a First Amendment right to burn the flag in *Texas v. Johnson* (1989) and, together with Justices Sandra Day O'Connor and David Souter, he drafted an opinion for the Court upholding a woman's right to abortion in *Planned Parenthood v. Casey* (1992).

DAVID HACKETT SOUTER

PERSONAL DATA
Born: September 17, 1939, in Melrose, Massachusetts
Parents: Joseph A. Souter, Helen A. Hackett Souter
Higher Education: Harvard University (B.A., magna cum laude, Phi Beta Kappa, 1961); Magdalen College, Oxford University, England (Rhodes Scholar, 1961-1963); Harvard Law School (LL.B., 1966)
Bar Admission: New Hampshire, 1966
Political Party: Republican
Marriage: None

PROFESSIONAL CAREER
Occupations: Lawyer, 1966-1978; Government Official, 1968-1978; Judge, 1978-
Official Positions: Assistant Attorney General, Criminal Division, State of New Hampshire, 1968-1971; Deputy Attorney General, New Hampshire, 1971-1976; Attorney General, New Hampshire, 1976-1978; Associate Justice, New Hampshire Superior Court, 1978-1983; President, Concord Hospital Board of Trustees, Concord, New Hampshire, 1978-1984; Vice President, New Hampshire Historical Society, ca. late 1970s-mid-1880s; Associate Justice, New Hampshire Supreme Court, 1983-1990; Judge, United States First Circuit Court of Appeals, 1990; Associate Justice, United States Supreme Court, 1990-

SUPREME COURT SERVICE
Nominated: July 25, 1990
Nominated By: George Bush
Confirmed: October 2, 1990
Confirmation Vote: 90-9
Oath Taken: October 9, 1990
Replaced: William J. Brennan Jr.
Significant Opinions: *Planned Parenthood of Pennsylvania v. Casey* (1992); *Board of Education v. Grumet* (1994)

Although David Souter lived with his parents in Massachusetts, he spent his summers at his

The Rehnquist Court, 1990 (Investiture of David H. Souter). From left; Byron R. White, William H. Rehnquist, Antonin Scalia, Sandra Day O'Connor, David H. Souter, Thurgood Marshall, Anthony M. Kennedy, Harry A. Blackmun, John Paul Stevens

maternal grandparents' farmhouse in the small town of Weare, New Hampshire. When he was 11, his grandparents died, and he moved with his parents to the farmhouse in Weare, where he continues to spend his summers.

A prodigious student, Souter went on to achieve honors at Harvard, from which he obtained both undergraduate and law degrees and which sent him to Oxford on a Rhodes Scholarship from 1961 to 1963. Souter returned to his native New Hampshire, however, where in 1966 he joined the law firm of Orr and Reno as an associate.

Souter, who was clearly interested in public service, devoted a portion of his private practice to *pro bono work, and when offered an opportunity to join the state attorney general's office in 1968, he quickly accepted. Souter soon impressed his superiors, including Warren G. Rudman, who as New Hampshire attorney general appointed Souter his deputy and whom Souter succeeded in that position in 1976.

Two years later, Souter began his judicial career, ascending quickly through the ranks of the state judiciary. In April 1990 President George Bush appointed him to the U.S. First Circuit Court of Appeals. Only three months later, on the recommendation of then Senator Warren Rudman, Bush nominated Souter to replace the retiring Justice William J. Brennan. Given Brennan's liberal record, speculation about his replacement focused on his successor's presumed conservative leanings. The Bush administration, with the bruising Robert Bork confirmation battle fresh in its memory, took care to choose a candidate with no paper trail that could be traced by liberal opponents. Indeed, although Souter had by that time served a dozen years as jurist, he had issued surprisingly few written opinions. Opposition to his nomination centered on his lack of experience on the federal bench, but he was easily confirmed.

Souter made a cautious start, writing only three opinions during his first term, the lowest number produced by any justice appointed in the last 20 years. He then began producing more and exerting — together with Justices Sandra Day

O'Connor and Anthony Kennedy — a moderating influence on the Court's more activist wing. The profound respect for history and *precedent he exhibited as a state judge may predispose him to side with those disinclined to roll back the liberal *jurisprudence advanced during the Warren and Burger years.

CLARENCE THOMAS

PERSONAL DATA

Born: June 23, 1948, in Pin Point, Georgia
Parents: M.C. Thomas, Leola Anderson
Higher Education: Holy Cross College (B.A., with honors, 1971); Yale Law School (LL.B., 1974)
Bar Admission: Missouri, 1974
Political Party: Republican
Marriages: 1971 to Kathy Grace Ambush, who bore Thomas a son and from whom he was divorced in 1984; May 1987 to Virginia Lamp

PROFESSIONAL CAREER

Occupations: Lawyer, 1974-1979; Government Official, 1974-1977, 1979-1990; Judge, 1990-
Official Positions: Staff Attorney, Missouri Attorney General's Office, 1974-1977; Legislative Assistant, Office of U.S. Senator John Danforth, 1979-1981; Assistant Secretary for Civil Rights, United States Department of Education, 1981-1982; Director, Equal Employment Opportunity Commission, 1982-1990; Judge, United States Court of Appeals for the District of Columbia Circuit, 1990-1991; Associate Justice, United States Supreme Court, 1991-

SUPREME COURT SERVICE

Nominated: July 1, 1991
Nominated By: George Bush
Confirmed: October 15, 1991
Confirmation Vote: 52-48
Oath Taken: November 1, 1991
Replaced: Thurgood Marshall
Significant Opinions: *Associated General Contractors v. Jacksonville* (1993); *Godinez v. Moran* (1993)

Born into poverty in the tiny Georgia community of Pin Point, south of Savannah, Thomas was only two when he and his two siblings were abandoned by their father. His mother struggled to support her children by working as a maid, but after the family's house burned down, Clarence and his brother were sent to live with his maternal grandfather in Savannah.

Myers Anderson was a devout Roman Catholic and a successful self-made businessman who provided Thomas and his brother with a middle-class lifestyle and a commitment to hard work. Following his grandfather's wishes that he become a priest, Thomas attended Immaculate Conception Seminary in northwest Missouri, but dropped out during his first year there, citing racism. After finishing college at another Catholic institution, he obtained a law degree at Yale, where he had been admitted in part because of the school's affirmative action program. His inability upon graduation to secure a position with any prestigious private law firm added to his sense of having been discriminated against. He finally accepted a position with the office of Missouri Attorney General John Danforth, where he avoided assignments that might suggest racial stereotyping. He also joined the African American conservative movement and the Republican Party.

After a brief stint in the private sector, in 1979 Thomas returned to work for Danforth, by then a U.S. senator. Thomas's prominence as an African American conservative brought him to the attention of the Reagan administration, where he performed the type of civil rights work he had previously eschewed. He advanced quickly through the ranks, and in 1990, Reagan's successor, George Bush, appointed Thomas to the highly visible District of Columbia Circuit Court of Appeals. After less than a year on the bench, he was nominated as Thurgood Marshall's replacement on the Supreme Court.

Thomas's confirmation hearings were tumultuous, marred at first by questions about his judicial qualifications and his unwillingness to be forthcoming about his attitudes toward controversial legal issues such as abortion. Then, shortly before the Senate confirmation vote was to take place, the news media announced that Anita Hill, one of his former employees at the Department of Education and the Equal Opportunity Commission, was charging that he had sexually harassed her when she worked for him.

The Senate Judiciary Committee reconvened, and the hearing of Hill's charges was nationally televised and widely followed in the print media. Three months after he had been nominated, Thomas was confirmed — but by the slimmest margin given any Supreme Court appointee in over one hundred years. Two weeks later he took his seat on the high bench, the second African American ever to do so. Since then, although he has remained reticent and aloof, his voting pattern indicates that he continues along the doctrinaire conservative path he had followed prior to his appointment to the Court.

RUTH JOAN BADER GINSBURG

PERSONAL DATA

Born: March 15, 1933, in Brooklyn, New York
Parents: Nathan Bader, Celia Amster Bader
Higher Education: Cornell University (B.A., Phi Beta Kappa, 1954); Harvard Law School, 1956-1958; Columbia University Law School (LL.B., Kent Scholar, 1959)
Bar Admissions: New York, 1959; District of Columbia, 1975
Political Party: Democrat
Marriage: June 23, 1954, to Martin D. Ginsburg, with whom she has had a daughter and a son

PROFESSIONAL CAREER

Occupations: Law Clerk, 1959-1961; Legal Researcher, 1961-1963; Educator, 1963-1980; Lawyer, late 1960s-1980; Judge, 1980-
Official Positions: Law Clerk, United States District Court for the Southern District of New York, 1959-1963; Research Associate, Columbia Law School project on international procedure, 1961-1962; Associate Director, Columbia international procedure project, 1962-1963; Assistant Professor, Rutgers University Law School, 1963-1966; Associate Professor, Rutgers University Law School, 1966-1969; Professor, Rutgers University Law School, 1969-1972; Professor, Columbia University Law School, 1972-1980; Counsel, American Civil Liberties Union Women's Right Project, 1972-1980; General Counsel, American

Civil Liberties Union, 1973-1980; Board of Directors, American Civil Liberties Union, 1974-1980; Judge, United States Court of Appeals for the District of Columbia Circuit, 1980-1993; Associate Justice, United States Supreme Court, 1993-

SUPREME COURT SERVICE

Nominated: June 14, 1993
Nominated By: Bill Clinton
Confirmed: August 3, 1993
Confirmation Vote: 96-3
Oath Taken: August 10, 1993
Replaced: Byron R. White
Significant Opinions: None

Ruth Joan Bader was one of two daughters born to descendants of Central European and Russian Jewish immigrants. After the age of one, she was raised as an only child when her older sister died of meningitis. She lost her mother to cancer the day before she graduated from high school.

At Cornell University, which she attended on scholarship, Ruth Bader met her future husband, Martin Ginsburg, whom she married upon graduation. When her husband was drafted for military service in 1959, Ginsburg went with him to Ft. Sill, Oklahoma, where she experienced her first serious episode of sex discrimination. Applying for a position with the Social Security administration, she revealed that she was pregnant and was downgraded, while the higher-ranking opening went to another woman who was also pregnant, but who hid her condition.

Ginsburg's husband resumed his legal education at Harvard after he was discharged from the military in 1956. Ginsburg also enrolled at Harvard Law School, one of only nine women in a class of 500. After her husband graduated and obtained a job with a New York City law firm, Ginsburg transferred to Columbia University Law School. Although she graduated at the top of her class in 1959, she was unable to obtain employment in private practice because of her gender. Instead, she pursued a distinguished career in academia that would last for the next 20 years.

When she was hired by Rutgers University in 1963, she was one of only two women to join the law school faculty, and when she became pregnant in 1965, she carefully disguised her condition by wearing oversized clothes. In the late 1960s the American Civil Liberties Union began referring sex discrimination cases to Ginsburg. She won five of the six sex discrimination cases that she argued before the United States Supreme Court, earning for herself a reputation as "the Thurgood Marshall of gender-equality law."

When President Jimmy Carter appointed Ginsburg to the influential District of Columbia Circuit, however, Ginsburg's activism was replaced by a more restrained attitude toward the law. Critics were concerned about her friendships with her conservative *appellate court colleagues Robert H. Bork and Antonin Scalia, as well as her public criticism of *Roe v. Wade* (1973). Although a longtime supporter of a woman's right to choose, she challenged the Burger Court's precipitousness and rationale for granting abortion constitutional protection.

Nonetheless, President Bill Clinton's 90-minute interview with Ginsburg in June 1993 convinced him that she remained pro-choice, an opinion verified during her untroubled confirmation hearings. With her appointment to the High Court, Ginsburg became the first Jewish justice to sit on the Court since the resignation of Abe Fortas in 1969, and only the second female Supreme Court justice in history.

STEPHEN GERALD BREYER

PERSONAL DATA

Born: August 15, 1938, in San Francisco, California
Parents: Irving G. Breyer, Anne R. Breyer
Higher Education: Stanford University (A.B., with great distinction, 1959); Magdalen College, Oxford University, England (Marshall Scholar, B.A., first in class, 1961); Harvard Law School (LL.B., magna cum laude, 1964)
Bar Admissions: California, 1966; District of Columbia, 1966; Massachusetts, 1971
Political Party: Democrat
Marriage: September 4, 1967, to Joanna Hare, who has borne Breyer two daughters and a son

PROFESSIONAL CAREER

Occupations: Law Clerk, 1964-1965; Lawyer, 1965-1981; Educator, 1967-1994; Government Official, 1965-1967, 1973-1975, 1979-1980, 1985-1989, 1990-1994; Judge, 1981-
Official Positions: Law Clerk to Justice Arthur J. Goldberg, United States Supreme Court, 1964-1965; Special Assistant for antitrust matters to the Assistant Attorney General, Department of Justice, 1965-1967; Assistant Professor, Harvard Law School, 1967-1970; Professor, Harvard Law School, 1967-1980; Assistant Special Prosecutor, Watergate Special Prosecution Force, 1973; Special Counsel, United States Senate Judiciary Committee, Subcommittee on Administrative Practices, 1974-1975; Trustee, University of Massachusetts, 1974-1981; Trustee, Dana Farber Cancer Institute, 1977; Professor, Kennedy School of Government, 1977-1980; Chief Counsel, United States Senate Judiciary Committee, 1979-1980; Lecturer, Kennedy School of Government, 1980-1994; Judge, United States First Circuit Court of Appeals, 1981-1990; Member, United States Sentencing Commission, 1985-1989; Chief Judge, United States First Circuit Court of Appeals, 1990-1994; Member, Judicial Conference of the United States, 1990-1994; Associate Justice, United States Supreme Court, 1994-

SUPREME COURT SERVICE

Nominated: May 13, 1994
Nominated By: Bill Clinton
Confirmation: July 29, 1994
Confirmation Vote: 87-9
Oath Taken: August 3, 1994
Replaced: Harry A. Blackmun
Significant Opinions: None

Stephen Breyer was not President Bill Clinton's first choice as a replacement for retiring Justice Harry Blackmun. In fact, Clinton had interviewed Breyer in 1993 as a potential successor to Justice Byron White, but the interview had not gone well (Breyer was recovering from injuries incurred in a bicycle accident), and Clinton turned instead to Ruth Bader Ginsburg. For Blackmun's replacement, Clinton stated that he wanted to appoint an individual with "real world" experience who could bring a fresh perspective to the Court. But other potential candidates were discarded in favor of Breyer, whose record is almost entirely academic, political, and judicial.

Breyer began his legal career serving as Justice Arthur Goldberg's law clerk in 1965, and he was responsible for helping Goldberg draft an important concurring opinion expanding on the nascent right of privacy in *Griswold v. Connecticut* (1965). From there Breyer went to the Justice Department, where he worked in antitrust enforcement and began to develop an expertise in government regulation that would later become his forte. As an academic and a judge, he would write four books on the subject.

Although he joined academia in 1967, Breyer never entirely left Washington, D.C. In addition to acting as a special Watergate prosecutor in 1973, he has served as counsel to the Senate Judiciary Committee, where he added to his credentials in administrative law. Subsequent distinguished service on the United States Sentencing Commission, together with 14 years on the First Circuit Court of Appeals — the last four as chief judge — gave him the judicial experience that may have helped to convince Clinton of Breyer's suitability.

On the sentencing commission and as a federal judge, Breyer exhibited no particular ideological orientation, only a dedication to pragmatism and consensus building. Given that the balance of power in the Rehnquist Court seems to rest with moderate conservatives — Justices Sandra Day O'Connor, Anthony Kennedy, and David Souter — it is probable that Clinton had just these qualities in mind when he chose Breyer to replace Justice Blackmun, who had played a significant role as middleman during the increasingly conservative Burger and Rehnquist eras.

SIGNIFICANT CASES

JOHNSON V. SANTA CLARA COUNTY

Citation: 480 U.S. 616 (1987)
Argued: November 12, 1986
Decided: March 25, 1987
Court Below: United States Ninth Circuit Court of Appeals
Basis for Review: *Writ of certiorari
Facts: In 1978 the Transportation Agency of Santa Clara County, California, instituted an affirmative action plan designed to rectify racial and gender imbalances among its workforce. Race and gender were only some of the factors to be taken into account, and the plan did not set quotas. Although he had achieved a slightly higher interview score, Johnson, a male employee, lost a promotion to road dispatcher — a position never held by a female — to a female co-worker.
Issue: Are gender-based voluntary affirmative action programs authorized under Title VII of the 1964 Civil Rights Act?
Outcome: The Supreme Court, citing the flexibility of Santa Clara's affirmative action plan, upheld it.
Vote: 6-3
Participating: Rehnquist, Brennan, White, Marshall, Blackmun, Powell, Stevens, O'Connor, Scalia
Opinions: Brennan for the Court; Stevens and O'Connor concurring; White dissenting; and Scalia, joined by Rehnquist and White, dissenting
Significance: *Johnson* marked the first time the Supreme Court upheld voluntary affirmative action programs instituted under Title VII to remedy the effects of past sex discrimination. A parallel decision in *United Steelworkers of America v. Weber* (1979) upheld similar programs intended to correct racial imbalances in the workplace.

MCCLESKEY V. KEMP

Citation: 481 U.S. 279 (1987)
Argued: October 15, 1986
Decided: April 22, 1987
Court Below: United States Eleventh Circuit Court of Appeals
Basis for Review: *Writ of certiorari
Facts: Warren McCleskey, an African American man, was convicted of having murdered a white Atlanta police officer and was sentenced to death. On appeal, McCleskey's lawyers presented statistical data demonstrating that in Georgia the death penalty was being administered in a racially

discriminatory fashion against African Americans — particularly those convicted of killing whites.
Issue: Do such statistical disparities demonstrate that Georgia's administration of the death penalty violates either the *Equal Protection Clause of the Fourteenth Amendment or the Eighth Amendment ban on cruel and unusual punishment?
Outcome: The Court rejected McCleskey's claim and upheld his death sentence.
Vote: 5-4
Participating: Rehnquist, Brennan, White, Marshall, Blackmun, Powell, Stevens, O'Connor, Scalia
Opinions: Powell for the Court; Brennan, joined by Marshall, Blackmun, and Stevens, dissenting; Blackmun, joined by Marshall, Stevens, and Brennan, dissenting; and Stevens, joined by Blackmun, dissenting
Significance: Justice Powell's opinion for the Court held that proof of discriminatory intent on the part of the Georgia legislature would be necessary to uphold a Fourteenth Amendment claim in cases such as McCleskey's. The statistics, he indicated, did not demonstrate a great enough disparity to make the death penalty in Georgia cruel and unusual punishment. Furthermore, a remedy to the situation they portrayed lay with the legislature, not with the courts. McCleskey's *habeas corpus petition would also be rejected by the Court four years later in *McCleskey v. Zant* (1991).

FIRST ENGLISH EVANGELICAL LUTHERAN CHURCH OF GLENDALE V. COUNTY OF LOS ANGELES

Citation: 482 U.S. 304 (1987)
Argued: January 14, 1987
Decided: June 9, 1987
Court Below: California Supreme Court
Basis for Review: Appeal
Facts: After buildings owned by the plaintiff church were destroyed by flooding, the county passed an ordinance prohibiting all rebuilding on the land the buildings had occupied. State courts ruled that the church could only seek compensation if the ordinance was found to be an unlaw-

ful *taking and the county did not rescind the ordinance (which it later did).
Issue: Can a government land use regulation, even one that is later withdrawn, be construed as a taking in violation of the Fifth Amendment?
Outcome: The Supreme Court overruled the court below, declaring that withdrawal of an ordinance is insufficient compensation; in addition, the local government must pay for any interference with the owner's use of private property occurring during the period between passage and rescission of such an ordinance.
Vote: 6-3
Participating: Rehnquist, Brennan, White, Marshall, Blackmun, Powell, Stevens, O'Connor, Scalia
Opinions: Rehnquist for the Court; Stevens, joined by Blackmun and O'Connor, dissenting
Significance: This case marks the first time that the Supreme Court found that land use regulation can constitute an exercise of *eminent domain for which the owner of the affected property is owed compensation. The Court made its ruling applicable even to regulations that prove to be only temporary, if they are found to effect a taking. On *remand, the lower courts found that the Los Angeles regulation did not constitute a taking.

CLUB ASSOCIATION V. CITY OF NEW YORK

Citation: 487 U.S. 1 (1988)
Argued: February 23, 1988
Decided: June 20, 1988
Court Below: New York Court of Appeals
Basis for Review: Appeal
Facts: Following the Supreme Court's 1984 decision in *Roberts v. United States Jaycees*, the City of New York drafted an ordinance that differentiated between clubs run by benevolent associations and religious corporations and large private clubs allowing greater public access. The latter were made subject to the city's human rights laws.
Issue: Does the city ordinance violate the First Amendment right to freedom of association?
Outcome: Owing to the greater public access already permitted at large, albeit private clubs, the Court upheld the city ordinance.
Vote: 9-0

Participating: Rehnquist, Brennan, White, Marshall, Blackmun, Stevens, O'Connor, Scalia, Kennedy

Opinions: White for the Court; O'Connor, joined by Kennedy, concurring; and Scalia concurring

Significance: As a direct result of this decision, many private clubs which had restricted their membership to men only began admitting women.

MORRISON V. OLSON

Citation: 487 U.S. 654 (1988)

Argued: April 26, 1988

Decided: June 29, 1988

Court Below: United States Court of Appeals for the District of Columbia Circuit

Basis for Review: Appeal

Facts: Title VI of the Ethics in Government Act, authorizing appointment of special prosecutors by courts and adopted in 1978, was a product of the Watergate scandal, in which a coverup of misdeeds by officials of the Nixon administration was investigated by special prosecutors. Under the act, the special prosecutor was to be appointed by a special court at the attorney general's request and could be removed by the attorney general only for good cause.

Issue: Does Title VI of the Ethics in Government Act violate the *separation of powers doctrine?

Outcome: Reasoning that the removal limitation on this executive branch official appointed by the judiciary did not unduly hamper executive authority, the Court upheld the law.

Vote: 7-1

Participating: Rehnquist, Brennan, White, Marshall, Blackmun, Stevens, O'Connor, Scalia (Kennedy not participating)

Opinions: Rehnquist for the Court; Scalia dissenting

Significance: With *Morrison*, the Court affirmed its willingness to accept limitations on the *removal power of the executive branch, as it had done in *Humphrey's Executor v. United States* (1935).

MISTRETTA V. UNITED STATES

Citation: 488 U.S. 361 (1989)

Argued: October 5, 1988

Decided: January 18, 1989

Court Below: United States District Court for the Western District of Missouri

Basis for Review: *Writ of certiorari

Facts: In an attempt to impose more uniformity on sentences handed down by federal courts, in 1984 Congress created the United States Sentencing Commission. This independent commission was to consist of seven members, at least three of them federal judges, to be appointed by the president from a list drawn up by the Judicial Conference of the United States. The president also was vested with the power to remove commission members.

Issue: Does the commission, which grants presidentially appointed federal judges policy making powers, violate the doctrine of *separation of powers?

Outcome: The structure of the commission was upheld without qualification.

Vote: 8-1

Participating: Rehnquist, Brennan, White, Marshall, Blackmun, Stevens, O'Connor, Scalia, Kennedy

Opinions: Blackmun for the Court; Scalia dissenting

Significance: Despite the unusual nature of the commission, it was not a court and was not controlled by the judiciary. The Court deemed it an "essentially neutral endeavor" requiring judicial participation. This successful body (which included future Supreme Court Justice Stephen Breyer) developed sentencing guidelines for all federal offenses over the course of four years of sessions.

RICHMOND V. J.A. CROSON CO.

Citation: 488 U.S. 469 (1989)

Argued: October 5, 1988

Decided: January 23, 1989

Court Below: United States Fourth Circuit Court of Appeals

Basis for Review: Appeal

Facts: Richmond, Virginia, enacted a business plan requiring its prime contractors to allocate 30 percent of the value of each contract to minority subcontractors.

Issue: Does such an affirmative action plan enacted by a state violate the *Equal Protection Clause of the Fourteenth Amendment?

Outcome: The Court struck the plan down as unconstitutional.

Vote: 6-3

Participating: Rehnquist, Brennan, White, Marshall, Blackmun, Stevens, O'Connor, Scalia, Kennedy

Opinions: O'Connor for the *plurality; Stevens and Kennedy concurring in part; Scalia concurring; Marshall, joined by Brennan and Blackmun, dissenting; and Blackmun, joined by Brennan, dissenting

Significance: Although Richmond claimed it had modeled its plan after the federal set-asides approved in *Fullilove v. Klutznick* (1980), in her opinion for a plurality of the Court Justice O'Connor stated that a different constitutional standard applied to affirmative action at the federal level. The Court applied *strict scrutiny to state affirmative action plans, requiring that they include an unspecified combination of justifying factors.

NATIONAL TREASURY EMPLOYEES UNION V. VON RAAB; SKINNER V. RAILWAY LABOR EXECUTIVES' ASSOCIATION

Citation: 489 U.S. 656 (1989) (*Von Raab*); 489 U.S. 602 (1989) (*Skinner*)

Argued: November 2, 1988

Decided: March 21, 1989

Court Below: United States Fifth Circuit Court of Appeals

Bases for Review: *Writs of certiorari

Facts: These cases, decided together, both addressed the constitutionality of drug testing of employees. In *Von Raab*, drug tests were administered to Customs Service employees seeking promotion to positions where they would be involved with drugs, guns, and classified materials. In *Skinner*, the Federal Railroad Administration proposed administering drug tests to employees involved in serious safety violations or accidents.

Issue: Do such drug tests violate the Fourth Amendment's prohibition on unreasonable search and seizure?

Outcome: In both cases, the Court upheld the procedures.

Vote: 5-4 (*Von Raab*); 7-2 (*Skinner*)

Participating: Rehnquist, Brennan, White, Marshall, Blackmun, Stevens, O'Connor, Scalia, Kennedy

Opinions: *Von Raab:* Kennedy for the Court; Marshall, joined by Brennan, dissenting; and Scalia, joined by Stevens, dissenting; *Skinner:* Kennedy for the Court; Stevens concurring; Marshall, joined by Brennan, dissenting

Significance: Although the Court found in both cases that the procedures employed by the government did implicate the Fourth Amendment, policy considerations of public safety — including the war on drugs — outweighed the need for the usually required showing of *probable cause.

WARD'S COVE PACKING CO. V. ATONIO

Citation: 490 U.S. 642 (1989)

Argued: January 18, 1989

Decided: June 5, 1989

Court Below: United States Ninth Circuit Court of Appeals

Basis for Review: *Writ of certiorari

Facts: Employees of an Alaska salmon cannery brought suit, claiming employment discrimination. In their *disparate impact case, the employees showed that while a high percentage of unskilled, low-paying cannery jobs were held by nonwhite employees, only a small percentage held skilled, higher paying non-cannery positions.

Issue: Are statistical data sufficient to make out a case of employment discrimination?

Outcome: Because the Court found that the employees' data was flawed, the Court held that the employees had failed to make out a case.

Vote: 5-4

Participating: Rehnquist, Brennan, White, Marshall, Blackmun, Stevens, O'Connor, Scalia, Kennedy

Opinions: White for the Court; Blackmun, joined by Brennan and Marshall, dissenting, and Stevens, joined by Brennan, Marshall, and Blackmun, dissenting

Significance: In *Ward's Cove*, the Rehnquist Court made several rulings that had far-reaching effects. Most significantly, the Court shifted the *burden of proof in Title VII employment discrimination cases from defendants to plaintiffs, holding that plaintiffs must show that the employment practices they challenge actually caused a statistical disparity. Defendants could then counter with a "business necessity" defense to any intentional discrimination. Congress reacted by passing the Civil Rights Act of 1991, which eliminated the business justification defense and once again shifted the burden of proof to defendants, thereby making it easier for women and minorities to prevail in employment discrimination suits.

MARTIN V. WILKS

Citation: 490 U.S. 755 (1989)
Argued: January 18, 1989
Decided: June 12, 1989
Court Below: United States Eleventh Circuit Court of Appeals
Basis for Review: *Writ of certiorari
Facts: African American fire fighters in Birmingham, Alabama, brought suit alleging the city engaged in racially discriminatory employment practices. Prior to approving *consent decrees instituting new, racially sensitive hiring and promotion policies, the federal court issued a notice of public hearing regarding the decrees. A group of white fire fighters then filed a reverse discrimination suit against the city, alleging that the consent decrees would result in discrimination against them.
Issue: Should the white fire fighters have been made parties to the original litigation?
Outcome: The Court found that the white firemen did have a stake in the outcome of the original lawsuit and ruled that they should have been allowed to join in that litigation. As they were not, they were not subject to the consent decrees.
Vote: 5-4
Participating: Rehnquist, Brennan, White, Marshall, Blackmun, Stevens, O'Connor, Scalia, Kennedy
Opinions: Rehnquist for the Court; Stevens, joined by Brennan, Marshall, and Blackmun, dissenting

Significance: The Court held, in effect, that it was the responsibility of plaintiffs in employment discrimination suits to bring all potentially affected parties into their action. This *holding was limited by the Civil Rights Act of 1991, thus making it more problematical for third parties to undermine consent decrees in employment discrimination cases.

PATTERSON V. MCLEAN CREDIT UNION

Citation: 491 U.S. 164 (1989)
Argued: February 29, 1988; reargued October 12, 1988
Decided: June 15, 1989
Court Below: United States Fourth Circuit Court of Appeals
Basis for Review: *Writ of certiorari
Facts: An African American woman brought suit for employment discrimination under Title 42, section 1981, of the 1866 Civil Rights Act. Her employer won in the lower court. After hearing *oral argument in her case, the Supreme Court ordered reargument on the issue of whether or not *Runyon v. McCrary* (1976), the last case to use section 1981 as a means of outlawing discrimination, should be overruled. *Runyon* had the effect of outlawing discrimination in all contracts, private and public, and the more conservative members of the Rehnquist Court were eager to curtail its broad sweep. Justices Harry Blackmun, John Paul Stevens, William Brennan, and Thurgood Marshall objected strenuously to the reargument order.
Issue: Should *Runyon's* interpretation of section 1821 be overruled?
Outcome: Citing the principle of *stare decisis, the Court declined to overrule Runyon.
Vote: 9-0
Participating: Rehnquist, Brennan, White, Marshall, Blackmun, Stevens, O'Connor, Scalia, Kennedy
Opinions: Kennedy for the Court; Brennan, joined by Marshall, Blackmun, and Stevens, concurring in the judgment and dissenting in part
Significance: Although it did not overrule *Runyon*, *Patterson* modified the earlier case by limiting the effect of section 1821 to the right

to make contracts. The statute did not, Justice Kennedy wrote for the Court, extend to breaches of existing contracts or to the imposition of discriminatory working conditions. The Civil Rights Act of 1991 in turn overruled this narrow reading of section 1821.

TEXAS V. JOHNSON

Citation: 491 U.S. 397 (1989)
Argued: March 21, 1989
Decided: June 21, 1989
Court Below: Texas Court of Criminal Appeals
Basis for Review: *Writ of certiorari
Facts: To protest policies of the Reagan administration, Johnson burned an American flag during the Republican National Convention in Dallas, Texas. He was convicted under a Texas statute making it a crime willfully to desecrate the flag. His sentence and fine were reversed on appeal.
Issue: Does flag burning constitute a form of symbolic speech protected by the First Amendment?
Outcome: Reasoning that flag burning is a form of "expressive conduct" intended to "convey a particularized message," Justice Brennan, writing for the Court, upheld the ruling below.
Vote: 5-4
Participating: Rehnquist, Brennan, White, Marshall, Blackmun, Stevens, O'Connor, Scalia, Kennedy
Opinions: Brennan for the Court; Rehnquist, joined by White and O'Connor, dissenting; and Stevens dissenting
Significance: Although the Court previously had ruled in favor of defendants in flag desecration cases, it had never before done so in such a direct fashion. Public reaction to *Johnson* was swift, and within months Congress passed the Flag Protection Act of 1989, but the Court held the act unconstitutional in *United States v. Eichman* (1990).

PENRY V. LYNAUGH

Citation: 492 U.S. 302 (1989)
Argued: January 11, 1989
Decided: June 26, 1989
Court Below: United States Fifth Circuit Court of Appeals

Basis for Review: *Writ of certiorari
Facts: Penry, who was moderately mentally retarded, was sentenced to death for rape and murder.
Issue: Does execution of the mentally retarded violate the Eighth Amendment's ban on cruel and unusual punishment?
Outcome: Because the trial court failed to advise the jury that it could take mitigating circumstances — for example, the fact that Penry's mental condition may have resulted from childhood beatings — into account, the Court reversed his sentence.
Vote: 5-4
Participating: Rehnquist, Brennan, White, Marshall, Blackmun, Stevens, O'Connor, Scalia, Kennedy
Opinions: O'Connor for the *plurality; Brennan, joined by Marshall, concurring in part and dissenting in part; Stevens, joined by Blackmun, concurring in part and dissenting in part; and Scalia, joined by Rehnquist, White, and Kennedy, concurring in part and dissenting in part
Significance: While emphasizing the importance of mitigating factors in sentencing mentally retarded individuals to death, the Court nonetheless held that unless such individuals are legally insane, imposition of the death penalty under such circumstances is constitutionally permissible.

STANFORD V. KENTUCKY

Citation: 492 U.S. 361 (1989)
Argued: March 27, 1989
Decided: June 26, 1989
Court Below: Kentucky Supreme Court
Basis for Review: *Writ of certiorari
Facts: Kevin Stanford was sentenced to death for a murder he committed when he was seventeen years, four months old.
Issue: Does application of the death penalty to juveniles violate the Eighth Amendment's ban on cruel and unusual punishment?
Outcome: Citing the fact that juveniles were sentenced to death at the time the Bill of Rights was drafted, and refuting the contention that application of *capital punishment to juveniles now would violate "evolving standards of

decency," the Court upheld Stanford's sentence.

Vote: 5-4

Participating: Rehnquist, Brennan, White, Marshall, Blackmun, Stevens, O'Connor, Scalia, Kennedy

Opinions: Scalia for the Court; O'Connor concurring; Brennan, Marshall, Blackmun, and Stevens, dissenting

Significance: In a gesture towards contemporary "standards of decency," the Rehnquist Court held that it would be unconstitutional for states to impose the death penalty on individuals who were under the age of sixteen at the time of their offenses.

ALLEGHENY COUNTY V. ACLU GREATER PITTSBURGH CHAPTER

Citation: 492 U.S. 573 (1989)

Argued: February 22, 1989

Decided: July 3, 1989

Court Below: United States Third Circuit Court of Appeals

Basis for Review: *Writ of certiorari

Facts: As a Christmas display, Allegheny County placed a creche, together with a banner reading "Gloria in Excelsis Deo," on its courthouse steps. Another display outside an office building, jointly owned by the county and the city of Pittsburgh, consisted of a Christmas tree, a menorah, and a sign saluting the holiday season.

Issue: Do such displays violate the doctrine of separation of church and state mandated by the First Amendment's *Establishment Clause?

Outcome: Because the Allegheny County creche display focused on religious symbols, rather than the general holiday season, the Court found it constitutionally impermissible. The display including the menorah, however, was found constitutionally permissible.

Vote: 5-4 (agreeing on unconstitutionality of the creche display); 6-3 (upholding the menorah display)

Participating: Rehnquist, Brennan, White, Marshall, Blackmun, Stevens, O'Connor, Scalia, Kennedy

Opinions: Blackmun for the *plurality; O'Connor, joined by Brennan and Stevens, concurring; Brennan, joined by Marshall and Stevens,

concurring in part and dissenting in part; Stevens, joined by Brennan and Marshall, concurring in part and dissenting in part; and Kennedy, joined by White and Scalia, concurring in part and dissenting in part

Significance: At the same time it struck down the Allegheny County display by one vote, the Court also voted 6 to 3 that a menorah, set in the context of other, secular symbols of the season displayed outside another government building, did not violate the Establishment Clause. The distinction in *Allegheny County* rests on earlier Supreme Court applications of the so-called "Lemon test" (enunciated in 1971 in *Lemon v. Kurtzman*) permitting government displays of religious symbols set in a context that does not imply excessive government entanglement of church and state.

WEBSTER V. REPRODUCTIVE HEALTH SERVICES

Citation: 492 U.S. 490 (1989)

Argued: April 26, 1989

Decided: July 3, 1989

Court Below: United States Eighth Circuit Court of Appeals

Basis for Review: Appeal

Facts: Missouri passed new restrictions on abortions, including a ban on the use of state property for abortions and a requirement that physicians test for the viability of any fetus they judged to be at least 20 weeks in gestation.

Issue: Does the Missouri abortion statute violate the constitutional framework of *Roe v. Wade* (1973)?

Outcome: Without overruling *Roe v. Wade*, the Court upheld the statute.

Vote: 5-4

Participating: Rehnquist, Brennan, White, Marshall, Blackmun, Stevens, O'Connor, Scalia, Kennedy

Opinions: Rehnquist for the *plurality; O'Connor and Scalia concurring; Blackmun, joined by Brennan and Marshall, concurring in part and dissenting in part; and Stevens concurring in part and dissenting in part

Significance: Although Justice Rehnquist argued

that upholding the statute required formal modification of *Roe v. Wade*, other justices declined to join in this view, finding arguments that justified the new law as a third-trimester regulation permissible under *Roe*. Antiabortionists and pro-choice supporters alike took *Webster* as a sign that the Court was willing not only to narrow *Roe*, but eventually to overturn it altogether.

MISSOURI V. JENKINS

Citation: 495 U.S. 33 (1990)
Argued: October 30, 1989
Decided: April 18, 1990
Court Below: United States Eighth Circuit Court of Appeals
Basis for Review: *Writ of certiorari
Facts: As a remedy for ongoing school segregation in a Kansas City, Missouri, school district, the federal district court devised a plan for "magnet" schools designed to attract suburban students back to city schools. The expensive new magnet schools were to be financed 75 percent by the state and 25 percent by the school district. The latter contribution exceeded limits set by the state, but the Court nonetheless ordered property taxes to be doubled within the district.
Issue: Does the federal court order impermissibly violate intergovernmental tax immunities?
Outcome: Declining to reach the constitutional issue, the Court approved an indirect method of permitting the district itself to raise the necessary taxes.
Vote: 9-0
Participating: Rehnquist, Brennan, White, Marshall, Blackmun, Stevens, O'Connor, Scalia, Kennedy
Opinions: White for the Court; Kennedy, joined by Rehnquist, O'Connor, and Scalia, concurring
Significance: *Jenkins* is a vivid illustration that difficulties in enforcing school desegregation while respecting state and local autonomy continue, hampered by constitutional barriers.

UNITED STATES V. EICHMAN

Citation: 496 U.S. 310 (1990)
Argued: May 14, 1990
Decided: June 11, 1990
Court Below: United States District Court for the Western District of Washington
Basis for Review: Appeal
Facts: Eichman was convicted under the 1989 Flag Protection Act for burning an American flag. On the basis of *Texas v. Johnson* (1989), the district court overturned his conviction.
Issue: Does the Flag Protection Act, which bans all forms of flag mistreatment — rather than singling out acts intended to convey an offensive message as did the statute at issue in *Johnson* — nonetheless violate the First Amendment's guarantee of *free expression?
Outcome: Stating that the government's interest as expressed in the legislation is "related to the suppression of free expression," the Supreme Court affirmed the decision below and overturned the Flag Protection Act.
Vote: 5-4
Participating: Rehnquist, Brennan, White, Marshall, Blackmun, Stevens, O'Connor, Scalia, Kennedy
Opinions: Brennan for the Court; Stevens, joined by Rehnquist, White, and O'Connor, dissenting
Significance: The government argued that because its statute had no content-based restrictions, it should be judged by a lower standard than *strict scrutiny. However, Justice Brennan, writing for the Court, indicated that a majority of the Supreme Court would always regard flag desecration laws as inherently constitutionally suspect.

CRUZAN V. DIRECTOR, MISSOURI DEPARTMENT OF HEALTH

Citation: 497 U.S. 261 (1990)
Argued: December 6, 1989
Decided: June 25, 1990
Court Below: Missouri Supreme Court
Basis for Review: *Writ of certiorari
Facts: Nancy Cruzan, who was in a permanent coma as the result of an automobile accident, was being kept alive by artificial nutrition. Her parents, citing Cruzan's previous informal declarations that she never wished to be kept alive in a vegetative state, sought court permission to have the artificial nutrition withdrawn, but their

request was rejected.

Issue: Do guardians of dying, incompetent patients have a constitutionally protected right to reject unwanted medical treatment on behalf of their wards?

Outcome: Citing the lack of evidence of a previous clear expression of the patient's wishes, the Supreme Court affirmed the decision below.

Vote: 5-4

Participating: Rehnquist, Brennan, White, Marshall, Blackmun, Stevens, O'Connor, Scalia, Kennedy

Opinions: Rehnquist for the Court; O'Connor, joined by Scalia, concurring; Brennan, joined by Marshall, Blackmun, and Stevens, dissenting

Significance: This was the Court's first case directly to address the constitutional rights of the dying. Justice Rehnquist, writing for the Court, upheld the state's right to demand clear evidence of incompetent patients' wishes — expressed prior to being rendered incapable of speaking for themselves — as a legitimate protection against potential abuses. Still, the Court did assume that such a patient has a constitutionally protected right to reject potentially life-saving treatment, whether in the face of imminent death or prolonged suffering. Furthermore, *Cruzan* indicated a willingness on the part of the Court to respect fully the prior wishes of a patient even after the onset of incompetence.

HODGSON V. MINNESOTA

Citation: 497 U.S. 417 (1990)
Argued: November 29, 1989
Decided: June 25, 1990
Court Below: United States Eighth Circuit Court of Appeals
Basis for Review: Appeal
Facts: A Minnesota statute, requiring that both parents be notified in advance of the procedure, imposed new restrictions on minors seeking abortions. The only exception to this requirement were minor females who obtained a court ruling stating that they were either mature enough to undergo abortion without parental notice or that such notice would not be in their best interests.
Issue: Is the parental notice requirement in advance of abortion constitutional?

Outcome: While a majority of the Court struck down the two-parent notification requirement, a different majority upheld the provision for judicial intervention.

Vote: 5-4 (against two-parent notification); 5-4 (in favor of the judicial alternative)

Participating: Rehnquist, Brennan, White, Marshall, Blackmun, Stevens, O'Connor, Scalia, Kennedy

Opinions: Stevens for the *plurality; O'Connor concurring; Marshall concurring in part and, joined by Brennan and Blackmun, dissenting in part; Scalia concurring in part and dissenting in part; and Kennedy, concurring in part and, joined by Rehnquist, White, and Scalia, dissenting in part

Significance: In *Hodgson*, the Court accepted even greater restrictions on abortion than it upheld in *Webster v. Reproductive Health Services* (1989). However, *Hodgson* also marked the first time that Justice O'Connor held such a restriction to be unconstitutional, as she did again the next year in *Rust v. Sullivan* (1991). In *Planned Parenthood of Pennsylvania v. Casey* (1992), she would join with Justices Kennedy and Souter to form a new coalition resisting the momentum to overturn *Roe v. Wade* (1973).

MARYLAND V. CRAIG

Citation: 497 U.S. 836 (1990)
Argued: April 18, 1990
Decided: June 27, 1990
Court Below: Maryland Court of Appeals
Basis for Review: *Writ of certiorari
Facts: Craig was convicted of the crime of child abuse after a trial at which her alleged victim testified by one-way closed circuit television, as permitted by state law.
Issue: Does the Maryland law permitting such remote testimony by children at criminal trials violate the Sixth Amendment *Confrontation Clause?
Outcome: Finding that the purposes of the Sixth Amendment — such as the right to cross-examine a witness — were met by this procedure, the Court upheld the Maryland statute.

Vote: 5-4
Participating: Rehnquist, Brennan, White, Marshall, Blackmun, Stevens, O'Connor, Scalia, Kennedy
Opinions: O'Connor for the Court; Scalia, joined by Brennan, Marshall, and Stevens, dissenting
Significance: *Craig* marked a significant departure from the customary interpretation of the Confrontation Clause, which provides the criminally accused a right to confront his or her accuser face-to-face. However, Justice O'Connor, writing for the Court, stressed that the right to confront an accuser face-to-face was mitigated in cases such as *Craig* by the state's interest in protecting children from being forced to confront persons who allegedly had harmed them.

METRO BROADCASTING, INC. V. FEDERAL COMMUNICATIONS COMMISSION

Citation: 497 U.S. 547 (1990)
Argued: March 28, 1990
Decided: June 27, 1990
Court Below: United States Court of Appeals for the District of Columbia Circuit
Basis for Review: *Writ of certiorari
Facts: Two federal affirmative action programs, set up to increase minority ownership of broadcast licenses, were challenged.
Issue: Do such programs — intended to promote affirmative action, rather than rectify past discrimination — violate the *equal protection principle?
Outcome: The Court upheld Congress's power to enact legislation prospectively favoring minority groups.
Vote: 5-4
Participating: Rehnquist, Brennan, White, Marshall, Blackmun, Stevens, O'Connor, Scalia, Kennedy
Opinions: Brennan for the Court; Stevens concurring; O'Connor, joined by Rehnquist, Scalia, and Kennedy, dissenting; and Kennedy, joined by Scalia, dissenting
Significance: By endorsing the notion that the federal government has more power than state governments in the area of affirmative action,

Metro Broadcasting extended *Fullilove v. Klutznick* (1980) to promote a policy to benefit minorities in the future, rather than remedy past or present harm.

PACIFIC MUTUAL LIFE INSURANCE CO. V. HASLIP

Citation: 499 U.S. 1 (1991)
Argued: October 3, 1990
Decided: March 4, 1991
Court Below: Alabama Supreme Court
Basis for Review: *Writ of certiorari
Facts: The Pacific Mutual Insurance Company challenged as excessive a one million dollar punitive damage award set by an Alabama jury in a case involving fraud on the part of one of the company's agents.
Issue: Do Alabama court procedures adequately protect rational decision-making on the part of juries, or do they violate the Fourteenth Amendment's *due process guarantee?
Outcome: Justice Blackmun, writing for the Court, upheld the procedures and the award.
Vote: 7-1
Participating: Rehnquist, White, Marshall, Blackmun, Stevens, O'Connor, Scalia, Kennedy (Souter not participating)
Opinions: Blackmun for the Court; Scalia and Kennedy concurring; O'Connor dissenting
Significance: As Justice Blackmun wrote, it traditionally has been the jury's role to determine punitive damage awards. But his opinion also suggested that in some cases the size of such awards could violate due process. This suggestion, together with an increase in public concern about the increasing size of punitive damage awards, has resulted in legislative attempts to address the issue and will almost certainly lead to other High Court battles concerning punitive damages.

RUST V. SULLIVAN

Citation: 500 U.S. 173 (1991)
Argued: October 30, 1990
Decided: May 23, 1991
Court Below: United States Second Circuit Court of Appeals
Basis for Review: *Writ of certiorari

Facts: In 1988 the Reagan administration imposed a gag order on family planning services that received federal funds. Formerly forbidden to perform abortions, the clinics now were also barred from providing clients with any information concerning abortions.

Issue: Do the new regulations violate the First Amendment's guarantee of *freedom of speech, as well as the client's right to abortion under *Roe v. Wade* (1973)?

Outcome: The new regulations were upheld.

Vote: 5-4

Participating: Rehnquist, White, Marshall, Blackmun, Stevens, O'Connor, Scalia, Kennedy, Souter

Opinions: Rehnquist for the Court; Blackmun, joined by Marshall, Stevens, and O'Connor, dissenting; and Stevens and O'Connor dissenting

Significance: While rebuffing the free speech argument against the regulations, the Court went to some pains to explain its disposition of the case in terms of the doctrine of unconstitutional conditions or conditional spending. Government was free, Justice Rehnquist wrote for the Court, to place conditions on the clinic to insure that government moneys were spent only for those purposes for which they were allocated. While the gag rule on doctors and other clinic personnel might be unconstitutional on its face, these individuals were still free to advise women about abortion in locations not associated with the program receiving federal funds.

CALIFORNIA V. ACEVEDO

Citation: 500 U.S. 565 (1991)
Argued: January 8, 1991
Decided: May 30, 1991
Court Below: California Court of Appeal
Basis for Review: *Writ of certiorari
Facts: Charles Acevedo pleaded guilty to possession of marijuana for purposes of sale after a denial of his motion to suppress evidence seized from a sealed container in his car trunk.

Issue: Which rule governs a police search of a closed container in an automobile: the *United States v. Ross* (1982) rule, permitting a search of the container if police have *probable cause to

search the car, or the *Arkansas v. Sanders* (1979) rule, which requires a *warrant if the closed container merely turns up in a vehicle?

Outcome: The Court upheld Acevedo's sentence and eliminated the warrant requirement for such searches.

Vote: 6-3

Participating: Rehnquist, White, Marshall, Blackmun, Stevens, O'Connor, Scalia, Kennedy, Souter

Opinions: Blackmun for the Court; Scalia concurring; White dissenting; and Stevens, joined by Marshall, dissenting

Significance: Commentators have speculated that this constriction of the probable cause standard could be extended to cover searches of closed containers found outside automobiles.

MASSON V. NEW YORKER MAGAZINE, INC.

Citation: 501 U.S. 496 (1991)
Argued: January 14, 1991
Decided: June 20, 1991
Court Below: United States Ninth Circuit Court of Appeals
Basis for Review: *Writ of certiorari
Facts: In a series of articles on Dr. Jeffrey Masson published in *The New Yorker* magazine, journalist Janet Malcolm allegedly deliberately misquoted him in such a manner as to libel him. The district court granted *summary judgment to *The New Yorker*, basing its ruling on *New York Times Co. v. Sullivan* (1964), which held that libelous remarks about public figures are only actionable in court if they are made with "knowledge of falsity " or "reckless disregard" for the truth. The *appellate court affirmed, stating that altered quotations are protected by the First Amendment so long as they contain the "substantial truth" of what was said.

Issue: Can deliberate alterations of actual statements made by public figures constitute libel?

Outcome: The Rehnquist Court reversed the ruling below.

Vote: 7-2

Participating: Rehnquist, White, Marshall, Blackmun, Stevens, O'Connor, Scalia, Kennedy, Souter

Opinions: Kennedy for the Court; White, joined

by Scalia, concurring in part and dissenting in part
Significance: In this case of *first impression, the Court ruled that a deliberate alteration can indeed constitute libel if it "results in a material change in the meaning conveyed by the statement," and *remanded the case. The jury found for Masson but could not agree on damages. A new trial finally resulted in a verdict for Malcolm.

BARNES V. GLEN THEATRE, INC.

Citation: 501 U.S. 560 (1991)
Argued: January 8, 1991
Decided: June 21, 1991
Court Below: United States Seventh Circuit Court of Appeals
Basis for Review: *Writ of certiorari
Facts: Two South Bend, Indiana, enterprises featuring totally nude dancers were convicted of having violated a state law prohibiting all intentional public nudity.
Issue: Does nude dancing constitute a form of expressive conduct eligible for First Amendment protection and therefore outside the Indiana statute?
Outcome: The Court upheld the statute.
Vote: 5-4
Participating: Rehnquist, White, Marshall, Blackmun, Stevens, O'Connor, Scalia, Kennedy, Souter
Opinions: Rehnquist for the Court; Scalia concurring; White, joined by Marshall, Blackmun, and Stevens, dissenting
Significance: Justice Rehnquist's opinion for the Court found the state statute to be a reasonable "time, place, and manner" restriction on speech, intended to protect against public nudity, not erotic dancing. The law, he stated, was "unrelated to the suppression of free expression," but as Justice White's dissent pointed out, the dancers' nudity was a significant — and expressive — part of their conduct.

PAYNE V. TENNESSEE

Citation: 501 U.S. 808 (1991)
Argued: April 24, 1991
Decided: June 27, 1991
Court Below: Tennessee Supreme Court

Basis for Review: *Writ of certiorari
Facts: Payne was tried and convicted of first degree murder, punishable by death in Tennessee. During the sentencing phase of the trial, a surviving victim's grandmother was permitted to talk about the impact on her grandson of the deaths of his mother and sister, both killed by Payne. In addition, in closing argument the prosecution discussed the effects of Payne's actions on the victims' family.
Issue: Is presentation at trial of such so-called "victim-impact" evidence violative of the Eighth Amendment?
Outcome: The Court upheld Payne's sentence.
Vote: 6-3
Participating: Rehnquist, White, Marshall, Blackmun, Stevens, O'Connor, Scalia, Kennedy, Souter
Opinions: Rehnquist for the Court; O'Connor, joined by White and Kennedy, concurring; Scalia, joined in part by O'Connor and Kennedy, concurring; Souter, joined by Kennedy, concurring; Marshall, joined by Blackmun, dissenting; and Stevens, joined by Blackmun, dissenting
Significance: In permitting both victim-impact testimony and prosecutorial references to victim impact, the Rehnquist Court overruled its own recent *precedents, *Booth v. Maryland* (1987) and *South Carolina v. Gathers* (1989).

SIMON & SCHUSTER V. CRIME VICTIMS BOARD

Citation: 502 U.S. 105 (1991)
Argued: October 15, 1991
Decided: December 10, 1991
Court Below: United States Second Circuit Court of Appeals
Basis for Review: *Writ of certiorari
Facts: Publisher Simon & Schuster sued the New York State Crime Board seeking an order declaring the state "Son of Sam" law (named for mass murderer David Berkowitz's pseudonym) unconstitutional. The law required all proceeds from works describing crimes committed by convicted criminals to be deposited in an escrow account for the benefit of crime victims.
Issue: Does the Son of Sam law violate First Amendment *free speech guarantees?

Outcome: The Court unanimously struck the statute down.
Vote: 8-0
Participating: Rehnquist, White, Blackmun, Stevens, O'Connor, Scalia, Kennedy, Souter (Thomas not participating)
Opinions: O'Connor for the Court; Blackmun and Kennedy concurring
Significance: The statute was struck down primarily because it singled out a particular type of speech by placing a burden on it which was not imposed on other types of speech. The Court conceded that the state had a compelling interest in making criminals compensate their victims, but found the Son of Sam law to be too broad, in that it also affected literature unrelated to the crimes from which the criminals sought to benefit.

HUDSON V. MCMILLIAN

Citation: 503 U.S. 1 (1992)
Argued: November 13, 1991
Decided: February 25, 1992
Court Below: United States Fifth Circuit Court of Appeals
Basis for Review: *Writ of certiorari
Facts: Inmate Hudson argued with McMillian, a corrections officer, who then beat Hudson while another officer helped and a supervisor looked on. While Hudson's suit against the officers was upheld by a magistrate, the *appellate court found that Hudson's injuries were not significant enough to support a claimed use of excessive force against him.
Issue: What constitutes proof of cruel and unusual punishment endured by a prison inmate?
Outcome: The Court held that proof of excessive force, even if it does not cause serious injury, can violate the Eighth Amendment.
Vote: 7-2
Participating: Rehnquist, White, Blackmun, Stevens, O'Connor, Scalia, Kennedy, Souter, Thomas
Opinions: O'Connor for the Court; Stevens and Blackmun concurring; Thomas, joined by Scalia, dissenting
Significance: In this clarification of the standards governing the *Cruel and Unusual Punishment

Clause, the Court held that it is the severity of the punishment, not of the resulting injury, that is determinative. The Court thus distinguished between claims based on the state of a prisoner's confinement and those based on abuse.

FREEMAN V. PITTS

Citation: 503 U.S. 467 (1992)
Argued: October 7, 1991
Decided: March 31, 1992
Court Below: United States Eleventh Circuit Court of Appeals
Basis for Review: *Writ of certiorari
Facts: In 1969, following a suit by African American students in federal court, the district court entered a desegregation order against the DeKalb County, Georgia, school system. In 1986 the school system filed a *motion to dismiss the ongoing litigation, which the district court granted, blaming the system's continued segregation on population shifts. The circuit court reversed this decision on appeal, citing *Green v. County School Board of New Kent County* (1968).
Issue: Can a district court relinquish control of a desegregation order before a school system has erased the vestiges of past segregation?
Outcome: The Supreme Court reversed the ruling below, granting district courts discretion as to when to withdraw from supervision of school desegregation efforts.
Vote: 8-0
Participating: Rehnquist, White, Blackmun, Stevens, O'Connor, Scalia, Kennedy, Souter (Thomas not participating)
Opinions: Kennedy for the Court; Scalia and Souter concurring; and Blackmun, joined by Stevens and O'Connor, concurring
Significance: By deferring to district courts in this case, the Rehnquist Court permitted them the opportunity to withdraw from school desegregation efforts before integration is achieved.

NEW YORK V. UNITED STATES

Citation: 112 S.Ct. 2408 (1992)
Argued: March 30, 1992
Decided: June 19, 1992

Court Below: United States Second Circuit Court of Appeals

Basis for Review: *Writ of certiorari

Facts: In 1985 Congress passed the Low-Level Radioactive Waste Policy Amendments Act (LLR-WPAA), a scheme for disposing of nuclear contaminants. The act holds each of the 50 states responsible for disposing of waste generated within its borders. States that fail to provide for permanent disposal of their nuclear wastes must "take title, or possession" of them. The state of New York sued, claiming the statute infringed on state *sovereignty, but the district court dismissed New York's complaint, and the circuit court affirmed the dismissal.

Issue: Does the LLRWPAA violate the Tenth Amendment's reservation to the states of those powers not expressly enumerated elsewhere in the Constitution?

Outcome: Reversing the lower courts, the Supreme Court struck the act down as unconstitutional.

Vote: 6-3

Participating: Rehnquist, White, Blackmun, Stevens, O'Connor, Scalia, Kennedy, Souter, Thomas

Opinions: O'Connor for the Court; White, joined by Blackmun and Stevens, concurring in part and dissenting in part; and Stevens concurring in part and dissenting in part

Significance: *New York v. United States* represents an attempt on the part of the Rehnquist Court to define its attitude toward *federalism. In *National League of Cities v. Usery* (1976), Justice Rehnquist had written an opinion for the Burger Court which, for the first time since the New Deal, struck down on grounds of federalism federal legislation enacted under the *Commerce Clause. Then, in *Garcia v. San Antonio Metropolitan Transit Authority* (1985), the Burger Court overruled *Usery* by a 5 to 4 vote. In *New York v. United States*, the Court was able to distinguish *Garcia* by pointing out that while the legislation at issue in the earlier cases affected both states and private parties, the LLRWPAA impacted only states and thus had a more direct connection with the Tenth Amendment.

R.A.V. V. ST. PAUL

Citation: 112 S.Ct. 2538 (1992)

Argued: December 4, 1991

Decided: June 22, 1992

Court Below: Minnesota Supreme Court

Basis for Review: *Writ of certiorari

Facts: In 1990 St. Paul, Minnesota, passed the St. Paul Bias-Motivated Crime Ordinance, aimed at combating racist speech and bias-related crime. R.A.V. was charged under the ordinance with burning a cross on an African American family's lawn.

Issue: Does the ordinance violate the First Amendment's *free speech protections?

Outcome: Reasoning that while the ordinance permissibly outlawed certain constitutionally unprotected "fighting words," but not others, the Court struck it down and reversed and *remanded R.A.V.'s case.

Vote: 9-0

Participating: Rehnquist, White, Blackmun, Stevens, O'Connor, Scalia, Kennedy, Souter, Thomas

Opinions: Scalia for the Court; White, joined by Blackmun, O'Connor, and Stevens, concurring; Blackmun concurring; Stevens, joined by White and Blackmun, concurring in part

Significance: *R.A.V.* illustrates the difficulty of drafting content-based legislation intended to regulate speech. Whereas restrictions on time, place, and manner, such as the ordinance prohibiting demonstrations aimed at private residences in *Frisby v. Schultz* (1988), have been upheld, the Court consistently has struck down overbroad regulations such as those under consideration in *R.A.V.* and *United States v. Eichman* (1990).

CIPOLLONE V. LIGGETT GROUP, INC.

Citation: 112 S.Ct. 2608 (1992)

Argued: October 8, 1991; reargued January 13, 1992

Decided: June 24, 1992

Court Below: United States Third Circuit Court of Appeals

Basis for Review: *Writ of certiorari

Facts: Rose Cipollone began smoking in 1942 when she was 16, and she continued to smoke for the next 41 years, even after she developed lung cancer. In 1983 she and her husband Anthony filed suit against a number of cigarette manufacturers, raising a number of *common law claims, such as failure to warn, conspiracy to defraud, breach of express warranty, and fraudulent misrepresentation. A series of appeals and *remands ensued. In 1990 a jury, citing the cigarette manufacturers' breach of express warranty and failure to warn consumers about the potentially harmful effects of smoking, awarded Cipollone's husband $400,000 in damages. (Rose Cipollone had died in the meanwhile). After the *circuit court affirmed this ruling, Liggett appealed to the Supreme Court.

Issue: Do the federal laws requiring warnings on cigarette packages *preempt state common law claims against cigarette manufacturers?

Outcome: The Court held that while federal law bars common law failure to warn claims, it does not preempt others. This ruling precipitated a retrial of *Cipollone*, but after the death of Anthony Cipollone, the Cipollone family withdrew their suit because of mounting legal costs.

Vote: 7-2

Participating: Rehnquist, White, Blackmun, Stevens, O'Connor, Scalia, Kennedy, Souter, Thomas

Opinions: Stevens for the Court; Blackmun, joined by Kennedy and Souter, concurring in part and dissenting in part; and Scalia, joined by Thomas, concurring in part and dissenting in part

Significance: *Cipollone* was the first smoker-death jury award to be upheld on appeal. It weaked the defenses to product liability claims not just of cigarette manufacturers, but also of other manufacturers who have in the past used federal regulations as a shield. Nonetheless, because of the Court's indeterminate pronouncement in *Cipollone*, tobacco litigation continues to appear on federal court *dockets.

INTERNATIONAL SOCIETY FOR KRISHNA CONSCIOUSNESS, INC. V. LEE

Citations: 112 S.Ct. 2701 (1992) (*ISKCON I*);

112 S.Ct. 2709 (1992) (*ISKCON II*); 112 S.Ct. 2711 (1992) (*ISKCON III*)

Argued: March 25, 1992

Decided: June 26, 1992

Court Below: United States Second Circuit Court of Appeals

Basis for Review: *Writ of certiorari

Facts: The Port Authority of New York and New Jersey, responsible for operation of the airports in the vicinity of New York City, passed a regulation prohibiting the solicitation of money and distribution of literature in airport terminals. The International Society for Krishna Consciousness (ISKON), a religious group, challenged the regulation as a violation of First Amendment rights.

Issue: Are airports *public fora where First Amendment rights are fully protected?

Outcome: In three separate opinions, the Court ruled as follows: because airports are not public fora, the ban on solicitation of money was permissible; and even if airport terminals are not public fora, the ban on distribution was not constitutional. (*ISKCON III* includes the views of Justices O'Connor, Kennedy, and Souter on these two decisions.)

Vote: 6-3 (*ISKCON I*); 5-4 (*ISKCON II*)

Participating: Rehnquist, White, Blackmun, Stevens, O'Connor, Scalia, Kennedy, Souter, Thomas

Opinions: *ISKCON I*: Rehnquist for the Court; O'Connor and Kennedy concurring; Souter, joined by Blackmun and Stevens, dissenting. *ISKCON II*: *Per curiam; Rehnquist, joined by White, Scalia, and Thomas, dissenting. *ISKCON III*: O'Connor and Kennedy, joined by Blackmun, Stevens, and Souter, concurring in part

Significance: This series of splintered decisions left the public forum doctrine established in *Hague v. Congress of Industrial Relations* (1939) in a state of confusion, with a bare majority of the Court distinguishing soliciting from distribution, and a minority of four holding these actions to be indistinguishable. In the end, the decision does seem to narrow the doctrine, coming down on the side of property owners, including the government.

UNITED STATES V. FORDICE

Citation: 112 S.Ct. 2727 (1992)
Argued: November 13, 1991
Decided: June 26, 1992
Court Below: United States Fifth Circuit Court of Appeals
Basis for Review: *Writ of certiorari
Facts: This lawsuit was commenced in 1975 when, two decades after *Brown v. Board of Education (II)* (1955), Mississippi continued to observe policies of racial segregation in its public colleges and universities. Subsequent voluntary adoption of racially neutral policies did not result in integration, however, and the suit proceeded to trial.
Issue: Is adoption of apparently neutral policies by public educational institutions sufficient to fulfill the requirements of *Brown II*?
Outcome: The Court found that the state had an affirmative duty actively to desegregate, not just implement integration on paper.
Vote: 8-1
Participating: Rehnquist, White, Blackmun, Stevens, O'Connor, Scalia, Kennedy, Souter, Thomas
Opinions: White for the Court; O'Connor and Thomas concurring; Scalia dissenting in part
Significance: In *Fordice*, the Court for the first time specified the nature of state responsibility to address continuing — if not legally mandated — segregation in public institutions of higher learning.

PLANNED PARENTHOOD OF PENNSYLVANIA V. CASEY

Citation: 112 S.Ct. 2791 (1992)
Argued: April 22, 1992
Decided: June 29, 1992
Court Below: United States Third Circuit Court of Appeals
Basis for Review: *Writ of certiorari
Facts: Five abortion clinics and a physician challenged several provisions of the Pennsylvania Abortion Control Act that were enacted between 1988 and 1989. These provisions, which included informed consent and elaborate reporting require-

ments, were permanently *enjoined by the district court. The circuit court, applying the "undue burden" test enunciated by Justice O'Connor in *Webster v. Reproductive Health Services* (1989), struck down only a spousal consent provision, upholding the others.
Issue: Are the provisions of the Pennsylvania act at issue unduly burdensome to women wishing to exercise their right to abortion?
Outcome: In a multiplicity of opinions, the Court upheld most of the provisions.
Vote: 5-4
Participating: Rehnquist, White, Blackmun, Stevens, O'Connor, Scalia, Kennedy, Souter, Thomas
Opinions: O'Connor, Kennedy, and Souter writing together for the Court; Stevens concurring in part and dissenting in part; Blackmun concurring in the judgment in part and dissenting in part; Rehnquist, joined by White, Scalia, and Thomas, concurring in part and dissenting in part; Scalia, joined by Rehnquist, White, and Thomas, concurring in part and dissenting in part
Significance: The true significance of *Casey*, which upheld a state's right to enact burdensome regulations on abortions, is that the case clearly stated that *Roe v. Wade* (1973) should not be overruled. Furthermore, this pronouncement was made by a new centrist coalition on the Rehnquist Court.

NIXON V. UNITED STATES

Citation: 113 S.Ct. 732 (1993)
Argued: October 14, 1992
Decided: January 13, 1993
Court Below: United States Court of Appeals for the District of Columbia Circuit
Basis for Review: *Writ of certiorari
Facts: Walter L. Nixon, a former federal district court judge, was *impeached by the Senate, which used a committee to take testimony and hear evidence. Nixon challenged this procedure as a failure of the Senate's constitutional duty to "try" all impeachments.
Issue: Do impeachment proceedings before less than the full Senate violate Article I, section 3, of the Constitution, providing that the "Senate

shall have sole Power to try all Impeachments"?
Outcome: Finding that the Senate has sole discretion over impeachment procedures, the Court
dismissed the case as a nonjusticiable *political
question.
Vote: 9-0
Participating: Rehnquist, White, Blackmun,
Stevens, O'Connor, Scalia, Kennedy, Souter,
Thomas
Opinions: Rehnquist for the Court; Stevens concurring; White, joined by Blackmun and Souter,
concurring
Significance: *Nixon* is only the second political
question case to be entertained by the Court since
it outlined the political question doctrine in *Baker
v. Carr* (1962). It is, above all, a demonstration
of the Rehnquist Court's commitment to upholding the *separation of powers.

ASSOCIATED GENERAL CONTRACTORS V. JACKSONVILLE

Citation: 113 S.Ct. 2297 (1993)
Argued: February 22, 1993
Decided: June 14, 1993
Court Below: United States Eleventh Circuit
Court of Appeals
Basis for Review: *Writ of certiorari
Facts: Nonminority contractors challenged a
Jacksonville, Florida, ordinance which set aside
10 percent of city business for minority contrac-
tors, saying that they would have bid on the con-
tracts had they not been restricted. The circuit
court found that because they had not been
harmed, the nonminority contractors had no
*standing to sue.
Issue: What constitutes standing to challenge
an affirmative action program?
Outcome: Reversing the court below, the
Rehnquist Court held that the affirmative action
program's barrier to competition constituted harm
enough to give the nonminority contractors
standing.
Vote: 7-2
Participating: Rehnquist, White, Blackmun,
Stevens, O'Connor, Scalia, Kennedy, Souter,
Thomas
Opinions: Thomas for the Court; O'Connor,

joined by Blackmun, dissenting
Significance: In this case, the Rehnquist Court,
customarily loyal to the concept of *federalism,
jettisoned this loyalty to increase judicial access
for opponents of affirmative action, a propensity
first shown in *Richmond v. J.A. Croson Co.*
(1989), which announced that such programs
would be subject to *strict scrutiny.

GODINEZ V. MORAN

Citation: 113 S.Ct. 2680 (1993)
Argued: April 21, 1993
Decided: June 24, 1993
Court Below: United States Ninth Circuit Court
of Appeals
Basis for Review: *Writ of certiorari
Facts: Richard Allen Moran killed three people,
including his ex-wife, before turning his gun on
himself and attempting suicide. Two days later,
while hospitalized for self-inflicted wounds, Moran
summoned the police and confessed to all three
killings. After he was diagnosed a depressive and
given medication, he appeared in court and
waived his right to counsel, indicating — mostly
monosyllabically — that he did not wish for any
mitigating evidence to be presented. And indeed,
while representing himself during sentencing, he
presented no defense and was sentenced to death.
After going off his medication while incarcerated, he petitioned the district court for a writ
of *habeas corpus and was denied, but the circuit court reversed his conviction.
Issue: Is the standard for determining a defendant's competency to stand trial the same as that
for determining his competency to plead guilty
and represent himself?
Outcome: The Court held that it is and upheld
Moran's conviction.
Vote: 7-2
Participating: Rehnquist, White, Blackmun,
Stevens, O'Connor, Scalia, Kennedy, Souter,
Thomas
Opinions: Thomas for the Court; Kennedy, joined
by Scalia, concurring; Blackmun, joined by
Stevens, dissenting
Significance: *Godinez* settled a long-standing dis-
pute among circuit courts as to the standard for

competency to plead guilty and to waive counsel. *Due process, said the majority, does not mandate a higher standard or a separate inquiry, but Justice Blackmun dissented, stating that this decision, in effect, meant Moran "volunteer[ed] himself for execution."

ST. MARY'S HONOR CENTER V. HICKS

Citation: 113 S.Ct. 2742 (1993)
Argued: April 20, 1993
Decided: June 25, 1993
Court Below: United States Eighth Circuit Court of Appeals
Basis for Review: *Writ of certiorari
Facts: Hicks, an African American correctional officer at St. Mary's, sued his former employer, alleging that employment discrimination had resulted in his discharge. The trial court, despite determining that St. Mary's proffered reasons for the firing were a pretext, nonetheless held that Hicks had failed to prove that his dismissal stemmed from discriminatory intent. The *appellate court reversed.
Issue: Can an employment discrimination plaintiff prevail if he can demonstrate that his employer's explanations constitute merely a pretext for discrimination?
Outcome: *Holding that a showing of pretext is insufficient to compel judgment for an employment discrimination plaintiff, the Supreme Court reversed the appellate court's ruling.
Vote: 5-4
Participating: Rehnquist, White, Blackmun, Stevens, O'Connor, Scalia, Kennedy, Souter, Thomas
Opinions: Scalia for the Court; Souter, joined by White, Blackmun, and Stevens, dissenting
Significance: Hicks contradicted 20 years of employment discrimination decisions, increasing the likelihood that claims of such discrimination will fail, given the paucity of direct evidence of discrimination.

SHAW V. RENO

Citation: 113 S.Ct. 2816 (1993)
Argued: April 20, 1993

Decided: June 28, 1993
Court Below: United States District Court for the Eastern District of North Carolina
Basis for Review: Appeal
Facts: White North Carolina voters challenged the boundaries drawn for their state's Twelfth Congressional District, which deliberately created a marginal African American majority by including the state's major cities. The district court dismissed their suit.
Issue: Can race-based districting give rise to a claim under the Fourteenth Amendment's *Equal Protection Clause?
Outcome: The Court found that it can.
Vote: 5-4
Participating: Rehnquist, White, Blackmun, Stevens, O'Connor, Scalia, Kennedy, Souter, Thomas
Opinions: O'Connor for the Court; White, joined by Blackmun and Stevens, dissenting; and Blackmun, Stevens, and Souter dissenting
Significance: Although the Court had ruled in United Jewish Organizations of Williamsburgh v. Carey (1977) that race could be used in legislative redistricting, in Shaw, it reasoned that the irregular appearance of the Twelfth District made it resemble "the most egregious racial gerrymandering of the past."

UNITED STATES V. JAMES DANIEL GOOD REAL PROPERTY

Citation: 114 S.Ct. 492 (1993)
Argued: October 6, 1993
Decided: December 13, 1993
Court Below: United States Ninth Circuit Court of Appeals
Basis for Review: *Writ of certiorari
Facts: James Daniel Good owned a house situated on four acres in Hawaii. In 1985 the state police searched his house, turning up drugs and drug paraphernalia. Good pleaded guilty to drug charges and served a year in jail, in addition to paying a fine. Four and one-half years after the initial seizure, the United States claimed Good's house and land under a federal forfeiture statute, and the property was seized without notice or hearing.

Issue: Does the forfeiture statute violate *due process?

Outcome: Because it did not provide for notice or a hearing, the Court struck the applicable law down as unconstitutional.

Vote: 5-4

Participating: Rehnquist, Blackmun, Stevens, O'Connor, Scalia, Kennedy, Souter, Thomas, Ginsburg

Opinions: Kennedy for the *plurality; Rehnquist, joined by Scalia and O'Connor, concurring in part and dissenting in part; and O'Connor and Thomas concurring in part and dissenting in part

Significance: *Good* curtailed the steady expansion of federal forfeiture law that had occurred over the preceding decade as a consequence of the government's war on drugs.

NATIONAL ORGANIZATION FOR WOMEN, INC. V. SCHEIDLER

Citation: 114 S.Ct. 798 (1994)

Argued: December 8, 1993

Decided: January 24, 1994

Court Below: United States Seventh Circuit Court of Appeals

Basis for Review: *Writ of certiorari

Facts: A *class action, filed on behalf of various pro-choice advocates, alleged that certain activities of antiabortion groups violated the Racketeer Influenced and Corrupt Organizations Act (RICO). RICO, passed by Congress in 1970, was originally intended to combat organized crime by attacking it financially. The district court dismissal of the case was affirmed on appeal.

Issue: Does RICO require that alleged acts of racketeering spring from a financial motive?

Outcome: Relying on the clear language of the statute, rather than its legislative history, the Court reversed the ruling below.

Vote: 9-0

Participating: Rehnquist, Blackmun, Stevens, O'Connor, Scalia, Kennedy, Souter, Thomas, Ginsburg

Opinions: Rehnquist for the Court; Souter, joined by Kennedy, concurring

Significance: By refusing to narrow the interpretation of RICO, the Court left pro-choice

activists with a powerful weapon. With *Scheidler*, the Court also may have intended to alert Congress to the potentially overly broad applications frequently lent this legislation in a variety of possibly unintended contexts.

J.E.B. V. ALABAMA *EX REL. T.B.

Citation: 114 S.Ct. 1419 (1994)

Argued: November 2, 1993

Decided: April 19, 1994

Court Below: Alabama Court of Civil Appeals

Basis for Review: *Writ of certiorari

Facts: Alabama filed a paternity suit against J.E.B. on behalf of T.B. The jury pool for the trial consisted of 24 women and 12 men. After the state used *peremptory challenges to strike all but one man from the pool, J.E.B. used peremptories to strike ten women and the one remaining man. J.E.B. subsequently was found to be the father of the child and ordered to make child support payments. State courts denied his appeals.

Issue: Does *equal protection under the Fourteenth Amendment mandate close scrutiny of sex-based peremptory challenges?

Outcome: Although the Court did not make clear what level of scrutiny applies in such instances, it declared discriminatory use of peremptory challenges unconstitutional and overturned the verdict against J.E.B.

Vote: 6-3

Participating: Rehnquist, Blackmun, Stevens, O'Connor, Scalia, Kennedy, Souter, Thomas, Ginsburg

Opinions: Blackmun for the Court; O'Connor and Kennedy concurring; Rehnquist dissenting; and Scalia, joined by Rehnquist and Thomas, dissenting

Significance: This decision is a logical extension of *Batson v. Kentucky* (1986), in which the Court first extended equal protection to peremptory challenges based on race.

HONDA MOTOR CO. V. OBERG

Citation: 114 S.Ct. 2331 (1994)

Argued: April 20, 1994

Decided: June 24, 1994

Court Below: Oregon Supreme Court

Basis for Review: *Writ of certiorari

Facts: An Oregon jury awarded Karl Oberg $919,390.39 in compensatory damages (later reduced to $735,512.32 because of his contributory negligence) and $5,000,000 in punitive damages for permanent and severe injuries incurred when his Honda all-terrain vehicle overturned. Honda challenged the latter award on grounds that Oregon granted juries almost unlimited discretion in awarding punitive damages.

Issue: Does the Fourteenth Amendment's *Due Process Clause require judicial review of the size of punitive damages awarded by juries?

Outcome: Finding that it does, the Court reversed the ruling against Honda in the court below and *remanded the case for further hearings.

Vote: 7-2

Participating: Rehnquist, Blackmun, Stevens, O'Connor, Scalia, Kennedy, Souter, Thomas, Ginsburg

Opinions: Stevens for the Court; Scalia concurring; Ginsburg, joined by Rehnquist, dissenting

Significance: *Oberg* is important for increasing judicial control over punitive damage awards, which have come under increasing public and legislative criticism. The decision also has implications for judicial oversight of other jury-imposed civil and criminal penalties.

BOARD OF EDUCATION V. GRUMET

Citation: 114 S.Ct. 2481 (1994)
Argued: March 30, 1994
Decided: June 27, 1994
Court Below: New York Court of Appeals
Basis for Review: *Writ of certiorari
Facts: The New York legislature passed a statute granting the Village of Kiryas Joel, a community consisting solely of members of the Jewish Satmar Hasidim sect, status as a separate school district. The purpose of the law was to permit education of the community's disabled children at a site set apart from the established public schools.
Issue: Does the New York law violate the *Establishment Clause of the First Amendment, mandating separation of church and state?
Outcome: Arguing that the legislation demon-

strated special treatment, rather than neutrality, the Court struck it down as unconstitutional.

Vote: 6-3

Participating: Rehnquist, Blackmun, Stevens, O'Connor, Scalia, Kennedy, Souter, Thomas, Ginsburg

Opinions: Souter for the Court; Blackmun concurring; Stevens, joined by Blackmun and Ginsburg, concurring; O'Connor and Kennedy concurring; Scalia, joined by Rehnquist and Thomas, dissenting

Significance: The court based this recent application of the *Lemon v. Kurtzman* (1971) test for separation of church and state on its finding that the special legislation at issue meant Kiryas Joel "did not receive its new governmental authority simply as one of many communities eligible for equal treatment under a general law."

INTERNATIONAL UNION, UNITED MINE WORKERS V. BAGWELL

Citation: 114 S.Ct. 2552 (1994)
Argued: November 29, 1993
Decided: June 30, 1994
Court Below: Virginia Supreme Court
Basis for Review: *Writ of certiorari
Facts: Union disobedience of a federal court *injunction during a strike at the Pittston Coal Company resulted in millions of dollars in fines, payable both to Pittston and to the court. When the strike was settled, the court vacated the fines payable to Pittston and dispatched John Bagwell to collect the others.
Issue: Were the fines payable to the court fines not for civil, but for criminal contempt, which should have accorded the union a jury trial?
Outcome: A unanimous Court held the union was entitled to the additional protection afforded by criminal procedures and vacated the fines.
Vote: 9-0
Participating: Rehnquist, Blackmun, Stevens, O'Connor, Scalia, Kennedy, Souter, Thomas, Ginsburg
Opinions: Blackmun for the Court; Scalia concurring; and Ginsburg, joined by Rehnquist, concurring
Significance: *Bagwell* announced a sweeping new

test for determining when contempt fines require criminal proceedings. As originally formulated in *Gompers v. Bucks Stove & Range Co.* (1911) and refined in *United States v. United Mine Workers* (1947), criminal procedural protections were not mandated for fines intended to compensate the complainant for damages or those conditioned upon a defendant's future noncompliance with court orders. Now, imposition of noncompensatory contempt fines issued for violation of any complex injunction requires criminal proceedings.

MCKENNON V. NASHVILLE BANNER PUBLISHING CO.

Citation: 115 S.Ct. 879 (1995)
Argued: November 2, 1994
Decided: January 23, 1995
Court Below: United States Sixth Circuit Court of Appeals
Basis for Review: *Writ of certiorari
Facts: After Christine McKennon was dismissed from her job with Nashville Banner Publishing when she was 62 years old, she filed suit against her former employer under the Age Discrimination in Employment Act of 1967 (ADEA). In a pretrial *deposition, she admitted to having secretly copied some of the publishing company's confidential documents in her last year of employment. While conceding discrimination for purposes of *summary judgment, the employer also claimed that had it known of McKennon's conduct, she would have been fired immediately. The district court's grant of summary judgment in favor of the employer was affirmed by the circuit court.
Issue: Does evidence of employee misconduct acquired after the employee is terminated preclude relief under ADEA?
Outcome: The Court ruled that it does not, reversing the decision below and *remanding the case for further hearings.
Vote: 9-0
Participating: Rehnquist, Stevens, O'Connor, Scalia, Kennedy, Souter, Thomas, Ginsburg, Breyer
Opinions: Kennedy for the Court

Significance: The Court's holding in *McKennon* underscores the Court's endorsement of the goals of ADEA, which is designed not only to compensate employees dismissed on account of discrimination, but to deter employers from engaging in discrimination.

HARRIS V. ALABAMA

Citation: 115 S.Ct. 1031 (1995)
Argued: December 5, 1994
Decided: February 22, 1995
Court Below: Alabama Supreme Court
Basis for Review: *Writ of certiorari
Facts: Louise Harris, on trial for murder, was sentenced by a jury to life in prison without parole. The trial judge, after determining that Harris's pecuniary motive for the murder canceled out any mitigating circumstances, overrode the jury's recommendation and imposed the death sentence. He did so under authority of the state capital sentencing law, which vests final authority in judges who, although they are required to consider jury recommendations, are not bound by them.
Issue: Does the Alabama sentencing statute violate the Eighth Amendment's ban on cruel and unusual punishment?
Outcome: Largely because the Alabama statute did not define the weight that is to be given to jury sentencing recommendations, the Court upheld it, as well as Harris's sentence.
Vote: 8-1
Participating: Rehnquist, Stevens, O'Connor, Scalia, Kennedy, Souter, Thomas, Ginsburg, Breyer
Opinions: O'Connor for the Court; Stevens dissenting
Significance: *Harris* is yet another instance in which the conservative majority on the Rehnquist Court is returning authority for death penalty policies and procedures to the states.

UNITED STATES V. LOPEZ

Citation: 115 S.Ct.1624 (1995)
Argued: November 8, 1994
Decided: April 26, 1995
Court Below: United States Fifth Circuit Court of Appeals

Basis for Review: *Writ of certiorari

Facts: When he was a high school senior, Alfonso Lopez Jr., was *indicted for having carried a concealed handgun to school in violation of the federal Gun-Free School Zones Act of 1990. The district court denied Lopez's motion to dismiss the indictment, concluding that the act is a valid exercise of Congress's authority to regulate activities affecting interstate commerce, but this decision was reversed on appeal.

Issue: Does the act exceed Congress's authority under the *Commerce Clause?

Outcome: A bare majority of the Rehnquist Court affirmed the *appellate court decision, declaring the act unconstitutional.

Vote: 5-4

Participating: Rehnquist, Stevens, O'Connor, Scalia, Kennedy, Souter, Thomas, Ginsburg, Breyer

Opinions: Rehnquist for the Court; Kennedy, joined by O'Connor, concurring; Thomas concurring; Stevens and Souter dissenting; Breyer, joined by Stevens, Souter, and Ginsburg, dissenting

Significance: For the first time in nearly 60 years, with *Lopez* the Supreme Court struck down federal legislation on *Commerce Clause grounds. Nineteen years earlier, in an opinion written by then Associate Justice Rehnquist in *National League of Cities v. Usery* (1976), the Court struck a blow for *federalism by declaring a federal minimum wage law unconstitutional. But *Usery*, which was decided on Tenth Amendment grounds, was overruled nine years later in *Garcia v. San Antonio Metropolitan Transit Authority* (1985). With *Lopez*, the Court seems to be endorsing state autonomy in a fashion not seen since the early New Deal era.

U.S. TERM LIMITS, INC. V. THORNTON

Citation: 115 S.Ct. 1842 (1995)

Argued: November 29, 1994

Decided: May 22, 1995

Court Below: Arkansas Supreme Court

Basis for Review: *Writ of certiorari

Facts: Arkansas passed a state constitutional amendment prohibiting persons who already had served a total of three terms in the United States House of Representatives or a total of two terms in the Senate from running in a subsequent federal congressional election.

Issue: Does the Arkansas amendment run afoul of the qualifications for congressional office set forth in Article I of the U.S. Constitution?

Outcome: The Court found that, in the absence of an amendment to the federal constitution, state limitations on federal congressional terms such as those propounded by Arkansas are unconstitutional.

Vote: 5-4

Participating: Rehnquist, Stevens, O'Connor, Scalia, Kennedy, Souter, Thomas, Ginsburg, Breyer

Opinions: Stevens for the Court; Kennedy concurring; Thomas, joined by Rehnquist, O'Connor, and Scalia, dissenting

Significance: Arkansas was only one of twenty-three states that had passed term limits legislation which was obliterated by *U.S. Term Limits*. The term limits movement took place in an atmosphere of resurgent enthusiasm for *states' rights, a position supported by the dissenters in this opinion who, in the words of Justice Thomas, view the individual states, not the "undifferentiated people of the nation as a whole," the source of federal authority.

ADARAND CONSTRUCTORS, INC. V. PENA

Citation: 115 S.Ct. 2097 (1995)

Argued: January 17, 1995

Decided: June 12, 1995

Court Below: United States Tenth Circuit Court of Appeals

Basis for Review: *Writ of certiorari

Facts: Although Adarand, a subcontractor, submitted the lowest bid on a federal highway project, it lost out to another company certified by the federal Small Business Administration as a business controlled by economically disadvantaged individuals. Because such certification frequently presumes the minority status of such individuals, Adarand sued, citing the *equal protection component of the Fifth Amendment's *Due Process Clause. However, both the district and *appellate courts ruled against Adarand.

Issue: Do the race-based presumptions inherent in federal subcontractor compensation programs violate equal protection?

Outcome: Overturning the ruling below, the Court held that federal programs employing racial classifications, such as those administered at the state and local level, must meet standards of *strict scrutiny in order to pass constitutional muster.

Vote: 5-4

Participating: Rehnquist, Stevens, O'Connor, Scalia, Kennedy, Souter, Thomas, Ginsburg, Breyer

Opinions: O'Connor for the Court; Scalia and Thomas concurring; Stevens, joined by Ginsburg, dissenting; Souter, joined by Ginsburg and Breyer, dissenting; Ginsburg, joined by Breyer, dissenting

Significance: Although Justice O'Connor's opinion for the Court did not disqualify the federal government from instituting and administering affirmative action programs, *Adarand* marks a significant retreat from the Court's endorsement in *Fullilove v. Klutznick* (1980) of minority set-asides as a remedy for past discrimination.

MISSOURI V. JENKINS

Citation: 115 S.Ct. 2038 (1995)
Argued: January 11, 1995
Decided: June 12, 1995
Court Below: United States Eighth Circuit Court of Appeals
Basis for Review: *Writ of certiorari
Facts: A federal district court had ordered the state of Missouri to help fund a model Kansas City desegregation plan featuring magnet schools. The state appealed.
Issue: Can federal courts require states to pay for school desegregation?
Outcome: The Rehnquist Court reversed the lower court's order.
Vote: 5-4
Participating: Rehnquist, Stevens, O'Connor, Scalia, Kennedy, Souter, Thomas, Ginsburg, Breyer
Opinions: Rehnquist for the Court; O'Connor and Thomas concurring; Souter, joined by

Stevens, Ginsburg, and Breyer, dissenting; Ginsburg dissenting

Significance: Forty years after the Warren Court, in *Brown v. Board of Education II* (1955), ordered that schools be desegregated with "all deliberate speed," *Jenkins* underscores the intractability of the problem. This decision also illustrates the Rehnquist Court's fundamental disagreement with such Burger Court decisions as *Swann v. Charlotte-Mecklenberg Board of Education* (1971), which mandate federal enforcement of state desegregation plans.

VERONIA SCHOOL DISTRICT V. ACTON

Citation: 115 S.Ct. 2386 (1995)
Argued: March 28, 1995
Decided: June 26, 1995
Court Below: United States Ninth Circuit Court of Appeals
Basis for Review: *Writ of certiorari
Facts: Together with his parents, James Acton, then a seventh grader in one of the Veronia, Oregon, district's schools, challenged a district policy requiring students to submit to random urinalysis prior to participating in interscholastic sports.
Issue: Does the school district's policy violate the Fourth Amendment prohibition against unreasonable search and seizure?
Outcome: Finding drug testing of prospective student athletes to be reasonable, the Court also found for the school district.
Vote: 6-3
Participating: Rehnquist, Stevens, O'Connor, Scalia, Kennedy, Souter, Thomas, Ginsburg, Breyer
Opinions: Scalia for the Court; Ginsburg concurring; O'Connor, joined by Stevens and Souter, dissenting
Significance: *Acton* — which caused the Court to reevaluate the standard for unreasonable search and seizure in light of America's war on drugs — left open the issue of whether public schools can randomly test students in general, or only those who want to participate in an extracurricular activity, such as an athletic program.

CAPITOL SQUARE REVIEW BOARD V. PINETTE

Citation: 115 S.Ct. 2440 (1995)
Argued: April 26, 1995
Decided: April 26, 1995
Court Below: United States Sixth Circuit Court of Appeals
Basis for Review: *Writ of certiorari
Facts: Ohio law designates Capitol Square, a state-owned plaza surrounding the statehouse in Columbus, a *public forum to be regulated by a review board. When the board denied the Ku Klux Klan permission to display an unattended cross during the 1993 Christmas season, the Klan sued. The federal district court ordered the board to issue a permit to the Klan, a ruling upheld by the *appellate court.
Issue: Would state authorization of the cross violate the First Amendment's *Establishment Clause?
Outcome: Because the Klan's unattended display of the cross in a traditional public forum constitutes a private expression of religious belief fully protected by the First Amendment, the Court ruled in favor of the Klan.
Vote: 7-2
Participating: Rehnquist, Stevens, O'Connor, Scalia, Kennedy, Souter, Thomas, Ginsburg, Breyer
Opinions: Scalia for the Court; Thomas concurring; O'Connor, joined by Souter and Breyer, concurring; and Souter, joined by O'Connor and Breyer, concurring; Stevens and Ginsburg dissenting
Significance: Together with *Rosenberger v. University of Virginia*, which was handed down the same day, *Pinette* indicates a new willingness on the part of the Court to permit state accommodation of religious expression.

MILLER V. ABRAMS

Citation: 115 S.Ct. 2475 (1995)
Argued: April 19, 1995
Decided: June 29, 1995
Court Below: United States District Court for the Southern District of Georgia
Basis for Review: Appeal
Facts: In the early 1990s, the Georgia state legislature drew up a plan to create a third congressional district containing a majority of African American voters. The district was intentionally drawn to include as many African Americans as possible, even though this required dividing towns and counties between congressional districts and resulted in a district that zigged and zagged across much of the state. Five white voters from this district challenged the plan by suing, among others, Georgia Governor Zell Miller.
Issue: Does the Georgia redistricting plan violate the Fourteenth Amendment's *Equal Protection Clause?
Outcome: The Court ruled the plan invalid.
Vote: 5-4
Participating: Rehnquist, Stevens, O'Connor, Scalia, Kennedy, Souter, Thomas, Ginsburg, Breyer
Opinions: Kennedy for the Court; O'Connor concurring; Stevens dissenting; Ginsburg, joined by Stevens, Breyer, and Souter in part, dissenting
Significance: In *Miller*, the Rehnquist Court introduced a new factor into the highly politicized debate about legislative districting: only a compelling justification can override a presumption of unconstitutionality that prohibits redistricting plans in which race is the "primary factor."

ROSENBERGER V. UNIVERSITY OF VIRGINIA

Citation: 115 S.Ct. 2510 (1995)
Argued: March 1, 1995
Decided: June 29, 1995
Court Below: United States Fourth Circuit Court of Appeals
Basis for Review: *Writ of certiorari
Facts: Ronald Rosenberger, the founder of a Christian student newspaper at the University of Virginia, a state institution, sued the university after it declined to subsidize the paper from a fund used to help support other student publications.
Issue: Would the university's financial support of the publication violate the First Amendment's requirement of separation of church and state?

POLITICAL COMPOSITION
of the Rehnquist Court

Justice & Total Term	Courts Served	Appointing President	Political Party
William H. Rehnquist (1972-1986)	Burger	Nixon	Republican
(As Chief Justice 1986-)	Rehnquist	Reagan	
William J. Brennan Jr. (1956-1990)	Warren Burger Rehnquist	Eisenhower	Democrat
Byron R. White (1962-1993)	Warren Burger Rehnquist	Kennedy	Democrat
Thurgood Marshall (1967-1991)	Warren Burger Rehnquist	Johnson	Democrat
Harry A. Blackmun (1970-1994)	Burger Rehnquist	Nixon	Republican
Lewis F. Powell Jr. (1972-1987)	Burger Rehnquist	Nixon	Democrat
John Paul Stevens (1975-)	Burger Rehnquist	Ford	Republican
Sandra Day O'Connor (1981-)	Burger Rehnquist	Reagan	Republican
Antonin Scalia (1986-)	Rehnquist	Reagan	Republican
Anthony M. Kennedy (1988-)	Rehnquist	Reagan	Republican
David H. Souter (1990-)	Rehnquist	Bush	Republican
Clarence Thomas (1991-)	Rehnquist	Bush	Republican
Ruth Bader Ginsburg (1993-)	Rehnquist	Clinton	Democrat
Stephen G. Breyer (1994-)	Rehnquist	Clinton	Democrat

Outcome: The Court found for Rosenberger.
Vote: 5-4
Participating: Rehnquist, Stevens, O'Connor, Scalia, Kennedy, Souter, Thomas, Ginsburg, Breyer
Opinions: Kennedy for the Court; O'Connor and Thomas concurring; Souter, joined by Stevens, Ginsburg, and Breyer, dissenting
Significance: *Rosenberger* marks the first time that the Court has approved direct state financing of a clearly religious activity.

VOTING PATTERNS

For the first time in five decades, the Court has a conservative majority. During Earl Warren's leadership, the Court was dominated by liberals, and while Warren Burger led the Court, a moderate core of justices held sway. With the retirements of William J. Brennan and Thurgood Marshall in 1990 and 1991, respectively, the Court lost two powerful liberal voices — although in recent years they had been raised more often in dissent — and gained a clearly conservative orientation. These justices were replaced by others with strong conservative credentials, David Souter and Clarence Thomas, leaving only one Democrat on the Rehnquist Court, Byron White. (Lewis F. Powell, the only other Democratic member of the early Rehnquist Court, retired less than a year after William Rehnquist assumed leadership of the Court.) For some years, however, White had exhibited a conservatism of his own, particularly in criminal matters, and until his retirement in 1993, this trend continued. In the 1991 and 1992 Court terms, for example, White agreed more frequently with William Rehnquist than with any other justice, 71.9 percent of the time in the 1991 term, and 78.9 percent of the time in the 1992 term.

The highest percentages of agreement during those terms, as well as the subsequent one, were achieved by the most conservative justices, Antonin Scalia and Clarence Thomas, who voted together more than 80 percent of the time during the years 1991-1994. Scalia and Thomas have tended, however, to be on the margins of what might be an emerging core of moderate conservatives, a coalition that first became apparent when Justices Sandra Day O'Connor, Anthony Kennedy, and David Souter jointly wrote the majority opinion reaffirming *Roe v. Wade* (1973) in *Planned Parenthood v. Casey* (1992). It seems probable that this group will be strengthened by Democrats Ruth Bader Ginsburg and Stephen Breyer — chosen by Bill Clinton as replacements for, respectively, Byron White and Harry Blackmun — at least in part because of their avowed support for a woman's right to abortion.

John Paul Stevens remains, as he has throughout his Supreme Court tenure, an independent. However, from 1991 to 1994 he consistently agreed with Blackmun more than 70 percent of the time, far more frequently than with any other justice. These figures, together with his history as a true centrist on the Burger Court, indicate that he, like Blackmun, will finally be accounted as one of the more liberal members of the Rehnquist Court.

Appendixes

APPENDIX A

CONSTITUTION OF THE UNITED STATES OF AMERICA

We the People of the United States, in Order to form a more perfect Union, establish Justice, insure domestic Tranquillity, provide for the common defence, promote the general Welfare, and secure the Blessings of Liberty to ourselves and our Posterity, do ordain and establish this Constitution for the United States of America.

ARTICLE I

Section 1. All legislative Powers herein granted shall be vested in a Congress of the United States, which shall consist of a Senate and House of Representatives.

Section 2. The House of Representatives shall be composed of Members chosen every second Year by the People of the several States, and the Electors in each State shall have the Qualifications requisite for Electors of the most numerous Branch of the State Legislature.

No Person shall be a Representative who shall not have attained to the age of twenty five Years, and been seven Years a Citizen of the United States, and who shall not, when elected, be an Inhabitant of that State in which he shall be chosen.

[Representatives and direct Taxes shall be apportioned among the several States which may be included within this Union, according to their respective Numbers, which shall be determined by adding to the whole Number of free Persons, including those bound to Service for a Term of Years, and excluding Indians not taxed, three fifths of all other Persons.][1] The actual Enumeration shall be made within three Years after the first Meeting of the Congress of the United States, and within every subsequent Term of ten Years, in such Manner as they shall by Law direct. The Number of Representatives shall not exceed one for every thirty Thousand, but each State shall have at Least one Representative; and until such enumeration shall be made, the State of New Hampshire shall be entitled to chuse three, Massachusetts eight, Rhode-Island and Providence Plantations one, Connecticut five, New-York six, New Jersey four, Pennsylvania eight, Delaware one, Maryland six, Virginia ten, North Carolina five, South Carolina five, and Georgia three.

When vacancies happen in the Representation from any State, the Executive Authority thereof shall issue Writs of Election to fill such Vacancies.

The House of Representatives shall chuse their Speaker and other Officers; and shall have the sole Power of Impeachment.

Section 3. The Senate of the United States shall be composed of two Senators from each State, [chosen by the Legislature thereof,][2] for six Years; and each Senator shall have one Vote.

Immediately after they shall be assembled in

---

[1] The part in brackets was changed by section 2 of the Fourteenth Amendment.
[2] The part in brackets was changed by the first paragraph of the Seventeenth Amendment.

Consequence of the first Election, they shall be divided as equally as may be into three Classes. The Seats of the Senators of the first Class shall be vacated at the Expiration of the second Year, of the second Class at the Expiration of the fourth Year, and of the third Class at the Expiration of the sixth Year, so that one third may be chosen every second Year; [and if Vacancies happen by Resignation, or otherwise, during the Recess of the Legislature of any State, the Executive thereof may make temporary Appointments until the next Meeting of the Legislature, which shall then fill such Vacancies.][3]

No Person shall be a Senator who shall not have attained to the Age of thirty Years, and been nine Years a Citizen of the United States, and who shall not, when elected, be an Inhabitant of that State for which he shall be chosen.

The Vice President of the United States shall be President of the Senate, but shall have no Vote, unless they be equally divided.

The Senate shall chuse their other Officers, and also a President pro tempore, in the Absence of the Vice President, or when he shall exercise the Office of President of the United States.

The Senate shall have the sole Power to try all Impeachments. When sitting for that Purpose, they shall be on Oath or Affirmation. When the President of the United States is tried, the Chief Justice shall preside: And no Person shall be convicted without the Concurrence of two thirds of the Members present.

Judgment in Cases of Impeachment shall not extend further than to removal from Office, and disqualification to hold and enjoy any Office of honor, Trust or Profit under the United States: but the Party convicted shall nevertheless be liable and subject to Indictment, Trial, Judgment and Punishment, according to Law.

Section 4. The Times, Places and Manner of holding Elections for Senators and Representatives, shall be prescribed in each State by the Legislature thereof; but the Congress may at any time by Law make or alter such Regulations, except as to the Places of chusing Senators.

The Congress shall assemble at least once in every Year, and such Meeting shall [be on the first Monday in December][4], unless they shall by Law appoint a different Day.

Section 5. Each House shall be the Judge of the Elections, Returns and Qualifications of its own Members, and a Majority of each shall constitute a Quorum to do Business; but a smaller Number may adjourn from day to day, and may be authorized to compel the Attendance of absent Members, in such Manner, and under such Penalties as each House may provide.

Each House may determine the Rules of its Proceedings, punish its Members for disorderly Behaviour, and, with the Concurrence of two thirds, expel a Member.

Each House shall keep a Journal of its Proceedings, and from time to time publish the same, excepting such Parts as may in their Judgment require Secrecy; and the Yeas and Nays of the Members of either House on any question shall, at the Desire of one fifth of those Present, be entered on the Journal.

Neither House, during the Session of Congress, shall, without the Consent of the other, adjourn for more than three days, nor to any other Place than that in which the two Houses shall be sitting.

Section 6. The Senators and Representatives shall receive a Compensation for their Services, to be ascertained by Law, and paid out of the Treasury of the United States. They shall in all Cases, except Treason, Felony and Breach of the Peace, be privileged from Arrest during their Attendance at the Session of their respective Houses, and in going to and returning from the same; and for any Speech or Debate in either House, they shall not be questioned in any other Place.

No Senator or Representative shall, during the Time for which he was elected, be appointed to any civil Office under the Authority of the United States, which shall have been created, or the Emoluments whereof shall have been encreased during such time; and no Person holding any Office under the United States, shall be a Member of either House during his Continuance in Office.

Section 7. All Bills for raising Revenue shall

---

[3] The part in brackets was changed by the second paragraph of the Seventeenth Amendment.
[4] The part in brackets was changed by section 2 of the Twentieth Amendment.

originate in the House of Representatives; but the Senate may propose or concur with Amendments as on other Bills. Every Bill which shall have passed the House of Representatives and the Senate, shall, before it become a Law, be presented to the President of the United States; If he approve he shall sign it, but if not he shall return it, with his Objections to that House in which it shall have originated, who shall enter the Objections at large on their Journal, and proceed to reconsider it. If after such Reconsideration two thirds of that House shall agree to pass the Bill, it shall be sent, together with the Objections, to the other House, by which it shall likewise be reconsidered, and if approved by two thirds of that House, it shall become a Law. But in all such Cases the Votes of both Houses shall be determined by yeas and Nays, and the names of the Persons voting for and against the Bill shall be entered on the Journal of each House respectively. If any Bill shall not be returned by the President within ten Days (Sundays excepted) after it shall have been presented to him, the Same shall be a Law, in like Manner as if he had signed it, unless the Congress by their Adjournment prevent its Return, in which Case it shall not be a Law.

Every Order, Resolution, or Vote to which the Concurrence of the Senate and House of Representatives may be necessary (except on a question of Adjournment) shall be presented to the President of the United States; and before the Same shall take Effect, shall be approved by him, or being disapproved by him, shall be repassed by two thirds of the Senate and House of Representatives, according to the Rules and Limitations prescribed in the Case of a Bill.

Section 8. The Congress shall have Power To lay and collect Taxes, Duties, Imposts and Excises, to pay the Debts and provide for the common Defence and general Welfare of the United States; but all Duties, Imposts and Excises shall be uniform throughout the United States;

To borrow Money on the credit of the United States;

To regulate Commerce with foreign Nations,

and among the several States, and with the Indian Tribes;

To establish an uniform Rule of Naturalization, and uniform Laws on the subject of Bankruptcies throughout the United States;

To coin Money, regulate the Value thereof, and of foreign Coin, and fix the Standard of Weights and Measures;

To provide for the Punishment of counterfeiting the Securities and current Coin of the United States;

To establish Post Offices and post Roads;

To promote the Progress of Science and useful Arts, by securing for limited Times to Authors and Inventors the exclusive Right to their respective Writings and Discoveries;

To constitute Tribunals inferior to the supreme Court;

To define and punish Piracies and Felonies committed on the high Seas, and Offences against the Law of Nations;

To declare War, grant Letters of Marque and Reprisal, and make Rules concerning Captures on Land and Water;

To raise and support Armies, but no Appropriation of Money to that Use shall be for a longer Term than two Years;

To provide and maintain a Navy;

To make Rules for the Government and Regulation of the land and naval Forces;

To provide for calling forth the Militia to execute the Laws of the Union, suppress Insurrections and repel Invasions;

To provide for organizing, arming, and disciplining, the Militia, and for governing such Part of them as may be employed in the Service of the United States, reserving to the States respectively, the Appointment of the Officers, and the Authority of training the Militia according to the discipline prescribed by Congress;

To exercise exclusive Legislation in all Cases whatsoever, over such District (not exceeding ten Miles square) as may, by Cession of particular States, and the Acceptance of Congress, become the Seat of the Government of the United States, and to exercise like Authority over all Places purchased by the Consent of the

Legislature of the State in which the Same shall be, for the Erection of Forts, Magazines, Arsenals, dock-Yards, and other needful Buildings;—And

To make all Laws which shall be necessary and proper for carrying into Execution the foregoing Powers, and all other Powers vested by this Constitution in the Government of the United States, or in any Department or Officer thereof.

Section 9. The Migration or Importation of such Persons as any of the States now existing shall think proper to admit, shall not be prohibited by the Congress prior to the Year one thousand eight hundred and eight, but a Tax or duty may be imposed on such Importation, not exceeding ten dollars for each Person.

The Privilege of the Writ of Habeas Corpus shall not be suspended, unless when in Cases of Rebellion or Invasion the public Safety may require it.

No Bill of Attainder or ex post facto Law shall be passed.

[No Capitation, or other direct, Tax shall be laid, unless in Proportion to the Census or Enumeration herein before directed to be taken.[5]]

No Tax or Duty shall be laid on Articles exported from any State.

No Preference shall be given by any Regulation of Commerce or Revenue to the Ports of one State over those of another; nor shall Vessels bound to, or from, one State, be obliged to enter, clear, or pay Duties in another.

No Money shall be drawn from the Treasury, but in Consequence of Appropriations made by Law; and a regular Statement and Account of the Receipts and Expenditures of all public Money shall be published from time to time.

No Title of Nobility shall be granted by the United States: And no Person holding any Office of Profit or Trust under them, shall, without the Consent of the Congress, accept of any present, Emolument, Office, or Title, of any kind whatever, from any King, Prince, or foreign State.

Section 10. No State shall enter into any Treaty, Alliance, or Confederation; grant Letters of Marque and Reprisal; coin Money; emit Bills of Credit; make any Thing but gold and silver Coin

a Tender in Payment of Debts; pass any Bill of Attainder, ex post facto Law, or Law impairing the Obligation of Contracts, or grant any Title of Nobility.

No State shall, without the Consent of the Congress, lay any Imposts or Duties on Imports or Exports, except what may be absolutely necessary for executing itís inspection Laws: and the net Produce of all Duties and Imposts, laid by any State on Imports or Exports, shall be for the Use of the Treasury of the United States; and all such Laws shall be subject to the Revision and Controul of the Congress.

No State shall, without the Consent of Congress, lay any Duty of Tonnage, keep Troops, or Ships of War in time of Peace, enter into any Agreement or Compact with another State, or with a foreign Power, or engage in War, unless actually invaded, or in such imminent Danger as will not admit of delay.

ARTICLE II

Section 1. The executive Power shall be vested in a President of the United States of America. He shall hold his Office during the Term of four Years, and, together with the Vice President, chosen for the same Term, be elected, as follows:

Each State shall appoint, in such Manner as the Legislature thereof may direct, a Number of Electors, equal to the whole Number of Senators and Representatives to which the State may be entitled in the Congress: but no Senator or Representative, or Person holding an Office of Trust or Profit under the United States, shall be appointed an Elector.

[The Electors shall meet in their respective States, and vote by Ballot for two Persons, of whom one at least shall not be an Inhabitant of the same State with themselves. And they shall make a List of all the Persons voted for, and of the Number of Votes for each; which List they shall sign and certify, and transmit sealed to the Seat of the Government of the United States, directed to the President of the Senate. The President of the Senate shall, in the Presence of the Senate and House of Representatives, open all the Certificates,

---

[5] The part in brackets was changed by the Sixteenth Amendment.

and the Votes shall then be counted. The Person having the greatest Number of Votes shall be the President, if such Number be a Majority of the whole Number of Electors appointed; and if there be more than one who have such Majority, and have an equal Number of Votes, then the House of Representatives shall immediately chuse by Ballot one of them for President; and if no Person have a Majority, then from the five highest on the list the said House shall in like Manner chuse the President. But in chusing the President, the Votes shall be taken by States, the Representation from each State having one Vote; a quorum for this Purpose shall consist of a Member or Members from two thirds of the States, and a Majority of all the States shall be necessary to a Choice. In every Case, after the Choice of the President, the Person having the greatest Number of Votes of the Electors shall be the Vice President. But if there should remain two or more who have equal Votes, the Senate shall chuse from them by Ballot the Vice President.]⁶

The Congress may determine the Time of chusing the Electors, and the Day on which they shall give their Votes; which Day shall be the same throughout the United States.

No Person except a natural born Citizen, or a Citizen of the United States, at the time of the Adoption of this Constitution, shall be eligible to the Office of President; neither shall any Person be eligible to that Office who shall not have attained to the Age of thirty five Years, and been fourteen Years a Resident within the United States.

In Case of the Removal of the President from Office, or of his Death, Resignation, or Inability to discharge the Powers and Duties of the said Office,⁷ the Same shall devolve on the Vice President, and the Congress may by Law provide for the Case of Removal, Death, Resignation or Inability, both of the President and Vice President, declaring what Officer shall then act as President, and such Officer shall act accordingly, until the Disability be removed, or a President shall be elected.

The President shall, at stated Times, receive for his Services, a Compensation, which shall neither be encreased nor diminished during the Period for which he shall have been elected, and he shall not receive within that Period any other Emolument from the United States, or any of them.

Before he enter on the Execution of his Office, he shall take the following Oath or Affirmation:⁷ "I do solemnly swear (or affirm) that I will faithfully execute the Office of President of the United States, and will to the best of my Ability, preserve, protect and defend the Constitution of the United States."

Section 2. The President shall be Commander in Chief of the Army and Navy of the United States, and of the Militia of the several States, when called into the actual Service of the United States; he may require the Opinion, in writing, of the principal Officer in each of the executive Departments, upon any Subject relating to the Duties of their respective Offices, and he shall have Power to grant Reprieves and Pardons for Offences against the United States, except in Cases of Impeachment.

He shall have Power, by and with the Advice and Consent of the Senate, to make Treaties, provided two thirds of the Senators present concur; and he shall nominate, and by and with the Advice and Consent of the Senate, shall appoint Ambassadors, other public Ministers and Consuls, Judges of the supreme Court, and all other Officers of the United States, whose Appointments are not herein otherwise provided for, and which shall be established by Law: but the Congress may by Law vest the Appointment of such inferior Officers, as they think proper, in the President alone, in the Courts of Law, or in the Heads of Departments.

The President shall have Power to fill up all Vacancies that may happen during the Recess of the Senate, by granting Commissions which shall expire at the End of their next Session.

Section 3. He shall from time to time give to the Congress Information of the State of the Union, and recommend to their Consideration such Measures as he shall judge necessary and expedient; he may, on extraordinary Occasions, convene both Houses, or either of them, and in Case of Disagreement between them, with Respect to the Time of Adjournment, he may adjourn them

---

⁶ The material in brackets has been changed by the Twelfth Amendment.
⁷ This provision has been affected by the Twenty-fifth Amendment.

to such Time as he shall think proper; he shall receive Ambassadors and other public Ministers; he shall take Care that the Laws be faithfully executed, and shall Commission all the Officers of the United States.

Section 4. The President, Vice President and all civil Officers of the United States, shall be removed from Office on Impeachment for, and Conviction of, Treason, Bribery, or other high Crimes and Misdemeanors.

ARTICLE III

Section 1. The judicial Power of the United States shall be vested in one supreme Court, and in such inferior Courts as the Congress may from time to time ordain and establish. The Judges, both of the supreme and inferior Courts, shall hold their Offices during good Behaviour, and shall, at stated Times, receive for their Services, a Compensation, which shall not be diminished during their Continuance in Office.

Section 2. The judicial Power shall extend to all Cases, in Law and Equity, arising under this Constitution, the Laws of the United States, and Treaties made, or which shall be made, under their Authority;—to all Cases affecting Ambassadors, other public Ministers and Consuls;—to all Cases of admiralty and maritime Jurisdiction;—to Controversies to which the United States shall be a Party;—to Controversies between two or more States;—between a State and Citizens of another State;[8]—between Citizens of different States;—between Citizens of the same State claiming Lands under Grants of different States, and between a State, or the Citizens thereof, and foreign States, Citizens or Subjects.[8]

In all Cases affecting Ambassadors, other public Ministers and Consuls, and those in which a State shall be Party, the supreme Court shall have original Jurisdiction. In all the other Cases before mentioned, the supreme Court shall have appellate Jurisdiction, both as to Law and Fact, with such Exceptions, and under such Regulations as the Congress shall make.

The Trial of all Crimes, except in Cases of Impeachment, shall be by Jury; and such Trial shall be held in the State where the said Crimes shall have been committed; but when not committed within any State, the Trial shall be at such Place or Places as the Congress may by Law have directed.

Section 3. Treason against the United States, shall consist only in levying War against them, or in adhering to their Enemies, giving them Aid and Comfort. No Person shall be convicted of Treason unless on the Testimony of two Witnesses to the same overt Act, or on Confession in open Court.

The Congress shall have Power to declare the Punishment of Treason, but no Attainder of Treason shall work Corruption of Blood, or Forfeiture except during the Life of the Person attained.

ARTICLE IV

Section 1. Full Faith and Credit shall be given in each State to the public Acts, Records, and judicial Proceedings of every other State. And the Congress may by general Laws prescribe the Manner in which such Acts, Records and Proceedings shall be proved, and the Effect thereof.

Section 2. The Citizens of each State shall be entitled to all Privileges and Immunities of Citizens in the several States.

A Person charged in any State with Treason, Felony, or other Crime, who shall flee from Justice, and be found in another State, shall on Demand of the executive Authority of the State from which he fled, be delivered up, to be removed to the State having Jurisdiction of the Crime.

[No Person held to Service or Labour in one State, under the Laws thereof, escaping into another, shall, in Consequence of any Law or Regulation therein, be discharged from such Service or Labour, but shall be delivered up on Claim of the Party to whom such Service or Labour may be due.][9]

Section 3. New States may be admitted by the Congress into this Union; but no new State shall be formed or erected within the Jurisdiction of any other State; nor any State be formed by the

---

[8] The Eleventh Amendment limited federal jurisdiction over civil litigation involving the states.
[9] This paragraph refers to slavery, abolished by the Thirteenth Amendment.

Junction of two or more States, or Parts of States, without the Consent of the Legislatures of the States concerned as well as of the Congress.

The Congress shall have Power to dispose of and make all needful Rules and Regulations respecting the Territory or other Property belonging to the United States; and nothing in this Constitution shall be so construed as to Prejudice any Claims of the United States, or of any particular State.

Section 4. The United States shall guarantee to every State in this Union a Republican Form of Government, and shall protect each of them against Invasion; and on Application of the Legislature, or of the Executive (when the Legislature cannot be convened) against domestic Violence.

ARTICLE V

The Congress, whenever two thirds of both Houses shall deem it necessary, shall propose Amendments to this Constitution, or, on the Application of the Legislatures of two thirds of the several States, shall call a Convention for proposing Amendments, which, in either Case, shall be valid to all Intents and Purposes, as Part of this Constitution, when ratified by the Legislatures of three fourths of the several States, or by Conventions in three fourths thereof, as the one or the other Mode of Ratification may be proposed by the Congress; Provided that no Amendment which may be made prior to the Year One thousand eight hundred and eight shall in any Manner affect the first and fourth Clauses in the Ninth Section of the first Article; and that no State, without its Consent, shall be deprived of its equal Suffrage in the Senate.

ARTICLE VI.

All Debts contracted and Engagements entered into, before the Adoption of this Constitution, shall be as valid against the United States under this Constitution, as under the Confederation.

This Constitution, and the Laws of the United States which shall be made in Pursuance thereof; and all Treaties made, or which shall be made, under the Authority of the United States, shall be the supreme Law of the Land; and the Judges in every State shall be bound thereby, any Thing in the Constitution or Laws of any State to the Contrary notwithstanding.

The Senators and Representatives before mentioned, and the Members of the several State Legislatures, and all executive and judicial Officers, both of the United States and of the several States, shall be bound by Oath or Affirmation, to support this Constitution; but no religious Test shall ever be required as a Qualification to any Office or public Trust under the United States.

ARTICLE VII

The Ratification of the Conventions of nine States, shall be sufficient for the Establishment of this Constitution between the States so ratifying the Same.

Done in Convention by the Unanimous Consent of the States present the seventeenth Day of September in the Year of our Lord one thousand seven hundred and Eighty seven and of the Independence of the United States of America the Twelfth. IN WITNESS whereof We have hereunto subscribed our Names,

George Washington,
President and deputy from Virginia.

New Hampshire:
John Langdon,
Nicholas Gilman.

Massachusetts:
Nathaniel Gorham,
Rufus King.

Connecticut:
William Samuel Johnson,
Roger Sherman.

New York:
Alexander Hamilton.

New Jersey:
William Livingston,
David Brearley,
William Paterson,
Jonathan Dayton.

Pennsylvania:
Benjamin Franklin,

Thomas Mifflin,
Robert Morris,
George Clymer,
Thomas FitzSimons,
Jared Ingersoll,
James Wilson,
Gouverneur Morris.
Delaware:
George Read,
Gunning Bedford Jr.,
John Dickinson,
Richard Bassett,
Jacob Broom.
Maryland:
James McHenry,
Daniel of St. Thomas Jenifer,
Daniel Carroll.
Virginia:
John Blair,
James Madison Jr.
North Carolina:
William Blount,
Richard Dobbs Spaight,
Hugh Williamson.
South Carolina:
John Rutledge,
Charles Cotesworth Pinckney,
Pierce Butler.
Georgia:
William Few,
Abraham Baldwin.
(Ratification of the Constitution was completed on June 21, 1788)

AMENDMENTS

AMENDMENT I
(First ten admendments ratified December 15, 1791.)
Congress shall make no law respecting an establishment of religion, or prohibiting the free exercise thereof; or abridging the freedom of speech, or of the press; or the right of the people peaceably to assemble, and to petition the Government for a redress of grievances.

AMENDMENT II
A well regulated Militia, being necessary to the security of a free State, the right of the people to keep and bear Arms, shall not be infringed.

AMENDMENT III
No Soldier shall, in time of peace be quartered in any house, without the consent of the Owner, nor in time of war, but in a manner to be prescribed by law.

AMENDMENT IV
The right of the people to be secure in their persons, houses, papers, and effects, against unreasonable searches and seizures, shall not be violated, and no Warrants shall issue, but upon probable cause, supported by Oath or affirmation, and particularly describing the place to be searched, and the persons or things to be seized.

AMENDMENT V
No person shall be held to answer for a capital, or otherwise infamous crime, unless on a presentment or indictment of a Grand Jury, except in cases arising in the land or naval forces, or in the Militia, when in actual service in time of War or public danger; nor shall any person be subject for the same offences to be twice put in jeopardy of life or limb; nor shall be compelled in any criminal case to be a witness against himself, nor be deprived of life, liberty, or property, without due process of law; nor shall private property be taken for public use, without just compensation.

AMENDMENT VI
In all criminal prosecutions, the accused shall enjoy the right to a speedy and public trial, by an impartial jury of the State and district wherein the crime shall have been committed, which district shall have been previously ascertained by law, and to be informed of the nature and cause of the accusation; to be confronted with the witnesses against him; to have compulsory process for obtaining witnesses in his favor, and to have the Assistance of Counsel for his defence.

AMENDMENT VII
In Suits at common law, where the value in controversy shall exceed twenty dollars, the right of

trial by jury shall be preserved, and no fact tried by a jury, shall be otherwise re-examined in any Court of the United States, than according to the rules of the common law.

AMENDMENT VIII

Excessive bail shall not be required, nor excessive fines imposed, nor cruel and unusual punishments inflicted.

AMENDMENT IX

The enumeration in the Constitution, of certain rights, shall not be construed to deny or disparage others retained by the people.

AMENDMENT X

The powers not delegated to the United States by the Constitution, nor prohibited by it to the States, are reserved to the States respectively, or to the people.

AMENDMENT XI

(Ratified February 7, 1795)

The Judicial power of the United States shall not be construed to extend to any suit in law or equity, commenced or prosecuted against one of the United States by Citizens of another State, or by Citizens or Subjects of any Foreign State.

AMENDMENT XII

(Ratified June 15, 1804)

The Electors shall meet in their respective states, and vote by ballot for President and Vice–President, one of whom, at least, shall not be an inhabitant of the same state with themselves; they shall name in their ballots the person voted for as President, and in distinct ballots the person voted for as Vice–President, and they shall make distinct lists of all persons voted for as President, and of all persons voted for as Vice–President, and of the number of votes for each, which lists they shall sign and certify, and transmit sealed to the seat of the government of the United States, directed to the President of the Senate;—The President of the Senate shall, in the presence of the Senate and House of Representatives, open all the certificates and the votes shall then be counted;—The person having the greatest number of votes for President, shall be the President, if such number be a majority of the whole number of Electors appointed; and if no person have such majority, then from the persons having the highest numbers not exceeding three on the list of those voted for as President, the House of Representatives shall choose immediately, by ballot, the President. But in choosing the President, the votes shall be taken by states, the representation from each state having one vote; a quorum for this purpose shall consist of a member or members from two-thirds of the states, and a majority of all the states shall be necessary to a choice. [And if the House of Representatives shall not choose a President whenever the right of choice shall devolve upon them, before the fourth day of March next following, then the Vice–President shall act as President, as in the case of the death or other constitutional disability of the President.—][11] The person having the greatest number of votes as Vice–President, shall be the Vice–President, if such number be a majority of the whole number of Electors appointed, and if no person have a majority, then from the two highest numbers on the list, the Senate shall choose the Vice–President; a quorum for the purpose shall consist of two–thirds of the whole number of Senators, and a majority of the whole number shall be necessary to a choice. But no person constitutionally ineligible to the office of President shall be eligible to that of Vice–President of the United States.

AMENDMENT XIII

(Ratified December 6, 1865)

Section 1. Neither slavery nor involuntary servitude, except as a punishment for crime whereof the party shall have been duly convicted, shall exist within the United States, or any place subject to their jurisdiction.

Section 2. Congress shall have power to enforce this article by appropriate legislation.

AMENDMENT XIV

(Ratified July 9, 1868)

Section 1. All persons born or naturalized in

---

[11] The section in brackets was superced by section 3 of the Twentieth Amendment.

the United States, and subject to the jurisdiction thereof, are citizens of the United States and of the State wherein they reside. No State shall make or enforce any law which shall abridge the privileges or immunities of citizens of the United States; nor shall any State deprive any person of life, liberty, or property, without due process of law; nor deny to any person within its jurisdiction the equal protection of the laws.

Section 2. Representatives shall be apportioned among the several States according to their respective numbers, counting the whole number of persons in each State, excluding Indians not taxed. But when the right to vote at any election for the choice of electors for President and Vice President of the United States, Representatives in Congress, the Executive and Judicial officers of a State, or the members of the Legislature thereof, is denied to any of the male inhabitants of such State, being twenty–one years of age,[12] and citizens of the United States, or in any way abridged, except for participation in rebellion, or other crime, the basis of representation therein shall be reduced in the proportion which the number of such male citizens shall bear to the whole number of male citizens twenty–one years of age in such State.

Section 3. No person shall be a Senator or Representative in Congress, or elector of President and Vice President, or hold any office, civil or military, under the United States, or under any State, who, having previously taken an oath, as a member of Congress, or as an officer of the United States, or as a member of any State legislature, or as an executive or judicial officer of any State, to support the Constitution of the United States, shall have engaged in insurrection or rebellion against the same, or given aid or comfort to the enemies thereof. But Congress may by a vote of two–thirds of each House, remove such disability.

Section 4. The validity of the public debt of the United States, authorized by law, including debts incurred for payment of pensions and bounties for services in suppressing insurrection or rebellion, shall not be questioned. But neither the United States nor any State shall assume or pay

any debt or obligation incurred in aid of insurrection or rebellion against the United States, or any claim for the loss or emancipation of any slave; but all such debts, obligations and claims shall be held illegal and void.

Section 5. The Congress shall have power to enforce, by appropriate legislation, the provisions of this article.

AMENDMENT XV
(Ratified February 3, 1870)

Section 1. The right of citizens of the United States to vote shall not be denied or abridged by the United States or by any State on account of race, color, or previous condition of servitude.

Section 2. The Congress shall have power to enforce this article by appropriate legislation.

AMENDMENT XVI
(Ratified February 3, 1913)

The Congress shall have power to lay and collect taxes on incomes, from whatever source derived, without apportionment among the several States, and without regard to any census or enumeration.

AMENDMENT XVII
(Ratified April 8, 1913)

The Senate of the United States shall be composed of two Senators from each State, elected by the people thereof, for six years; and each Senator shall have one vote. The electors in each State shall have the qualifications requisite for electors of the most numerous branch of the State legislatures.

When vacancies happen in the representation of any State in the Senate, the executive authority of such State shall issue writs of election to fill such vacancies: *Provided,* That the legislature of any State may empower the executive thereof to make temporary appointments until the people fill the vacancies by election as the legislature may direct.

This amendment shall not be so construed as to affect the election or term of any Senator chosen before it becomes valid as part of the Constitution.

[12] See the Ninteenth and Twenty-sixth Amendments.

AMENDMENT XVIII
(Ratified January 16, 1919)

[Section 1. After one year from the ratification of this article the manufacture, sale, or transportation of intoxicating liquors within, the importation thereof into, or the exportation thereof from the United States and all territory subject to the jurisdiction thereof for beverage purposes is hereby prohibited.

Section 2. The Congress and the several States shall have concurrent power to enforce this article by appropriate legislation.

Section 3. This article shall be inoperative unless it shall have been ratified as an amendment to the Constitution by the legislatures of the several States, as provided in the Constitution, within seven years from the date of the submission hereof to the States by the Congress.][13]

AMENDMENT XIX
(Ratified August 18, 1920)

The right of citizens of the United States to vote shall not be denied or abridged by the United States or by any State on account of sex.

Congress shall have power to enforce this article by appropriate legislation.

AMENDMENT XX
(Ratified January 23, 1933)

Section 1. The terms of the President and Vice President shall end at noon on the 20th day of January, and the terms of Senators and Representatives at noon on the 3d day of January, of the years in which such terms would have ended if this article had not been ratified; and the terms of their successors shall then begin.

Section 2. The Congress shall assemble at least once in every year, and such meeting shall begin at noon on the 3d day of January, unless they shall by law appoint a different day.

Section 3.[14] If, at the time fixed for the beginning of the term of the President, the President elect shall have died, the Vice President elect shall become President. If a President shall not have been chosen before the time fixed for the beginning of his term, or if the President elect shall have failed to qualified, then the Vice President

elect shall act as President until a President shall have qualified; and the Congress may by law provide for the case wherein neither a President elect nor a Vice President elect shall have qualified, declaring who shall then act as President, or the manner in which one who is to act shall be selected, and such person shall act accordingly until a President or Vice President shall have qualified.

Section 4. The Congress may by law provide for the case of the death of any of the persons from whom the House of Representatives may choose a President whenever the right of choice shall have devolved upon them, and for the case of the death of any of the persons from whom the Senate may choose a Vice President whenever the right of choice shall have devolved upon them.

Section 5. Sections 1 and 2 shall take effect on the 15th day of October following the ratification of this article.

Section 6. This article shall be inoperative unless it shall have been ratified as an amendment to the Constitution by the legislatures of three–fourths of the several States within seven years from the date of its submission.

AMENDMENT XXI
(Ratified December 5, 1933)

Section 1. The eighteenth article of amendment to the Constitution of the United States is hereby repealed.

Section 2. The transportation or importation into any State, Territory, or possession of the United States for delivery or use therein of intoxicating liquors, in violation of the laws thereof, is hereby prohibited.

Section 3. This article shall be inoperative unless it shall have been ratified as an amendment to the Constitution by conventions in the several States, as provided in the Constitution, within seven years from the date of the submission hereof to the States by the Congress.

AMENDMENT XXII
(Ratified February 27, 1951)

Section 1. No person shall be elected to the office

---

[13] The Eighteenth Amendment was repealed by section 1 of the Twenty-first Amendment.
[14] See the Twenty-fifth Amendment.

of the President more than twice, and no person who has held the office of President, or acted as President, for more than two years of a term to which some other person was elected President shall be elected to the office of the President more than once. But this Article shall not apply to any person holding the office of President when this Article was proposed by the Congress, and shall not prevent any person who may be holding the office of President, or acting as President, during the term within which this Article becomes operative from holding the office of President or acting as President during the remainder of such term.

Section 2. This article shall be inoperative unless it shall have been ratified as an amendment to the Constitution by the legislatures of three–fourths of the several States within seven years from the date of its submission to the States by the Congress.

AMENDMENT XXIII
(Ratified March 29, 1961)

Section 1. The District constituting the seat of Government of the United States shall appoint in such manner as the Congress may direct:

A number of electors of President and Vice President equal to the whole number of Senators and Representatives in Congress to which the District would be entitled if it were a State, but in no event more than the least populous State; they shall be in addition to those appointed by the States, but they shall be considered, for the purposes of the election of President and Vice President, to be electors appointed by a State; and they shall meet in the District and perform such duties as provided by the twelfth article of amendment.

Section 2. The Congress shall have power to enforce this article by appropriate legislation.

AMENDMENT XXIV
(Ratified January 23, 1964)

Section 1. The right of citizens of the United States to vote in any primary or other election for President or Vice President, for electors for President or Vice President, or for Senator or Representative in Congress, shall not be denied or abridged by the United States or any State by reason of failure to pay any poll tax or other tax.

Section 2. The Congress shall have power to enforce this article by appropriate legislation.

AMENDMENT XXV
(Ratified February 10, 1967)

Section 1. In case of the removal of the President from office or of his death or resignation, the Vice President shall become President.

Section 2. Whenever there is a vacancy in the office of the Vice President, the President shall nominate a Vice President who shall take office upon confirmation by a majority vote of both Houses of Congress.

Section 3. Whenever the President transmits to the President pro tempore of the Senate and the Speaker of the House of Representatives his written declaration that he is unable to discharge the powers and duties of his office, and until he transmits to them a written declaration to the contrary, such powers and duties shall be discharged by the Vice President as Acting President.

Section 4. Whenever the Vice President and a majority of either the principal officers of the executive departments or of such other body as Congress may by law provide, transmit to the President pro tempore of the Senate and the Speaker of the House of Representatives their written declaration that the President is unable to discharge the powers and duties of his office, the Vice President shall immediately assume the powers and duties of the office as Acting President.

Thereafter, when the President transmits to the President pro tempore of the Senate and the Speaker of the House of Representatives his written declaration that no inability exists, he shall resume the powers and duties of his office unless the Vice President and a majority of either the principal officers of the executive department or of such other body as Congress may by law provide, transmit within four days to the President pro tempore of the Senate and the Speaker of the House of Representatives their written declaration that the President is unable to discharge the powers and duties of his office. Thereupon Congress shall decide the issue, assembling within forty–eight hours for that purpose if not in session. If the Congress, within twenty–one days after receipt of the latter written declaration, or, if Congress is not in session, within twenty–one days after Congress is required to assemble, determines by two–thirds vote of both Houses that the President is unable to discharge the powers and duties of his office, the Vice President shall continue to discharge the same as Acting President; otherwise, the President shall resume the powers and duties of his office.

AMENDMENT XXVI
(Ratified July 1, 1971)
Section 1. The right of citizens of the United States, who are eighteen years of age or older, to vote shall not be denied or abridged by the United States or by any State on account of age.
Section 2. The Congress shall have power to enforce this article by appropriate legislation.

AMENDMENT XXVII
(Ratified May 7, 1992)
No law varying the compensation for the services of the Senators and Representatives shall take effect, until an election of Representives shall have intervened.

APPENDIX B

UNITED STATES CODE ANNOTATED, 1995

TITLE 28, JUDICIARY AND JUDICIAL PROCEDURE 1995
SECTIONS CONCERNING U.S. SUPREME COURT JURISDICTION

§ 1251. ORIGINAL JURISDICTION

(a) The Supreme Court shall have original and exclusive jurisdiction of all controversies between two or more States.

(b) The Supreme Court shall have original but not exclusive jurisdiction of:

(1) All actions or proceedings to which ambassadors, other public ministers, consuls, or vice consuls of foreign states are parties;

(2) All controversies between the United States and a State;

(3) All actions or proceedings by a State against the citizens of another State or against aliens.

§ 1253. DIRECT APPEALS FROM DECISIONS OF THREE-JUDGE COURTS

Except as otherwise provided by law, any party may appeal to the Supreme Court from an order granting or denying, after notice and hearing, an interlocutory or permanent injunction in any civil action, suit or proceeding required by any Act of Congress to be heard and determined by a district court of three judges.

§ 1254. COURTS OF APPEALS; CERTIO-RARI; CERTIFIED QUESTIONS

Cases in the courts of appeals may be reviewed by the Supreme Court by the following methods:

(1) By writ of certiorari granted upon the petition of any party to any civil or criminal case, before or after rendition of judgment or decree;

(2) By certification at any time by a court of appeals of any question of law in any civil or criminal case as to which instructions are desired, and upon such certification the Supreme Court may give binding instructions or require the entire record to be sent up for decision of the entire matter in controversy.

§ 1257. STATE COURTS; CERTIORARI

(a) Final judgments or decrees rendered by the highest court of a State in which a decision could be had, may be reviewed by the Supreme Court by writ of certiorari where the validity of a treaty or statute of the United States is drawn in question or where the validity of a statute of any State is drawn in question on the ground of its being repugnant to the Constitution, treaties, or laws of the United States, or where any title, right, privilege, or immunity is specially set up or claimed under the Constitution or the treaties or statutes of, or any commission held or authority exercised under the United States.

(b) for the purposes of this section, the term "highest court of State" includes the District of Columbia Court of Appeals.

§ 1258. SUPREME COURT OF PUERTO RICO; CERTIORARI

Final judgments or decrees rendered by the Supreme Court of the Commonwealth of Puerto Rico may be reviewed by the Supreme Court by writ of certiorari where the validity of a treaty or statute of the United States is drawn in question or where the validity of a statue of the Commonwealth of Puerto Rico is drawn in question on the ground of its being repugnant to the Constitution, treaties, or laws of the United

States, or where any title, right, privilege, or immunity is specially set up or claimed under the Constitution or the treaties or statutes of, or any commission held or authority exercised under, the United States.

§ 1259. COURT OF APPEALS FOR THE ARMED FORCES; CERTIORARI

Decisions of the United States Court of Appeals for the Armed Forces may be reviewed by the Supreme Court by writ of certiorari in the following cases:

(1) Cases reviewed by the Court of Appeals for the Armed Forces under section 867(a)(1) of title 10.

(2) Cases certified to the Court of Appeals for the Armed Forces by the Judge Advocate General under section 867(a)(2) of title 10.

(3) Cases in which the Court of Appeals for the Armed Forces granted a petition for review under section 867(a)(3) of title 10.

(4) Cases, other than those described in paragraphs (1), (2), and (3) of this subsection, in which the Court of Appeals for the Armed Forces granted relief.

APPENDIX C

RULES OF THE SUPREME COURT OF THE UNITED STATES

PART I.
THE COURT

RULE 1
Clerk

.1. The Clerk shall maintain the Court's records and shall not permit any of them to be removed from the Court building except as authorized by the Court. Any pleading, paper, or brief filed with the Clerk and made a part of the Court's records may not thereafter be withdrawn from the official Court files. After the conclusion of the proceedings in this Court, any original records and papers transmitted to this Court by any other court will be returned to the court from which they were received.

.2. The office of the Clerk will be open, except on a federal legal holiday, from 9 a.m. to 5 p.m., Monday through Friday, unless otherwise ordered by the Court or the Chief Justice. See 5 U. S. C. § 6103 for a list of federal legal holidays.

RULE 2
Library

.1. The Court's library is available for use by appropriate personnel of this Court, members of the Bar of this Court, Members of Congress and their legal staffs, and attorneys for the United States, its departments and agencies.

.2. The library will be open during such times as

the reasonable needs of the Bar may require. Its operation shall be governed by regulations made by the Librarian with the approval of the Chief Justice or the Court.

.3. Library books may not be removed from the building, except by a Justice or a member of a Justice's legal staff.

RULE 3
Term

.1. The Court will hold a continuous annual Term commencing on the first Monday in October. See 28 U. S. C. § 2. At the end of each Term, all cases pending on the docket will be continued to the next Term.

.2. The Court at every Term will announce the date after which no case will be called for oral argument at that Term unless otherwise ordered.

RULE 4
Sessions and Quorum

.1. Open sessions of the Court will be held beginning at 10 a.m. on the first Monday in October of each year, and thereafter as announced by the Court. Unless otherwise ordered, the Court will sit to hear arguments from 10 a.m. until noon and from 1 p.m. until 3 p.m.

.2. Any six Members of the Court constitute a quorum. See 28 U. S. C. §1. In the absence of a quorum on any day appointed for holding a session of the Court, the Justices attending, or if no Justice is present, the Clerk or a Deputy Clerk may announce that the Court will not meet until there is a quorum.

.3. The Court in appropriate circumstances may direct the Clerk or the Marshal to announce recesses.

PART II.
ATTORNEYS AND
COUNSELORS

RULE 5
Admission to the Bar

.1. It shall be requisite for admission to the Bar of this Court that the applicant shall have been admitted to practice in the highest court of a State, Commonwealth, Territory or Possession, or of the District of Columbia for the three years immediately preceding the date of application and shall have been free from any adverse disciplinary action whatsoever during that 3-year period, and that the applicant appears to the Court to be of good moral and professional character.

.2. Each applicant shall file with the Clerk (1) a certificate from the presiding judge, clerk, or other authorized official of that court evidencing the applicant's admission to practice there and the applicant's current good standing, and (2) a completely executed copy of the form approved by the Court and furnished by the Clerk containing (i) the applicant's personal statement and (ii) the statement of two sponsors (who must be members of the Bar of this Court and who must personally know, but not be related to, the applicant) endorsing the correctness of the applicant's statement, stating that the applicant possesses all the qualifications required for admission, and affirming that the applicant is of good moral and professional character.

.3. If the documents submitted demonstrate that the applicant possesses the necessary qualifications, has signed the oath or affirmation, and has paid the required fee, the Clerk will notify the applicant of acceptance by the Court as a member of the Bar and issue a certificate of admis-

sion. An applicant who so desires may be admitted in open court on oral motion by a member of the Bar of this Court, provided that all other requirements for admission have been satisfied.

.4. Each applicant shall take or subscribe to the following oath or affirmation: I, _____, do solemnly swear (or affirm) that as an attorney and as a counselor of this Court, I will conduct myself uprightly and according to law, and that I will support the Constitution of the United States.

.5. The fee for admission to the Bar and a certificate under seal is $100, payable to the Marshal, U. S. Supreme Court. The Marshal shall maintain the proceeds as a separate fund to be disbursed by the Marshal at the direction of the Chief Justice for the costs of admissions, for the benefit of the Court and the Supreme Court Bar, and for related purposes.

.6. The cost for a duplicate certificate of admission to the Bar under seal is $10, payable to the Marshal, U. S. Supreme Court. The proceeds shall be maintained by the Marshal as provided in paragraph .5 of this Rule.

RULE 6
Argument Pro Hac Vice

.1. An attorney not admitted to practice in the highest court of a State, Commonwealth, Territory or Possession, or of the District of Columbia for the requisite three years, but who is otherwise eligible for admission to practice in this Court under Rule 5.1, may be permitted to argue *pro hac vice*.

.2. An attorney, barrister, or advocate who is qualified to practice in the courts of a foreign state may be permitted to argue *pro hac vice*.

.3. Oral argument *pro hac vice* will be allowed only on motion of the attorney of record for the party on whose behalf leave is requested. The motion must briefly and distinctly state the appropriate qualifications of the attorney who is to argue *pro hac vice*. It must be filed with the Clerk, in the form prescribed by Rule 21, no later than the date on which the respondent's or appellee's brief on the merits is due to be filed and must be accompanied by proof of service pursuant to Rule 29.

RULE 7

Prohibition Against Practice

. l. The Clerk shall not practice as an attorney or counselor while holding office.

.2. No law clerk, secretary to a Justice, or other employee of this Court shall practice as an attorney or counselor in any court or before any agency of government while employed at the Court; nor shall any person after leaving employment in this Court participate, by way of any form of professional consultation or assistance, in any case pending before this Court or in any case being considered for filing in this Court, until two years have elapsed after separation; nor shall a former employee ever participate, by way of any form of professional consultation or assistance, in any case that was pending in this Court during the employee's tenure.

RULE 8

Disbarment and Disciplinary Action

.1. Whenever it is shown to the Court that a member of the Bar of this Court has been disbarred or suspended from practice in any court of record, or has engaged in conduct unbecoming a member of the Bar of this Court, that member will be suspended from practice before this Court forthwith and will be afforded the opportunity to show cause, within 40 days, why a disbarment order should not be entered. Upon response, or upon the expiration of the 40 days if no response is made, the Court will enter an appropriate order.

.2. The Court may, after reasonable notice and an opportunity to show cause why disciplinary action should not be taken, and after a hearing if material facts are in dispute, take any appropriate disciplinary action against any attorney who practices before it for conduct unbecoming a member of the Bar or for failure to comply with these Rules or any Rule of the Court.

RULE 9

Appearance of Counsel

.1. An attorney seeking to file a pleading, motion, or other paper in this Court in a representative capacity must first be admitted to practice before this Court pursuant to Rule 5. The attorney whose name, address, and telephone number appear on the cover of a document being filed will be deemed counsel of record, and a separate notice of appearance need not be filed. If the name of more than one attorney is shown on the cover of the document, the attorney who is counsel of record must be clearly identified.

.2. An attorney representing a party who will not be filing a document must enter a separate notice of appearance as counsel of record indicating the name of the party represented. If an attorney is to be substituted as counsel of record in a particular case, a separate notice of appearance must also be entered.

PART III.
JURISDICTION ON WRIT OF CERTIORARI

RULE 10

Considerations Governing Review on Writ of Certiorari

.1. A review on writ of certiorari is not a matter of right, but of judicial discretion. A petition for a writ of certiorari will be granted only when there are special and important reasons therefor. The following, while neither controlling nor fully measuring the Court's discretion, indicate the character of reasons that will be considered:

   (a) When a United States court of appeals has rendered a decision in conflict with the decision of another United States court of appeals on the same matter; or has decided a federal question in a way in conflict with a state court of last resort; or has so far departed from the accepted and usual course of judicial proceedings, or sanctioned such a departure by a lower court, as to call for an exercise of this Court's power of supervision.

   (b) When a state court of last resort has decided a federal question in a way that conflicts with the decision of another state court of last resort or of a United States court of appeals.

   (c) When a state court or a United States court of appeals has decided an important question of federal law which has not been, but should be, settled by this Court, or has decided a federal question in a way that conflicts with applicable decisions of this Court.

.2. The same general considerations outlined above will control in respect to a petition for a writ of certiorari to review a judgment of the United States Court of Military Appeals.

RULE 11

Certiorari to a United States Court of Appeals Before Judgment

A petition for a writ of certiorari to review a case pending in a United States court of appeals, before judgment is given in that court, will be granted only upon a showing that the case is of such imperative public importance to justify deviation from normal appellate practice and to require immediate settlement in this Court. 28 U. S. C. § 2101(e).

RULE 12

Review on Certiorari; How Sought; Parties

.1. The petitioner's counsel, who must be a member of the Bar of this Court, shall file, with proof of service as provided by Rule 29, 40 copies of a printed petition for a writ of certiorari, which shall comply in all respects with Rule 14, and shall pay the docket fee prescribed by Rule 38. The case then will be placed on the docket. It shall be the duty of counsel for the petitioner to notify all respondents, on a form supplied by the Clerk, of the date of filing and of the docket number of the case. The notice shall be served as required by Rule 29.

.2. Parties interested jointly, severally, or otherwise in a judgment may petition separately for a writ of certiorari; or any two or more may join in a petition. A party who is not shown on the petition for a writ of certiorari to have joined therein at the time the petition is filed with the Clerk may not thereafter join in that petition. When two or more cases are sought to be reviewed on a writ of certiorari to the same court and involve identical or closely related questions, a single petition for a writ of certiorari covering all the cases will suffice. A petition for a writ of certiorari shall not be joined with any other pleading.

.3. Not more than 30 days after receipt of the petition for a writ of certiorari, counsel for a respondent wishing to file a cross-petition that would otherwise be untimely shall file, with proof of service as prescribed by Rule 29, 40 printed copies of a cross-petition for a writ of certiorari, which shall comply in all respects with Rule 14, except that materials printed in the appendix to the original petition need not be reprinted, and shall pay the docket fee pursuant to Rule 38. The cover of the petition shall clearly indicate that it is a cross-petition. The cross-petition will then be placed on the docket subject, however, to the provisions of Rule 13.5. It shall be the duty of counsel for the cross-petitioner to notify the cross-respondent, on a form supplied by the Clerk, of the date of docketing and of the docket number of the cross-petition. The notice shall be served as required by Rule 29. A cross-petition for a writ of certiori may not be joined with any other pleading, and the Clerk shall not accept any pleading so joined. The time for filing a cross-petition may not be extended.

.4. All parties to the proceeding in the court whose judgment is sought to be reviewed shall be deemed parties in this Court, unless the petitioner notifies the Clerk of this Court in writing of the petitioner's belief that one or more of the parties below has no interest in the outcome of the petition. A copy of the notice shall be served as required by Rule 29 on all parties to the proceeding below. A party noted as no longer interested may remain a party by promptly notifying the Clerk, with service on the other parties, of an intention to remain a party. All parties other than petitioners shall be respondents, but any respondent who supports the position of a petitioner shall meet the time schedule for filing papers which is provided for that petitioner, except that a response to the petition shall be filed within 20 days after its receipt, and the time may not be extended.

.5. The clerk of the court having possession of the record shall retain custody thereof pending notification from the Clerk of this Court that the record is to be certified and transmitted to this Court. When requested by the Clerk of this Court to certify and transmit the record, or any part of it, the clerk of the court having possession of the record shall number the documents to be certified and shall transmit therewith a numbered list specifically identifying each document transmitted. If the record, or stipulated portions thereof, has been printed for the use of the court below, that printed record, plus the proceedings in the court below, may be certified as the record unless one of the parties or the Clerk of this Court otherwise requests. The record may consist of certified copies, but the presiding judge of the lower court who believes that original papers of any kind should be seen by this Court may, by order, make provision for their transport, safekeeping, and return.

RULE 13

Review on Certiorari; Time for Petitioning

.1. A petition for a writ of certiorari to review a judgment in any case, civil or criminal, entered by a state court of last resort, a United States court of appeals, or the United States Court of Military Appeals shall be deemed in time when it is filed with the Clerk of this court within 90 days after the entry of the judgment. A petition for a writ of certiorari seeking review of a judgment of a lower state court which is subject to discretionary review by the state court of last resort shall be deemed in time when it is filed with the Clerk within 90 days after the entry of the order denying discretionary review.

.2. A Justice of this Court, for good cause shown, may extend the time to file a petition for a writ of certiorari for a period not exceeding 60 days.

.3. The Clerk will refuse to receive any petition for a writ of certiorari which is jurisdictionally out of time.

.4. The time for filing a petition for a writ of certiorari runs from the date the judgment or decree sought to be reviewed is rendered, and not from the date of the issuance of the mandate (or its equivalent under local practice). However, if a petition for rehearing is timely filed in the lower court by any party in the case, the time for filing the petition for a writ of certiorari for all parties (whether or not they requested rehearing or joined in the petition for rehearing) runs from the date

of the denial of the petition for rehearing or the entry of a subsequent judgment. A suggestion made to a United States court of appeals for a rehearing in banc pursuant to Rule 35(b), Federal Rules of Appellate Procedure, is not a petition for rehearing within the meaning of this Rule.

.5. A cross-petition for a writ of certiorari shall be deemed in time when it is filed with the Clerk as provided in paragraphs .1, .2, and .4 of this Rule, or in Rule 12.3. However, a cross-petition which, except for Rule 12.3, would be untimely, will not be granted unless a timely petition for a writ of certiorari of another party to the case is granted.

.6. An application to extend the time to file a petition for a writ of certiorari must set out the grounds on which the jurisdiction of this Court is invoked, must identify the judgment sought to be reviewed and have appended thereto a copy of the opinion and any order respecting rehearing, and must set forth with specificity the reasons why the granting of an extension of time is thought justified. For the time and manner of presenting the application, see Rules 21, 22, and 30. An application to extend the time to file a petition for a writ of certiorari is not favored.

RULE 14

Content of the Petition for a Writ of Certiorari

.1. The petition for a writ of certiorari shall contain, in the order here indicated:

(a) The questions presented for review, expressed in the terms and circumstances of the case, but without unnecessary detail. The questions should be short and concise and should not be argumentative or repetitious. They must be set forth on the first page following the cover with no other information appearing on that page. The statement of any question presented will be deemed to comprise every subsidiary question fairly included therein. Only the questions set forth in the petition, or fairly included therein, will be considered by the Court.

(b) A list of all parties to the proceeding in the court whose judgment is sought to be reviewed, unless the names of all parties appear in the caption of the case. This listing may be done in a footnote. See also Rule 29.1 for the required listing of parent companies and nonwholly owned subsidiaries.

(c) A table of contents and a table of authorities, if the petition exceeds five pages.

(d) A reference to the official and unofficial reports of opinions delivered in the case by other courts or administrative agencies.

(e) A concise statement of the grounds on which the jurisdiction of this Court is invoked showing:

(i) The date of the entry of the judgment or decree sought to be reviewed;

(ii) The date of any order respecting a rehearing, and the date and terms of any order granting an extension of time within which to file the petition for a writ of certiorari;

(iii) Express reliance upon Rule 12.3 when a cross-petition for a writ of certiorari is filed under that Rule and the date of receipt of the petition for a writ of certiorari in connection with which the cross-petition is filed; and

(iv) The statutory provision believed to confer on this Court jurisdiction to review the judgment or decree in question by writ of certiorari.

(f) The constitutional provisions, treaties, statutes, ordinances, and regulations involved in the case, setting them out verbatim, and giving the appropriate citation therefor. If the provisions involved are lengthy, their citation alone will suffice at this point and their pertinent text must be set forth in the appendix referred to in subparagraph .1(k) of this Rule.

(g) A concise statement of the case containing the facts material to the consideration of the questions presented.

(h) If review of a judgment of a state court is sought, the statement of the case shall also specify the stage in the proceedings, both in the court of first instance and in the appellate courts, at which the federal questions sought to be reviewed were raised; the method or manner of raising them and the way in which they were passed upon by those courts; and such pertinent quotation of specific portions of the record or summary thereof, with specific reference to the places in the record where the matter appears (e. g., ruling on excep-

tion, portion of court's charge and exception thereto, assignment of errors) as will show that the federal question was timely and properly raised so as to give this Court jurisdiction to review the judgment on a writ of certiorari. When the portions of the record relied upon under this subparagraph are voluminous, they shall be included in the appendix referred to in subparagraph .1(k) of this Rule.

(i) If review of a judgment of a United States court of appeals is sought, the statement of the case shall also show the basis for federal jurisdiction in the court of first instance.

(j) A direct and concise argument amplifying the reasons relied on for the allowance of the writ. See Rule 10 .

(k) An appendix containing, in the following order:

(i) The opinions, orders, findings of fact, and conclusions of law, whether written or orally given and transcribed, delivered upon the rendering of the judgment or decree by the court whose decision is sought to be reviewed.

(ii) Any other opinions, orders, findings of fact, and conclusions of law rendered in the case by courts or administrative agencies, and, if reference thereto is necessary to ascertain the grounds of the judgment or decree, of those in companion cases. Each document shall include the caption showing the name of the issuing court or agency, the title and number of the case, and the date of entry.

(iii) Any order on rehearing, including the caption showing the name of the issuing court, the title and number of the case, and the date of entry.

(iv) The judgment sought to be reviewed if the date of its entry is different from the date of the opinion or order required in sub-subparagraph (i) of this subparagraph.

(v) Any other appended materials.

If what is required by subparagraphs .1(f), (h), and (k) of this Rule to be included in or filed with the petition is voluminous, it may be presented in a separate volume or volumes with appropriate covers.

.2. The petition for a writ of certiorari and the appendix thereto, whether in the same or a separate volume, shall be produced in conformity with Rule 33. The Clerk shall not accept any petition for a writ of certiorari that does not comply with this Rule and with Rule 33, except that a party proceeding *in forma pauperis* may proceed in the manner provided in Rule 39.

.3. All contentions in support of a petition for a writ of certiorari shall be set forth in the body of the petition, as provided in subparagraph .1(j) of this Rule. No separate brief in support of a petition for a writ of certiorari will be received, and the Clerk will refuse to file any petition for a writ of certiorari to which is annexed or appended any supporting brief.

.4. The petition for a writ of certiorari shall be as short as possible and may not exceed the page limitations set out in Rule 33.

.5. The failure of a petitioner to present with accuracy, brevity, and clearness whatever is essential to a ready and adequate understanding of the points requiring consideration will be a sufficient reason for denying the petition.

RULE 15

Brief in Opposition; Reply Brief; Supplemental Brief

.1. A brief in opposition to a petition for a writ of certiorari serves an important purpose in assisting the Court in the exercise of its discretionary jurisdiction. In addition to other arguments for denying the petition, the brief in opposition should address any perceived misstatements of fact or law set forth in the petition which have a bearing on the question of what issues would properly be before the Court if certiorari were granted. Unless this is done, the Court may grant the petition in the mistaken belief that the issues presented can be decided, only to learn upon full consideration of the briefs and record at the time of oral argument that such is not the case. Counsel are admonished that they have an obligation to the Court to point out any perceived misstatements in the brief in opposition, and not later. Any defect of this sort in the proceedings below that does not go to jurisdiction may be deemed waived if not called to the attention of the Court by the respondent in the brief in opposition.

.2. The respondent shall have 30 days (unless enlarged by the Court or a Justice thereof or by the Clerk pursuant to Rule 30.4) after receipt of a petition within which to file 40 printed copies of an opposing brief disclosing any matter or ground as to why the case should not be reviewed by this Court. See Rule 10. The brief in opposition shall comply with Rule 33 and with the requirements of Rule 24 governing a respondent's brief, and shall be served as prescribed by Rule 29. A brief in opposition shall not be joined with any other pleading. The Clerk shall not accept a brief which does not comply with this Rule and with Rule 33, except that a party proceeding *in forma pauperis* may proceed in the manner provided in Rule 39. If the petitioner is proceeding *in forma pauperis*, the respondent may file 12 typewritten copies of a brief in opposition prepared in the manner prescribed by Rule 34.

.3. A brief in opposition shall be as short as possible and may not exceed the page limitations set out in Rule 33.

.4. No motion by a respondent to dismiss a petition for a writ of certiorari will be received. Objections to the jurisdiction of the Court to grant a writ of certiorari may be included in the brief in opposition.

.5. Upon the filing of a brief in opposition, the expiration of the time allowed therefor, or an express waiver of the right to file, the petition and brief in opposition, if any, will be distributed by the Clerk to the Court for its consideration. However, if a cross-petition for a writ of certiorari has been filed, distribution of both it and the petition for a writ of certiorari will be delayed until the filing of a brief in opposition by the cross-respondent, the expiration of the time allowed therefor, or an express waiver of the right to file.

.6. A reply brief addressed to arguments first raised in the brief in opposition may be filed by any petitioner, but distribution and consideration by the Court under paragraph .5 of this Rule will not be delayed pending its filing. Forty copies of the reply brief, prepared in accordance with Rule 33 and served as prescribed by Rule 29, shall be filed.

.7. Any party may file a supplemental brief at any time while a petition for a writ of certiorari is pending calling attention to new cases or legislation or other intervening matter not available at the time of the party's last filing. A supplemental brief must be restricted to new matter. Forty copies of the supplemental brief, prepared in accordance with Rule 33 and served as prescribed by Rule 29, shall be filed.

RULE 16
Disposition of a Petition for a Writ of Certiorari

.1. After consideration of the papers distributed pursuant to Rule 15, the Court will enter an appropriate order. The order may be a summary disposition on the merits.

.2. Whenever a petition for a writ of certiorari to review a decision of any court is granted, the Clerk shall enter an order to that effect and shall forthwith notify the court below and counsel of record. The case will then be scheduled for briefing and oral argument. If the record has not previously been filed, the Clerk of this Court shall request the clerk of the court having possession of the record to certify it and transmit it to this Court. A formal writ shall not issue unless specially directed.

.3. Whenever a petition for a writ of certiorari to review a decision of any court is denied, the Clerk shall enter an order to that effect and shall forthwith notify the court below and counsel of record. The order of denial will not be suspended pending disposition of a petition for rehearing except by order of the Court or a Justice.

PART IV.
OTHER JURISDICTION

RULE 17
Procedure in an Original Action

.1. This Rule applies only to an action within the Court's original jurisdiction under Article III of the Constitution of the United States. See also 28

U. S. C. § 1251 and the Eleventh Amendment to the Constitution of the United States. A petition for an extraordinary writ in aid of the Court's appellate jurisdiction must be filed in accordance with Rule 20.

.2. The form of pleadings and motions prescribed by the Federal Rules of Civil Procedure should be followed in an original action to be filed in this Court. In other respects those Rules, when their application is appropriate, may be taken as a guide to procedure in an original action in this Court.

.3. The initial pleading in any original action shall be prefaced by a motion for leave to file, and both the pleading and motion must be printed in conformity with Rule 33. A brief in support of the motion for leave to file, which shall also comply with Rule 33, may also be filed with the motion and pleading. Sixty copies of each document with proof of service as prescribed by Rule 29, are required, except that when an adverse party is a State, service shall be made on both the Governor and the attorney general of that State.

.4. The case will be placed on the docket when the motion for leave to file and the pleading are filed with the Clerk. The docket fee provided by Rule 38 must be paid at that time.

.5. Within 60 days after the receipt of the motion for leave to file and the pleading, an adverse party may file, with proof of service as prescribed by Rule 29, 60 printed copies of a brief in opposition to the motion. The brief shall comply with Rule 33. When the brief in opposition has been filed, or when the time within which it may be filed has expired, the motion, pleading, and briefs will be distributed to the Court by the Clerk. The Court may thereafter grant or deny the motion, set it down for oral argument, direct that additional pleadings be filed, or require that other proceedings be conducted.

.6. A summons issuing out of this Court in an original action shall be served on the defendant 60 days before the return day set out therein. If the defendant does not respond by the return day, the plaintiff may proceed *ex parte*.

.7. Process against a State issued from the Court in an original action shall be served on both the Governor and the attorney general of that State.

RULE 18

Appeal from a United States District Court

.1. A direct appeal from a decision of a United States district court, when authorized by law, is commenced by filing a notice of appeal with the clerk of the district court within 30 days after the entry of the judgment sought to be reviewed. The time may not be extended. The notice of appeal shall specify the parties taking the appeal, shall designate the judgment, or part thereof, appealed from and the date of its entry, and shall specify the statute or statutes under which the appeal is taken. A copy of the notice of appeal shall be served on all parties to the proceeding pursuant to Rule 29 and proof of service must be filed in the district court with the notice of appeal.

.2. All parties to the proceeding in the district court shall be deemed parties to the appeal, but a party having no interest in the outcome of the appeal may so notify the Clerk of this Court and shall serve a copy of the notice on all other parties. Parties interested jointly, severally, or otherwise in the judgment may appeal separately; or any two or more may join in an appeal.

.3. Not more than 60 days after the filing of the notice of appeal in the district court, counsel for the appellant shall file, with proof of service as prescribed by Rule 29, 40 printed copies of a statement as to jurisdiction and pay the docket fee prescribed by Rule 38. The jurisdictional statement shall follow, insofar as applicable, the form for a petition for a writ of certiorari prescribed by Rule 14. The appendix must also include a copy of the notice of appeal showing the date it was filed in the district court. The jurisdictional statement and the appendices thereto must be produced in conformity with Rule 33, except that a party proceeding *in forma pauperis* may proceed in the manner prescribed in Rule 39. A Justice of this Court may, for good cause shown, extend the time for filing a jurisdictional statement for a period not exceeding 60 days. An application to extend the time to file a jurisdictional statement must set out the basis of jurisdiction in this Court, must identify the judgment to be reviewed, must include a copy of the opinion, any order respecting rehearing, and the notice of appeal, and must set forth specific reasons why the granting of an extension of time is justified. For the time and manner of presenting the application, see Rules 21, 22, and 30. An application to extend the time to file a jurisdictional statement is not favored.

.4. The clerk of the district court shall retain possession of the record pending notification from the Clerk of this Court that the record is to be certified and transmitted. See Rule 12.5.

.5. After a notice of appeal has been filed, but before the case is docketed in this Court, the parties may dismiss the appeal by stipulation filed in the district court, or the district court may dismiss the appeal upon motion of the appellant and notice to all parties. If a notice of appeal has been filed but the case has not been docketed in this Court within the time prescribed for docketing or any enlargement thereof, the district court may dismiss the appeal upon the motion of the appellee and notice to all parties and may make any order with respect to costs as may be just. If an appellee's motion to dismiss the appeal is not granted, the appellee may have the case docketed in this Court and may seek to have the appeal dismissed by filing a motion pursuant to Rule 21. If the appeal is dismissed, the Court may give judgment for costs against the appellant.

.6. Within 30 days after receipt of the jurisdictional statement, the appellee may file 40 printed copies of a motion to dismiss, to affirm, or, in the alternative, to affirm and dismiss. The motion shall comply in all respects with Rules 21 and 33, except that a party proceeding *in forma pauperis* may proceed in the manner provided in Rule 39. The Court may permit the appellee to defend a judgment on any ground that the law and record permit and that would not expand the relief granted.

.7. Upon the filing of the motion, or the expiration of the time allowed therefor, or an express waiver of the right to file, the jurisdictional statement and motion, if any, will be distributed by the Clerk to the Court for its consideration.

.8. A brief opposing a motion to dismiss or affirm may be filed by an appellant, but distribution to the Court under paragraph .7 of this Rule will not be delayed pending its receipt. Forty copies, prepared in accordance with Rule 33 and served as prescribed by Rule 29, shall be filed.

.9. Any party may file a supplemental brief at any time while a jurisdictional statement is pending, calling attention to new cases, new legislation, or other intervening matter not available at the time of the party's last filing. Forty copies, prepared in accordance with Rule 33 and served as prescribed by Rule 29, shall be filed.

.10. After consideration of the papers distributed under this Rule, the Court may summarily dispose of the appeal on the merits, note probable jurisdiction, or postpone jurisdiction to the hearing on the merits. If not disposed of summarily, the case will stand for briefing and oral argument on the merits. If consideration of jurisdiction is postponed, counsel, at the outset of their briefs and at oral argument, shall address the question of jurisdiction.

RULE 19

Procedure on a Certified Question
.1. A United States court of appeals may certify to this Court a question or proposition of law concerning which it desires instruction for the proper decision of a case. The certificate submitted shall contain a statement of the nature of the case and the facts on which the question or proposition of law arises. Only questions or propositions of law may be certified, and they must be distinct and definite.

.2. When a case is certified by a United States court of appeals, this Court, on application or on its own motion, may consider and decide the entire matter in controversy. See 28 U. S. C. § 1254(2).

.3. When a case is certified the Clerk will notify the respective parties and docket the case. Counsel shall then enter their appearances. After docketing, the certificate shall be submitted to the Court

for a preliminary examination to determine whether the case shall be briefed, set for argument, or dismissed. No brief may be filed prior to the preliminary examination of the certificate.

.4. If the Court orders that the case be briefed or set for argument, the parties shall be notified and permitted to file briefs. The Clerk of this Court shall then request the clerk of the court from which the case originates to certify the record and transmit it to this Court. Any portion of the record to which the parties wish to direct the Court's particular attention shall be printed in a joint appendix prepared by the appellant in the court below under the procedures provided in Rule 26, but the fact that any part of the record has not been printed shall not prevent the parties or the Court from relying on it.

.5. A brief on the merits in a case on certificate shall comply with Rules 24, 25, and 33, except that the brief of the party who is the appellant below shall be filed within 45 days of the order requiring briefs or setting the case for argument.

RULE 20

Procedure on a Petition for an Extraordinary Writ
.1. The issuance by the Court of an extraordinary writ authorized by 28 U. S. C. §1651(a) is not a matter of right, but of discretion sparingly exercised. To justify the granting of any writ under that provision, it must be shown that the writ will be in aid of the Court's appellate jurisdiction, that there are present exceptional circumstances warranting the exercise of the Court's discretionary powers, and that adequate relief cannot be obtained in any other form or from any other court.

.2. The petition in any proceeding seeking the issuance by this Court of a writ authorized by 28 U. S. C. §§1651(a), 2241, or 2254(a), shall comply in all respects with Rule 33, except that a party proceeding *in forma pauperis* may proceed in the manner provided in Rule 39. The petition shall be captioned "*In re* [name of petitioner]" and shall follow, insofar as applicable, the form of a petition for a writ of certiorari prescribed by Rule 14. All contentions in support of the petition shall be included in the petition. The case will be placed on the docket when 40 printed copies, with proof of service as prescribed by Rule 29 (subject to subparagraph .4(b) of this Rule), are filed with the Clerk and the docket fee is paid.

.3. (a) A petition seeking the issuance of a writ of prohibition, a writ of mandamus, or both in the alternative, shall set forth the name and office or function of every person against whom relief is sought and shall set forth with particularity why the relief sought is not available in any other court. There shall be appended to the petition a copy of the judgment or order in respect of which the writ is sought, including a copy of any opinion rendered in that connection, and any other paper essential to an understanding of the petition.

(b) The petition shall be served on the judge or judges to whom the writ is sought to be directed and shall also be served on every other party to the proceeding in respect of which relief is desired The judge or judges and the other parties may, within 30 days after receipt of the petition, file 40 printed copies of a brief or briefs in opposition thereto, which shall comply fully with Rule 15. If the judge or judges who are named respondents do not desire to respond to the petition, they may so advise the Clerk and all parties by letter. All persons served shall be deemed respondents for all purposes in the proceedings in this Court.

.4. (a) A petition seeking the issuance of a writ of habeas corpus shall comply with the requirements of 28 U. S. C. §§2241 and 2242, and in particular with the provision in the last paragraph of §2242 requiring a statement of the "reasons for not making application to the district court of the district in which the applicant is held." If the relief sought is from the judgment of a state court, the petition shall set forth specifically how and wherein the petitioner has exhausted available remedies in the state courts or otherwise comes within the provisions of 28 U. S. C. § 2254(b). To justify the granting of a writ of habeas corpus, the petitioner must show exceptional circumstances warranting the exercise of the Court's discretionary powers and must show

that adequate relief cannot be obtained in any other form or from any other court. These writs are rarely granted.

(b) Proceedings under this paragraph .4 will be *ex parte*, unless the Court requires the respondent to show cause why the petition for a writ of habeas corpus should not be granted. A response, if ordered, shall comply fully with Rule 15. Neither the denial of the petition, without more, nor an order of transfer to a district court under the authority of 28 U. S. C. § 2241(b), is an adjudication on the merits, and therefore does not preclude further application to another court for the relief sought.

.5. When a brief in opposition under subparagraph .3(b) has been filed, when a response under subparagraph .4(b) has been ordered and filed, when the time within which it may be filed has expired, or upon an express waiver of the right to file, the papers will be distributed to the Court by the Clerk.

.6. If the Court orders the case to be set for argument, the Clerk will notify the parties whether additional briefs are required, when they must be filed, and, if the case involves a petition for a common law writ of certiorari, that the parties shall proceed to print a joint appendix pursuant to Rule 26.

PART V.
MOTIONS AND
APPLICATIONS

RULE 21
Motions to the Court

.1. Every motion to the Court shall clearly state its purpose and the facts on which it is based and (except for a motion to dismiss or affirm under Rule 18) may present legal argument in support thereof. No separate brief may be filed. A motion shall be as short as possible and shall comply with any applicable page limits. For an application addressed to a single Justice, see Rule 22.

.2. (a) A motion in any action within the Court's original jurisdiction shall comply with Rule 17.3.

(b) A motion to dismiss or affirm under Rule 18, a motion to dismiss as moot (or a suggestion of mootness), a motion for permission to file a brief *amicus curiae*, and any motion the granting of which would be dispositive of the entire case or would affect the final judgment to be entered (other than a motion to docket and dismiss under Rule 18.5 or a motion for voluntary dismissal under Rule 46) shall be printed in accordance with Rule 33 and shall comply with all other requirements of that Rule. Forty copies of the motion shall be filed.

(c) Any other motion to the Court may be typewritten in accordance with Rule 34, but the Court may subsequently require the motion to be printed by the moving party in the manner provided by Rule 33.

.3. A motion to the Court shall be filed with the Clerk and must be accompanied by proof of service as provided by Rule 29. No motion shall be presented in open court, other than a motion for admission to the Bar, except when the proceeding to which it refers is being argued. Oral argument will not be permitted on any motion unless the Court so directs.

.4. A response to a motion shall be made as promptly as possible considering the nature of the relief asked and any asserted need for emergency action, and, in any event, shall he made within 10 days of receipt, unless otherwise ordered by the Court or a Justice or by the Clerk under the provisions of Rule 30.4. A response to a printed motion shall be printed if time permits. In an appropriate case, however, the Court may act on a motion without waiting for a response.

RULE 22

Applications to Individual Justices

.1. An application addressed to an individual Justice shall be submitted to the Clerk, who will promptly transmit it to the Justice concerned.

.2. The original and two copies of any application addressed to an individual Justice shall be filed in the form prescribed by Rule 34, and shall be accompanied by proof of service on all parties.

.3. The Clerk in due course will advise all counsel concerned, by means as speedy as may be appropriate, of the disposition made of the application.

.4. The application shall be addressed to the Justice allotted to the Circuit within which the case arises. When the Circuit Justice is unavailable for any reason, the application addressed to that Justice will be distributed to the Justice then available who is next junior to the Circuit Justice; the turn of the Chief Justice follows that of the most junior Justice.

.5. A Justice denying the application will note the denial thereon. Thereafter, unless action thereon is restricted by law to the Circuit Justice or is out of time under Rule 30.2, the party making the application, except in the case of an application for an extension of time, may renew it to any other Justice, subject to the provisions of this Rule. Except when the denial has been without prejudice, a renewed application is not favored. Any renewed application may be made by sending a letter to the Clerk of the Court addressed to another Justice to which must be attached 12 copies of the original application, together with proof of service pursuant to Rule 29.

.6. A Justice to whom an application for a stay or for bail is submitted may refer it to the Court for determination.

RULE 23

Stays

.1. A stay may be granted by a Justice of this Court as permitted by law.

.2. A petitioner entitled thereto may present to a Justice of this Court an application to stay the enforcement of the judgment sought to be reviewed on writ of certiorari. 28 U. S. C. §2101(f).

.3. An application for a stay must set forth with particularity why the relief sought is not available from any other court or judge thereof. Except in the most extraordinary circumstances, an application for a stay will not be entertained unless the relief requested has first been sought in the appropriate court or courts below or from a judge or judges thereof. An application for a stay must identify the judgment sought to be reviewed and have appended thereto a copy of the order and opinion, if any, and a copy of the order if any, of the court or judge below denying the relief sought, and must set forth with specificity the reasons why the granting of a stay is deemed justified. The form and content of an application for a stay are governed by Rule 22.

.4. The judge, court, or Justice granting an application for a stay pending review by this Court may condition the stay on the filing of a supersedeas bond having an approved surety or sureties. The bond shall be conditioned on the satisfaction of the judgment in full, together with any costs, interest, and damages for delay that may be awarded. If a part of the judgment sought to be reviewed has already been satisfied, or is otherwise secured, the bond may be conditioned on the satisfaction of the part of the judgment not otherwise secured or satisfied, together with costs, interest, and damages.

PART VI.
BRIEFS ON THE MERITS AND ORAL ARGUMENT

RULE 24
Briefs on the Merits; In General

.1. A brief of a petitioner or an appellant on the merits must comply in all respects with Rule 33, and must contain in the order here indicated:

(a) The questions presented for review, stated as required by Rule 14. The phrasing of the questions presented need not be identical with that set forth in the petition for a writ of certiorari or the jurisdictional statement, but the brief may not raise additional questions or change the substance of the questions already presented in those documents. At its option, however, the Court may consider a plain error not among the questions presented but evident from the record and otherwise within its jurisdiction to decide.

(b) A list of all parties to the proceeding in the court whose judgment is sought to be reviewed, unless the caption of the case in this Court contains the names of all parties. This listing may be done in a footnote. See also Rule 29.1, which requires a list of parent companies and nonwholly owned subsidiaries.

(c) A table of contents and a table of authorities, if the brief exceeds five pages.

(d) Citations of the opinions and judgments delivered in the courts below.

(e) A concise statement of the grounds on which the jurisdiction of this Court is invoked, with citation of the statutory provision and of the time factors upon which jurisdiction rests.

(f) The constitutional provisions, treaties, statutes, ordinances, and regulations which the case involves, setting them out verbatim and giving the appropriate citation therefor. If the provisions involved are lengthy, their citation alone will suffice at this point, and their pertinent text, if not already set forth in the petition for a writ of certiorari, jurisdictional statement, or an appendix to either document, shall be set forth in an appendix to the brief.

(g) A concise statement of the case containing all that is material to the consideration of the questions presented, with appropriate references to the joint appendix, *e. g.* (J. A. 12) or to the record, *e. g.* (R. 12).

(h) A summary of the argument, suitably paragraphed, which should be a succinct, but accurate and clear, condensation of the argument actually made in the body of the brief. A mere repetition of the headings under which the argument is arranged is not sufficient.

(i) The argument, exhibiting clearly the points of fact and of law being presented and citing the authorities and statutes relied upon.

(j) A conclusion, specifying with particularity the relief which the party seeks.

.2. The brief filed by a respondent or an appellee must conform to the foregoing requirements, except that no statement of the case need be made beyond what may be deemed necessary to correct any inaccuracy or omission in the statement by the other side. Items required by subparagraphs .1(a), (b), (d), (e), and (f) of this Rule need not be included unless the respondent or appellee is dissatisfied with their presentation by the other side.

.3. A brief on the merits shall be as short as possible and shall not exceed the page limitations set out in Rule 33. An appendix to a brief must be limited to relevant material, and counsel are cautioned not to include in an appendix arguments or citations that properly belong in the body of the brief.

.4. A reply brief shall conform to those portions of this Rule that are applicable to the brief of a respondent or an appellee, but, if appropriately divided by topical headings, need not contain a summary of the argument.

.5. A reference to the joint appendix or to the record set forth in any brief must be accompanied by the appropriate page number. If the reference is to an exhibit, the page numbers at which the exhibit appears, at which it was offered in evidence, and at which it was ruled on by the judge must be indicated, *e. g.* (Pl.Ex. 14; R.199, 2134).

.6. A brief must be compact, logically arranged with proper headings, concise, and free from burdensome, irrelevant, immaterial, and scandalous matter. A brief not complying with this paragraph may be disregarded and stricken by the Court.

RULE 25
Brief on the Merits; Time for Filing
.1. Counsel for the petitioner or appellant shall file with the Clerk 40 copies of a brief on the merits within 45 days of the order granting the writ of certiorari or of the order noting or postponing probable jurisdiction.

.2. Forty copies of the brief of the respondent or appellee must be filed with the Clerk within 30 days after the receipt of the brief filed by the petitioner or appellant.

.3. A reply brief, if any, must be filed within 30 days after receipt of the brief for the respondent or appellee, or must actually be received by the Clerk not later than one week before the date of oral argument, whichever is earlier. Forty copies are required.

.4. The periods of time stated in paragraphs .1 and .2 of this Rule may be enlarged as provided in Rule 30. If a case is advanced for hearing, the time for filing briefs on the merits may be abridged as circumstances require pursuant to the order of the Court on its own motion or a party's application.

.5. A party desiring to present late authorities, newly enacted legislation, or other intervening matter that was not available in time to have been included in a brief may file 40 printed copies of a supplemental brief, restricted to new matter and otherwise presented in conformity with these Rules, up to the time the case is called for oral argument, or by leave of the Court thereafter.

.6. No brief will be received through the Clerk or otherwise after a case has been argued or submitted, except from a party and upon leave of the Court.

.7. No brief will be received by the Clerk unless it is accompanied by proof of service as required by Rule 29.

RULE 26
The Joint Appendix
.1. Unless the parties agree to use the deferred method allowed in paragraph .4 of this Rule, or the Court so directs, the petitioner or appellant, within 45 days after the entry of the order granting the writ of certiorari, or noting or postponing jurisdiction, shall file 40 copies of a joint appendix, printed as prescribed by Rule 33. The joint appendix shall contain: (1) the relevant docket entries in all the courts below; (2) any relevant pleading, jury instruction, finding, conclusion, or opinion; (3) the judgment, order, or decision sought to be reviewed; and (4) any other parts of the record which the parties particularly wish to bring to the Court's attention. Any of the foregoing items which have already been reproduced in a petition for a writ of certiorari, jurisdictional statement, brief in opposition to a petition for a writ of certiorari, motion to dismiss or affirm, or any appendix to the foregoing complying with Rule 33 need not be reproduced again in the joint appendix. The petitioner or appellant shall serve

three copies of the joint appendix on each of the other parties to the proceeding.

.2. The parties are encouraged to agree to the contents of the joint appendix. In the absence of agreement, the petitioner or appellant shall, not later than 10 days after receipt of the order granting the writ of certiorari, or noting or postponing jurisdiction, serve on the respondent or appellee a designation of parts of the record to be included in the joint appendix. A respondent or appellee who deems the parts of the record so designated not to be sufficient shall, within 10 days after receipt of the designation, serve upon the petitioner or appellant a designation of additional parts to be included in the joint appendix, and the petitioner or appellant shall include the parts so designated. If the respondent or appellee has been permitted by this court to proceed *in forma pauperis* the petitioner or appellant may seek by motion to be excused from printing portions of the record deemed unnecessary.

In making these designations, counsel should include only those materials the Court should examine. Unnecessary designations should be avoided. The record is on file with the Clerk and available to the Justices. Counsel may refer in their briefs and in oral argument to relevant portions of the record not included in the joint appendix.

.3. When the joint appendix is filed, the petitioner or appellant shall immediately file with the Clerk a statement of the cost of printing 50 copies and shall serve a copy of the statement on each of the other parties to the proceeding pursuant to Rule 29. Unless the parties otherwise agree, the cost of producing the joint appendix shall initially be paid by the petitioner or appellant; but a petitioner or appellant who considers that parts of the record designated by the respondent or appellee are unnecessary for the determination of the issues presented may so advise the respondent or appellee who then shall advance the cost of printing the additional parts, unless the Court or a Justice otherwise fixes the initial allocation of the costs. The cost of printing the joint appendix shall be taxed as costs in

the case, but if a party unnecessarily causes matter to be included in the joint appendix or prints excessive copies, the Court may impose the costs thereof on that party.

.4. (a) If the parties agree, or if the Court shall so order, preparation of the joint appendix may be deferred until after the briefs have been filed. In that event, the petitioner or appellant shall file the joint appendix within 14 days after receipt of the brief of the respondent or appellee. The provisions of paragraphs .1, .2, and .3 of this Rule shall be followed, except that the designations referred to therein shall be made by each party when that party's brief is served.

(b) If the deferred method is used, the briefs may make reference to the pages of the record involved. In that event, the printed joint appendix must also include in brackets on each page thereof the page number of the record where that material may be found. A party desiring to refer directly to the pages of the joint appendix may serve and file typewritten or page-proof copies of the brief within the time required by Rule 25, with appropriate references to the pages of the record involved. In that event, within 10 days after the joint appendix is filed, copies of the brief in the form prescribed by Rule 33 containing references to the pages of the joint appendix, in place of or in addition to the initial references to the pages of the record involved, shall be served and filed. No other change may be made in the brief as initially served and filed, except that typographical errors may be corrected.

.5. The joint appendix must be prefaced by a table of contents showing the parts of the record which it contains, in the order in which the parts are set out therein, with references to the pages of the joint appendix at which each part begins. The relevant docket entries must be set out following the table of contents. Thereafter, the other parts of the record shall be set out in chronological order. When testimony contained in the reporter's transcript of proceedings is set out in the joint appendix the page of the transcript at which the testimony appears shall be indicated in brackets immediately before the statement which is set out. Omissions in the transcript or in any other document printed in the joint appendix must be indicated by asterisks. Immaterial formal matters (captions, subscriptions, acknowledgments, etc.) shall be omitted. A question and its answer may be contained in a single paragraph.

.6. Exhibits designated for inclusion in the joint appendix may be contained in a separate volume or volumes suitably indexed. The transcript of a proceeding before an administrative agency, board, commission, or officer used in an action in a district court or court of appeals shall be regarded as an exhibit for the purposes of this paragraph.

.7. The Court by order may dispense with the requirement of a joint appendix and may permit a case to be heard on the original record (with such copies of the record, or relevant parts thereof, as the Court may require), or on the appendix used in the court below, if it conforms to the requirements of this Rule.

.8. For good cause shown, the time limits specified in this Rule may be shortened or enlarged by the Court, by a Justice thereof, or by the Clerk under the provisions of Rule 30.4.

RULE 27
The Calendar

.1. The Clerk shall from time to time prepare calendars of cases ready for argument. A case will not normally be called for argument less than two weeks after the brief of the respondent or appellee is due.

.2. The Clerk will advise counsel when they are required to appear for oral argument and will publish a hearing list in advance of each argument session for the convenience of counsel and the information of the public.

.3. On the Court's own motion, or on motion of one or more parties, the Court may order that two or more cases, involving what appear to be the same or related questions, be argued together as one case or on any other terms as may be prescribed.

RULE 28
Oral Argument

.1. Oral argument should emphasize and clarify the written arguments appearing in the briefs on the merits. Counsel should assume that all Justices of the Court have read the briefs in advance of oral argument. The Court looks with disfavor on oral argument read from a prepared text.

.2. The petitioner or appellant is entitled to open and conclude the argument. A cross-writ of certiorari shall be argued with the initial writ of certiorari as one case in the time allowed for that one case and the Court will advise the parties who will open and close.

.3. Unless otherwise directed, one-half hour on each side is allowed for argument. Counsel is not required to use all the allotted time. A request for additional time to argue must be presented by a motion to the Court under Rule 21 not later than 15 days after service of the petitioner's or appellant's brief on the merits and shall set forth with specificity and conciseness why the case cannot be presented within the half-hour limitation. Additional time is rarely accorded.

.4. Only one attorney will be heard for each side, except by special permission granted upon a request presented not later than 15 days after service of the petitioner's or appellant's brief on the merits. The request must be presented by a motion to the Court under Rule 21 and shall set forth with specificity and conciseness why more than one attorney should argue. Divided argument is not favored.

.5. In any case, and regardless of the number of counsel participating, counsel having the opening must present the case fairly and completely and not reserve points of substance for rebuttal.

.6. Oral argument will not be allowed on behalf of any party for whom no brief has been filed.

.7. By leave of the Court and subject to paragraph .4 of this Rule, counsel for an *amicus curiae* whose brief has been duly filed pursuant to Rule 37 may, with the consent of a party, argue orally on the side of that party. In the absence of consent, counsel for an *amicus curiae* may orally argue only by leave of the Court on a motion particularly setting forth why oral argument is thought to provide assistance to the Court not otherwise available. The motion will be granted only in the most extraordinary circumstances.

PART VII.
PRACTICE AND PROCEDURE

RULE 29
Filing and Service of Documents;
Special Notifications
.1. Any pleading, motion, notice, brief, or other document or paper required or permitted to be presented to this Court, or to a Justice, shall be filed with the Clerk. Every document, except a joint appendix or brief *amicus curiae*, filed by or on behalf of one or more corporations, shall include a list naming all parent companies and subsidiaries (except wholly owned subsidiaries) of each corporation. This listing may be done in a footnote. If there is no parent or subsidiary company to be listed, a notation to this effect shall be included in the document. If a list has been included in a document filed earlier in the particular case, reference may be made to the earlier document and only amendments to the listing to make it currently accurate need to be included in the document currently being filed.

.2. To be timely filed, a document must actually be received by the Clerk within the time specified for filing; or be sent to the Clerk by first-class mail, postage prepaid, and bear a postmark showing that the document was mailed on or before the last day for filing; or, if being filed by an inmate confined in an institution, be deposited in the institution's internal mail system on or before the last day for filing and be accompanied by a notarized statement or declaration in compliance with 28 U. S. C. §1746 setting forth the date of deposit and stating that first-class postage has been prepaid. If the postmark is missing or not legible, the Clerk shall require the person who mailed the document to submit a notarized statement or declaration in compliance with 28

U. S. C. §1746 setting forth the details of the mailing and stating that the mailing took place on a particular date within the permitted time. A document forwarded through a private delivery or courier service must be received by the Clerk within the time permitted for filing.

.3. Any pleading, motion, notice, brief, or other document required by these Rules to be served may be served personally or by mail on each party to the proceeding at or before the time of filing. If the document has been produced under Rule 33, three copies shall be served on each other party separately represented in the proceeding. If the document is typewritten pursuant to Rule 34, service of a single copy on each other party separately represented shall suffice. If personal service is made, it may consist of delivery at the office of counsel of record, either to counsel or to an employee therein. If service is by mail it shall consist of depositing the document in a United States post office or mailbox, with first-class postage prepaid, addressed to counsel of record at the proper post office address. When a party is not represented by counsel, service shall be made upon the party, personally or by mail.

.4. (a) If the United States or any department, office, agency, officer, or employee thereof is a party to be served, service must also be made upon the Solicitor General, Department of Justice, Washington, D. C. 20530. If a response by the Solicitor General is required or permitted within a prescribed period after service, the time does not begin to run until the document actually has been received by the Solicitor General's office. When an agency of the United States is authorized by law to appear on its own behalf as a party, or when an officer or employee of the United States is a party, the agency, officer, or employee must also be served, in addition to the Solicitor General; and if a response is required or permitted within a prescribed period the time does not begin to run until the document actually has been received by the agency, the officer, the employee, and the Solicitor General's office.

(b) In any proceeding in this Court wherein the constitutionality of an Act of Congress is drawn in question, and the United States or any department, office, agency, officer, or employee thereof is not a party, the initial pleading, motion or paper filed in this Court shall recite that 28 U. S. C. § 2403(a) may be applicable, and the document must be served on the Solicitor General, Department of Justice, Washington, D. C. 20530. In a proceeding from any court of the United States, as defined by 28 U. S. C. §451, the initial pleading, motion, or paper shall also state whether or not that court, pursuant to 28 U. S. C. §2403(a), has certified to the Attorney General the fact that the constitutionality of an Act of Congress was drawn into question.

(c) In any proceeding in this Court wherein the constitutionality of any statute of a State is drawn into question, and the State or any agency, officer, or employee thereof is not a party, the initial pleading, motion, or paper filed in this Court shall recite that 28 U. S. C. § 2403(b) may be applicable and shall be served upon the attorney general of that State. In a proceeding from any court of the United States, as defined by 28 U. S. C. § 451, the initial pleading, motion, or paper shall state whether or not that court, pursuant to 28 U. S. C. §2403(b), has certified to the state attorney general the fact that the constitutionality of a statute of that State was drawn into question.

.5. Proof of service, when required by these Rules, must accompany the document when it is presented to the Clerk for filing and must be separate from it. Proof of service may be shown by any one of the methods set forth below, and must contain, or be accompanied by, a statement that all parties required to be served have been served, together with a list of the names, addresses, and telephone numbers of counsel indicating the name of the party or parties each counsel represents. It is not necessary that service on each party required to be served be made in the same manner or evidenced by the same proof.

(a) By an acknowledgment of service of the document in question, signed by counsel of record for the party served.

(b) By a certificate of service of the document

in question, reciting the facts and circumstances of service in compliance with the appropriate paragraph or paragraphs of this Rule, and signed by a member of the Bar of this Court representing the party on whose behalf service is made.

(c) By a notarized affidavit or declaration in compliance with 28 U. S. C. §1746, reciting the facts and circumstances of service in accordance with the appropriate paragraph or paragraphs of this Rule, whenever service is made by any person not a member of the Bar of this Court.

RULE 30
Computation and Enlargement of Time

.1. In computing any period of time prescribed or allowed by these Rules, by order of the Court, or by an applicable statute, the day of the act, event, or default from which the designated period of time begins to run shall not be included. The last day of the period shall be included, unless it is a Saturday, a Sunday, a federal legal holiday, or a day on which the Court building has been closed by order of the Court or the Chief Justice, in which event the period extends until the end of the next day which is not a Saturday, a Sunday, a federal legal holiday or a day on which the Court building has been closed. See 5 U. S. C. § 6103 for a list of federal legal holidays.

.2. Whenever a Justice of this Court or the Clerk is empowered by law or these Rules to extend the time for filing any document or paper, an application seeking an extension must be presented to the Clerk within the period sought to be extended. However, an application for an extension of time to file a petition for a writ of certiorari or to docket an appeal must be submitted at least 10 days before the specified final filing date. If received less than 10 days before the final filing date, the application will not be granted except in the most extraordinary circumstances.

.3. An application to extend the time within which a party may file a petition for a writ of certiorari or docket an appeal shall be presented in the form prescribed by Rules 13.6 and 18.3, respectively. An application to extend the time within which to file any other document or paper may be presented in the form of a letter to the Clerk setting forth with specificity the reasons why the granting of an extension of time is justified. Any application seeking an extension of time must be presented and served upon all other parties as provided in Rule 22, and, once denied may not be renewed.

.4. An application to extend the time for filing a brief, motion, joint appendix, or other paper, for designating parts of a record to be printed in the appendix, or for complying with any other time limit provided by these Rules (except an application for an extension of time to file a petition for a writ of certiorari, to docket an appeal, to file a reply brief on the merits, to file a petition for rehearing, or to issue a mandate forthwith) shall in the first instance be acted upon by the Clerk, whether addressed to the Clerk, to the Court, or to a Justice. Any party aggrieved by the Clerk's action on an application to extend time may request that it be submitted to a Justice or to the Court. The Clerk shall report action under this Rule to the Court in accordance with instructions that may be issued by the Court.

RULE 31
Translations
Whenever any record to be transmitted to this Court contains any material written in a foreign language without a translation made under the authority of the lower court, or admitted to be correct, the clerk of the court transmitting the record shall immediately advise the Clerk of this Court to the end that this Court may order that a translation be supplied and, if necessary, printed as a part of the joint appendix.

RULE 32
Models, Diagrams, and Exhibits
.1. Models, diagrams, and exhibits of material forming part of the evidence taken in a case, and brought to this Court for its inspection, shall be placed in the custody of the Clerk at least two weeks before the case is to be heard or submitted.

.2. All models, diagrams, and exhibits of material placed in the custody of the Clerk must be removed by the parties within 40 days after the case is decided. When this is not done, the Clerk shall notify counsel to remove the articles forthwith. If they are not removed within a reasonable time thereafter, the Clerk shall destroy them or make any other appropriate disposition of them.

RULE 33
Printing Requirements
.1. (a) Except for papers permitted by Rules 21, 22, and 39 to be submitted in typewritten form (see Rule 34), every document filed with the Court must be printed by a standard typographic printing process or be typed and reproduced by offset printing, photocopying, computer printing, or similar process. The process used must produce a clear, black image on white paper. In an original action under Rule 17, 60 copies of every document printed under this Rule must be filed; in all other cases, 40 copies must be filed.

(b) The text of every document including any appendix thereto, produced by standard typographic printing must appear in print as 11-point or larger type with 2-point or more leading between lines. The print size and typeface of the United States Reports from Volume 453 to date are acceptable. Similar print size and typeface should be standard throughout. No attempt should be made to reduce or condense the typeface in a manner that would increase the content of a document. Footnotes must appear in print as 9-point or larger type with 2-point or more leading between lines. A document must be printed on both sides of the page.

(c) The text of every document, including any appendix thereto, printed or duplicated by any process other than standard typographic printing shall be done in pica type at no more than 10 characters per inch. The lines must be double spaced. The right-hand margin need not be justified, but there must be a margin of at least three-fourths of an inch. In footnotes, elite type at no more than 12 characters per inch may be used. The document should be printed on both sides of the page, if practicable. It shall not be reduced in duplication. A document which is photographically reduced so that the print size is smaller than pica type will not be received by the Clerk.

(d) Whether printed under subparagraph (b) or (c) of this paragraph, every document must be produced on opaque, unglazed paper 6⅛ by 9¼ inches in size, with type matter approximately 4⅛ by 7⅛ inches and margins of at least three-fourths of an inch on all sides. The document must be firmly bound in at least two places along the left margin (saddle stitch or perfect binding preferred) so as to make an easily opened volume, and no part of the text shall be obscured by the binding. Spiral and other plastic bindings may not be used. Appendices in patent cases may be duplicated in such size as is necessary to utilize copies of patent documents.

.2. Every document must bear on the cover, in the following order, from the top of the page: (1) the number of the case or, if there is none, a space for one; (2) the name of this Court; (3) the Term; (4) the caption of the case as appropriate in this Court; (5) the nature of the proceeding and the name of the court from which the action is brought (e. g.,. "Petition for Writ of Certiorari to the United States Court of Appeals for the Fifth Circuit"; or, for a merits brief, "On Writ of Certiorari to the United States Court of Appeals for the Fifth Circuit"); (6) the title of the paper (e. g., "Petition for Writ of Certiorari" "Brief for Respondent," "Joint Appendix"); (7) the name of the member of the Bar of this Court who is counsel of record for the party concerned, and upon whom service is to be made, with a notation directly thereunder that the attorney is the counsel of record together with counsel's office address and telephone number. (There can be only one counsel of record noted on a single document.) The individual names of other members of the Bar of this Court, or of the Bar of the highest court of a State, and, if desired, their post office addresses, may be added, but counsel of record must be clearly identified. Names of persons other than attorneys admitted to a state Bar may not be listed. The foregoing must be displayed in an appropriate typographic manner and, except for the identification of counsel, may not be set in type smaller than 11-point or uppercase pica.

.3. Every document produced under this Rule shall comply with the page limits shown below and shall have a suitable cover consisting of heavy paper in the color indicated. Counsel must be certain that there is adequate contrast between the printing and the color of the cover.

The document limitations on page 495 are exclusive of the questions presented page, the subject index, the table of authorities, and the appendix. Verbatim quotations required by Rule 14.1(f), if set forth in the text of the brief rather than the appendix, are also excluded. A motion for leave to file a brief *amicus curiae* filed pursuant to Rule 37 must be printed with the brief.

A document filed by the United States, by any department, office, or agency of the United States, or by any officer or employee of the United States represented by the Solicitor General shall have a gray cover.

A joint appendix and any other document shall have a tan cover.

In a case filed under the original jurisdiction of the Court, the initial pleading and motion for leave to file and any accompanying brief shall have white covers. A brief in opposition to the motion for leave to file shall have an orange cover; exceptions to the report of a special master shall have a light blue cover, if filed by the plaintiff and a light cover, if filed by any other party; and a reply brief to any exceptions shall have a yellow cover.

.4. The Court or a Justice, for good cause shown, may grant leave to file a document in excess of the page limits, but these applications are not favored. An application to exceed page limits shall comply in all respects with Rule 22 and must be submitted at least 15 days before the filing date of the document in question, except in the most extraordinary circumstances.

.5. Every document which exceeds five pages (other than a single joint appendix) shall, regardless of the method of duplication, contain a table of contents and a table of authorities (*i. e.*, cases alphabetically arranged, constitutional provisions, statutes, textbooks, etc.) with correct references to the pages in the document where they are cited.

The Rules of the Supreme Court include the specific requirements for all official documents submitted to the Court.

Type of Document	Page Limits		Color of the Cover
	Typo-graphic Printing	Typed and Double Spaced	
a. Petition for a Writ of Certiorari (Rule 14.4); Jurisdictional Statement (Rule 18.3); or Petition for an Extraordinary Writ (Rule 20.2)	30	65	White
b. Brief in Opposition (Rule 15.3); Motion to Dismiss or Affirm (Rule 18.6); Brief in Opposition to Mandamus or Prohibition (Rule 20.3(b)); or Response to a Petition for Habeas Corpus (Rule 20.4)	30	65	Orange
c. Reply to Brief in Opposition (Rule 15.6); or Brief Opposing a Motion to Dismiss or Affirm (Rule 18.8)	10	20	Tan
d. Supplemental Brief (Rules 15.7 and 18.9)	10	20	Tan
e. Brief on the Merits by Petitioner or Appellant (Rule 24.3)	50	110	Light Blue
f. Brief on the Merits by Respondent or Appellee (Rule 24.3)	50	110	Light Red
g. Reply Brief on the Merits (Rule 24.4)	20	45	Yellow
h. Brief on *Amicus Curiae* at the Petition Stage (Rule 37.2)	20	45	Cream
i. Brief on an *Amicus Curiae* on the Merits in Support of the Petitioner or Appellant or in Support of Neither Party (Rule 37.3)	30	65	Pastel or Pale Green
j. Brief of an *Amicus Curiae* on the Merits in Support of the Respondent or Appellee (Rule 37.3)	30	65	Green
k. Petition for Rehearing (Rule 44)	10	20	Tan

.6. The body of every document at its close shall bear the name of counsel of record and such other counsel identified, on the cover of the document in conformity with paragraph .2(7) of this Rule, as may be desired. One copy of every motion or application (other than a motion to dismiss or affirm under Rule 18) must in addition be signed by counsel of record at the end thereof.

.7. The Clerk shall not accept for filing any document presented in a form not in compliance with this Rule, but shall return it indicating to the defaulting party any failure to comply. The filing, however shall not thereby be deemed untimely provided that new and proper copies are promptly substituted. If the Court finds that the provisions of this Rule have not been adhered to, it may impose, in its discretion, appropriate sanctions including but not limited to dismissal of the action, imposition of costs, or disciplinary sanction upon counsel.

RULE 34
Form of Typewritten Papers
.1. Any paper specifically permitted by these Rules to be presented to the Court without being printed shall, subject to Rule 39.3, be typewritten on opaque, unglazed paper 8¹/₂ x 11 inches in size and shall be stapled or bound at the upper left hand corner. The typed matter, except quotations, must be double spaced. Copies, if required, must be produced on the same type of paper. All copies presented to the Court must be legible.

.2. The original of any motion or application (except a motion to dismiss or affirm under Rule 18.6) must be signed in manuscript by the party proceeding *pro se* or by counsel of record who must be a member of the Bar of this Court.

RULE 35
Death, Substitution, and Revivor; Public Officers
.1. In the event a party dies after filing a notice of appeal to this Court, or after filing a petition for a writ of certiorari, the authorized representative of the deceased party may appear and, upon motion, be substituted as a party to the proceeding. If the representative does not voluntarily become a party, any other party may suggest the death on the record and on motion seek an order requiring the representative to become a party within a designated time. If the representative then fails to become a party, the party so moving, if a respondent or appellee, shall be entitled to have the petition for a writ of certiorari or the appeal dismissed or the judgment vacated for mootness as may be appropriate. A party so moving who is a petitioner or appellant shall be entitled to proceed as in any other case of nonappearance by a respondent or appellee. The substitution of a representative of the deceased, or the suggestion of death by a party, must be made within six months after the death of the party, or the case shall abate.

.2. Whenever a case cannot be revived in the court whose judgment is sought to be reviewed because the deceased party has no authorized representative within the jurisdiction of that court, but does have an authorized representative elsewhere, proceedings shall be conducted as this Court may direct.

.3. When a public officer, who is a party to a proceeding in this Court in an official capacity, dies, resigns, or otherwise ceases to hold office, the action does not abate and any successor in office is automatically substituted as a party. Proceedings following the substitution shall be in the name of the substituted party, but any misnomer not affecting the substantial rights of the parties shall be disregarded.

.4. A public officer who is a party to a proceeding in this Court in an official capacity may be described as a party by the officer's official title rather than by name, but the Court may require the name to be added.

RULE 36
Custody of Prisoners in Habeas Corpus Proceedings
.1. Pending review in this Court of a decision in a habeas corpus proceeding commenced before a court, Justice, or judge of the United States, the person having custody of the prisoner shall not transfer custody to another person unless the transfer is authorized in accordance with the provisions of this Rule.

.2. Upon application by a custodian showing a need therefor, the court, Justice, or judge rendering the decision under review may authorize transfer and the substitution of a successor custodian as a party.

.3. (a) Pending review of a decision failing or refusing to release a prisoner, the prisoner may be detained in the custody from which release is sought or in other appropriate custody or may be enlarged upon personal recognizance or bail, as may appear fitting to the court, Justice, or judge rendering the decision, or to the court of appeals or to this Court or to a judge or Justice of either court.

(b) Pending review of a decision ordering release, the prisoner shall be enlarged upon personal recognizance or bail, unless the court, Justice, or judge rendering the decision, or the court of appeals, or this Court, or a judge or Justice of either court, shall otherwise order.

.4. An initial order respecting the custody or enlargement of the prisoner, and any recognizance or surety taken, shall continue in effect pending review in the court of appeals and in this Court unless for reasons shown to the court of appeals or to this Court, or to a judge or Justice of either court, the order is modified or an independent order respecting custody, enlargement, or surety is entered.

RULE 37

Brief of an Amicus Curiae

.1. An *amicus curiae* brief which brings relevant matter to the attention of the Court that has not already been brought to its attention by the parties is of considerable help to the Court. An *amicus* brief which does not serve this purpose simply burdens the staff and facilities of the Court and its filing is not favored.

.2. A brief of an *amicus curiae* submitted prior to the consideration of a petition for a writ of certiorari or a jurisdictional statement, accompanied by the written consent of all parties, may be filed only if submitted within the time allowed for filing a brief in opposition to the petition for a writ of certiorari or for filing a motion to dis-

miss or affirm. A motion for leave to file a brief *amicus curiae* when consent has been refused is not favored. Any such motion must be filed within the time allowed for the filing of the brief *amicus curiae*, must indicate the party or parties who have refused consent, and must be printed with the proposed brief. The cover of the brief must identify the party supported.

.3. A brief of an *amicus curiae* in a case before the Court for oral argument may be filed when accompanied by the written consent of all parties and presented within the time allowed for the filing of the brief of the party supported, or, if in support of neither party within the time allowed for filing the petitioner's or appellant's brief. A brief *amicus curiae* must identify the party supported or indicate whether it suggests affirmance or reversal, and must be as concise as possible. No reply brief of an *amicus curiae* and no brief of an *amicus curiae* in support of a petition for rehearing will be received.

.4. When consent to the filing of a brief of an *amicus curiae* in a case before the Court for oral argument is refused by a party to the case, a motion for leave to file indicating the party or parties who have refused consent, accompanied by the proposed brief and printed with it, may be presented to the Court. A motion will not be received unless submitted within the time allowed for the filing of an *amicus* brief on written consent. The motion shall concisely state the nature of the applicant's interest and set forth facts or questions of law that have not been, or reasons for believing that they will not be, presented by the parties and their relevancy to the disposition of the case. The motion may in no event exceed five pages. A party served with the motion may file an objection thereto concisely stating the reasons for withholding consent which must be printed in accordance with Rule 33. The cover of an *amicus* brief must identify the party supported or indicate whether it supports affirmance or reversal.

.5. Consent to the filing of a brief of an *amicus curiae* is not necessary when the brief is presented an behalf of the United States by the Solicitor

General; on behalf of any agency of the United States authorized by law to appear on its own behalf when submitted by the agency's authorized legal representative; on behalf of a State, Territory, or Commonwealth when submitted by its Attorney General; or on behalf of a political subdivision of a State, Territory, or Commonwealth when submitted by its authorized law officer.

.6. Every brief or motion filed under this Rule must comply with the applicable provisions of Rules 21, 24, and 33 (except that it shall be sufficient to set forth in the brief the interest of the *amicus curiae*, the argument, the summary of the argument, and the conclusion); and shall be accompanied by proof of service as required by Rule 29.

RULE 38
Fees
In pursuance of 28 U. S. C. §1911, the fees to be charged by the Clerk are fixed as follows:

(a) For docketing a case on a petition for a writ of certiorari or on appeal or docketing any other proceeding, except a certified question or a motion to docket and dismiss an appeal pursuant to Rule 18.5, $300.00.

(b) For filing a petition for rehearing or a motion for leave to file a petition for rehearing, $200.00.

(c) For the reproduction and certification of any record or paper, $1.00 per page; and for comparing with the original thereof any photographic reproduction of any record or paper, when furnished by the person requesting its certification, $.50 per page.

(d) For a certificate under seal, $25.00.

(e) For a check paid to the Court, Clerk, or Marshal which is returned for lack of funds, $35.00.

NOTES OF DECISIONS
Acceptance of petitions
1. Acceptance of petitions
Clerk of the Court would be directed not to accept any further petitions for extraordinary writs from petitioner in noncriminal matters unless he paid the required docketing fee and submitted his petition in compliance with rule governing printing requirements where petitioner

had filed 23 claims for relief, including 18 petitions for certiorari, nine of which had been filed in the last three terms, and Supreme Court had denied all petitions without recorded dissent; although petitioner had exhibited frequent filing patterns with respect to petitions for writ of certiorari, Court would limit sanctions to the type of relief requested by petitioner, petition for extraordinary writ. In re Whitaker, U.S. 199

RULE 39
Proceedings in Forma Pauperis
.1. A party desiring to proceed in *forma pauperis* shall file with the pleading a motion for leave to proceed in *forma pauperis*, together with the party's notarized affidavit or declaration (in compliance with 28 U. S. C. §1746) in the form prescribed by the Federal Rules of Appellate Procedure, Form 4. See 28 U. S. C. §1915. If the United States district court or the United States court of appeals has appointed counsel under the Criminal Justice Act of 1964, as amended, the party need not file an affidavit or declaration in compliance with 28 U. S. C. §1746, but the motion must indicate that counsel was appointed under the Criminal Justice Act. See 18 U. S. C. §3006A(d)(6). The motion shall also state whether or not leave to proceed in *forma pauperis* was sought in any other court and, if so, whether leave was granted.

.2. The motion, and affidavit or declaration if required, must be filed with the petition for a writ of certiorari, jurisdictional statement, or petition for an extraordinary writ, as the case may be, and shall comply in every respect with Rule 21, except that it shall be sufficient to file a single copy. If not received together, the documents will be returned by the Clerk.

.3. Every paper or document presented under this Rule must be clearly legible and, whenever possible, must comply with Rule 34. While making due allowance for any case presented under this Rule by a person appearing *pro se*, the Clerk will refuse to receive any document sought to be filed that does not comply with the substance of these Rules, or when it appears that the document is obviously and jurisdictionally out of time.

.4. When the papers required by paragraphs .1 and .2 of this Rule are presented to the Clerk, accompanied by proof of service as prescribed by Rule 29, they as to be placed on the docket without the payment of a docket fee or any other fee.

.5. The respondent or appellee in a case filed *in forma pauperis* may respond in the same manner and within the same time as in any other case of the same nature, except that the filings of 12 copies of a typewritten response, with proof of service as required by Rule 29, will suffice whenever the petitioner or appellant has filed typewritten papers. The respondent or appellee may challenge the grounds for the motion to proceed *in forma pauperis* in a separate document or in the response itself.

.6. Whenever the Court appoints a member of the Bar to serve as counsel for an indigent party in a case set for oral argument, the briefs prepared by that counsel, unless otherwise requested, will be printed under the supervision of the Clerk. The Clerk will also reimburse appointed counsel for any necessary travel expenses to Washington, D. C., and return in connection with the argument.

.7. In a case in which certiorari has been granted or jurisdiction has been noted or postponed, this Court may appoint counsel to represent a party financially unable to afford an attorney to the extent authorized by the Criminal Justice Act of 1964, as amended, 18 U. S. C. §3006A.

.8. If satisfied that a petition for a writ of certiorari, jurisdictional statement, or petition for an extraordinary writ, as the case may be, is frivolous or malicious, the Court may deny a motion for leave to proceed *in forma pauperis*.

RULE 40

Veterans, Seamen, and Military Cases
.1. A veteran suing to establish reemployment rights under 38 U. S. C. §2022, or under any other provision of law exempting a veteran from the payment of fees or court costs, may file a motion to proceed upon typewritten papers under Rule 34, except that the motion shall ask leave to proceed as a veteran, and the affidavit shall set forth the moving party's status as a veteran.

.2. A seaman suing pursuant to 28 U. S. C. §1916 may proceed without the prepayment of fees or costs or furnishing security therefor, but a seaman is not relieved of printing costs nor entitled to proceed on typewritten papers.

.3. An accused person petitioning for a writ of certiorari to review a decision of the United States Court of Military Appeals pursuant to 28 U. S. C. §1259 may proceed without the prepayment of fees or costs or furnishing security therefor and without filing an affidavit of indigency, but is not relieved of the printing requirements under Rule 33 and is not entitled to proceed on typewritten papers except as authorized by the Court on separate motion.

PART VIII.
DISPOSITION OF CASES

RULE 41
Opinions of the Court
Opinions of the Court will be released by the Clerk in preliminary form immediately upon delivery. Thereafter the Clerk shall cause the opinions of the Court to be issued in slip form and shall deliver them to the Reporter of Decisions who shall prepare them for publication in the preliminary prints and bound volumes of the United States Reports.

RULE 42
Interest and Damages
.1. If a judgment for money in a civil case is affirmed, whatever interest is allowed by law shall be payable from the date the judgment below was entered. If a judgment is modified or reversed with a direction that a judgment for money be entered below, the mandate will contain instructions with respect to the allowance of interest. Interest will be allowed at the same rate that similar judgments bear interest in the courts of the State in which judgment was entered or was directed to be entered.

.2. When a petition for a writ of certiorari, an appeal, or application for other relief is frivolous, the Court may award the respondent or appellee just damages and single or double costs. Damages or costs may be awarded against the petitioner, appellant, or applicant, or against the party's attorney or against both.

RULE 43
Costs

.1. If a judgment or decree is affirmed by this Court, costs shall be paid by the petitioner or appellant, unless otherwise ordered by the Court.

.2. If a judgment or decree is reversed or vacated by this Court, costs shall be allowed to the petitioner or appellant, unless otherwise ordered by the Court.

.3. The fees of the Clerk and the costs of printing the joint appendix are the only taxable items in this Court. The cost of the transcript of the record from the court below is also a taxable item, but shall be taxable in that court as costs in the case. The expenses of printing briefs, motions, petitions, or jurisdictional statements are not taxable.

.4. In a case involving a certified question, costs shall be equally divided unless otherwise ordered by the Court; but if a decision is rendered on the whole matter in controversy, see Rule 19.2, costs shall be allowed as provided in paragraphs .1 and .2 of this Rule.

.5. In a civil action commenced on or after July 18, 1966, costs under this Rule shall be allowed for or against the United States, or an officer or agent thereof, unless expressly waived or otherwise ordered by the Court. See 28 U. S. C. §2412.

.6. When costs are allowed in this Court, the Clerk shall insert an itemization of the costs in the body of the mandate or judgment sent to the court below. The prevailing side shall not submit a bill of costs.

.7. If appropriate, the Court may adjudge double costs.

RULE 44
Rehearing

.1. A petition for the rehearing of any judgment or decision of the Court on the merits shall be filed within 25 days after the entry of the judgment or decision, unless the time is shortened or enlarged by the Court or a Justice. Forty printed copies, produced in conformity with Rule 33, must be filed (except when the party is proceeding *in forma pauperis* under Rule 39), accompanied by proof of service as prescribed by Rule 29 and the filing fee required by Rule 38. The petition must briefly and distinctly state its grounds. Counsel must certify that the petition is presented in good faith and not for delay; one copy of the certificate shall bear the manuscript signature of counsel. A petition for rehearing is not subject to oral argument, and will not be granted except at the instance of a Justice who concurred in the judgment or decision and with the concurrence of a majority of the Court.

.2. A petition for the rehearing of an order denying a petition for a writ of certiorari shall be filed within 25 days after the date of the order of denial and shall comply with all the form and filing requirements of paragraph .1 of this Rule, including the payment of the filing fee if required, but its grounds must be limited to intervening circumstances of a substantial or controlling effect or to other substantial grounds not previously presented. Counsel must certify that the petition is restricted to the grounds specified in this paragraph and that it is presented in good faith and not for delay. One copy of the certificate shall bear the manuscript signature of counsel or of a party not represented by counsel. A petition without a certificate shall be rejected by the Clerk. The petition is not subject to oral argument.

.3. No response to a petition for rehearing will be received unless requested by the Court, but no petition will be granted without an opportunity to submit a response.

.4. Consecutive petitions and petitions that are out of time under this Rule will not be received.

RULE 45
Process; Mandates

.1. All process of this Court shall be in the name of the President of the United States.

.2. In a case coming from a State court, the mandate shall issue 25 days after the entry of judgment, unless the time is shortened or enlarged by the Court or a Justice, or unless the parties stipulate that it be issued sooner. The filing of a petition for rehearing, unless otherwise ordered, will stay the mandate until disposition of the petition. If the petition is then denied, the mandate shall issue forthwith.

.3. In a case coming from a United States court, a formal mandate will not issue unless specially directed; instead, the Clerk will send the court a copy of the opinion or order of this Court and a certified copy of the judgment (which shall include provisions for the recovery of costs, if any are awarded). In all other respects, the provisions of paragraph .2 of this Rule apply.

RULE 46
Dismissing Cases
.1. Whenever all parties, at any stage of the proceedings, file with the Clerk an agreement in writing that a case be dismissed, specifying the terms with respect to the payment of costs, and pay to the Clerk any fees that may be due, the Clerk, without further reference to the Court, shall enter an order of dismissal.

.2. (a) A petitioner or appellant in a case in this Court may file a motion to dismiss the case, with proof of service as prescribed by Rule 29, and must tender to the Clerk any fees and costs payable. An adverse party may, within 15 days after service thereof, file an objection, limited to the quantum of damages and costs in this Court alleged to be payable or, in a proper case, to a showing that the moving party does not represent all petitioners or appellants. The Clerk will refuse to receive any objection not so limited.

(b) When the objection goes to the standing of the moving party to represent the entire side, the party moving for dismissal, within 10 days thereafter, may file a reply, after which time the matter shall be submitted to the Court for its determination.

(c) If no objection is filed, or if upon objection going only to the quantum of damages and costs in this Court, the party moving for dismissal, within 10 days thereafter, tenders the whole of such additional damages and costs demanded, the Clerk, without further reference to the Court, shall enter an order of dismissal. If, after objection as to the quantum of damages and costs in this Court, the moving party does not respond with a tender within 10 days, the Clerk shall report the matter to the Court for its determination.

.3. No mandate or other process shall issue on a dismissal under this Rule without an order of the Court.

PART IX.
APPLICATION OF TERMS AND EFFECTIVE DATE

RULE 47
Term "State Court"
The term "state court" when used in these Rules includes the District of Columbia Court of Appeals and the Supreme Court of the Commonwealth of Puerto Rico. See 28 U. S. C. §§ 1257 and 1258. References in these Rules to the common law and statutes of a State include the common law and statutes of the District of Columbia and of the Commonwealth of Puerto Rico.

RULE 48
Effective Date of Amendments
These Rules adopted December 5, 1989, shall be effective January 1, 1990.

GLOSSARY

Note: References to other terms in the Glossary are in italics.

Abstention doctrine: A policy that permits federal courts to decline to exercise *jurisdiction* over certain constitutional questions related to state laws so the questions can be decided in a state court proceeding. The doctrine is invoked in cases involving ambiguous state statutes awaiting definitive interpretation by a state supreme court whose decision may resolve the constitutional questions.

Admiralty law: The body of law that governs actions occurring on or related to the sea and other navigable waters.

Advisory opinion: A formal but not legally binding opinion rendered by a court of law at the request of an interested party or a governing body. Citing the need for *separation of powers*, courts customarily decline to issue such opinions, as the Jay Court did in 1793 when President George Washington asked the justices to interpret a U.S. treaty with France.

Affidavit: Any written statement sworn to before an officer of the court or a notary public.

Alien: Any foreign-born individual who may be a resident of the United States, but who has not qualified as a citizen.

Appellant: Any party who appeals the decision of a lower court to a higher *appellate* court.

Appellate jurisdiction: The power of a superior court to review an appeal from one of the parties of a judicial action taken by a lower court, particularly for a legal error, and to revise that court's judgment if such error is found.

Appellee: The party who prevailed in a lower court and who, if the case is appealed to a higher court, argues against setting aside the original judgment.

Apportionment: The determination of the number of elected representatives that a geographic area, such as a state, county, or other electoral district, is permitted to send to a legislative body. Apportionment also refers to the allotment of *direct taxes* on the basis of state population.

Assistance of Counsel Clause: The portion of the Sixth Amendment to the Constitution that provides: "In all criminal prosecutions, the accused shall enjoy the right to... have the Assistance of Counsel for his defence."

Attainder, Bill of: Any legislative act that imposes criminal punishment on an individual without a trial or other judicial proceeding to determine guilt or innocence.

Black letter law: Generally accepted, unambiguous legal principles, so called because they once appeared in bold type in legal treatises.

Breach of promise: A failure to perform something that was promised as part of an agreement with another individual or entity; most often it is used in connection with a promise to marry.

Brief: Written arguments concerning the facts and law of a case. Briefs are submitted to a court by lawyers on each side of a suit, usually in advance of *oral argument.*

Burden of proof: The duty of a party to provide evidence to support his or her interpretation of contended facts or issues in a case so as to convince the court or a jury and thus prevail at trial.

Capital case (or punishment): A criminal offense that is punishable by death.

Certification: The procedure that allows a United States court of appeals to request from the Supreme Court an immediate review of a case for specific *questions of law.* This method of invoking Supreme Court *jurisdiction* is rarely employed and is reserved for issues considered too pressing or too central to the public welfare to await a full hearing of the appeal in the lower court.

Certification of division of opinion: An early procedure for obtaining Supreme Court review of a case when the judges of a lower *appellate* court were deadlocked.

Certiorari, writ of: The primary means by which a case is brought before the Supreme Court. If the petition for certiorari is granted, the Court issues a *writ* requesting the court below to forward a complete record of the legal proceedings in the case as the first step in the process of hearing an appeal.

Circuit: Any geographical area that is designated a judicial division. Currently, for example, courts in the federal Second Circuit hear cases in New York, Connecticut, and Vermont.

Circuit court: One of several courts that have *jurisdiction* over cases heard in its geographic area, which may be a state or several states. Originally circuit courts had both *original* and *appellate jurisdiction,* but in 1891 the old circuit

courts became solely trial courts and appellate work was transferred to the circuit courts of appeals, renamed United States courts of appeals in 1948.

Circuit duty (or riding): Originally, it was the responsibility of Supreme Court justices to help staff circuit court benches in their respective districts, which they did each year by riding through their designated circuits and hearing cases in the various federal courts located there. This practice, which the justices found onerous, was completely abolished in 1911.

Citizen: An individual who resides in a state. For the purposes of *diversity jurisdiction,* a corporation is deemed a citizen of the state in which it maintains its principal place of business.

Citizenship Clause: The portion of section 1 of the Fourteenth Amendment to the Constitution that provides: "All persons born or naturalized in the United States... are citizens of the United States and of the State wherein they reside."

Class action: A type of law suit brought by representatives of a large group of persons who share a common interest in the issues at stake. All members who join such a group are bound by the judgment in the case.

Commerce Clause (also commerce power): article I, section 8, clause 3 of the Constitution provides that: "The Congress shall have Power... To Regulate Commerce with foreign Nations, and among the several States, and with the Indian Tribes."

Commercial speech: Speech connected with advertising and business. Commercial speech was not deemed to be protected by the First Amendment until the 1970s, when the Supreme Court ruled that publication of such matters as advertising by lawyers and of prescription drugs was governed by the *free speech* doctrine. Commercial speech, however, is still granted a lesser degree of First Amendment protection than noncommercial speech in such areas as journalism or politics.

Common law: Judge-made law, as distinct from legislative enactments. Common law is based on legal *precedent* and is handed down in the form of opinions in previous cases. In the aggregate, these opinions form a system of laws, also called common law, which was originally administered in the royal courts of England. English common law became the basis of American *jurisprudence*. American, legal practice, like the English version, once included two systems of law, one administering common law, the other *equity*, or laws based on fundamental principles of fairness.

Compact Clause: Article I, section 10, clause 3 of the Constitution provides that: "No State shall, without the Consent of Congress... enter into any Agreement or Compact with another State...."

Compelling state interest: Justification for *state action* alleged to violate the First Amendment or a person's right to *equal protection* under the law.

Complaint: The initial set of papers, setting out the facts on which a claim for relief is based, filed with a court to begin a legal case.

Confrontation Clause: The portion of the Sixth Amendment to the Constitution that provides: "In all criminal prosecutions, the accused shall enjoy the right... to be confronted with the witnesses against him...."

Consent decree: An agreement by a defendant to cease activities that the government alleges to be illegal. Once signed, a consent decree results in the government's discontinuing its legal action against the defendant.

Contempt of court (or Congress): Actions that hinder the administration of justice. Contempt can be either civil (failing to perform something ordered by a court) or criminal (willfully disobeying an order or obstructing a court or the Congress).

Contracts Clause: Article I, section 10, clause 1 of the Constitution provides that: "No State shall... pass any... Law impairing the Obligation of Contracts...."

Cruel and Unusual Punishment Clause: The Eighth Amendment to the Constitution prohibits the infliction of "cruel and unusual punishments." Although the clause prohibits penalties disproportionate to the offenses they are intended to punish, the death penalty is not considered per se cruel and unusual if it is administered with adequate safeguards to protect against its arbitrary or discriminatory application.

Declaratory judgment: A binding judgment of a court that sets out the rights of the parties without requiring them to perform any action and without granting any further relief.

Demurrer: During a trial, a formal objection to the legal sufficiency, or adequacy of the plaintiff's written allegations. A demurrer can result in a judgment for the defendant.

Deposition: Oral testimony of a witness taken out of court and committed to writing.

Derivative suit: A suit brought on behalf of a corporation by its shareholders.

Dictum (plural: dicta): A statement in a judge's written opinion that does not form a part of his or her judgment in the case; unlike the *holding* of an opinion, dicta are not binding as *precedent* on future cases.

Direct tax: A tax, such as an income or property tax, levied directly on the taxpayer, as compared to a sales tax, which applies to commodities at the point of sale before they reach the taxpayer. (Compare *indirect tax*.)

Disparate impact: A type of employment discrimination which does not involve an act of intentional discrimination against an individual, but which is the result of a policy whose potential effect, often demonstrated by statistics, may be the same.

Diversity jurisdiction: The basis for granting federal courts the power to hear cases between *citizens* of different states, or between citizens and *aliens*.

Docket: A list of cases on a court calendar.

Dormant Commerce Clause: An interpretation of the Constitution's *Commerce Clause* that recognizes some aspects of commerce between states to be subject to regulation at the state, rather than the federal, level.

Double Jeopardy Clause: The portion of the Fifth Amendment to the Constitution that provides: "No person shall... be subject for the same offence to be twice put in jeopardy of life or limb...." The prohibition against double jeopardy bars double prosecution and double punishment for the same offence, but it applies only to criminal cases and only when there is no appeal of a conviction.

Due Process Clause: A portion of the Fifth Amendment to the Constitution that provides: "No person shall be... deprived of life, liberty, or property, without due process of law...." Originally, the due process clause applied only to the federal government, but it was extended to the states by section 1 of the Fourteenth Amendment to the Constitution, which provides that: "No state shall... deprive any person of life, liberty, or property, without due process of law."

Eminent domain: The power of federal, state, or municipal governments to take private property for public use. Eminent domain is limited by the *Takings Clause* of the Fifth Amendment, which requires the government to compensate for such an appropriation of property.

Enabling legislation: Laws providing authorities with the power to implement and enforce other statutes.

Enjoin: To order that a given action be ended or avoided. Such orders are usually backed by court *injunctions*.

Enumerated powers: The powers specifically granted to any branch of the federal government by the Constitution. Article I enumer-

ates those powers given to Congress, article II those given to the executive branch, and article III those given to the judiciary.

Equal Protection Clause: The portion of section 1 of the Fourteenth Amendment to the Constitution that provides: "No State shall... deny to any person within its jurisdiction the equal protection of the laws." This clause has been interpreted to mean that no individual or class of individuals can be denied rights enjoyed by other persons or classes who exist in similar circumstances.

Equity: In one definition, equity is generally equivalent to justice. The term is also the name of a legal system which, in contrast with *common law*, is based on general principles of fairness rather than on established procedural rules.

Error, Writ of [Obsolete]: A method of reviewing a lower court decision that involves a *federal question* whereby the Supreme Court would issue a command, or *writ*, to the lower court to forward the record in the case, which the Supreme Court would then scrutinize for errors in application of the law.

Establishment Clause: The portion of the First Amendment to the Constitution that provides: "Congress shall make no law respecting an establishment of religion...."

Excise tax: A tax levied on the performance of an act, such as manufacturing, or on the enjoyment of a privilege, such as consumption of commodities. A sales tax.

Exclusionary rule: The rule that prevents the use in criminal proceedings of any evidence obtained in an unconstitutional manner in violation of the Fourth Amendment's prohibition against unreasonable searches and seizures.

Executive privilege: The privilege of the executive branch of the federal government under the doctrine of *separation of powers* to refuse to disclose information that would impair proper functioning of the president or other members of the branch.

Executive power: The authority to execute laws that is granted to the executive branch by article I of the Constitution.

Ex parte: A legal proceeding brought by or for the benefit of one party, where no opposing party is present. Often such cases concern absent or incompetent parties. *Ex parte Milligan* (1866), for example, concerned the death sentence imposed on Milligan, then imprisoned for alleged anti-Union activities during the Civil War.

Ex post facto laws: Statutes making a given act, which was not designated a crime at the time it was committed, punishable as a crime. Such laws are prohibited by article I, section 9, clause 3 of the Constitution.

Ex rel.: This term is used in a legal proceeding brought by a state on behalf of an individual. Thus in *J.E.B. v. Alabama ex rel. T.B.* (1994), the state of Alabama filed a paternity suit for T.B. against J.E.B. Usually, the state believes a larger public interest or good will be served by the outcome of the case and the precedent it sets.

Extradition: The surrender by a state or country to another *sovereign* entity of an individual accused or convicted of an offense outside the borders of the state or country holding the individual.

Extrajudicial activities (or duties): Participation of Supreme Court justices in activities outside their judicial duties. An example of extrajudicial activity was Chief Justice Salmon P. Chase's perennial quest for the presidency of the United States. In his case, the activity was thought to compromise the authority of the Court.

Federal question doctrine: The jurisdiction of federal courts over cases arising under the Constitution, federal laws, or treaties, as stipulated in article III, section 2 of the Constitution.

Federalism: A system of government that divides power between local governments and a central government.

Felony: A category of crimes that includes murder and rape which often are punishable with heavy fines or lengthy jail terms. (Compare *misdemeanor.*)

Felony murder: An unintended homicide committed in the course of another *felony*. Felony murder is punishable as first degree murder.

First impression (case of): The expression used to describe the first instance in which a specific *question of law* is presented for determination in court.

Foreign corporation (or individual): For purposes of litigation, a party that is a *citizen* of another state or country.

Free Exercise Clause: The portion of the First Amendment to the Constitution that provides: "Congress shall make no law... prohibiting the free exercise [of religion]...."

Free Speech Clause: The portion of the First Amendment to the Constitution that provides: "Congress shall make no law... abridging the freedom of speech, or of the press...."

Friendly suit: Litigation brought by mutual agreement between parties who appear formally as antagonists, but who actually seek a binding judgment on an issue that concerns them.

Grand jury: A jury empaneled to determine if the facts and allegations presented by prosecutors in criminal cases are sufficient to warrant a trial. If so, the grand jury *indicts* the defendant. A grand jury usually consists of 23 individuals, while a *petit jury* consists of 12 or fewer jurors.

Guarantee Clause: The provision of article IV, section 4 of the Constitution that provides: "The United States shall guarantee to every State in this Union a Republican Form of Government...."

Habeas Corpus: A judicial procedure for determining whether there is a legal basis for holding someone in custody. In criminal law habeas corpus is used to challenge a convict's confinement.

Holding: The legal principal underlying a court decision; it is the part of a decision that is legally binding as precedent on subsequent similar cases. (Compare *Dictum.*)

Immunity: An exemption from prosecution granted to a witness in exchange for his testimony or evidence. There are also different kinds of immunity — executive, legislative, or judicial — that are based on the status of the party.

Impeachment: A criminal proceeding against a public official conducted by a quasi-judicial body. The term also applies to an attempt to undermine a witness's credibility.

Implied powers: Those powers not expressly granted in the Constitution that are nonetheless necessary for carrying out those other powers *enumerated* in the Constitution.

Incorporation doctrine: The doctrine that holds that nearly all of the guarantees of the Bill of Rights are binding on the states as well as the federal government through the *Due Process Clause* of the Fourteenth Amendment.

Indirect tax: A tax, like a franchise tax, that is imposed on a right or privilege, rather than on a tangible product. (Compare *Direct tax.*)

Indictment: A formal written accusation drawn up by a prosecutor and issued by a *grand jury* against an individual charged with a criminal offense.

Injunction: An order issued by a court requiring a defendant to cease or refrain from specified acts.

In re: Meaning "in the matter of," In re in the title of a case signifies a nonadversarial judicial proceeding concerning a matter, such as an estate, requiring only a legal decision, not litigation.

Intergovernmental immunities: A doctrine usually pertaining to taxes, under which the states

and the federal government are not subject to one another's revenue laws.

Intermediate scrutiny: The standard under the *Equal Protection Clause* used by federal courts to determine the constitutionality of government actions based on gender, such as the Oklahoma liquor law at issue in *Craig v. Boren* (1976), which permitted young women but not young men to purchase beer containing 3.2% alcohol. Using intermediate scrutiny, the Court found the Oklahoma law invalid.

Judicial activism: A theory of judging based not on legal *precedent* but on a more subjective determination of what is right for a party or for the larger society. Many decisions of the Warren Court, such as the landmark school desegregation case, *Brown v. Board of Education* (1954), have been criticized as exercises of judicial activism. (Compare *Judicial restraint.*)

Judicial restraint: A theory of judging based on *precedent* and deference to the legislative branch's power to take the more active role in changing the law. (Compare *Judicial activism.*)

Judicial review: The power of the United States Supreme Court and the highest state courts to determine the constitutionality of legislation and executive branch actions.

Jurisdiction: The power to hear and decide cases. The concept of jurisdiction can be specific to various types of cases (e.g., trial versus *appellate jurisdiction*) or to geographic entities (e.g., the United States Second Circuit Court of Appeals hears appellate cases in New York, Connecticut, and Vermont), but the term includes every type of judicial action regardless of where it is entertained.

Jurisprudence: The philosophy or form of a legal system rather than its content, such as statutes and judicially determined case law.

Justiciability: The capacity of an issue to be determined by a court. The term applies to true controversies, rather than hypothetical issues not subject to binding judicial decisions. (See, e.g., *Mootness* and *Ripeness*.)

Laissez faire: A philosophy of judging based on the economic theory of the same name, which favors individualism and market forces and is hostile to government regulation.

Legal fiction: An assumed fact, which may or may not be true, that is adopted by a court to aid it in disposing of a case. For example, in order to reach a decision regarding which laws apply to taxation of personal property, a court may assume that the property in question is located in an individual's primary residence, even though it may not be.

Magistrate: Minor officials with limited judicial powers, such as justices of the peace.

Mandamus, Writ of: An extraordinary *writ* issued by courts when other legal remedies have failed compelling an official to perform some necessary duty.

Maritime law: see *Admiralty law*

Military power: The authority of the executive branch conferred by article II, section 2, clause 1 of the Constitution, which provides: "The President shall be Commander in Chief of the Army and Navy of the United States, and of the Militia of the several States, when called into the actual Service of the United States...."

Misdemeanor: Any criminal offense — loitering for instance — that is less serious than a *felony* and carries a lesser punishment.

Mistrial: The result of a trial being terminated before a verdict is returned. A mistrial usually happens because of a deadlocked jury or some incurable fundamental error that could influence the outcome in a manner prejudicial to the defendant.

Mootness: A constitutional doctrine asserting that an action cannot be justiciable if a plaintiff no longer has the problem for which he sought judicial resolution. For example, if a complainant who has filed a suit claiming that the admissions policy of a school has discriminated against him is then admitted before the case is resolved, the issue would be declared moot. (Compare *Ripeness*.)

Motion: An application to a court requesting a judicial ruling, usually regarding a pending action.

Necessary and Proper Clause: The provision in article I, section 8, clause 18 of the Constitution that provides: "The Congress shall have Power.... To make all Laws which shall be necessary and proper for carrying into Execution the foregoing [enumerated] Powers, and all other Powers vested by this Constitution in the Government of the United States, or in any Department or Officer thereof."

Noncapital case: see *Capital* case

Oral argument: Speech delivered by a lawyer in an *appellate* proceeding to persuade the court to decide the case in favor of a client.

Original intent: A philosophy of constitutional interpretation that attempts to interpret the words of the Constitution according to the perceived intentions of its creators.

Original jurisdiction: The authority to hear a case — usually in the form of adversarial litigation — from its inception and to pass judgment on the *questions of law* the case presents.

Per curiam: A written opinion that expresses the decision of the court but which is unsigned by any of the presiding judges.

Peremptory challenge: The right before trial to exclude prospective jurors without giving reasons for doing so. Most *jurisdictions* grant each party a set number of peremptory challenges in both civil and criminal cases. When these are exhausted, jurors may only be stricken for a reason the judge finds acceptable.

Petitioner: see *Appellant*

Petit jury: An ordinary trial jury, traditionally consisting of 12 individuals (fewer in some *jurisdictions*) who determine factual issues in civil and criminal proceedings.

Plurality: A court opinion endorsed by fewer than a majority of the judges, but which nonetheless conveys a judgment about the case with which the majority agrees. In plurality opinions, the judges, while agreeing in an outcome, often write separate opinions describing the different reasoning that brought them to the same result.

Police power: The authority granted governments, usually state and local, to restrict individual rights in order to promote the public welfare. While it does include law enforcement, police power is a broader concept that embraces such disparate areas as land use regulation and minimum wage laws.

Political question: An issue that a court finds inappropriate for judicial resolution because the proper resolution lies with the executive or the legislative branch of government.

Precedent: A previously decided case that is accepted as authority in subsequent judicial decisions. In all but cases of *first impression*, precedents provide the bases for judges' rulings on *questions of law*; the *common law* thus grows by a process of accretion.

Preemption: The precedence of federal legislation over state legislation. Federal laws governing interstate commerce, for example, always prevail over conflicting state regulations concerning the same matter.

Prima facie: Customarily applied to a case which is sufficient on its face; i.e. bearing enough evidence and no obvious defects, so that it can survive the defendant's attempts to dismiss it before trial.

Prior restraint: A prohibition — usually on the government's part — against the communication or publication of information not yet released. Prior restraint is generally prohibited under the First Amendment to the Constitution.

Privileges and Immunities Clause: Section 1 of the Fourteenth Amendment to the Constitution provides that: "No State shall make or enforce any law which shall abridge the privileges or immunities of citizens of the United States...."

Probable cause: A reasonable knowledge or belief on the part of police that criminal activity has taken place. A demonstration of probable cause is necessary to obtain a *warrant* or to uphold the validity of a warrantless search and seizure or arrest. The Fourth Amendment to the Constitution states that, "No Warrants shall issue, but upon probable cause, supported by Oath or affirmation, and particularly describing the place to searched, and the persons or things to be seized."

Pro bono: Legal services that are performed by attorneys free of charge, often for poor defendants.

Procedural due process: Safeguards, such as the right to counsel, that are meant to protect individual liberty and private property from arbitrary government intrusion. Procedural due process is provided for in the Sixth and Fourteenth Amendments to the Constitution.

Public forum: Under First Amendment constitutional doctrine government may not prohibit speech-related activities, such as demonstrating and leafleting, in areas traditionally provided to or used by the public for speaking, such as public parks and city sidewalks.

Question of fact: A disputed factual contention that will be decided by the finder of fact, usually a jury or a judge. (Compare *Question of law*.)

Question of law: A disputed legal contention reserved for resolution by a judge. (Compare *Question of fact*.)

Quorum: The number of members of an organization needed to be present at a meeting in order to transact business. Under its rules, the Supreme Court requires six members to be present before a case can be heard.

Rational basis: The most lenient test used under the *Equal Protection Clause* to determine if a challenged government action is reasonably related to a legitimate government end.

Reapportionment: see *Apportionment*

Recuse: To disqualify a judge or jury from hearing a case because of potential bias or conflict of interest that might affect the outcome.

Remand: To send back for further deliberation. *Appellate* courts remand cases to trial courts for new hearings, to be based on judgments delivered on appeal.

Remove: Transfer a case from its original court to another court upon the defendant's petition. Usually such transfers take place from state to federal court.

Removal power: This is one-half of the president's power of appointment and removal, granted by the Constitution in article II, section 2, clause 2, which provides that the president "by and with the Advice and Consent of the Senate, shall appoint... Judges of the supreme Court . . . ." It is limited by article III, section 1, which provides that: "Judges, both of the supreme and inferior Courts, shall hold their Offices during good Behaviour...."

Reserved powers: Those powers not specifically delegated to the federal government or denied the states in the Constitution which are therefore reserved to the states or to the people of the United States, as spelled out in the Tenth Amendment. (Compare *Enumerated powers*.)

Respondent: see *Appellee*

Restrictive covenant: A restriction in a deed or agreement concerning real property that limits the use of the property in some fashion. Restrictive covenants concerning sales of real estate to African Americans, for example, were finally outlawed by *Jones v. Alfred B. Mayer, Co.* (1968).

Ripeness: The constitutional doctrine that requires federal courts to forego decisions in any case that has not developed (ripened) into a true controversy. A federal court would not, for example, hear a case concerning the hypothetical impact of, say, a new environmental statute on an individual's property value before that individual has tried to sell his property. (Compare *Mootness*.)

Sedition: Illegal action, such as certain types of treasonous communications during wartime, intended to disrupt or overthrow the government.

Seditious libel: The publication of any words or documents intended to incite the public to overthrow the government.

Selective exclusiveness: A pragmatic doctrine holding that the power to regulate interstate commerce does not rest solely with the federal government, but that some areas are more properly controlled at the state level. (Compare *preemption*.)

Self-incrimination Clause: The portion of the Fifth Amendment to the Constitution that provides: "No person... shall be compelled in any criminal case to be a witness against himself...."

Separation of powers: The doctrine that none of the three branches of government — executive, legislative, or judicial — is allowed to infringe upon the powers reserved to the other branches. For example, in this theory courts are supposed to refrain from rewriting legislation they have struck down when they decide a case.

Seriatim: In succession, one by one. Originally, every Supreme Court justice issued his own opinion in reverse order of seniority, a style of delivery known as seriatim opinions.

Sovereignty: The supreme power of an independent government — at both the state and the national levels — which enables it to control its internal affairs without foreign intervention.

Speech and Debate Clause: Article I, section 6, clause 1 of the Constitution provides that, "for any Speech or Debate in either House, they [senators and representatives] shall not be questioned in any other Place." Thus the clause grants a limited legislative *immunity*.

Standing: The right of an individual or entity, by virtue of his having a stake in the outcome, to challenge another in a judicial proceeding. Courts will not hear cases brought by persons who will be affected only hypothetically by their decisions.

Stare decisis: The *common law* policy of adhering in subsequent similar cases to principles set forth in precedents, or previously decided cases.

State action: Generally, those activities of state or federal governments that violate the rights of an individual protected by the *Due Process Clause* of the Fourteenth Amendment and by the various federal civil rights acts.

States' rights: The *sovereignty* of a state or states in the face of federal government power. The concept of states' rights is commemorated in the Tenth Amendment to the Constitution, which declares: "The powers not delegated to the United States by the Constitution, nor prohibited by it to the States, are reserved to the States respectively, or to the people." (See also *Reserved powers*.)

Stay: A court order issued to halt or suspend a judicial proceeding while some related matter is resolved. For example, the Supreme Court can stay an *injunction* issued by a lower court while the Court is reviewing an appeal of the case giving rise to the injunction.

Strict construction: An interpretation of laws, especially the Constitution, that adheres closely to the clear — and sometimes literal — meaning of the words, rather than to their implications.

Strict scrutiny: A test of whether a statute that creates *suspect categories* of individuals, particularly those based on race or ethnicity, is constitutional. In order to pass the test of strict scrutiny, a law must be not only necessary to achieve a *compelling state interest*, but also the least intrusive means of doing so.

Subpoena: A written order compelling the appearance of a witness at a judicial proceeding. Any officer of the court, including a lawyer, can issue a subpoena. Often, subpoenas require witnesses to produce documents pertinent to an unresolved controversy in advance of trial.

Substantive due process: This doctrine, rooted in the *Due Process Clause* of the Fourteenth Amendment, holds that the Constitution confers on individuals certain inalienable rights — above all the right to be free from arbitrary government intrusion. Such rights are insured by *procedural due process*, which guarantees a fair trial before an individual is deprived of property or liberty.

Summary judgment: A judgement rendered in a civil case prior to delivery of the verdict. Such a judgement results when the judge grants one party's *motion* for summary judgement claiming that there is no outstanding factual issue that would prevent that party from prevailing. A grant of summary judgement thus prevents the issues involved from ever being considered by the jury (or the judge, in the absence of a jury) and usually ends the trial.

Supremacy Clause: The second clause of article VI of the Constitution, which provides in part: "This Constitution, and the Laws of the United States which shall be made in Pursuance thereof... shall be the supreme Law of the Land." It provides the basis for the federal government's supremacy over the states.

Suspect category (or classification): When a given law denies *equal protection* to individuals based on their race, *alienage*, national origin, religion, or sometimes economic status and legitimacy, it is said to have created suspect categories. Unless the government can show, under the court's *strict scrutiny*, that such categories are reasonable to achieve the law's legitimate purpose, the law will be declared unconstitutionally discriminatory. For example, while it is permissible to use age as a criterion for setting different punishments for the same offense, a law employing national origin for the same purpose would be considered inherently suspect and presumed to be unconstitutional.

Takings Clause: Also called the *Eminent Domain* Clause, this section of the Fifth Amendment to the Constitution provides, "private property [shall not] be taken for public use, without just compensation."

Taxing and Spending Clause (or power): This portion of article I, section 8, clause 1 of the Constitution that provides: "The Congress shall have Power To lay and collect Taxes, Duties, Imposts and Excises, to pay the Debts and provide for the common Defence and general Welfare of the United States."

Test case: An action selected from a number of similar cases pending in the same court and brought by several plaintiffs against one defendant (or by one plaintiff against several defendants) to test the right to recovery by all plaintiffs who are in the same situation with regard to the contested issues. All parties in a test case agree in advance to be bound by the outcome of the case. *Plessy v. Ferguson* (1896), which was selected to test the validity of the "separate but equal" justification for segregation, is one example of a significant test case.

Tort: A civil wrong or injury, as distinct from a crime. A tort is usually remedied with a court award of money damages. Examples of tort actions include those based on claims of pro-fessional malpractice and product liability. A breach of contract is not considered a tort.

Transactional immunity: *Immunity* from future prosecution for any criminal offense related to testimony a witness is legally compelled to give. (Compare *Use immunity*.)

Treaty power: The power granted the president of the United States in article II, section 2, clause 2 of the Constitution, which provides: "He shall have Power, by and with the Advice and Consent of the Senate, to make Treaties, provided two-thirds of the Senators present concur...."

Unenumerated powers: see *Enumerated powers*

Use immunity: *Immunity* from future prosecution in a criminal proceeding specifically growing out of the witness's compelled testimony or its consequences. Use immunity is thus not as broad as *transactional immunity*, which extends to any offenses the witness may have committed if they are related to his or her testimony. In 1970 Congress replaced the latter with the former, finding that immunity from related subsequent criminal prosecutions was all that was required by the Fifth Amendment's prohibition against *self-incrimination*.

Warrant: An official order, usually written, and usually authorizing a police search or an arrest.

Writ: A court order requiring performance of a specified act, or giving authority for its performance.

SOURCES FOR FURTHER STUDY

Abraham, Henry J. *The Judiciary: The Supreme Court in the Governmental Process*. 8th ed. Dubuque, Iowa: Brown, 1991.

—. *Justices and Presidents: A Political History of Appointments to the Supreme Court*. 3d ed. New York: Oxford University Press, 1991.

Bates, Ernest S. *The Story of the Supreme Court*. South Hackensack, N.J.: Fred B. Rothman & Co., 1982.

Baum, Lawrence. *The Supreme Court*. 4th ed. Washington, D.C.: CQ Press, 1992.

Bickel, Alexander M. *The Least Dangerous Branch: The Supreme Court at the Bar of Politics*. Indianapolis: Bobbs-Merrill, 1962, 1986.

—. *The Supreme Court and the Idea of Progress*. New York: Harper & Row, 1970.

Brigham, John. *The Cult of the Court*. Philadelphia: Temple University Press, 1987.

Choper, Jesse H. *Judicial Review and the National Political Process: A Functional Reconsideration of the Role of the Supreme Court*. Chicago: University of Chicago Press, 1980.

—. *The Supreme Court and Its Justices*. Chicago: American Bar Association, 1987.

Cox, Archibald. *The Court and the Constitution*. Boston: Houghton Mifflin, 1988.

—. *The Role of the Supreme Court in American Government*. New York: Oxford University Press, 1976.

Currie, David P. *The Constitution in the Supreme Court: The First Hundred Years, 1789-1888*. Chicago: University of Chicago Press, 1986.

—. *The Constitution in the Supreme Court: The Second Century, 1888-1986*. Chicago: University of Chicago Press, 1990.

Cushman, Clare, ed. *The Supreme Court Justices: Illustrated Biographies, 1789-1993*. Washington, D.C.: Congressional Quarterly, 1993.

Documentary History of the Supreme Court of the United States, 1789-1800. 4 vols. New York: Columbia University Press, 1985-1992.

Elliott, Stephen P., ed. *A Reference Guide to the United States Supreme Court*. New York: Facts on File, 1986.

Epstein, Lee, and Thomas G. Walker. *Constitutional Law for a Changing America: Institutional Powers and Constraints*. Washington, D.C., CQ Press, 1992.

Epstein, Lee, et al. *The Supreme Court Compendium: Data, Decisions, and Developments*. Washington, D.C.: Congressional Quarterly, 1994.

Frank, John Paul. *Marble Palace: The Supreme Court in American Life*. New York: Alfred A. Knopf, 1958.

Freund, Paul A. *On Understanding the Supreme Court*. Boston: Little, Brown, 1949; New York: Greenwood, 1977.

Friedman, Leon, ed. *The Justices of the United States Supreme Court: Their Lives and Major Opinions.* Vol. 5, *The Burger Court, 1969-1978.* New York: Chelsea House, 1979.

Friedman, Leon, and Fred Israel, eds. *The Justices of the Supreme Court 1789-1969: Their Lives and Major Opinions.* 4 vols. New York: Chelsea House, 1969.

Goldstein, Joseph. *The Intelligible Constitution: The Supreme Court's Obligation to Maintain the Constitution as Something We the People Can Understand.* New York: Oxford University Press, 1992.

Haines, Charles Grove. *The Role of the Supreme Court in American Government and Politics, 1789-1835.* New York: Russell & Russell, 1960.

Hall, Kermit L. *The Magic Mirror: Law in American History.* New York: Oxford University Press, 1989.
—. ed. *The Oxford Companion to the Supreme Court of the United States.* New York: Oxford University Press, 1992.

History of the Supreme Court of the United States. The Oliver Wendell Holmes Devise. New York: Macmillan, 1971-1988.
—. Vol. I: Julius Goebel Jr. *Antecedents and Beginnings to 1801.* 1971.
—. Vol. II: George L. Haskins and Herbert A. Johnson. *Foundations of Power: John Marshall, 1801-15.* 1981.
—. Vol. III-IV: G. Edward White. *The Marshall Court and Cultural Change, 1815-35.* 1988.
—. Vol. V: Carl B. Swisher. *The Taney Period, 1836-64.* 1974.
—. Vol. VI: Charles Fairman. *Reconstruction and Reunion, 1864-88, Part One.* 1971.
—. Vol. VII: Charles Fairman. *Reconstruction and Reunion, 1864-88, Part Two.* 1987.
—. Supplement to Vol. VII: Charles Fairman. *Five Justices and the Electoral Commission of 1877.* 1988.
—. Vol. IX: Alexander M. Bickel and Benno C. Schmidt Jr. *The Judiciary and Responsible Government, 1910-1921.* 1984.

Krislov, Samuel. *The Supreme Court in the Political Process.* New York: Macmillan, 1965.

Kurland, Phillip B., and Gerhard Casper, eds. *Landmark Briefs and Arguments of the Supreme Court of the United States: Constitutional Law.* Arlington, Va.: University Publishers of America, 1977-

MacKenzie, John P. *The Appearance of Justice.* New York: Scribner's, 1974.

McCloskey, Robert Green. *The American Supreme Court.* Chicago: University of Chicago Press, 1960.
—. *The Modern Supreme Court.* Cambridge, Mass.: Harvard University Press, 1972.

Martin, Fenton. *How to Research the Supreme Court.* Washington, D.C.: Congressional Quarterly, 1992.

Martin, Fenton, and Robert U. Goehlert. *The U.S. Supreme Court: A Bibliography.* Washington, D.C.: CQ Press, 1990.

Mendelson, Wallace. *The Supreme Court: Law and Discretion.* Indianapolis: Bobbs-Merrill, 1967.

O'Brien, David M. *Storm Center: The Supreme Court in American Politics.* 2d ed. New York: W.W. Norton & Co., 1990.

Rehnquist, William H. *The Supreme Court: How It Was, How It Is.* New York: Morrow, 1987.

Rohde, David W., and Harold J. Spaeth. *Supreme Court Decision Making.* San Francisco: Freeman, 1976.

Rostow, Eugene V. *The Sovereign Prerogative: The Supreme Court and the Quest for Law.* New Haven: Yale University Press, 1962; New York: Greenwood, 1974.

Schmidhauser, John R. *The Supreme Court: Its Politics, Personality and Procedures.* New York: Holt, Rinehart, & Winston, 1960.

Schubert, Glendon A. *Constitutional Politics: The Behavior of the Supreme Court Justices and the Constitutional Policies That They Make.* New York: Holt, Rinehart, & Winston, 1960.

Schwartz, Bernard. *A History of the Supreme Court.* New York: Oxford University Press, 1993.

—. *The Reins of Power: A Constitutional History of the United States.* New York: Hill and Wang, 1963.

Segal, Jeffrey A., and Harold J. Spaeth. *The Supreme Court and the Attitudinal Model.* New York: Cambridge University Press, 1993.

Shnayerson, Robert. *The Illustrated History of the Supreme Court of the United States.* New York: Abrams, 1986.

Siegan, Bernard H. *The Supreme Court's Constitution.* New Brunswick, N.J.: Transaction, 1987.

Spaeth, Harold J. *Supreme Court Policy Making.* San Francisco: Freeman, 1974.

Streamer, Robert J. *Chief Justice: Leadership and the Supreme Court.* Columbia: University of South Carolina Press, 1986.

Swindler, William Finley. *Court and Constitution in the Twentieth Century.* 2 vols. Indianapolis: Bobbs-Merrill, 1969, 1974.

Swisher, Carl Brent. *The Supreme Court in Modern Role.* Rev. ed. New York: New York University Press, 1965.

Tribe, Laurence H. *God Save This Honorable Court: How the Choice of the Supreme Court Justices Shapes Our History.* New York: Random House, 1985.

Urofsky, Melvin I. *A March of Liberty: A Constitutional History of the United States.* New York: Alfred A. Knopf, 1988.

Wagman, Robert J. *The Supreme Court: A Citizen's Guide.* New York: Pharos Books, 1993.

Walker, Thomas G., and Lee Epstein. *The Supreme Court: An Introduction.* New York: St. Martin's Press, 1992.

Wasby, Stephen L. *The Supreme Court in the Federal Judicial System.* 3d ed. Chicago: Nelson-Hall, 1988.

Wiecek, William M. *Liberty under Law: The Supreme Court in American Life.* Baltimore: Johns Hopkins University Press, 1988.

Witt, Elder. *Congressional Quarterly's Guide to the U.S. Supreme Court.* 2d ed. Washington, D.C.: Congressional Quarterly, 1990.

Woodward, Bob, and Scott Armstrong. *The Brethren: Inside the Supreme Court.* New York: Simon & Schuster, 1979.

Index of Cases

H

I

J

K

GENERAL INDEX

Note: For specific cases, see the **Index of Cases,** which begins on p. 519. In the **General Index,** page numbers in boldface denote the biographies of associate justices. Under the heading for each associate justice will be found the titles of the cases he or she participated in as well as high-level political offices held before or after serving on the Court. Under the heading for each chief justice will be found the titles of the significant cases the Court decided during his tenure as well as subheadings for his role as chief justice, the associate justices who served under him, his early life, public life, and voting patterns on the Court during his tenure. Subject entries in this index include terms, issues, concepts, events, and proper names. Subentries are used to guide the reader to more specific information. Whenever appropriate, cross-references are given to cases, which appear in *italics* and will be found in the **Index of Cases,** as well as other headings in this index. Definitions of legal terms are found in the glossary (pp. 503-513), which is not indexed here.

A

abolitionists, 77

abortion, xvii, xxv, xxviii, xxix, 231, 330, 377, 381, 390, 407, 409, 420, 426, 430, 437, 439, 441, 446. *See also Akron v. Akron Center for Reproductive Health, Inc.; Harris v. McRae; Planned Parenthood of Pennsylvania v. Casey; Roe v. Wade; Rust v. Sullivan; Thornburgh v. American College of Obstetricians and Gynecologists; Webster v. Reproductive Health Services.*

Abrams, Jacob, 214

abstention doctrine, 353

Acevedo, Charles, 441

Acheson, Dean, 297

Acton, James, 453

Adams, John, 4, 6, 7, 30, 31, 38, 48, 197; criticism of, 26; election of 1800, 41; election to presidency, 25-26; nominations to the U.S. Supreme Court, xviii, xix, 32, 33, 42, 46, 48, 60; vice president, 22

Adams, John Quincy, 51, 54, 58, 90 election of 1824, 44-45; nominations to the U.S. Supreme Court, 56, 57; Secretary of State, 44

admiralty law, 35, 60, 108, 146, 167

advisory opinion, xi, 17, 208

affidavit, 389

affirmative action, xvii, xxviii, 326, 378, 381, 414, 416, 420, 431, 434, 440, 447. See also *Associated General Contractors v. Jacksonville; Fullilove v. Klutznick; Johnson v. Santa Clara County; Local 28 of the Sheet Metal Workers' International Association v. Equal Employment Opportunity Commission; Metro Broadcasting, Inc. v. Federal Communications Commission; Regents of the University of California v. Bakke; Richmond v. J.A. Croson Co.; United Steel Workers of America v. Weber.*

Afghanistan, 371

Age Discrimination in Employment Act, 451

Agnew, Spiro T., 316, 370

Agricultural Adjustment Administration, 240

Agriculture Adjustment Act, 245, 251, 261, 268, 286

Alabama, admitted to the Union, 40; secession from the Union, 80

Alien Enemies Act, 26, 28, 31, 38

Alien Friends Act, 26, 28, 31, 38

Alien Registration Act, 296

alienage, 385

aliens, rights of, 178. *See also De Geofroy v. Riggs.*

alimony, 405. *See also Orr v. Orr.*

American Civil Liberties Union (ACLU), 430

American Communist Party, 301, 309, 336, 337, 338, 339, 341, 343, 351, 354, 355, 357, 359. *See also* Communists.

American Federation of Labor (AFL), 209, 247, 331

American Railway Union, 160, 181

American Revolution. *See* Revolutionary War.

American Socialist Party, 213

American Sugar Refining Company, 180

amicus curiae, xiv

Anderson, Robert, 80

Anti-Federalists, 2, 5, 51, 55, 56, 71; concerns about state court authority, 3; *Hayburn's Case,* 15; limitation of the federal government, 25; sedition trials of outspoken —, 14; state sovereignty, 16. *See also* Republican Party.

Anti-Masons, 75

Anti-Saloon League, 211

E

I

T